The Routledge Handbook of Sociolinguistics Around the World

Drawing on examples from a wide range of languages and social settings, *The Routledge Handbook of Sociolinguistics Around the World* is the first single-volume collection surveying current and recent research trends in international sociolinguistics. With over 30 chapters written by leading authorities in the region concerned, all continents and their respective regions are covered. This book will serve as an important tool to help widen the perspective on sociolinguistics to readers of English.

Divided into parts covering: the Americas, Asia, Australasia, Africa and the Middle East, and Europe, the book provides readers with a solid, up-to-date appreciation of the interdisciplinary nature of the field of sociolinguistics in each area. It clearly explains the patterns and systematicity that underlie language variation in use, as well as the ways in which alternations between different language varieties mark personal style, social power and national identity.

Sociolinguistics Around the World is the ideal resource for all students on undergraduate sociolinguistics courses and researchers involved in the study of language, society and power.

Martin J. Ball is Hawthorne-BoRSF Endowed Professor, and Director of the Hawthorne Research Center, at the University of Louisiana at Lafayette. Dr Ball has written and edited over 120 academic publications including *Clinical Sociolinguistics* and *The Handbook of Clinical Linguistics*.

Contributors: David Atkinson, Yasemin Bayyurt, William O. Beeman, Mercedes Bengoechea, Richard Benton, Sally Boyd, David Bradley, Zhanna Burstein-Feldman, Dominique Caubet, Peter Collins, Bruce Connell, Serafín M. Coronel-Molina, Jeroen Darquennes, Probal Dasgupta, Winifred V. Davies, Nadine Di Vito, Mark Donohue, Ina Druviete, Alek D. Epstein, José Antonio Flores Farfán, Victor A. Friedman, Elaine Gold, Nanette Gottlieb, Robert D. Greenberg, Victoria Gulida, Bill Haddican, Jen Hay, Kirk Hazen, Christina M. Higgins, Nina Kheimets, Agnieszka Kiełkiewicz-Janowiak, Miklós Kontra, Shulamith Kopeliovich, Margaret Maclagan, Rajend Mesthrie, Catherine Miller, France Mugler, Jiří Nekvapil, Sandi Michele de Oliveira, Mair Parry, Viviana Quintero, Madhavi Sardesai, Jane Stuart-Smith, Joel Walters, Lionel Wee, Dafna Yitzhaki, Valerie Youssef, David Zeitlyn, and Minglang Zhou.

The Routledge Handbook of Sociolinguistics Around the World

Edited by
Martin J. Ball

Routledge
Taylor & Francis Group

LONDON AND NEW YORK

First published 2010
by Routledge
2 Park Square, Milton Park, Abingdon, Oxon OX14 4RN

Simultaneously published in the USA and Canada
by Routledge
270 Madison Avenue, New York, NY 10016

Routledge is an imprint of the Taylor & Francis Group, an informa business

© 2010 selection and editorial matter, Martin J. Ball; individual chapters,
the contributors

Typeset in Bembo by
Taylor & Francis Books
Printed and bound in Great Britain by
CPI Antony Rowe, Chippenham, Wiltshire

British Library Cataloguing in Publication Data
A catalogue record for this book is available from the British Library

Library of Congress Cataloging in Publication Data
A catalog record for this book has been requested

ISBN 978-0-415-42278-9 (hbk)
ISBN 978-0-203-86965-9 (ebk)

Contents

Tables

Contributors

David Atkinson is Senior Lecturer in Spanish at the University of Limerick, Ireland. His research interests include Language and Power/Critical Discourse Analysis; Language Policy and Language Planning; The Politics of Language in the Spanish-speaking World; Popular music in Spain; Language and the Media; Language teaching methodology and language learning. His work on Catalonia has appeared in many journals since 1997. These include *Journal of Multilingual and Multicultural Development*; *Journal of Language Problems and Language Planning; International Journal of Iberian Studies* and *Journal of Language and Politics*.

Martin J. Ball is Hawthorne-Board of Regents Endowed Professor, and Director of the Hawthorne Research Center in the Department of Communicative Disorders, at the University of Louisiana at Lafayette. He is an honorary professor at the University of Wales Institute, Cardiff. His main research interests include sociolinguistics, clinical phonetics and phonology, and the linguistics of Welsh. He has authored and edited twenty-five books, 40 contributions to collections and over eighty refereed articles in academic journals. His books include *The Use of Welsh, The Celtic Languages,* and *Clinical Sociolinguistics*.

Yasemin Bayyurt is an Associate Professor in the Department of Foreign Language Education at Boğaziçi University, Istanbul, Turkey. Her research interests include language planning and policy, Teaching Turkish as a Foreign Language, Teaching English as an International Language, Cross-cultural Communication, Computer-Mediated Communication, and general issues in sociolinguistics and pragmatics. Her publications include articles in various refereed journals and books in the field. She has recently co-edited a book on Teaching Turkish as a Foreign Language.

William O. Beeman is Professor and Chair of the Department of Anthropology at the University of Minnesota. He is past President of the Middle East Section of the American Anthropological Association and Former Director of Middle East Studies at Brown University. He has worked throughout the Middle East, especially in Iran,

Central Asia and the Persian Gulf region. His books include *Language, Status and Power in Iran*, and *The Great Satan vs. the Mad Mullahs: How the United States and Iran Demonize Each Other*.

Mercedes Bengoechea is Senior Lecturer in Sociolinguistics and has been Dean of the Faculty of Filosofía y Letras (Universidad de Alcalá, Spain) for six years. She is also a member of the Advisory Language Committee of the Instituto de la Mujer (Ministry of Social Affairs) since 1994; and has been the co-ordinator of the Annual Report of the Spanish National Observatory on Gender Violence. Her research has focused on feminist theory and practice, language and gender, linguistic ideologies, the use of non-standard language in literature and the media. She is now working on feminist linguistic policies of Spanish.

Richard Benton has studied, written about and lectured on language policy, the revitalization of minority and indigenous languages and related subjects in the Pacific, Southeast Asia, Europe and North America since becoming involved in efforts to revitalize the Māori language while a student in the late 1950s. He led research programmes on education, language, law and development at the New Zealand Council for Educational Research and the Universities of Waikato (where he retired as a Research Professor in 2007) and Auckland.

Sally Boyd received a BA from Bryn Mawr College and an MA in linguistics from the University of Pennsylvania during the 1970s. She received a PhD in linguistics in 1988 at the University of Gothenburg, Sweden. During the 1990s she was research fellow at the Center for research on migration and ethnic relations, Stockholm University. She was promoted to professor of general linguistics in Gothenburg in 2000. Her research interests focus on multilingualism in Europe from a sociolinguistic perspective.

David Bradley, based at La Trobe University in Australia, does research on the socio-historical linguistics of various East and Southeast Asian languages and on language endangerment, maintenance and policy. He is author or editor of thirty books including Language Endangerment and Language Maintenance (RoutledgeCurzon 2002). He has been visiting professor at universities in Thailand, France and the UK, is honorary professor and Director of the Institute for Minority Development at Yuxi Normal University in China.

Zhanna Burstein-Feldman holds a PhD in English Linguistics from Bar-Ilan University. Her research interests include first language attrition, language and identity, and second language learning in minorities. She has conducted research on language teaching in Israel and on immigrants (funded by the Israeli Education Ministry the German-Israel Research Foundation). She is currently working on language and social identity issues in second generation Russian immigrant children.

Dominique Caubet is University Professor of North African (Maghribi) Arabic at INALCO (Institute of Oriental Languages), Paris. Her research interests include general linguistics (aspect, tense, modality, nominal determination, negation, enunciative particles), sociolinguistics from codeswitching to youth languages and the social status of minority languages in the Maghreb and in the European diaspora (France and the

Netherlands). She has published a reference description of Moroccan Arabic, several books and numerous articles.

Peter Collins is an Associate Professor in the Department of Linguistics at the University of New South Wales in Australia. His research interests include corpus linguistics, Australian English, and descriptive grammar. He has published books and articles on grammar, sociolinguistics, introductory linguistics, clefts and modality and his articles have appeared in such journals as *English World-Wide, Journal of Pragmatics, World Englishes, Linguistics, Word, Australian Journal of Linguistics, Functions of Language, English Studies*, and *International Journal of Corpus Linguistics*.

Bruce Connell is based at Glendon College, York University in Toronto, where he is a member of the Centre for Research in Language Contact. His main areas of interest include: endangered languages in Africa and causes of language endangerment; maintenance of minority languages; the phonetics of tone and phonetic variation; and language variation and change and comparative historical linguistics. His research focuses mainly on the Mambiloid group and other languages of the Nigeria-Cameroon borderland, and languages of the Niger Delta.

Serafín M. Coronel-Molina is an Assistant Professor at Indiana University. He is an educational linguist and sociolinguist. Dr. Coronel-Molina received his B.A. from the Ricardo Palma University in Peru; his M.A. from the Ohio State University, and his Ph. D. from the University of Pennsylvania. He has published articles in Quechua, English and Spanish, and presented papers internationally. His research is of an interdisciplinary nature, drawing on fields as diverse as sociolinguistics, linguistic anthropology, politics of language and pragmatics.

Jeroen Darquennes is an assistant professor in German and general linguistics at the University of Namur. He is affiliated to the Fryske Akademy/Mercator Research Centre in Ljouwert/Leeuwarden (the Netherlands). Together with Ulrich Ammon (Duisburg) and Sue Wright (Portsmouth) he is the editor of *Sociolinguistica, The International Yearbook of European Sociolinguistics* (de Gruyter). His main research interests lie in the sociolinguistic and contact linguistic study of language policy and planning in European language minority settings.

Probal Dasgupta is based in the Centre for Applied Linguistics at the University of Hyderabad, India. He has taught in New York, San Francisco, Melbourne, Kolkata, Pune, and Hyderabad. He was Editor of *Indian Linguistics* (1982–87), and currently co-edits *Language Problems and Language Planning* (1990-, Benjamins). His publications include: (2002, with Amares Datta and Udayon Misra) *English at the Crossroads: the Postcolonial Situation*; (1995, with Jayant Lele and Rajendra Singh) *Explorations in Indian Sociolinguistics*; (1993) *The Otherness of English: India's Auntie Tongue Syndrome*.

Winifred V. Davies is Reader in German at Aberystwyth University, Wales (UK). She has published on variation and language attitudes in Germany, teachers' language awareness, differences between lay and academic discourse about language, and the contribution of linguistic myths to the construction of sociolinguistic norms. A major recent publication was *The Making of Bad Language: Lay linguistic stigmatisations in German, past and present* (Peter Lang 2006) (co-authored with Nils Langer).

Nadine Di Vito is Director of the Romance Language Program in the Department of Romance Languages and Literatures at the University of Chicago. She specializes in sociolinguistics and discourse analysis, especially as they relate to second language acquisition and teaching. Her book, *Patterns Across Spoken and Written French: Empirical Research on the Interaction Among Forms, Functions, and Genres* (1997), focuses on the frequency and contextual use of particular grammatical structures. In addition to published writings, she has developed and analyzed several corpora of authentic French spoken discourse and is collaborating with a colleague to create a first- and second-year French language method with these data as its central core.

Mark Donohue works at the Australian National University. His focus is the languages of Indonesia and Papua New Guinea. Focusing on morphosyntax, phonology and historical linguistics, he has published grammars from this area. Since a great tool in understanding synchronic grammar is an understanding of the language's history, so he devotes a fair amount of time investigating the historical relations of the languages, and developing tools for understanding the linguistic past of Melanesia and the Pacific.

Ina Druviete is Professor at the University of Latvia (General Linguistics) and author of more than 200 articles on sociolinguistics, language policy and linguistic rights. She is one of the main authors of linguistic legislation in Latvia, has served as the Minister of Education and Research (2004–6), has been a Member of the Latvian Parliament since 2002. She is an editorial board member of the journal *Language Policy* and the series *Studies in World Language Problems*. Currently she is Deputy President of the European Federation of National Institutions for Languages (EFNIL).

Alek D. Epstein has written extensively on the history of Israel, intellectuals' influence on the emergence of civil society and on the sociological and educational aspects of multiculturalism and multilingualism. He has published several books and more than 100 manuscripts in four languages in various scientific journals and collections. Pieces of research, co-authored with Nina Kheimets, were published in *Language in Society; Language Problems and Language Planning; Journal of Multilingual and Multicultural Development; International Studies in Sociology of Education; Journal of International Migration and Integration*.

José Antonio Flores Farfán is Professor of Linguistics at the Centro de Investigaciones y Estudios Superiores en Antropología Social in Mexico City. His research interests include language contact, pragmatics, language ideologies and intervention. He has been active in the field of Native American Indian Education for a decade, designing and teaching courses for indigenous and non-indigenous people. He has published widely on the linguistics and sociolinguistics of indigenous languages in Mexico, including the Otomi and the Nahuas. Flores Farfán is a leading expert in Nahuatl, and has done extensive research on sociolinguistics, language ideologies, pragmatics and language revitalization and reversal.

Victor A. Friedman is Andrew W. Mellon Professor in the Slavic Department and the Department of Linguistics at the University of Chicago. He also holds an associate appointment in the Department of Anthropology and is Director of the Center for East European and Russian/Eurasian Studies. His main research interests are grammatical categories as well as sociolinguistic issues related to contact phenomena, standardization, ideology, and identity in the Caucasus and the Balkans. His research has been supported by Guggenheim, ACLS, NEH, Fulbright-Hays, and others.

Elaine Gold is a Lecturer in the Department of Linguistics at the University of Toronto. Her research interests include topics in Canadian English and Yiddish in the areas of Sociolinguistics, Historical Linguistics and Language Contact. Her most recent publications investigate the ubiquitous tag *eh?* in Canadian English, and *Bungi*, a Scottish-Cree dialect of Manitoba.

Nanette Gottlieb FAHA is Professor of Japanese Studies in the Japan Program, School of Languages and Comparative Cultural Studies at the University of Queensland in Brisbane, Australia. Her recent work includes *Language and Society in Japan* (2005) and *Linguistic Stereotyping and Minority Groups in Japan* (2006). She is currently working on a study of the challenges to language policy in Japan brought about by increased immigration and new technologies, funded by the Australian Research Council.

Robert D. Greenberg is a Professor of Linguistics in the Department of Anthropology at Hunter College, and Associate Dean of the School of Arts and Sciences. He is also Adjunct Professor in the Department of Slavic Languages and Literatures at Yale University. He is a specialist in South Slavic languages and linguistics, and has worked primarily on sociolinguistic issues in the former Yugoslavia. His publications include numerous books and articles on South Slavic and Balkan Slavic topics. His most recent book is *Language and Identity in the Balkans* (Oxford University Press, second edition, 2008).

Victoria Gulida is senior lecturer in the Department of General Linguistics, St. Petersburg State University. She is responsible for the Master's programme in sociolinguistics and in charge of the summer field practice for the Department. Starting with a PhD in experimental research of speech prosody, she then turned to sociolinguistics to study urban dialectology, ongoing language shift (in the Azov Sea area) and ideas of early Soviet sociolinguists. Her publications include articles on urban dialects and language change, Soviet sociolinguistic heritage and recent sociolinguistic developments in St. Petersburg. Her current project examines prosodic aspects of power and distance variability.

Bill Haddican is a lecturer in language variation and change in the Department of Language and Linguistic Science at the University of York. His research focuses on language change, syntax and language contact in Basque and English dialects. He has published on these areas in leading journals, including *Language Variation and Change, Language in Society,* and *Estudios de Sociolinguistica.*

Jennifer Hay is Associate Professor in the Department of Linguistics at the University of Canterbury in Christchurch, New Zealand. She has research interests in New Zealand English, sociophonetics, laboratory phonology and morphology. Her articles have appeared in leading journals, including *Language, Lingua, Language Variation and Change, Journal of Phonetics, Yearbook of Morphology, Annual Review of Anthropology, Journal of Pragmatics, Corpora,* and *Trends in Cognitive Science.*

Kirk Hazen is Professor in the Department of English at West Virginia University. He focuses his research on language variation in American English, primarily writing about Southern US varieties and English in Appalachia. He promotes sociolinguistic goals by presenting dialect diversity programs to numerous communities, including future health professionals, social workers, and service organizations.

Christina M. Higgins is an assistant professor in the Department of Second Language Studies at the University of Hawai'i at Mānoa, where she teaches courses in socio-linguistics, English as a global language, discourse analysis, and qualitative research methods. Her research in Tanzania has focused on codeswitching, linguistic and cul-tural hybridity in popular culture, language and advertising, and culturally relevant communication in HIV/AIDS education.

Nina Kheimets' dissertation examined language policy and language practice in Israeli higher education institutions in a comparative perspective, as well as the role of immigrant intellectual elites' construction of collective identities and subcultures in Israel.

Agnieszka Kiełkiewicz-Janowiak is an associate professor and a lecturer in socio-linguistics at the School of English, Adam Mickiewicz University, in Poznań, Poland. Her current research interests are lifespan sociolinguistics, and language and gender. She is the author of *'Women's language'? – a socio-historical view: Private writings in early New England* (Motivex, 2002) and *A socio-historical study in address: Polish and English* (Peter Lang, 1992). She is now working on a book on age-related issues in language and communication.

Miklós Kontra is Professor of Linguistics at the University of Szeged and Head of the Department of Sociolinguistics in the Linguistics Institute of the Hungarian Academy of Sciences, Budapest. His primary interests lie in variation in Hungarian; the contact varieties of Hungarian in Slovakia, Ukraine, Rumania, Serbia, Croatia, Slovenia and Austria; Hungarian-American bilingualism; educational linguistics and Linguistic Human Rights. Among other volumes he has edited *Language Contact in East-Central Europe* (= *Multilingua*, Volume 19–1/2, 2000).

Shulamith Kopeliovich emigrated from Russia to Israel in 1995. She received her PhD from the Department of English, Bar-Ilan University. Her dissertation 'Reversing Language Shift in the Immigrant Family' examines controversial social and linguistic processes involved in the intergenerational transmission of a heritage language. She conducted post-doctoral research at The Hebrew University of Jerusalem. Her research areas include heritage language maintenance, family language policy, codeswitching and convergence, Jewish education.

Margaret Maclagan is an Associate Professor of Communication Disorders at the University of Canterbury, Christchurch, New Zealand. Her major research interests have included a long-term study of the sound changes over time in New Zealand English and in Māori. Her current research include the relationship between English and Māori in the pronunciation of Māori speakers, and the relevance of sound change for speech-language therapists. She is a co-author of two books which consider New Zealand English from a sociolinguistic perspective.

Rajend Mesthrie is Professor of Linguistics at the University of Cape Town, where he holds a National Research Foundation (SARCHI) research chair. He is also the current President of the Linguistics Society of Southern Africa. He has published in the fields of Sociolinguistics, with special reference to language contact and variation in South Africa. His most recent publication is *World Englishes* (with Rakesh Bhatt, CUP 2008).

Catherine Miller is a Senior Research Fellow at CNRS-IREMAM, University of Aix en Provence, France. Her research includes Arabic sociolinguistics, language policies, contact and change in Arabic-speaking countries and the role of language in collective identity construction. She has worked on Sudan, Egypt and currently Morocco. She has published five books and numerous articles in various journals, including *Linguistics, Revue des Mondes Arabes et Musulmans, MAS-GELLAS* and numerous edited books. She is presently working on socio-cultural changes in Arab cities.

France Mugler has worked at the University of the South Pacific in Fiji for almost twenty years. She has an interest in sociolinguistics and has done research on some of the Indian languages spoken in Fiji, including Fiji Hindi, Gujarati, and South Indian languages. She and Jan Tent have conducted two surveys of language use and attitudes in Fiji and written on Fiji English. With Jan Tent and Paul Geraghty, she is co-author of a dictionary of English for Fiji.

Jiří Nekvapil teaches sociolinguistics, discourse analysis and general linguistics at the Department of Linguistics at Charles University in Prague. He has published extensively in these areas. His current research focuses on theories of language planning, Language Management Theory, ethnomethodologically informed analysis of media discourse, and the use of languages in multinational companies. His most recent book is *Language Management in Contact Situations* (Peter Lang Publishing Group 2009, co-editor together with T. Sherman).

Sandi Michele de Oliveira is Associate Professor of Portuguese (Institute for English, Germanic and Romance Studies; University of Copenhagen). Research interests include address forms and broader issues in pragmatics, as well as the multidisciplinary approaches to the negotiation amd construction of identity through language use. Recent works have appeared in *The ISA Handbook in Contemporary Sociology, The Multilingual Internet* and *Formas y fórmulas de tratamiento en el mundo hispánico,* as well as in such journals as the *Journal of Historical Pragmatics, National Identities* and *Journal of Computer-Mediated Communication.* A book presenting a model for the analysis of address is in preparation.

Mair Parry is Professor Emeritus and Senior Research Fellow in Italian Linguistics at the University of Bristol, UK. Her research interests focus on the current sociolinguistic situation in Italy, particularly non-standard varieties, and the syntax of the dialects of Italy, both early and modern. Publications include *The Dialects of Italy* (jointly edited with Martin Maiden, Routledge, 1997) and a sociolinguistic and grammatical analysis of an urban dialect on the Piedmontese-Ligurian border (*Parluma 'd Còiri,* 2005).

Viviana Quintero is a PhD candidate in Linguistic Anthropology at the University of Michigan. She received her BA from Brown University in American Civilization. Her research interests include the semiotics of language ideologies in language-shifting communities and the discursive and interdiscursive production of indigeneities. She is writing a dissertation on how indigenous people in northern highland Ecuador perceive, enact, and regiment spatio-temporal, political-economic, and sartorial distinctions through diverse discursive practices.

Madhavi Sardesai is lecturer in linguistics in the department of Konkani of Goa University, India. She was awarded her PhD in 2007 from Goa University for her research, 'A Comparative Linguistic and Cultural Study of Lexical Influences on Konkani'. She is closely associated with the Konkani Language and literary movement, and was executive editor of *Jaag*, the Konkani Literary Monthly from 1995 to 1996, and its editor from 2007. She has published three books (in Konkani), and has several essays and research articles (in Konkani and English) to her credit.

Jane Stuart-Smith is Reader in English Language at the University of Glasgow. She is the author of a number of articles on: variation and change in Glaswegian accent, the impact of the media on language change, the phonetics and phonology of British varieties of Panjabi, the acquisition of literacy in Panjabi/English bilingual children, and historical linguistics and sound-change. She is author of *Phonetics and Philology: Sound Change* (2004), and co-editor of *The Edinburgh Companion to Scots* (2003). She is now writing a monograph on the influence of the media on language change (*Mediating the local: language change and the media*).

Joel Walters is Professor of Linguistics at Bar-Ilan University. His research on bilingualism has been funded by the Israel Science Foundation, the Netherlands-Israel Research Program, and the German-Israel Research Foundation. A current project on language acquisition and social identity in bilingual preschool children is funded by BMBF, the German Ministry of Education. His book *Bilingualism: The Sociopragmatic-Psycholinguistic Interface* was published by Erlbaum in 2005.

Lionel Wee is an Associate Professor in the Department of English Language and Literature at the National University of Singapore. His research interests include language policy, language ideologies, metaphor in discourse, Singapore English, and general issues in sociolinguistics and pragmatics. His articles have appeared in *Applied Linguistics, English World-Wide, Journal of Pragmatics, Journal of Sociolinguistics, Language Policy, Language in Society*, and *Language and Communication*. He is currently working on a book about language rights.

Dafna Yitzhaki is a lecturer in Linguistics at Bar Ilan University and a post-doctoral fellow in Language Policy at the University of the Free State, South Africa. Her PhD dissertation analyzed institutional-level language policy and practice in Israel with respect to Arabic in legal, educational and media domains. Her research interests include societal bilingualism, language policy and Language Rights.

Valerie Youssef is Professor of Linguistics in the Dept. of Liberal Arts, University of the West Indies, St. Augustine, Trinidad and Tobago. Her main areas of teaching and research have been sociolinguistics, language acquisition and learning and discourse analysis. She has published in a range of journals including *Language in Society, Journal* *of Child Language, Language and Communication,* and *Journal of Pidgin and Creole Languages.* She has published *The Languages of Tobago* with Winford James and *Writing Rage: Unmasking Violence in Caribbean Discourse* with Paula Morgan. The latter won an Award from UWI Press in 2008 for Most Outstanding Interdisciplinary text.

David Zeitlyn is Professor of Anthropology at University of Kent, Canterbury, UK. His research interests include sociolinguistics, life writing, and diaries in contexts of restricted literacy. Current work includes projects examining endangered languages on the Nigeria-Cameroon border, focusing on Mambiloid languages (funded by Arts and Humanities Research Council, UK). His articles have appeared in *Research on Language and Social Interaction, Journal of the Royal Anthropological Institute* and *Africa.* He is currently preparing a book on divination and working with Cameroonian studio photographers to archive their negatives.

Minglang Zhou is Associate Professor and Director of the Chinese program in the School of Languages, Literatures and Cultures at the University of Maryland, College Park. He has published five volumes and many articles on multilingualism and ethnicity in China. He has recently won a 2009 American Philosophical Society Fellowship for his project on *Between integration and segregation: Changing models of nation-state building and language education for minorities in China.*

Foreword

This is an ambitious undertaking, particularly since – as the editor notes in his Introduction – 'sociolinguistics' is interpreted very broadly here, embracing those macro-level topics more usually found under the sociology-of-language rubric.[1] There are other sociolinguistic and variationist handbooks, but none attempts such wide coverage nor, more particularly, the geographical breadth that is found here. The contributors comprise a felicitous mix of established and up-and-coming scholars, and many are simply the best qualified for their particular assignments.

In Part I ('the Americas'), the most notable features have to do with the cultural and linguistic diversity found in countries where increasingly beleaguered indigenous populations have had to contend with massive waves of immigration. The Canadian context is unique here, inasmuch as there are *two* substantial European 'mainstream' groups whose fortunes have intertwined with those of the aboriginal 'first nations' and, latterly, with the 'allophones'. Attention to the indigenous 'others' is, in fact, a recurring strength throughout this handbook – we note in this first part the belated focus upon the languages and cultures of the 'Indians', many of which are now in the gravest danger. (Of the 53 surviving autochthonous varieties in Canada, for example, only three can be considered healthy – and the strongest of these, Cree, has only 60,000 speakers.) As the chapters dealing with South and Central America imply, a further difficulty is that only *some* indigenous varieties have been studied at all well; we need much more work on Caribbean creoles, for instance, and investigations that will take us beyond Quechua.

Part II presents eight Asian studies, and there are several important themes. In the Chinese and Asian contexts, for instance, policies of linguistic standardization for official or 'scheduled' varieties must contend with a very large number of other languages, many of which have very large numbers of speakers. Furthermore, these 'minority' languages are often endangered varieties and so any linguistically informed attempts at revitalization are enormously complex. Another common theme is the vexed question of minorities-within-minorities. The Georgian linguistic and cultural claims made vis-à-vis Russia are not ones that the newly independent country has always been ready to extend to its own Ossetian and Abkhazian enclaves, for example. (Similarly, nationalist arguments for Québec sovereignty have not generally been sensitive to those made by indigenous peoples – notably, the James Bay Cree – within the province.) A third theme – which, like the previous ones, can of course be detected elsewhere in this book, too – is the apparently paradoxical staying power of imperialist languages in former colonies, where the multiplicity of indigenous varieties has often given those European mediums a curiously neutral status. And a fourth theme of importance is the ever-recurring question of distinctions between 'language' and 'dialect', distinctions that can have much more to do with political pressures and requirements than with textbook definitions. (This theme is importantly taken up in the European section (Part V), where we are reminded that while, linguistically, there is a Scandinavian language that unites speakers in Norway, Sweden and Denmark, political realities mean that each area has its own separate 'language'. It is political imperatives, too, that now fuel scholarly efforts to create two separate languages from Serbo-Croatian.)

Studies of Australasia and the South Pacific highlight once again the ramifications of contact between a large number of indigenous varieties and a smaller – but more powerful – assortment of imported ones. In Australia and New Zealand, we also see the development of particularized varieties of English, of regional standards. Beyond these two imperial transplants, and putting aside New Guinea as well, we are still left with a vast area with about two dozen countries and some 250 languages. Language decline and the many local illustrations of borrowings – from stronger to weaker varieties – are central features in this landscape. New Guinea is singled out for special treatment here, as it often is: with about 1,000 languages in 50 families, the region is the most richly diverse in the world. If we also bear in mind that no single variety has more than a quarter of a million speakers, that the island is politically divided, that it has undergone several different colonizations, that one of its most important languages is in fact a creole (Tok Pisin), and that this creole is – more than any one European variety – the overarching rival that puts smaller languages on the endangered list, we are even more overwhelmed by the cultural and linguistic complexity of the area. New Guinea is a natural language laboratory where almost all aspects of sociolinguistics and the sociology of language can be investigated, but where the sheer contextual breadth means that relatively little has, in fact, been done.

Africa is the most linguistically rich continent, a New Guinea writ large, and the authors of the five chapters here have therefore had to be particularly selective in their coverage – particularly since this part *also* includes some discussion of the Semitic language regions that extend well beyond North Africa, into the Near East. In West and Central Africa, we find a huge number of languages; indeed, about one-quarter of *all* the languages of the world are found here, as well as some 85 per cent of all African varieties. The 325 languages of East Africa represent every African family. Most people, then, are multilingual – and yet most countries officially endorse only one or two languages (although post-apartheid South Africa recognizes 11). Realization of this simple fact alone is enough to suggest a great many intriguing linguistic questions, and several of the authors here argue that foundational work remains to be done in a great many quarters. More pointedly, they suggest that such work will revitalize and lead to re-examination of existing (largely American and European) conceptions of quite basic features ('speech community', 'dialect', and other central and elemental topics). Elsewhere in this part we are given useful discussions of Hebrew, that most famous of all 'revival' scenarios, and of Arabic, whose complexity within and across regions provided Ferguson with one of his four 'defining instances' of *diglossia*.

Given the richness of the Americas, Africa, Asia and the Pacific, it may seem a little unbalanced that there should be more chapters in the final part ('Europe') than in any of the others. Practically speaking, however, it is simply the case that European contexts have been much more thoroughly investigated. One of the interesting features in Part V is the reminder that a unique language is not always associated with a specific cultural identity: German, English, French, Spanish and other widely scattered varieties are each officially recognized in many parts of the world, and it is largely through dialectal variation that particular local stamps have been put on such 'large' languages. Another feature found across settings is the increasing clout of English; even national languages are susceptible here. The fact, for instance, that Irish is the only Celtic language with its own country does not mean that English has been halted at the customs post; and the ubiquitous presence of English in the Netherlands is also relevant here. We are also reminded in this part that national languages that now seem quite strong are typically recent developments: at the time of the French Revolution, for example, only half the population of *l'hexagone* – some say only one-third – spoke French. And 'seem' is apparently the key word here, at least in the minds of many francophones: a language that once grew and stretched through extensive borrowing is now marked by its insecurity in the face of English. Standardized Italian, too, is historically young, and several peninsular dialects remain important today. The Iberian region is also rich in dialectal variation (Valencian, Galician, and so on), but is perhaps most notable for the interplay of *languages* (Castilian, Basque, Catalan, Portuguese), a linguistic dynamic in which the minority varieties are very much stronger and better established than most of those elsewhere – but where, as in Eastern Europe, they had to endure a long period of political repression.

In Eastern Europe itself, sociolinguistic investigations are only now coming into their own, a consequence of the long-standing limitations imposed during the Soviet era. However, the linguistic and cultural richness of this region – and we can certainly include the Balkans, Russia and all the former Soviet satellite states here – suggests that many important insights can be expected in future. These do not all reflect favourable or desirable developments, by the way: post-Soviet and post-Yugoslavian nationalisms have not always been tolerant of cultural and linguistic diversity. Finally, mention should be made of the situation in the Baltic States, where newly-independent polities must grapple with large numbers of Russian speakers, relics, as it were, of earlier imperialist days. The tensions here are reflected chiefly at the level of language legislation, with its implications for rights and obligations in many public spheres – most importantly, perhaps, in education.

It is apparent, I hope, from this brief and selective overview that readers can expect a well-informed and timely assessment of the sociolinguistic and sociology-of-language situation in a large number of geographic settings. These are all of considerable intrinsic interest, but – as I have implied here – the treatments also reveal important and recurring themes. Every regional setting is unique, but the uniqueness does not rest upon the presence of cultural and linguistic elements found nowhere else; it rests, rather, upon the particular combinations and weightings of features that are, in fact, quite common around the world.

John Edwards
St Francis Xavier University
April 2009

Note

1 It is a little restrictive to suggest, as the author of Chapter 20 does, that the sociology of language is 'a field of study that investigates the effects that languages have on society'. Most scholars would argue for a more reciprocal relationship here, to say the least.

Introduction

Martin J. Ball

It is generally recognized that the term *sociolinguistics* was coined by Currie (1952) in an article exploring the relationship between speech and social status, which is of course still one of the main aims of the field (see Chambers 2002, for a fuller description of Currie's work). Currie's paper did not present any new data, but was basically a discussion of how some of the trends then present in linguistics, especially in dialectology, could be developed into a new field of investigation. Currie had correctly noted a trend in American dialectology where, unlike in Europe, work was not restricted to rural areas. It may be that the urban situation prompted more forcefully the realization of the importance of social factors. However this may be, McDavid (1948) published a study of postvocalic-r usage in South Carolina that contained information on social differences. At the time, this was not seen as an end in itself; McDavid comments, "A social analysis proved necessary because the data proved too complicated to be explained by merely a geographical statement" (ibid.: 194). This clearly implies that at this stage the social analysis was not the primary impetus behind the study; but this attitude gradually changed over the following fifteen years or so.

In the mid-1950s, attacks on the traditional methods of dialectology were being made by sociologists who had developed a refined methodology for sampling and investigating communities. Pickford (1956) particularly pointed out the use that such a methodology would be to dialectologists, criticizing their then current findings on grounds of lacking reliability and validity.

As reported in Petyt (1980), studies of urban communities became more frequent, including Putnam and O'Hern (1955) who investigated black speech in Washington, DC, De Camp (1958–59) who worked in San Francisco, and Levine and Crockett (1966) on North Carolina speech. This last study was conducted earlier than the publication date suggests, and showed considerable methodological advances over previous studies. Sampling and fieldwork techniques were more rigorously designed—taking into consideration the contributions of sociology—and this work laid down the framework for many future studies. Levine and Crockett found considerable variation in the use of postvocalic-r in North Carolina, and were able to correlate this variation with both linguistic and social factors—something that became a major concern in variationist sociolinguistics.

Another important paper of this period was Fischer (1958). He criticized the term *free variation* then in common use as an "explanation" for variable usage of certain linguistic features. He concluded that many examples of what was termed free variation were in fact "socially conditioned variants" (ibid.: 51).

Sociolinguistics came to a much greater degree of prominence (and, subsequently, popularity) within linguistics with the work of Labov in the mid-sixties. The work on Martha's Vineyard (Labov 1963) and in New York City (Labov 1966) developed and refined methodology and analysis, and laid the foundations for the explosion of research in this field.

Variationist sociolinguistics soon spread outside the United States, and Trudgill (1979) is a good example of the application of Labov's techniques, in this case to the city of Norwich in England. Moreover, the interests of sociolinguists also broadened from the more micro-level investigation correlating social and linguistic variables, to more macro-level concerns. These latter have included topics such as the areas of bi- and multi-lingualism together with diglossia and code-switching, language and culture, language and power/language and gender, language change, and language planning. This last area has become ever more important in recent times with the apparent threat of extinction to a large number of the world's languages (Crystal 2000), and within this topic we can also include the study of language obsolescence and death (research pioneered by Dorian 1981), and language revitalization (see Fishman 1991). Indeed, the breadth of interests in sociolinguistics is evidenced by the need recently for two large handbooks to be produced to provide current guides to the field: one in traditional sociolinguistics (Coulmas 1998) and the other in language variation and change (Chambers *et al.* 2002).

As it is now 50 or so years that scholars have been investigating the interaction of language and society under the heading of sociolinguistics, it is perhaps a good point at which to examine the current state of the art internationally. This collection does this, through a series of 33 chapters examining sociolinguistics around the world. The book is a survey of current and recent research trends in international sociolinguistics, rather than an account of regional and social dialects and patterns of language use in different countries. Each chapter, written by a leading authority in the region concerned, looks at current sociolinguistic research in that region. Traditional variationist sociolinguistics has been taken as the core of the subject, added to which are the areas of bi- and multilingualism together with diglossia and code-switching, language and culture, language and power, and language planning. It was decided to exclude the study of conversation/discourse and other areas more usually subsumed under the heading of pragmatics or discourse studies. The contents naturally differ from chapter to chapter, just as the research interests of different regions differ. It will also be noted that there are some lacunae. Some chapters deal primarily with just a few areas within a larger region; some regions have been omitted altogether. This reflects mostly the bias of where research has been conducted and so the gaps reflect geographical areas where sociolinguistic research has not been carried out, or where very little has been undertaken and no author could be found to write about it.

The aim of this book is to fill a gap in the sociolinguistics literature. There have been many studies of sociolinguistic variation in specific locales, volumes of sociolinguistic field-work, theory, and applications. However, there is no published single-volume collection surveying sociolinguistic work around the world. Furthermore, sociolinguistic studies published in languages other than English are often inaccessible to students and researchers in the anglophone world. Therefore, this collection will serve as an important tool to widen the perspective on sociolinguistics to readers of English.

References

Chambers, J. K. (2002) *Sociolinguistic Theory*, 2nd edn, Oxford: Blackwell.

Chambers, J. K., Trudgill, P. and Schilling-Estes, N. (eds.) (2002) *The Handbook of Language Variation and Change*, Oxford: Blackwell.

Coulmas, F. (ed.) (1998) *The Handbook of Sociolinguistics*, Oxford: Blackwell.

Crystal, D. (2000) *Language Death*, Cambridge: Cambridge University Press.

Currie, H. C. (1952) "A projection of sociolinguistics: the relationship of speech to social status," *The Southern Speech Journal*, 18, 28–37.

De Camp, D. (1958–59) "The pronunciation of English in San Francisco," *Orbis*, 7, 372–91; 8, 54–77.

Dorian, N. C. (1981) *Language Death: The Life Cycle of a Scottish Gaelic Dialect*, Philadelphia, PA: University of Pennsylvania Press.

Fischer, J. L. (1958) "Social influences on the choice of a linguistic variant," *Word*, 14, 47–56.

Fishman, J. A. (1991) *Reversing Language Shift*, Clevedon: Multilingual Matters.

Labov, W. (1963) "The social motivation of a sound change," *Word*, 19: 273–309. Revised as Chapter 1, in *Sociolinguistic Patterns*, Philadelphia, PA: University of Pennsylvania Press, 1972, pp. 1–42.

——(1966) *The Social Stratification of English in New York City*, Washington, DC: Center for Applied Linguistics.

Levine, L. and Crockett, H. (1966) "Speech variation in a Piedmont community: postvocalic-r," *Sociological Inquiry*, 36, 204–26.

McDavid, R. I. Jr. (1948) "Postvocalic /-r/ in South Carolina: a social analysis," *American Speech*, 23, 194–203.

Petyt, K. M. (1980) *The Study of Dialect: An Introduction to Dialectology*, London: André Deutsch.

Pickford, G. R. (1956) "American linguistic geography: a sociological approach," *Word*, 12, 211–33.

Putnam, G. N. and O'Hern, E. M. (1955) "The status significance of an isolated urban dialect," Supplement to *Language* (Language Dissertation 53).

Trudgill, P. (1979) *The Social Differentiation of English in Norwich*, Cambridge: Cambridge University Press.

Part I

The Americas

Sociolinguistics in the United States of America

Kirk Hazen

Introduction

In the US, sociolinguistics is not a single discipline guided by a coherent motivation towards a unified goal. Instead, it is a loose federation of fields examining the intersections of language and society. These fields are sampled in this chapter, drawing primarily from contemporary sociolinguistic journals. Some fields appear more prevalently in the US than perhaps in other countries. For example, variationist sociolinguistics, drawing from the influence of Labov (1963) and Weinreich, Labov, and Herzog (1968), has a major presence in the US. However, the focus in this chapter remains broad as handbooks exist on such specialties within sociolinguistics: For example, Chambers, Trudgill, and Schilling-Estes (2002) and Bayley and Lucas (2007) are overviews of the field of variationist sociolinguistics.

Numerous studies in this chapter push forward sociolinguistics by rebuilding theoretical frameworks laid decades earlier. For example, Eckert (2003) focuses on the concept of the "authentic speaker," the supposed "pure" vernacular speaker. Recognizing that sociolinguistics has been a fractured field since its inception, Bucholtz (2003) follows Eckert's article with a view that authenticity is often designed with nostalgia as the theme; for a remedy, she argues for a more self-reflective sociolinguistics.

Beyond surveying the vast sociolinguistic work conducted in the US,[1] the intent here is to provide some of Bucholtz's suggested reflection on the enterprise of sociolinguistics in the US. Its goals and progress should be regularly reassessed to provide the best possible scholarship for the two main focus areas, the sociolinguistics of society and the sociolinguistics of language (following Fasold 1987; 1990). This chapter is divided into these two broad sections.

Sociolinguistics of society

Region and dialectology

The touchstone work in modern dialectology is Labov, Ash, and Boberg (2006), as it provides a sketch of phonological differences for most of North America. Most other studies focus specifically on geographical locations. For example, Murray (2002) characterizes St. Louis as a Midwestern city containing both Southern and Northern features, although Murray does assert that it is developing a stronger Northern dialectological profile.

Most regional studies build from quality scholarship of past decades. In a reinvestigation of Labov's germinal study of Martha's Vineyard (1963), Blake and Josey (2003) provide a diachronic perspective on the /ay/ diphthong,[2] a pivotal vowel in Labov's argument for synchronic observation of diachronic processes. Labov (1963) correlated the raised variants of /ay/ and /aw/ with local identity[3] on the island and illustrated that the different generations demonstrated language change in progress. Blake and Josey argue that orientation to local culture has diminished in the interim, hence removing the oppositional identity behind marking /ay/ raising in Labov (1963). Pope, Meyerhoff, and Ladd (2007) provide a differing report on the status of Martha's Vineyard: They validate the inferencing of the apparent-time method and argue for the continuing robustness of social indexing for the (ay) and (aw) variables. Pope *et al.* find the social indexing of (ay) and (aw) on Martha's Vineyard to be very similar to what it was in the early 1960s.

Some variables have become staples of modern research. One is the low-back merger. In a sociophonetic study, Majors (2005) examines the merger (e.g. *caught~cot*) in Missouri speech, finding that it is an active sound change spreading in the region, although residents of St. Louis appear to be resisting the merger. Irons (2007) conducted acoustic analysis of the low-back merger in English for 114 native, nonurban Kentuckians. He proposes a profile of the region where the merger is expanding because of the glide loss of /ò/ in Southern US phonology. The same explanation could be applied to adjacent West Virginia, where Southern West Virginia speakers demonstrate a higher rate of merger than Northern West Virginia speakers despite the merger being complete in western Pennsylvania (Hazen 2005).

Another widely studied set of features is the Northern Cities Shift (e.g. Labov 1994; Labov *et al.* 2006). Evans (2004) investigates how the Northern Cities Shift affects the transplanted Appalachian variety in Ypsilanti, MI. She acoustically analyzes /æ/ raising for 28 speakers. Social network and sex were significant social factors, with women leading in /æ/ raising, as were less tightly integrated speakers. Labov and Baranowski (2006) investigated a component of the Northern Cities Shift where two vowels are on a collision course to see how close vowels can be and maintain a phonemic distinction. The means of duration for 48 speakers in the inland North were examined for /è/ and merged /o/. Overall, a 50 millisecond difference was a result of the word class itself and not simply phonetic factors. Gender differences were clearly shown in the backing and lowering of /è/, with women leading the change.

Contact across national borders is also recognized in the regional literature. Although contact with Canadians has supposedly transferred Canadian raising with /ai/ and /au/ to Vermont, Roberts (2007) finds the variability for these two vowels to suggest otherwise. In an acoustic analysis of 19 speakers, Roberts finds that /ai/ is influenced by both age and gender with the oldest males having the front central variants predominantly; younger speakers generally have a lowered variant. In addition, the /ai/ vowel does not follow the linguistic constraint of raising before only voiceless obstruents but instead is raised (not lowered) before all sounds.

Not all regional studies are phonetic in nature. Burkette (2007) investigates English in Ashe County, North Carolina, in the Appalachian mountains. She focuses on the use of conversational narrative to create community and display identity through the analysis of two grammatical variables: a-prefixing (*they said he's a-coming down*) and nonstandard past tense (*And they said he run till he dropped*). At the Northern end of Appalachia, Johnstone, Andrus, and Danielson (2006) examine the sociolinguistic history of Pittsburgh, Pennsylvania, using an intersectional analysis of historical records, ethnography, discourse analysis, and sociolinguistic interviews. They track the evolution of linguistic features from markers of social class to markers of "place." Taking up what most researchers refer to as the Northern Subject Rule (e.g. Hazen 2000a), José (2007) investigates the variable use of verbal −s with third-person plural subjects analyzed in Indiana and compared with varieties in Appalachia. Migration of features appears to be the case in José's data, as universalist explanations are rejected.

With the increasing recognition of diversity in African-American English, Charity (2007) investigates regional differences in low socioeconomic status of African-American children's speech. Charity utilized sentences primed with standard English features, which are often variable for African-American speakers, such as the omission of final consonants (e.g. *best* → *bes'*) or the copula (e.g. *She is pretty* → *she pretty*). New Orleans children were found to have higher vernacular rates than those in either Cleveland or Washington, DC.

Ethnicity

The most studied dialects in the US are the varieties spoken by African Americans. Accordingly, articles dealing with these varieties are referred to throughout this chapter. Although theoretical concerns arise in articles on ethnicity, US scholars are also concerned with applied results of their work. For example, Rickford, Sweetland, and Rickford (2004) provide an exhaustive bibliography of scholarship on education and African-American English and other vernaculars. For an overview of sociolinguistic work in education, including many articles involving ethnicity, see Hazen (2007b).

The areas of ethnic sociolinguistic study are now mature enough to receive quality summary articles reassessing progress made in recent decades. Thomas (2007) provides both a summary and detailed description of the phonological and phonetic characteristics of African-American Vernacular English (AAVE). He notes that the distribution of the scholarship is not evenly divided among the possible subfields of study and recommends areas where work is most critically needed.

The southeastern US is a frequently studied region for ethnic differences. Fridland (2003) examines /ai/ ungliding for African-American and European-American Southerners, specifically describing /ai/ ungliding in prevoiceless environments (e.g. *bike*). Most previous literature describes African-American communities avoiding ungliding in this environment. However, Fridland reveals that for her 30 speakers, glide weakening, rather than full monophthongization, is a regular feature regardless of ethnicity. She finds that African Americans have this feature in all phonetic environments.

In connection with the construction of identities, Sweetland (2002) investigates ethnic crossing through a case study of a 23-year-old white US female who consistently uses AAVE features. She argues for a reassessment of how academic linguists construe race, language, and crossing; Sweetland adopts a broader view of ideologies of the speaker (and other qualitative evidence) to assess whether crossing is viewed as authentic or not.

Over the past decade numerous investigations into the history of African-American English have been made (e.g. Kautzsch 2002). Mallinson and Wolfram (2002) investigate language variation patterns in an ethnically diverse Appalachian mountain enclave community. Their examination of diagnostic phonological and morphological variables from interviews with three African Americans reveals "that earlier African American English largely accommodated local dialects while maintaining a subtle, distinctive ethnolinguistic divide" (ibid.: 743).

Numerous studies have reexamined the development of AAVE in the US (e.g. Wolfram and Thomas 2002). Wolfram (2003) argues for the regional accommodation of earlier AAVEs which subsequently maintained a similar substrate of language variation patterns. He argues that the regional accommodation of AAVE has given way to younger generations moving towards more nationally generalized AAVE norms.

Dubois and Horvath (2003) study Creole African-American English in Louisiana. They focus on its maintenance of traditional language variation patterns in the face of massive sociocultural change: For example, the Creole African-American speakers have maintained glide reduction. Dubois and Horvath conclude that social intercourse has not changed significantly since the nineteenth century, and that only with speakers going off to college have social networks changed enough to alter language variation patterns.

Thomas and Carter (2006) examine prosodic rhythms of 20 African Americans and 20 European Americans from North Carolina. No significant difference was found between the two groups, with both being stress-timed. Their study provides a good overview and introduction to the study of prosodic rhythm for sociolinguists. They also examine ex-slave narratives and find them to be between stress-timed and syllable-timed, hence more similar to Jamaican English.

African-American English has had a broad influence on US culture. In an overview of the different studies of hip-hop language, Cutler (2007) explores what constructs *authenticity*, how identity is built with hip-hop language, and what local scenes the language represents. Cutler emphasizes that the study of hip-hop language is conducted by a range of disciplines, from cultural studies to musicology (see Alim 2004, for an extensive study).

Despite the emphasis on varieties of African-American English, the US is a diverse nation with a wide variety of ethnic dialects. The largest non-European-American ethnic group is the Latino community, and sociolinguists are increasingly recognizing this demographic fact. For example, Shenk (2007) examines how Mexican–American bilinguals use their linguistic resources to authenticate their ethnic identities. From the study of a friendship group, issues of authenticity of Mexicanness develop from the interaction of three topics: purity of bloodline, purity of nationality, and Spanish linguistic fluency. Shenk recognizes speakers' own ideologies in creating authentic ethnic practices.

At times, the interactions of different ethnic groups provide fertile ground for study. Reyes (2005) explains the strategies through which Asian-American teens employ African-American slang and the value of that slang. By closely examining metapragmatic discussions of slang, she finds that slang and identities constructed from its use are able to establish divisions, not only between generations, but also between different teenage groups.

US sociolinguists have also increasingly examined ethnicity of Native Americans. For example, Meek (2006) examines the linguistic features of "Hollywood Indian English" used to depict Native Americans in public media. Meek finds that it relies on grammatical features normally associated with "baby talk" and "foreigner talk." From these depictions, it is easy to see how they are covertly racist portrayals.

Sexuality and gender

The sociolinguistic study of sexuality is a burgeoning field and has made considerable strides in the past decade. The sociolinguistic study of language and gender continues to develop from its earlier days. Both can be examined as separate fields, but many scholars who examine one of them assess the role of the other.

Schilling-Estes (2002) provides an overview of the development and contemporary status of sociolinguistic gender research in the US. A wide range of diverse topics and methods fall under the umbrella of language and gender research: For example, working with written survey results, Fuller (2005) tracks the progression of the female title *Ms.* through the American lexicon.

Bucholtz and Hall (2004) debate the role of identity-based vs. desire-based research, arguing that such a binary choice restricts the possibilities in studying the sociolinguistics of sexuality. They argue that sexuality should be understood as a broad sociocultural phenomenon. The scholarship of language and sexuality ranges from studies of sexual orientation to that of eroticism, e.g. Del-Teso-Craviotto (2006) investigates the socio-linguistics of eroticism in online chat rooms. Studies of orientation and desire do not always focus on queer studies: e.g. Kiesling (2005) addresses how homosocial, as contrasted with homosexual, desire is created through men's language.

In reviewing the literature on perceptual language cues of sexual orientation, Munson and Babel (2007) address an idea widely believed by the general public. They do find that some speakers represent their sexual orientation through their speech, but that the phonetic parameters of homosexual or bisexual speech are not complete approximations of opposite-sex qualities. They also go further to discuss the implications from the literature for fields such as language acquisition and language processing.

In a study of gender in a Native American community, Innes (2006) investigates Muskogee women's linguistically active role in public spheres. Innes argues that what Muskogee women call "gossip" is a powerful genre for the culture since it maintains appropriate social behavior.

Herring and Paolillo (2006) explore the language interaction of gender and genre in blogs. In 127 entries from 44 blogs, they took up two subgenres of blogs, the *diary* and the *filter*.[4] Through a quantitative analysis of stylistic features, they found that the diaries contained more 'female' stylistic features, and the filters contained more 'male' stylistic features, regardless of author gender. Other gendered characteristics of traditional written and spoken genres did carry over into the blogs, demonstrating the fluid construction of gender among competing social forces.

Language change/age

In alignment with the roots of the field (Labov 1963; Weinreich *et al.* 1968), US socio-linguists continue to focus on language change within speech communities. This tradi-tion of examining diachronic variation through synchronic means remains a focus in the US. Additionally, researchers have begun to investigate the role age plays as a social factor (e.g. Rose 2006).

Innovations in recent research also develop from research on language change across the lifespan (see Sankoff and Blondeau 2007). For example, Cameron (2005) tracks the co-occurrence of age segregation and sex segregation throughout the life span of Puerto Rican Spanish speakers. He demonstrates that gender is constructed differently and fluidly across different spans of a person's life.

Wolfram, Carter, and Moriello (2004) examine newly established Hispanic popula-tions in North Carolina and the extent to which they accommodate to local norms. Through an instrumental acoustic analysis of the /ai/ diphthong, the authors study 18

11

speakers of Hispanic English to find no accommodation to a fully unglided vowel but glide weakening for the more rural Hispanic English speakers.

In looking at the transmission problem of language change, Jacewicz, Fox, and Salmons (2006) explore the role of prosodic prominence in chain shifts through regional acoustic analysis and perceptual experiments. Vowels in the most prominent prosodic positions require more effort; prominent vowels are consequently longer and have a greater frequency change over their duration. The authors find that emphatic productions are more prominent with women, and that correspondingly, their vowels are longer, more diphthongal, and rated as better, regardless of speaker or listener.

Continuing his work on language change over 40 years, Labov (2007) compares the transmission of linguistic change within a speech community to the diffusion across communities. He finds that transmission faithfully preserves the language variation patterns while diffusion does not. He concludes from this finding that the key difference between diffusion and transmission is the language learning abilities of children (transmission) versus adults (diffusion).

Community groupings

One recurring concern within sociolinguistics is how speakers group themselves in socially meaningful ways: Do our methodologies appropriately model those interactions? Accordingly, researchers focus on speech communities,[5] communities of practice, social networks, individuals, and other divisions (see Chambers *et al.* 2002).

Some researchers start with the basics. Beckett (2003) argues for a closer examination of individual variation when examining sociolinguistic variables across a speech community, using data from rural, Southern, African-American speakers. Carpenter and Hilliard (2005) also examine the relationship between the group and the individual in a study of four generations on Roanoke Island, NC.

Social networks are the focus of a study by Dodsworth (2005). Dodsworth develops an original network-based technique, attribute networking, to study 24 speakers of a suburb of Columbus, Ohio, through two variables: /l/ vocalization and the phonetic realization of the word *the* before vowels. For attribute networking, Dodsworth explains that "a critical assumption underlying attribute networking is that nodes or subsets of nodes which are structurally important in the aggregate network are the most salient aspects of social identity in the community" (ibid.: 229). Dodsworth aims to develop an improved approach to sociolinguistic variation which would "combine the interpretive power of subjective perceptions with the replicability of quantitative data" (ibid.: 226).

In examining Reform American Judaism, Levon (2006b) grapples with the concept of the *mosaic* identity of American Jews, that their identity as Jews is transformed because of multiple group affiliations conflicting with each other. By conducting an analysis of language style of two synagogue members, specifically focusing on word-final /t/, Levon finds that speakers compartmentalize their Jewish identity to contexts specifically set up to be Jewish. Benor (2001, 2004) also provides thorough analyses of Jewish speech styles, how they can be altered, and how they can be acquired.

Dodsworth (2008) adopts an alternative technique for establishing connections between individual language variation patterns and community social structures. She concludes that individuals do not negotiate style within a single model of society shared by all speakers. By making this move, Dodsworth takes the realistic approach that our language modules only connect to the social information in our minds (not the external world), and that our minds are not collectively aligned. For additional work on style, readers should consult Eckert and Rickford (2001).

Multilingualism

Although, from a historical perspective, US sociolinguistics has been predominantly focused on English, recent research has focused more evenly on other languages in the United States.

In an examination of the nature of lexical and structural borrowing, Brown (2003) studies bilingual morphemes in the speech of 22 French-English speakers. However, the balance between French and English has been shifting in Louisiana for each generation, and accordingly, the characteristics of English dominance have shifted over time. Her data of morphological reanalysis suggest that a complex interplay of competing grammars results from a shifting bilingual community.

Through participant observation, Barrett (2006) investigates how language ideology affects language interactions. He specifically focuses on a bilingual divide in Texas: English-speaking Anglo employees and their Spanish-speaking peers. Barrett finds that Spanish serves as a tool for solidarity and resistance for the Spanish speakers, but that the Anglo managers do not accommodate themselves to the Spanish-speaking employees. Instead the Anglo managers used English with scatterings of mock Spanish: When miscommunications occurred, the managers held the Spanish-speaking employees responsible. Barrett concludes that racial segregation and inequality are fostered by these competing functions.

The lexical boundaries between languages are a productive site for sociolinguistic research. Cacoullos and Aaron (2003) conduct a corpus study of New Mexican Spanish discourse to examine whether or not the use of single English words are nonce loans or code-switches. The authors demonstrate the utility of variationist methodology by demonstrating different grammatical conditions for New Mexican Spanish and English in the discourse, even though the rate of bare nouns is similar. They find that these items are loan words. Torres (2002) investigates the use of bilingual discourse markers in Brentwood, NY. She focuses on the integration of English discourse markers into Spanish narratives by English-dominant and Spanish-dominant Puerto Ricans. Examining 60 Spanish narratives, Torres takes up the difficult case of whether the English discourse markers are instances of code-switching or borrowing: She finds that they demonstrate a continuum of code-switching and borrowing, indicating a change in progress for New York Puerto Rican Spanish.

Flores-Ferrán (2004) examines subject personal pronouns in a contact variety of Puerto Rican residents of New York City through quantitative investigation of 41 speakers. Overall, the New York City speakers closely matched the variation found in Puerto Rico, despite the native-born New York City Puerto Ricans' use of explicit subject personal pronouns. Flores-Ferrán finds little evidence for an English contact hypothesis. In a review of the literature, Flores-Ferrán (2007) provides a summary of Spanish subject personal pronoun research since 1969.

Wolford (2006) focuses on spontaneous speech samples of 126 Latino students from Philadelphia and compares them to similar samples from 28 African-American students and 28 white students. She examined English variables including gender variation of third-person possessive personal pronouns (e.g. *her* for *his*), periphrastic *of* possessives (e.g. *the friend of my brother*), and attributive *−s* possessives (e.g. *my cousin house*). Wolford finds that speaker sex and origin of speaker (Mexico or Puerto Rico) were significant external factors. Girls favored periphrastic *of* and a subgroup of boys favored absence of possessive *–s*, and overall substrate effects from Spanish were mediated by social factors such as gender. She views contact between Puerto Rican and African Americans in Philadelphia as contributing to the social differences.

Social intersections and effects comprise one important component of multilingual studies. Lindemann (2002) provides an account of how negative attitudes towards nonnative speakers hinder communication. In a study of a map task involving 12 pairs of Koreans and Americans, Lindemann finds that the Americans with negative attitudes towards the Koreans engage in avoidance and problematizing strategies, in turn rating the communication as less successful. However, not all such interactions are negative. For example, Sunaoshi (2005) finds that despite the lack of cultural connections between Japanese and US Southern employees, they are able to find means to creatively use communicative resources to create meaning.

Major (2004) focuses on communicative competence for second language phonology in terms of gender and style. He studied phonological variables including palatalization, *of* reduction to /ë/, and /n/ assimilation in <can>. He also investigates (ING).[6] Forty-eight speakers of American English, Japanese, and Latin American Spanish were tested, and he found that nonnative speakers learn gender differences of the target language earlier than stylistic differences.

Queen (2004) provides a fascinating examination of an understudied area in sociolinguistics, the area of translation. Queen discusses what is possible by means of a sociolinguistic analysis of translations of African-American English into German films. She finds that the concepts are transferable to the extent that the cultures contain similar organizations of ideas. Through the study of African-American English dialogue of 32 films, Queen finds that stylistic variation in the original films is erased in dubbed film, as are regional differences. She notes that urban youth-street culture is indexed in dubbed films, and therefore concludes that this trait is shared across national borders.

Perception studies

In sociolinguistics in the US, researchers often employ perception studies to estimate how listeners interpret social factors. Perceptual studies are a methodological choice, but they are grouped in this chapter under social factors since most US sociolinguists who use them do so to study social factors, working mostly with regional divisions and sexual orientation. Following in the footsteps of Preston (1999), Benson (2003) analyzes folk perceptions to address the question of US dialect boundaries, providing a more complete picture of speech communities: for example, perceptual studies show that Ohioans from central and northwestern Ohio want to maintain a nonSouthern identity.

Fridland, Bartlett, and Kreuz (2004) investigate perceptual differences for Southerners from Memphis, TN, through vowel formant positions. Focusing on the difference between front vowel shifts vs. back vowel shifts, they examine whether or not listeners are more perceptually aware of changes in which they are participating. Their results suggest "that there is a degree of correlation between productive and perceptual aspects of vowel quality" (ibid.: 13). They conclude that listeners make judgments based on minor phonetic cues and that speakers' productive and perceptual systems are tightly connected.

Clopper and Pisoni (2004) examined forced-choice perception tests where listeners with greater dialect experience—having lived in three or more states—performed better than those who had lived in only one state. In addition, they found that residents of an area significantly outperformed nonresidents across all dialect regions. Clopper and Pisoni (2006) find that listeners could make the large divisions between dialect varieties (Northeastern, Southern, Western) but not smaller subdivisions. Naïve listeners correctly categorized speakers with 26 percent overall accuracy. Familiarity with the dialect variety, as a result of mobility, increased the listeners' ability to distinctively distinguish varieties. Clopper and Pisoni (2006) emphasize that having category labels for the different varieties made a crucial difference for listeners.

Bucholtz, Bermudez, Fung, Edwards, and Vargas (2007) conducted the first detailed perceptual dialectological study of California. They find that the most salient linguistic boundary is between the northern and southern regions, although, reminiscent of Clopper and Pisoni (2006), category labels ranging from "surfers" to "hicks" played a role in the social map.

By digesting many studies on perception of African-American and European-American voices, Thomas and Reaser (2004) induce that Americans can accurately recognize the ethnicity of a speaker, even in the absence of stereotypical morphosyntactic features. They provide a high quality review of the literature, and sociolinguists working with this topic should start with this article to assess the previous literature. To approach an answer to the question of what cues listeners do use to identify ethnicity, Thomas and Reaser conducted an experiment involving features of a European-American vernacular from Hyde County, North Carolina (see Wolfram and Thomas 2002). They included 24 speakers in all: 12 African Americans and 6 European Americans from Hyde County and 6 other inland speakers. Thomas and Reaser (2004) demonstrate that African Americans with atypical features are difficult for listeners to identify.

In a study of men's speech, Levon (2006a) presents the results of an experiment designed to elucidate what people listen to in determining a speaker's sexuality. He found that altering the phonetic qualities of the variables, pitch range and syllable duration, was insufficient to change listeners' perceptions, but he also found that perceptions of sexuality are ideologically linked to perceptions of personality and personhood.

Sociolinguistics of language

Phonology and phonetics

The realm of phonology has been productive for US sociolinguistics (e.g. Labov 1994, 2001; Labov *et al.* 2006), and numerous works mentioned throughout this chapter contain phonetic and phonological analyses because they allow for fine-grained linguistic tools to explore social factors. In addition, the complexity of phonology lends itself to detailed accounts of language variation in the mind.

Podesva (2007) contributes to sociophonetics by investigating voice quality through the examination of falsetto phonation. In a case study of one gay, male, US English speaker, Podesva finds that the social context, and hence the construction of style and speaker identity, modulate falsetto phonation which is more frequent, longer, and characterized by higher fundamental frequency (f0) levels and wider f0 ranges. Podesva bridges a wide range of disciplines by connecting sociophonetics with the social construction of meaning in discourse by situating phonetic forms in their discursive contexts.

15

Raymond, Dautricourt, and Hume (2006) perform a highly detailed quantitative account of word internal /t,d/ deletion, using linguistic and extra-linguistic variables. They found influences from speech rate, fluency, word form and word predictability, prominence, and aspects of local phonological process. They conclude that word-internal deletion is not a single event, but two different linguistic processes: In syllable onsets, it is gestural lenition; in syllable codas, deletion of /t,d/ was sensitive to segmental context. Overall, word internal deletion was widespread.

Morphology and syntax

Some sociolinguistic studies focus on morphological and syntactic language variation patterns. Within African-American English, these linguistic factors have been the primary areas of study (Thomas 2007), but this trend has not been true for other varieties.

Bayley, Lucas, and Rose (2002) examine American Sign Language variation in the l-handshape[7] with more than 5,000 tokens across the United States. This language variation pattern is conditioned by multiple social and linguistic factors, including grammatical function and preceding and following segments, although assimilation is a second order constraint to grammatical function. Importantly, on the social-theoretical front, signers of every region of the US demonstrate similar language variation patterns with the l-handshape and thus can be seen as a single, albeit geographically discontinuous, speech community.

Yaeger-Dror, Hall-Lew, and Deckert (2002) find speech community and register to be important domains of variation for *not* contraction. *Not*-contraction (e.g. *isn't*) was favored in the North and Aux-contraction (e.g. *is not* → *'s not*) was favored in the Southeast and Southwest. Trüb (2006) conducts a corpus investigation into writings by Southern plantation overseers, dissecting the linguistic constraints on verbal paradigms. She finds that the patterning of idiolects has to be kept in consideration when interpreting the results from the group.

Weldon (2003) takes up the study of the copula in the Creolist debate of AAVE. She quantitatively analyzes copula variability in Gullah, a creole of the Sea Islands of South Carolina. Gullah demonstrates high rates of the zero form in all subject environments, but for first-person singular subjects, the zero form and *'m* are evenly distributed, a traditional creole trait. For Gullah, deletion is a strictly grammatical process. It should be noted that phonological constraints on copula absence in the US are present in some communities but not others (Hazen 2000b, 2004; Dannenberg 2002). Although not all of her results show statistically significant differences, the patterning of the grammatical constraint mirrors those of AAVE, and Weldon (2003) sees these patterns as supporting the Creolist hypothesis.

Angermeyer and Singler (2003) take up the prescriptivist saw of case and NP position in phrases such as *me and you* (as subject) and *between you and I*. Through a sociolinguistic experiment and observation of television usage, Angermeyer and Singler find three separate and stable patterns: a vernacular pattern (*me and X*), a standard pattern (*X and me*); and a polite form (*X and I*). The distribution of these patterns appears to have been stable for four centuries.

Lexicon

Since its early connections with dialectology (Hazen 2007a), sociolinguistics in the US has maintained a concern for changes in lexical usage. However, given the complexity of human language, numerous studies concentrating on lexical items also must contend with phonological, morphosyntactic, and social influences which guide the choice of some words over others.

Some of lexical studies are focused on shifts in the usage of specific words away from traditional denotations. Henderson (2003) explores the difficulties of treating ethnic slurs in dictionaries, highlighting the special status editors give the word *nigger*. In a study with a narrow focus but wide appeal, and drawing from sources ranging from media to student surveys, Kiesling (2004) investigates the word *dude* and finds that the "casual and cool stance" of *dude* plays an important role in some men's homosociality in the US.

Baranowski (2002) focuses on current usage of epicene pronouns in American and British English. He provides a thorough review of previous research and then explores the prevalence of gender-neutral *he*, singular *they*, and the collocation *he or she* in two written corpora. Baranowski finds that the traditional *he* is no longer predominant, but instead that singular *they* has taken its place. American writers were also found to be more conservative than their British counterparts.

Frequently studied lexical changes involve the system of quotatives. Buchstaller (2006) provides a concise yet comprehensive overview of quotative studies before comparing *be like* and *go* in US and British English. She argues that the verb *go* is not new to the quotative system and has been rendered as either prominent or not depending on local trends. Buchstaller further finds that *be like* is not replacing *go* but instead suggests that social psychological factors might explain the variation in the data. In the study of a computerized corpus of quotatives, Barbieri (2007) examines the effect of sex and speaker age on the performance *be like*, *go*, *be all*, and *say* in modern, spoken American English. She finds that sex differences are more vigorous for those under 40, with age negatively correlated with use of *be like* for women. The same finding was not true for men. Equally valuable in Barbieri's (2007) study is the summary of previous studies of quotatives. Cukor-Avila (2002) investigates quotatives in African-American Vernacular English in east-central Texas. She finds that adolescents are propagating the form *be like* in all quotative contexts, but that the grammatical and discourse constraints remain constant.

Mental grammar and language acquisition

One of the accomplishments of modern sociolinguistics is that other, more traditional fields of linguistics have begun to study language variation from their particular perspectives (see Hazen 2007a). Here, the three works exemplified focus on language acquisition and the organization of the mental grammar.

Bybee (2002) promotes the exemplar model to demonstrate how frequency effects can account for how rapidly an ongoing change progresses. In examining /t,d/ deletion, Bybee challenges models of language change employing underlying phonemic forms and the constraints of bound morphemes for /t,d/ deletion. By detailing how sociolinguistic information might be stored in the lexicon, Bybee (2007) further contributes to knowledge of the mental grammar.

Gahl and Garnsey (2004) examine the interaction of grammar and usage, reporting a case of pronunciation variation that reflects contextual probabilities of syntactic structures. Their results are consistent with the notion that knowledge of grammar includes knowledge of probabilities of syntactic structures, and that this knowledge affects language production.

In reassessment of language acquisition, Clark and Wong (2002) argue for the importance of pragmatics in the acquisition of the lexicon. Through both linguistic and non-linguistic means, adults offer language-acquiring children pragmatic directions on every level of language use. Direct offers of lexical information are important at early stages, and children use this directly offered pragmatic information in their attention to lexical meanings and relations. Working from evidence drawn from experimental results and natural conversation, Clark and Wong present this pragmatic view as an alternative to constraint-based accounts of lexical acquisition.

Pragmatics, discourse, and conversation

In recent work, perhaps the most productive area of linguistics for sociolinguists is the study of language "above the sentence." The fields of pragmatics and discourse analysis have produced articles stemming from diverse methodologies on an extensive range of topics.

Through the study of discourse, scholars have expanded the repertoire of what factors can constitute "society." Modan (2002) develops an argument of how the conceptualized notion of space can be rendered as a sociolinguistic battlefield for those in authority. In examining a discussion of public discourse about public toilets, Modan finds that the authoritative powers use language practices such as presupposition, deixis, and contrast between the "core" of the community and those on the fringes. These practices are coupled with themes of filth and geography to create a moral space to locate core members of the community and immigrant members.

Politicized speech is another area of concentration for sociolinguists. Duranti (2006) conducts discourse analysis of a California Congressional campaign, focusing on semantic, pragmatic, and discursive strategies. These strategies—"(i) constructing a narrative of belonging; (ii) casting the present as a natural extension of the past; and (iii) exposing potential contradictions in order to show how to solve them"—are found to be more prevalent of candidates who cast themselves as "independent". Other forms of political speech are analyzed when Gaudio (2003) argues against any "natural" privileging of conversation over other speech forms. Through analysis of the conflation of space, capitalism, conversation, and coffeehouses, Gaudio argues that purportedly ordinary conversations "are inextricably implicated in the political, economic, and cultural-ideological processes of global capitalism" (ibid.: 659).

A more traditional technique of analysis is the discourse marker, which has been used for both ethnic and gender analysis. Wharry (2003) studies discourse markers of African-American English in sermons. Fuller (2005) examines the colloquial use of *like* with an eye to sociolinguistically describing its semantic and pragmatic characteristics. Fuller finds that discourse *like* responds to the interactional needs of the speaker, being employed to mark both focus and inexactness.

Some sociolinguistic studies adjoin other fields of communication studies by examining rhetoric and trends in media. In the analysis of American TV shows, Richardson (2006) investigates the sociolinguistic representation of the rhetorical act of 'spin' in *The West Wing*. In another study of a popular TV show, Tagliamonte and Roberts (2005) examine the use of intensifier *so* in *Friends* between 1994 and 2002. They examined both the variable in real time, over the duration of the show, and tested the viability of using media data as a surrogate for "real-world" data. They conclude that media data accurately reflected the trends found throughout North America.

Framing in discourse is the focus for Gordon (2002) when she investigates role reversal of a mother–daughter conversational dyad. These speakers maintain multiple and overlapping frames which connect back to their shared experiences. These frames carry different metamessages, such as *play* vs. *real life* or the footing of the participants. Gordon also illustrates how prior texts can be material for framing.

Schiffrin (2002) analyzes the life story of one Holocaust survivor to locate and explicate two sets of relationships: one with the mother and one with a collective of friends. Schiffrin demonstrates how life-stories place local relations within more archetypal roles such as victim, survivor, or bystander. Schiffrin's article also provides a richly textured view of how powerful events echo through sociolinguistic variation.

In an innovative study, Keating and Mirus (2003) examine how the internet shapes language practice in the Deaf community. As the authors remark, "For the first time, deaf people can communicate using manual visual language, in many cases their native language, across space and time zones" (ibid.: 693). Keating and Mirus find that signers transform their normal communication practices through trial and error, often limiting sign space, altering the production of signs, slowing signing speed down, and layering redundancy. They conclude that signers now have a new frontier to explore and in which to develop new genres of signing.

Conclusion

The breadth of research topics and research methods covered in this chapter illustrates the plethora of fields in the US. From acoustic phonetics to discourse analysis, US sociolinguists employ the entire repertoire of modern linguistic methodology to English, Spanish, ASL, and other languages. In the future, sociolinguistic scholars in their disparate subfields should attempt to understand the roots of their differences and emphasize their common goals to ensure efficient research with the limited resources available to us. By examining our current state and evaluating the research outside of our own sub-specialties, we can construct a fuller, more connected body of scholarship in order to understand the ways in which we, as humans, use language.

Notes

1 Most likely, a similar survey of modern US sociolinguistic research could be written with a completely different set of references, and thus works cited herein should not be seen as the sum total of US research.
2 The vowel labels and the ethnicity labels are the ones used by the authors cited in this chapter, and they fluctuate therefore from study to study.
3 For a reinterpretation of local identity, see Hazen (2002).
4 Filters are blogs which pull content from the internet into specific categories (e.g. politically filtered blogs), sometimes with commentary.
5 Speech communities are often discussed in perceptual sociolinguistic studies (see below).
6 Majors identifies (ING) as a phonological variable (morphophonological in a footnote), but other researchers have found it to be strictly a morphological variable (Labov 2001; Hazen 2008), although it is certainly socially sensitive.
7 The 1-handshape is the use of the hand with the index finger extended and the others closed. This handshape is used in the first person singular pronoun and can be altered in numerous ways (e.g. more than one finger can be extended). See for a demonstration: http://commtechlab.msu.edu/sites/aslweb/O/W2608.htm.

19

References

Alim, H. S. (2004) *You Know My Steez: An Ethnographic and Sociolinguistic Study of Style Shifting in a Black American Speech Community*, Publications of the American Dialect Society, 89, Durham, NC: Duke University Press.

Angermeyer, P. S. and Singler, J. V. (2003) "The case for politeness: pronoun variation in co-ordinate NPs in object position in English," *Language Variation and Change*, 15, 171–210.

Baranowski, M. (2002) "Current usage of the epicene pronoun in written English," *Journal of Sociolinguistics*, 6, 378–97.

Barbieri, F. (2007) "Older men and younger women: a corpus-based study of quotative use in American English," *English World-Wide*, 28, 23–45.

Barrett, R. (2006) "Language ideology and racial inequality: competing functions of Spanish in an Anglo-owned Mexican restaurant," *Language in Society*, 35, 163–204.

Bayley, R. and Lucas, C. (2007) *Sociolinguistic Variation: Theories, Methods, and Applications*, New York: Cambridge University Press.

Bayley, R., Lucas, C. and Rose, M. (2002) "Phonological variation in American Sign Language: the case of l handshape," *Language Variation and Change*, 14, 19–54.

Beckett, D. (2003) "Sociolinguistic individuality in a remnant dialect community," *Journal of English Linguistics*, 31, 3–33.

Benor, S. (2001) "The learned /t/: phonological variation in Orthodox Jewish English," in T. Sanchez and D. Johnson (eds.) *Penn Working Papers in Linguistics: Selected Papers from NWAV 29*, Philadelphia, PA: University of Pennsylvania Linguistics, pp. 1–16.

——(2004) "Second style acquisition: language and newly orthodox Jews," unpublished PhD dissertation, Stanford University, CA.

Benson, E. (2003) "Folk linguistic perceptions and the mapping of dialect boundaries," *American Speech*, 78, 307–30.

Blake, R. and Josey, M. (2003) "The /ay/ diphthong in a Martha's Vineyard community: what can we say 40 years after Labov?" *Language in Society*, 32: 451–85.

Brown, B. (2003) "Code-convergent borrowing in Louisiana French," *Journal of Sociolinguistics*, 7, 3–23.

Bucholtz, M. (2003) "Sociolinguistic nostalgia and the authentification of identity," *Journal of Sociolinguistics*, 7, 398–416.

Bucholtz, M., Bermudez, N., Fung, V., Edwards, L. and Vargas, R. (2007) "Hella Nor Cal or totally So Cal? The perceptual dialectology of California," *Journal of English Linguistics*, 35, 325–52.

Bucholtz, M. and Hall, K. (2004) "Theorizing identity in language and sexuality research," *Language in Society*, 33, 469–515.

Buchstaller, I. (2006) "Diagnostics of age-graded linguistic behaviour: the case of the quotative system," *Journal of Sociolinguistics*, 10, 3–30.

Burkette, A. (2007) "Constructing identity: grammatical variables and the creation of a community voice," *Journal of Sociolinguistics*, 11, 286–96.

Bybee, J. (2002) "Word frequency and context of use in the lexical diffusion of phonetically conditioned sound change," *Language Variation and Change*, 14, 261–90.

——(2007) "From usage to grammar: the mind's response to repetition," *Language*, 82, 711–33.

Cacoullos, R. T. and Aaron, J. E. (2003) "Bare English-origin nouns in Spanish: rates, constraints, and discourse functions," *Language Variation and Change*, 15, 289–328.

Cameron, R. (2005) "Aging and gendering," *Language in Society*, 34, 23–61.

Carpenter, J. and Hilliard, S. (2005) "Shifting parameters of individual and group variation African American English on Roanoke Island," *Journal of English Linguistics*, 33, 161–84.

Chambers, J., Trudgill, P. and Schilling-Estes, N. (2002) *The Handbook of Language Variation and Change*, Malden, MA: Blackwell.

Charity, A. H. (2007) "Regional differences in low SES African-American children's speech in the school setting," *Language Variation and Change*, 19, 281–93.

Clark, E. V. and Wong, A. D. W. (2002) "Pragmatic directions about language use: offers of words and relations," *Language in Society*, 31, 181–212.

Clopper, C. G. and Pisoni, D. B. (2004) "Homebodies and army brats: some effects of early linguistic experience and residential history on dialect categorization," *Language Variation and Change*, 16, 31–48.

——(2006) "Effects of region of origin and geographic mobility on perceptual dialect categorization," *Language Variation and Change*, 18, 193–221.

Cukor-Avila, P. (2002) "She say, she go, she be like: verbs of quotation over time in African American Vernacular English," *American Speech*, 77, 3–31.

Cutler, C. (2007) "Hip-hop language in sociolinguistics and beyond," *Language and Linguistics Compass*, 1, 519–38.

Dannenberg, C. (2002) *Sociolinguistic Constructs of Ethnic Identity: The Syntactic Delineation of Lumbee English*, Durham, NC: Duke University Press.

Del-Teso-Craviotto, M. (2006) "Language and sexuality in Spanish and English dating chats," *Journal of Sociolinguistics*, 10, 460–80.

Dodsworth, R. (2005) "Attribute networking: a technique for modeling social perceptions," *Journal of Sociolinguistics*, 9, 225–53.

——(2008) "Sociological consciousness as a component of linguistic variation," *Journal of Sociolinguistics*, 12, 34–57.

Dubois, S. and Horvath, B. M. (2003) "The English vernacular of the Creoles in Louisiana," *Language Variation and Change*, 15, 255–88.

Duranti, A. (2006) "Narrating the political self in a campaign for U.S. Congress," *Language in Society*, 35, 467–97.

Eckert, P. (2003) "Sociolinguistics and authenticity: an elephant in the room," *Journal of Sociolinguistics*, 7, 392–97.

Eckert, P. and Rickford, J. R. (2001) *Style and Sociolinguistic Variation*, New York: Cambridge University Press.

Evans, B. (2004) "The role of social network in the acquisition of local dialect norms by Appalachian migrants in Ypsilanti, Michigan," *Language Variation and Change*, 16, 153–66.

Fasold, R. W. (1987) *The Sociolinguistics of Society*, Cambridge, MA: Blackwell.

——(1990) *The Sociolinguistics of Language*, Cambridge, MA: Blackwell.

Flores-Ferrán, N. (2004) "Spanish subject personal pronoun use in New York City Puerto Ricans: can we rest the case of English contact?" *Language Variation and Change*, 16, 49–73.

——(2007) "A bend in the road: subject personal pronoun expression in Spanish after 30 years of sociolinguistic research," *Language and Linguistics Compass*, 1, 624–52.

Fridland, V. (2003) "'Tie, tied, and tight': the expansion of /ai/ monophthongization of African-American and European-American speech in Memphis, Tennessee," *Journal of Sociolinguistics*, 7, 279–98.

Fridland, V., Bartlett, K. and Kreuz, R. (2004) "Do you hear what I hear? Experimental measurement of the perceptual salience of acoustically manipulated vowel variants by Southern speakers in Memphis, TN," *Language Variation and Change*, 16, 1–16.

Fuller, J. (2005) "The use and meanings of the female title Ms.," *American Speech*, 80, 180–206.

Gahl, S. and Garnsey, S. M. (2004) "Knowledge of grammar, knowledge of usage: syntactic probabilities affect pronunciation variation," *Language*, 80, 748–75.

Gaudio, R. P. (2003) "Coffeetalk: Starbucks™ and the commercialization of casual conversation," *Language in Society*, 32, 659–91.

Gordon, C. (2002) "'I'm Mommy and you're Natalie': role-reversal and embedded frames in mother–child discourse," *Language in Society*, 31, 679–720.

Hazen, K. (2000a) "Subject–verb concord in a post-insular dialect: the gradual persistence of dialect patterning," *Journal of English Linguistics*, 28, 127–44.

——(2000b) *Identity and Ethnicity in the Rural South: A Sociolinguistic View Through Past and Present Be*, Publications of the American Dialect Society No. 83, Durham, NC: Duke University Press.

——(2002) "Identity and language variation in a rural community," *Language*, 78, 240–57.

——(2004) "Some cases for the syllable in Southern English," *Southern Journal of Linguistics* 28, 164–80.

21

——(2005) "Mergers in the mountains," *English World Wide*, 26, 199–221.

——(2007a) "The study of variation in historical perspective," in R. Bayley and C. Lucas (eds.) *Sociolinguistic Variation: Theory, Methods, and Applications*, Cambridge: Cambridge University Press, pp. 70–89.

——(2007b) "Variationist approaches to language and education," in N. Hornberger and K. King (eds.) *The Encyclopedia of Language and Education*, 2nd edn, vol. 10, *Research Methods in Language and Education*, Berlin: Springer, pp. 85–98.

——(2008) "'ING': a vernacular baseline for English in Appalachia," *American Speech*, 83, 116–40.

Henderson, A. (2003) "What is in a slur?," *American Speech*, 78, 52–74.

Herring, S. C. and Paolillo, J. C. (2006) "Gender and genre variation in weblogs," *Journal of Sociolinguistics*, 10, 439–59.

Innes, P. (2006) "The interplay of genres, gender, and language ideology among the Muskogee," *Language in Society*, 35, 231–59.

Irons, T. L. (2007) "On the status of low back vowels in Kentucky English: more evidence of merger," *Language Variation and Change*, 19, 137–80.

Jacewicz, E., Fox, R. and Salmons, J. (2006) "Prosodic prominence effects on vowels in chain shifts," *Language Variation and Change*, 18, 285–316.

Johnstone, B., Andrus, J. and Danielson, A. E. (2006) "Mobility, indexicality, and the enregisterment of 'Pittsburghese'," *Journal of English Linguistics*, 34, 77–104.

José, B. (2007) "Appalachian English in southern Indiana? The evidence from verbal -s," *Language Variation and Change*, 19, 249–80.

Kautzsch, A. (2002) *The Historical Evolution of Earlier African American English*, New York: Walter de Gruyter.

Keating, E. and Mirus, G. (2003) "American Sign Language in virtual space: interactions between deaf users of computer-mediated video communication and the impact of technology on language practices," *Language in Society*, 32, 693–714.

Kiesling, S. F. (2004) "Dude," *American Speech*, 79, 281–305.

——(2005) "Homosocial desire in men's talk: balancing and re-creating cultural discourses of masculinity," *Language in Society*, 34, 695–726.

Labov, W. (1963) "The social motivation of language change," *Word*, 19, 273–309.

——(1994) *Principles of Linguistic Change*, Vol. I, Oxford: Blackwell.

——(2001) *Principles of Linguistic Change*, Vol. II, Oxford: Blackwell.

——(2007) "Transmission and diffusion," *Language*, 83, 344–87.

Labov, W., Ash, S. and Boberg, C. (2006) *Atlas of North American English*, The Hague: Mouton de Gruyter.

Labov, W. and Baranowski, M. (2006) "50 msec," *Language Variation and Change*, 18, 223–40.

Levon, E. (2006a) "Hearing 'gay': prosody, interpretation, and the affective judgments of men's speech," *American Speech*, 81, 56–78.

——(2006b) "Mosaic identity and style: phonological variation among Reform American Jews," *Journal of Sociolinguistics*, 10, 181–204.

Lindemann, S. (2002) "Listening with an attitude: a model of native-speaker comprehension of non-native speakers in the United States," *Language in Society*, 31, 419–41.

Major, R. C. (2004) "Gender and stylistic variation in second language phonology," *Language Variation and Change*, 16, 169–88.

Majors, T. (2005) "Low back vowel merger in Missouri speech: acoustic description and explanation," *American Speech*, 80, 165–79.

Mallinson, C. and Wolfram, W. (2002) "Dialect accommodation in a bi-ethnic mountain enclave community: more evidence on the development of African American," *Language in Society*, 31, 743–75.

Meek, B. A. (2006) "And the Injun goes 'How!': representations of American Indian English in white public space," *Language in Society*, 35, 93–128.

Modan, G. (2002) "Public toilets for a diverse neighborhood: spatial purification practices in community development discourse," *Journal of Sociolinguistics*, 6, 487–513.

Munson, B. and Babel, M. (2007) "Loose lips and silver tongues, or, projecting sexual orientation through speech," *Language and Linguistics Compass*, 1, 416–49.

Murray, T. E. (2002) "Language variation and change in the urban Midwest: the case of St. Louis," *Language Variation and Change*, 14, 347–61.

Podesva, R. J. (2007) "Phonation type as a stylistic variable: the use of falsetto in constructing a persona," *Journal of Sociolinguistics*, 11, 478–504.

Pope, J., Meyerhoff, M. and Ladd, R. D. (2007) "Forty years of language change on Martha's Vineyard," *Language*, 83, 615–27.

Preston, D. (1999) *Handbook of Perceptual Dialectology*, Amsterdam: Benjamins.

Queen, R. (2004) "'Du hast jar keene Ahnung': African American English dubbed into German," *Journal of Sociolinguistics*, 8, 515–37.

Raymond, W. D., Dautricourt, R. and Hume, E. (2006) "Word-internal /t,d/ deletion in spontaneous speech: modeling the effects of extra-linguistic, lexical, and phonological factors," *Language Variation and Change*, 18, 55–98.

Reyes, A. (2005) "Appropriation of African American slang by Asian American youth," *Journal of Sociolinguistics*, 9, 509–32.

Richardson, K. (2006) "The dark arts of good people: how popular culture negotiates 'spin' in NBC's *The West Wing*," *Journal of Sociolinguistics*, 10, 52–69.

Rickford, J. R., Sweetland, J. and Rickford, A. E. (2004) "African American English and other vernaculars in education: a topic-coded bibliography," *Journal of English Linguistics*, 32, 230–320.

Roberts, J. (2007) "Vermont lowering? Raising some questions about /ai/ and /au/ south of the Canadian border," *Language Variation and Change*, 19, 181–97.

Rose, M. (2006) "Language, place and identity in later life," unpublished PhD dissertation, Stanford University.

Sankoff, G. and Blondeau, H. (2007) "Language change across the lifespan, /r/ in Montreal French," *Language*, 83, 560–88.

Schiffrin, D. (2002) "Mother and friends in a Holocaust life story," *Language in Society*, 31, 309–53.

Schilling-Estes, N. (2002) "American English social dialect variation and gender," *Journal of English Linguistics*, 30, 122–37.

Shenk, P. S. (2007) " 'I'm Mexican, remember?' Constructing ethnic identities via authenticating discourse," *Journal of Sociolinguistics*, 11, 194–220.

Sunaoshi, Y. (2005) "Historical context and intercultural communication: interactions between Japanese and American factory workers in the American South," *Language in Society*, 34, 185–217.

Sweetland, J. (2002) "Unexpected but authentic use of an ethnically-marked dialect," *Journal of Sociolinguistics*, 6, 514–36.

Tagliamonte, S. and Roberts, C. (2005) "So weird; so cool; so innovative: the use of intensifiers in the television series 'Friends'," *American Speech*, 80, 280–300.

Thomas, E. R. (2007) "Phonological and phonetic characteristics of African American Vernacular English," *Language and Linguistics Compass*, 1, 450–75.

Thomas, E. R. and Carter, P. M. (2006) "Prosodic rhythm and African American English," *English World-Wide*, 27, 331–55.

Thomas, E. R. and Reaser, J. (2004) "Delimiting perceptual cues used for the ethnic labeling of African American and European American voices," *Journal of Sociolinguistics*, 8, 54–87.

Torres, L. (2002) "Bilingual discourse markers in Puerto Rican Spanish," *Language in Society*, 31, 65–83.

Trüb, R. (2006) "Nonstandard verbal paradigms in earlier white Southern American English," *American Speech*, 81, 250–65.

Weinreich, U., Labov, W. and Herzog, M. (1968) "Empirical foundations for a theory of language change," in W. Lehmann and Y. Malkiel (eds.) *Directions for Historical Linguistics*, Austin, TX: University of Texas Press, pp. 95–188.

Weldon, T. L. (2003) "Copula variability in Gullah," *Language Variation and Change*, 15, 37–72.

Wharry, C. (2003) "Amen and hallelujah preaching: discourse functions in African American sermons," *Language in Society*, 32, 203–25.

Wolford, T. E. (2006) "Variation in the expression of possession by Latino children," *Language Variation and Change*, 18, 1–14.

Wolfram, W. (2003) "Reexamining the development of African American English: evidence from isolated communities," *Language*, 79, 282–316.

Wolfram, W., Carter, P. and Moriello, B. (2004) "Emerging Hispanic English: new dialect formation in the American South," *Journal of Sociolinguistics*, 8, 339–58.

Wolfram, W. and Thomas, E. R. (2002) *The Development of African American English*, Oxford: Blackwell.

Yaeger-Dror, M., Hall-Lew, L. and Deckert, S. (2002) "*It's not* or *isn't it*? Using large corpora to determine the influences on contraction strategies," *Language Variation and Change*, 14, 79–116.

2

Sociolinguistics in Canada

Elaine Gold

Introduction

Canada, a vast country with a relatively small population, is extremely rich in languages. There are two official languages, English and French, many indigenous language families, and increasing numbers of immigrant languages. More than 200 mother tongues were reported in the 2006 census (Statistics Canada 2007).

Table 2.1 lists the official languages and some of the larger immigrant and aboriginal languages. Anglophones make up 58 per cent of the population and francophones 22 per cent overall; allophones, those reporting neither French nor English as their mother tongue, constitute one-fifth of the population. About 200,000 Canadians report an aboriginal language as their mother tongue.

These languages are not spread evenly across the country. Most of the French speakers live in the province of Quebec; the 5.9 million francophones there make up 80 per cent of the population. There are francophones in every other province, with the largest group outside of Quebec, 490,000, in Ontario. Francophones form a particularly large minority in New Brunswick, where the 233,000 French speakers make up one-third of the population.

Table 2.1 Mother tongues spoken in Canada rounded to the nearest thousand

Official languages (2006 census)		Immigrant languages (2006 census)		Aboriginal languages (2001 census)	
English	18,056,000	Chinese languages	1,034,000	Cree	77,000
French	6,892,000	Italian	477,000	Inuktitut	30,000
		German	467,000	Ojibway	22,000
		Punjabi	383,000	Dene	10,000
		Spanish	362,000	Montaignais-Naskapi	10,000
		Arabic	287,000		
		Tagalog	286,000		
		Portuguese	229,000		
		Polish	218,000		

Most of the speakers of immigrant languages live in or near the large urban centres of Toronto, Montreal and Vancouver; the speakers of aboriginal languages live mostly in rural areas, particularly in northern Canada and in the west. For a good background on the languages of Canada, consult the volume *Language in Canada* (Edwards 1998).

The main focus of this chapter is on research into the variation and status of Canadian English and Canadian French and the contact between them. A brief section at the end outlines some current research on gender and language. It is impossible to adequately cover all of the sociolinguistic research in Canada in this limited space; only some of the current research and recent publications on these topics have been included.

Canadian English

This section outlines four areas of research in Canadian English: the nation-wide Dialect Topography project; several projects focused on the urban centres of Toronto, Montreal, and Winnipeg; research on the regional dialects of Newfoundland and the Maritimes; and projects from the Sociolinguistics Laboratory in Ottawa, which bridge research in Canadian English and Canadian French. A recent issue of the *Canadian Journal of Linguistics* (Avery *et al.* 2006), devoted to Canadian English, contains papers on many of these topics.

Dialect topography surveys

Much of the sociolinguistic research into Canadian English has been based upon surveys. The Survey of Canadian English (Scargill and Warkentyne 1972) was the earliest, providing data from 14,000 students and their parents from across the country. This was followed by two extensive surveys in Ottawa and Vancouver that examined variation in lexicon, pronunciation, grammar and language attitudes across age, socio-economic levels and formality of speech (Woods 1980; Dodds de Wolf *et al.* 2004). These surveys together gave strong evidence for the homogeneity of speech across Canadian urban centres and pointed to common patterns of change. They underline the unique position of Canadian English in its combination of British and American elements and its ready acceptance of variation.

Jack Chambers of the University of Toronto has made an enormous contribution to variation studies of Canadian English through his Dialect Topography research. This project began in 1991 with a survey of the Golden Horseshoe region of Ontario, a region that includes Toronto and has over five million residents. Since that time the same survey has been conducted in locations across Canada: in Montreal, the Ottawa Valley, Quebec City, Greater Vancouver, the Eastern Townships, New Brunswick and again in the Golden Horseshoe, in 2000 (Chambers 1998; Chambers and Heisler 1999; Boberg 2004). The survey has also been conducted on the American side of the Canadian border in the states of New York, Washington, Vermont and Maine. The project results are available on the Dialect Topography website (www.dialect.topography.chass.utoronto.ca) which is designed for easy analysis of the data for the independent variables of age, location, sex, social class, occupational mobility, regionality, education and language use. This research project is contributing to an understanding of trends in language change in Canadian English as well as variation between regions in Canada and between Canadian and American speech.

Urban studies

Sali Tagliamonte, at the University of Toronto, has created a corpus of 1.8 million words of Toronto English based on speech samples from over 200 Toronto-born men and women between the ages of 8 and 92. This corpus has provided data for tracking change in Toronto speech, including young people's use of quotatives, intensifiers and tags such as *like, really, so, right,* and *whatever* (Tagliamonte and D'Arcy 2007).

Tagliamonte is expanding the Toronto corpus by collecting data from two other groups: established populations in rural communities, and immigrants within Toronto. She plans to investigate whether changes observed in the Toronto corpus are also occurring in these populations.

While Tagliamonte charted the use of tags in a corpus of collected speech, Elaine Gold, at the University of Toronto, investigated the use of the tag *eh* through self-reporting surveys. *Eh* is widely considered a marker of Canadian speech, and is found in a very broad range of speech acts, from set expressions, such as *Thanks, eh?* and *I know, eh?* to opinions, exclamations, questions, commands and interjections in narratives.

Gold's survey of University of Toronto students indicates that contemporary reported usage is as high as that reported in the earlier Canadian surveys and that the same types of expressions are reported to be used most frequently, that is, *eh* following opinions and exclamations (Gold 2008). The research also suggests that new immigrants quickly pick up *eh* and view it as marker of Canadian nationality.

James Walker and Michol Hoffman of York University, have initiated a project entitled 'Ethnicity and Language in Toronto' to investigate the effects of language contact in Toronto's multicultural milieu. Walker and Hoffman are considering variables of ethnic origin, generation, and degree of affiliation to one's ethnic group, in their investigation of the ways in which ethnic identity is expressed through linguistic variation.

Research has also been underway on the ethnic enclaves of Montreal. Charles Boberg, at McGill University, heads a project at the McGill Dialectology and Sociolinguistics Laboratory entitled 'English as a Minority Language: Ethnolinguistic Variation and the Phonetics of Montreal English'. This research focuses on pronunciation variation in native English speakers from the three largest Anglophone ethnic groups: people of British/Irish, Italian, and East-European Jewish ancestry. Boberg has found that these groups can be distinguished by their pronunciation of English, even after several generations of living in Montreal.

There are currently two other research projects at the McGill Dialectology and Sociolinguistics Laboratory. The 'North American Regional Vocabulary Survey', focuses on vocabulary that reflects contemporary popular culture, such as words for fast food and modern technology. Through the 5000 responses collected to date, variation can be traced within Canada and between Canada and the United States. The second project 'The Phonetics of Canadian English', uses students at McGill University, who come from across Canada, as a resource to investigate regional differences in the phonetics of Canadian English.

The phonetics of Canadian English continue to be the focus of much research. Robert Hagiwara, at the University of Manitoba, is overseeing 'The Winnipeg Vowel Project', a project which is investigating the phenomena of Canadian Raising and the Canadian Vowel Shift in Winnipeg. Canadian raising, the process of raising the onsets of the diphthongs [aj] and [aw] before voiceless consonants, and Canadian shift, the backward shift of front lax vowels, are discussed in several articles in 'Canadian English in a Global Context' (Avery *et al.* 2006) and in Boberg (2005).

27

English of Newfoundland and the Maritimes

The most distinctive dialects of Canadian English are found in eastern Canada, the areas first settled by English speakers. Newfoundland English was the first Canadian English dialect to be the subject of a regional dictionary (Story *et al.* 1990) and has been of much interest to sociolinguists. Gerard Van Herk holds the Canada Research Chair in Regional Language and Oral Text at Memorial University in Newfoundland and is investigating issues of language retention during this time of rapid change for Newfoundland English. Sandra Clarke, also at Memorial University, researches variation in Newfoundland Vernacular English, identity issues, and Newfoundland residents' attitudes towards their own dialect (Clarke 1997).

The eastern provinces are well known for their dialect pockets and the range of language contacts: from the influence of Irish English in Newfoundland, to Scottish Gaelic in Cape Breton, French influence in New Brunswick, and German and New England influence in Nova Scotia. Less known is the speech of the black communities of Nova Scotia. Shana Poplack and Sali Tagliamonte investigated the speech of two communities of African-Canadians in Nova Scotia, whose history dates back over 200 years. Their quantitative study of grammatical traits of African Nova Scotian English (ANSE) provides strong evidence that the African American Vernacular English (AAVE) of the early nineteenth century was closer to the standard English of its time than contemporary AAVE is to today's standard varieties (Poplack and Tagliamonte 2001).

The Sociolinguistics Laboratory, University of Ottawa

The interviews from the ANSE research are housed at the University of Ottawa's Sociolinguistics Laboratory, which is directed by Shana Poplack. The University of Ottawa is a bilingual university situated in Canada's capital city, on the provincial border between English-speaking Ontario, and French-speaking Quebec. The Laboratory has a special research focus on language change arising from language contact and has investigated many issues in both Canadian English and Canadian French. The Laboratory has developed extensive corpora in Canadian English and Canadian French, and has collections of English and French grammar texts and usage guides dating from the sixteenth century.

The English corpora include interviews with 463 residents of the Ottawa-Hull region, and 164 anglophones native to Montreal and Quebec of different ethnic and socioeconomic backgrounds. There is also a collection of African diaspora English which includes, in addition to the ANSE recordings, interviews from the African-American community in Samana, Dominican Republic, and recordings of ex-slave speech. These recordings are supplemented by a collection of early African-American correspondence written from Sierra Leone, Liberia and the United States, most of which has never been published (Van Herk and Walker 2005).

The Canadian French corpora include over 500,000 words of vernacular Quebec French from recordings of speakers born between 1846 and 1945; these recordings are an important resource for the study of language change in Quebec. There are also two corpora of contemporary spoken French: 3.5 million words from informal conversations with 120 francophones native to the Ottawa-Hull region, and over one million words of interviews with Ottawa teachers of French and their students.

Poplack is currently supervising projects investigating the influence of prescriptive norms on Canadian French and the effects of language contact with French on Canadian

English spoken in Quebec. One issue being investigated is whether there has been more influence of French on Quebec English since the introduction of the French Language Charter in 1977, which legislated widespread use of French in business and education in Quebec. Early results from this project suggest that there is surprisingly little evidence of French influence on the grammar of Quebec English, and a relatively low rate of French borrowings.

Canadian French

The following discussion of current research in Canadian French is divided into two parts: the first part describes studies of Quebec French; the second, research into three varieties of French outside of Quebec – Acadian French, Ontario French and the French of Alberta. Major topics of research include language variation, language contact with English, and issues of language identity in minority contexts.

Quebec French

France Martineau at the University of Ottawa researches the historical sociolinguistics of Quebec French in its centuries of development in Canada and its origins in con-tinental French (Martineau and Mougeon 2003). Martineau is currently involved in two major projects. The first, 'Modeling Change: The Paths of French', involves a large international, cross-disciplinary team. The project's goal is to examine the evolution of French from its beginnings in the Middle Ages through to the seventeenth and eighteenth centuries when it began to be established in Canada. A corpus is being developed to reflect a wide range of social spheres; this will allow research into the dif-fering levels of influence that various social groups have had on language change. This project will also examine the development of diverging French norms, changes in lin-guistic and cultural identities, and the role of language in bilingual and multilingual societies.

In the second project, Martineau is working with Alain Desrochers and Yves Charles Morin to investigate the development of, and variation in, Quebec French from the 1700s to the 1900s. This research is based on the informal French found in letters written between family members in those centuries, which provides evidence both for grammatical variation and for issues of language and identity.

Diane Vincent is the director of the Laboratory of Sociopragmatics (LaSic) at Laval University in Quebec City. LaSic has a special focus on Quebec French and on discourse in the workplace, and houses the largest corpus of spontaneous oral French speech in Quebec, made up of 300 hours of Montreal francophone speech. This comprises three corpora: the 1971 Sankoff-Cedergren corpus of 60 sociolinguistic interviews; the 1984 corpus of follow-up surveys with the informants from 1971, and the 1994 Montreal corpus, which includes some interviews with informants from the earlier surveys along with family and workplace discourse recordings. These corpora have provided data for research on language change in real time, such as changes in the personal pronoun paradigm (Blondeau 2001). The workplace recordings have supported research into the interactions between health care professionals and their patients, which include lying and rebukes (Vincent et al. 2007).

French outside of Quebec

Ontario French

Raymond Mougeon of Glendon College, York University, is currently involved in two major projects that build on years of research in the field. His main focus is on Ontario French – both that used by speakers with French as their first language, and that learned by students enrolled in French immersion programs. Mougeon's projects are in association with the Centre for Research on Language Contact, at York University, a research centre with a multidisciplinary approach to language contact.

The first of Mougeon's projects is entitled 'A Real-Time Study of Linguistic Change in Ontario French'; his co-investigators are Terry Nadasdi from the University of Alberta and Katherine Rehner from the University of Toronto. This study is based on two corpora, one collected in 1978 and the other in 2004–05, of the speech of francophone students enrolled in French language high schools in four Ontario communities. The communities were chosen for their different sizes of French population and the different amounts of French–English language contact. The research incorporates a range of sociolinguistic variables, including the social and ethno-linguistic backgrounds of the students and their parents, the students' use of French in and outside of school, and the students' linguistic identity.

Mougeon's other focus has been on the speech of anglophone students enrolled in French immersion high school programs in Ontario. His research group has compared the sociolinguistic variation of the French of immersion students with variation in the French of francophone students their own age, to see if the L2 students are acquiring native-like sociolinguistic variation and are affected by the same social factors as are the L1 speakers (Mougeon et al. 2004). The same team of researchers is investigating the treatment of variation in French in the classroom and plan to amass corpora both of teachers' speech in the classroom and of the teaching materials used.

Acadian French

Much sociolinguistic research has been done on varieties of Acadian French, both inside and outside of the province of New Brunswick. A recent issue of the *Canadian Journal of Linguistics* is devoted to this topic (Balcom et al. 2008). Louise Beaulieu of the Université de Moncton and Wladyslaw Cichocki, of the University of New Brunswick are currently collaborating on research into morphosyntactic variation in the Acadian French of north-east New Brunswick. Their work focuses on features considered unique to Acadian French, such as the third person plural verbal inflection–*ont*. They have also looked at the variation found in the rural areas where these dialects are spoken (Beaulieu and Cichocki 2005). This work was based on a corpus of adult Acadian speech that Beaulieu collected; she is currently developing a corpus of pre-adolescent Acadian speech. Cichocki also researches the social factors responsible for regional variation of phonetic features of Acadian French based on dialect atlas data (Péronnet et al. 1998).

Both Gisèle Chevalier and Sylvia Kasparian at the Université de Moncton are engaged in research on Acadian French. Kasparian is currently investigating verbal constructions in the French of south-east New Brunswick; Chevalier is focusing on language contact between Acadian French and English (Chevalier 2002).

Ruth King of York University and Terry Nadasdi of the University of Alberta are investigating Acadian French outside of New Brunswick in a project entitled 'Acadian

French in Time and Space'. This project focuses on grammatical variation in the Acadian French spoken in the provinces of Prince Edward Island and Newfoundland, based on corpora collected by King. King's earlier research has shown a number of morpho-syntactic differences between Acadian French and Quebec French and has looked at the linguistic results of language contact in Acadian communities (King 2000). The current project includes diachronic data to allow for the reconstruction of earlier stages of Atlantic Canada Acadian French. This will allow comparisons with the development of Quebec French and Cajun French in Louisiana and help trace the evolution of French in North America and the consequences of French–English language contact in all areas. Sylvie Dubois of Louisiana State University and France Martineau of Université d'Ottawa are collaborating on this project as well.

French in Alberta

The topic of English–French language contact has also been investigated in the minority French communities of Alberta. Douglas Walker, at the University of Calgary, has focused on the effects of language contact on the retention and pronunciation of Canadian French. His research is part of an international project on the usage, varieties and structure of contemporary French (Walker 2003).

French language and identity

The minority status of French in Canada has precipitated much discussion of issues of language and identity. Monica Heller and Normand Labrie at the University of Toronto edited a collection of papers on discourse and identity in French Canada (Heller and Labrie 2003). Annette Boudreau at the Université de Moncton works on linguistic identity, language maintenance and revitalization in Acadian French communities (Boudreau 2005); Boudreau and Lise Dubois at the Université de Moncton have two papers on Acadian French in the Heller and Labrie collection. Boudreau is part of the Research Group on Cultures in Contact at the Université de Moncton, and, with Dubois, is working on a comparison of the attitudes of English and French speakers to their own and to the other official language. Boudreau and Dubois are also co-researchers on a large research project headed by Heller at the University of Toronto that is exploring the changing relation-ships between language and identity in Canadian Francophone communities in this time of rapid change and increased mobility of information and people. One aspect of this project is a comparison of the changes in vernacular and standard French in Ontario and New Brunswick.

Language and gender

Many Canadian scholars have researched issues of language and gender. Henry Rogers and Ron Smyth of the University of Toronto have been investigating sociophonetic variation in vowel and consonant articulation with respect to gender, gender identity and sexual orientation. In particular, they have focused on identifying the phonetic characteristics that make speech sound gay. They found several acoustic correlates that listeners use to judge a voice as gay-sounding: longer and higher frequency of fricatives /s/ and /z/; longer aspiration of voiceless stops; a clearer /l/. Similar characteristics have been associated

31

with female speech and Rogers and Smyth suggest that young boys with gay-sounding speech have subconsciously acquired phonetic characteristics of women's speech (Smyth *et al.* 2003).

Susan Ehrlich at York University also works on language and gender. Ehrlich's recent work focuses on the way that language is used in legal settings, in particular the discourse of testimony and judicial decisions associated with cases of sexual harassment and rape. Ehrlich argues that underlying preconceptions in courtroom language affect the outcome of the trials (Ehrlich 2001).

Deborah James at the University of Toronto researches gender differences in language use. Her earlier work looked at the different ways in which men and women use derogatory terms (James 1998). James has amassed a large corpus of graffiti taken from washroom walls, and she is currently analyzing the similarities and differences in men's and women's use of graffiti.

Another scholar in the field of language and gender is Bonnie McElhinny at the University of Toronto (McElhinny 2003). One focus of her work is the different interactional styles of men and women in the workplace. McElhinny has studied the speech of women who are working in traditionally male-dominated workplaces, such as police departments, to see whether women adapt more 'masculine' styles of interaction.

Conclusion

This is a brief overview of some of the sociolinguistic research being carried out in Canada today. Research into Canadian English and Canadian French is increasing; both fields have had conferences dedicated specifically to them in the past few years. Many Canadian linguists are currently working on issues of language maintenance and revitalization, in particular among the aboriginal languages of Canada. With the latest statistics showing that one in five Canadians has a mother tongue other than English or French, topics of multilingualism, language contact, language retention and language and identity will doubtless continue to be important areas of research for Canadian sociolinguists.

References

Avery, P., Chambers, J. K., D'Arcy, A., Gold, E., and Rice, K. (eds) (2006) 'Canadian English in a global context', *Canadian Journal of Linguistics*, 51, 99–347.
Balcom, P., Beaulieu, L., Butler, G.R., Cichocki, W., King, R. (eds) (2008) 'Acadian French/Le français acadien', *Canadian Journal of Linguistics*, 53, 1–138.
Beaulieu, L. and Cichocki, W. (2005) 'Innovation et maintien dans une communauté linguistique du nord-est du Nouveau-Brunswick', *Francophonies d'Amérique*, 19, 155–75.
Blondeau, H. (2001) 'Corpora comparability and changes in real time within the paradigm of the personal pronouns in Montreal French', *Journal of Sociolinguistics*, 5, 453–74.
Boberg, C. (2004) 'The dialect topography of Montreal', *English World-Wide*, 25, 171–98.
——(2005) 'The Canadian shift in Montreal', *Language Variation and Change*, 17, 133–54.
Boudreau, A. (2005) 'Le français en Acadie: maintien et revitalisation du français dans les provinces Maritimes', in A. Valdman, J. Auger and D. Piston-Hatlen (eds) *Le français en Amérique du Nord: État present*. Ste-Foy: Presses de l'Université Laval, pp. 439–54.
Chambers, J. K. (1998) 'Inferring dialect from a postal questionnaire', *Journal of English Linguistics*, 26, 222–46.

Chambers, J. K. and Heisler, T. (1999) 'Dialect topography of Quebec City English', *Canadian Journal of Linguistics*, 44, 23–48.

Chevalier, G. (2002) 'La concurrence entre les marqueurs "well" et "ben" dans une variété métissée du français acadien', *Cahier de sociolinguistique de Rennes*, 7, 65–81.

Clarke, S. (1997) 'Language in Newfoundland and Labrador: past, present and future', *Journal of the Canadian Association of Applied Linguistics*, 19, 11–34.

Dodds de Wolf, G., Fee, M. and McAlpine, J. (eds) (2004) *The Survey of Vancouver English: A Sociolinguistic Study of Urban Canadian English*, by R. Gregg *et al.*, Kingston: Strathy Language Unit, Queen's University.

Edwards, J. (ed.) (1998) *Language in Canada*, Cambridge: Cambridge University Press.

Ehrlich, S. (2001) *Representing Rape: Language and Sexual Consent*, London: Routledge.

Gold, E. (2008) 'Canadian eh? From eh to zed', *Anglistik: International Journal of English Studies*, 19, 141–56.

Heller, M. and Labrie, N. (eds) (2003) *Discours et identités. La francité canadienne entre modernité et mondialisation*, Bruxelles: Éditions Modulaires Européennes.

James, D. (1998) 'Gender-linked derogatory terms and their use by women and men', *American Speech*, 73, 399–420.

King, R. (2000) *The Grammatical Basis of Lexical Borrowing: A Prince Edward Island French Case Study*, Philadelphia, PA: John Benjamins.

Martineau, F. and Mougeon, R. (2003) 'Sociolinguistic research on the origins of ne deletion in European and Quebec French', *Language*, 79, 118–52.

McElhinny, B. (2003) 'Theorizing gender in sociolinguistics and linguistic anthropology', in J. Holmes and M. Meyerhoff (eds) *The Language and Gender Handbook*, Oxford: Blackwell, pp. 21–42.

Mougeon, R., Rehner, K. and Nadasdi, T. (2004) 'The learning of spoken French variation by immersion students from Toronto, Canada', in R. Bayley and V. Regan (eds) *The Acquisition of Sociolinguistic Competence*, Special Issue of *The Journal of Sociolinguistics*, 8, 408–32.

Péronnet, L., Babitch R. M., Cichocki, W. and Brasseur, P. (1998) *Atlas linguistique du vocabulaire maritime acadien*, Québec: Presses de l'Université Laval.

Poplack, S. and Tagliamonte, S. (2001) *African American English in the Diaspora*, Oxford: Blackwell.

Scargill, M. H. and Warkentyne, H. J. (1972) 'The survey of Canadian English: a report', *The English Quarterly*, 5, 47–104.

Smyth, R., Jacobs, G. and Rogers, H. (2003) 'Male voices and perceived sexual orientation: an experimental and theoretical approach', *Language in Society*, 32, 329–50.

Statistics Canada (2007) Data. Online. Available at: www.statcan.ca/Daily/English/071204/d071204a.htm (accessed 2 January 2007).

Story, G. M., Kirwin, W. J., and Widdowson, J. D. A. (eds) (1990) *Dictionary of Newfoundland English*, 2nd edn with supplement, Toronto: University of Toronto Press.

Tagliamonte, S. A. and D'Arcy, A. (2007) 'Frequency and variation in the community grammar: tracking a new change through the generations', *Language Variation and Change*, 19, 1–19.

Van Herk, G. and Walker, J.A. (2005) '*S* marks the spot? Regional variation and early African American correspondence', *Language Variation and Change*, 17, 113–31.

Vincent, D., Laforest, M. and Bergeron, A. (2007) 'Lies, rebukes and social norms: on the unspeakable in interactions with health-care professionals', *Discourse Studies*, 9, 226–45.

Walker, D. (2003) 'Aperçu de la langue française en Alberta (Canada)', in E. Delais-Roussarie and J. Durand (eds) *Corpus et variation en phonologie du français. Méthodes et analyses*, Toulouse: Presses Universitaires du Mirail, pp. 279–300.

Woods, H. B. (1980) *The Ottawa Survey of Canadian English*, Kingston: Strathy Language Unit, Queen's University.

3

Sociolinguistics in Mexico

Defining new agendas

José Antonio Flores Farfán

Introduction

Sociolinguistics in Mexico is a relatively recent development. It dates back to the 1970s and 1980s, when the first publications with the sociolinguistic label started to appear (Perissinotto 1975; Hamel *et al.* 1982; Lastra 1992). At least three research traditions have been developed which can be considered as sociolinguistic practice. First, *anthropological linguistics*, which pre-dates the other two and goes back to the beginning of the twentieth century and has had continuity ever since the founders of the discipline launched their work, considering Mexico an open laboratory for the development of its research agenda (Boas 1963). Second, *variationist sociolinguistics*, as represented today by work on urban sociolinguistics, specifically of Mexico City Spanish (see Butragueño 2000). The latter is the most recent addition to this myriad of research. Last but not least, there is the *socio-linguistics of conflict* between the immense number of indigenous languages of the country and Spanish. What the first two traditions have in common is their focus on one single language, indigenous languages and Spanish, respectively. The third tradition at least appeals to bilingualism, even when ironically not always studying the multiple linguistic expressions of bilingualism as a social practice. In this chapter, I will provide a sketch of such sociolinguistic studies and their caveats, pinpointing to the enormous wealth of sociolinguistic topics waiting to be taken into consideration. For example, there are few, if any, investigations on the immigrated languages of Indo-European or other origins (for exceptions, see Hancock 1980; Lastra 1992, 2005; Lipski 2007).

The sociolinguistics of Spanish

Spanish is the only official, standard language of a total population of over 120 million people in Mexico. Linguistic investigations of Spanish supersede what has been carried out with Mexican indigenous languages in different respects, for instance, regarding the study of sociolinguistic variability, even when this is a very recent attempt. In the case of indigenous languages, such study is almost nonexistent. Following a Labovian paradigm, research in and around Spanish has concentrated on internal linguistic variability, with the advantage of going beyond impressionistic descriptions of Mexican Spanish (social) dialectology. Although presenting different advantages with respect to previous philological traditions, such as vindicating the realistic Labovian approach on data and its emphasis on language use, the fascination with a quantitative model is pervasive (see Butragueño 2000).

Perhaps the most interesting premise that the sociolinguistics of Spanish advances is its appeal to a conflict model which alludes to the power differentials which guide any sociolinguistic process. Yet this has hardly gone beyond a theoretical formulation following Milroy (1987) and Milroy and Milroy (1995) (see Butragueño 2000). In short, variationist sociolinguistics in Mexico is still a research program, with a few preliminary case studies, ranging from the investigation of "linguistic leaders," to courtesy strategies in Mexican Spanish (ibid.).

On the other hand, almost no sociolinguistic investigations have been developed on the Spanish that indigenous people speak (for an attempt, see Zimmermann 1986), not to speak of immigrants. What has been investigated is the influence of indigenous languages on monolingual Spanish, yet overwhelmingly limited to philological approaches on the lexicon and its impact on the phonetics of Mexican or Yucatec Spanish.[1] Even such interesting cases as the latter, in which the influence of Yucatec Maya is notable, have been treated as marginal phenomena, subsidiary to internal "systemic" constraints (Lope Blanch 1987), even when this and maybe other Mexican Spanish varieties such as Oaxaca Spanish (see Garza Cuarón 1987), at least partially resemble what in the contact literature is termed a semi-Creole (Lipski 2007).

The sociolinguistics of Mexican indigenous languages

Parallel to its ethnic complexity, Mexico is one of the fifth most diverse countries of the world linguistically speaking. It occupies the first place in linguistic diversity in the American continent in terms of number of speakers as well as in variety of languages. Of over 120 million people, the indigenous population is estimated between 10 and 20 percent, that is, roughly 10 to 20 million people speak an indigenous language. The country's sociolinguistic complexity is evidenced by the non-total agreement between scholars regarding the number of its languages or even linguistic families. No matter how unconscious this may be, quantitative figures are the subject of intense political manipulation and ideologies, thus different research traditions tend to either overestimate or underestimate the number of Mexican languages. Compare the top figure of almost 300 languages suggested by the Summer Institute of Linguistics (SIL) (www.sil.org) with the official figures provided by the Mexican state, which range from 62 up to 100 languages. According to a reliable source (Suárez 1983), Mexico has representatives of eight extant linguistic families (including the Uto-Aztecan, the Mayan, and the Otomanguean, together with three other linguistic families represented by isolates; namely, Huave, Purepecha, and Seri, plus Totonac-Tepehua, and Mixe Zoque).

In contrast to situations with highly endangered languages such as in the United States, in Mexico, monolingualism exists in specific enclaves of indigenous languages, a meaningful index of historical entrenchment of several of these communities and their vibrant existence.[2] Yet, this does not mean they are not endangered. Since these languages have been less investigated from a sociolinguistic point of view, I will devote the rest of this chapter to reviewing the state of the art in the sociolinguistics of Mexican indigenous languages.

A handful of indigenous languages have enjoyed sociolinguistic investigation, notably Nahuatl (e.g. Hill and Hill 1986), Maya Yucatec (e.g. Pfeiler 1998), Otomi (e.g. Zimmermann 1986), Mazahua (e.g. Pellicer 2005), Tzotzil (e.g. Haviland 1988), Zapotec (e.g. Saynes 2000), and Yaqui (e.g. Moctezuma-Zamarrón 1998).

The one-sided monolingual perspective on which most of these investigations have developed their practice is difficult to overcome for a number of reasons. For example, in my initial work on the verbal interaction in Hñahñu (Otomi) markets (Flores Farfán 1983), the investigation was carried out in Spanish, since I am not a Hñahñu speaker. However, one of the main results was that researching in the indigenous language would open up another perspective that would allow a much more comprehensive picture of the complex sociolinguistic reality of this (and other) indigenous groups, characterized as a situation of conflictive diglossic bilingualism, leading to language shift. Even when such a trend does exist, evidenced in that some of these communities already have Spanish as their mother tongue, revisiting Hñahñu shows that there are ways of resisting the intromission of Spanish. For example, Hñahñu was found to be linked to important emotional and even instrumental functions, such as being a secret language to conceal information leading to decision-making in the communal assemblies in which Hñahñus negotiate specific demands with the Mexican state (see Franco Pellotier 1997). Thus in the subsequent phases of my work, learning the indigenous languages became a must, starting with varieties of Nahuatl, supposedly the single best-known indigenous language, or rather, *languages*, of the country. This allowed me to start understanding ways of resisting and overcoming the ever present possibility of language displacement and shift. To understand such less investigated processes, that is, the entrenchment and resistance of several indigenous communities and their languages, or diglossic reversals, a historical perspective becomes useful and even necessary.

Historical sketch of Mexican indigenous languages sociolinguistics

Even when there is extensive documentation spanning the whole colonial period and important archeological and ethnohistorical information, it is still hard to reconstruct part of the sociolinguistic history of Mexican indigenous languages. Three languages enjoy such extensive documentation. The most extensive of all is Nahuatl, a language which became the most widely used lingua franca in pre-Hispanic times. Other linguae francae probably included Yucatec Maya, Mixtec, Zapotec and Purepecha. All these languages coincided with the so-called languages of civilization in Mesoamerica.[3]

Limited Mesoamerican prehistoric evidence of loanwords in several Mesoamerican languages points to the loose political organization of Classical times (c. 330 AD), as Suárez (1983: 157) suggests. Most loanwords reflect existing power differentials of the time. For instance the widespread use of *cacao* as common currency, the general use of the base 20 numeral system, or toponyms such as Nahuatl *Atitlan* show Aztec domination in what today is Guatemala in Quichean (Mayan) languages. Yet contacts were mostly limited to the ruling classes (ibid.: 158), and the grammars and other materials produced by missionaries reflect this fact, since it was with the (male!) elites that Spaniards mostly interacted (see Flores Farfán 2007).

While paying tribute and under military control this non-apparent independence was present in all separate cultural and linguistic entities of the so-called Aztec empire. This group dominated vast parts of Mesoamerica some 300 years before the Spanish invasion. This fact prefigures today the high linguistic diversification in most Mexican languages, except in some of those which were not subjugated by the Aztecs. Even when Nahuatl had the status of the lingua franca which the Spaniards chose for evangelization and administration of the new colonies up until the eighteenth century—a fact which ironically contributed to Nahuatl maintenance—this is an excellent example of permitting a multilingual status in highly stratified systems in general and in particular in the expression of the Aztec state.

The history of Nahuatl illustrates the sociolinguistic situation of Mexican indigenous languages in different periods, including the pre-Hispanic one, when there were a series of double-nested diglossias (see Fasold 1990), or better polyglossia, in which Nahuatl occupied the high pole of the diglossic relationships, both internally (with respect to other Nahuatl varieties or languages) as well as externally (with respect to other languages). Linguistic evidence of this complex pre-Hispanic organization, which to a certain extent continued in colonial times, is evidenced in the existence of native terms which refer to this diglossic differentiation: *Macehuallatoli* "speech of the people, the common people, the *campesino*," as opposed to *Pillatolli* in Classical Nahuatl, "the speech of the elite," the high varieties in which most early sources of the sixteenth century were written, now extinct (see Flores Farfán 2004).

Moreover, to understand the conflictive multilingual pre-Hispanic *ethos*, consider that Nahuatl means "something pristine, pleasant, intelligible to the ear" (Karttunen 1983), something that the Aztecs spread throughout the Mesoamerican world as part of their sociolinguistic policy. This included devising derogatory names for speakers of other languages, including Nahua languages, such as *Cohuixca*, or *Pipil* "lizard" and "girlie speech," when referring to speakers in the Balsas (Guerrero) Nahuatl and those of today's Salvador, respectively; or *Popoluca* "unintelligible tongue," *Chontal* "foreigner," *Otomitl* "barbarian," etc. (Heath 1972), names that still prevail today.

Despite the extensive intrusion of Spaniards during the first half-century of the colony, Nahuatl did not really undergo much change in its structure, a fact interpreted as an effect of limited social contact. New words (neologisms), descriptive explanations (circumlocutions), or adapting old words to new meanings (semantic extensions) prevailed in this phase. Few if any nouns were borrowed, although specific key domains of Nahuatl culture such as religious terminology were forcibly rooted out. In the second stage, which goes up to the first half of the seventeenth century, resistance to borrowing decreased, yet loanwords were limited to nouns, and bilingualism started to expand. The third stage is characterized by opening up the Nahuatl language to all types of borrowing, including verbs and almost any type of Spanish material (see Lockhart 1992; Flores Farfán 1999), together with the generalization of one-sided bilingualism. This tendency has prevailed and been taken to a high level in modern times, in which massive borrowing is possible, seeing the birth of new types of Nahuatl in processes reminiscent of pidgin formation. These processes have emerged in relation to Nahuatl shift (Flores Farfán 2006).

In modern Nahuatl, shift has occurred in several Nahua communities, as in the Balsas region, as represented by extremely Hispanicized communities reaching the brink of linguistic extinction, such as the contemporary successors of Milpa Alta speakers in today's Mexico City, the last location where Nahuatl is still spoken in the Valley of Mexico, or Chilacachapa Nahuatl (ibid.). However, Nahuatl is alive and well in several villages, although endangered. All this leads to a fifth or even sixth stage, characterized by movement to resist language shift, as in the Balsas region. Linked to internal commerce and ritual ties at the community level, diglossic reversals can and indeed do exist not only in Nahuatl communities, but also in several other languages; such a process of course is not exclusive to Mexico.

Moreover, even if stage theories suggest a systematic account of the historical order in which Spanish has impacted Mesoamerican languages, and eventually replaced them, the most interesting sociolinguistic phenomena have not yet been deciphered by such large-scale macro-characterizations (Flores Farfán 2001). In sum, chronologies are not linear, static or homogeneous phenomena (e.g. Lockhart 1992). Local differences are present in isolated communities in which a single interpretation cannot be mechanically applied. For instance, a wide spectrum of speakers exists, including quasi- and pseudo-speakers, depending on variables such as age, gender, degree of Hispanicization and even political affiliation (Flores Farfán 1999). Thus within a single region and even within communities themselves extreme shift together with monolingualism in the indigenous tongue exists, challenging any attempt at linear characterizations.

In general, what is true for Nahuatl is valid, *mutatis mutandis*, for several indigenous languages which have experienced extreme diversification processes, most notably the Otomanguean family. Today Nahuatl is supposedly the language with more speakers in Mexico (circa 2 million), but is isolated in several different areas with no contact what-soever, Spanish becoming the lingua franca. But both the name Nahuatl itself and the idea of Nahuatl as a single language are likely to have originated in pre- and post-colonial monolingual ideologies, still prevalent in academia and among the general public. Nahuatl is a set of languages (e.g. speakers give it different names, contingent on the region in question, Mexicano being the most common). This fact has an effect on Mexican indigenous demolinguistics, situating Maya Yucatec in first place, numerically speaking. Interestingly Maya Yucatec is the opposite case as compared to Nahuatl or Otomanguean languages (e.g. Mixtec or Zapotec). Yucatec Maya (and also a few others such as Purepecha) is a relatively uniform language, a fact reinforcing awareness and consciousness of linguistic and cultural intelligibility and internal solidarity ties. This situation is to a certain extent pre-figured by the pre-Hispanic complexity of these lan-guages and their sociolinguistic colonial and modern history, which link linguistic diversification to a subordinated position, while languages such as Yucatec or Purepecha were actually spoken in independent states, at least in certain periods of history, expressed by high levels of linguistic uniformity.

Today the field of Mexican sociolinguistics has dramatically reconfigured itself, espe-cially associated with the field of language endangerment, which has become the most important focus of linguistic research both at the local and global levels. This calls for new ways of approaching the issue of multilingualism.

Future directions

The question of developing specific intervention proposals for research in the field of language revitalization has become central and a whole rhetoric has appeared regarding endangered languages worldwide. In Mexico, there are few revitalization projects or even studies on revitalization processes (see Saynes 2000). Inspired by models such as research in action or action research, we have developed a pilot program in which the revitalization effort is focused upon members of the community and the production and dissemination of a revitalization corpus. The main approach to the revitalization issue is going beyond the colonial heritage present in received descriptive and even documentary linguistics, developing a Mexican sociolinguistics, which would have as one of its main tenets developing an approach along the lines of what could be termed "militant sociolinguistics." A brief example of such an exercise follows.

The Linguistic and Cultural Revitalization, Maintenance and Development Project

The Linguistic and Cultural Revitalization, Maintenance and Development Project is a pilot program developed in Mexico for over a decade now. As the title suggests, it is oriented to the defense of endangered languages and cultures, a key issue of which is the active participation of speakers. In the quest to balance power, an intercultural approach is taken. Revitalizing is not a one-person job, but a collective endeavor, so the corpus planning phase stems from *co-authorships*, in which each and every participant plays a role contributing specific complementary skills, such as speaker–artist–researcher. These teams look to recreate ethnic contents in multimodal, high quality formats (e.g. 3D animation), recasting local genres with a high didactic potential, such as riddles. Stemming from the ethnic group's epistemology itself (Nahuas, Mayas, Mixtec), riddles are language nests of the indigenous culture. The materials are hosted by a Mesoamerican trickster, the opossum (*Tlakwaatsiin, Tlacuache*), who plays around with the deepest content of the indigenous culture, such as those depicted in the ancient codexes, bringing together old and modern knowledge. The status planning phase includes audio, video and books in bilingual form, in which the indigenous language occupies the most prominent place, even subordinating the colonial to the endangered language, providing status and reversing extremely negative stereotypes towards the threatened tongue. The model is thought of as a playful, joyful one, openly attempting to actively capture interlocutors, especially children, utilizing attractive, trendy formats. We have pursued such goals via informal workshops developing an exercise towards a different ecology of preferred language choices, implying a new ecology in terms of the research relationship alluded to. This is favored by triggering participation via video shows which are conducted in the indigenous tongue to which members of the whole community are invited to attend on special occasions such as community festivities. Based on the use of such multimodal incentives, and the production of culturally sensitive materials, an indirect methodology of language revitalization is used in informal settings in which the participation of children is a spontaneous prerogative of the audience. It is detached from school rituals, and not limited to a single medium such as the written code. This allows the emergence of children's voices without forcing participation. In this way children are motivated to share their own knowledge and even produce more materials collaboratively, replying to the riddles or tongue-twisters or producing new ones. In turn, their participation is encouraged through the distribution of books, audio tapes or the videos themselves, disseminating materials that will reach and hopefully be used in local households, a key sphere for the reproduction and revitalization of endangered languages and cultures (Flores Farfán 2001).

Notes

1 Mexican Spanish refers to the variety spoken in Mexico City, representing the prestige variety utilized in the media, while Yucatec Spanish, spoken in the Yucatán Peninsula, is often mocked by speakers of Mexican Spanish.

2 However, monolingualism can also be the expression of interethnic exploitation, as suggested for Huastec Nahuatl, in which *Mestizos* (the Spanish-speaking dominant group) prevent indigenous people from learning Spanish in order to perpetuate their subordination (Stiles 1982).

3 Mesoamerica is conceived as a common cultural and linguistic area which geographically spanned from today's Central Mexico down to El Salvador and Honduras, with such shared traits as monumental architecture and highly sophisticated systems of writing, together with elaborated social stratifications expressed in, for instance, honorific speech and shared linguistic abilities, such as the use of a lingua franca and the existence of multilingual individuals. Common linguistic traits traditionally include shared vocabulary for specific cultural and material objects, which has led scholars to speak of Mesoamerica as a linguistic area or *Sprachbund* (see Campbell *et al.* 1986). Another trait that came into open conflict with colonizers' ideologies was the existence of polytheistic societies.

References

Boas, F. (1963) *Introduction to Handbook of American Indian Languages*, Washington, DC: Georgetown University Press.

Butragueño, P. M. (ed.) (2000) *Estructuras en contexto. Estudios de variación lingüística*, México: El Colegio de México.

——(2006) "Líderes lingüísticos en la Ciudad de México," in P. M. Butragueño (ed.) *Líderes lingüísticos: Estudios de variación y cambio*, México: El Colegio de México, pp. 185–208.

Campbell, L., Kaufman, T. and Smith Stark, T. C. (1986) "Mesoamerica as a linguistic area," *Language Journal of the Linguistics Society of America*, 62, 530–70.

Fasold, R. (1990) *The Sociolinguistics of Society*, Oxford: Basil Blackwell.

Flores Farfán, J. A. (1983) "Interacciones verbales de compra-venta en mercados otomíes del Valle del Mezquital," in *Anales del CIESAS 1983*, México: CIESAS.

——(1999) *Cuatreros Somos y Toindioma Hablamos. Contactos y Conflictos entre el Náhuatl y el Español en el Sur de México*, México: CIESAS.

——(2001) "Culture and language revitalization, maintenance and development in Mexico," *International Journal of the Sociology of Language*, 152, 185–97.

——(2004) "Classical Nahuatl: outlining its sociolinguistic complexity," in T. Stolz (ed.) *Alte Sprachen, Diversitas Linguarum*, 8, Bochum: Universitätsverlag Dr. N. Brockmeyer, pp. 167–78.

——(2006) "En los márgenes del contacto náhuatl-español. Los últimos estertores del náhuatl," *Signos Lingüísticos*, 4, 9–32.

——(2007) "La variación lingüística en las artes mexicanas (con especial énfasis en el náhuatl)" in Z. Otto, G. James and E. Riduejo (eds.) *Missionary Linguistics III: Morphology and Syntax. Selected Papers from the Third and Fourth International Conferences on Missionary Linguistics*, Amsterdam: John Benjamins, pp. 59–74.

Franco Pellotier, V. M. (1997) "Revalorización lingüística en sociedades indígenas: uso del video en comunidades ñañhu," M.A. thesis, ENAH, México.

Garza Cuarón, B. (1987) *El español hablado en la Ciudad de Oaxaca, México: caracterización fonética y léxica*, México: El Colegio de México.

Hamel, R. E., Lastra de Suarez, Y. and Muñoz, H. (eds.) (1982) *Sociolingüística latinoamericana. Congreso Mundial de Sociología, México, 1982*, México: UNAM.

Hancock, I. F. (1980) *The Texas Seminoles and their Language*, (Papers – African and Afro-American Studies and Research Center, Series 2; No. 1), Austin, TX: University of Texas at Austin.

Haviland, J. B. (1988) "Minimal maxims: cooperation and natural conversation in Zinacantan," *Mexican Studies / Estudios Mexicanos*, 4, 79–114.

Heath, S. B. (1972) *La Política del Lenguaje en México. De la Colonia a la Nación*, México: INI, SEP.

Hill, J. H. and Hill, K. C. (1986) *Speaking Mexicano: Dynamics of a Syncretic Language in Central Mexico*, Tucson, AZ: The University of Arizona Press.

Karttunen, F. (1983) *An Analytical Dictionary of Nahuatl*, Austin, TX: University of Texas at Austin.

Lastra, Y. (1992) *Sociolingüística para hispanoamericanos. Una introducción*, México: El Colegio de México.

——(2005) "Mexico and Central America," in U. Ammon, N. Dittmar, K. Mattheier and P. Trudgill (eds.) *Sociolinguistics/Soziolinguistik: An International Handbook of the Science of Language and Society/Ein Internationales Handbuch zur Wissenschaft von Sprache und Gesellschaft*, 2nd edn, vol. 3, Berlin: Mouton de Gruyter, pp. 2073–81.

Lipski, J. M. (2007) "El español de América en contacto con otras lenguas," in M. Lacorte (ed.) *Lingüística aplicada del español*. Online. Available at: www.personal.psu.edu/jml34/contacts.pdf.

Lockhart, J. (1992) *The Nahuas: A Social and Cultural History of the Indians of Central Mexico, Sixteenth through Eighteenth Centuries*, Stanford, CA: Stanford University Press.

Lope Blanch, J. M. (1987) *Estudios sobre el español de Yucatán*, México: UNAM.

Milroy, J. and Milroy, L. (1995) *Authority in Language: Investigating Language Prescription and Standardization*, New York: Routledge.

Milroy, L. (1987) *Language and Social Networks*, 2nd edn, Oxford: Basil Blackwell.

Moctezuma-Zamarrón, J. L. (1998) "Yaqui-Mayo language shift," doctoral thesis, the University of Arizona.

Pellicer, S. D. (2005) "Stages of bilingualism: local conversational practices among Mazahuas," in Margarita Hidalgo (ed.) *Mexican Indigenous Languages at the Dawn of the 21st Century*, Berlin: Mouton de Gruyter.

Perissinotto, G. A. (1975) *Fonología del español hablado en la Ciudad de México: Ensayo de un método socio-lingüístico*, trans. Raúl Ávila, México: El Colegio de México.

Pfeiler, B. (1998) "El xe'ek y la hach maya: Cambio y futuro del maya ante la modernidad cultural en Yucatán," in A. Koechert and T. Stolz (eds.) *Convergencia e individualidad. Las lenguas Mayas entre hispanización e indigenismo*, Hannover: Verlag für Ethnologie, pp. 125–40.

Saynes, V. F. (2000) "Zapotec language shift and reversal in Juchitan, Mexico," doctoral thesis, University of Arizona.

Stiles, N. (1982) "Nahuatl in the Huasteca hidalguense: a case study in the sociology of language," doctoral thesis, University of Saint Andrews.

Suárez, J. A. (1983) *The Mesoamerican Indian Languages*, Cambridge: Cambridge University Press.

Zimmermann, K. (1986) "El español de los otomíes del Valle del Mezquital," in *Actas del II Congreso Internacional sobre el español de América*, México: UNAM, pp. 234–40.

4

The sociolinguistics of indigenous languages in South America

Serafín M. Coronel-Molina and Viviana Quintero

Introduction

This chapter reviews some of the empirical sociolinguistic research conducted on South America's indigenous speech communities in the past ten years. Because of the great number of sociolinguistic works on Andean indigenous speech communities and our expertise in the Andean sociolinguistic landscape, we discuss mainly research findings on the Quechua speech communities of Ecuador, Peru, Bolivia, and Chile. However, where appropriate and relevant, we also refer to representative sociolinguistic research on other South American indigenous communities, such as the Aymara, the Mapudungu (also known as Mapuche), the Guaraní, and various Amazonian language communities.

Like sociolinguistic work conducted elsewhere, much of the work carried out on South American indigenous language communities has been propelled by larger and broader concerns for social and educational policy and reforms. The need for these policies and reforms emerged from convergent social, political–economic, and political circumstances that helped determine the kinds of sociolinguistic issues researchers investigated. Indigenous language communities are embedded within postcolonial nations, which not long ago were reluctant to recognize themselves as multilingual, multiethnic, and pluricultural. A number of indigenous communities have demanded social, economic, political, and educational reforms through political mobilizations and social movements. Moreover, indigenous people's migration from the countryside to cities, from the 1950s to the present, has driven much of the sociolinguistic research that tries to clarify and solve language-related social problems. Not surprisingly, the primary goal of this research has been to determine the ethnolinguistic vitality of indigenous languages as a first step to assessing bilingual education programs and other language planning efforts.

In what follows, we first provide brief geographic and demographic profiles of major South American indigenous language communities. In the second section, we cite key works in language contact, variation, and change for these language communities. Next we discuss recent trends in the sociolinguistics of bilingualism, migration, and identity in the Andean region. In the penultimate section, we provide an overview of recent empirical work in language policy and planning, intercultural bilingual education, and literacy. In the final section, we summarize the current state of sociolinguistic work on the South American indigenous communities covered in this review. We also offer suggestions for future work.

Brief geographic and demographic profiles of major South American indigenous language communities

The sociolinguistic landscape of South America is diverse and complex, with multi-lingual, pluricultural and multiethnic communities residing throughout the following countries: Argentina, Bolivia, Brazil, Chile, Colombia, Ecuador, French Guiana, Guyana, Paraguay, Peru, Surinam, Uruguay, and Venezuela. Ninety percent of the South American population speaks Spanish or Portuguese. Spanish is the official language of most South American countries. Brazil, which contains nearly 50 percent of the South American population, claims Portuguese as its official language. Other languages—English, French, German, Dutch, Italian and Japanese—are also spoken throughout this continent. Spanish, Portuguese, and, increasingly, English are considered prestige languages, while indigenous languages are, overall, neglected or devalued. In this section, we consider briefly the geographic distribution and demographic details of major indigenous language families and communities in South America.

The Andes stretch from southern Colombia to northern Chile and Argentina and from the Pacific coast of Ecuador and Peru to the jungles of the Amazon rainforest. In total, this area encompasses six different modern-day countries: Colombia, Ecuador, Peru, Bolivia, Chile and Argentina. The number of Quechua speakers fluctuates between eight and 12 million speakers. Mapudungu, another Andean language, is spoken by the Mapuche of Chile and Argentina. About 330,000 people throughout this region speak the Mapudungu dialects (Zúñiga 2006). The Guaraní reside in Paraguay, Brazil, and Bolivia, and they number approximately 5 million (Adelaar 2006).

Amazonia is home to 300 languages, most of them endangered (Dixon and Aikhenvald 1999). These Amazonian language communities live in Ecuador, Peru, Bolivia, and Brazil. Research on Amazonian languages is deeply involved with documentation and descriptive linguistic work. Amazonian languages are usually spoken by small groups of people. Besides language documentation, sociolinguistic surveys are needed to assess language attitudes of these often-small speech communities as well as their complex linguistic ecologies (Everett 2003).

Language contact phenomena: structural processes and outcomes

In this section, we briefly review research in the language contact and language variation and change frameworks. First, we discuss the linguistic and sociolinguistic outcomes of Andean language contact phenomena. Then we conclude with a few representative works on language contact involving the other languages.

Language contact in the Andes goes back to ancient times, even before the arrival of the Incas and the establishment of *Tawantinsuyu*. Quechua and Aymara, in particular, have been in long-term contact with other languages and continue to coexist with them. Since the arrival of the Spaniards in the 1500s, Quechua, Aymara, and other lesser-known

43

indigenous languages have been in contact and conflict with Spanish. The Andean case is a typical diglossic situation with asymmetrical relationships of power, distribution, use, and prestige.

Contact linguistics has greatly influenced Andean sociolinguistic scholarship. Seminal works on Andean contact linguistics include Adelaar and Muysken (2004); Cerrón-Palomino (2003); Chirinos (2001); De Granda (2002); Heggarty (2007, 2008); and Torero (2002). These and the others mentioned in this section provide essential linguistic information on the structural effects and patterns of language contact phenomena between indigenous languages and Spanish, and between the indigenous languages themselves.

One of the pioneering works of Andean language contact and variation is Escobar's (1978) book. He depicts the variations of Spanish resulting from long-term contact with Andean and Amazonian indigenous languages. He also explores the sociolinguistic features of Standard Spanish spoken in Lima, the capital of Peru. Andean Spanish, considered a long-term effect of language contact, has been a dominant area of study. Cerrón-Palomino's scholarship covers more than 30 years of research on the contact and conflict of Quechua and Aymara with Spanish since colonial times (see Cerrón-Palomino 2000, 2006, 2008). Other scholars contributing to Peruvian Andean Spanish include A. M. Escobar (2000); de los Heros (2001); Klee and Caravedo (2005); and Sánchez (2003). For research on Ecuadorian Andean Spanish, refer to Haboud (2005); Muysken (2005); Olbertz (2008); and Palacios (2006). For Quechua-Spanish bilingual usage of evidentiality, see Faller (2002), Feke (2004), and Sánchez (2004). For Ecuadorian Quichua-Spanish language contact, see Haboud (1998) and Yánez Cossío (2001); for Ecuadorian Media Lengua, see Muysken (1997) and Gómez-Rendón (2005).

For details on Guarani-Spanish language contact, see Choi (1998), de Granda (1999), and Palacios (2000, 2005). For language contact studies in Amazonia, see Dixon and Aikhenvald (1999) and Aikhenvald (2002).

Bilingualism, migration, and identity

South American indigenous speech communities have experienced long-term linguistic and cultural contact with European languages and communities for more than 500 years. As noted in the previous section, dynamic and complex configurations of bi- and multilingualism and other language contact phenomena have resulted from these sociolinguistic encounters. In this section, we identify two closely related directions in recent sociolinguistic studies of language and identity of South American indigenous speech communities. The first addresses how migration and its concomitant adaptive mechanisms and effects, both positive and negative, affect ethnolinguistic vitality. The purported goal is to assess the degree to which a speech community undergoes language shift or maintains its native linguistic repertoire. The second, closely related to the first, seeks to reveal speakers' ethnic, gender, and class-based identities and subjectivities from their experiences of linguistic and cultural dislocation. Themes broached in this section include migration, language shift and maintenance, and the discursive construction of ethnic and gender identities.

Rural-to-urban migration and its role in language shift and language maintenance have been long-standing preoccupations in Andean sociolinguistics. For instance, Marr (1998) finds that Andean indigenous migrants to Peru's capital city, Lima, often fail to pass on Quechua to their city-born children and grandchildren. Relying on ethnographic fieldwork and sociolinguistic interviews, he argues that migration by itself may not be a direct cause of language shift. Rather, other mediating factors, particularly speakers' attitudes toward Quechua and Spanish, can lead to language shift or maintenance. In a similar context of internal rural-to-urban migration, Gugenberger (1999) discusses how southern Peruvian Quechua speakers manage to preserve their language in Arequipa, a predominantly Peruvian Spanish-speaking city. She finds a disjuncture between speakers' commentaries on their uses of Quechua and Spanish and their language practices in their homes and neighborhoods. In a recent sociolinguistic ethnography involving transnational migration, Mamani Morales (2005) documents the extent to which Bolivian indigenous migrants in northern Chile maintain Aymara in their daily communicative practices. He concludes that Aymara has ceased to be functional in the daily life of most of the migrant residents, except for a handful of elderly who use it intermittently in family affairs but fail to transmit it to the younger generation.

Sociolinguists have also carried out comparative research that highlights the differences along a rural-to-urban continuum and their role in assessing ethnolinguistic vitality. For instance, Sichra (2003) gauges the ethnolinguistic vitality of two Bolivian Quechua-speaking communities with varying degrees of rurality. Combining ethnographic and sociolinguistic detail, she examines speakers' language attitudes toward Quechua and Spanish and their code-switching practices. Using both sociolinguistic surveys and census data, Lenk (2007) examines the ethnolinguistic vitality of two Ecuadorian Quichua-speaking communities, one rural, the other urban. She finds that an individual's networks of linguistic contacts are crucial in maintaining a stable bilingual environment.

Using a nation-wide sociolinguistic survey, Haboud (1998) examines the distribution and use of Ecuadorian Quichua and Spanish throughout the Ecuadorian highlands. Her work not only assesses the current ethnolinguistic vitality of Ecuador's Quichua-speaking indigenous communities, but also examines the linguistic effects of long-term Quichua-Spanish contact. Among her findings, Haboud reports that indigenous women are losing Quichua to Spanish at a faster rate than indigenous men—a remarkable finding that contradicts the commonly held sociolinguistic view that men are more likely than women to shift from their native language to a dominant one. Zavala and Bariola (2008), on the other hand, find that Shipibo women who have migrated to Lima, Peru, from the Peruvian Amazonian rainforest are not just maintaining their native language, but also using it more than men, especially in communal meetings. Indeed, these findings about the relationships among bilingualism, gender, and migration highlight the need for more data on multiplex interactions between women and men and between women.

It is not surprising that sociolinguists dealing with present-day indigenous speech communities are becoming increasingly interested in revealing speakers' identities and subjectivities through narrative or discourse analysis, especially in light of continuous migration and recent indigenous-led social movements throughout Latin America. For instance, Sichra (2005) analyzes the attitudes and ideologies toward bilingualism of Bolivian indigenous intellectuals and activists with high levels of ethnolinguistic loyalty and awareness. Through their narratives, she shows us these speakers' contradictory, ambivalent attitudes and feelings in their self-reflections as urban bilingual speakers. With a comparative perspective, Howard (2007) examines the role of language ideologies of Quechua and Spanish in the discursive construction of cultural identities in contemporary Andean societies. She uses critical discourse analysis (CDA) to analyze oral testimonies of interviewees with diverse social positions and Quechua and Spanish language competencies. This important and remarkable work grows out of her wide-ranging and decades-long fieldwork throughout the Andes.

As demonstrated in this section, numerous studies describe the sociolinguistic situation of Quechua and Spanish in various Andean regions. However, we still need more sociolinguistic portrayals of how present-day indigenous speech communities make sense of centuries-long Quechua-Spanish language contact and differentiation as they engage in domestic and international migration. We need to examine how speakers construe, produce, and negotiate heterogeneous linguistic practices arising from the lingua-cultural interplay of Quechua and Spanish.

Language policy and planning, bilingual intercultural education, and literacy

In this section, we discuss the most recent studies in the fields of language policy and planning (LPP), bilingual intercultural education (BIE), and literacy. We have grouped these fields to stress not only their interventionist bent, which aims to influence the linguistic behaviors and practices of speech communities, but also the multiple vectors of human agency and the "messiness" that often accompany such interventions. In the past ten years, these fields have experienced significant reconceptualizations in their theoretical and methodological approaches.

Until recently, the field of language policy and planning was conceived chiefly from a top-down perspective, in which key players—national governments and nongovernmental organizations—proposed, enacted, and evaluated official national or regional language and educational policy. However, research has shown that it is important to include the perspectives of the people and the communities most affected by these policies. Thus a bottom-up approach has begun to be incorporated into the overall framework, in which speakers and their communities take part in the decision-making and implementation of new language and educational policies. To contextualize and capture the dynamics resulting from joint efforts between top-down organizations and bottom-up community groups, scholars are increasingly relying on ethnography. For instance, Coronel-Molina (2007), through interviews and participant-observation, highlights the top-down activities of Peru's High Academy of the Quechua Language to revitalize Quechua use throughout the Andes. He concludes that the Academy is so ideologically bound that it inhibits its own efforts to promote and revitalize the language.

Likewise, recent studies in bilingual intercultural education and literacy are influenced by similar theoretical and methodological orientations and emphases. King (2001) takes a similar look at BIE in the Saraguro region of the Ecuadorian Andes, studying the uses that two different indigenous communities have for Quichua, and what the language means to them in their daily lives. She finds that even within the same geographic region, different communities have different cultural needs and uses for their native language. In similar fashion, García (2005) points to another disconnect between the state and indigenous communities. In Peru, the state has created an idealized vision of a BIE program. The indigenous communities, on the other hand, have a different view of what they need. In recent years, they have begun speaking up more and demanding more input into the design of the educational curriculum. They clearly recognize the role that the educational system has in forming them into citizens of the state, but they also want to remain citizens of their own communities.

A major focus in intercultural bilingual education in South America is the role of education in constituting ethnic and national identities and producing citizens. Conducting fieldwork in a Bolivian teacher's college, Luykx (1999) explores how female indigenous students study the state-mandated curriculum to become teachers of the state-operated BIE program. Luykx shows how this environment becomes a contested site of identity production between indigenous students and their mainstream teachers who want to convert them from indigenous Aymaras into *mestiza* citizens. Hornberger (2000) addresses similar themes, discussing the top-down versus bottom-up definitions of "interculturality" and its impact on the BIE curriculum. Interculturality in the educational realm aims to transform a "standardizing education" into one that allows for the expression and practice of cultural and linguistic diversity. Hornberger analyzes data from her own fieldwork to explore this concept and determine whether such a sea change has been possible, or might yet be possible.

In other South American indigenous communities, intercultural bilingual education and other language policy and planning initiatives have underscored the need for educational initiatives to effect language revitalization. For example, Corvalán (1998, 1999) outlines the paths that both LPP and BIE have taken in Paraguay with regard to Guaraní and Spanish. While the first article expands on the more purely sociocultural implications of BIE, the second examines LPP and its impact on the sociolinguistic aspects of bilingualism in education. Gynan (2001) focuses mainly on the successes that both language planning and BIE have enjoyed in Paraguay. Choi (2004) discusses how Guaraní came to be revalorized and made an official language after nearly 500 years of Spanish domination. She then offers a comparison of two studies she carried out in 1990 and 2000 to determine whether the National Plan for Bilingual Education and Maintenance is having the desired effect of maintaining and even expanding the use of Guaraní in daily life.

Most synthetic studies center their attention on the Andean region, dealing with LPP and BIE in Peru, Ecuador and Bolivia. Among these synthetic works, Albó and Anaya's (2004) monograph highlights how BIE has developed in Bolivia among the Quechua and Aymara populations, and the social and political uses to which they are putting their newfound knowledge and literacy skills. In this regard, they seem to declare BIE a success story, for the most part, in Bolivia. Hornberger and López (1998) do not make the same claims for BIE and LPP in Peru and Bolivia, but they present a cogent view of how the multilingual nature of much of the indigenous population is changing educational policy and practice. In contrast, Godenzzi (2008) discusses how LPP evolves across the Andean region, how it purportedly addresses linguistic rights, and how this planning plays out in the educational arena, while King and Haboud (2002) discuss similar themes for Ecuador. Hornberger and Coronel-Molina (2004) take on a much larger and more ambitious project: rather than focusing only on education, their overview of LPP across the Andes addresses language maintenance and revitalization of Quechua. They provide a historical overview of not only formal language policy and planning issues, but also informal, *ad hoc* practices that have affected the outcomes of these policies (see López 2005, for BIE in Bolivia, López and Rojas 2006, for BIE in Latin America, and López 2006, for LPP from an ecological perspective).

Similar conclusions abound in studies of literacy practices in South American indigenous speech communities, especially the indigenous communities in Amazonia. Aikman's (1999) monograph illustrates the literacy experiences of the Arakmbut, an indigenous people living in the Peruvian Amazonian rainforest. Aikman offers a bottom-up perspective, examining the complex relationship that this community has with the state, as brought about by state-mandated education. She shows us how these people develop their own version of literacy, taking what they are taught and subverting it in

47

ways that are culturally relevant to them. Tacelosky (2001) considers the Peruvian Amazonian community, the Shipibo, and their experiences with state-run bilingual education. Despite the transitional bilingual education program active in this community, Tacelosky finds that, contrary to his expectations, the Shipibo do not appear to be giving up their language in favor of Spanish; rather, they are keeping their own language while acquiring Spanish literacy. In another example, de la Piedra (2003) finds that literacy as taught to rural Peruvian Quechua speakers has little basis in their daily lives and ways of understanding the world, and they do not adopt traditional literacy in any functional way.

In studying mother tongue literacy among Bolivian women, Howard-Malverde (1998) finds that the women experienced a disjuncture between the top-down expectations and policy design, on one hand, and the community's perceptions and expectations towards literacy, on the other. Zavala (2002) examines how a decontextualized literacy taught by the state affects a small Peruvian Andean community, alienating the learners who see no real need for either Quechua or Spanish literacy. Salomon and Apaza (2006) discover that Quechua and Aymara peoples around Lake Titicaca have made "mainstream" literacy serve viable functions in their daily lives, despite the strong disjuncture between state-taught Spanish literacy and both their native languages and the rural Spanish they speak.

Zavala, Niño-Murcia and Ames (2004) and Hornberger (1997) have each compiled anthologies on literacy, underscoring the need to understand first how a community views and uses literacy, either in its native language or in the dominant language or both, before simply imposing or mandating BIE or any language policy. In a similar vein, López and Jung's (1998) collection of essays focuses on the distinction between spoken and written literacy, and its impact on language revitalization efforts. In a recent review, Sichra (2008) attends to indigenous or native literacy practices in the Andes, whether these are oral, alphabetic or symbolic.

In conclusion, as this selective review has shown, several solid ethnographic studies examine the status of language policy and planning issues regarding South American indigenous languages. However, one of the major conclusions of every study is that its results and findings are relevant almost exclusively to the population studied, although they do suggest some broad generalizations. Given the specific and local application of findings to language policy and planning issues, we need more ethnographic studies that inform or shape culturally relevant services and programs for indigenous speakers and their communities.

Conclusion

In this review chapter, we have provided a broad and critical glimpse into the state of recent empirical sociolinguistic research into diverse indigenous speech communities in South America. We hope that this review will stimulate and motivate further studies of language contact, bilingualism and identity, and applied sociolinguistics.

As stated earlier, educational concerns and developments have propelled much of the sociolinguistic research highlighted here. This has been especially true in the Andes—the area on which the review focused. As a result, much of the linguistic and sociolinguistic work emerging from this area is descriptive and applied. In studies of bilingualism and identity, we suggest more analysis of interactional data, not just interview data, to understand how speakers deploy their linguistic repertoires to enact and negotiate their identities and subjectivities with others. In other words, we need speaker-centered ethnographies of language shift and bilingualism. In studies of intercultural bilingual education and literacy, we need to conduct more ethnographic studies that combine both top-down and bottom-up approaches. In doing so, we can better understand the agentive power and intricacies of mapping and advancing visions, goals, and strategies among the governments, institutions, communities and individuals involved in these efforts.

References

Adelaar, W. F. H. (2006) "Guaraní," in K. Brown (ed.), *Encyclopedia of Language and Linguistics*, Oxford: Elsevier, pp. 165–66.

Adelaar, W. F. H. and Muysken, P. (2004) *The Languages of the Andes*, Cambridge: Cambridge University Press.

Aikhenvald, A. Y. (2002) *Language Contact in Amazonia*, New York: Oxford University Press.

Aikman, S. (1999) *Intercultural Education and Literacy: An Ethnographic Study of Indigenous Knowledge and Learning in the Peruvian Amazon*, Amsterdam: John Benjamins.

Albó, X. and Anaya, A. (2004) *Niños alegres, libres, expresivos: La audacia de la educación intercultural bilingüe en Bolivia*, La Paz: UNICEF/CIPCA Cuadernos de Investigación 58.

Cerrón-Palomino, R. (2000) *Lingüística aimara*, Cuzco: Centro Bartolomé de las Casas.

——(2003) *Lingüística quechua*, Cuzco: Centro Bartolomé de las Casas.

——(2006) *El chipaya o la lengua de los hombres del agua*, Lima: Fondo Editorial de la Pontificia Universidad Católica del Perú.

——(2008) *Quechumara: estructuras paralelas del quechua y del aimara*, La Paz: Plural.

Chirinos, A. (2001) *Atlas lingüístico del Perú*, Cuzco: Centro Bartolomé de las Casas.

Choi, J. K. (1998) "Languages in contact: a morphosyntactic analysis of Paraguayan Spanish from a historical and sociolinguistic perspective," unpublished thesis, Georgetown University.

——(2004) "La planificación lingüística y la revaloración del guaraní en el Paraguay: comparación, evaluación e implicación," *Language Problems & Language Planning*, 28, 241–59.

Coronel-Molina, S. M. (2007) "Language policy and planning, and language ideologies in Peru: the case of Cuzco's High Academy of the Quechua Language (Qheswa simi hamut' ana kuraq suntur)," unpublished thesis, University of Pennsylvania.

Corvalán, G. (1998) "La educación escolar bilingüe del Paraguay: avances y desafíos," *Revista Paraguaya de Sociologia*, 35, 101–18.

——(1999) "Políticas lingüísticas, integración y educación en el Paraguay," *Ñemity: Revista Bilingüe de Cultura*, 37, 18–24.

de Granda, G. (1999) *Español y lenguas indoamericanas en Hispanoamérica. Estructuras, situaciones y transferencias*, Valladolid: Universidad de Valladolid.

——(2002) *Lingüística de contacto. Español y quechua en el área andina suramericana*, Lima: Pontificia Universidad Católica del Perú.

de la Piedra, M. T. (2003) "Literacy practices among Quechua-speakers: the case study of a rural community in the Peruvian Andes," unpublished thesis, University of Texas, Austin.

de los Heros, S. (2001) *Discurso, identidad y género en el castellano peruano*, Lima: Pontificia Universidad Católica del Perú.

Dixon, R. M. W. and Aikhenvald, A.Y. (eds.) (1999) *The Amazonian Languages*, Cambridge: Cambridge University Press.

Escobar, A. (1978) *Variaciones sociolingüísticas del castellano en el Perú*, Lima: Instituto de Estudios Peruanos.

Escobar, A. M. (2000) *Contacto social y lingüístico: el español en contacto con el quechua en el Perú*, Lima: Pontificia Universidad Católica del Perú.

Everett, D. L. (2003) "Documenting languages: the view from Brazilian Amazon," in P. Austin (ed.), *Language Documentation and Description*, vol. 1, Papers from the First Conference Sponsored by the Hans Rausing Endangered Languages Project. London: School of Oriental and African Studies, pp. 140–58.

Faller, M. (2002) "Semantics and pragmatics of evidentials in Cuzco Quechua," unpublished thesis, Stanford University.

Feke, M. S. (2004) "Quechua to Spanish cross-linguistic influence among Cuzco Quechua-Spanish bilinguals: the case of epistemology," unpublished thesis, University of Pittsburgh.

García, M. E. (2005) *Making Indigenous Citizens: Identities, Education, and Multicultural Activism in Peru*, Stanford, CA: Stanford University Press.

Godenzzi, J. C. (2008) "Language policy and education in the Andes," in S. May and N. H. Hornberger (eds.) *Encyclopedia of Language and Education*, 2nd edn, vol. 1, *Language Policy and Political Issues in Education*, New York: Springer, pp. 315–29.

Gómez-Rendón, J. (2005) "La media lengua de Imbabura," in H. Olbertz and P. Muysken (eds.) *Encuentros y conflictos: Bilingüismo y contacto de lenguas en el mundo andino*, Madrid/Frankfurt am Main: Iberoamericana/Vervuert, pp. 39–57.

Gugenberger, E. (1999) "Entre el quechua y el castellano: manifestaciones del conflicto de identidades etnolingüísticas en un pueblo joven de Arequipa," *Lexis*, 23, 257–300.

Gynan, S. N. (2001) "Language planning and policy in Paraguay," *Current Issues in Language Planning*, 2, 53–118.

Haboud, M. (1998) *Quichua y castellano en los andes ecuatorianos. Los efectos de un contacto prolongado*, Quito: Abya-Yala/EBI-GTZ.

——(2005) "El gerundio de anterioridad entre bilingües quichua-castellano y monolingües hispanohablantes de la Sierra ecuatoriana," *UniverSOS: Revista de Lenguas Indígenas y Universos Culturales*, 2, 9–38.

Heggarty, P. (2007) "Linguistics for archaeologists: principles, methods and the case of the Incas," *Cambridge Archaeological Journal*, 17, 311–40.

——(2008) "Linguistics for archaeologists: a case-study in the Andes," *Cambridge Archaeological Journal*, 18, 35–56.

Hornberger, N. H. (ed.) (1997) *Indigenous Literacies in the Americas: Language Planning from the Bottom Up*, New York: Mouton de Gruyter.

——(2000) "Bilingual education policy and practice in the Andes: ideological paradox and intercultural possibility," *Anthropology and Education Quarterly*, 31, 173–201.

Hornberger, N. H. and Coronel-Molina, S. M. (2004) "Quechua language shift, maintenance, and revitalization in the Andes: the case for language planning," *International Journal of the Sociology of Language*, 167, 9–67.

Hornberger, N. and López, L. (1998) "Policy, possibility and paradox: indigenous multilingualism and education in Peru and Bolivia," in J. Cenoz and F. Genesee (eds.) *Beyond Bilingualism: Multilingualism and Multilingual Education*, Clevedon: Multilingual Matters, pp. 206–42.

Howard, R. (2007) *Por los linderos de la lengua: Ideologías lingüísticas en los Andes*, Lima: Instituto de Estudios Peruanos/Instituto Francés de Estudios Peruanos/Fondo Editorial/Pontificia Universidad Católica del Perú.

Howard-Malverde, R. (1998) "'Grasping awareness': mother-tongue literacy for Quechua speaking women in Northern Potosí, Bolivia," *International Journal of Educational Development*, 18, 181–96.

King, K.A. (2001) *Language Revitalization Processes and Prospects: Quichua in the Ecuadorian Andes*, Clevedon: Multilingual Matters.

King, K. A. and Haboud, M. (2002) "Language planning and policy in Ecuador," *Current Issues in Language Planning*, 3, 359–424.

Klee, C.A. and Caravedo, R. (2005) "Contact-induced language change in Lima, Peru: the case of clitic pronouns," in D. Eddington (ed.) *Selected Proceedings of the 7th Hispanic Linguistics Symposium*, Somerville, MA: Cascadilla Proceedings Project, pp. 12–21.

Lenk, S. (2007) "Can minority languages survive in a situation of sustained bilingualism? Ethnolinguistic vitality and language behavior among indigenous speakers of Quichua in Ecuador," unpublished thesis, University of Pittsburgh.

López, L. E. (2005) *De resquicios a boquerones: La educación intercultural bilingüe en Bolivia*, La Paz: PROEIB-Andes/Plural.

——(ed.) (2006) *Diversidad y ecología del lenguaje en Bolivia*, La Paz, Bolivia: PROEIB-Andes/Plural.

López, L. E. and Jung, I. (eds.) (1998) *Sobre las huellas de la voz: Sociolingüística de la oralidad y la escritura en su relación con la educación*, Madrid/Cochabamba/Bonn: Morata/PROEIB-Andes/DSE.

López, L. E. and Rojas, C. (2006) *La EIB en América Latina bajo examen*, La Paz: Banco Mundial/GTZ/Plural.

Luykx, A. (1999) *The Citizen Factory: Schooling and Cultural Production in Bolivia*, Albany, NY: SUNY Press.

Mamani Morales, J. C. (2005) *Los rostros del aymara en Chile. El caso de Parinacota*, La Paz: Plural Editores/PINSEIB/PROEIB Andes.

Marr, T. (1998) "The language left at Ticlio: social and cultural perspectives on Quechua language loss in Lima, Peru," unpublished thesis, University of Liverpool.

Muysken, P. (1997) "Media lengua," in S. G. Thomason (ed.) *Contact Languages: A Wider Perspective*, Amsterdam: John Benjamins, pp. 365–426.

——(2005) "A modular approach to sociolinguistic variation in syntax: the gerund in Ecuadorian Spanish," in L. Cornips and K. P. Corrigan (eds.) *Syntax and Variation: Reconciling the Biological and the Social*, Amsterdam: John Benjamins, pp. 31–53.

Olbertz, H. (2008) "*Dar* + gerund in Ecuadorian Highland Spanish: contact-induced grammaticalization," *Spanish in Context*, 5, 89–109.

Palacios, A. (2000) "El sistema pronominal del español Paraguayo: un caso de contacto de lenguas," in J. Calvo (ed.) *Contacto de lenguas en América: El español en el candelero*, Madrid/Frankfurt am Main: Iberoamericana/Vervuert.

——(2005) "Lenguas en contacto en Paraguay: español y guaraní," in C. Ferrero Pino and N. Lasso-von Lan (eds.) *Variedades lingüísticas y lenguas en contacto en el mundo de habla hispana*, Bloomington, IN: Books Library, pp. 44–52.

——(2006) "Cambios inducidos por contacto en el español de la sierra ecuatoriana: la simplificación de los sistemas pronominales (procesos de neutralización y elisión)," *Tópicos del Seminario*, 15, 197–229.

Salomon, F. and Apaza, E. C. (2006) "Vernacular literacy on the Lake Titicaca high plains, Peru," *Reading Research Quarterly*, 41, 304–26.

Sánchez, L. (2003) *Quechua-Spanish Bilingualism: Interference and Convergence in Functional Categories*, Amsterdam: John Benjamins.

——(2004) "Functional convergence in the tense, evidentiality, and aspectual system of Quechua-Spanish bilinguals," *Bilingualism: Language and Cognition*, 7, 147–62.

Sichra, I. (2003) *La vitalidad del quechua: Lengua y sociedad en dos provincias de Cochabamba*, La Paz, Bolivia: PROEIB-Andes/Plural Editores.

——(2005) "De eso no se habla pero se escucha: conociendo y reconociendo el bilingüismo urbano," in H. Olbertz and P. Muysken (eds.) *Encuentros y conflictos: Bilingüismo y contacto de lenguas en el mundo andino*, Madrid/Frankfurt am Main: Iberoamericana/Vervuert, pp. 153–70.

——(2008) "Language diversity and indigenous literacy in the Andes," in B. V. Street and N. H. Hornberger (eds.) *Encyclopedia of Language and Education*, 2nd edn, vol. 2, *Literacy*. New York: Springer, pp. 283–97.

Tacelosky, K. (2001) "Bilingual education and language use among the Shipibo of the Peruvian Amazon," *Journal of Multilingual and Multicultural Development*, 22, 39–56.

Torero, A. (2002) *Idiomas de los andes: Lingüística e historia*, Lima: Editorial Horizonte/Institut Français des Études Andines.

Yánez Cossío, C. (2001) *Dos lenguas en contraste. Quichua-Español*, Quito: Abya-Yala.

Zavala, V. (2002) *(Des)encuentros con la escritura. Escuela y comunidad en los Andes peruanos*, Lima: Red para el Desarrollo de las Ciencias Sociales en el Perú.

Zavala, V. and Bariola, N. (2008) "'Enra kopiai, non kopiai': gender, ethnicity, and language use in a Shipibo community in Lima," in M. Niño-Murcia and J. Rothman (eds.), *Bilingualism and Identity: Spanish at the Crossroads with Other Languages*, Amsterdam: John Benjamins, pp. 151–74.

Zavala, V., Niño-Murcia, M. and Ames, P. (eds.) (2004) *Escritura y sociedad: Nuevas perspectivas teóricas y etnográficas*, Lima: Red para el Desarrollo de las Ciencias Sociales en el Perú.

Zúñiga, F. (2006) "Mapudungun," in K. Brown (ed.) *Encyclopedia of Language and Linguistics*, Oxford: Elsevier, pp. 487–8.

5

Sociolinguistics of the Caribbean

Valerie Youssef

Introduction

The insular Caribbean spans the region from Florida to the northern coast of South America. It is flanked on the west by Central America. The islands are often grouped according to their official languages as hispanophone, francophone or anglophone and they include some few small Dutch-official territories, e.g. St. Maarten and Saba. The Anglophone grouping is the largest and has attracted the most sociolinguistic interest. A list of territories of the region is included in Table 5.1. It is useful to survey how the region is constituted before proceeding to a fuller description of sociolinguistic work on the Anglophone Caribbean, which must be our focus in a chapter of quite limited length.

The Greater Antilles encompasses three islands (one constituted of two very distinct countries):

1 Cuba (population 11,300,000; Spanish-speaking).
2 The Dominican Republic (population approximately 8,500,000, also Spanish-speaking) and Haiti (French Creole-speaking/French official). Haiti has been little investigated from a sociolinguistic perspective but the work of Rachelle Doucet (e.g. Schieffelin and Doucet 1994) is a notable exception.
3 Jamaica (population 2,800,000: Anglophone Creole-speaking/English official).

In the region as a whole, there continues to be a major focus on Jamaican Creole, and its interface with Jamaican English (e.g. Devonish 1998; Patrick 1999; Beckford-Wassink 1999, 2001) though the Creole continuum model is conceptualized very differently from the way in which it was regarded in the 1960s (cf. De Camp 1971).

The Lesser Antilles is made up of smaller islands. Martinique and Guadeloupe are the major Francophone territories, with Francophone Creole and French as distinct codes within them. US territories to the north are the US Virgin Islands and Puerto Rico, and within these, creolized English and Spanish respectively battle with the dominion of American English. The Bahamas is a member of the economic union of the Caribbean though geographically north of the region.

Table 5.1 Caribbean population and languages, 2001

Country	Population	Official language	Spoken languages
Antigua and Barbuda	66,970	English	English, local dialects
Aruba	70,007	Dutch	Papiamentu, Dutch, English, Spanish
Bahamas	303,611	English	English, Creole
Barbados	275,330	English	English
Bay Islands, Honduras	49,151	Spanish	Spanish, English, Creole, Amerindian 'dialects'
Belize	256,062	English	English, Spanish, Mayan, Garifuna, Creole
Bermuda	63,503	English	English, Portuguese
British Virgin Islands	20,812	English	English
Cancun	400,000	Spanish	Spanish, English
Cayman Islands	40,900	English	English
Cuba	11,217,100	Spanish	Spanish
Curacao	130,000	Dutch	Dutch
Dominica	70,786	English	English, French patois
Dominican Republic	8,581,477	Spanish	Spanish, some English
Grenada	89,227	English	English, French patois
Guadeloupe	431,170	French	French, Creole patois
Haiti	6,964,549	French	French, Creole
Isla Cozumel	50,000	Spanish	Spanish
Isla de Margarita	350,000	Spanish	Spanish
Jamaica	2,665,636	English	English, Creole

Belize in Central America is usually included within sociolinguistic discussions of the region (e.g. Young 1973; Le Page and Tabouret-Keller 1985) as is Guyana on the South American continent (e.g. Rickford 1979; Edwards 1990). Belize has a unique linguistic situation with several indigenous languages being of sociolinguistic import (e.g. Bonner 2001; Escure 1982).

The hispanophone territories have not attracted much attention among sociolinguists, perhaps because of their 'lack' of Creole languages save for Papiamentu in Aruba and Bonaire.

From Creole continuum to acts of identity and beyond

The history of modern Creole sociolinguistics in the Caribbean was landmarked in 1968 with a conference at the Mona campus of the University of the West Indies, which resulted in the publishing of Dell Hymes's (1971) seminal edited volume of papers from that meeting. Chapters in that volume are still reference points today, including of course David De Camp's famous Introduction, reviewing the field and describing what he then called a post-Creole continuum, as well as Labov's work debating the existence of one or two underlying systems. Dennis Craig's seminal work on language education is also included and he later developed it further (Craig 1999, 2006).

Following that closely came Bickerton's (1975) *Dynamics of a Creole System*, in which he used an implicational scale model to demonstrate shift across the continuum as revealed by his Guyanese data. Bickerton did not have sociolinguistic concerns but his study has been considered significant, although his view of language shift as a uni-dimensional flow from Creole to Standard has become inadequate for the complex of present-day development and change. This work contains an Introduction by Richard Allsopp which demonstrates how a co-existent systems model is inapplicable since language features do not shift uniformly in the contact sub-systems entailed.

At the same time as the 1969 conference a series of scholars including such eminent present-day creolists as Walter Edwards, Pauline Christie, Hubert Devonish and Donald Winford were undertaking Caribbean linguistics research in the UK under the supervision of Robert Le Page. Le Page was involved in a research project concerned to describe the vernaculars of all the Caribbean territories and into which his students fitted well. They included Christie (1969) for Dominica, Winford for Trinidad (1972) and Edwards (1975) and Devonish (1978) for Guyana. Each of these works was sociolinguistic in its approach. Devonish took up a lifelong battle for the instrumentalization of Creole vernaculars at this time.

Winford's (1972) work was the first major application of classical Labovian methodology, to the Trinidad sociolinguistic complex. Out of the work came the first quantitatively based recognition that the Trinidad Creole predicate system formed a distinct system from the Standard English system and that speakers used it and modified their speech towards the Standard in predictable ways, with certain overt markers being highly stigmatized and others less overt and more admissible to semi-formal speech levels. Winford showed that the application of a variable rule type description to Creole communities would be a fraught one given the separateness of the contact systems.

Later, he observed that what speakers shared was not always the precise forms that they commanded and certainly not the incidence of their usage but norms for interaction (Winford 1988). He brought discussion of what constitutes a speech community into a Caribbean frame of reference, in the context of which it has continued to prove challenging (cf. Patrick 1999).

Returning to Le Page, he had spent time working at the then University College of the West Indies in Jamaica from 1950 to 1960 and was later to contribute his own theory to sociolinguistic investigation through his work in Belize and St. Lucia and the formulation of his *Acts of Identity* theory (Le Page and Tabouret-Keller 1985).

In 2007, we came full circle with a workshop at Stanford to celebrate Le Page's work, under the aegis of leading creolist and Stanford Professor, John Rickford. It reconsidered Le Page's work and legacy (Christie 2007), and reassessed its contribution to sociolinguistic models and theory (Edwards 2007).

Le Page stressed the active role of the speaker in selecting language in the multi-dimensional socio-cultural milieu s/he inhabits as s/he aligns him/herself selectively closer to or further away from others in this space. He individualized language choice and attempted to find an analytical frame to apply on a large scale. While the analytic power of cluster analysis remained problematic, the major sociolinguistic theories that followed after, namely accommodation theory (Giles and Smith 1979), social network theory (Milroy 1980) and communities of practice theory (e.g. Eckert and McConnell-Ginet 1992), include ideas that were integral to Le Page's work. None of these has been applied to the Caribbean region on a large scale.

The other major work in the Labovian paradigm was Rickford's (1979) on Guyana. He used a later model and also compared the quantitative and implicational scale models. He discerned that the former worked better for phonological variables and the latter for highly differentiated grammatical variables. Since both Guyana and Trinidad have large Indian populations, it is unsurprising that studies therein have found ethnic differentiation as well as socio-economic. Gender was not studied by Winford in Trinidad, but Sidnell

(1999) found similar patterns of gender variation to Rickford in Guyana, which he explained in the enduring quality of gender relations in the rural Indo-Guyanese community investigated by them both.

It is important for us to remember that language situations such as those of Jamaica, Guyana and Tobago are not parallelled across the Caribbean, where several varieties, including both Barbados and Trinidad do not exhibit a basilect and therefore do not strictly conform to the Creole continuum construct.

Allsopp's Caribbean Lexicography Project which began in the 1970s culminated in his *Dictionary of Caribbean English Usage* (Allsopp 1996), a work which has demonstrated the profound fusion of cultures within Caribbean lexicon well into the local Standard varieties.

Transitioning

Since 1990, the Labovian model, and the Creole continuum construct have been modified further. Peter Patrick's (1999) work on urban Jamaica applies it in a more current frame, negating the association of a continuum with decreolization and arguing for a multidimensional frame of investigation. He conducted his sociolinguistic survey of Kingston, Jamaica (Patrick 1992), based on interviews, English to Patwa translations and SE reading tests along with a language attitude survey. He focuses on the mesolect and argues for its distinct, though heterogeneous character. Patrick has also discussed the application of the speech community conceptualization to his data and argued for a heterogeneous language consciousness which stretches the boundaries of the concept.

Youssef's work on Trinidad language use (e.g. 1991) has resulted in her coinage of the term 'varilingualism' to describe the systematic code-mixing behaviour which mesolectal speakers use from the earliest stages of language development as appropriate to stylistic and social factors. This term, also applied to the adult language situation in Tobago (e.g. Youssef 1996), interrogates the character of mesolectal interaction with the acrolect, and argues for a stabilization of the contact varieties, with each variety having discrete and particular functions.

In recent years, we have witnessed some spreading of attention to the smaller islands (including Aceto 2003 and the range of territories examined in Aceto and Williams's edited volume, 2003). This work demonstrates the individuality of linguistic development of each island community, which non-Caribbean linguists are sometimes not aware of. There are two articles on the Bahamas in the volume in question, the first (Childs *et al.* 2003) investigates phonological variation in both black and white communities and demonstrates an increasingly common duality whereby there is both mutual accommodation and an ethnic divide. McPhee's chapter describes the TMA system in Bahamian Creole (McPhee 2003).

Cutler's chapter describes language use in The Turks and Caicos islands, specifically on the language varieties of Grand Turk (Cutler 2003). Her study is grammatical and concludes that the vernacular is close to the acrolect and might be closer to American-African varieties than to Caribbean ones. She indicates the need for comparison of the islands. The chapter on Anguilla (Williams 2003) is narrow since it focuses on the language of a single clear-skinned family in the village of Island Harbour. What he shows, however, is that their distinctive variety is losing ground such that young family members share more features of Anguillan Creole English. Van Herk's chapter is an entertaining comparison between two radically different Barbadian speakers (Van Herk 2003); in its very lack of typicality, however, it does not take us far into Barbadian description. Other insightful works on Barbados include Blake (1997) which deals with dialectal difference according to both race and class and Isaacs (2006).

Aceto himself carried out his major work on Barbuda and writes a chapter in which he explains the existence of a basilect in this territory, which did not experience plantation slavery (Aceto 2003). He explains it in a distinction which he makes between 'Immigrant Creole varieties' and 'autonomous' or deep Creole ones. There are two chapters on Carriacou by Fayer (Fayer 2003) and by Kephart (Kephart 2003). The latter is a useful linguistic sketch of the territory.

In the past decade, there has been major focus on Trinidad and Tobago, with a concern in particular for adequate description of Tobago, e.g. James and Youssef (2002, 2008), Youssef and James (2008). Work has also emerged on the language of Bequia (St. Vincent and the Grenadines) and Meyerhoff and Walker (2007) have noted that native speakers abroad may superficially adopt foreign 'twangs' beneath which there is only superficial restructuring of grammar. This kind of comparison is needed for the region as a whole as its diasporic communities are growing apace. The territory has received considerable study (Meyerhoff and Walker 2006, 2007), has been used to re-examine the creole continuum construct and has demonstrated the extent of differentiation among language varieties, even in such a small close community.

There has also been continued work on St. Lucia (e.g. Simmons-McDonald 1996; Garrett 2003) and Dominica (Christie 1990, 1994; Paugh 2005) both of which continue to be classified as Francophone *and* Anglophone Creole territories since they are English official, with middle-level Anglophone mesolectal creoles spreading their domains of usage, but with continuing basilectal French Creole varieties. I discuss this work in the following sub-section.

Developing trends and tendencies

In the past decade there has been a major shift in the concerns of sociolinguistic literature of the region which merits discussion in its own right. Sociolinguistics generally has observed a shift in the concerns of major conferences to admit considerable work in corpus linguistics and discourse analysis. There has been a recognition that sociolinguistics can be carried out using corpus tools for speed and accuracy of analysis and the tremendous embracing of discourse analysis reflects the insurgence of micro-analysis as a means of reaching further into the macro. These trends are mirrored in writing on the Caribbean.

Corpus linguistics

For corpus linguistics, the work of Mark Sebba and Susan Dray on Jamaican Creole is significant. From working initially on British Black English and on London Jamaican, they have extended their studies to collecting data based on the language of written street signs in Jamaica (Dray 2002; Sebba and Dray 2004). Because these signs are written in Creole, they give insight into the language of the street. They have grappled with the close interface between Creole and standard in the written form and on the relative contribution of their work to sociolinguistics (Sebba and Dray 2003). They have tagged into their corpora writing styles to distinguish conscious and unconscious writing strategies (Devonish 1996) and have flagged demographic information to compare orthographic tendencies across social parameters such as age, social level and education. Their work is significant for demonstrating how an orthography naturally develops and delineates its importance to the development of descriptive grammars for Creoles.

In addition, the International Corpus of English (ICE), work that is based in Freiburg under the aegis of Christian Mair (cf. Mair and Sand 1998), has produced a corpus for Jamaica and is now beginning a corpus for Trinidad to supplement and diversify the Caribbean base (for a first mention, Deuber and Youssef 2007). This corpus, unlike the Lancaster one, is drawn from spoken language as well as written language with a precise focus on local Standard English. Because of the fluidity of this variety, however, the corpus includes a range of language close to the acrolect, which serves the functions of Standard and is liberally mixed with it. This might seem problematic for a purist corpus of SE but speaks to a need to move away from a traditional creole continuum framework, for it demonstrates the complexity of linguistic inter-relationships close to the acrolect and a spreading of Creole into the domains of Standard. It delineates a linguistic reality with which we must grapple as the description of post-colonial Englishes develops. These varieties will have to be recognized as entities which draw on the essential language of the people. The removal of colonial powers has led to the Standard language being represented globally by non-native speakers. These varieties have to be grafted on to the ever-developing Standard language 'tree'. Beyond corpus linguistics, studies of the Jamaican acrolect such as Irvine's (2004) attest to a variability at that level in phonology that has not formerly been admitted.

Mair (2007) has expressed a reserved view of the role of corpus evidence in sociolinguistic studies. He delineates analytic differences in corpus linguistics having an absolute corpus size, being rooted in the public domain (as distinct from the academic) and having an emphasis on collocational patterns and corpus-internal variability rather than the relationship between dependent linguistic variables and independent social ones. Despite these differences, the one area can clearly complement the other and his recognition that Caribbean Standards no longer draw heavily on a British influence but rather on American varieties and the local mesolect itself is significant.

The twenty-first century sees us integrating post-colonial English (Schneider 2007) into our linguistic reality, charting its course of development and its structural features. When Platt et al. (1984) wrote of the New Englishes, they were still marginalized but the very course of time and continuum-oriented investigations have shown that Standard too is a dynamic entity that must change its shape and perforce recognize non-English influence.

Discourse analysis

The plethora of work on discourse analysis across the Caribbean in the past decade ranges across media and medicine (e.g. Shields-Brodber 2006), law and justice (Evans 2007), to the stuff of ordinary conversation, from greetings to routines to face-saving (Mühleisen and Migge 2005). It embraces developmental interaction (Tessoneau 2005; Youssef 2005) and classroom language (Bryan 2001; Youssef 2006), never with a focus on Standard so much as on conversation building and its cultural ramifications. It embraces literary discourse (Lalla 2006; Schneider and Wagner 2006), which is forging new ground in its discussion of the representation of Creole use in both direct speech and narrative.

Today an authenticity is being recognized in literary representation which allows for power-solidarity relations and other situational dynamics coming through in the alternation of codes and for alternative meanings, at once Creole and Standard, being exploited (Lalla 2006: 184–5). There is developing discussion of the use of Creole in narrative and the force that this can achieve in writing (cf. Mühleisen 2002).

Shields–Brodber (2006) makes the point that Creole has long since become a public variety insofar as it has been adopted into educated speech. With an increasing number of call-in shows of all kinds, the speakers and those who question them must needs produce Creole to relate effectively. Indeed, if they do not deal in it effectively, exploitation results, as Evans' study (2007) of language use in the law courts of St. Lucia is able to show. Broadly, then, the domains of Creole enactment are spreading.

2005 witnessed the publication of a volume on politeness and face-saving in Creoles (Mühleisen and Migge 2005), a landmark study in itself. The papers are based on fieldwork and span territories such as Jamaica, Trinidad, Barbados and Guyana as well as Guadeloupe and the Maroon communities of Surinam and French Guyana. They are significant for placing the language varieties in precise socio-cultural contexts which delineate at once specific cultural norms and universal social-psychological tendencies. The developmental studies in this volume are significant for this duality also. Youssef argues that face-saving is a universal phenomenon established from the pre-school stage and manifested differentially in different cultures. Tessoneau shows how at every stage and level face-work is critical, and how in the country regions of Guadeloupe the appropriate balance between Creole and French is a major part of this.

The papers range beyond language per se to 'rude sounds' (Figueroa 2005: 76) in a discussion of use of the famous 'kiss teeth', 'suck teeth' or plain 'steups' characteristic of disapproval in Anglophone Caribbean territories. This discussion takes its own distinct place in the shift in focus to the language of every man in the public sphere.

Beyond this work, of course, it is important to recognize that studies of conversation have been very evident in recent Caribbean sociolinguistic literature. We can summarize by referring to Shields–Brodber's (2001) work on the nature of the performance floor, a jointly constructed and often public sharing of floor space, which uses Jamaican data as the source. Youssef has worked on conversational structure both among university students (Youssef 2001) and among small children with their teachers (Youssef 2006). The first work gives a clear indication of the ways in which conversational roles change dependent on the exact composition of the group, while the latter shows how prejudice can be levelled against the vernacular by unsensitized teachers.

The ways in which written discourse in its various dimensions has impacted on sociolinguistic investigation and theory are brought out clearly in Mühleisen's (2002) volume. She argues from a Faircloughian (Fairclough 1992) perspective that the representation of Creole in discourse is itself a reflection and creator of perspectives on the languages and their speakers, and explains changing attitudes to both in the evolution of their representation.

Since she has done considerable work on language attitudes, specifically in Trinidad and in reference to Winford's (1976) earlier work on teacher attitudes (e.g. Mühleisen 2002), studies of this kind are summarized also. Mühleisen speaks to the distinction between 'staging' and 'performing' identity in her own interviewees, reflecting the longstanding dichotomy between stated attitudes towards the vernacular, in this case positive, running counter to evidence from its actual use.

An important study of attitudes to Jamaican Creole is that of Beckford-Wassink (1999), which demonstrates an expected ambivalence, with the Creole being perceived as more or less appropriate for different situations. Attitude studies like this one, however, make it unsurprising that code-switching and mixing are becoming increasingly normative as speakers balance the functional values of the contact codes of their exposure.

58

Code-mixing

The trend towards discussion of code-mixing is as illuminating as the shift to discussion of new Standard varieties. The Creole continuum construct is being consistently modified to show that we are witnessing stabilization of the contact varieties as a result of the functional role that each plays in the language complexes in which we live. The term coined by Carrington (1980) – Caribbean sociolinguistic complex, which acknowledges the multidimensional space within which Creole languages and official Standards function – has taken on increased meaning over the past 20 years and has effectively modified the continuum construct.

As long ago as 1991, Youssef coined the term 'varilingualism' to describe that competence whereby individuals learn to mix codes according to appropriacy levels, learnt through their individual language exposure and the term has also been useful in describing adult language competence and use (Youssef 1996). As time passes, more and more attention is being paid to this phenomenon. A very recent work by Isaacs (2006) describes code-mixing for St. Lucia as what she conceives of as 'a new discourse strategy' (ibid.: 226). She does not speculate too much on the reasons for it, but Youssef is less hesitant, finding its source in speakers working out their identity through the effective mixing of codes, each being critical to their identity even as the varieties fulfil distinct functions in creole societies as a whole.

Other kinds of Creole societies show different kinds of code-switching behaviour, because of the multidimensionality of their structure. Migge (2007) describes the situation in the Eastern Maroon community of Surinam and French Guiana wherein negotiating interpersonal social meanings involves local community language as well as Creole and standard variation.

In the past decade there has been more and more evidence of young people code-switching (e.g. Bryan 2001) as well as of children learning to use the contact varieties effectively in role play beyond the censure of their elders (Paugh 2005). A greater focus on language socialization itself (e.g. Garrett and Baquedano-López 2002) has allowed ethnographic research which brings awareness of code-specific mores among children into focus. Like Paugh in Dominica, Garrett (2005), has been able to show children's awareness of the French Creole as the language of 'cursing' in St. Lucia despite the censure normally entailed in its use.

Conclusion

All in all, the interest level which first crystallized among Caribbean and non-Caribbean scholars in the late 1960s has never abated, due to the complex nature of the sociolinguistic communities under investigation and also to ongoing change in the relationship of the vernaculars to the official languages of each territory. These changes reflect an increasing democratization of Creole societies and an affirmation of Creoles not only as languages in their own right but as representative of peoples whose voices can now be freely heard.

There is a clear stemming of the tide in the progression of generations from basilect to acrolect. Stabilization may never occur but each language variety in each community has now a proven representational and functional value for its speakers. If the region has yet to embrace Standard English truly as its own, that recognition is inevitable, however hard the description of that local variety may be. Code-mixing is a function of our Caribbean identities, but the capacity to separate the varieties as necessary is also within many speakers' capacities. Where it is not, there should be no censure for twenty-first century realities deny the potential for existence of a simplistic mono-varietal speech mode anywhere around the globe.

References

Aceto, M. (2003) 'What are Creole languages? An alternative approach to the Anglophone Atlantic world with special emphasis on Barbudan Creole English', in M. Aceto and J. P. Williams (eds) *Contact Englishes of the Eastern Caribbean*, Amsterdam: John Benjamins, pp. 121–40.

Aceto, M. and Williams, J. P. (2003) *Contact Englishes of the Eastern Caribbean*, Amsterdam: John Benjamins.

Allsopp, R. (1975) *Dynamics of a Creole System*, Cambridge: Cambridge University Press.

——(1996) *Dictionary of Caribbean English Usage*, Cambridge: Cambridge University Press.

Beckford-Wassink, A. (1999) 'Historic low prestige and seeds of change: attitudes towards Jamaican Creole', *Language in Society*, 28, 57–92.

——(2001) 'Theme and variation in Jamaican Creole', *Language Variation and Change*, 13, 135–59.

Bickerton, D. (1975) *Dynamics of a Creole System*, Cambridge: Cambridge University Press.

Blake, R. (1997) '"All o' we is one": race, class and language in a Barbados community', unpublished PhD dissertation, Stanford University, CA.

Bonner, D. (2001) 'Garifuna children's language shame: ethnic stereotypes, national affiliation and transnational immigration as factors in language choice in Southern Belize', *Language in Society*, 30, 81–96.

Bryan, B. (2001) 'Defining the role of linguistic markers in manufacturing classroom consent', in P. Christine (ed.) *Due Respect: Papers on English and English-related Creoles in the Caribbean in Honour of Robert Le Page*, Jamaica: University of the West Indies Press, pp. 79–96.

Carrington, L. (1980) 'Images of Creole space', *Journal of Pidgin and Creole Languages*, 7, 93–9.

Childs, B., Reaser, J. and Wolfram, W. (2003) 'Defining ethnic varieties in the Bahamas: phonological accommodation in black and white enclave communities', in M. Aceto and J. P. Williams (eds) *Contact Englishes of the Eastern Caribbean*, Amsterdam: John Benjamins, pp. 1–28.

Christie, P. (1969) 'A sociolinguistic study of some Dominican Creole speakers', DPhil dissertation, University of York, UK.

——(1990) 'Language as expression of identity in Dominica', *International Journal of the Sociology of Language*, 85, 61–9.

——(1994) 'Language preference in two communities in Dominica, West Indies', *La Linguistique*, 7–16.

——(2007) 'Introduction to Robert Le Page's work', paper presented at a workshop on 'Creoles, Acts of Identity and Education: Celebrating Robert Le Page's contribution to Sociolinguistics', Stanford University, CA, 15 July.

Craig, D. (1971) 'Education and Creole English in the West Indies', in D. Hymes (ed.) *Pidginization and Creolization of Languages*, Cambridge: Cambridge University Press, pp. 371–91.

——(1999) *Teaching Language and Literacy: Policies and Procedures for Vernacular Situations*, Guyana: Education and Development Services Inc.

——(2006) *Teaching Language and Literacy to Caribbean Students: From Vernacular to Standard*, Jamaica: Ian Randle Publishers

Cutler, C. (2003) 'English in the Turks and Caicos Islands: a look at Grand Turk', in M. Aceto and J. P. Williams (eds) *Contact Englishes of the Eastern Caribbean*, Amsterdam: John Benjamins, pp. 51–80.

De Camp, D. (1971) 'Towards a generative analysis of a post-creole speech continuum', in D. Hymes (ed.) *Pidginization and Creolization of Languages*, Cambridge: Cambridge University Press, pp. 349–70.

Deuber, D. and Youssef, V. (2007) 'Teacher language in Trinidad: a pilot corpus study of direct and indirect Creolisms in the verb phrase', paper presented at Corpus Linguistics 2007, University of Birmingham, 27–30 July.

Devonish, H. (1978) 'The selection and codification of a widely understood and publicly usable language variety in Guyana, to be used as a vehicle of national development', DPhil dissertation, University of York, UK.

——(1996) 'Vernacular languages and writing technology transfer: "The Jamaican Case"', in P. Christie (ed.) *Caribbean Language Issues Old and New*, Jamaica: UWI Press, pp. 101–11.

——(1998) 'On the existence of autonomous language varieties in Creole continuum situations', in P. Christie, B. Lalla, V. Pollard and L. Carrington (eds) *Studies in Caribbean Language 11*, Trinidad: Society for Caribbean Linguistics.

Dray, S. (2002) '"A yard we deh": the uses of Creole on roadside texts in Jamaica', paper presented at the 14th Biennial Conference of the Society for Caribbean Linguistics, August 2002, University of the West Indies, St. Augustine, Trinidad and Tobago.

Eckert, P. and McConnell-Ginet, S. (1992) 'Think practically and look locally: language and gender as community-based practice', *Annual Review of Anthropology*, 21, 461–90.

Edwards, W. (1975) 'Sociolinguistic behaviour in rural and urban circumstances in Guyana', DPhil dissertation, University of York, UK.

——(1990) 'Morphosyntactic acculturation at the rural/urban interface in Guyana', *American Speech*, 65, 99–113.

——(2007) 'Le Page's theoretical framework and its influence on recent sociolinguistic models', paper presented at a Workshop on 'Creoles, Acts of Identity and Education: Celebrating Robert Le Page's Contribution to Sociolinguistics'. Stanford University, CA, 15 July.

Escure, G. (1982) 'Contrastive patterns of intra-group and inter-group interaction in the Creole continuum of Belize', *Language in Society*, 11, 239–64.

Evans, S. (2007) 'An examination of the processes of cautioning Kweyol-speaking suspects by police officers in St. Lucia', paper presented at Linguistics Research Day, Dept. of Liberal Arts, UWI, St. Augustine, May.

Fairclough, N. (1992) *Discourse and Social Change*, Cambridge: Polity Press.

Fayer, J. (2003) 'The Carriacou Shakespeare Mas: linguistic creativity in a Creole community', in M. Aceto and J. P. Williams (eds) *Contact Englishes of the Eastern Caribbean*, Amsterdam: John Benjamins, pp. 211–26.

Figueroa, E. (2005) 'Rude sounds: Kiss Teeth and negotiation of the public sphere', in S. Mühleisen and B. Migge (eds) *Politeness and Face in Caribbean Creoles*, Amsterdam: John Benjamins, pp. 73–100.

Garrett, P. (2003) 'An English Creole that isn't: on the sociohistorical origins and linguistic classification of the vernacular English of St. Lucia', in M. Aceto and J. Williams (eds) *Contact Englishes of the Eastern Caribbean*, Amsterdam: John Benjamins, pp. 155–210.

——(2005) 'What language is good for: language socialization, language shift, and the persistence of code specific genres in St. Lucia', *Language in Society*, 34, 327–61.

Garrett, P. and Baquedano-López, P. (2002) 'Language socialization: reproduction and continuity, transformation and change', *Annual Review of Anthropology*, 31, 339–61.

Giles, H. and Smith, P. (1979) 'Accommodation theory: optimal levels of convergence', in H. Giles and R. St. Clair (eds) *Language and Social Psychology*, Baltimore, MD: University Park Press, pp. 45–65.

Hymes, D. (1971) *Pidginization and Creolization of Languages*, Cambridge: Cambridge University Press.

Irvine, A. (2004) 'A good command of the English language: phonological variation in the Jamaican acrolect', *Journal of Pidgin and Creole Languages*, 19, 41–76.

Isaacs, M. (2006) 'Asou down-there: code-mixing in a bilingual community', in *Exploring the Boundaries of Caribbean Creole Languages*, Jamaica: University of the West Indies Press.

James, W. and Youssef, V. (2002) *The Languages of Tobago: Genesis, Structure and Perspectives*, Trinidad: School of Continuing Studies, University of the West Indies, St. Augustine.

——(2008) 'The phonological systems of the Creoles of Trinidad and Tobago', in *Mouton Handbook of Varieties of English*, The Hague: Mouton de Gruyter.

Kephart, R. (2003) 'Creole English on Carriacou: a sketch and some implications', in M. Aceto and J. P. Williams (eds) *Contact Englishes of the Eastern Caribbean*, Amsterdam: John Benjamins, pp. 227–39.

Labov, W. (1971) 'The notion of "system" in Creole languages', in D. Hymes (ed.) *Pidginization and Creolization of Languages*, Cambridge: Cambridge University Press, pp. 447–72.

Lalla, B. (2006) 'Creole representation in literary discourse', in H. Simmons-McDonald and I. Robertson (eds) *Exploring the Boundaries of Caribbean Creole Languages*, Jamaica: University of the West Indies Press, pp. 173–87.

Le Page, R. and Tabouret-Keller, A. (1985) *Acts of Identity: Creole-Based Approaches to Language and Ethnicity*, Cambridge: Cambridge University Press.

Mair, C. (2007) 'Corpus linguistics meets sociolinguistics: the role of corpus evidence in the study of sociolinguistic variation and change', paper presented at ICAME 28, Stratford-upon-Avon.

Mair, C. and Sand, A. (1998) 'Caribbean English: structure and status of an emerging variety', in R. Borgmeier, H. Grabes and A. H. Jucker (eds) *Anglistentag 1997 Giessen: Proceedings*, pp. 187–98.

McPhee, H. (2003) 'The grammatical features of TMA auxiliaries in Bahamian Creole', in M. Aceto and J. P. Williams (eds) *Contact Englishes of the Eastern Caribbean*, Amsterdam: John Benjamins, pp. 29–50.

Meyerhoff, M. and Walker, J. A. (2006) 'Zero copula in the Caribbean: evidence from Bequia', *American Speech*, 81, 146–63.

——(2007) 'The persistence of variation in individual grammars: copula absence in urban sojourners and their stay-at-home peers, Bequia (St. Vincent and the Grenadines)', *Journal of Sociolinguistics* 11, 346–66.

Migge, B. (2007) 'Code-switching and social identities in the Eastern Maroon community of Suriname and French Guiana', *Journal of Sociolinguistics*, 11, 53–73.

Milroy, L. (1980) *Language and Social Networks*, Oxford: Blackwell.

Mühleisen, S. (2002) *Creole Discourse: Exploring Prestige Formation and Change across Caribbean English-lexicon Creoles* (Creole Language Library 24), Amsterdam: John Benjamins.

Mühleisen, S. and Migge, B. (2005) *Politeness and Face in Caribbean Creoles*, Amsterdam: John Benjamins.

Patrick, P. (1992) 'Linguistic variation in Urban Jamaican Creole: a sociolinguistic study of Kingston, Jamaica', PhD dissertation, University of Pennsylvania.

——(1999) *Urban Jamaican Creole: Variation in the Mesolect*, Amsterdam: John Benjamins.

Paugh, A. (2005) 'Multilingual play: children's code-switching, role play and agency in Dominica, West Indies', *Language in Society*, 34, 63–86.

Platt, J. T., Weber, H. and Lian, H. M. (1984) *The New Englishes*, London: Routledge and Kegan Paul.

Rickford, J. (1979) 'Variation in a Creole continuum: quantitative and implicational approaches', unpublished PhD dissertation, University of Pennsylvania.

Schieffelin, B. and Doucet, R. (1994) 'The "real" Haitian Creole: ideology, metalinguistics, and orthographic choice', *American Ethnologist*, 21, 176–200.

Schneider, E. (2007) *Postcolonial English: Varieties around the World*, Cambridge: Cambridge University Press.

Schneider, E. and Wagner, S. (2006) 'The variability of literary dialect in Jamaican Creole: Thelwell's "Harder they Come"', *Journal of Pidgin and Creole Languages*, 21, 45–95.

Sebba, M. and Dray, S. (2003) 'Is it Creole, is it English, is it valid? Developing and using a corpus of unstandardized written language', in P. Lang (ed.) *Corpus Linguistics by the Lunes: A Festschrift for Geoffrey Leech*, Frankfurt am Main, pp. 223–39.

——(2004) 'Developing and using a corpus of written Creole', paper presented at Sociolinguistics Symposium 15, Newcastle-upon-Tyne, UK, 1–4 April.

Shields-Brodber, K. (2001) 'Contrapuntal conversation and the performance floor', in *Due Respect: Papers on English and English-related Creoles in the Caribbean in Honour of Professor Robert le Page*, Mona, Jamaica: UWI Press, pp. 208–18.

——(2006) 'Is the pain in your belly-bottom? Extending the boundaries of Jamaican Creole to non-native users', in H. Simmons-McDonald and I. Robertson (eds) *Exploring the Boundaries of Caribbean Creoles*, Jamaica UWI Press, pp. 188–210.

Sidnell, J. (1999) 'Gender and pronominal variation in an Indo-Guyanese Creole-speaking community', *Language in Society*, 28, 367–99.

Simmons-McDonald, H. (1996) 'Language education policy: the case for Creole in formal education in St. Lucia', in P. Christie (ed.) *Caribbean Language Issues Old and New*, Jamaica: UWI Press, pp. 120–42.

Tessoneau, A. L. (2005) 'Learning respect in Guadeloupe: greetings and politeness rituals', in S. Mühleisen and B. Migge (eds) *Politeness and Face in Caribbean Creoles*, Amsterdam: John Benjamins, pp. 255–82.

Van Herk, G. (2003) 'Barbadian lects: beyond Meso', in M. Aceto and J. P. Williams (eds) *Contact Englishes of the Eastern Caribbean*, Amsterdam: John Benjamins, pp. 241–64.

Williams, J. (2003) 'The establishment and perpetuation of Anglophone white enclave communities in the Eastern Caribbean: the case of Island Harbor, Anguilla', in M. Aceto and J. P. Williams (eds) *Contact Englishes of the Eastern Caribbean*, Amsterdam: John Benjamins, pp. 95–119.

Winford, D. (1972) 'A sociolinguistic description of two communities in Trinidad', unpublished. DPhil dissertation, University of York, UK.

——(1976) 'Teacher attitudes towards language variation in a Creole community', *International Journal of the Sociology of Language*, 8, 45–75.

——(1988) 'The Creole continuum and the notion of the speech community as the locus of language', *International Journal of the Sociology of Language*, 71, 91–105.

Young, C. (1973) 'Belize Creole: a study of the creolized English spoken in the city of Belize, in its cultural and social setting', unpublished. DPhil dissertation, University of York, UK.

Youssef, V. (1991) 'Variation as a feature of language acquisition in the Trinidad context', *Language Variation and Change*, 3, 71–101.

——(1996) 'Varilingualism: the competence behind code-mixing in Trinidad and Tobago', *Journal of Pidgin and Creole Languages*, 11, 1–22.

——(2001) 'Working out conversational roles through questioning strategies', in P. Christie (ed.) *Due Respect: Papers on English and English-related Creoles in the Caribbean in Honour of Professor Robert le Page*, Jamaica: UWI Press, pp. 155–83.

——(2005) '"May I have the bilna?" The development of face-saving in young Trinidadian children', in S. Mühleisen and B. Migge (eds) *Politeness and Face in Caribbean Creoles*, Amsterdam: John Benjamins, pp. 228–54.

——(2006) 'Issues of face-saving in the pre-school classroom', in H. Simmons-McDonald and I. Robertson (eds) *Exploring the Boundaries of Caribbean Creole Languages*, Jamaica: UWI Press, 147–69.

Youssef, V. and James, W. (2008) 'The morphosyntactic systems of the Creoles of Trinidad and Tobago', *Mouton Handbook of Varieties of English*, The Hague: Mouton de Gruyter.

Part II

Asia

6

Sociolinguistic research in China

Minglang Zhou

Introduction

China is generally understood to include the geographic areas of the Mainland, Hong Kong, Macau, and Taiwan, though this notion is now challenged by some people in Taiwan. This chapter focuses on sociolinguistic research by linguists in Mainland China because significant sociolinguistic studies conducted in Hong Kong, Macau, and Taiwan are usually available in English while such work conducted in Mainland China seldom is.

China is characterized by enormous linguistic diversity. It is estimated that over 120 languages are spoken, being members of the Sino-Tibetan, Altaic, Austroasiatic, Austronesian, Indo-European, and other unidentified families of languages (Zhou 2003: 23–6). In addition, there are numerous dialects within each language. For example, as a member of the Sino-Tibetan family, Chinese alone is divided into eight major dialects, including Mandarin, Wu, Min, Yue, Kejia, Huizhou, Xiang, and Gan, all of which are, in turn, further divided into numerous subdialects (Norman 1988: 181–244). To a large extent, sociolinguistic research in China is centered on the contact and tension among these languages and dialects, and on the goal of pursuing a common or standard language (*Putonghua*) as is the case in many multilingual states (Chen 1999; Zhou 2003, 2006; Zhou and Sun 2004). For this reason, this chapter examines China's sociolinguistic research over the past five decades at both the macro- and micro-level.

Historical background

China's search for a common language, an attempt with a long history, was re-energized at the end of the nineteenth century as part of the building of a modern China, but the effort gathered full steam when the People's Republic of China (PRC) was established in 1949 (Norman 1988: 133–5; Chen 1999: 13–33). In this social and political context, sociolinguistic research in the 1950s explored a number of questions: What is a standard language?, How does a standard language develop?, What is the relationship between a standard variety and the non-standard varieties/dialects?, What is the relationship between a common language and local or minority languages?

Early research focused extensively on the standard language, for the majority language and minority languages, within a single ethnic community. Guided by Stalin's views on linguistics, Wang Li *et al.* (1956) tried to answer some of the above questions in the first few years of the PRC. The authors of this collection justified selecting the Beijing variety (Mandarin) as the base for *Putonghua*, by arguing that a common language develops from its local varieties, and the selected local variety must be the one spoken by the people of the nation's political and economic center. In the case of Chinese, that is Beijing. These researchers viewed the development of the common language as a process of both absorbing linguistic elements from the other varieties and building new linguistic elements and as a process of the eventual replacing of the existing non-standard varieties. Thus, in corpus planning, the development of terminology was characterized by controlled input from locally spoken varieties of Chinese, from classic Chinese, and from foreign loan words. These sociolinguistic views underpinned China's early language policy, which assumed that *Putonghua* would eventually replace Chinese dialects.

At the same time, with the guidance of Soviet linguistic advisors, linguists working on minority languages also tried to apply the same model to each minority language (Zhou 2003: 171–98). During the first stage, seven hundred Chinese linguists surveyed many minority languages, examining the difference between languages and dialects. They developed two criteria: the ratio of cognates, and the correspondence between the two phonological systems in question. If the two examined targets shared more than 50 percent cognates in their basic vocabulary, and their two phonological systems had extensive systematic correspondence, they were generally identified as varieties of the same language. Otherwise they would be considered to be different languages.

Further, these linguists identified a variety, within each language, as the standard on which a writing system might be created. Taking a step beyond purely linguistic descriptions of local varieties, they examined the relationship between the varieties and the political, economic, and social contexts in an ethnic community in which the varieties were used, and recommended the one variety with the most political and economic potential as the standard for the common language within that community. Studies then expanded to cover issues concerning the enrichment of the standard variety, its standardization, and the addition of Chinese loanwords to it (Fu [1959] 1995: 257–88). At that time, the above sociolinguistic research was a state undertaking, comparable to the Manhattan Project to develop nuclear weapons in the US in the 1940s.

By 1958, as the PRC adopted a monolingual stance in its language policy, it was clear that *Putonghua* was to become not only the common language for Chinese-dialect speakers but also for minority-language speakers (Zhou 2003: 60–77). During this stage, with an eye on the spread of *Putonghua*, some researchers examined how two languages, or varieties, behaved in contact situations. For example, when comparing contact between two Chinese varieties, as well as between Chinese and a minority language, Wang Jun ([1964] 2004: 33–85) noted that when two forms coexisted in vocabulary, phonology or syntax, one of the forms would eventually replace the other. He suggested that standardization should take advantage of this natural tendency and facilitate variations moving toward the common language—*Putonghua*. Such studies reflected the sociolinguistic reality at a time when Chinese elements were actively introduced into minority languages and *Putonghua* elements into various Chinese dialects.

Emergence of sociolinguistic research in China

No significant linguistic research was carried out during the political chaos in China from the mid-1960s to the end of the 1970s. When China reopened in 1979, the notion of sociolinguistics was formally introduced for the first time (see Y. Chen 1980, 1983). At the same time, many researchers carried out studies on the sociolinguistic aspects of language use and variation, without explicit reference to the new concept. This paper examines two such studies before looking into the ways that sociolinguistics was understood, because different interpretations led to different research paradigms from the mid-1980s to the mid-1990s.

In a study of variations in the Nanjing dialect, Bao Mingwei (1980) found that some sounds in free variations in the local dialect, such as that between [l] and [n], became contrastive as in *Putonghua*. Though not mentioning sociolinguistics, Bao's study deviated from China's traditional dialectological studies and used sociolinguistic factors. Unlike the traditional approach, which selected one or a few older speakers as the survey informants, Bao sampled over 40 informants of different ages, some of whom represented two or three generations of the same family. Bao also selected a few families whose older generations were native speakers of Nanjing dialect, and a few families whose older generations were not native speakers, in order to compare family influence and social influence on younger generations' language choice. Unfortunately, without an explicit sociolinguistic framework, Bao failed to report how he selected the sample, to describe his sample, and to present data reflecting the difference in age cohorts and family linguistic backgrounds. Consequently he did not answer some of his own sociolinguistic research questions.

In the other study of 33 phonological variables (such as zero ↔ [n], zero ↔ [dz]), Shi and Jiang (1987) sampled 500 middle-aged speakers of Shanghai dialect with three social variables: age (two groups: 35–45 and 46–55), gender, and education (three groups: primary, secondary, and higher). The results were tabulated in relation to age cohorts, gender and education. Significant gender and educational differences were found in the use of many of these phonological variables, while age differences were usually not found, given the age range of the sample. At that time, the authors might not have known fully the development of sociolinguistics outside China, but they took a huge step in applying general sociological methods in linguistic research.

Meanwhile, "sociolinguistics" was formally introduced by Chen Yuan in his two books, entitled *Language and Social Life* (Y. Chen 1980) and *Sociolinguistics* (Y. Chen 1983). Chen's work covered the origin of language, language as thought, language as communication, language and socio-economic class, language change and social life, language contact, language and international relations, and more. These topics involved the fields of sociolinguistics, linguistic anthropology, and communications studies. In Chen's view (ibid.: 1), "Sociolinguistics studies language change from changes in social life on the one hand, and studies changes in social life from language change." Chen's work helped to inspire further studies of the relationship between language and society in China. In responding to one or the other clause of Chen's two-clause definition of sociolinguistics, two paradigms emerged. One examined language and society in the dialectological tradition, and the other in the linguistic anthropological tradition.

Linguists specializing in dialectology began to examine extensively sociolinguistic issues in dialectology, a move that is viewed as taking the development of dialectology to a new level (You 2005). These studies had two orientations: (1) examining the relationship among different dialects or varieties in urban areas, particularly newly arising industrial cities; and (2) examining the relationship between linguistic variation and social variables in Chinese dialects.

In the 1960s and 1970s, China saw the rise of some industrial cities in previously undeveloped areas where the population exploded from a few thousand to a half million or more. Changes in dialects and development of dialects have long been associated with waves of immigration (Zhou and You 1986: 15–63), but researchers wanted to know what happens when a number of dialects merge into a community marked by this kind of rapid immigration. Studying dialects in Dukou city (now Panzhihua in Sichuan Province), which started to develop in 1963, Liang Deman (1985) found some interesting phenomena. First, a *lingua franca* appeared as a variety of *Putonghua* marked by both the linguistic features of each group's native dialect and the local dialect. Second, the *lingua franca* was used by most younger immigrants and by all of the children of immigrants. Third, each group maintained its own dialect in a zone within the city, usually in a unit or *danwei*, such as a company, a factory or a college. And fourth, all dialects saw phonological, lexical, and syntactical changes induced by other dialects spoken in that city.

Complementing Liang's work, Guo Youpeng (1990) surveyed language use in a rising automobile-manufacturing city, Shiyan in Hubei Province. His study showed the frequency of *Putonghua* use in department stores (81.5–85.5 percent), on buses (75–78 percent), and at home (64 percent) as well as the difference in *Putonghua* use between genders (3–4 percent higher for women) and between age cohorts (53 percent of the middle-aged and older, 75 percent of young adults, and 95 percent of children). As Liang did, Guo also found dialect zones within the city. Guo discovered that speakers of certain dialects (such as those from Shanghai, Guangzhou, and Xi'an) resisted the spread of *Putonghua* in their zones, and that the local dialect had no impact on the immigrant dialects. Liang did not do further research on the latter topics, probably because he was unaware of their sociolinguistic significance.

Meanwhile, some dialectologists began to examine the relationship between social variables and linguistic variations. Lin Tao (1982) demonstrated that what was usually considered free variation ([v] → [β]) in Beijing dialect actually is not sociolinguistically free. This variation was generally found among younger speakers who tended to use [β] instead of [v]. He believed that this variation served a social function. Cao Zhiyun (1985) also showed that what appeared to be free variations, such as [tɕ] → [ts], [ɕ] → [s], etc., actually served multiple sociolinguistic functions: representing femininity, marking age difference (girls used the variants more than women did), and signifying the coming of puberty as teenage boys gave up these variants.

The early transition of research from dialectology to sociolinguistics saw problems in methodology, with one possible exception in the study by Guo (1990), who sampled subjects and language use with a good research design. Other studies either failed to report how they sampled their informants or how they obtained the data. Those who did report the methodology relied on one or a few selected informants for their data. This was the accepted methodology in Chinese dialectology, but it became questionable when employed for sociolinguistic research (for further comment, see You 2005).

Given the broad interpretation of sociolinguistics, a lot of research was devoted to the anthropological paradigm in the 1980s and 1990s (see Xu 2006). Research in this tradition can be traced back to the work of Luo Changpei, who published a book, *Language and Culture*, in 1950 (reprinted in 1989) (Luo [1950] 1989). However, research in this tradition flourished largely as a response to the introduction of sociolinguistics. Research in this area developed in three distinctive but related directions: Luo's tradition, folk linguistics, and ethnic linguistics.

Following Edward Sapir, Luo ([1950] 1989) studied the relationship between language and culture by examining word formation, linguistic loans, history of place names, kinship terms, and the origin of family names. Zhou and You (1986) extended that research to the relationship between dialect geography and human geography, dialect and local literature/drama, language and agriculture, and so on. For example, they found that dialect maps often matched historical, government administrative maps at the prefecture level, though not at the provincial level. Zhou and You demonstrated that a political and economic center helped to unify dialects within its jurisdiction, but they did not realize that this evidence was closely related to the Soviet model that China adopted for minority language development in the 1950s. Other researchers, such as Shen Xilung (1995), focused on language and thought, language and worldviews, language and cultural values, language and religion, and Chinese language and Chinese psychology.

In another perceived aspect of sociolinguistics, some researchers saw a close relationship between language and folklore. They not only found employment of linguistic features in folklore but also the representation of folklore in language (see Qu 1996; Wang 2000). Chinese folklore reflects both cults and taboos in cultural rituals that are associated with linguistic features of Chinese. For example, the character, *fu* (luck), is always hung upside down at the door. When people comment on this, they say, "*Fu dao le*," which means both "The word, luck, is upside down" and " Luck has arrived" because "*dao*" is a homonym. Sharing a single pear is taboo, particularly between a couple, because "to share a pear" and "to separate" are homonyms (*fen li*) in Chinese. These studies showed, among other things, the deployment of meta-linguistic awareness in everyday language use.

The third direction unfolded in the relationship between language and ethnicity. Studies focused on the linguistic features in language contact that mark ethnicity in the language rather than in language use. Zhang (2002: 51–66) suggested that, from word formation, we could trace the history of cultivated plants in an ethnic community and across ethnic communities. One criterion is whether plant names are phonological loans, such as *putao* (grapes) and *danbagu* (tobacco), or derived from existing morphemes, such as *fanqie* (*fan* "foreign" + *qie* "eggplant" = tomato) and *yangyu* (*yang* "foreign" + *yu* "taro" = potato). Phonological loans suggest that no similar plants existed in that community at the time the new plant was introduced from another community, whereas derived forms indicate that similar plants had existed. Applying this approach to language contact, Zhang found extensive evidence of linguistic, cultural, and ethnic exchanges among various ethnic groups in China.

On the other hand, some researchers adopted this paradigm to study the (im)migration and assimilation of ethnic groups in China. Examining various, non-native elements in the Chinese spoken in Hui (Muslim) communities, Yang (1996: 4) argued that there are different Chineses, just as there are different Englishes, and Hui Chinese is one such unique Chinese for three reasons. First, Hui Chinese retains Persian and Arabic elements in the basic lexicon, such as "sky, heaven, god" (*asima* vs. *tian*), "servant" (*bandai* vs. *puren*), and "friend" (*duositi* vs. *pengyou*). Second, Hui Chinese maintains unique phonological patterns that are different from the local Chinese dialects. For example, word final nasal consonants are usually dropped in Hui Chinese, as such as "*mama*" (*ana* vs. *anian*) and "untie" (*ayina* vs. *yinian*). Hui Chinese uses low-rising tones where the Han Chinese uses falling tones. Third, Hui Chinese uses Chinese expressions grammatically and semantically differently from Han Chinese. For instance, "*youshui*" in Hui Chinese means "to take a bath or bathed" whereas in Han Chinese it means "there is water." "*Kanshou*" is used as an adjective or noun to mean "loyal or loyalty to Quaran" in Hui Chinese, but it is a noun or verb meaning "watch, monitor" in Han Chinese.

In short, these studies are strongly oriented toward anthropological linguistics as represented by the title of the collected papers from China's third symposium on socio-linguistics: *Multidisciplinary Studies of Language and Culture* (Chen and Tan 1993), which contains numerous articles on language and culture.

If linguists starting from the micro level suffered from some confusion about the orientation of sociolinguistic research during this period, linguists whose starting point was on the macro level concentrated more on language contact, language shift, bilingu-alism, and language policy. Research in this area is represented by Dai Qingxia's *An Introduction to Sociolinguistics* (1993a), which covered topics in language and ethnic iden-tity; language and ethnic relations; language attitudes; language and gender, age, class, and profession; and variation of languages across national borders. Dai (ibid.: 3) unam-biguously defined sociolinguistics with a macro-level branch focusing on language policy, language planning, and language relations, and with a micro-level branch examining linguistic variations among individuals and within communities.

Given China's multilingual context where Chinese has been the dominant language for a long time, one of these linguists' first questions is, "What happens to the languages in contact?" Research on language contact (see Dai *et al.* 1990; Institute of Minority Languages 1990) examined Chinese loanwords into minority languages and varieties of Chinese spoken by native speakers of minority languages. These loans may be categor-ized into the diachronic and the synchronic. The former are usually nativized while the latter maintain their Chinese forms with little or no nativization. Earlier loans of basic vocabulary underwent nativization from Chinese to minority languages, such as the fol-lowing examples: *fandian* (meal + shop in Chinese) → *janbhuanb* (shop + meal in Miao) "restaurant" and *caiyou* (vegetable + oil) → *youlceab* (oil + vegetable) "vegetable oil." Contemporary loans often don't undergo this process, as shown in this example from Chinese to Miao *si mian ba fang* (four + sides + eight + direction) → *sih mianh bal huangd* (four + sides + eight + direction) "every direction." These two kinds of loans may occur in combination in the same contexts (Dai *et al.* 1990: 190–8). On the other hand, the varieties of Chinese spoken by minority-language speakers as a second language are found to have hybrid structures in word formation and syntax. The transfer of the first language into the second language is commonly found in phonology, morphology, and syntax. For example, Chinese spoken in Leishan County in eastern Guizhou Province demonstrates the transfer in all three areas (Institute of Minority Languages 1990: 63–9). The local Miao language does not have phonological forms corresponding to the [an], [iɛn], and [yɛn] finals (a term for the combination of a nuclear and coda used in Chinese linguistics) in Chinese. As a result, [iɛn], and [yɛn] diachronically became [ɛn], but syn-chronically just drop the nasal [n] in the local variety of Chinese. The local Miao has a morphological form [yɛn] "capably," which is similar to the Chinese morphological form [xɛn] "very." Replacing the Chinese, the Miao form is found both as [yɛn] + verb and as [yɛn] + noun in the local variety of Chinese. Syntactically, the local Miao places adver-bials after the verb, but standard Chinese places them before the verb. The Miao verb + adverbial structure is found in the local Chinese, such as "*Ni zuo gan xian*" (you + go + first) instead of "*Ni xian zuo*" (you + first + go).

Researchers noted that these loans and transfers all took place in communities where bilingualism is practiced. Examining bilingualism in Qiang communities in southwestern

China, Sun Hongkai (1988) observed that the process of language contact saw language shift from monolingualism to early bilingualism, then to later bilingualism, and finally to monolingualism. There are several dimensions of the shift. First, it took place from one geographic area to another, usually from towns to rural areas. Second, within the same area, it spread from communities with more contact with Chinese speakers to communities with less such contact. Third, within a community, it spread from public domains to private domains, and it spread from younger people to older people. The shift to monolingualism began when the native language was no longer spoken by older people in the home domain. This observation is largely true of language contact and bilingualism in China. However, Dai Qingxia (1993a: 134–5) noted that, in some communities in Yunnan, where the native language of the community was no longer spoken at home, some children learned it from other children in school as a second language.

Migration, social changes, the economy, and language policy all have a significant impact on language contact, language shift and bilingualism (Dai 1994: 72–6). The Qiang community that Sun (1988) studied is a typical example of the interplay of migration, social changes, and language policy. Bilingualism there was triggered by migration of the Han into the Qiang territory, and was further accelerated when the Qing Imperial Court replaced the local system of chieftains with imperial magistrates, and forced linguistic and cultural assimilation. Extensive economic and political influence was also found to be connected to language contact and bilingualism, particularly involving languages across borders (see Dai 1993b). For example, minority languages such as Jingpo (Kachin) had more loans from English than from Chinese before 1949, but Chinese became the only source of loans after 1949. Similarly, we can note Soviet influence on Turkic languages spoken in China, though that influence did not fade away until the late 1950s, when the Sino-Soviet relationship deteriorated. However, no other language has influenced China's minority languages as rapidly or extensively as Chinese has because of the PRC's monolingual policies implemented from the late 1950s to the late 1970s, and the legislation of *Putonghua* as the official language since 1982.

Development of sociolinguistic research

Since the late 1990s, the notion of sociolinguistics in China has become closer to that in the international sociolinguistic community. Research methodology has also been improving, sometimes in innovative ways. The maturing of sociolinguistics in China may be attributed to three factors (Xu 2006). First, Chinese scholars have had more access to international scholarship in sociolinguistics by reading both English publications and Chinese translations. Second, some scholars have visited their colleagues in North America and Europe or earned doctoral degrees in (socio)linguistics abroad. Third, William Labov, John Gumperz, William Bright and other internationally prominent sociolinguists have visited China and had scholarly exchanges with their Chinese colleagues at the beginning of the new century. During this period, sociolinguistic research demonstrates direct employment and innovative use of introduced sociolinguistic concepts and methods in the Chinese context, focusing on majority–minority relations, and those between *Putonghua* and other varieties of Chinese from the macro and micro levels.

The fruit of efforts to utilize concepts and methods from international scholarship in the study of majority–minority language relations appeared around the turn of the new century. Holistically, Zhou Qingsheng (2000) reexamined China's sociolinguistics within the framework of international sociolinguistic scholarship. He tried to make a connection between the notion of modern sociolinguistics and Mohist canons, the latter of which make a distinction between language and language use. From this starting point, he evaluated his and others' research in relation to China's multilingualism and language planning. He generally saw China's sociolinguistic situations as products of history, culture, and language policies, of which the last played the most crucial role in shaping and reshaping language contact, shift, and variation.

At the same time, Huang Xing (2000) studied the maintenance of minority languages by investigating their vitality in ten domains. Huang revised McConnell and Gendron's (1998) eight domains of vitality, adopting six of them—administration, legislature, courts, schools, media and religion—and creating four new ones—economy, information technology, publication, and literature and (performing) arts—in place of the domains of manufacturing industries and sales/service. Huang's revision reflected China's sociolinguistic situation more realistically. For example, whether a minority language has an official status and the political power to obtain the resources for publication, and lately for information technology, makes a crucial difference in its vitality. It is all decided by China's language policy and by ethnic politics. Further, Huang developed an index of language-vitality prospects, an index that predicts future vitality instead of measuring current vitality. Measuring on a scale of 0–3, with three as the best prospect, this index utilizes six factors: language-use status (How wide is the user community?); language planning status (Which level of administration is responsible?); degree of language standardization; function of the written language; degree of concentration of the speakers in a community; and cross-border relations (Is it spoken in another country as an official or non-official language?).

The same efforts are seen in investigating majority–minority language relations in specific communities. Following the development of studies of language contact in the international community, such as the work by Appel and Muysken (1987), Yuan Yan (2001) extensively investigated language contact, language shift, and bilingualism in the Atsang community in south-western China. Yuan's work differs significantly from previous research by Chinese scholars in two respects. First, in addition to diachronic evidence, she looked into the synchronic dynamics of language contact. She found competitions between Dai loans and Chinese loans in Atsang, which borrows from both Dai and Chinese for the same word. She also predicted the results of the competition based on the age of the users of the loans, saying that the loans used by the younger speakers would win. Second, Yuan also looked, beyond the language, at the users, and found a pattern of language attrition similar to that in immigrants in the US: proficiency in listening and speaking → proficiency in listening but not in speaking → no proficiency in listening and speaking within four generations. Yuan's work shows the power of conceptualization in sociolinguistic research.

Most such studies have been carried out in rural areas in China. When a study involves urban areas, researchers need to re-conceptualize their approaches. Ding Qingshi (2007) adopted Gumperz's notion of a "speech community" in redefining his approach to the study of minority language use in Beijing. He proposed three categories of minority-language speech communities: permanent communities, work-unit communities, and scattered-residence communities. The permanent communities have a history in Beijing, at least, for over two hundred years. The work–unit communities are the products of China's planned economy where government offices, schools, and businesses developed their own employee housing, schools, hospitals, public security, shops, etc. around their work-sites. These communities are closed and serve only the employees and their families. The scattered-residence communities are those where speakers of the same language do not reside in the same physical community. Ding is not the first to put forward the idea of the work-unit speech community (see Liang 1985; Yang 2002), but is the first to investigate language use in the three different speech communities. Though failing to generalize from this comparison, Ding showed that: (1) even if living in their small permanent communities, members have lost their native languages over time; (2) in the work-unit communities, many of the second generation are still minority-Chinese language bilingual speakers; and (3) in scattered-residence communities, only some are bilingual speakers. Obviously, if it is physically dense, a small speech community of a minority language may slow down but cannot prevent the shift to the majority language.

Language contact and language shift may eventually lead to endangerment of the lesser-used languages. Responding to world-wide attention, China started a dialogue on endangered languages at the turn of the century. This dialogue raised two key questions. First, how do we view the phenomenon of language endangerment, and what can we do about it? The dominant view is that the right language policy may slow down the endangerment, but cannot stop it because language choice and use are essentially individual rights. Thus, the two crucial measures are: (1) documenting and publishing endangered languages; and (2) developing a phonetic spelling system for speakers of an endangered language to maintain their own language (Sun 2001). The second question is: What is an endangered language? Some argued for using the population of a language community as the criterion, while other claimed that age cohorts of the remaining speakers are better indicators. Dai (2004: 4–5) uses case studies to show three main criteria: (1) the percentage (80 percent or more) of speakers shifting to a second language; (2) that the shifters belong to the younger generations; and (3) the attrition rate of speaking ability among the remaining speakers. In China, many other studies now have been carried out that contribute to the understanding of language endangerment.

Progress in sociolinguistic research on the relationship between *Putonghua* and Chinese dialects was made during the same period. Guo Xi ([1999] 2004) investigated Chinese sociolinguistics from three new perspectives while systematically examining it within the international sociolinguistic framework. First, he saw a direct relationship during the whole twentieth century between China's political and economic system, on the one hand, and language change and use, on the other, the former of which had decided the rate of change, the sources of loans, the adoption of codes, and differences in style and discourses. Second, he suggested that China's language policies enriched both community and individual linguistic repertoires, which simplified the social choice of codes, but complicated individuals' choices of codes and code switches. Third, he explored the impact of globalization on the Chinese language, the effects of which are seen in lexical, phonological, and syntactical loans from English as well as from Chinese spoken in Taiwan, Hong Kong, and Singapore. Guo (ibid.: 89) believes that sociolinguistic research in China should serve as the basis for language policy-making.

Four decades of socialist, planned economy shaped China's social structures as well as its sociolinguistic situations. With this fact in his mind, Yang Jinyi (2002) focused on the relationship between such social structures and language use in industrial cities. Taking an innovative approach that is not available to most sociolinguists, Yang was able to use the household registration databases at police stations to trace over a half million people's family origin and codes. He found that, being a closed community, work-units (*danwei*) formed dialect and/or variety islands that were isolated speech communities in industrial cities. In the competition among *Putonghua*, the local dialect, and the employees' native varieties, the initial workplace language often became the first language for the second and third generations of the work-unit-centered speech communities. These speech communities where *Putonghua* varieties are usually spoken have expanded in the last decade as *Putonghua* spreads nationally.

At the same time, dialect islands in rural China present a different picture. Cao Zhiyun (2006) found that two-thirds of over 1,500 dialect islands in the Wu and Hui dialect zones in south-east China have disappeared, mostly in the past two decades. This has happened in two ways: by being dissolved and by being submerged. In the dissolving mode, the dialect of the isolated speech community gradually changes toward the strong, neighboring dialect, while in the submerging mode, speakers shifted to *Putonghua* varieties and/or to a strong, local dialect in a few generations. Cao suggested that migration, marriage across speech-community boundaries, education, and mass media all contributed to the disappearance of dialect islands. It appears that not only do dialect speakers shift to *Putonghua,* but dialects also change in the direction of *Putonghua*. *Putonghua* spread introduces variations into dialects, variations that usually move toward *Putonghua* lexically, phonologically, and syntactically (see Cao 2000; J. Guo 2006).

The above sociolinguistic changes took place during a time when the state became more accommodating and launched the largest sociolinguistic survey to inform policy-making. Abandoning the goal of replacing dialects with *Putonghua* in the 1990s, the state language-policy accepted the coexistence of *Putonghua* and Chinese dialects, but assigned them different functions and domains (see L. Guo 2004; Chen 2005: 102–12). To understand the actual sociolinguistic situation in China, the PRC State Language Commission did a national survey of language use and attitudes between 1999 and 2001 (for the full report, see China 2006). This survey consisted of a household survey (one questionnaire for the head of the household and questionnaires for a few other members of each household), and a special survey that involved questionnaires specifically for government employees, sales and commercial employees, medical professionals, teachers, college students, secondary-school students, and media and press employees. The survey was carried out nationally in 17 major Chinese dialect zones, including 98 subdialect zones and communities of 110 minority languages. Researchers collected 475,000 valid questionnaires from 165,000 households and 40,000 valid questionnaires from professionals and students. The survey yielded a significant amount of useful results, some of which are shown in Table 6.1.

In addition to providing a good picture of China's language use and attitudes at the beginning of the twenty-first century, this survey systematically trained thousands of linguists in survey methodology (see China 1999). It will have significance for China's sociolinguistic research, but a discussion of the strengths and weaknesses of this survey is beyond the scope of this chapter.

Table 6.1 Language use in China at the turn of the century (%)

Codes/Users	All	Male	Female	Urban	Rural	Age 1	Age 2	Age 3	Age 4
Putonghua	53.06	56.76	49.22	66.03	45.06	70.12	52.74	40.59	30.97
Chinese dialects	86.38								
Minority language	5.46								

Source: China (2006: 1–4).

Note: Age 1 = 15–29; Age 2 = 30–44; Age 3 = 45–59; Age 4 = 60–69.

Conclusion

Significant progress has been made in sociolinguistic research in China in the past two decades. However, further progress depends on innovations in methodology as well as on breakthroughs in theory. Sociolinguists in China are now beginning to reflect on their research methodologies. Wang Yuanxin (2007) has recently published the journals compiled by his doctoral students during their sociolinguistic research in the field in northwestern China. These journals explore the methodological issues encountered in their socio-linguistic fieldwork. Such reflections are helpful, but are not significant without theoretical considerations. Innovations in methodology rely largely on new conceptualizations because the former eventually serves the latter. Knowing this, Xu Daming (2004) tried to redefine the concept of speech community, which has been used without serious challenge since Gumperz ([1968] 1972) put it forward in the 1960s. Xu defines speech community as naturally existing sociolinguistic being or entity, which is identified by the ways language is used in socially bound contexts. With this concept, researchers should examine a speech community in terms of communicative intensity, conventions in code-choice, and (shared) values of language variation, which require innovations and improvements in methodology.

In addition to work in theory and methodology, China's sociolinguists have also made efforts to establish platforms for scholarly exchange and promotion of research. In 2003, they founded the Sociolinguistic Society of China, which holds an annual meeting and publishes bi-annually *The Journal of Chinese Sociolinguistics*. The journal publishes cutting-edge articles by international scholars, such as J. Gumperz and C. Myers-Scotton, and research by scholars in greater China. For example, it has included sociolinguistic research done in Taiwan, Hong Kong, and Macau, such as Ang Uijin's (2003) work on language attitudes and language change in Taiwan; Wang Peiguang's (2003) work on language use and attitudes in Hong Kong, and Gan Yu'en's (2003) work on creolization in Macau. At the same time, using laboratories at the Universities of Pennsylvania and Ottawa as his models, Xu Daming established a sociolinguistic laboratory at Nanjing University. In the past few years, Xu's laboratory has held annual workshops on urban sociolinguistic research, workshops that facilitate exchanges between young sociolinguists and leading scholars from China and other countries.

In conclusion, all these efforts will undoubtedly smooth the integration of China's sociolinguistic research into the international sociolinguistic research community though there are still some gaps.

Acknowledgments

I am grateful for the advice and suggestions of Sun Hongkai, Zhou Qingsheng, Xu Daming, You Yujie, Guo Xi, Cao Zhiyun, and Yang Jingyi, but I am solely responsible for the contents of this chapter and any errors it may contain.

References

Ang, U. J. (2003) "Taiwan Quanzhou qiang yang yuanyin de bengkui yu yuyin biaojixing" [Phonetic markedness and the collapse of central vowels of Quanzhou dialect in Taiwan], *The Journal of Chinese Sociolinguistics*, 1, 34–51.

Appel, R. R. and Muysken, P. C. (1987) *Language Contact and Bilingualism*, London: Edward Arnold.

Bao Mingwei, W. (1980) "Liushi nian lai Nanjing fangyin xiang *Putonghua* kaolung qingkuang de kaocha" [A study of phonological developments of Nanjing dialect towards *Putonghua* in the last 60 years], *Zhongguo Yuwen* [Chinese Language], 157, 241–5.

Cao, Z. Y. (1985) "Beijing hua yuyin li de xingbie chayi" [Gender differences in the phonology of Beijing dialect], *Hanyu Xuexi* [Chinese Studies], 6, 31.

——(2000) "Shengcun haishi xiaowang: Hanyu fangyan mianlin de juece" [To survive or to die: Chinese dialects face a choice], in Z. T. Chen *et al.* (eds.) *Shiji Zhijiao de Zhongguo Yingyong Yuyanxue Yanjiu* [Applied Linguistic Research in China at the Turn of the Century], Beijing: Huayu Jiaoxue Press, pp. 139–48.

——(2006) "Lun fangyan dao de xiaowang: yi Wu and Hui qu wei li" [On the disappearance of dialect islands: a case study of the islands in Wu and Hui dialect communities], in Institute of Applied Linguistics (ed.) *Theory and Practice of Language Planning*, Beijing: Language Press, pp. 1–7.

Chen, J. M. and Tan, Z. M. (eds.) (1993) *Yuyan yu Wenhua Duoxueke Yanjiu* [Multidisciplinary Studies of Language and Culture], Beijing: Beijing Language University Press.

Chen, P. (1999) *Modern Chinese: History and Sociolinguistics*, Cambridge: Cambridge University Press.

Chen, Y. (1980) *Yuyan Yu Shenghuo* [Language and Social Life], Shanghai: Xuelin Press.

——(1983) *Shehui Yuyanxue* [Sociolinguistics], Beijing: Sanlian Press.

Chen, Z. T. (2005) *Yuyan Guihua Yanjiu* [Studies on Language Planning], Beijing: Shangwu Press.

China (1999) *Zhongguo Uyuyan Wenzi Shiyong Qingkuang Diaocha: Daochayuan Shouce* [A Handbook for China's Language Use Survey Implementers], Beijing: Language Press.

——(2006) *Zhongguo Uyuyan Wenzi Shiyong Qingkuang Diaocha Ziliao* [China's Language Use Survey Data], Beijing: Language Press.

Dai, Q. X. (1993a) *Shehui Yuyanxue Jiaocheng* [An Introduction to Sociolinguistics], Beijing: Central University for Nationalities Press.

——(ed.) (1993b) *Kuajing Yuyan Yanjiu* [Studies on Languages Across Borders], Beijing: Central University for Nationalities Press.

——(1994) *Minzu he Yuyan* [Language and Ethnicity], Beijing: Central University for Nationalities Press.

——(2004) *Zhongguo Binwei Yuyan Gean Yanjiu* [Case Studies of Endangered Languages in China], Beijing: Minzu Press.

Dai, Q. X., Bi, X. and Wang, Q. R. (1990) *Yuyan Guanxi yu Yuyan Gongzuo* [Language Relationship and Language Work], Beijing: Central University for Nationalities Press.

Ding, Q. S. (2007) *Shequ Yuyan yu Jiating Yuyan: Beijing Shaoshu Minzu Shequ Yuyan Diacha Yanjiu zhi Yi* [Community Language and Family Language: A Study of Language Use in Minority Communities and Families in Beijing], Beijing: Minzu Press.

Fu, M. J. ([1959] 1995) *Fu Maoji Xiansheng Minzu Yuwen Lunji* [Collection of Fu Maoji's Papers on Minority Language Work], Beijing: Chinese Social Sciences Press.

Gan, Y. E. (2003) "Siyi hua: yizhong Erhua de huanhe fangyan" [The Siyi dialect: a creolized Cantonese variety], *The Journal of Chinese Sociolinguistics*, 1, 95–100.

Gumperz, J. ([1968] 1972) "The speech community," in P. P. Gigliou (ed.) *Language and Social Context*, London: Penguin Books, pp. 219–31.

Guo, J. (2006) "Analysis of the (u)–variation in the 'Town Speech' of Lishui," *Journal of Asian Pacific Communication*, 16, 335–49.

Guo, L. S. (2004) "The relationship between *Putonghua* and Chinese dialects," in M. Zhou and H. K. Sun (eds.) *Language Policy in the People's Republic of China: Theory and Practice since 1949*, Boston: Kluwer, pp. 45–54.

Guo, X. ([1999] 2004) *Zhongguo Shehui Yuyanxue* [Sociolinguistics in China], Hangzhou: Zhejiang University Press.

Guo, Y. P. (1990) "Hubei Shiyan shi *Putonghua* yu fangyan de shiyong qingkuang" [*Putonghua* and dialect use in Shiyan City, Hubei], *Zhongguo Yuwen* [Chinese Language], 219, 427–32.

Huang, X. (2000) *Shaoshu Minzu Yuyan Huoli Yanjiu* [A Study of Minority Language Vitalities], Beijing: Central University for Nationalities.

78

Institute of Minority Languages (ed.) (1990) *Hanyu yu Shaoshu Minzu Yu Guanxi Yanjiu* [Studies of the Relationship between Chinese and Minority Languages], Beijing: Central University for Nationalities Press.

Liang, D. M. (1985) "Sichuan sheng Dukou shi fangyan de xianzhuang he weilai" [Current status and outlook of dialects in Dukou, Sichuan], *Fangyan* [Dialects], 4, 291–6.

Lin, T. (1982) "*Putonghua* le de v, [[v] in *Putonghua*], " *Hanyu Xuexi* [Chinese Studies], 6, 1–5.

Luo, C. P. ([1950] 1989) *Yuyan yu Wenhua* [Language and Culture], Beijing: Language Press.

McConnell, G. D. and Gendron, J-D. (1998) *International Atlas of Language Vitality*, 4. Quebec: International Center for Research of Language Planning, Laval University.

Norman, J. (1988) *Chinese*, Cambridge: Cambridge University Press.

Qu, Y. B. (1996) *Zhoungguo Minsu Yuyanxue* [Chinese Folklore Linguistics], Shanghai: Shanghai Wenyi Press.

Shen, X. L. (1995) *Zhongguo Zhuantong Wenhua he Yuyan* [Traditional Chinese Culture and Language], Shanghai: Shanghai Educational Press.

Shi, Y. J. and Jiang, J. P. (1987) "Shanghai shiqu zhongnianren yuyin gongshi chayi de wubai ren diaochu" [A survey of synchronic phonological variations among 500 middle-aged people in Shanghai City], in Z. L. Li and B. H. Xu (eds) *Yuyan Yanjiu Jikan* [Collection of Linguistic Research Papers], Shanghai: Fudan University Press, pp. 271–96.

Sun, H. K. (1988) "Lun Qiangzu shuangyuzhi: Jiantan Hanyu to Qiangyu de yingxiang," *Minzu Yuwen* [Minority Languages], 4, 55–65.

——(2001) "Guanyu binwei yuyan wenti" [On endangered languages], *Yuyan Jiaoxue yu Yanjiu* [Language Teaching and Research], 1, 1–7.

Wang, J. ([1962] 2004) *Wang Jun Yuyanxue Lunwenji* [Collection of Wang Jun's Linguistic Papers], Beijing: Commercial Press.

Wang, L., Shao, R., Yu, M., Zhou, Y., Liu, J. *et al.* (1956) *Hanzu de Gongtongyu he Biaozhunyin* [The Common Language and Standard Pronunciation for the Han People], Shanghai: China Books.

Wang, P. G. (2003) "Shehui yuyan yinsu yu yugan de yanjiu: Xianggang ren dui chunjie huoyu yugan de diaocha" [A survey of Spring Festival greetings in Hong Kong], *The Journal of Chinese Sociolinguistics*, 1, 78–86.

Wang, Y. X. (2007) *Yuyan Tianye Diaocha Shilu* [Journals of Language Fieldwork], Beijing: Central University for Nationalities.

Wang, Z. X. (2000) *Yuyan Minsu* [Linguistic Folklore], Wuhan: Hubei Educational Press.

Xu, D. M. (2004) "Yanyu shequ lilun" [Speech community theory], *The Journal of Chinese Sociolinguistics*, 2, 18–28.

——(2006) "Zhongguo shehui yuyanxue de xin fazhan" [New developments in sociolinguistics in China], *Nanjing Shehui Kexue* [Nanjing Social Sciences], 2, 128–34.

Yang, J. Y. (2002) "Zhongguo xinxing gongye qu yuyan zhongtai yanjiu" [Research on language status in new industrial cities in China], *Yuwen Yanjiu* [Language Research], 1, 13–21 and 2, 28–32.

Yang, Z. W. (1996) *Huzu Yuyan Wenhua* [Linguistic Culture of the Hui (Muslim) People], Yinchuan: Ningxia People's Press.

You, Y. J. (2005) "Shehui yuyanxue yu Hanyu fangyanxue de xin jieduan" [A new stage of sociolinguistics and Chinese dialectology], in D. Q. Liu (ed.) *Yuyanxue Qianyan yu Hanyu Yanjiu* [Cutting-edge Research in Linguistics and Chinese Language], Shanghai: Shanghai Educational Press, pp. 332–46.

Yuan, Y. (2001) *Yuyan Jiechu yu Yuyan Yanbian: Atsang Yu Gean diacha Yanjiu* [Language Contact and Language Change: A Case Study of Atsang], Beijing: Central University for Nationalities Press.

Zhang, G. J. (2002) *Yuyan yu Minzu Wuzhi Wenhua Shi* [Language and Ethnic Material-Cultural History], Beijing: Minzu Press.

Zhou, M. (2003) *Multilingualism in China: The Politics of Writing Reforms for Minority Languages, 1949–2002*, Berlin: Mouton de Gruyter.

——(ed.) (2006) *Journal of Asian Pacific Communication (Special Issue: Language Planning and Varieties of (Modern Standard) Chinese)*, 16.

Zhou, M. and Sun, H. K. (eds.) (2004) *Language Policy in the People's Republic of China: Theory and Practice since 1949*, Boston: Kluwer.

Zhou, Q. S. (2000) *Yuyan yu Ren* [Language and Man: A Sociolinguistic Perspective on the Chinese Nation], Beijing: Central University for Nationalities Press.

Zhou, Z. H. and You, Y. J. (1986) *Fangyan yu Zhongguo Wenhua* [Dialects and Chinese Culture], Shanghai: Shanghai People's Press.

7

Sociolinguistics in South Asia

Probal Dasgupta and Madhavi Sardesai

Introduction

That formal grammar as an enterprise began in South Asia, and reached the height of its early excellence in the work of Panini, is likely to be familiar to all readers. But the need to contextualize formal grammar in a social and philosophical matrix was seen at the very inception of the formal grammar enterprise. This is a less familiar fact and deserves attention. In order to focus on issues of such generality, this exposition develops a few key moments in South Asian sociolinguistic inquiry at length. The option of mentioning all major sociolinguists of the region and providing an annotated bibliography for each of them – the only alternative that suggests itself – would amount to allowing unmentioned exogenous texts to set the agenda instead of examining the local praxis on its own terms, an unacceptable dilution of the complexity of a South Asian debate of potential global interest.

One contemporary South Asian sociolinguist who offers a particularly far-reaching update on the issue of just where the validity of linguistic form choices is to be ascertained is E. Annamalai. In the most accessible collection of his relevant writings (Annamalai 2001), he offers a line of reasoning that is worth presenting here in some detail. This argument may serve as one point of entry into contemporary South Asian inquiry at the society–language interface.

For a different point of entry, one more focused on the study of power and rooted in the distinctive realities of language development in Pakistan, see Rahman (1990, 1995, 2001). Power and access are also key factors in the thinking of distinguished socio-linguists from Bangladesh (Maniruzzaman 1991) and Sri Lanka (Kandiah 1981). In some of these countries, ethnic conflict (see Kandiah 2001, for one approach to this) has directly shaped the trajectories of languages – and, correspondingly, the paths of socio-linguistic inquiry. Historical linguistics has also played a major role (Maniruzzaman 1977; Singh and Maniruzzaman 1983; see Singh 1992, for further elaboration of certain issues).

The many regional languages in South Asia

Annamalai suggests a bifocal view of multilingualism in South Asia: the elites learn English at school in addition to their South Asian language(s), while others pick up their languages at home, at work and on the streets. Societal bilingualism and constant code switching expressing multiple identities, Annamalai argues, encourage code convergence and more generally a fluid verbal repertoire within which language boundaries are freely crossed. Taking this overall scene as a given, he finds a fundamental change in the role of languages involved in political control and social mobility since India became independent in 1947. His argument focuses on India; some of the reasoning carries over to other South Asian societies, but the present summary will continue to refer to India for expository accuracy.

The old functional distribution that was based on sharing has given way to a more hierarchical relation between the languages within each of the linguistic states India put in place from 1956 onwards. This shift changes the terms of the multilingual arrangement. A pyramid has replaced the old mosaic.

One might imagine that the context of the democratic economy in which these processes play out would at least enable social mobility. In that case one might lament linguistic dedifferentiation and the demise of static societies, but one would expect robust new individuals in a modern economy to make sense of their cultural inheritance on a new basis, which the social scientist would then codify in keeping with the modern rationality reshaping their context.

But Annamalai argues that the new set-up has in fact created structural factors making social mobility difficult for many. Minority speakers in most of India's linguistic states, in particular, have tended to find that discrimination against them by the majority community is based not on language competence (a matter of achievement) but on language identification (a matter of ascription).

Faced with this factor undermining the convergence of rational choice with a public good, minority speakers find themselves encouraged to join dominant language identities even at the cost of either social submergence within the state's dominant language – dialectalization – or language loss. But minority speakers often discover – belatedly – that only keeping their mother tongue alive will ensure group survival in an electoral system based on the ethnic and caste differentiation of constituencies.

The millennia-old South Asian reality of minority languages being stably maintained has thus been losing ground, through such dynamics, to new linguistic forces in independent India. The informally picked up neighbourhood multilingualism that used to run stable inter-communal equations in the Indian countryside no longer does so. Schooling has made the children of the elite passively trilingual – with English for reading and with Hindi for receiving mass entertainment. Language boundaries have become sharper due to corpus planning, the 'modernization' of regional languages emphasizing the purity of each language anchored in a separate past. That the older cross-language communication continuum is no longer a socially recognized reality inhibits linguistic convergence and code mixing.

Status planning has also made an impact. The educational system of the new linguistic state is so run that proficiency in the standard dialect of its regional language turns into an upper-class characteristic, superimposing class on an older map of castes and regions. The interplay of the ritual status and the economic status of castes now works through the rural–urban distinction, a newly significant intervening variable – class being a city-driven phenomenon in modern India.

To understand what it means for informally acquired multilingualism to give way to schooled multilingualism, one must consider the quantitative effects of schooling. In this country where bilingualism is widely regarded as normal, there is a low incidence of reported bilingualism given its more than 200 languages: only 9.7 per cent in the 1961 census (treated as the canonical year because of later restructuring of language reporting in the census). But this figure is not low relative to the 24.02 per cent figure for literacy.

While the census does not enable us to correlate bilinguals and literates, indirect methods provide an answer. Pointing to the fact that tribal literacy (8.56 per cent) and tribal bilingualism (15.73 per cent) are respectively lower and higher than the national averages (24.02 per cent; 9.7 per cent), Annamalai shows that orally acquired bilingualism is the norm in India, like oral acquisition of knowledge in general. (The word 'tribal' for indigenous peoples is still socially accepted as the default term in the South Asian context.)

What schooling contributes to multilingualism in this land of non-universal literacy, Annamalai shows, is a quarter of that 9.7 per cent bilingualism. About half the bilinguals whose second language is Hindi, and nearly all the bilinguals for whom it is English, learn it at school. But schooling does not implement independent India's three language formula: regional languages have not spread, through schooling, beyond their state boundaries.

Outside schooling, the continued efficacy of informal second language learning is only a one-way street – and disproportionately affects tribals. Nationally, bilingualism is mainly urban; but among tribals it is overwhelmingly rural and is associated with language shift. Between 1961 and 1981, nearly half the speakers of tribal languages shifted from a tribal to a non-tribal first language.

Annamalai innovatively argues that it would be a mistake to view this development simply in terms of mother tongue loss in a context shaped by power. He observes that language shift affects not just the mother tongue but the verbal repertoires of the individuals and groups concerned. He reexamines power at the level of the self-identifications of the individual and collective players whose rational decisions drive the process. What particularly deserves attention is his account of just how a classical India that maximized language maintenance has given way to a modern India that makes language shift normal.

Classical India, Annamalai argues, had a robust system for language maintenance that reflected at least the following interacting factors. Philosophically, the system relied on traditional conceptualizations of accepting difference. Socially, it was able to count on stratification, on restricted scope for upward mobility (via language choice or other acquired characteristics), and on kinship systems confined within small caste groups. Economically, its feudal and agrarian management of land use was not conducive to economic mobility by choice. Politically, oligarchic and colonial governance concentrated all the power in some non-local language (Persian, Sanskrit, English) whose acquisition was expensive and socially closed. Such a set-up forced tribals into language shift, but robustly maintained the non-tribal languages.

The pressures of a democratically governed modern socio-economic system have pushed segments of the non-tribal Indian population today into selective assimilation and dissimilation. Annamalai's account of these processes emphasizes the new power of the regional language in each linguistic state. To cope with this power, minority language speakers in the state learn the regional language and in practice assimilate as individuals. But they theoretically dissimilate, maintaining their mother tongues at the community level, taking advantage of the constitutional provision encouraging them to establish minority language-based schools – which, however, teach all non-language subjects in

English so that the children's upward mobility is assured. The Constitution makes this possible; it says nothing about the medium of instruction in such schools.

The regional languages are pitted against each other in the dynamics of this process, leaving the national players English (the ex-colonial language) and Hindi (the constitutionally designated official language of the nation) in a different league. Annamalai argues that public policy initiatives will have to respond to these processes on the ground. He argues that minorities have focused on surviving as communities and have thus been forced into linguistic assimilation to the dominant state language at the level of individual behaviour, but that this does not reflect informed rational choice. In his view, social science analysis and activism against the loss of languages (and the consequent cultural denudation of the planet) will have to raise public awareness at the mainstream level for these processes to be articulated – and modified.

One language for the nation?

If we turn to Hindi and English, the nationwide languages of India, we will comment only on Hindi, avoiding the disarray in which we find the state of the linguistic study of the role of English in the contemporary world and in South Asia. For some discussion of the background of English in modern India, we refer the reader to Dasgupta (1993). In this section, we introduce the reader to Lachman Khubchandani's (1997) influential take on diglossia – a key that will help open up the English and Hindi spaces for serious investigation when informed participants in public debates feel willing and able to take on those long neglected challenges – and to the way Khubchandani, using diglossia theory as one of his tools, thematizes some of Mahatma Gandhi's not very widely known linguistic initiatives that had to do with Hindi. We make this choice in order to familiarize the reader with canonical material from the time when the crucial moves in the fashioning of the linguistic landscape of South Asia were being made. The global public's understanding of Gandhi's interventions needs to take on board his approach to issues of language. But we turn first to Khubchandani on diglossia.

Khubchandani (1997: 136) characterizes South Asian plurilingualism as follows: 'Patterns of verbal communication are marked by the fluidity of codes, depending upon the relevance of identity among its speakers even across the so-called language boundaries.' He allows that theories of diglossia may need a different take in the case of 'unilingual standardized societies' where 'variations due to stratification may be limited to a narrow spectrum of speech behavior' (ibid.: 137). But he argues that:

> This spectrum becomes much wider when the society is either multilingual with its members controlling several different languages, or is made up of fluid speech groups, with its members claiming different speech identities in response to changing contexts. Such a linguistic spectrum may operate across the language boundaries delineated by grammarians and other custodians of language.
>
> (ibid.: 137)

This is a point he makes in direct consonance with Gandhi's negative view of the role of such custodians.

The case at stake is that of the loose-knit language (or linguistic agglomeration) for which the only neutral term was and still is 'Hindustani' and on which the superstructures of 'Hindi' and 'Urdu' have been erected. Khubchandani's study employs the code fluidity version of the diglossia concept in the context of making sense of the 'superposed homogeneity in communication patterns' and the 'varying degrees of diglossic complementation among many speech varieties' in the north-central Hindustani region (ibid.: 139). He notes that this overall population includes native speakers of markedly different varieties of Hindustani – Braj Bhasha, Bangru, Bundelkhandi – and of distinct languages such as Punjabi, Dogri, Pahari, Rajasthani, Marwari, Awadhi, Chattisgarhi, Bhojpuri, Maithili and Magahi; speakers continue to use these varieties/languages for primary communication (ibid.: 139). However, in this region, 'The verbal repertoire in the community is hierarchically structured [on the basis of Hindustani-focused standardization], with many speech varieties enjoying different status and privileges according to overt identity pressures.'

Overtly, what one observes is population segments in this region claiming Hindi as their mother tongue. Khubchandani's (ibid.: 139–40) division of this population into five broad categories displaying different domains of diglossic complementation is helpful:

1 Bilinguals of the north-central region who view their own primary speech in terms of substandard variations of the prestigious Hindi standard.
2 Bilinguals who use primary speech varieties in their intimate rural milieu and Hindi in modern settings.
3 Bilinguals who use primary varieties for all oral communication and relegate standard Hindi to written use.
4 Illiterate monolinguals who only speak – in primary varieties – but say they belong to the Hindi fold.
5 'Real' users who speak and write standard Hindi (a variety called Khari Boli) and nothing but standard Hindi.

However, this does not correspond to self-descriptions. Many residents of Khubchandani's 'fluid zone' (ibid.: 139) have declared Hindi and Urdu as their mother tongues but in practice use it as what may be called an 'associate native speech' variety (ibid.: 141); they are, in fact, bilingual, but describe and often see themselves as monolingual. 'For them, switching linguistic codes from native speech to Hindi-Urdu is similar to the switching of styles … in a monolingual situation' (ibid.: 141). These language attitudes and cohesive tendencies in communicative patterns have resulted in a striking situation:

> *Many different languages* of the Fluid Zone, stretching from Pashto (an Iranian language) to Maithili (an East Indo-Aryan language, structurally close to Bengali), are identified by their speakers as mere dialects or style *variants of one language* amalgam, Hindi-Urdu. On the other hand, the *two socio-cultural styles* of the same speech – Khariboli, belonging to the same region – are identified as *distinct language institutions*: Hindi and Urdu.
>
> (ibid.: 141, italics ours)

These standardized codes of high Hindi and high Urdu are instances of 'restricting domains of communication through distinct orthographies and literary traditions' (ibid.: 145). This is the point at which Khubchandani takes us back to Gandhi's unsuccessful intervention:

> Efforts to amalgamate Hindu-Urdu were made in undivided India through the elevation of Hindustani (to be written in both Devanagari and Perso-Arabic scripts).

Propagated by Gandhiji and others, it did not succeed due to the growing animosity between the Hindu and Muslim pressure groups expressed through Sanskritized Hindi and Perso-Arabicized Urdu.

(ibid.: 145)

Gandhi's intervention deserves independent attention. Gandhi used *Hindi* and *Hindustani* as synonyms to indicate that he proposed to include the Urdu component within the description 'Hindi'. In his 1918 presidential address at the eighth session of the Hindi Sahitya Sammelan (the Hindi Literature Conference) at Indore, Gandhi offered the following definition: 'Hindi is that language which is spoken in the North by Hindus and Muslims, and which is written in Nagari or in Persian script. This Hindi is neither heavily Sanskritized in its vocabulary, nor is it copiously laden with Persian words' (Gandhi 1947: 11). In other words, what he had in mind was a compromise between what became the later articulations of official Hindi in partitioned India and official Urdu in Pakistan.

Returning to the issue in his 1935 presidential address at the twenty-fourth session – again at Indore – of the Hindi Sahitya Sammelan, Gandhi characterized Hindi as 'that language which is spoken naturally and without effort by both Hindus and Muslims' (ibid.: 44). Stressing that his use of the compound name *Hindi-Hindustani* was intended to indicate his inclusive concept of Hindi, Gandhi went on to say:

There is no difference between Hindustani and Urdu [or between Hindustani and Hindi]. The language becomes Hindi when written in Devanagari and Urdu when written in Arabic … One who is too meticulous about using Sanskrit or Perso-Arabic vocabulary in one's speech only does harm to the nation.

(ibid.: 44)

Seven years later, writing in the 23 January 1942 issue of *Harijan Sevak*, Gandhi focused on his use of the neutral designation *Hindustani* for the language that he hoped would be used by all Indians as a national link language. He wrote:

There is no independent language bearing this name [Hindustani] which is different from Urdu and Hindi … The term truly signifies both Hindi and Urdu. By bringing both of these together we need to forge a language which would be of use to all. A language of this kind does not exist today in writing. However, crores[1] of Hindus and Muslims in the North currently communicate in this language. But as this language has no written form, it is incomplete. And what is written manifests two separate streams which day by day are moving away from each other. Hence *Hindustani* has come to signify Hindi and Urdu. That is, both Hindi and Urdu can call themselves Hindustani provided they do not boycott each other, and also attempt to blend with each other, retaining their individual characteristics and sweetness. Today Hindustani lacks an organization that could bring together the two streams that are running away from each other.

(ibid.: 118–19)

This was the gap that Gandhi himself tried to fill by establishing a Hindustani Prachar Sabha (Society for Promoting Hindustani) on 3 May 1942 (ibid.: 144–7).

His thinking and mobilization differed in two major respects from the government-sponsored official language teaching set-up that in fact prevailed after 1947. First of all,

Gandhi took it that no existing product would do the job, and that one would have to go through a process to arrive at a viable Hindustani language. He argued for active participation by the public in the forging of such a 'just' link language for a diverse nation as part of the nation-building project. He proposed that supporters of the idea of a national language should learn both the Sanskritized Hindi version and the Persianized Urdu version of this language. Such a speech community would, in his view, eventually deliver the Lokbhasha, 'the people's language' (ibid.: 123) – a second respect in which his proposals differed from the later regime of Hindi as the Rajbhasha, 'the language of government'.

The point of having a specific organization for developing such a Hindustani language was that the political organization steering the struggle for independence – the Indian National Congress – could not take on the character of a cultural community. But the commitment of the Indian National Congress to the cause in Gandhi's time was explicit. Its Nagpur Congress (1925) had resolved to conduct the proceedings of its General Body and its Executive in Hindustani, indicating that Gandhi's Hindustani proposal was not an unsupported personal idea comparable to his nature-oriented medical preferences. Why, then, did Gandhi choose to launch the idea at a Hindi Sahitya Sammelan in 1918 rather than work within the political framework of the Indian National Congress?

As in many of Gandhi's decisions, the point was not simply to act, but to direct the action in dialogue with a real or potential adversary. His Hindustani movement would have to compete with the idea of Sanskritized Hindi, written in the Nagari script shared with Sanskrit, as the only legitimate national language for a primarily Hindu India. Hence his decision to initiate his project of persuasion in the context of a Hindi movement which Gandhi hoped to persuade out of business.

The Hindi Sahitya Sammelan, 'Hindi Literature Conference', established in Allahabad in 1910 and the Nagari Pracharini Sabha, 'Nagari Script Promotion Society', established in Banaras in 1893, were the most important organizations promoting the Hindi language written in the Nagari script. They were acting in the context of a northern Indian educational ethos that treated the learning of Urdu at school as normal for Hindu children – an ethos that a new Nagari-scripted Hindi-speaking nationalism proposed to reverse in favour of a Sanskritic, Hinduism-driven mobilization of Hindi as a national language for India.

The battle for linguistic neutrality was an important dimension of the larger struggle against the separatist agenda that in fact prevailed and led to the partition of the subcontinent, the bloodbaths of the 1940s and other consequences. That Gandhi launched a cultural and linguistic movement for an inclusive national language is less well known than the fact that he lost the battle in the wider political arena. In this context, it is important to revisit the terms in which his 1942 Hindustani Prachar Sabha formulated its project.

Note the work that the definition of Hindustani is supposed to do in the founding document of this society for the promotion of Hindustani:

> Hindustani is that language which is understood and spoken by all people – Hindus and Muslims – in the North Indian towns and villages where it is the language of everyday communication. This language is written in both the Nagari and the Persian script and its literary forms are known today by the names of Hindi and Urdu.

> (ibid.: 147–8)

What merits attention, when we look back, is the proposal to take the core unity of the spoken language as the Hindustani Prachar Sabha's point of departure. 'Hindustani' as a unifying designation for the language – in the context of an explicit recognition of the separate acrolect codifications that had taken place under the descriptions 'Hindi' and 'Urdu' – was supposed to help articulate the agenda for a speech community merging the two codifications.

Note the contrast between the classical Indian ethos that Gandhi's articulation drew upon and the post-1947 ethos that Annamalai's account delineates for us. Khubchandani, the sociolinguist who has used the term 'ethos' most often, argues that the communicative ethos undervalued language codifications, and that the modern custodians of languages have tried, with only partial success, to reverse this towards a monolingual ethos that the traffic in India tends not to favour.

Note

1 Editor's note: a crore equals 10,000,000.

References

Annamalai, E. (2001) 'Managing multilingualism in India: political and linguistic manifestations', in *Language and Development*, vol. 8, New Delhi: Sage.

Dasgupta, P. (1993) 'The otherness of English: India's Auntie tongue syndrome', *Language and Development*, vol. 1, New Delhi: Sage.

Gandhi, M. K. (1947) *Rastrabhasha Hindustani*, Ahmedabad: Navajeevan.

Kandiah, T. (1981) 'Lankan English schizoglossia', *English Worldwide*, 2, 63–72.

——(2001) *A History of Ethnic Conflict in Sri Lanka: Recollection, Reinterpretation and Reconciliation*, Oxford: Oxford University Press.

Khubchandani, L. M. (1997) 'Indian diglossia', in L. M. Khubchandani, *Revisualizing Boundaries: A Plurilingual Ethos*, New Delhi: Sage.

Maniruzzaman (1977) 'Controlled historical reconstruction based on five Bengali dialects', PhD dissertation, University of Mysore, India.

——(1991) *Studies in the Bangla Language*, Dhaka: Adiabad Sahitya Bhaban and Bhasha Tattva Kendra.

Pillai, K. R. (1971) *The Vakyapadiya: Critical Texts of Cantos I and II*, Delhi: Motilal Banarsidass.

Rahman, T. (1990) *Pakistani English*, Islamabad: National Institute of Pakistan Studies, Quaid-i-Azam University.

——(1995) 'Cultural imperialism and the pragmatics of Urdu in Pakistan', *Journal of Central Asia*, 17, 16–44.

——(2001) 'Language, knowledge and inequality', in A. Abbi, R. S. Gupta, and A. Kidwai (eds) *Linguistic Structure and Language Dynamics in South Asia*, Delhi: Motilal Banarsidass, pp. 185–96.

Singh, U. N. (1992) *On Language Development and Planning: A Pluralistic Paradigm*, New Delhi: Munshiram Manoharlal' (with Indian Institute of Advanced Study, Shimla).

Singh, U. N. and Maniruzzaman (1983) *Diglossia in Bangladesh and Language Planning*, Kolkata: Gyan Bharati.

8

Sociolinguistics in Japan

Nanette Gottlieb

Introduction

In 1987, in an important article entitled 'Japanese Sociolinguistics', Janet S. Shibamoto listed the major areas of sociolinguistic research in Japan as the writing system, loanword usage, standardization, honorification, language and sex, and bilingualism and minority languages (Shibamoto 1987). These categories in general remain the major areas of research in the field, but social, technological and academic developments over the intervening 20 years mean that the emphasis in many of them has changed. In this chapter, I discuss the manner in which recent research on Japanese sociolinguistics has responded to social changes and what the pressing concerns are today.

Sociolinguistics in Japan is said to have officially begun when the Kokuritsu Kokugo Kenkyūjo (National Institute for Japanese Language, NIJL, known in English until 2001 as the National Language Research Institute) was established in 1949 (Shibamoto 1987). Research work on what we would normally think of as aspects of sociolinguistics had long preceded that date, of course, but the key word here is 'official'. The setting up of the Institute within what was then called the Ministry of Education[1] marked official recognition at government level and the allocation of funds to enable large-scale research projects on the national language. The primary brief of the Institute is to provide the basic information needed to support the discussion and formulation of language policy, which was done first by the Kokugo Shingikai (National Language Council) and more recently (since 2001) by the Kokugo Bunkakai (National Language Subdivision) of the Agency for Cultural Affairs' Bunka Shingikai (Committee for Cultural Affairs). The Kokuritsu Kokugo Kenkyūjo compiles annual bibliographies of research published in the fields of Japanese language (*Kokugo Nenkan*) and Teaching Japanese as a Foreign Language (*Nihongo Kyōiku Nenkan*). Other useful research aids it provides for sociolinguists include a database of newspaper articles relating to language from 2002 on, searchable electronically on its website.

One noteworthy feature of research on sociolinguistics over the past 20 years is that Japanese scholars, particularly those either currently studying or working in English-speaking academic institutions or those who have done so in the past, have published a wide range of studies in English as well as Japanese, thus opening their work up to the wider community of sociolinguistic researchers. In addition, a collection of important articles by Shibata Takeshi, considered by many to be the founder of sociolinguistics research in Japan, was translated into English and published in 1998 (see Kunihiro *et al.* 1998). Taking into account also the work of non-Japanese scholars, we now have a substantial and growing body of English-language work making a significant contribution to studies of Japanese sociolinguistics, and for that reason I have included many English-language studies in this chapter.

Background information

I begin with a brief introduction to where and how Japanese is spoken. Most of Japan's 128 million inhabitants speak and write Japanese as their native language; a small percentage speaks it as a foreign or second language. While regional dialects do of course remain, Standard Japanese (based on the speech of the Yamanote area of Tokyo and designated as the standard in 1916) is spoken and understood throughout the country. Unlike other major languages spoken in the region such as Chinese and English, the diasporic footprint of Japanese is not broad: outside Japan, the language is spoken by descendants of earlier waves of migrants in parts of North and South America and Hawaii, and as a legacy of Japan's colonial period in parts of Asia (particularly Taiwan). It is also spoken in small expatriate communities of business people, students and academics around the world and by an estimated 10 million current and former learners of Japanese as a foreign language.

In any discussion of recent trends in Japanese sociolinguistics, it is important first to understand two key things: the make-up of the lexicon, and the nature of the orthography. The Japanese lexicon consists of approximately two-thirds loanwords and one-third words of Japanese origin (*wago*). Of the loanwords, the majority are *kango* (words of Chinese origin), borrowed from Chinese over centuries of linguistic and cultural contact and now an integral part of the lexicon, where they are perceived as being more formal in tone than words of Japanese origin. The remainder of the loanwords, estimated to account for between 6 and 10 per cent of the lexicon, are *gairaigo*, loanwords from languages other than Chinese (predominantly English).

The writing system consists of a combination of three scripts: ideographic characters (*kanji*) adopted originally from China and two phonetic scripts, *hiragana* and *katakana*, developed over time from the characters. These are supplemented by Arabic numerals and, in certain contexts (often as a design feature), the Roman alphabet. Characters are used to write nouns and the stems of inflected words; *hiragana*, to show Japanese pronunciation where required and for the copula, pronouns and grammatical features such as inflections and postpositions; *katakana*, for non-Japanese loanwords and for emphasis; and Arabic numerals, when numbers are written horizontally rather than vertically. Current script policy as set down in the Jōyō Kanji Hyō (List of Characters for General Use, in force since 1981[2]) stipulates the teaching in schools of 1,945 of the most commonly occurring characters, although in practice it is necessary to know a much larger number (around 3,000) to read newspapers and advertisements. A feature of this multifaceted script use is its flexibility; as we shall see, technology-mediated divergent uses of orthography form the focus of an important new area of sociolinguistic research.

Salient areas of social change over the past 20 years which have opened up new areas of sociolinguistic research include technological advances in electronic text production, an increase in immigration levels, and the regional focus on the importance of English. The invention and rapid uptake in the 1980s of character-capable stand-alone word processors were followed in the 1990s with similar software packages for computers, which in turn enabled Japan to construct a substantial native-language presence on the Internet. Recent years have seen the emergence of mobile texting: Japan today leads the world in use and development of the mobile Internet. Immigration levels, while still small by comparison with other developed countries – legal immigrants account for just under 2 per cent of the population – have increased markedly since the early 1980s. As a result, it has become important to look at ways of providing education in Japanese as a second language for newcomer children in Japanese schools. And finally, the Japanese government has expended large amounts of money over the past 20 years on two initiatives meant to increase the ability of Japanese students to communicate effectively in English: the Japan Exchange and Teaching (JET) program, initiated in 1987, which brings native speakers of English (and occasionally other languages) to work in high school English classrooms alongside Japanese teachers, and a five-year Action Plan to Cultivate Japanese with English Abilities, begun in 2003, which is currently in the process of implementing defined strategies intended to enhance and expand the communicative teaching of English. One of the hottest language policy topics in Japan today is the planned introduction of compulsory English teaching into the primary school curriculum.

The Shibamoto article referred to earlier (Shibamoto 1987), which I commend to readers seeking an overview of earlier sociolinguistic research in Japan, highlighted what had been until 1987 the major themes in the area: to recap, they were the writing system, loanword usage, standardization and honorifics, supplemented by a growing interest in language and gender, and in bilingualism and minority languages. The first four of these had earlier been identified as the primary foci of Japanese sociolinguistics by Shibata Takeshi and formed the stuff of the national surveys conducted by the Kokuritsu Kokugo Kenkyūjo. Those same areas remain important foci today, although in each case the emphasis has shifted in line with the social developments outlined above, as we shall see.

The writing system

Research on the writing system has expanded to include analysis of the impact of computer technology on written Japanese. Some of this work has focused on the forms of the characters in electronic dictionaries; some has branched out into reflection on (and, in many cases, empirical examination of) broader changes observed in the way people write when they use computers, such as increases in the number of characters used by comparison with handwriting, revival of more complex characters not included on the List of Characters for General Use, mistaken use of homophonous characters through over-hasty acceptance of the choices thrown up by the computer, and so on. An extensive body of publications in Japanese, mostly qualitative but a few based on empirical studies, documented and analysed these phenomena in the late 1980s and 1990s (e.g. Kabashima 1988; Ogino 1994); for work in English, see Gottlieb (2000). More recent years have seen a growing body of research studies on the language used in *keitai* (mobile phone) messaging and in online chat rooms (e.g. Tanaka 2001), as well as on some of the specialized forms of electronic writing used to assert membership of cliquish identity groups such as *kogaru* (fashion-mad teens) (see, e.g. Miller 2004).

91

Loanwords

Loanword usage remains an important focus of concern, with a notable shift of interest from the pronunciations or orthographic representations of foreign words to the problem of finding Japanese equivalents to replace them in public discourse. Here political developments external to the academic research community have played a part: in 2002, the then Prime Minister Koizumi, in response to concern – particularly among older people – over the perceived overuse in government documents of loanwords where Japanese equivalents exist, sought the Education Minister's help in setting up a committee within the Kokuritsu Kokugo Kenkyūjo to carry out an extensive study of the matter. Committee members, drawn from academe, literary circles and the media, produced four reports between 2003 and 2006 recommending the replacement of certain loanwords with Japanese equivalents (for full details, see Kokuritsu Kokugo Kenkyūjo 2006; the reports themselves are also available online in Japanese at www.kokken.go.jp/public/gairaigo/index.html). Torikai Kumiko, a member of the committee, has reported that it was not an easy task and that in some cases, particularly in the information technology, health and welfare sectors, it proved impossible to suggest Japanese terms, owing to the rapid influx of new terminology from English (Torikai 2005).

Dialects

In the area of language standardization and variety, research since the 1980s has reflected the resurgence of official interest at policy level in local dialects as an interesting adjunct to (not substitute for) the standard language, after a policy of regionalism emerged during the latter part of that decade. During the 1990s, a report by the Kokugo Shingikai announced that dialects, far from being targeted for eradication as had happened earlier during the twentieth century, should be valued as an important element in the overall picture of 'a rich and beautiful national language'. The report stressed the importance of continuing research into the dialects, giving particular mention to the dialect surveys and atlases produced by the Kokuritsu Kokugo Kenkyūjo and various university research centres (Kokugo Shingikai 1995: 432). The Kokuritsu Kokugo Kenkyūjo has since published most of a planned 20-volume dialect database consisting of transcriptions and recordings of dialect passages spoken by elderly persons (both male and female) from across Japan. Most data having been obtained during the period 1977–85, however, this collection throws no particular light on dialect use today, particularly on the use of dialects by younger speakers or outside their originating areas. It is nevertheless useful as a record of dialects spoken by a particular age group – at least in the specified locations – for the twentieth century.

Honorifics

Recent research on honorifics has mirrored a concurrent concern expressed in school curricula with fostering the communicative aspects of language. Kikuchi (1994), for example, emphasizes the pragmatics of honorifics over the linguistic structures involved; Usami (2002) likewise discusses politeness at the discourse level. This approach resonates with a report of the Kokugo Shingikai, which advised that knowing when the use of honorifics was appropriate to achieve smooth communication was more important than focusing only on the correct forms (Kokugo Shingikai 2000), a departure from the earlier prescriptive emphasis on form alone. A fine English-language study on honorifics is Wetzel (2004), in particular, her chapter on *keigo* common sense which focuses on language ideology in Japan as it relates to honorifics. Of the wide range of excellent work on politeness theory, in particular, on different cultural understandings of what politeness means, space permits me to mention only one here. Haugh (2004) compares Japanese and English understandings of politeness, maintaining that while different cultures may share common elements in their understanding of politeness, overarching definitions and hence expressions of politeness differ in quite specific ways.

Language and gender

Two areas which Shibamoto flagged as new and of growing interest in 1987 were studies of gender and language and studies of minority languages and bilingualism. In the first of these, research predicated upon the traditional view of 'women's language' as a natural and historically sanctified category, a distinctive feature of language in Japan usually conceptualized as having been present from its earliest times, continues in some quarters. The work of Ide Sachiko (e.g. Ide and McGloin 1990), with a strong focus on women's language and honorifics, is prominent in this area, but she is far from alone: Horii (1992), for example, canvasses the language used by women in sectors dominated by female employees (clothing and service industries, in this case) and identifies specific terms as being 'women's language'. Not everyone agrees, however, and female scholars in both Japan and elsewhere have published excellent studies aiming to demonstrate the disconnect between ideology and real-life practice. In the recent work on women and language, we find the very strong theme that 'women's language' as prescribed in textbooks and other sources does not resonate with the lived experience of Japanese women, not even in Tokyo where it might most be expected to do so.

To take one example: Endō Orie, in her *Onna no Kotoba no Bunkashi* (A Cultural History of Women's Language, 1997), argues vigorously for 'women's language' as an imposed rather than 'natural' category, sifting through literary and other sources from the Nara Period (710–94) to the present and including fieldwork which produced a digital database of the speech of women in the workplace to support her thesis. Her findings are that evidence for gender-based linguistic differences cannot be found until as late as the sixteenth century. That the expectations of women's speech began to diverge from men's at this point she attributes to the gradual erosion of women's earlier (Nara period) status under the influence of a combination of male-oriented military culture, Confucian thought and Buddhism. Subsequent prescription of the norms of female speech was bolstered during the Edo Period (1603–1867) by the Confucian view of women as inferior to men and during the modern period (1868–) by the perceived imperatives of nationalism and consumerism. Today, however, Endō posits, following an examination of the increasing erasure of gendered speech differences among contemporary young women, Japan is experiencing a return to the gender-neutral speech patterns of the Nara and Heian Periods. Endō's examination of the manner in which women are represented in dictionaries has also been influential in the expanding body of work on this topic.

Other research in the same vein but more strongly informed by postmodern theory has likewise sought to remove the burden of prevailing ideological freight from sociolinguistic studies of women's speech and elucidate some of the ways in which real women actually speak. A good example which showcases scholarship of this kind is Okamoto and Shibamoto Smith (2004), a collection of essays by Japanese and non-Japanese scholars living both in Japan and elsewhere which celebrates both the post-1970s feminist excavation of 'women's language' as an unquestioned category and the expanding body of literature on diversity in Japanese language. An added advantage of this collection is that it focuses not just on women's language: several chapters also contest the uncritical acceptance of 'men's language' as an irreducible category. The chapters range over theoretical and literary aspects and conclude with a set of studies of language usage among very diverse groups including provincial farm workers, lesbians, middle-aged PTA mothers, male and female high school students and men in different parts of the country. The emphasis on empirical analysis of actual discourse data in recent work is a particularly welcome development.

Minority languages and bilingualism

In Shibamoto's second new area, the nascent body of research on minority languages and bilingualism was certainly not large in 1987. Since then, the growth of interest in this area of research as a consequence of social developments has been noteworthy. With regard to the indigenous Ainu language, for example, the decade or more of activism leading up to the passing of the Law for the Promotion of Ainu Culture in 1997 led to a renewed interest in the language. Linguistically oriented studies have included Tamura (2000) and other comparative studies or dictionaries. In the historical field, Refsing (1998) presents a collection of writings on the Ainu-Indo-European controversy over the origins of Ainu. Work with a stronger sociolinguistic emphasis, most of it – significantly – in English, includes de Chicchis (1995) and Gottlieb (2005). At the other end of the archipelago, we find this trend replicated: much (though not all) Japanese-language work has focused on linguistic rather than sociolinguistic aspects of language in Okinawa while English-language work includes sociolinguistic studies by Heinrich (2004) and Osumi (2001).

An increase in migration levels since the early 1980s has seen growing numbers of children in Japanese schools whose first language is not Japanese, and this has spawned a great deal of work on the problems they face; particularly notable here is the work coming out of Waseda and Ochanimizu universities produced by graduate students training as educators in the TJFL area. Bilingualism has been the topic of fine publications in both Japanese (e.g. Maher and Yashiro 1991) and English (e.g. Noguchi and Fotos 2001) by both Japanese and non-Japanese scholars, most of them focusing on the language situations and experiences of particular ethnic populations. Kanno (2003) is a notable longitudinal study focusing on the identity construction of bilingual Japanese students who return to Japan for higher education after several years abroad and how their choices in language use (between English and Japanese) direct that identity construction. Most recently, in a study of linguistic landscaping, Backhaus (2007) examines the use of multiple languages on street and other signs in Tokyo as an indicator of multilingualism in the city. Sanada and Shōji (2005) offers a useful Japanese-language resource which presents in encyclopaedic form a wide range of issues relating to multilingualism within the Japanese context.

One of the most pressing topics in sociolinguistics over the past 20 years has been the contentious issue of the role of English in Japanese society, in the wake of large injections of cash and policy interest by the Japanese government in the form of the afore-mentioned

Japan Exchange and Teaching (JET) program instituted in 1987 and the five-year Action Plan to Cultivate Japanese with English Abilities begun in 2003. Much of the research literature here focuses on the teaching of English in Japanese schools from both applied linguistics and wider sociolinguistic perspectives. Of particular interest for the light it throws on language attitudes within Japan is the heated debate which followed a mild suggestion in a government report that English might one day become the second official language of Japan. This provoked a large number of polemical publications. Funabashi (2000), for instance, argued strongly in support both of the idea of a second official language and of the value of English to Japanese society at large, while Tsuda (2000) strongly attacked the proposal, seeing it as a form of English linguistic nationalism likely to create a social wedge in Japan between those who are proficient in English and those who are not.

Language planning and language policy

Language planning and language policy in general continue to be topics of interest. In the four decades following World War II, Japanese-language research on language policy focused mainly on the nature of the language policies being developed and implemented in Japan during that period, documenting and analyzing the ideological and political struggles which preceded the establishment of the policies in force today, most of which relate to the writing system. Much of the more recent research, however, has either focused on delving into Japan's language policies in its pre-war colonies of Taiwan and Korea (e.g. Seki 2005) or has been an overview history of twentieth-century language policy development in general. The work of Yasuda Toshiaki is of particular interest here: Yasuda (2006), for example, examines the role of 'kokugo gakusha' (scholars of the national language) in the formation and continuation of the ideology of the national language and of language policy debates. Recent English-language studies of language policy include Carroll (2001) on language policy in the 1990s, Gottlieb (1995) on the twentieth-century script reforms, and Gottlieb (2001, 2005) on the wider scope of language planning and language policy.

Conclusion

As this short chapter has shown, research on the interaction of language and society in Japan is diverse and wide-ranging in its scope and I have merely skimmed the surface here. However, I trust that the themes introduced in this chapter will be sufficient to give interested readers an insight into some of the major topics of interest in socio-linguistics in Japan today. In coming years we can expect to see the thrust towards research on multilingualism continue, along with the interest in the impact of new media tech-nologies on language – as technology diversifies and extends, so too will creative use of language not consonant with the kind of language use envisaged by Japan's current language policies. This is likely to lead to an increased concern with how literacy is to be interpreted in twenty-first-century Japan. If the recent empirically based studies of gender and language are correct in their contention that the supposedly traditional differences between men's and women's speech are being ironed out under the influence of women's progress into the workforce, we may see less of an emphasis on studies of 'women's language' and more work on honorific expressions mediated by workforce position regardless of gender. The early twenty-first century in Japan is a linguistically exciting time as the assumptions and structures of the past are increasingly challenged by a slow but steady move away from the previous policy emphases on monolingualism and writing by hand. Language ideology remains a powerful force, however, and the clashes between what has always been seen as the natural order of things and what is actually happening promise to provide fertile ground for sociolinguistic investigation in the years ahead.

Notes

1 Renamed in 2001 the Ministry of Education, Culture, Sports, Science and Technology (MEXT) following a reorganization of ministries into larger entities.
2 Available online at: www.bunka.go.jp/kokugo/frame.asp?tm=20081007111519 (accessed 7 October 2008).

References

Backhaus, P. (2007) *Linguistic Landscapes: A Comparative Study of Urban Multilingualism in Tokyo*, Clevedon: Multilingual Matters.

Carroll, T. (2001) *Language Planning and Language Change in Japan*, Richmond: Curzon.

De Chicchis, J. (1995) 'The current state of the Ainu language', in J. Maher and K. Yashiro (eds) *Multilingual Japan*, Clevedon: Multilingual Matters, pp. 103–24.

Endō, O. (1997) *Onna no Kotoba no Bunkashi* [A Cultural History of Women's Language], Tokyo: Gakuyō Shobō. Translated into English as *A Cultural History of Japanese Women's Language*, Ann Arbor, MI: Center for Japanese Studies, University of Michigan, 2006.

Funabashi, Y. (2000) *Aete Eigo Kōyōgoron* [Taking a Risk: The Debate on English as an Official Language], Tokyo: Bungei Shunjū.

Gottlieb, N. (1995) *Kanji Politics: Language Policy and Japanese Script*, London: Kegan Paul International.

——(2000) *Word-processing Technology in Japan: Kanji and the Keyboard*, Richmond: Curzon.

——(2001) 'Language planning and policy in Japan', in N. Gottlieb and P. Chen (eds) *Language Planning and Language Policy: East Asian Perspectives*, Richmond: Curzon, pp. 21–48.

——(2005) *Language and Society in Japan*, Cambridge: Cambridge University Press.

Haugh, M. (2004) 'Revisiting the conceptualisation of politeness in English and Japanese', *Multilingua*, 23, 85–109.

Heinrich, P. (2004) 'Language planning and language ideology in the Ryūkyū Islands', *Language Policy*, 3, 153–79.

Horii, R. (1992) *Hataraku Josei no Kotoba* [The Language of Working Women], Tokyo: Meiji Shoin.

Ide, S. and McGloin, N. (eds) (1990) *Aspects of Japanese Women's Language*, Tokyo: Kuroshio.

Kabashima, T. (1988) 'Wapuro wa nihongo o kaeru ka' [Will word processors change Japanese?] *Nihongogaku*, 7, 22–9.

Kanno, Y. (2003) *Negotiating Bilingual and Bicultural Identities: Japanese Returnees betwixt Two Worlds*, Mahwah, NJ: Lawrence Erlbaum.

Kikuchi, Y. (1994) *Keigo* [Honorifics], Tokyo: Kadokawa Shoten.

Kokugo Shingikai (1995) 'Atarashii jidai ni ōjita kokugo shisaku ni tsuite' [Toward a language policy for a new era], in Kokuritsu Kokugo Kenkyūjo (eds) *Kokugo Nenkan 1995* [Japanese Language Yearbook 1995], Tokyo: Shūei Shuppan, pp. 427–51.

——(2000) *Gendai Shakai ni okeru Kei-i Hyōgen: Kokugo Shingikai Tōshin* [Report of the National Language Council: Honorifics in Today's Society]. Online. Available at: www.bunka.go.jp/kokugo/frame.asp?tm=20040306100053 (accessed 14 May 2007).

Kokuritsu Kokugo Kenkyūjo (eds) (2006) *Shin 'Kotoba' Shiriizu 19: Gairaigo to Gendai Shakai* [New 'Language' Series 19: Loanwords and Contemporary Society], Tokyo: Kokuritsu Insatsukyoku.

Kunihiro, T., Inoue, F. and Long, D. (eds) (1998) *Takesi Sibata: Sociolinguistics in Japanese Contexts*, Berlin: Mouton de Gruyter.

Maher, J. and Yashiro, K. (eds) (1991) *Nihon no Bairingarizumu* [Bilingualism in Japan], Tokyo: Kenkyūsha Shuppan.

Miller, L. (2004) 'Those naughty teenage girls: Japanese kogals, slang, and media assessments', *Journal of Linguistic Anthropology*, 14, 225–47.

Noguchi, M. and Fotos, S. (eds) (2001) *Studies in Japanese Bilingualism*, Clevedon: Multilingual Matters.

Ogino, T. (1994) 'Waapuro to gengo seikatsu' [Word processors and our linguistic life], *Gendai no Esupuri*, 319, 102–14.

Okamoto, S. and Shibamoto Smith, J. (eds) (2004) *Japanese Language, Gender, and Ideology: Cultural Models and Real People*, Oxford: Oxford University Press.

Osumi, M. (2001) 'Language and identity in Okinawa today', in M. Noguchi and S. Fotos (eds) *Studies in Japanese Bilingualism*, Clevedon: Multilingual Matters, pp. 68–97.

Refsing, K. (ed.) (1998) *Origins of the Ainu Language: The Ainu Indo-European Controversy*, Richmond: Curzon.

Sanada, S. and Shōji, H. (eds) (2005) *Nihon no Tagengo Shakai* [Japan's Multilingual Society], Tokyo: Iwanami Shoten.

Seki, G. (2005) *Nihon no Shokuminchi Gengo Seisaku Kenkyu?* [A Study of Japan's Colonial Language Policies], Tokyo: Akashi Shoten.

Shibamoto, J. (1987) 'Japanese sociolinguistics', *Annual Review of Anthropology*, 16, 261–78.

Tamura, S. (2000) *The Ainu Language*, Tokyo: Sanseido.

Tanaka, Y. (2001) 'Keitai denwa to denshi meeru no hyōgen' [Language use in cell phone texting and e-mail], in Y. Hida and T. Sato (eds) *Gendai Nihongo Kōza* [Contemporary Japanese Series], vol. 2, *Hyōgen* [Language Use], Tokyo: Meiji Shoin, pp. 98–127.

Torikai, K. (2005) 'The challenge of language and communication in twenty-first century Japan', *Japanese Studies*, 25, 249–56.

Tsuda, Y. (2000) *Eigo Heta no Susume: Eigo shinkō wa mō suteyō* [In Defence of Poor English: Let Us Abandon Our Trust in English], Tokyo: BesutoSeraazu.

Usami, M. (2002) *Discourse Politeness in Japanese Conversation: Some Implications for a Universal Theory of Politeness*, Tokyo: Hitsuji Shobō.

Wetzel, P. (2004) *Keigo in Modern Japan: Polite Language from Meiji to the Present*, Honolulu: University of Hawaii Press.

Yasuda, T. (2006) *'Kokugo' no Kindaishi – Teikoku Nihon to kokugo gakusha-tachi* [The Modern History of the National Language – Imperial Japan and the National Language Scholars], Tokyo: Chūō Kōron Shinsha.

9

Burma, Thailand, Cambodia, Laos and Vietnam

David Bradley

Introduction

The political history of this region is diverse. Burma was an independent kingdom, then gradually became a British colony between 1826 and 1886. Indochina was colonized by France, administered as five colonies: Cochin China (southern Vietnam) and Cambodia from 1864, Annam (central Vietnam) from 1874, Tonkin (northern Vietnam) from 1885, and Laos from 1893. Thailand was never a colony; however, the French took Laos from Thailand in 1893 and part of Cambodia in 1907. The whole area was occupied by Japan from 1942 to 1945. Burma achieved independence in 1948, with the Indochina countries gaining independence during the 1950s.

For an overview of the structure, orthographies and interaction styles of the five national languages, see Bradley *et al.* (1998). For detailed language maps with population, genetic classification and references, see Moseley and Asher (2007).

Burma

Burmese or Myanmar is the national and official language; it has been written since 1111 in an Indic script adapted from Mon. Allott (1985) outlines language policy in Burma. The Myanmar Language Commission makes corpus decisions; they published the standard Burmese dictionary (Myanmar Language Commission 1991), the standard Burmese-English dictionary (Myanmar Language Commission 1993), and various books on grammar and spelling. Burmese spelling has been reformed twice since 1885: in the 1890s, mainly to remove superfluous graphic final 'w' from the combination used to write the vowel /o/, and in the 1970s, mainly to systematize the spelling of words formerly written with long final 'ny' according to their modern pronunciation: those pronounced /in/ are now written with short final 'ny', while those pronounced /i/, /e/ or /ɛ/ are written with the original long final 'ny'; in many such words, the literary High form has /i/ and the spoken Low form has /ɛ/.

There is substantial variation in standard Burmese phonology; this has never been documented or discussed. One striking example is a change in progress: /wuʔ/ and /wun/ are merging with /wiʔ/ and /win/; this is near-categorical in casual Rangoon speech, but not noted in any published source. Similarly, the aspirated /sʰ/ is variably merging into the unaspirated /s/, though this is less advanced. Another example is juncture voicing, which is completely productive in some morphosyntactic environments such as medially within compound nouns, between the numeral 'one' and a following numeral classifier and between the verb and following grammatical elements, but much more variable in other environments, such as initial /t/ → [d] in the numeral 'one' followed by a numeral classifier. However, the orthography continues to write the conservative forms in nearly all such cases.

Another type of variation is the reconvergence of various regional varieties of Burmese, such as Arakanese, Tavoyan, Intha, and so on, which are gradually losing some of their distinctive phonological and lexical properties. For example, southern Arakanese dialects use Burmese /i/ after initial /m/ and /n/ in words which are /mi/ or /ni/ in Burmese, such as 'fire' /mì/ and 'red' /ni/; these are /mèin/ and /nein/ in the rest of Arakanese (Bradley 1985b).

Burmese is a diglossic language; the High has archaic grammatical forms which differ from the Low spoken forms (Okell and Allott 2001). In most cases, the system is the same, as for the demonstratives /i/ 'this' and /tʰo/ 'that' in High, versus /di/ and /ho/ in Low. In a few cases there is more than one High form corresponding to one Low form, such as the High realis relative markers /θí/ and /θɔ́/ versus Low /tɛ́/, or High continuative realis /i/ and noncontinuative realis /θi/ versus Low realis /tɛ/. There are three reflexive constructions: one with /mímí/ is only High, one with Pronoun + /ko/ + Pronoun is only Low, and one with /kókoko/ is used in both (Bradley 2005). Some High forms like the plural /mjà/ tend to spread into spoken contexts, but forms such as the Low plural /twe/ or /te/ are not used in literary contexts. Domains for Low Burmese are increasing, as discussed in Saw Tun (2005). High is used in nearly all written contexts, in formal public speeches and in radio news broadcasts, but Low is used in everyday conversation, television news broadcasts, comics, some poetry, letters to close friends, and increasingly in other informal written contexts. A severe educational problem is that schools teach High Burmese, including to minority children in remote areas who have no exposure to and little use for it.

Studies of discourse phenomena in Burmese are limited, but Hopple (2005) discusses topicalization and San San Hnin Tun (2005) discusses discourse particles.

The other 134 recognized ethnic groups of Burma all have distinct languages; seven have separate states, and many have substantial populations and well-established writing systems, but none may be used in official education. Religious organizations such as Buddhist temples and Christian churches often teach literacy in some of these languages, and there used to be limited government support for the development of literacy materials in the seven state minority languages, especially Shan, Kachin and Karen, but this has stopped. Most material in minority languages is prepared in neighbouring countries (Thailand, China, India, where many of the same groups also live) for use in Burma.

A third of the population speaks a minority language as mother tongue and Burmese as a second language. Many have difficulties with certain segments of Burmese, such as the dental fricative /θ/, often replaced by [t] or other approximations, or the diphthongs such as /ei/ and /ou/, absent from most minority languages and often replaced by monophthongs [e] and [o] in second-language usage. In some areas, Burmese is replacing minority languages, for example, among much of the Mon and some of the Karen population in the Irrawaddy delta region, and many minority languages are endangered.

During the colonial period, English was very widely spoken, but levels have declined drastically. Burmese speakers often transfer Burmese phonology into their English; for example, the diphthong /ai/ occurs only in nasal /ain/ or stop-final /ai?/ syllables in Burmese, and most Burmese speakers of English replace English /ai/ with Burmese nasalized /ain/.

Thailand

Thai is the national and official language of Thailand, mother tongue dialect of over 26 million people in the central region, a second dialect for about 27 million in north-eastern Thailand who speak closely-related Lao, about eight million in the north who speak Kham Myang or Northern Thai, and about seven million in the south who speak Pak Tai. It is a second language for other people in Thailand. Thai is understood by Lao speakers in Laos and many Shan in Burma. Smalley (1994) surveyed the sociolinguistic situation in Thailand.

Since 1933, Thailand has a Royal Institute responsible for standardizing the Thai language. It produced the standard dictionary (1950, 1982, 2003) and is now drafting a national language policy. There was a conference to discuss this in July 2008. Thai script was originally based on Khmer script, adapted since 1283 to write Thai. The main body implementing the standardization and spread of Thai is the Ministry of Education, especially through its Khurusapha (textbook printing office). Also involved are the Office of National Identity and various other bodies. Diller (1991) gives an overview of the stages of policy formulation.

The major stereotyped variable in central Thai is /r/, which is very often replaced by /l/; both can be deleted in initial clusters. Other variables include /s/, which can also be realized as [θ], and /kʰw/ → /f/ among others. Variation in /r/ is so extensive that teaching children which words are spelled with r is a major educational problem. All these variables show the typical pattern of social and stylistic stratification (Beebe 1975), with /s/ → [θ] less advanced and mainly restricted to lower-status Bangkok speakers. Within Central Thai, there are also sub-regional forms such as the western merger of the rising tone into the falling tone, variably reseparated according to the standard distinction.

Differences between Thai and regional varieties of the north, north-east and south are much greater. Northern Thai is known as Kham Myang ('city words'), Yuan or Nyuan, and its separate writing system is often referred to as the Lanna ('million rice fields') script, from the name of the former Northern Thai kingdom; Lanna script is undergoing a folkloristic revival. In the north-east of Thailand, also known as Isan, the local speech is various varieties of Lao, more similar to the standard variety of the national language of Laos than to standard central Thai, but literacy is in Thai. The Thai Buddhist population of southern Thailand speaks Pak Tai, which is more conservative than Central Thai in some ways; for example, it retains /r/. Diller (1985) refers to 'segmentally subjugated' Southern Thai, retaining a regional tone pattern but variably using standard central Thai segments. There is also tonally subjugated Northern Thai, with a Central Thai tone system superimposed on Northern Thai segments, variably used in Chiangmai. All speakers of regional varieties of Thai have extensive variation depending on interlocutors and domains, and shift to standard Thai in formal contexts and when writing.

Thai has a very old stratum of Chinese loans including most numerals. Many Khmer loans including honorific vocabulary but also everyday words like *tamruat* 'police', a large number of Pali loans relating to Buddhism and the massive influx of recent English loans are written in ways reflecting their source but pronounced with integration into Thai phonology. Most English loanwords have falling tone on the final syllable.

Studies of discourse phenomena in Thai are relatively advanced. For an overview, see Somsonge (2002) and more recently Usitara (2006).

The largest linguistic minorities are the Malay in the south, the Khmer in the north-east and the Chaozhou or Teochiu Chinese in all urban areas; most maintain their languages, though not necessarily literacy in them. There are over twenty recognized mountain minority groups, some growing rapidly due to migration from Burma. Many of these, such as the Karen, Lahu, Lisu, Akha, Shan, Khmu and others, are much more numerous in adjacent countries; a few live only in Thailand. Often such groups have various names: the Lahu (own name) are also called Museu in Thai and formerly Lohei in Chinese. There are various NGOs assisting their development and the preservation of their languages and cultures, such as IMPECT (Inter Mountain Peoples Education and Culture in Thailand), AFECT (Akha Association for Education and Culture in Thailand) and others.

A number of small minority groups whose languages are endangered, such as Chong, Thavung, Gong and Bisu, have community-based language maintenance programs assisted by scholars at Thai universities (especially Mahidol University) and funded by the Thailand Research Fund. Government policy requires orthographies for minority languages taught in schools to be based on Thai script, and Thai-script versions of Malay and various other minority languages have been developed and implemented. However, some minority groups prefer other pre-existing orthographies.

English is widely learned as a foreign language, and spoken with a distinctive Thai accent. For example, English 'sh' /ʃ/ is consistently replaced by Thai /tɕʰ/ (similar to English 'ch' /tʃ/) as there is no /ʃ/ in Thai; final /l/ is normally replaced by /n/; and so on. The only quantified study of Thai English phonology and morphosyntax is Bradley and Bradley (1984).

Laos

Lao is the national language of Laos and the regional Thai dialect of Isan or north-eastern Thailand, with about 2.8 million first-language speakers in Laos from a total population of just over 5.6 million, and 27 million in Thailand. Most minority people in Laos speak Lao as a second language, and some ethnic Lao live in north-eastern Cambodia and north-western Vietnam. Some post-1975 Lao refugees in western countries are ethnic Lao; more are from Hmong or other minority groups.

Lan Xang ('million elephants') is a traditional name for the Lao kingdom; the Lao script used in Laos has been in use for over 500 years and is also called the Lan Xang script. It is based on Thai script but more rounded; thus it is ultimately derived from the Khmer script. After 1975, written Lao was reformed to make spelling conform closely to speech. For example, Luang Phrabang, the old royal capital, is now written Luang Phabang with the unpronounced medial *r* omitted. The letters of the Lao Tham script are more similar to Khmer; this is used for some religious and astrological purposes. Lao has five main regional subvarieties with quite different tone systems: Southern Laos; Vientiane (in Lao, *Wiang chan* 'moon city' or 'sandalwood city'), central Laos and much of north-eastern Thailand; Luang Phabang and northern Laos; north-eastern Laos (sometimes further subdivided); and Korat in the south-western part of north-eastern Thailand. Many villages of Lao are scattered across the central plain of Thailand, after the forced relocations of captured populations brought back from what is now Laos by Thai kings in the eighteenth and nineteenth centuries. These groups often call themselves Lao plus some specifier, such as Lao Wiang for the Lao from the Vientiane area, Lao Dan for those from the border area, and so on. The standard language is the Vientiane dialect, and this is widely understood throughout the country; other regional Lao varieties are less widely known, though the Luang Phabang variety of the former royal capital retains some prestige due to its former status.

In recent years, Lao has had a massive influx of Thai loanwords adjusted to Lao phonology, and this trend is increasing. For example, the Thai word *prachum* 'meeting' is borrowed as Lao *pasum*. This shows the regular pattern of Lao lacking medial /r/ and the regular change of Thai /tɕʰ/ to Lao /s/, also seen in *xang* 'elephant' versus Thai *chang*. Lao /s/ from earlier /tɕʰ/ is transliterated as 'x' to distinguish it from original /s/. See Enfield (2002, 2003) for some sociolinguistic observations on Lao syntax.

All Lao speakers can understand Thai media including radio, television and written Thai; many Thai textbooks are used in Laos. Speakers of standard central Thai have difficulty understanding most kinds of Lao, due to lack of exposure and the sociolinguistic dynamics of the region. However, some Lao songs from north-eastern Thailand are very popular throughout Thailand, and also understood by Thai as well as Lao speakers.

In 2002, 49 ethnic groups were officially recognized in Laos; this number and the exact inventory and official names have fluctuated slightly since 1975. The overall categories are Lao Lum who are the Lao (about half the total population) and other Thai-related groups (about an eighth), Lao Theung 'jungle Lao' who are the minorities of the low hills, mostly speaking Mon-Khmer languages (about a quarter), and Lao Sung, minorities of the high mountains (about an eighth). Sometimes an additional category of Lao Thai is used to distinguish the various groups speaking related Thai languages from the ethnic Lao. Lao Sung includes the Hmong (own name) or Meo and Mien (own name) or Yao in the north. Many Lao Theung groups are very small, especially in the south. Policy for minorities is supportive of their rights (Godineau 2003), but educational policy does not allow teaching in any language other than Lao (Bradley 2003). Bradley (1996) gives details of the situation of the groups speaking Tibeto-Burman languages in northern Laos, which is typical for other groups as well.

Many of the Hmong minority of Laos are now refugees in western countries. The Hmong messiah Yang Shong Lue developed a new writing system (Smalley *et al.* 1990), which is now used by his followers outside Laos, such as in Australia (Eira 2002). However, most Hmong still use a missionary romanization.

Laos has very few trained indigenous linguists, and they do not do sociolinguistic work. Since 1975, it has been extremely difficult for outsiders to do research in Laos. Virtually no work on variation or discourse has ever been done there. The most urgent sociolinguistic issue is the disappearance of minority languages. Because no survey has ever documented the linguistic diversity of Laos, additional languages or dialects are still occasionally located, such as the Kri dialect of Maleng in the south, found during an environmental impact study for a new dam, or the Iduh language related to Khmu in the north-east. Both were found in the mid-1990s.

The official foreign language remains French, but its knowledge and use have been gradually decreasing since 1954; English is now the preferred foreign language among younger people.

Cambodia

Khmer is the national language of Cambodia, spoken by over ten million people including all ethnic Khmer in Cambodia, over a million in the Mekong delta of Vietnam, over 800,000 along the northern border of Cambodia in north-eastern Thailand and among post-1975 refugees in the west. However, many ethnic Khmer who were resettled to central Thailand after Thai invasions in the early nineteenth century have now assimilated completely and no longer identify as Khmer. The vast majority of people in Cambodia is ethnic Khmer, and nearly all the rest speak Khmer as a second language; some small minorities are losing their own languages. Apart from the urban ethnic Chinese and some small Austronesian-speaking groups in the north-east, most of those who are not ethnic Khmer have related Mon-Khmer mother tongues.

About half the post-1975 refugees from Cambodia are ethnic Chinese, and the ethnic Chinese population of Cambodia has decreased greatly since 1975. In the south-east of the country, there is a substantial Vietnamese minority, which increased after 1979.

Since 609, Khmer has been written in a script derived from Indic sources, representing the pronunciation of the Angkor period. There was a brief and unpopular flirtation with romanization from 1943 to 1945. Over more than a millennium, Khmer speech has undergone radical sound changes, so that the same original written symbol for a vowel may now be pronounced completely differently depending on whether it is preceded by an originally voiced or voiceless consonant. These vowel splits were conditioned by a difference of phonation, breathy in syllables starting with an originally voiced consonant versus normal in syllables starting with an originally voiceless consonant, still found in some regional varieties of Khmer but absent from the standard speech of the capital, Phnom Penh.

As a result, standard Phnom Penh Khmer has a remarkably rich vowel system. Starting from the written system with nine long and short vowels and three long and short diphthongs, there are nine short and ten long monophthongs and 13 diphthongs, with a contrast of five vowel heights for front vowels. There is a great deal of sociolinguistic variation in the vowel system of Phnom Penh speakers, which is discussed and quantified by Naraset (2002).

Khmer has extensive Indic lexical borrowings, including both Hindu and Theravada Buddhist strata; these are superposed on its basic Mon-Khmer lexicon. Khmer is also the source of a substantial amount of formal vocabulary in Thai and Lao; Thai and Lao orthographies, among others in the area, are derived from the Khmer script. After the decline of Angkor, the flow of loanwords eventually reversed, and Khmer started to borrow Thai words. During nearly a century of French rule, the elite learned French and many French loanwords entered the language. The Khmer Rouge discarded much of the Indic and other formal and foreign vocabulary, some brought back after 1979. Most recently, some English loanwords have started to enter Khmer as well.

A National Commission worked from 1915 to standardize Khmer spelling, finally publishing a two-volume dictionary in 1939 and 1943. The Ministry of Education set up a Textbook Committee in 1932 and has published a wide range of textbooks and literature. In 1947, a National Cultural Commission was established to coin new words, and later published a French-Khmer dictionary. In 1955, Khmer finally replaced French as the medium of education. During the Khmer Rouge period, language policy mainly consisted of eliminating all but the most basic stratum of vocabulary, proscribing pronouns reflecting differences of status and most formal and foreign words, and requiring the use of the most basic vocabulary, often from rural sources. For example, only /hop/ was acceptable for 'eat', with 11 other words banned. Much, but not all, of the former lexicon was brought back into use after 1979. Currently, the Ministry of Education is responsible for language policy (Thel Thong 1985).

The minorities in Cambodia include speakers of over a dozen Mon–Khmer languages more or less closely related to Khmer, mainly in the north-east but also some moribund Pearic group languages scattered around the country which are very closely related to Khmer and in close contact with it for over a millennium. Minority policy in Cambodia is virtually nonexistent, and there is no government support for minority languages. If anything, some minorities were a special target of the Khmer Rouge, such as the urban ethnic Chinese and the Moslem Cham in the north-east, who speak an Austronesian language. These Cham came from the coast of Vietnam about 400 years ago, when their area was conquered by the Vietnamese. One village of Cham from north-eastern Cambodia were taken to Bangkok about 150 years ago to work as silk weavers; they are still Moslem, still live in the same area around the Jim Thompson house and some still weave silk, but no longer speak Cham.

French was widely learned during and after the colonial period. From 1970 to 1975 and from the 1980s, English became the dominant foreign language; Rado *et al.* (1986) discuss the characteristic English of Khmer refugees overseas, but there has not been much study of L2 English inside Cambodia.

Vietnam

Vietnamese is the national language of Vietnam and the first language of over 66 million people there. The ethnic Vietnamese gradually spread from the northern coast into the centre and south of the country over the last millennium. Vietnamese is also spoken as a second language by most of the other ethnic groups of Vietnam. Substantial Vietnamese minorities moved to south-eastern Cambodia and southern Laos during the French colonial period, and into north-eastern Thailand at various times: first, after the French colonization of Vietnam in the mid-nineteenth century, then around 1954 and after 1975. There is also a small Jing or Vietnamese nationality in south-western Guangxi, China, and after 1975 over a million refugees in Western countries. Overall, there are at least two million speakers of Vietnamese outside the country.

In Vietnamese, the term for ethnic Vietnamese people is *Kinh*; this is also the source of the Chinese term *Jing*. *Viet* is the traditional local and Chinese name for the political entity and the language, pronounced *Yue* in modern Mandarin Chinese. *Nam* 'south' is one of a very large number of Chinese loanwords in Vietnamese; northern Vietnam was part of China until 939. The Chinese influence was pervasive, in all areas of Vietnamese culture, and on the syntax and phonology of Vietnamese, not just the lexicon. For example, Vietnamese uses a numeral plus classifier construction preceding the noun, as in Chinese.

The traditional Vietnamese *chữ nôm* 'southern language' script used Chinese characters to write Vietnamese, but in 1910, the *quốc-ngữ* 'national language' romanization devised by the Jesuit Alexandre de Rhodes in the early seventeenth century officially replaced it, and knowledge of *chữ nôm* has almost disappeared. Work on language policy started late in Vietnam, and went on separately in north and south from 1954 to 1975. Finally, in 1979 a Standardization Conference was convened by the Institute of Linguistics and the Ministry of Education to reunify the lexicon of language (Nguyen 1985).

The standard dialect of Hanoi has six tones, written with diacritics in the romanized orthography, but the two falling-rising tones – lower *hỏi,* and higher *ngã* – are merged in central and southern dialects. Some vowel distinctions are also written with sup diacritics, so the orthography may have two diacritics over some vowels. Syllable-final palatals /c/, /ɲ/ merge with /t/, /n/ in central and southern dialects. The pitch values of tones in the central Vietnamese of Hue, the former capital, are fairly distinctive: higher *ngang* and *huyền* tones, lower *sắc* tone and so on (Vu 1981); some rural subvarieties of central Vietnamese have only four tones. Speakers of non-northern dialects variably adjust toward the standard in formal contexts, and always write in the standard.

Much of the learned vocabulary of Vietnamese is borrowed from Chinese, or more recently from French and most recently from English. However, basic vocabulary such as numerals shows that Vietnamese is a Mon-Khmer language.

Over 80 per cent of the population of Vietnam are ethnic-majority Vietnamese, and there are 53 recognized minority ethnic groups. There were 34 only in the former north (apart from small numbers of refugees from the north in the south after 1954), and 18 only in the former south. One group formerly known as Van Kiêu in the north and Bruu in the south was on both sides of the former border; it is now called Bruu-Van Kiêu. The 1.1 million Mường in the uplands of north central Vietnam speak a language closely related to Vietnamese. Very closely related to Mường and Vietnamese are the seven languages of the Chưt ethnic group of Vietnam and the Arem (formerly Bo) ethnic group of Laos, all with tiny speaker populations and numerous subgroup names which are sometimes cited as separate languages. Many of the other minority groups also speak more distinct Mon-Khmer languages, but there are also some Austronesian languages in the south and some Tibeto-Burman and Thai languages in the north.

Romanized orthographies based on the principles of the Vietnamese romanization are in use for many of these languages. Some of Vietnam's minorities are also found in adjacent countries, such as the Nung and Tay (total over 2.3 million, the latter formerly known as Thô) who also live in China where they are known as Zhuang. The Ha Nhi also live in China and Laos where they are known as Hani. The Meo of Vietnam are known as Miao in China, as Maew in Thailand and Laos, and often as Hmong from their own name.

French was widely learned during the colonial period. From the 1960s, English became the dominant foreign language. From the early 1960s, 'bamboo English', a contact pidgin, developed between American soldiers and local people, but this has disappeared. Rado *et al.* (1986) discuss the characteristic English of Vietnamese refugees overseas. There is also a large and growing literature on L2 English inside Vietnam.

Much of the original sociolinguistic research on languages of Vietnam is now published in Vietnamese inside Vietnam, and so is not widely accessible.

Conclusion

A great deal remains to be done to investigate the sociolinguistic situation in these five countries; for an overview, see Bradley (2006). In particular, there has been little quantified study of variation, especially in minority languages, though extensive variation is present. More has been done on issues relating to multilingualism, language and culture, some aspects of discourse studies, and research on second-language English, which is now the dominant foreign language. One strength of sociolinguistics in the area is the study of language planning (Bradley 1985a). A feature of all national languages of the area is a complex set of socially stratified pronouns and other vocabulary, not discussed for reasons of space. The major sociolinguistic problem is that most minority languages in the area are endangered, and many may disappear this century (Bradley 2007).

References

Allott, A. J. (1985) 'Language policy and language planning in Burma', in D. Bradley (ed.) *Language Policy, Language Planning and Sociolinguistics in South-East Asia*, Canberra: Pacific Linguistics A-67, pp. 131–54.

Baker, C. J. and Phongpaichit, P. (2005) *A History of Thailand*, New York: Cambridge University Press.

Beebe, L. M. (1975) 'Occupational prestige and consonant cluster simplification', *International Journal of the Sociology of Language*, 5, 43–62.

Bradley, D. (ed.) (1985a) *Language Policy, Language Planning and Sociolinguistics in South-East Asia*, Canberra: Pacific Linguistics A-67.

——(1985b) 'Arakanese vowels', in G. Thurgood, J. A. Matisoff and D. Bradley (eds) *Linguistics of the Sino-Tibetan Area: The State of the Art*, Canberra: Pacific Linguistics C-87, pp. 180–200.

——(1996) 'Tibeto-Burman languages in PDR Lao', *Linguistics of the Tibeto-Burman Area*, 19, 19–27.

——(1997) 'Democracy in Burma?', *Asian Studies Review*, 21, 19–31.

——(2003) 'Language and culture of minority groups', in Y. Godineau (ed.) *Laos and Ethnic Minority Cultures: Promoting Heritage*, Paris: UNESCO, pp. 45–68.

——(2005) 'Reflexives in literary and spoken Burmese', in J. Watkins (ed.) *Studies in Burmese Linguistics*, Canberra: Pacific Linguistics 570, pp. 67–86.

——(2006) 'Sociolinguistics in South-east Asia', in U. Ammon, N. Dittmar, K. Mattheier and P. Trudgill (eds) *Soziolinguistik*, vol. 3, Berlin: Mouton de Gruyter, pp. 2007–13.

——(2007) 'East and South-east Asia', in C. Moseley (ed.) *Encyclopedia of the World's Endangered Languages*, London: Routledge, pp. 349–422.

Bradley, D. and Bradley, M. (1984) *Problems of Asian Students in Australia: Language, Culture and Education*, Canberra: Australian Government Publishing Service.

Bradley, D., Roberts, J., Cummings, J., Ramly, A., Woods, P., Sarwao Rini, K., Wolff, J. U. and Xuan Thu, N. (1998) *South-east Asian Phrasebook*, Melbourne: Lonely Planet.

Diller, A. V. (1985) 'High and Low Thai: views from within', in D. Bradley (ed.) *Language Policy, Language Planning and Sociolinguistics in South-East Asia*, Canberra: Pacific Linguistics A-67, pp. 51–76.

——(1991) 'What makes Central Thai a national language?', in C. J. Reynolds (ed.) *National Identity and Its Defenders*, Monash Papers on South-east Asia No. 25, Clayton, VIC: Centre of South-east Asian Studies, Monash University, pp. 87–132.

Eira, C. (2002) 'Language maintenance at the micro level: Hmong ex-refugee communities', in D. Bradley and M. Bradley (eds) *Language Endangerment and Language Maintenance*, London: Routledge-Curzon, pp. 230–56.

Enfield, N. J. (2002) 'Cultural logic and syntactic productivity: associated posture constructions in Lao', in N. J. Enfield (ed.) *Ethnosyntax: Explorations in Grammar and Culture*, Oxford: Oxford University Press, pp. 231–58.

——(2003) *Linguistics Epidemiology: Semantics and Grammar of Language Contact in South-east Asia*, London: RoutledgeCurzon.

Evans, G. (1998) *The Politics of Ritual and Remembrance: Laos since 1975*, Honolulu: University of Hawaii Press.

Evans, G. and Rowley, K. (1990) *Red Brotherhood at War: Vietnam, Cambodia and Laos since 1975*, rev. edn, New York: Verso.

Godineau, Y. (ed.) (2003) *Laos and Ethnic Minority Cultures: Promoting Heritage*, Paris: UNESCO.

Hopple, P. (2005) 'Topicalization in Burmese expository discourse', in J. Watkins (ed.) *Studies in Burmese Linguistics*, Canberra: Pacific Linguistics 570, pp. 161–83.

Moseley, C. and Asher, R. E. (eds) (2007) *Atlas of the World's Languages*, 2nd edn, London: Routledge.

Myanmar Language Commission (1991) *Myanmar Dictionary* [in Burmese], Yangon: Myanmar Language Commission.

——(1993) *Myanmar-English Dictionary*, Yangon: Myanmar Language Commission.

Naraset, P. (2002) 'Variation in Khmer as spoken in Phnom Penh', PhD thesis, La Trobe University, Australia.

Nguyen, D. (1985) 'Terminology work in Vietnam', in D. Bradley (ed.) *Language Policy, Language Planning and Sociolinguistics in South-East Asia*, Canberra: Pacific Linguistics A-67, pp. 119–30.

Okell, J. and Allott, A. J. (2001) *Burmese/Myanmar Dictionary of Grammatical Terms*, Richmond, Surrey: Curzon.

Rado, M., Foster, L. and Bradley, D. (1986) *English Language Needs of Migrant and Refugee Youth*, Canberra: Australian Government Publishing Service.

Royal Institute (1950) *Royal Institute Dictionary* [in Thai], Bangkok: Royal Institute.

——(1982) *Royal Institute Dictionary* [in Thai], rev. edn, Bangkok: Royal Institute.

——(2003) *Royal Institute Dictionary* [in Thai], Bangkok: Royal Institute.

San San Hnin Tun (2005) 'Discourse particles in Burmese', in J. Watkins (ed.) *Studies in Burmese Linguistics*, Canberra: Pacific Linguistics 570, pp. 185–99.

Saw Tun (2005) 'Modern Burmese writing: an examination of the status of colloquial Burmese', in J. Watkins (ed.) *Studies in Burmese Linguistics*, Canberra: Pacific Linguistics 570, pp. 201–19.

Smalley, W. A. (1994) *Linguistic Diversity and National Unity: Language Ecology in Thailand*, Chicago: University of Chicago Press.

Smalley, W. A., Vang, Chia Khua, Yang, Gnia Yee and Moua, Mitt (1990) *Mother of Writing: The Origin and Development of a Hmong Messianic Script*, Chicago: University of Chicago Press.

Somsonge, B. (2002) 'Discourse studies in Thailand', *Discourse Studies*, 4, 501–10.

Thel Thong (1985) 'Language policy and language planning of Cambodia', in D. Bradley (ed.) *Language Policy, Language Planning and Sociolinguistics in South-East Asia*, Canberra: Pacific Linguistics A-67, pp. 103–17.

Usitara, J. (2006) 'A discourse study of the Northern Thai legends based on their structure', PhD thesis, La Trobe University, Australia.

Vickery, M. (2007) *Cambodia: A Political Survey*, Phnom Penh: Éditions Funan.

Vu, T. P. (1981) 'The acoustic and perceptual nature of tones in Vietnamese', PhD thesis, Australian National University, Canberra.

10

Malaysia, Singapore, Indonesia, Philippines

Lionel Wee

Introduction

Though South-east Asia is an area rich in sociolinguistic diversity – as exemplified by the four countries[1] that are the focus of this chapter – a focus on English is hard to avoid since, as we shall see, this language figures prominently in many sociolinguistic issues that concern the region. Malaysia (with a population of 22 million) and Indonesia (population 240 million) are both Islamic states that recognize Malay (known as Bahasa Malaysia and Bahasa Indonesia in the respective countries) as the sole official language, in spite of their linguistic heterogeneity. Malaysia has many speakers of Tamil and Mandarin. Indonesia has speakers of Javanese and Aceh, in addition to many other local languages. Both countries also privilege an ethnic-religious-linguistic nexus where the links between being Malay, Muslim, and a speaker of Malay are treated as being almost ineluctable. This is an ideological construction, of course, that has considerable implications for individuals and communities that do not display the privileged conglomeration of features. For example, all Malays are assumed to be Muslims, and any Malay who decides to change his/her religion (apostasy) faces great difficulty in getting the new religious affiliation officially recognized. And in Indonesia, it is only in the post-Soeharto era that ethnic Chinese were even allowed a restricted display of their culture, such as a Chinese language television channel with limited broadcast time.

The Philippines (population 76 million), in contrast, is a Catholic state that treats Filipino (Tagalog) and English as co-official languages. Though expectations regarding the kind of features that constitute the Philippine identity are less strongly defined, the situation here is no less ideological in that there are ongoing battles regarding the relative statuses of Filipino and English. The former is resisted by many on the basis that it is a language that represents just one out of eight major linguistic groups (the other seven being Bikol, Cebuango, Hiligaynon, Ilokano, Pampangan, Pangasinan and Warray), while the latter is perceived as a Western language that came into the country as a result of American colonial rule.

In the case of Singapore, a small secular state of 3.2 million people, four official languages are recognized: English, Malay, Mandarin and Tamil. Non-official languages include other

Chinese languages such as Cantonese, Hokkien, and Teochew, as well as other Indian languages, such as Bengali and Hindi. Among the official languages, only the last three are also official mother tongues (languages assigned by the state as representative of a community's ethnic identity): Malay for the Malays, Mandarin for the Chinese, and Tamil for the Indians. English is not accepted by the state as a mother tongue on the grounds that it needs to remain ethnically neutral for a number of reasons. One, it serves as an inter-ethnic lingua franca. Two, as the major language of socio-economic mobility, its ethnically neutral status ensures that the distribution of economic advantages is not seen as being unduly associated with a specific ethnic group, which would otherwise raise the danger of inter-ethnic tension. And three, as in the case of the Philippines (as well as Malaysia and Indonesia), English is treated as a language that essentially marks a non-Asian 'other'.

All four countries were historically subject to colonial rule, a fact that continues to have effects beyond the formal institution of a colonial regime. Thus, the widespread presence of English in Singapore, Malaysia and the Philippines, to the point where nativized varieties have developed, is the result of British (for Singapore and Malaysia) and American (for the Philippines) domination. No nativized variety of English can be said to have emerged (yet) in Indonesia (a former Dutch colony). However, given the status of English as the world's global language (Crystal 1997: 360), it is not surprising that English is Indonesia's most important foreign language.

In fact, the strong association between English and the forces of globalization means that all four countries are faced with the need to manage similar issues: Can the indigenous Asian languages find some social and economic value that allows them to carve out a space in relation to English? Is it possible or even desirable for English to be considered an Asian language? What changes to the relationship between linguistic and non-linguistic factors (such as ethnicity, religious affiliation or class) are likely? Language choice and shift in the region are increasingly influenced by utilitarian concerns, and English is probably the language most prominently associated with these. As a result, a class division between the English 'haves' and 'have-nots' is a potentially serious social problem, suggesting a strong need for further research into the commodification of language, and its implications for community and culture. These are centrally sociolinguistic issues as they all concern the social distribution and valuation of linguistic resources. English figures prominently in these issues simply because for many people in South-east Asia, it is either a language that holds the promise of a 'better life', one that poses a threat to traditional values, or both.

Language policy and planning

Language policy and planning (LPP) is perhaps the most convenient place to start appreciating the sociolinguistic dilemmas faced by these countries. This is because most states tend to have explicit formulations regarding what would be considered a desirable target sociolinguistic situation. And while LPP can occur at a variety of levels, most studies in this field have historically focused on that of the state. LPP in South-east Asia is no exception, as seen in the collection of chapters in Brown and Ganguly (2003), for example. The chapters focus on how state-level policies have impacted ethnic relations within individual countries. They also aim to distinguish successful policies – defined as those which promote economic and social justice, as well as ethnic stability (ibid.: 6) – from less successful ones.

The chapter by Bertrand in this collection deals specifically with LPP in Indonesia, and the author remarks that:

> Bahasa Indonesia spread among Indonesia's population through its adoption as the language of government, business, and education ... The gradual implementation of national language policies can reassure minority groups that the official language does not pose a threat. Furthermore, the promotion of an official language for purposes that are distinct from those of local language may be more acceptable to ethnic groups.
>
> (2003: 290)

Bertrand's remarks concern the ecological relationship between local minority languages and the national language, suggesting that minority languages and the national language can co-exist if there is a clear sociolinguistic division of labour that prevents the languages from competing in the same social domains.

But even the national language has to construct its own ecology in relation to the global powerhouse that is English. This issue is given specific consideration by Rappa and Wee (2006) who highlight three possible relationships between languages that LPP commonly adopt: (1) *equivalence*, where distinct languages are treated as equals; (2) *displacement*, where one language replaces another; and (3) *complementarity*, where distinct languages serve non-overlapping functions. (Bertrand's remarks above obviously fall under the category of 'complementarity'.) However, Rappa and Wee also point out that LPP is deeply influenced by state narratives, which are highly ideological and hence constrain in significant ways the kinds of policies that can be considered acceptable. For example, Malaysia's adoption of an affirmative action *bumiputera* policy aims at ensuring that the Malay identity and language are not just protected but flourishing. This has created a strong sensitivity towards how Bahasa Malaysia is faring in relation to English. National pride demands that the language be seen as equivalent to English. A relationship of complementarity (particularly if this relegates Malay to a cultural heritage marker while associating English with science and technology) appears unacceptable. Hence, the Malay language academy was tasked in 1995 with promoting the language in all fields, including science and technology, to demonstrate that it is capable of functioning in domains that typically use English. However, this move has been difficult to sustain because the state is also grappling with the problem of ensuring that its graduates remain competitive in the global economy, a problem compounded by the fact that there are still concerns over the ability of these graduates to communicate proficiently in English.

An important, even urgent, research agenda for LPP in South-east Asia, then, would be to investigate the state's ability to manage ethnic relations while also attending to the country's socio-economic development. Dealing with these issues requires the sensitive handling of complex ethnolinguistic relations between various local communities, as well as managing the presence of the English language, including the development of so-called 'New Englishes'.

New Englishes

The emergence of distinct forms of English, or 'New Englishes', is a phenomenon of major sociolinguistic interest, since different countries have in place different sociolinguistic and language-contact conditions, which may influence the kind of New English that develops. While earlier studies tended to assume that New Englishes are best analyzed by comparing them with more established varieties, more recent works are acknowledging the relevance of surrounding socio-political conditions, and arguing that these may need to be recognized as varieties of English in their own right.

This dynamical scenario where English moves over time from being a primarily foreign language to being a completely indigenous variety is the point of departure for Schneider's (2003) ambitious attempt to outline the different phases of development that a speech community undergoes as it grapples with English. Schneider proposes five such phases: (1) *foundation* (where English is used on a regular basis in a country that was not English-speaking before); (2) *exonormative stabilization* (where a community of expatriate native speakers provide normative stability); (3) *nativization* (where traditional realities, identities, and sociopolitical alignments undergo major shifts to reflect a changed reality and the concomitant development of a new sociolinguistic identity); (4) *endonormative stabilization* (where there is adoption and even acceptance of an indigenous linguistic norm); and (5) *differentiation* (where an attitude of linguistic independence and confidence prevails, reflected in the sense that there is no need to compare the indigenous variety to others).

English in the Philippines occupies phase three of Schneider's framework, nativization. This is because the promotion of Filipino 'restricts the range of uses of English and, more importantly, successfully bars it from the role of symbolizing identities, national or otherwise' (ibid.: 261), but at the same time, there is strong resentment against English, which is seen as a significant class marker (ibid.: 263). In contrast, Singapore occupies phase four, endonormative stabilization. This is because Singaporean English has come to be the means of expression of a 'novel identity merging European and Asian components' since 'English is the only bond shared by everybody' and 'the ethnic languages ... are distinct from and thus not supported by the dialectal home varieties' (ibid.: 264). This weakens the 'usefulness of the indigenous languages and, conversely, strengthens that of English' (ibid.: 264).

Schneider's phases provide a useful framework for understanding various country-specific studies. For example, as a country undergoing nativization, English in Philippine society may be widely used among the elite but it is much less common among the masses. And the formulation of the education system in the Philippines will need to bear this in mind if it is to be of any material value to its students. Thus, Tupas (2003, p. 18) observes that the use of English as a medium of education in the Philippines has exacerbated rather than mitigated the socio-economic disparity between the elite and the masses, because the language actually 'has very limited use in most communities'. Citing Canieso-Doronilla (1998), Tupas argues that this has effectively rendered 'whole populations of Filipinos illiterate', and calls instead for a broader notion of literacy, one that situates the development of communication skills and the use of resources within the needs of the local communities themselves. And with regard to a phase four country like Singapore, it is precisely because a new indigenous norm has emerged that one can and should expect resistance from the more conservative members of the society (Schneider 2003: 250). Thus, the highly conservative Singaporean state has recently expressed concerns that the growing popularity of the local variety of English (Singlish) will undermine the ability of Singaporeans to acquire 'good' English. This has led the state to initiate, in 2000, the Speak Good English Movement (SGEM). The SGEM, rather unfortunately, equates the promotion of 'good' English with the elimination of Singlish, thus confusing two otherwise independent goals (Chng 2003; Wee 2005). There is strong sociolinguistic irony here. The emergence of the indigenous norm should be seen as a sign of LPP success since English has taken root to the point where Singaporeans are comfortable with the language. But because of the general tendency to disparage New Englishes as deficient versions of more standard varieties, much effort is instead being spent by the state in an attempt to get rid of Singlish, under the mistaken belief that colloquial and standard varieties cannot co-exist.

Detailed studies of the relationships between emerging New Englishes and their more established counterparts can therefore help us better understand how social evaluations of languages change, and how such changes are both reflections of, and contributing factors to, the wider political economy of language.

Language choice and language shift

Whether as a direct result of state-level LPP or not, language use patterns are important indices of ongoing societal changes and community attitudes. Consequently, a large number of studies have focused on the issue of language choice and shift. But since language shift is rarely 'across the board' but, rather, unevenly distributed in different social settings (Fishman 1991: 45), these studies have quite reasonably dealt with data drawn from specific social domains, especially the family.

An interesting finding in the case of the family is that there appear to be changing language choices across generational lines. Li, Saravanan and Ng Lee Hoon (1997), for example, focus on language shift in Teochew families in Singapore, and note that the use of Teochew, a Chinese dialect originally from Guangdong, China, decreases as the participants get younger. The shift is primarily triggered by parents, who prefer using Mandarin to help their children educationally, since, as the official mother tongue of the Chinese community, Mandarin is also a school subject. And the children themselves use a combination of Mandarin and English with their peers. The authors suggest that there is '[a] general trend in Singapore society today that younger generations have given up their ethnic languages and adopted the "national" language such as Mandarin and English as their primary language of communication, even in the family domain' (ibid.: 376). Li et al. (ibid.: 380) suggest that these changes in language use result from speakers prioritizing the instrumental value of a language over the sentimental or symbolic value.

Similarly, Ting and Sussex (2002), in a study involving the Foochow community in Sarawak, Malaysia, note that the vitality of this Chinese dialect (originally from Fujian, China) is being eroded, especially in non-Foochow dominant areas. They point to 'a generational shift in language allegiance away from Foochow towards Mandarin Chinese and English in the home domain, the bastion of dialect use' (ibid.: 11), and conclude that language choice is increasingly based on 'utilitarian reasons such as communicative efficiency, compliance with institutional and national language policies, and gaining acceptance from outgroups' (ibid.: 12–13).

Even in Indonesia, Lamb and Coleman (2008: 201) point out that after the fall of Soeharto in 1998 and the devolution of power to the regions, one might have expected a resurgence in the use of local languages. But instead 'it appears to be English which is filling the ecological spaces' since 'the language not surprisingly occupies an important space in the developing mindset of many young Indonesians, going far beyond its actual practical value in daily life'. More importantly, they note that:

The way in which [English] is being acquired is through individuals acting auton-omously with the object of transforming themselves by joining an exclusive club of cosmopolitan English-speaking Indonesians ... turning the language into a luxury consumer product, sold by high-street language schools and profit-seeking pub-lishing companies. More seriously, while the intention is that English serves the nation, paradoxically it may deepen existing social divisions and help divert the attention of the elite from the problems and preoccupations of the rural poor.

Community and culture

The value (instrumental, sentimental, etc.) placed on a language is part of a wider issue: the revaluation of linguistic practices, and the impact on how these practices are con-strued as authentic manifestations of particular cultural identities. As communities in South-east Asia grapple with the forces of globalization – whether these are represented as the institution of a centralized education system, the growing presence of a global language, or the commodification of language – we might expect debates over what should legitimately be counted as authentic to become increasingly vigorous, providing fertile grounds for research into the role that language plays in identity construction.

Such shifts in the ideological loads of linguistic practices can be observed in Singapore, where the official mother tongue of the Chinese community, Mandarin, has – in addi-tion to serving as an ethnic identity marker – also recently acquired an important eco-nomic value because of China's economic development (Bokhorst-Heng 1998, 1999). This raises a number of interesting problems, which remain unresolved. First, how should differences between the Singapore and Chinese varieties of Mandarin be resolved? As a local identity marker, one might expect an endonormative position to be adopted, but as a language intended to facilitate economic exchanges with a much more powerful economy, one might expect a move toward exonormativity. Second, Mandarin's eco-nomic value also affects its relationship with the other mother tongues. As languages emblematic of different ethnic identities and different kinds of cultural heritage, Man-darin, Malay and Tamil were ostensibly of equal significance. But the economic value of Mandarin raises the possibility that less economically valuable mother tongues might start losing speakers to more economically valuable ones. Such fears are already in evidence, as members of the Malay community, for example, have voiced concerns that many Malays appear to be more interest in learning Mandarin than Malay (Wee 2003: 218).

Another interesting discussion of how changes to linguistic practices are ideologically informed comes from Kuipers (1998). This is a detailed ethnographic study of language ideology and social change on the Indonesian island of Sumba, populated by the Weyewa, for whom ritual speech represents an important genre whereby fluent speakers gain social prestige. The performance of ritual speech is traditionally tied to the speaker's attributes as a bold, assertive, and charismatic individual. Eloquent speakers were rewar-ded with opportunities to participate in important political and religious events. Under the Indonesian schooling system, however, the rich variety of ritual speech forms (pla-cating ancestral spirits, performances of founding myths) has been simplified such that only laments are taught. Consequently, for many younger Weyewa, laments have come to represent the entire category of ritual speech. Furthermore, because these laments are taught in the classroom as part of the local language curriculum, they undergo a shift in

113

their ideological functions: performances are no longer aimed at placating ancestral spirits or gaining political influence; rather, they are intended to please competition judges, impress government officials or entertain tourists (ibid.: 147). The more traditional expressions of ritual speech are increasingly seen as anachronisms, and (older) Weyewa men who insist on using such speech forms are perceived as 'crude' or 'rough' (ibid.: 63).

Kuipers' discussion of ritual speech reminds us that the relationship between language use and religious practice is clearly an area that would benefit from further research, given the diversity of languages and religions involved in the region. At present, however, most writings appear to take the form of macro socio-historical overviews (Kratz 2001a, 2001b; Chew 2006). Chew (2006) is a useful study of language and religion in Singapore, which correlates societal language shifts with changing religious affiliations and practices.

While such macro-level studies are important, they need to be complemented by more detailed micro descriptions of language use in religious contexts. We need answers to questions such as the following: How are actual linguistic practices incorporated into religion? Are they limited to very specific activities (sermons, religious study groups, translations)? Aside from the wish to attract newer members, what other motivations for language choice might there be? Is there any opposition from more conservative members? How much of a consideration is language for individuals who are deciding whether to adopt a particular religion?

Conclusion

The foregoing discussion has hopefully illustrated that sociolinguistic research in Malaysia, Singapore, Indonesia, and the Philippines is both vibrant and varied, as befits the highly diverse nature of the countries themselves. Having said this, there are other directions for future research that are also worth considering.

First, a major effect of globalization is the rise of the 'transnational community', where identity formations result as local ways of participating in broader understandings of community are negotiated. Such communities 'operate in the global context but are the projects of locally based communities' (Delanty 2003: 158). The notion of a transnational community is obviously related to that of diasporic identities, and here, it is worth noting that the community of Sri Lankan Malays has in recent times gained support from the Malaysian High Commission in Sri Lanka to help them acquire the standard Malay that they have 'lost' as a result of contact with Sinhala and Tamil (Lim and Ansaldo 2006). Such an activity may lead to structural changes in the creolized Malay that is currently spoken in Sri Lanka. But it could also herald a sense of transnational affiliation that might have repercussions on religious identification, such as a heightened sense of obligation to be a Muslim. In a similar vein, the Singapore government is attempting to cultivate in Singaporeans a sense of national cohesion as more educated and affluent Singaporeans live and work in overseas communities. The possible use of Singlish as such a national identity marker becomes sociolinguistically intriguing, since in such transnational contexts the government's anti-Singlish stance becomes much more difficult to sustain.

Second, while the issue of language rights has been quite prominent in European and African sociolinguistics, it has been far less pronounced with regard to South-east Asia. But the marginal and contested status of ethnic Chinese in Indonesia, as well as the resentment in the Philippines that English very clearly marks the elite–masses distinction, indicates that attention to language in relation to issues of social justice is very much needed. This is not to suggest that the research agenda should unequivocally adopt the rights perspective. Rather, contributions that combine empirical studies with conceptual rigor drawn from political theorizing can usefully add to the ongoing debates surrounding the feasibility of language rights and the exploration of alternatives to the rights paradigm.

Finally, while the notion of reflexivity has been broadly theorized by linguistic anthropologists as well as social theorists (see Adams 2006 and Agha 2007 for useful overviews), there is still scope for further work on how reflexivity is socially *distributed* as a form of cultural capital (cf. Skeggs 2002). Such work would have to start with prevailing ideologies about what kinds of linguistic performances can count as legitimate manifestations of reflexivity, and possibly link these to the utilitarian concerns (noted above) that motivate much of language choice and shift in South-east Asia.

Note

1 For further information regarding demography and linguistic diversity, see Gordon (2005) and Rappa and Wee (2006).

References

Adams, M. (2006) 'Hybridizing habitus and reflexivity: towards an understanding of contemporary identity?', *Sociology*, 40, 511–28.

Agha, A. (2007) *Language and Social Relations*, Cambridge: Cambridge University Press.

Bertrand, J. (2003) 'Indonesia', in M. E. Brown and S. Ganguly (eds) *Fighting Words: Language Policy and Ethnic Relations in Asia*, Cambridge, MA: MIT Press, pp. 263–90.

Bokhorst-Heng, W. (1998) 'Language and imagining the nation in Singapore', PhD dissertation, University of Toronto.

——(1999) 'Language is more than a language', *Centre for Advanced Studies (CAS) Research Paper Series*, Singapore: National University of Singapore.

Brown, M. E. and Ganguly, S. (eds) (2003) *Fighting Words: Language Policy and Ethnic Relations in Asia*, Cambridge, MA: MIT Press.

Canieso-Doronilla, M. (1998) 'The emergence of schools of the people and the transformation of the Philippine educational system', *UP-CIDS Chronicle*, 3, 63–97.

Chew, P. (2006) 'Language use and religious practice: the case of Singapore', in O. Tope and J. Fishman (eds) *Explorations in the Sociology of Language and Religion*, Amsterdam: John Benjamins, pp. 214–35.

Chng, H. H. (2003) '"You see me no up": Is Singlish a problem?', *Language Problems & Language Planning*, 27, 45–62.

Crystal, D. (1997) *English as a Global Language*, Cambridge: Cambridge University Press.

Delanty, G. (2003) *Community*, London: Routledge.

Fishman, J. A. (1991) *Reversing Language Shift*, Clevedon: Multilingual Matters.

Gordon, R. G. Jr. (ed.) (2005) *Ethnologue: Languages of the World*, 15th edn, Dallas, TX: SIL International.

Kratz, E. U. (2001a) 'Christianity in Southeast Asia', in J. F. A. Sawyer, J.M. Y. Simpson and R. E. Asher (eds) *Concise Encyclopedia of Language and Religion*, Amsterdam: Elsevier, pp. 41–2.

——(2001b) 'Islam in Southeast Asia', in J. F. A. Sawyer, J. M. Y. Simpson and R. E. Asher (eds) *Concise Encyclopedia of Language and Religion*, Amsterdam: Elsevier, pp. 65–6.

Kuipers, J. C. (1998) *Language, Identity and Marginality in Indonesia*, Cambridge: Cambridge University Press.

Lamb, M. and Coleman, H. (2008) 'Literacy in English and the transformation of self and society in post-Soeharto Indonesia', *International Journal of Bilingual Education and Bilingualism*, 11, 189–205.

Li, W., Saravanan V., and Ng Lee Hoon, J. (1997) 'Language shift in the Teochew community in Singapore: a family domain analysis', *Journal of Multilingual and Multicultural Development*, 18, 364–84.

Lim, L. and Ansaldo, U. (2006) 'Keeping Kirinda vital: the endangerment-empowerment dilemma in the documentation of Sri Lanka Malay', in E. Aboh and M. van Staden (eds) ACLC (Amsterdam Centre for Language & Communication) Working Papers 1, pp. 51–66.

Rappa, A. and Wee, L. (2006) *Language Policy and Modernity in Southeast Asia: Malaysia, the Philippines, Singapore, and Thailand*, New York: Springer.

Schneider, E. (2003) 'The dynamics of new Englishes: from identity construction to dialect birth', *Language*, 79, 233–81.

Skeggs, B. (2002) 'Techniques for telling the reflexive self', in T. May (ed.) *Qualitative Research in Action*, London: Sage.

Ting, S. H. and Sussex, R. (2002) 'Language choice among the Foochows in Sarawak, Malaysia', *Multilingua*, 21, 1–15.

Tupas, T. R. F. (2003) 'History, language planners, and strategies of forgetting: the problem of consciousness in the Philippines', *Language Problems & Language Planning*, 27, 1–25.

Wee, L. (2003) 'Linguistic instrumentalism in Singapore', *Journal of Multilingual and Multicultural Development*, 24, 211–24.

——(2005) 'Intra-language discrimination and Linguistic Human Rights: the case of Singlish', *Applied Linguistics*, 26, 48–69.

11

A sociolinguistic profile of Turkey, Northern Cyprus and other Turkic states in Central Asia

Yasemin Bayyurt

Introduction

Turkey is a geopolitically important region located between Asia and Europe. It is one of the largest countries in Europe and the Middle East with an area of approximately 775,000 sq. km. The official language of the country is Turkish, but in Turkey, there are also more than 50 languages spoken and one-third of these languages are Turkic. In her report on languages spoken in Turkey, Schlyter (2005: 1903) notes:

> Besides standard Turkish and its dialects, there are spoken varieties of Azerbaijanian, Turkmen, Uyghur, Uzbek, Kirghiz, Kazakh, Crimean and Kazan Tatar, Bashkir, Noghay, Karachay-Balkar and Kumuk. Other language families represented in Turkey are Indo-European (Kurdish dialects – mainly Kurmanji but also Zaza – Ossetic, Armenian, Greek, Albanian, Polish, Russian, German, Romani, Judeo-Spanish (Ladino), etc.), Finno-Ugric (Estonian), Semitic (Arabic and Neo-Aramaic dialects, Hebrew) and Caucasian languages (Georgian, Laz, Abkhaz, Circassian, Cheeneh-Ingush, etc.).

Turkish is the most commonly spoken as well as culturally and politically the most important of the Turkic languages.[1] In Turkey, the number of non–Turkish-speaking people does not exceed 10–15 per cent of the whole population (approximately 67 million). The majority of native speakers of Turkish live in Turkey and North Cyprus. There are also smaller groups of Turkish-speaking people living in Greece, Bulgaria, the Republic of Macedonia, Kosovo, Albania, and other parts of Europe. In addition, Turkish is spoken as a native language by several millions of immigrants in Germany, the Netherlands, Sweden, Norway and other countries in Western and North-west Europe (Jørgensen 2003).

Sociolinguistic studies of Turkish and other Turkic languages

In general, linguistics as a discipline started to attract the attention of Turkish scholars in the early 1950s. During the past two decades, however, sociolinguistics has become a popular area of research. The first sociolinguistic inquiry in Turkey seems to have taken place as early as 1928, when the language reform involving alphabet change and purification of the Turkish language took place. Language reform was supported and initiated by Mustafa Kemal Atatürk (the 'father' of the Turkish Republic) himself. As König (2004, 1) summarizes: 'Turkish language reform is a revolutionary act realized in a very short period eliminating the diglossic language situation which had been a barrier in the communication of different groups in the community.' Studies focusing on bilingualism and migration, language maintenance and shift, dialect changes, language choice and code-switching, culture and language, language in interaction, language and gender followed language planning and policy studies.

Language planning: Turkish language reform

Language planning is one of the important activities of a government when determining the educational and linguistic policies of a country (Kaplan and Baldauf 1997). In language planning, historical, political, ethnic, racial, social, and economic issues involving the current relationships among groups living in a country should be taken into consideration. However, language planning intended to solve current conflicts may sometimes cause later conflicts (Wiley 1996: 106).

Turkish language reform (henceforth TLR) is one of the most significant language reform movements in the world. It involved script reform and purification of the Turkish language, which meant eliminating foreign words and structures, mainly those taken from Arabic and Persian. As Doğançay-Aktuna indicates: 'These linguistic modifications would … aid in nation building and modernization by moving from eastern influences to western ones, because the latter were seen as a requirement for national development' (2004: 7).

Within the boundaries of the Ottoman Empire, Turks were one of many linguistic and ethnic groups. Because of their nomadic tradition, they were exposed to various cultures and languages, but they managed to keep their own language free from foreign influences (ibid.). Around the eleventh century, Turks accepted Islam as a religion, and the Turkish emperors of the time decided to replace the Uyghur alphabet with the Arabic alphabet (Clauson 2002). After the Ottoman Empire was established, the Ottoman elite started to use words and structures from Arabic and Persian influenced by 'religious, scientific and literary traditions and prestige of these languages' (Doğançay-Aktuna 2004: 5–6). While Ottoman Turkish emerged as the language used in divan (court) literature by the Arabic/Persian educated elite, Anatolian Turkish remained the language spoken by the poor and uneducated and illiterate Anatolian people (Doğançay-Aktuna 1995, 2004; Akıncı and Bayyurt 2003; Akıncı 2006). This diglossic situation continued until TLR. Anatolian Turkish was the 'purer' form of Turkish, free from the influence of Persian and Arabic. It was used as a means of expression by poets of the time, who considered themselves to be the voice of the people of Anatolia, in reaction to the Ottoman court, whose language was incomprehensible to the people of Anatolia.

TLR occurred in two major phases: the first phase was alphabet reform, that is, the adoption of the Latin alphabet to replace the Arabic script; and the second phase was the authentication or 'Turkification' of the Turkish lexicon and grammar by purification from foreign influence, especially the influence of Arabic and Persian (Doğançay-Aktuna 2004).

The alphabet reform

When establishing the Turkish Republic, Atatürk gave priority to language reform as part of the foundation of the new nation. He wanted to separate the Turkish language from the structural and lexical influence of Arabic and Persian. His aim in so doing was to 'break the ties with the Islamic east and to facilitate communication domestically as well as with the Western World' (Lewis 1999: 27).

In the middle of the nineteenth century, during the so-called Tanzimat Period, the modernist intellectuals of the Ottoman Empire started to criticize the Arabic alphabet, which was an obstacle to the elimination of illiteracy and use of the Turkish language in everyday life. There were two opposing views: to modify the alphabet so that it expressed Turkish sounds better, or to replace it with the Latin alphabet. The majority of scholars at that time supported the second view, that the Arabic alphabet needed to be replaced. At the same time, many schools and many teachers thought that it was necessary to teach schoolchildren verses from the Koran rather than giving them a modern education, which would help them to become literate more easily. Journalism was newly developing and the drafting of a daily newspaper required a satisfactory technique for printing. The intellectuals and writers of that time had to face many difficulties when using Arabic letters to express themselves in the Turkish language. Therefore, they depended on certain modifications of the Arabic letters to represent Turkish sounds correctly in print. Meanwhile, the Latin alphabet was becoming more and more popular because it provided a modern writing system compared to the Arabic writing system. Because of their diplomatic relations with western European countries, diplomats of the Ottoman Empire were obliged to use the Latin alphabet for foreign correspondence via telegram and mail. The first telegram from Istanbul to Italy was sent on 9 September 1855. Since the telegram could encode only the Latin alphabet, Ottoman Turks began using Latin characters 70 years before TLR. During the first few years of the newly born Turkish Republic, despite the prevalence of the Arabic alphabet and talk about sacrilege to the Koran and loss of cultural traditions, the number of supporters of the Latin alphabet continued to increase. At first, there were more urgent economic and political reforms to be accomplished; therefore, Atatürk set aside the question of script reform for five years.

On 1 November 1928, as the initial stage of language reform, the Turkish Grand National Assembly passed the Law on the Adoption and Implementation of the Turkish Alphabet (number 1353),[2] thus accepting a 29-letter Turkish alphabet. The motivation for the TLR was twofold. The first involved the change of the alphabet from Arabic to Latin. The second involved the purification of Turkish lexicon and grammar from foreign elements (Levend 1972). As Brendemoen states:

> Atatürk's aim was to 'liberate' the Turkish language from foreign elements, or rather from Arabic and Persian elements, which represented the old culture from which he wanted to rescue the country and language, and to replace them with pure Turkish elements
>
> (1998: 243)

The use of the new alphabet became obligatory on 1 December 1928, for print media, and 1 January 1929, for administrative offices and affairs of state. In a period of two months, the Arabic alphabet had become part of the past.

119

As Schlyter states:

> Turkish language reform was part of Atatürk's general political plan to make Turkish society less dependent on its Islamic past and to lay the ground for a modern civic state characterized by economic progress and social welfare. The change of alphabet was an important symbolic step towards this goal.
>
> (2005: 1907)

Although this was an effective precaution against the domination of Persian and Arabic in Turkish, the elimination of a foreign vocabulary and the creation of new lexical items based solely on Turkic language material were not an easy task. It created further complications and debate among scholars and other interested people (Doğançay-Aktuna 1995, 2004; Lewis 1999). In 1932, a language convention took place to continue to purify and modernize Turkish. As a result of long discussions and debates, a special language association was initiated, the *Türk Dil Kurumu* (Turkish Language Association).[3] Its major task was to 'Turkify' the language by proposing Turkish equivalents of foreign words, structures, and lexical items and to carry out scholarly work on the Turkish language. The TDK's efforts were supported by civic leaders and many other public figures (Doğançay-Aktuna 2004).

The consequences of the TLR and present-day Turkish

The success of the TLR is the result of extremely authoritative methods and the tacit approval of the population. It was successful because the linguistic conditions were ideal in Turkey. There were relatively few differences among the dialects of Anatolia and at the same time there was considerable migration within Turkey to the big cities, particularly to Istanbul, whose speech was used as a model for the standard language (König 1987).

Script reform is usually presented as the most important phase of the TLR. However, the second phase, the purification of Turkish from foreign structures and lexical elements, is also important and could not have been carried out without the first phase.

Considering the present state of the Turkish language, we can say that the script reform was very successful, thanks to Atatürk and his colleagues. However, the second stage of the reform, the purification of Turkish language from foreign elements, has only partially been achieved. The TDK's efforts to promote standardization and codification of modern Turkish language via publications, including dictionaries, spelling guides, modern literary texts, and academic publications, have been successful. However, the Turkish lexicon is still influenced by foreign languages. The difference from earlier times in the Turkish Republic is that languages like Arabic and Persian have lost their influence, while English and French have taken over. In the past few decades, English and French words have entered into the lexicon of Turkish to a great extent (Sağlam 2008). If an urgent plan for a second TLR is not activated, the Turkish language will be full of foreign structures, words, and phrases in the next decade or so. This is partially due to the unplanned spread of English in Turkey via education (English is the medium of instruction in many schools); print and broadcast media (TV characters often use foreign words and phrases even when Turkish equivalents exist); and technology (the terminology of the Internet, SMS, and other applications is usually in English).[4]

Varieties of Turkish, Northern Cypriot Turkish and Turkic languages

A variety of spoken Turkish may be heard within the borders of Turkey, and outside of Turkey there are additional varieties of spoken Turkish as well as other Turkic languages.

Varieties of modern spoken Turkish in Turkey

The standard spoken variety of modern Turkish language is 'Istanbul Turkish', which is characterized by certain structural, lexical and phonological properties distinguishing it from other local varieties of Turkish language (Uğur 2002). However, at present, due to immigration from Eastern, South-eastern and other regions of Turkey to Istanbul, it is no longer possible to call the variety of Turkish that is spoken in the streets of Istanbul 'Istanbul Turkish'. In contrast, it is a blend of different varieties and dialects of Turkish that are spoken all over Turkey (Gedik 2003; Söylemez 2004). Although this is the case, these varieties do not have clear distinctions because of constant language contact between regions and immigration from rural areas to big cities. As Gedik (2003) indicates, the urbanization level is very high (65 per cent) in Turkey. According to her findings: 'The level of urbanization increased about three fold from approximately 20% in 1950 to about 60% in 2000.' Therefore, it is difficult to trace dialect variation in such a highly mobile society.

In order to talk about a standard variety we need to base our argument on a large corpus of modern spoken Turkish. If a standard variety of spoken Turkish is needed, how it is spoken in the media and how it is passed on to younger generations should be considered, refined, and selectively promoted. Otherwise, 'Istanbul Turkish' as a standard variety will continue to be a *myth* without any clear evidence of how people are using Turkish in their formal and informal daily encounters (Bayyurt 2000; Bayyurt and Bayraktaroğlu 2001). As already mentioned, before the TLR there was a diglossic situation comprised of Ottoman Turkish spoken by the elite and educated people in Istanbul and the major cities of the Empire and ordinary people's Anatolian Turkish. which was spoken in Anatolia and other regions of the Empire. Ottoman Turkish was almost incomprehensible to the Anatolian people because it was full of foreign, predominantly Arabic and Persian, structures and lexical items. The TLR was successful in eliminating these differences and making Modern Turkish almost totally mutually comprehensible to both highly educated people and to people with little or no education. Work still needs to be done to identify the characteristics of standard and other varieties of spoken Turkish. Collecting samples of spoken Turkish from all over Turkey and establishing a large corpus of spoken Turkish would help reveal the distinctive features of spoken varieties, including Istanbul Turkish, Central Anatolian Turkish, Black Sea Regional Turkish, and others. It is also important to note that TV and other media do not seem to promote the use of a standard variety. Since the advent of private independent TV channels in the lives of Turkish people, television has played an important role in the integration of nonstandard varieties of Turkish increasingly into people's linguistic repertoire. Analyzing daytime live TV programmes might also be helpful in understanding the present situation of spoken Turkish. These programmes allow phone-in participation of viewers from all over Turkey. Açıkalın (2004) carried out a comparative longitudinal study on adolescents' language use between 1989 and 1999 and confirmed that television played an important role in their adoption of non-standard forms. In the beginning of her study, all TV channels were owned and operated by the state. However, after 1990, private independent channels started broadcasting. Açıkalın states, 'Today, nonstandard linguistic expressions are generously used by the young TV personalities on private TV channels. Therefore, the diffusion of nonstandard linguistic expressions is inevitable' (ibid.: 154).

Language contact and varieties of Northern Cypriot Turkish and other Turkic languages

Not much research has focused on language contact and varieties of Turkish. As Schlyter indicates:

> The diffusion of Turkic-speaking people in and around Anatolia ... was not, naturally enough, confined to the territory of modern Turkish Republic. Consequently, Turkic varieties which are close to Turkey Turkish and most of which are recognized as Turkish dialects can be found beyond the Turkish borders, above all on Cyprus and in the Balkans.
>
> (2005: 1905)

For example, in Bulgaria, the Turkish-speaking community constitutes 9–10 per cent (about 800,000) of the whole population. Although there has been massive emigration and change of populations, extensive language contact continues between local people in the region and the Turkic-speaking newcomers. Schlyter also notes cases of language change in southern Moldavia where the Gagauz people, an Eastern Orthodox Turkic group, live. They speak a variety of Turkish that is widespread in the area, influenced by contact with other languages in the region. The variety of Northern Cypriot Turkish seems to be an extension of Anatolian Turkish. As Demir and Johanson indicate, the local variety spoken in Northern Cyprus today

> [is] naturally confined to the island, and its contact with external cultural centers has been rather restricted. The dialect has thus developed without a strong influence from standard Turkish. As a result, a Cypriot Turkish dialect with specific characteristic properties has emerged.
>
> (2006: 1)

However, Northern Cypriot Turkish went through several stages of influence from Anatolian Turkish at different intervals. For example, after 1974, Northern Cyprus experienced periods of intensive language contact as a result of immigration and an influx of university students. This caused standard Turkish, Anatolian dialects, and Northern Cypriot Turkish dialects to come into closer contact with one another. For further analysis of Northern Cypriot Turkish, see Demir and Johanson (2006), Imer and Çelebi (2006), Kocaman (2006), Osam and Kelepir (2006), and Vancı-Osam (2006).

Csató and Karakoç (2006) list the varieties of Turkic languages as follows:

- South Western or Oghuz: Turkish, Gagauz, Azerbaijanian, Turkmen, Kashkay;
- North Western or Kipchak: Kazakh, Karakalpak, Noghay, Kirghiz, Tatar, Bashkir, Crimean Tatar, Kumyk, Karachay, Balkar, Karaim;
- South Eastern or Uyghur: Uzbek, Uyghur;

   North Eastern or Siberian: Yakut, Altay, Khakas, Tuvan, Shor, Tofa;
   Chuvash;
   Khala.

These varities of Turkic languages are not necessarily mutually intelligible. As one goes further East, Turkic languages become less intelligible to Turkish people. In other words, Turkish and Azeri are more mutually intelligible than Turkish and Uyghur. Turkic languages do not share important common features, such as a common script. For example, Kazakhs use the Cyrillic alphabet and Uyghurs use Arabic script. For more information about Turkic languages and linguistics, see Boeschoten and Johanson (2006), Clauson (2002), Csató (2003, 2006, 2007), Csató-Johanson and Johanson (2006), Décsy (1998), Gronbech (1997), Karakoç (2007), Karakoç and Rehbein (2004), Menges (1968), and Schlyter (2003, 2005).

Language maintenance and language shift

Studies of language maintenance and shift in Turkish sociolinguistics can be grouped as follows:

1 Studies of immigrant groups that moved to Turkey from the Balkans, Turkic states of Central Asia, and other parts of the world (Karahan 2004).
2 Studies of Turkish immigrant communities in different parts of the world:
   (a) immigrants from Turkey (Yağmur 1997, 2004; Akıncı and Yağmur 2000; Jørgensen 2003)
   (b) immigrants from Northern Cyprus (Issa 2006; Osam 2006).

These studies analyze patterns of language maintenance and shift, code-switching, code-mixing, language attrition in first, second, and later generations of Turkish immigrant societies in Europe and other parts of the world.

Conclusion

In this chapter, studies of Turkish sociolinguistics and Turkic languages have been outlined and summarized. Most of the literature up to the present has been about language planning. It seems that lots of unexplored areas remain, such as dialect variation, language contact, language maintenance and shift, language and gender, language and identity, and language change. Additional topics for investigation include standardization in a highly mobile society and the spread of non-standardized language use via media and technology. It is also important to develop links among modern Turkish speakers and those of other Turkic languages in order to increase mutual intelligibility. Finally, questions about the future of the Turkish language in a global world have yet to be answered.

Notes

1 A list of Turkic Languages includes: Turkish, Gagauz, Azerbaijanian, Turkmen, Kashkay, Kipchak, Kazakh, Karakalpak, Noghay, Kirghiz, Tatar, Bashkir, Crimean Tatar, Kumyk, Karachay, Balkar,

Karaim, Uyghur: Uzbek, Uyghur, Yakut, Altay, Khakas, Tuvan, Tofa, and so on (see Csató-Johanson and Johanson, 2006; Csató and Karakoç 2006).
2 Türk Harflerinin Kabul ve Tatbiki Hakkında Kanun. Online. Available at: www.mevzuat.adalet. gov.tr/html/463.html (accessed 26 October 2008).
3 Henceforth TDK (www.tdk.gov.tr).
4 It is important to note that careful foreign language planning is needed in Turkey as well, but this issue is beyond the scope of the present chapter. For further reading, see Bear (1985), Doğançay-Aktuna (1998), Kızıltepe and Doğançay-Aktuna (2005), and Sebüktekin (1981).

References

Açıkalın, I. (2004) 'The perpetuity trend of nonstandard linguistic forms', *International Journal of the Sociology of Language*, 165, 143–54.
Akıncı, M. A. (2006) 'La réforme de l'écriture en Turquie', in R. Honvault-Ducrocq (ed.) *L'orthographe en questions*, Rouen: Publications des Universités de Rouen et du Havre, Dyalang, pp. 299–319,
Akıncı, M. A. and Bayyurt, Y. (2003) 'From Arabic to Latin Alphabet: the Turkish Script Reform', paper presented at 'Literacies and Scripts Symposium', AILA Literacies Group, Multiliteracies: the Contact Zone, Ghent University, Ghent, Belgium, 22–27 September.
Akıncı, M. A. and Yağmur, K. (2000) 'Language use and attitudes of Turkish immigrants in France and their subjective ethnolinguistic vitality perceptions', paper presented at the 10th International Conference on Turkish Linguistics, 16–18 August, Boğaziçi University, Istanbul, Turkey.
Bayyurt, Y. (2000) 'Türkçe'de "resmiyet" kavramına TV sohbet programları çerçevesinden bir bakış', in Z. Kulelioğlu (ed.) *Dilbilim Araştırmaları 2000*, İstanbul: Simurg Yayıncılık, pp. 17–37.
Bayyurt, Y. and Bayraktaroğlu, A. (2001) 'The use of pronouns and terms of address in Turkish service encounters', in A. Bayraktaroğlu. and M. Sifianou (eds) *Linguistic Politeness: A Case of Greek and Turkish*, Amsterdam: John Benjamins, pp. 209–40.
Bear, J. (1985) 'Historical factors influencing attitudes towards foreign language learning in Turkey', *Journal of Human Sciences of Middle East Technical University*, 1, 27–36.
Boeschoten, H. and Johanson, L. (2006) *Turkic Languages in Contact* [Turcologica 61], Wiesbaden: Harrassowitz.
Brendemoen, B. (1998) 'The Turkish language reform', in L. Johanson and É. Á. Csató Johanson (eds) *The Turkic Languages*, London: Routledge, pp. 242–7.
Clauson, G. (2002) *Studies in Turkic and Mongolic Linguistics*, London: Routledge.
Csató, É. Á. (2003) 'Copied features of Turkic reflexives', *Orientalia Suecana*, LI–LII, 67–73.
——(2006) 'Copying word order properties', in H. Boeschoten and L. Johanson (eds) *Turkic Languages in Contact* [Turcologica 61], Wiesbaden: Otto Harrassowitz, pp. 152–7.
——(2007) 'Connectivity by means of finite elements in mono- and bilingual Turkish discourses', in J. Rehbein, C. Hohenstein and L. Pietsch (eds) *Connectivity in Grammar and Discourse*, Amsterdam: Benjamins, pp. 199–227.
Csató, É. Á., Isaksson, B. and Jahani, C. (eds) (2004) *Linguistic Convergence and Areal Diffusion Case Studies from Iranian, Semitic and Turkic*, London: Routledge.
Csató-Johanson, É.Á. and Johanson, L. (eds) (2006) *The Turkic Languages*, London: Routledge.
Csató-Johanson, É.Á. and Karakoç, B. (2006) 'Noghay', in É. Á. Csató-Johanson and L. Johanson (eds), *The Turkic Languages*, London: Routledge, pp. 333–43.
Décsy, G. (1998) *The Turkic Protolanguage: A Computational Reconstruction*, Bloomington, IN: Eurolingua.
Demir, N. and Johanson, L. (2006) 'Dialect contact in Northern Cyprus', *International Journal of the Sociology of Language*, 181, 1–9.
Doğançay-Aktuna, S. (1995) 'An evaluation of the Turkish language reform after 60 years', *Language Problems and Language Planning*, 19, 221–47.
——(1998) 'The spread of English in Turkey and its current sociolinguistic profile', *Journal of Multilingual and Multicultural Development*, 19, 24–39.

——(2004) 'Language planning in Turkey: yesterday and today', *International Journal of the Sociology of Language*, 165, 5–32.

Gedik, A. (2003) 'Differential urbanization in Turkey: 1955–2000', paper presented at 43rd Congress of the European Regional Science Association (ERSA), Jyväskylä, Finland, 27–30 August.

Gronbech, V. (1997) *Preliminary Studies in Turkic Historical Phonology (Uralic and Altaic)*, London: Routledge.

Imer, K. and Çelebi, N. (2006) 'The intonation of Turkish Cypriot dialect: a contrastive and socio-linguistic interpretation', *International Journal of the Sociology of Language*, 181, 69–82.

Issa, T. (2006) 'An ethnographic case study of code switching and language choice: the uses of Cypriot Turkish in London', *International Journal of the Sociology of Language*, 181, 83–106.

Jørgensen, J. N. (ed.) (2003) *Bilingualism and Social Change: Turkish Speakers in North Western Europe*, Clevedon: Multilingual Matters.

Kaplan, R. B. and Baldauf, R. B. (1997) *Language Planning: From Practice to Theory*, Clevedon: Multilingual Matters.

Karahan, F. (2004) 'Ethnolinguistic vitality, attitudes, social network and codeswitching: the case of Bosnian-Turks living in Sakarya, Turkey', *International Journal of the Sociology of Language*, 165, 59–92.

Karakoç, B. (2007) 'Connectivity by means of finite elements in monolingual and bilingual Turkish discourse', in J. Rehbein, C. Hohenstein and L. Pietsch (eds) *Connectivity in Grammar and Discourse*, Amsterdam: Benjamins, pp. 199–227.

Karakoç, B. and Rehbein, J. (2004) 'On contact-induced language change of Turkish aspects: langua-ging in bilingual discourse', in C. B. Dabelsteen and J. N. Jørgensen (eds) *Languaging and Language Practices*, Copenhagen: Copenhagen Studies in Bilingualism 36, pp. 125–49.

Kızıltepe, Z. and Doğançay-Aktuna, S. (2005) 'English in Turkey', *World Englishes*, 24, 253–65.

Kocaman, A. (2006) 'Language in the press in Turkish Cypriot dialect', *International Journal of the Sociology of Language*, 181, 11–21.

König, G. (2004) 'Introduction', *International Journal of the Sociology of Language*, 165, 1–3.

König, W. D. (1987) 'On some sociolinguistic aspects of language reform in Turkey', in H. Boeschoten and L. Verhoeven (eds) *Turkish Linguistics Today*, Leiden: Brill, pp. 259–70.

Levend, Agah Sırrı (1972) *Türk Dilinde Gelişme ve Sadeleşme Evreleri*, 3rd edn, Ankara: Türk Dil Kurumu Yayınları.

Lewis, G. (1999) *Turkish Language Reform: A Catastrophic Success*, Oxford: Oxford University Press.

Menges, K. H. (1968) *The Turkic Languages and People: An Introduction to Turkic Studies*, Wiesbaden: Otto Harrasowitz.

Osam, N. (2006) 'Turkish Cypriot women and their attitudes towards foreign words: a case of language loyalty', *International Journal of the Sociology of Language*, 181, 57–67.

Osam, N. and Kelepir, M. (2006) 'Bibliography of studies on Turkish Cypriot dialect', *International Journal of the Sociology of Language*, 181, 107–17.

Sağlam, M. Y. (2008) 'Yabancı Sözcükler Karşısında Türkçenin Gücü', paper presented at 8th International Symposium on Language, Literature and Stylistics, Izmir University of Economics, 14–16 May, Izmir, Turkey.

Schlyter, B. N. (2003) 'Sociolinguistic changes in transformed Central Asian societies', in J. Maurais and M. A. Morris (eds) *Languages in a Globalising World*, Cambridge: Cambridge University Press, pp. 157–87.

——(2005) 'Turkey', in U. Ammon, N. Dittmar, K. J. Mattheier and P. Trudgill (eds) *Sociolinguistics: An International Handbook of the Science of Language and Society*, Berlin: Mouton de Gruyter, pp. 1903–11.

Sebüktekin, H. (1981) *Yüksek Öğretim Kurumlarımızda Yabancı Dil ızlenceleri* [Foreign Language Curricula in Institutes of Higher Education], Istanbul: Boğaziçi University Publications.

Söylemez, Ü. (2004) 'Urbanization and language shift in Turkey: the change processes at work in the transition from rural to urban settings', *International Journal of the Sociology of Language*, 165, 93–113.

Uğur, F. (2002) 'İstanbul Türkçesi ve Ğ' [Istanbul Turkish and soft G], *Radikal*, 14 April.

Vancı-Osam, Ü. (2006) 'The impact of oral language features in written language in Cypriot Turkish', *International Journal of the Sociology of Language*, 181, 23–42.

Wiley, T. G. (1996) 'Language planning and policy', in S. L. McKay and N. H. Hornberger (eds) *Sociolinguistics and Language Teaching*, New York: Cambridge University Press, pp. 103–47.

Yağmur, K. (1997) *First Language Attrition among Turkish Speakers in Sydney*, Tilburg, The Netherlands: Tilburg University Press.

——(2004) 'Language maintenance patterns of Turkish immigrant communities in Australia and western Europe: the impact of majority attitudes on ethnolinguistic vitality perceptions', *International Journal of the Sociology of Language*, 165, 121–42.

12

Sociolinguistics in the Caucasus

Victor A. Friedman

Introduction

As a geo-political region, the Caucasus can be divided into the North Caucasus and the South Caucasus (Transcaucasia). Transcaucasia consists of the Republics of Georgia, Armenia, and Azerbaijan—including polities whose status is still disputed as of this writing: Abkhazia and South Ossetia in Georgia and Nagorno-Karabakh, which seceded from Azerbaijan to join Armenia in 1988, followed by a war lasting until 1994. In strictly geographic terms, Georgia and Azerbaijan also include some north Caucasian slopes in their territory. In the south, the political borders of Turkey to the west and Iran to the east form a convenient demarcation, although speakers of relevant languages extend into and/or migrated to both these countries. The geo-political North Caucasus is entirely within the Russian Federation and consists of a series of Republics (from west to east): Adygea, Karachay-Cherkessia, Kabardino-Balkaria, North Ossetia (Alania), Ingushetia, Chechnya, and Daghestan. Adygea is surrounded by Krasnodar Kraj, which, with Stavropol Kraj and Kalmykia, forms the northern administrative border of the remaining North Caucasian republics, whose southern borders are defined by Georgia and Azerbaijan. The Black Sea defines the western border, and to the east is the Caspian.[1]

The Caucasus, long known for its linguistic diversity, is home to three indigenous language families as well as representatives of Indo-European, Altaic, and Afro-Asiatic. The indigenous families are Kartvelian (South Caucasian), Nakh-Daghestanian (North-east Caucasian), and Abkhaz-Adyge (North-west Caucasian). These three were assumed to form a larger Ibero-Caucasian family, but that idea is no longer generally accepted owing to the lack of any plausible reconstruction. Attempts to unite the North Caucasian languages into a single family present serious problems of data and methodology. The time depth for North-east Caucasian alone is estimated as approximately that of Indo-European (Nichols 1992: 14).

The Kartvelian languages are Georgian, Svan, Mingrelian, and Laz. The North-west Caucasian languages are Abaza, Abkhaz, Adyge (West or Lower Circassian), Kabardian (Cherkes, East or Upper Circassian), and Ubykh. Tevfik Esenç, the last fluent Ubykh-speaker, died in Turkey in 1992, and Abkhaz-Abaza and Circassian are sometimes each

127

treated as single languages. The Nakh (or Vaynakh) languages are Chechen, Ingush, and Tsova-Tush (Bats'bi). Chechen and Ingush also form a continuum with the transitional Galanchozh dialects being claimed by both. The Daghestanian languages can be divided into three groups: Avaro-Ando-Tsezic, Lak-Dargic, and Lezgic. The Andic languages are Andi, Akhwakh, Bagwalal, Botlikh, Chamalal, Godoberi, Karata, and Tindi; the Tsezic languages are Tsez (Dido), Bezhta, Hinukh, Hunzib (Kapusha), and Khwarshi, while Avar constitutes its own sub-group. Lak is unique in the Lak-Dargic group, its dialects being relatively close to one another, while the dialects of Dargwa (Dargi) are differentiated between a core and peripheral dialects, some of which latter—Kubachi, Kaitag, Megeb, and Chirag—are sometimes considered separate languages (Tsirkha and Itsari are likewise peripheral but counted as Dargwa). The main sub-group in Lezgic is the Samurian: Lezgian, Rutul, Tsakhur, Agul, Tabasaran, Budukh, and Kryz. Archi, Udi, and Khinalug, are each so peripheral that their relationship within the rest of Daghestanian was, until recently, considered isolated. Of these, Archi is closest to Samurian, Udi is peripheral, and it now appears that Khinalug is a separate branch of Nakh-Daghestanian subsequently influenced by Lezgic.

Of the Altaic languages, Azeri and Turkish belong to the Oghuz Turkic group, while Karachay-Balkar, Kumyk, Nogai, and Tatar are Kipchak Turkic.[2] Almost all are Muslim. Ossetian, one of two surviving North-east Iranian languages (the other, Yaghnobi, is spoken in Tajikistan), has two dialects, Digor (Muslim) in North Ossetia and Iron (Christian and Muslim), the basis of standard Ossetian, in both North and South Ossetia as well as Georgia proper. Talysh and Kurdish are North-west Iranian, while Tat (Northern or Caucasian Tat) is South-west Iranian (like Persian).[3] Armenian is an isolate within Indo-European (with its own church), as is Greek (Orthodox, Pontic dialect). Armenian has two standards, Eastern, which is official in Armenia, and Western, which is the variant used by the Armenian diaspora and those in Turkey whose ancestors survived the massacres of the early twentieth century. We can also mention here Lomavren (Bosha), a para-Romani language whose grammar is Armenian with significant Indic vocabulary. Finally Assyrian (Neo-Aramaic) is North-west Semitic and spoken by Christians using Syriac as their liturgical language.

All the republics except Daghestan have titular linguistic nationalities, with speakers of other languages as minorities.[4] All Kartvelian-speakers in Georgia are counted as (and most consider themselves to be) ethnic Georgians and most live in Georgia except the Laz, who have a distinct consciousness and, with the exception of a single village in Georgia, are across the border in Turkey. The estimates are 350,000 for Mingrelian, and between 80,000 and 35,000 for Svan. Both use Georgian as their literary language. Estimates for Laz vary from 90,000–250,000. The Laz are Muslim, and like other Muslim linguistic minorities in Turkey, have no language rights. Other Kartvelian-speakers are mostly Georgian Orthodox, except the Adjarians, who are Muslim Georgian-speakers with an autonomous (but not breakaway) republic in south-western Georgia. They currently identify as Georgian on the basis of language, although under Ottoman rule they identified as Turks on the basis of religion. Tsova-Tush survives in the village of Zemo Alvani in Georgia (estimated at 3000). Unlike most other Nakh-speakers, who are Muslim, Tsova-Tush-speakers are Christian. The Mskhetian Turks are Muslim Turkish-speakers from Georgia who were deported by Stalin.

The Daghestanian languages are all spoken in Daghestan, except Budukh, Kryz (Azerbaijan only), and Udi (two villages in Azerbaijan and one in Georgia); Lezgian, Rutul, and Tsakhur are spoken in both Azerbaijan and Daghestan, while Bezhta and Hunzib are spoken in Daghestan and Georgia. Daghestanian-speakers are mostly Muslim, except Udi-speakers, who are Armenian or Georgian Christians. Nogai is spoken in Karachay-Cherkessia and Chechnya in addition to Daghestan (where it is one of 14 official languages together with Kumyk, Azeri, Tat, Chechen, Russian and 8 Daghestanian languages: Avar, Dargwa, Lezgian, Tabasaran, Lak, Tsakhur, Rutul, and Agul).[5] Chechen is also spoken in Ingushetia and Ingush in Chechnya and Alania. Azeri extends into Iran, Armenia, and Georgia, Georgian into Turkey, Azerbaijan, and North Ossetia, and Armenian is also spoken in Georgia, Azerbaijan, and parts of the North Caucasus. Abaza is spoken in Karachay-Cherkessia, and Ossetian is spoken in Georgia and Ingushetia in addition to its titular republics. Useful atlases of the Caucasian languages include Korjakov (2006) and Gippert and Schulze (2008).

History of sociolinguistic research in the Caucasus

Although the Caucasus is intimately connected with the beginnings of recorded history, the crucial events for the current sociolinguistic situation were the Russian conquest and annexation of the nineteenth century, the subsequent Soviet renewal of Russian hegemony after the October 1917 Revolution and its aftermath (during which the Caucasian republics were briefly independent), and the break-up of the USSR in 1989 and its reconstitution as the Russian Federation plus the CIS. As a result of Russian conquest in the nineteenth century, an estimated 1.2 million Muslims left the region, and an estimated 800,000 survivors settled in Ottoman Turkey. During the same period, the Russian Empire engaged in an intense campaign of Russification, aimed even at languages such as Georgian, which had a Christian majority and a literary tradition five centuries older than that of the Slavs. As Wixman (1980: 21–30, 121–69) argues, Soviet nationality policy was also ultimately aimed at Russification. Part of that goal was the creation of modern national identities, with concomitant standard languages, to serve as vehicles of literacy, modernization and, eventually, Russification.

Given the political system, Soviet sociolinguistics was dedicated to serving the ends of the state. Studies focused on questions of language planning and bilingualism, usually comparing non-Russian languages with "the language of inter-nationality communication," i.e., Russian.[6] Russification was framed as "mutual enrichment" and "mutual influence" while western sociolinguistics was labeled "bourgeois" and its results "falsifications" (e.g. Treskov 1982: 133–4). As Kreindler presciently observed of late Soviet sociolinguistics:

> There is a frantic, almost hysterical quality in the campaign waged on behalf of one of the most powerful world languages, which by all logic would seem in no need of special support. The spirit as well as much of the rhetoric of the campaign bears remarkable resemblance to the tsarist Russification campaigns in the last decades of the regime.
>
> (1985: 356)

Under Soviet rule, studies of social variation were discouraged on ideological grounds: a classless society with perfect gender equality that was moving forward on the road to the elimination of all social (including, ultimately, national or ethnic) distinctions does not support investigations of actually existing class, gender, regional, and other social differences (unless aimed at eliminating them). Madieva (1975) looked at differences in the acquisition of Russian by Avar-speakers according to traditional sociolinguistic parameters such as education, age, and social group (farmers, functionaries, students)—but not gender—at work, school, and home, complete with graphs and percentages. Unsurprisingly, younger, more urban, more educated Avars are more likely to use Russian. Madieva concludes that special efforts must be made to prepare children in a non-Russian environment to learn Russian, and that the development of bilingualism among Avars (which includes a complete shift to Russian among some) is in keeping with the Program of the Communist Party of the Soviet Union.

The four most important sociolinguistic works for the Caucasus during the Soviet period are Lewis (1972), Wixman (1980), Kreindler (1985), and Kirkwood (1989). For Daghestan, Džidalaev (2005) covers a broad range of topics spanning the Soviet and post-Soviet periods. For Circassian, Smeets (1994) gives a thorough and realistic survey through the Soviet period. He observes that while in 1920 there were more Circassian-speakers in Turkey than in the Caucasus, 70 years later language preservation was better in the Russian Federation than in Turkey, where there was no support of Muslim minority languages. Nonetheless, because urban Circassian-speakers are a minority in their republics, Russian being the dominant language in cities, Smeets cautions that Circassian faces the fate of Breton in France or Friulian in Italy. Weitenberg (1990) gives a useful survey of both Western and Eastern Armenian language reform. T'.A. Łaragyulyan (Agayan 1981: 1–119) and H.L. Zak'aryan (Agayan 1981: 120–271) give concrete data on modern colloquial Eastern Armenian, and, interestingly, Zak'aryan finds that despite the huge impact of Russian on colloquial Armenian due to Soviet policies, the degree of use of Russian loans in colloquial speech diminishes with increase in academic education and degree of association with language work—from most to least likely to use loans: workers, officials, natural scientists, social scientists, language professionals. Puristic tendencies have also been documented recently for Georgian (Apridonidze 2003).

Variationist studies, pragmatics, discourse, and conversation

For the most part, studies of variation in the Caucasus are in their infancy or pre-natal stage. Many languages of the Caucasus are only now being adequately described, and considerable effort is directed at such basic tools as grammars and dictionaries as well as problems of dialectology. Questions of discourse, pragmatics, and conversation have been minimally explored. The extremely promising project on language contact and variation in the Dargic regions of central Daghestan by Helma van den Berg was aborted by Helma's tragic death in 2003.

Although Vitkovskaja (2005) contains abstracts of articles with promising titles on discourse, communicative structures, politeness, etc., in Circassian, Karachay-Balkar, Abkhaz, and Ossetian—as well as the usual Russian-oriented "bilingualism" studies—in fact, there is very little concrete data. Solncev and Mixal'čen'ko (1996) present 17 abstracts (out of over 130) that pertain to sociolinguistics in the North Caucasus and Azerbaijan. Of these, nine deal with North-west Caucasian (one includes Ossetian), four treat Daghestan, one for Azerbaijan and one for the three breakaway republics (Abkhazia, South Ossetia, and Nagorno-Karabakh), one gives an overview of the shift from Arabic to Latin to Cyrillic orthographies in the North Caucasus, and one provides a comparative survey of Daghestan, Karachay-Cherkessia, and Kabardino-Balkaria. A number of the abstracts promote the use of Russian, either as an inter-nationality language (Daghestan) or as a means of conflict resolution in the breakaway republics. The article on Azerbaijan notes the decline of

Russian and the advance of English, criticizes the new Latin alphabet, and notes the use of Armenian in Nagorno-Karabakh and the "greater role" of minority languages. The articles on North-west Caucasian deal with language policy, language planning, and discourse phenomena, mainly formulae. Alekseev and Perexval'skaja (2000) and Balamamedov (1992) contain useful conversational data from Daghestan. After the fall of the USSR, it was common to hear complaints that the Soviet system had destroyed Russian stylistics by forcing clichéd and wooden language on all writers. Almost nothing has been written on speech registers in the Caucasus, although Rayfield (1992) gives a trenchant account of polemical style in Georgian in the Soviet period and in 1990.

Language contact, bi-/multilingualism, diglossia, code-switching

Although the Caucasus is sometimes described as a *Sprachbund*, Tuite (1999) argues that it does not fit the model of areas such as the Balkans, which originally gave rise to the concept. The Caucasus is not characterized by a single lingua franca and does not share the kind of morphosyntactic features that are typical of linguistic areas. That said, however, we can point to the fact that glottalization is shared by all the indigenous and— more significantly—most of the non-indigenous languages (or some of their dialects), and a number of bilateral or areally restricted multilateral contact-induced phenomena have been noted, mostly calques and lexical borrowings, but also, e.g. convergence in the use of personal pronouns (Nichols 1992; Džidalaev 2005).

One could argue that as an area where languages accumulate without being replaced, the nature of linguistic areality differs from that of the Balkans, where the time-depth of accumulation is shallower, the expansion of lingue franche has been more uniform, and complete replacement of pre-Indo-European languages has occurred. Of course, the linguistic elephant in the room when discussing language contact in the Caucasus is Russian.

In the Soviet period, language contact studies were dominated by a Russifying agenda. The 2002 Russian census (Russia 2004) gives data on the knowledge of the language and of declared nationality and of Russian, but also provides some data for assessing multilingualism, e.g. Table 4.5 gives figures for the 24 nationalities over 400,000 (including Avar, Armenian, Azeri, Chechen, Dargi, Ingush, Karbardian, Kumyk, Lezgian, Ossetian, Tatar) for knowledge of 50 languages other than Russian including also Adyge, Greek, Georgian, Karachay-Balkar, Lak, Nogai, Tabasaran, Tat. Table 4.6 gives the breakdown of these figures by administrative division, including the republics.

The 1999 Azerbaijan census (Azerbaijan 2006) gives data for knowledge of ethnic language, Azeri, Russian and English (Table 5.2). Of the ethnicities enumerated (figures in thousands of a total of 7953.4 of which 7205.5 were Azeri), Avar (50.9), Lezgian (178), Udi (4,1), Talysh (76.8), Tat (10.9 Muslims and 8.9 Mountain Jews), Tsakhur (15.9), and Georgian ([Ingilo] 14.9), are covered in Clifton (2002, 2003), as are Budukh (3000 Jarceva et al. 1999: 228), Kryz (10–15,000 Jarceva et al. 2001: 154), and Khinalug (2500 in 1976 and the same in Jarceva et al. 2005: 319), which were not included in the census separately.[7] Mentioned in the census but not covered in Clifton are Armenians (120.7; down from 390.5 in 1989), Tatars (30), Turks (43.4), and Kurds (13.1).[8] For most nationalities, reported fluency in the ethnic languages was 95 percent or greater.[9]

The 2001 Armenian census (Armenia 2003) gives figures for Armenian, Yezidian,[10] Russian, Ukrainian and "other" mother tongues all correlated with nationality and broken down by rural and urban. Other tables give correlations of ethnicity with gender, education, age, urban/rural, using a different set of ethnicities: Armenians (3,145,354 = 97.89 percent), Assyrian (3409), Yezidian (40,620), Greek (1176), Russian (14,660), Ukrainian (1633), Kurdish (1519), Other (4640).

The 2002 Georgian census (Georgia 2002) gave only ethnicities broken down by municipalities. The total figures were Georgian (3,661,173), Abkhaz (3527), Ossetian (38,028), Armenian (248,929), Russian (67,671), Azeri (284,761), Greek (15,166), Ukrainian (7039), Kist (7110),[11] and Yezid (18,329).

Nichols (1998) gives an excellent presentation of verticality in Caucasian multilingualism prior to the Russian conquest, which I quote here:

> [I]n highland villages many people knew the language(s) of lower villages, but not vice versa. This was because markets and winter pasture were to be found in the lowlands, while the highlands afforded few economic advantages. The male population of highland villages was largely transhumant and spent perhaps half of its working life in the lowlands. Naturally, under these conditions, lowlands languages tended to gradually spread uphill, reducing highlands languages to islands and eventually replacing them entirely. At present and for all known history and known prehistory, languages with large numbers of speakers have both lowland and highland ranges and a generally elongate vertical distribution; these are economically advantageous and/or culturally prestigious languages that have spread uphill. Languages with small numbers of speakers, including several one-village languages, are mostly found in the highlands. This pattern apparently predominated during the Little Ice Age (late middle ages to mid-19th century), a period of global cooling in which highland farms and pastures were economically precarious and the lowlands more prosperous. Prior to that, there is evidence that highland communities were larger and more prosperous and their languages spread downhill, and that highland communities formed and maintained lowland colonies. Chechen-Ingush isoglosses, and the discontinuous distribution of language families like Chechen-Ingush, Avar, and Lak all point in this direction. Overall, then, geography and size of speech community are correlated, and this is explained by verticality, economy, and climate change.

After conversions to Islam, Arabic served as a lingua franca for educated classes. In the northern lowlands of Daghestan Kumyk was used, in the southern lowlands Azeri, while the Avar Koine *bolmats'* "army language" was used in the north-east highlands, Lak in the central highlands, Tabasaran and Dargwa to the south-west. Peoples living along the Caucasus ridge are likely to know languages from both sides of the ridge. Since political organization was by clan, lineage, and commune—although there were at various times an Avar khanate, a Lak shamkhalate, Kajtag and Tabasaran utsmiates, etc.—allegiances were fluid and determined by desire and necessity. These coupled with patterns of endogamy contributed to a linguistically complex situation. We can also note that in the Muslim-majority republics of the Caucasus, as elsewhere in the Muslim ex-USSR, there is a resurgence and revival of Arabo-Perso-Turkic loans that had been eliminated by Soviet Russifying policies.

Language status, language planning, language and identity

Although a few languages of the Caucasus have long literary traditions and others have varying degrees of earlier written documentation, modern identity formation is connected with the nation-state-building processes of the nineteenth and twentieth centuries that affected other parts of Europe and the former USSR. A primary source of identity for peoples in the North Caucasus was the fact of being a mountaineer as opposed to a lowlander. Attempts at polities in the North Caucasus approached language issues in terms of potential lingue franche (Arabic, Kumyk, Azeri; under Shamil, Avar) rather than a mono-ethnic nation-state language. Even today, multiplicity of languages can lead to a multiplicity of identities that are not necessarily language-determined. Friedman (1998) discusses how identity in Daghestan has been determined by ruling polity, economic access, or school language rather than home language.

The 1926 Soviet census attempted to measure objectively the linguistic and ethnic composition of the USSR's population, but every subsequent Soviet census reduced the number of language and identity categories from the decade before in connection with the ideology of gradually creating a single Soviet (and de facto Russophone) nationality. For the 2002 census, social scientists at the Russian Academy of Sciences worked with the Bureau of Statistics to create the most complete and accurate possible list of language and ethnic categories. Unfortunately, in Daghestan, where access to resources and power continue to be allotted by ethnicity (e.g. the larger the ethnicity, the more seats in parliament), ethnic elites risked erosion of their power bases if speakers of unwritten languages declared their ethnicity on the basis of mother tongue and/or declared their home language rather than school language as mother tongue. In response, a rumor was spread that Moscow politicians and scholars were seeking to destabilize Daghestan and dismember it. As Tiškov and Kisriev (2005: 286) state: "Many interpreted this as requiring that they affirm their Avaro-Dargi and general Dagestanian loyalty." As a result, the 2002 census fails to reflect the true ethno-linguistic picture of Daghestan.

For example, in 2002, Botlikh, which numbered 3379 in 1926 and 4100 in 1938, had zero declaring Botlikh nationality and 54 in Daghestan declaring Botlikh mother tongue. Tiškov and Kisriev (2005: 279–80) give the following linguistic estimates: Andi (c. 40,000), Archi (1200), Akhwakh (6000+), Bagwalal (5000+), Bezhta (6500), Botlikh (4500), Hinukh (under 1000), Godoberi (c. 4000), Hunzib (c. 800), Tsez (c. 8000), Karata (c. 7500), Tindi (c. 10,000), Khwarshi (2500), Chamalal (c. 10,000), Kubachi (23,000) (see also M.E. Alekseev's articles on these languages in Mixal'čen'ko et al. 2003, where he cites estimates of 20,000 for Kaitag; the estimate for Megeb was 1500 in 1982). The official 2002 figures for the other Daghestanian languages of Daghestan are Avar (784,840), Lak (153,373), Lezgian (397,310), Rutul (29,383), Tsakhur (9771), Agul (29,399), Tabasaran (128,391), and Dargwa (503,523).

For the North Caucasus, Mixal'čen'ko et al. (2002, 2003) is an extraordinary resource. Included are all the indigenous languages of the North Caucasus as well as the main Turkic (Karachay-Balkar, Kumyk, Nogai, Tatar) and Iranian (Ossetian and Tat) languages. Kabardino-Cherkessian (Circassian) is treated as one language, Kubachi and Kaitag each have separate entries, but Azeri is not included despite being official in Daghestan. Census statistics are from 1989 and the partial census of 1994. Each entry has 20 sections: (1) language names; (2) detailed statistical and geographic data, e.g. numbers of monolinguals, numbers and ages of bilinguals by gender, numbers considering the language native broken down by declared ethnicity; (3) general linguistic data including classification, distinctive structural and typological features, dialects, contact languages, and regional variants; (4) literacy and orthography (both current and historical); (5) status including attitudes of speakers, regional literature, legal status (including texts); (6) literature, including languages into which and from which works are translated, publication

133

statistics; (7) use in religion and ideology; (8) literary categories (including textbooks) with statistics; (9) periodical press; (10–18) use in education, mass media (radio, TV, film, records, tapes, theater), federal, regional, and local government, courts, legislative bodies, means of production, marketing and retail; (19) resources including both bibliography and list of experts; and (20) additional observations.

For Azerbaijan, the studies in Clifton (2002, 2003) give rigorously thorough socio-linguistic profiles of minority languages, including extensive data for language use, language status, bi- and multi-lingualism, locations and types of communities, distinctions of age, gender, education, etc. Arzumanli's introductory article, however, uses 1989 census figures. The language articles are exemplary of what needs to be done for the Caucasus as a whole. At the same time, however, the relative retreat of Russian also needs to be studied. Anecdotal evidence indicates that it is currently more in use in urban areas of Azerbaijan than generally acknowledged.

Gippert and Schulze (2008) are leading a team doing sociolinguistic research in Georgia. Georgian nationalist anxieties have some claiming Svan and Mingrelian as dialects of Georgian, while other activists are agitating for language rights. In the context of Abkhaz and South Ossetian secession, the notion of minority language rights for non-Georgian Kartvelian-speakers provokes extreme anxiety. Tabidze (1999) provides a brief sociolinguistic introduction to Georgian.

For Armenian, Zolyan (2002) and Zak'aryan (1996) are recent works dealing with language policy, and Krjuchkova (1994) contains articles on language laws in the North Caucasian republics.

Orthographies are bound up with both religion and identity. When writing their native languages in the Caucasus, Muslim peoples used Arabic, Christian peoples used Georgian, Armenian, or Cyrillic, and Jewish peoples used Hebrew orthography.[12] Under the Soviets, all the languages of the Caucasus that had literary status, except Georgian and Armenian, were given Latin alphabets between 1923 and 1934 and most of these were changed to Cyrillic 1938–39 (Wixman 1980: 145).[13] The move to Latinization was modernizing and secularizing, and it cut Muslim peoples off from Islamic tradition (and Jews from Hebrew). In the case of Turkic peoples, Latinization was also associated with pan-Turkic ideology. The switch to Cyrillic was blatantly Russifying. Not only were the orthographies poorly designed, using up to four letters for a single sound, and not only did they use different letters for the same sounds in related languages, but Russian loanwords were often written exactly as in Russian with no respect for native phonotactics. All Cyrillicizing alphabets contained the letters necessary for spelling Russian words in Russian even if the letters had no other use. Azeri switched back to Latin in 1991, with a small reform in 1992, but no other such reforms have taken place.

Given the importance of religion to identity and its relation to linguistic phenomena, it is unfortunate that no religious data has been gathered on Russian territory since the suppressed census of 1937 (Stepanov 2005: 49–52). Of the Transcaucasian republics, only Georgia included census data on religion in its post-independence census, and that only by region.

Language endangerment

With the exception of the titular languages of the three Transcaucasian republics, all of the indigenous and long-present languages of the Caucasus are endangered or potentially endangered. At issue is not necessarily the absolute number of speakers but rather the fragile ecology of these languages owing to processes of modernization, urbanization, and the on-going effects of Russification or official language dominance. Caucasian endangered languages generally display vitality in the villages and morbidity in the towns, where Russian (or Georgian, Azeri, or Armenian in Transcaucasia) is the lingua franca, the language of higher education, the key to upward mobility and prosperity, and the majority urban language and the unmarked language in public contexts. In 2007, out of approximately 70 majors in the Daghestanian Languages Department of Daghestan State University (where Russian is the language of instruction)—a group representing the future of Daghestanian linguistics and language pedagogy in the republic—only four were from urban backgrounds (fieldwork observation). Another factor in language endangerment in the Caucasus is violence and its consequences. There are three crucial periods that have altered the linguistic landscape of the Caucasus by disrupting patterns of language transmission: the Russian wars of conquest in the mid-nineteenth century, the famines and Stalin's deportations of the mid-twentieth century, and the wars, rebellions, pogroms, and ethnic cleansings of the end of the twentieth century. Even in rural areas some small languages are losing ground to slightly larger ones owing to the breakdown of endogamy: Comrie (2008), citing D. Forker, observes that Hinukh is losing ground to Bezhta and Tsez owing to intermarriage.

Conclusion

Any field of sociolinguistic research in the region will prove fruitful for the future. Issues such as language standardization, language policy, linguistic identity, and to some extent language vitality and language contact are better served at this point than variationist studies, conversational analysis, code-switching, etc., and so one could point to precisely those areas with the most gaping lacunae in the Soviet period as areas still in need of the most work. At the same time, however, those areas that have traditionally been the focus of Caucasian sociolinguistics will also benefit from increased attention. In this respect, the shortcomings and/or absence of recent official census data both point to the most problematic areas and leave open the possibility of future advances.

Acknowledgments

I am grateful to Winfried Boeder, Jasmine Dum-Tragut, June Farris, Jost Gippert, Johanna Nichols, and Wolfgang Schulze, as well as John Colarusso, Anaïd Donabedian, Alice Harris, and Fatima Tlisova who responded to my queries and helped me track down sources. All errors are my responsibility.

Notes

1 Krasnodar, Stavropol and parts of Kalmykia are sometimes included in historical accounts of the region.
2 Schulze (2004: 9) includes Kalmyk (Mongol) transhumants (20,000) in northern Daghestan and Trukhman (Karapapakh; East Oghuz, 5000 in 14 villages) in southern Daghestan.
3 The term *Tat* was used by (originally nomadic) Turkic-speaking peoples to refer to (Iranian-speaking) settled farmers from Crimea to Central Asia. As a language name, it currently applies to

two different diasystems: Northern Tat mentioned above, and Southern Tat, a group of dialects spoken in Iranian Azerbaijan that are North-west Iranian. See below on religion for Iranian-speakers.

4 Of indigenous and long-present languages of the North Caucasus outside Daghestan, only Abaza and Nogai are non-titular. North Caucasian titular nationalities are minorities or barely majorities in "their" republics owing to emigrations, deportations, and/or gerrymandering that favored Russians (Wixman 1980; Russia 2004).

5 Russian is no longer an official language in the Transcaucasian republics and is still official in all North Caucasian republics, along with titular languages. The 1990 constitution of Daghestan names "all the languages of Daghestan" as official, but the language law names only these 13 and Russian. Attempts to publish in Andi, Tsez, Mingrelian, and Laz beyond strictly linguistic works have also been made. Tsakhur had literary status 1934–38 and regained it in 1990. Agul and Rutul have been in the process of standardization since 1990.

6 Šagirov, Tabulova and Sujunčev (1978) is a rare exception for the Caucasus, with articles comparing the North-west Caucasian languages with each other and with Karachay-Balkar and Ossetian without reference to Russian.

7 The total for "Other" was 9600. Lezgic-speakers in Azerbaijan use Azeri as the language of literacy and some declared Azeri nationality. Only 336 declared Rutul nationality in Azerbaijan in 1989, but the number is probably ten times that. Most declare Lezgian nationality.

8 Also Russians (141.7) and Ukrainians (29).

9 Mountain Jews 88.2 percent, Tatars 87.5 percent, Kurds 57 percent, Ukrainians 32.4 percent.

10 In the Caucasus, Yezidis are Kurmanji-Kurdish-speakers whose religion is syncretic with elements from Zoroastrianism and Islam. They consider themselves and their language to be distinct from Muslim Kurds (who are also Kurmanji-speakers). The ethnonym is otherwise applied to Zoroastrians in Iran and India (where they are called Parsi) and refers to a group of North-west Iranian dialects distinct from Kurdish.

11 K'ists (or K'istis) are Chechen-speakers.

12 Mountain Jews speak Tat, Georgian Jews speak Georgian. Judeo-Tat is distinct from Muslim Tat, Judeo-Georgian is an ethnolect of Georgian like the English of American Jews for English. Judeo-Tat was treated like other written languages of Daghestan and Azerbaijan. Of the Christian peoples, Caucasian Albanian (Agwan, Alwan, no relation to Balkan Albanian) had a written tradition with its own script as old as Georgian and Armenian, and the language was a lingua franca in what is now north-western Azerbaijan and adjacent parts of Georgia and Daghestan. We now know that Udi is the remnant of that language.

13 Digor Ossetian and Kara Nogai were abolished instead of Cyrillicized, Abkhaz was switched from Latin to Georgian in 1938 and Cyrillic in 1954.

References

Agayan, E. B. (ed.) (1981) *Zamanakakic' hayeren xosakc'akan lezown*, Yerevan: Armenian Academy of Sciences.

Alekseev, M. E. and Perexval'skaja, E. A. (2000) "Kubačincy i kubačinskij (urbugskij) jazyk," in V. Ju. Mixal'čen'ko, T. B. Krjuškova, O. A. Kazakevč, and N. G. Kolesnik (eds.) *Jazyki Rossijskoj federacii i novogo zarubež'ja: Status i funkcii*, Moscow: Editorial URSS, pp. 211–19.

Apridonidze, S. (2003) "Purism and normalization of language in Georgia: traditions and tendencies," in J. Brincat, W. Boeder, T. Stolz (eds.) *Purism in Minor Languages, Endangered Languages, Regional Languages, Mixed Languages*, Bochum: Brockmeyer. 171–97.

Armenia (2003) *The Results of 2001 Census of the Republic of Armenia*, Yerevan: National Statistical Service of the Republic of Armenia.

Azerbaijan (2006) *Statistical Yearbook of Azerbaijan*, Baku: State Statistical Committee of Azerbaijan Republic.

Balamamedov, A. K. (1992) *Osnovy social'noj lingvistiki (Funkcionirovanie jazykov Dagestana)*, Maxachkala: Daghestan State University.

Clifton, J. M. (ed.) (2002, 2003) *Studies in Languages of Azerbailjan*, 2 vols, St. Petersburg, Russia: SIL International.

Comrie, B. (2008) "Linguistic diversity in the Caucasus," *Annual Review of Anthropology*, 37.

Džidalaev, N. S. (2005) *Sociolingvističeskie problemy dagestancev i dagestanskix jazykov*, Maxachkala: DNC RAN.

Friedman, V. A. (1998) "A Balkanist in Daghestan: annotated notes from the field," *The Anthropology of East Europe Review*, 16, 115–29.

Georgia (2002) Census results. Online. Available at: www.statistics.ge/main.php?pform=145&plang=1 (accessed 31 July 2008).

Gippert, J. and Schulze, W. (2005) Georgian Project. Online. Available at: www.volkswagenstiftung.de/ foerderung/auslandsorientiert/mittelasien-kaukasus/bewilligungen-2005.html (accessed 31 July 2008).

——(2008) Atlas. Caucasian Languages. Online. Available at: www.titus.uni-frankfurt.de/didact/ karten/kauk/kaukasm.htm (accessed 31 July 2008).

Jarceva, V. N., Vinogradov, V. A. and Poceluevskij, E. A. (eds.) (1999, 2001, 2005) *Jaziki Rossijskoj Federacii i sosednyix gosudarstv*, 3 vols, Moscow: Nauka.

Korjakov, Ju. B. (2006) *Atlas kavkazsix jazykov*, Moscow: Russian Academy of Sciences.

Kirkwood, M. (1989) *Language Planning in the Soviet Union*, London: Macmillan.

Kreindler, I. T. (ed.) (1985) *Sociolinguistic Perspectives on Soviet National Languages*, Berlin: Mouton de Gruyter.

Krjuchkova, T. B. (ed.) (1994) *Jazykovye problemy Rossijskoj Federacii i zakony o jazykax*, Moscow: Russian Academy of Sciences.

Lewis, E. G. (1972) *Multilingualism in the Soviet Union*, The Hague: Mouton.

Madieva, N. B. (1975) "O nekotoryx social'nyx funkcijax avarsko-russkogo dvujazyčija v Dagestane," in Ju. L. Deševriev (ed.) *Sociolingvističeskie problemy razvivajuščixsja stran*, Moscow: Nauka, pp. 321–8.

Mixal'čen'ko, V. Ju., McConnell, G. D. and Kolesnik, N. G. (eds.) (2002, 2003) *Pis'mennye jazyki mira: Jazyki Rossijskoj Federacii*, 2 vols, Moscow: Russian Academy of Sciences.

Nichols, J. (1992) "The Caucasus as a linguistic area, 1: Personal pronouns," in G. B. Hewitt (ed.) *Caucasian Perspectives*, London: Lincom Europa, pp. 343–58.

——(1998) "An overview of languages of the Caucasus." Online. Available at: www. popgen.well.ox. ac.uk/eurasia/htdocs/nichols/nichols.html (accessed 31 July 2008).

Rayfield, D. (1992) "The language of abuse and the abuse of language – polemics in Georgian," in G. B. Hewitt (ed.) *Caucasian Perspectives*, Munich; Lincom Europa, pp. 265–77.

Russia (2004) *Itogi vserossijskoj perepisi naselenij 2002 goda: Tom 4, Nacional'sny sostav i vladenie jazykam*, Moscow: Federal Bureau of Statistics, Russian Federation.

Šagirov, A. K., Tabulova V. N. and Sujunčev, X. I. (eds.) (1978) *Voprosy vzaimnovlijanija i vzaimnoobogaščenija jazykov*, Čerkessk: Karačaevo-Čerkesskij nauchno issledovatel'nyj institut istorii, filologii i ėkonomiki.

Schulze, W. (2004) "Das Alte im Neuen: Sprachliche Überlebensstrategien im Ostkaukasus," in P. Schrijver and P. A. Mumm (eds.) *Sprachtod und Sprachgeburt. Schriftenreihe des Zentrum für historische Sprachwissenschaft*, Bremen: Hempen, pp. 251–77.

Smeets, R. (1994) "The development of literary languages in the Soviet Union: the case of Circassian," in I. Fodor and C. Hagège (eds.) *Language Reform: History and Future*, vol. 6, Hamburg: Buske, pp. 513–40.

Solncev, V. M. and Mixal'čen'ko, V. Ju. (eds.) (1996) *Sociolingvističeskie problemy v raznyx regionax mira*, Moscow: Russian Academy of Sciences.

Stepanov, V. V. (2005) "The All-Russia 2002 census: ways to measure the identity of large and small groups," *Anthropology and Archeology of Eurasia*, 44, 34–94.

Tabidze, M. (1999) "Sociolinguistic aspects of the development of Georgian," *Lund University Department of Linguistics Working Papers*, 47, 201–10.

Tiškov, V. A. and Kisriev, E. F. (2005) "Množestvennye indentičnosti meždu teoriej i politikoj (primer Dagestana)," in V.A. Tiškov (ed.) *Mnogoètničnye soobščestva v uslovijax transformacij: opyt Dagestana*, Moscow: Russian Academy of Sciences, pp. 255–87.

Treskov, S. I. (1982) "Vzaimoobogashchenie jazykov narodov SSSR i kritika burzhuaznyx falsifikatorov," in K. V. Baxnjan (ed.) *Aktual'nye problemy funkcionirovanija jazykov v socialisticheskom obshchestve*, Moscow: AN SSSR, pp. 122–44.

Tuite, K. (1999) "The myth of the Caucasian Sprachbund: the case of ergativity," *Lingua*, 108, 1–26. Online. Available at: www.caucasology.com/amirani.htm (accessed 31 July 2008).

Vitkovskaja, L.V. (ed.) (2005) *Kavkaszkij tekst: nacional'nyj obraz mira kak konceptual'naja polikul'turnaja sistema*, Pjatigorsk: Pjatigoskij gosudarstvennyj lingvističeski universitet.

Weitenberg, J. J. S. (1990) "Reform movements in Armenia," in I. Fodor and C. Hagège (eds.) *Language Reform: History and Future*, vol. 5, Hamburg: Buske, pp. 393–408.

Wixman, R. (1980) *Language Aspects of Ethnic Patterns and Processes in the North Caucasus*, Chicago: Department of Geography, University of Chicago.

Zak'aryan, H. L. (1996) "The language law of the republic of Armenia and problems of All-Armenian language policy," in D. Sakayan (ed.) *Proceedings of the Fifth International Conference on Armenian Linguistics*, Delmar, NY: Caravan, pp. 355–60.

Zolyan, S. (2002) "Hayastani lezvakan iravičakě ew HH lezvakan k'ałak'akanut'yuně," in A. E. Sargsyan (ed.) *Hanralezvabanut'yan dasěnt'ac'*, vol. 2, Yerevan: Armenian Academy of Sciences, pp. 43–8.

13

Sociolinguistics in the Iranian world

William O. Beeman

Introduction

The Iranian language sphere consists of three currently recognized "core" varieties, and a number of peripheral varieties that diverge significantly enough to be thought of as separate "languages." The core varieties are Standard Modern Persian,[1] Dari and Tajik. Other Iranian languages are Kurdish, of which there are several varieties; Baluchi; Modern Sogdian, known today as Yaghnobi; and a variety of so-called Eastern Iranian languages, including Nuristani, Pashto, Pasha'i. Included as well are the languages of the Pamir mountains: Shugni (Shugnani), Yazgulami, Ishkashimi and Wahkhi.

There have been a number of informal debates among Persian language specialists concerning the status of Tajik and Dari vs. standard Modern Persian. All linguists know that speech communities utilize a continuum of varieties of speech, and that the term "language" is more a political appellation than a scientifically accurate descriptor. The range of variation in Persian, Dari and Tajik communities is quite extensive, embodying regionalisms and borrowings from other language families. The term "register" has a special status in describing languages in that it represents a speech variety that is marked for particular specific occasions. Whereas Modern Persian and Dari are very close in form, Tajik has more divergent discourse structures. Based on fieldwork carried out in Tajikistan, I theorize that standard Persian as spoken in Iran has become a special register of Tajik marked for formal occasions such as political speech making, wedding orations, news broadcasts, and elevated scientific discourse. In this way the opposition between all the varieties of colloquial Tajik and standard Persian in Tajikistan resembles the diglossic opposition between *dhimotiki* and *katherevusa* in modern Greek. In the discussion below I provide several examples, and speculate on the concretization and meaning of such shifting diglossia in the use of vocal speech registers.

A controlled comparison of "Persian," "Dari" and "Tajik" is not very productive, since there is considerable regional variation within the three varieties. It is far more productive to explore the social and cultural relationships between these language varieties, and to provide a sketch of the development of these varieties in recent years.

When used for self-identification purposes, speech variables can be used to identify one's self and others as belonging to a specific community, to indicate membership in a particular social class, or to reinforce one's gender identity. When used to identify context, speech variables distinguish between literary and conversational genres. They also mark particular culturally defined situations, such as public, private, academic, legal, formal, informal, and many others. When used strategically, they can be used to indicate relative personal relations, such as status, formality, and intimacy. They can also be used to indicate attitudes such as humor, sarcasm, irony, subordination, superordination, admiration, flattery, and others. Variables are *polysemic* in the sense that they can be used to indicate more than one thing. For example, a particular variable may indicate at the same time that one is an upper-class male in a formal situation showing admiration toward one's companions in interaction. I have documented some of these dynamics for standard Persian in other publications (Beeman 1986, 1987).

Modern varieties of standard Iranian

As will be seen below, historical vagaries have split the Persian-speaking community of the ancient empires into the semi-distinct communities of Persian, Dari and Tajik speakers. I say "semi-distinct" because although these three varieties have been formalized through both academic and political processes, they remain mutually intelligible. Outside of the region, there is some confusion as to whether the varieties constitute one language with slight variations or distinct "languages." Brian Spooner raises this question in his paper: "Are we teaching Persian? or Farsi? or Dari? or Tojiki [sic]?" (1994). Spooner's article also highlights the curious Farsi/Persian distinction in nomenclature for the language that prevails today outside academic circles.[2]

What is clear is that the three varieties have diverged largely because of shifts in historical and political boundaries over many centuries. The Modern Persian that emerged during the eleventh and twelfth centuries spread throughout the great Iranian empires of the fifteenth to the nineteenth centuries, eventually being separated from each other during the period of European colonization, and the establishment of the nation-state system. The European political world mandated the creation of hard boundaries separating polities from each other. Frequency of communication became denser for the populations living within these new borders, and their speech varieties developed a separate character. This process was long ago noted by historical linguists, and in particular by Leonard Bloomfield in his classic (1933) work, *Language*, where he noted this political and social phenomenon as the reason for divisions in different varieties of Modern German.[3]

The broadest division in Persian is seen between modern Iranian Persian and Tajik, as will be shown below. The development of formalized modern Tajik is the result of a particular political and historical process situated through the control of the Tajik-speaking area, first, by Russia, then by the Soviet Union and, finally, under separate states in the post-Soviet period. The containment of Tajik speakers within these political boundaries brought this variety of Persian into closer interaction with Central Asian Turkic languages, notably Uzbek, and with Russian, which colored and changed this variety (cf. Atkin 1994; Subtelny 1994). Modern Iranian Persian was influenced by Azerbaijani Turkish through the Qajar court, and by contact with Western European languages, notably French, and in the post-World War II period by English (cf. Beeman 1992; Meskoob 1992).

Since the basic grammatical structure of all varieties is essentially the same, Persian, Dari and Tajik have usually been treated under one rubric, with the differences between the individual variations noted (cf. Lazard 1970). However, in recent years with the emergence of Tajikistan as an independent state, some newer studies have focused on the Tajik variety in a comprehensive manner (Rzehak 1999, 2001; Hillman 2000; Baizoyev and Hayward 2004; Ido 2005; Perry 2005).[4] The classic sketch of Tajik grammar by Rastorgueva (1963) from the Soviet period reflects the national language ideology of the Soviet Union, in which Tajik was conceptually separated from other varieties of Persian.[5]

Tajik, Dari and Persian are "languages" in the sense that they have concretized canonical forms that are transmitted through institutionalized schooling and reference works, however, as mentioned above, structurally they are all varieties of Persian.

The history of all three varieties may be surprising to speakers of Modern Persian in Iran. In fact, Modern Persian in its literary form emerged first in Bukhara (present-day Uzbekistan) during the Samanid Empire (ninth–tenth centuries CE). The term Dari derives from the phrase *Fārsi-ye Darbāri*, or "Court Persian." The term also dates from the Samanid Empire, although today it refers both to the variety of Persian spoken in Afghanistan, and to the variety spoken by Zoroastrians in Yazd and Kerman in Iran (also known as Gabri). Although its speakers have been active for millennia, Tajik, with its present name and in its present written form as mentioned above, is a twentieth-century creation—an artifact of the Soviet Union and its cultural policies, and some divergence between the two varieties is attributable to this political process (cf. Bashiri 1997a, 1997b).

Persian, Dari and Tajik encompass the kinds of variation referred to in the previous section, and there is much overlap in particular variable features. Some speakers of "Persian" in Khorasan communicate colloquially in a variety that is virtually identical with speakers in Heart, Samarkand or Dushanbeh. If we take Persian and Tajik as antipodes on a scale of variability, with Dari as an intermediate form, we can see some important dynamic relationships between the varieties.

There is a directionality in the relationship between the two varieties. Persian is seen by all speech communities as a prestige standard, and Tajik and Dari as colloquial forms. Dari, as spoken in Afghanistan, is seen as a stigmatized variety for many of its speakers when they find themselves in a primarily Persian-speaking setting. Afghan residents in Iran will often resort to using a foreign language such as English rather than speak Dari. To reinforce this notion of hierarchy, it is worth noting that speakers of Persian varieties rarely learn Tajik or Dari forms, whereas educated Tajik and Dari speakers all acquire some command of Persian forms.

It is important to note that Persian, Tajik and Dari are mutually intelligible. This is in stark contrast to their non-intelligibility with some other Iranian "languages" mentioned at the beginning of this discussion, such as Kurdish or Baluchi, and some varieties that are commonly referred to as "dialects" such as Tati or Kashi. The Pamir "languages" of the Gorno-Badakhshan region of Tajikistan are also unintelligible to Persian/Tajik/Dari speakers, despite the fact that these varieties have borrowed large amounts of standard Persian vocabulary. Shugni, or Shugnani, for example, no longer maintains any numbers above 10, the higher numbers being borrowed from Persian/Tajik.

Orthographic systems contribute to perceptions of intelligibility between the "languages." Tajik is written in Cyrillic characters despite some attempts to introduce Arabic script since Tajikistan's independence at the break-up of the Soviet Union in 1989. This leads many people to believe that the languages are less mutually intelligible than they actually are. This phenomenon is not uncommon elsewhere. Hindi/Urdu and Serbian/

Table 13.1 Relations between Persian, Tajik and Dari

	Persian	*Tajik*	*Dari*
Orthography	Arabic	Cyrillic	Arabic
Literature	Extensive	Moderate	Scant
Relative prestige	High	Moderate	Low

Croatian are examples of mutually intelligible varieties that differ primarily in their orthographic systems.

The existence of literature in the languages in question also contributes to the sense of difference. The extensive literature in Persian compared to the other two contributes to poetry—serves to concretize the idea of Tajik as a separate language.

Table 13.1 illustrates some of the differences between the formal languages discussed above.

Markers of Persian and Tajik

There are certain linguistic variables that tend to mark Persian and Tajik. Though it is not possible to specify every difference in this brief presentation, they fall into several broad categories roughly corresponding to standard linguistic descriptive categories.

Phonology

A simpler phonological structure tends to characterize varieties identified as Tajik as opposed to those identified as Persian. In theory, both varieties have the same vowel and consonant structure as described in standard Persian grammatical literature. However, Tajik in general has a tendency to centralize vowels, particularly in unstressed syllables, and in grammatical prefixes ([mi-] and [be-]) and in personal suffixes (i.e. [-æm]). The phoneme /o/ in Persian seems quite unstable in Tajik, and is frequently realized as either [u] or [ə].[6] There is a tendency for the prominent /a/ in Persian varieties to be realized as [o] or [ɔ] in Tajik varieties. Some of the same tendencies are seen in Dari, but Dari is generally closer in pronunciation to standard Persian. One generalizable difference is that Dari nearly universally realizes Persian /v/ as [w].

Morphology

Speakers of varieties identified as Persian generally see Tajik and Dari varieties as embodying completely recognizable, albeit occasionally archaic forms. In general, Indo-European root forms are favored over Arabic forms in Tajik and Dari varieties, although many transmitted Arabic vocabulary items are found. The third person singular pronoun /vai/ predominates over /u/ ("he, she") in Tajik, /besyor/ over /xeili/ ("very") and other similar preferences. Tajik differs from Persian and Dari in its increased number of Russian borrowings; and Arabic and Western European borrowings in Persian varieties add to the color of language use in Iran, but even with these different patterns of borrowing there is a high degree of overlap in the vocabulary of the three varieties.

Syntax

Two very distinct constructions differentiate Tajik varieties from Persian and Dari varieties in spoken language. The first involves the question construction. Tajik uses a terminal question particle [mi], probably as a result of *Sprachbund* influence from Turkish varieties in the region as in the following

    1 *šəmo zæn dorid mi ?* "Do you have a wife?"

Persian and Dari varieties would eliminate the question particle.[7]

The second involves the use of the verb *istadæn* "to stand" in many Tajik constructions foreign to Persian varieties. In particular, with the truncated infinitive in Tajik progressive verb constructions where *daštæn* with the present tense would be used in Persian constructions. There are both literary and colloquial constructions, and even further regional variations on these colloquial constructions. In the examples below (Table 13.2), one widely used set of colloquial forms is provided.

Table 13.2 "We are eating" in Tajik and Persian

English	Tajik	Persian
We are eating (now)	Mo xorda istadæ-im (lit.)	Ma darim mixorim
	Mo istadæ-im xur (colloq.)	
We were eating	Mo xorda istadæ budim (lit.)	Ma daštim mixordim
We had been eating	Mo xorda istadæ budæ-im	Ma daštim mixordim

Finally, there is an unusual use of a gerund construction with the suffix [-gi] in Tajik conditional constructions that rarely if ever occurs in Persian constructions where conditional forms collapse with normal indicative forms, see Table 3.3.[8]

Table 13.3 "We would eat," etc. in Tajik and Persian constructions

English	Tajik	Persian
We would eat	Mo mikhordagistim (lit.)	Ma mixorim
	Mo mikhordagim (colloq.)	
We would be eating	Mo xorda istadægistim (lit.)	Ma mixordim
	Mo xorda istadægim (colloq.)	
We would have eaten	Mo xordagistim (lit.)	Ma daštim mixordim
	Mo xordagim (colloq.)	
We would have been eating	Mo khorda istadægi budæ-im	Ma daštim mixordim

It should be noted that the past participle with the [-gi] suffix is widely used as a kind of impersonal construction in Tajik forms.

    2 *Vai ketobo xondægi, ræft.* "Having read, he left."

Note that in the above, the translation of the tense of the first clause depends on the tense of the verb. Viz.:

    3 *Vai ketobo xondægi, miravæd.* "Reading the book, he goes."

Colloquially, this construction is also used as a simple past tense:

4 *Shoma ketobo xondægi?* "Did you read the book?"

This [-gi] construction is seen in Persian forms, but is fully nominalized in most cases (e.g. *zendegi* "living, life"), having presumably lost its function in verb constructions.

Contexts for Persian in Tajik: shifting diglossia

Looking at the previous section we can see that the primary areas where differences in Tajik and Persian varieties exist is in phonology and syntax. Morphology seems not to be a dimension of particular attention for speakers who possess both varieties. It is first important to understand that virtually all speakers of Tajik are bilingual (Russian and Tajik) and many are trilingual (Russian, Uzbek or Kyrgyz, and Tajik). Thus Tajik usage is already embedded in a framework of variety choice that is quite complex, and it is shifting in the post-Soviet period. The government of Tajikistan has tended to emphasize the use of Tajik as a national identity marker, and increasingly that is how it is treated by speakers as well. Thus, in the first instance, the choice to speak Tajik is already an expression of social and cultural identity (cf. Schoeberlein-Engel 1994). Beyond this lies the choice of what variety and style of Tajik to adopt for a given situation. This "shifting diglossia" is not only normative, but also dynamic over time, as will be seen below.

Given that Tajik speakers all acquire some command of Persian forms, it is important to note where and under what conditions the tendency to use these different varieties of Persian is exercised.

In general, the Tajik situation tends toward *diglossia* as described by Ferguson (1959) in his classic article of the same title. This resembles the opposition between *dhimotiki* and *katherevousa* in Modern Greek.

Tajik speakers will demonstrate pronunciation and syntactic structures that tend toward formal Persian in literature, and in formal, public situations. They will tend toward Tajik constructions in face-to-face conversation and in informal, private situations, as discussed below.

Curiously, and perhaps because the two varieties are so very close, Dari speakers do not generally command standard Persian pronunciation or intonation in spoken forms. Written Dari approximates standard literary Persian. However, it should be noted that Dari speakers also find their use of language embedded in a situation of multi-lingual choice, with Pashto, Uzbek, Baluchi, Pasha'i and a multitude of smaller varieties competing as primary forms of communication

Literary usages in Tajik and Dari include journalistic writing, official government documents as well as some fiction, academic writing, non-fiction and poetry that emulates classic styles. Poetry in particular forms a touchstone for speakers of all varieties that keeps the most formal variety in this diglossic situation alive and active. Virtually every individual in Iran, Afghanistan and Tajikistan above the age of 6 knows at least a few lines of classical Persian poetry in standard Persian, complete with its pronunciation norms.

Formal usages include political speeches, public addresses and formal social occasions, such as weddings. Toasting at banquets can also involve highly Persianized speech, especially on the part of the "toastmaster" who must introduce each individual making a toast. It must also be noted that individuals wishing to appear erudite to others will adopt Persianized forms in their speech, at times to absurd degrees, indulging in a kind of *hypercorrection* (cf. Labov 1972) that can create an effect precisely opposite to that which they aspire.

In Tajikistan, Tajik forms dominate in personal contact situations. An individual using formal Persian elements in everyday speech risks alienating his or her intimate friends. A few of my Tajik friends studied in Tehran, and having learned standard urban Iranian Persian are seen as somewhat pretentious when they use elements of this variety in everyday conversation in Dushanbeh. Having myself learned Persian in Iran, I have been told by my Tajik friends, "I don't speak Iranian," even as we are carrying out a perfectly normal, mutually comprehensible conversation. Likewise people have listened to me speak, and then commented on the "beauty" of my language, just because I am speaking a predominantly Iranized form of Persian, which "reads" for the hearers as the formal register of their own speech. This for me clearly marks a cognitive recognition of a formal standard for Tajik speakers.

Colloquialized Tajik forms are used not only in conversation, but also in playwriting and colloquial literature as well as in comic strips, the most popular forms of journalism, and the lyrics of popular songs.

However, it must be recognized that the divergence of formal Persian registers from colloquial speech can be very great. Television is an important form of information and entertainment for most citizens in Tajikistan, but many rely on news broadcasts in Russian because they cannot understand the formal Persian register of the Tajik news broadcasts. President Rakhmanov is actually quite a skilled political speaker (in my opinion) because he manages to use a variety of speech in his public addresses that hits a medium between the use of Tajik and formal Persian forms.

Other varieties of Tajik are found in Uzbekistan, notably in Samarqand, Bukhara and the Boysun region in the Surkhandarya region of the country. Unfortunately for Tajik speakers, the government of Uzbekistan is engaged in a systematic eradication of the language by closing schools, university faculties, publications and media outlets. The Bukhara, Samarqand and Boysun varieties of Tajik differ from each other in pronunciation and in some morphological respects, however, historically, the people of these regions all had knowledge of classical Persian to serve as a touchstone for the mutual interpretation of these regional differences. In a field trip to these regions in 2003, I discovered that the speech of young people, who have lost access to formal Persian/Tajik instruction in schools, and exposure to the language in the media, was becoming unintelligible to Tajik speakers outside of their own region.

As Tajikistan becomes more accessible to scholars, it is clear that much more research needs to be undertaken on the interrelationship between Tajik and Persian varieties of speech. The historical and genetic relationships are in need of clarification and further investigation. Since there is relatively little in terms of formal structure separating the two varieties, most of the differences lie in the social realm. I hope that this small preliminary set of observations will start scholars thinking about the sociolinguistic dimensions of the relationship between the two speech communities.

Ta'arof: discourse marking of status and politeness

Persian, Dari and Tajik all embody an important pragmatic practice—the marking of relative status in speech. This is a component both of formality and politeness, and is routinely practiced by all competent speakers of the language.

145

Substitutions are made for common verbs, pronouns and forms of address to indicate "other raising" and "self-lowering" in polite discourse. Thus the verb "to say" has the neutral form: *goftan*, the other-raising form, *farmudan* (literally, "to command") and the self-lowering form *'arz kardan* (literally, "to petition"). There are a number of other-raising second-person singular pronouns varying in degrees of politeness starting with *shoma* (the 2nd person plural form), and proceeding to *jenāb-e āli* ("your honor") and advancing to even more elevated epithets. The neutral first-person pronoun is *man*, and a common self-lowering form is *bandeh* ("slave"). The contrast can be seen in Table 13.4.

Table 13.4 Lowering and raising pronouns

	Self-lowering (first person)	*Other raising (second person)*
Speak	Bandeh 'arz mikonam	Jenāb-e āli mifarmayid
Give	Bandeh taqdim mikonam	Jenāb-e āli lotf mikonid

The variations in these verbal formulas are extensive, and they are part of the repertoire of all competent speakers of Persian, Dari and Tajik.[9]

Conclusion: self-identification, context identification and strategic action

In this chapter I have tried to give a sense of the development of shifting diglossia in the three main varieties of Persian as they have developed historically in Iran, Afghanistan, and Central Asia. The varieties are mutually intelligible, but because they have diverged over time, and through historical circumstance, the differences between them have come to have more than linguistic significance.

Differences in language variety choice, as we would expect from standard sociolinguistic research, have come to provide the means for identity solidarity within the various communities. As Gregory Bateson once noted: "One of the ways a Frenchman indicates that he is French is by speaking French" (Bateson 2000: 9). The first broad self-identification mechanism for people of the region is to speak Persian, Dari or Tajik as opposed to some other language, like Russian, Uzbek or Pashto. The second is to speak a regional variety with its characteristic pronunciation and word usage.

Since the varieties of Persian also embody formal and informal registers that exist as antipodes on a gradated scale, one can mark social situations and events through the use of linguistic choice within the framework of phonological, morphological and syntactic variations available. One can abandon features that mark informal spoken Tajik in favor of the more standard Persian forms in more formal situations, and retain them in more colloquial intimate situations. Finally, one can mark formality, status and increase politeness through the use of pragmatic word choice in the rituals of *ta'arof*. As mentioned above, complex speech events such as weddings and political meetings are good places to observe a variety of these markings existing side by side as individuals move between public and private interaction modes.

Finally, because these choices exist, they can be used strategically for rhetorical purposes. President Hamid Karzai of Afghanistan must always choose between Dari and some other language (usually Pasto, or English) in his public appearances. Further, he must choose a level of formality when he does speak Dari. President Rakhmanov of Tajikistan has evolved a highly studied rhetorical strategy in his use of Tajik in public settings, adjusting his speech by topic and context between a formal and an informal standard.

Thus the linguistic landscape throughout the region mirrors the complexity of the social and historical landscape. It is difficult to predict the future development of Persian, Dari and Tajik, but the realignment of political boundaries and alliances throughout the region will have an important effect on the development of all of these languages. One interesting development is already taking place in the writing system of all these nations as a result of computerized communication. All previous official schemes to Romanize Persian script have failed, however hundreds of thousands of email messages are being written in Romanized Persian, Tajik and Dari. There is no standard—in some ways every writer devises their own scheme—but in time conventions will develop, and there will be a common Romanized script.

Notes

1 The widely, but incorrectly used term *Farsi* is the name of the language *in* Persian, the correct English name for the language. *Farsi* is analogous to *Deutsch* for German, *Français* for French or *Russki* for Russian.
2 See note 1 above.
3 The different varieties of Persian discussed in this chapter are, in my estimation, no more widely separated in form or intelligibility than the numerous varieties of Modern German.
4 Baizoyev and Hayward (2004) and Hillman's (2000) work as well as Rzehak (1989) are oriented to teaching Tajik. Ido and Perry have provided comprehensive descriptions of Tajik. Rzehak has provided not only a description of Tajik, but also a historical sketch of the gradual diversion of the varieties.
5 There are numerous works describing the grammar and structure of Modern Iranian Persian. A review of these is beyond the scope of this discussion.
6 Rastorgueva describes this phenomenon extensively (1963: 4).
7 Note, however, that the [-mi] particle is eliminated if the initial question particle /oyo/ is used in Tajik constructions. In the Badakhshan region of Afghanistan, Tajik varieties take precedence over Dari in many areas.
8 Cf. Rastorgueva (1963: 76–7) for a more complete analysis.
9 See Beeman (1986) and Sprachman (2002) for many more examples, and Asdjodi (2001) for a comparison with Chinese.

References

Asdjodi, M. (2001) "A comparison between ta'arof in Persian and limao in Chinese," *International Journal of the Sociology of Language*, 148, 71–92.
Atkin, M. (1994) "Tajiks and the Persian world," in B. Manz (ed.) *Central Asia in Historical Perspective*, Boulder, CO: Westview Press, pp. 127–43.
Baizoyev, A. and Hayward, J. (2004) *A Beginner's Guide to Tajiki*, New York: RoutledgeCurzon.
Bashiri, I. (1997a) "The languages of Tajikistan in perspective." Online. Available at: www.angelfire.com/rnb/bashiri/Tajling/Tajling.html.
——(1997b) "Samanid renaissance and establishment of Tajik identity." Online. Available at: www.angelfire.com/rnb/bashiri/Samanid/Samanid.html.
Bateson, G. (2000) *Steps to an Ecology of Mind*, Chicago: University of Chicago Press.
Beeman, W. O. (1986) *Language, Status and Power in Iran*, Bloomington, IN: Indiana University Press.
——(1987) "Affectivity in Persian Language Usage," in B. Good, M. J. Good, and M. M. J. Fischer (eds.) *Affect and Healing in Middle Eastern Cultures*, Special Issue, *Culture, Medicine and Psychiatry*, 11, 403–24.

147

——(1992) "Review of Meskoob, *Shahrokh, Iranian Nationality and the Persian Language* (John Perry's edition; Michael J. Hillmann's Tr)," *Iranian-Studies*, 28, 86–8.

——(2001) "Emotion and sincerity in Persian discourse: accomplishing the representation of inner states," *International Journal of the Sociology of Language*, 148, 31–57.

Bloomfield, L. (1933) *Language*, New York: H. Holt and Company.

Ferguson, C. A. (1959) "Diglossia," *Word*, 15, 325–40.

Hillman, M. C. (2000) *Tajiki Textbook and Reader*, Springfield, VA: Dunwoody Press.

Ido, S. (2005) *Tajik*, Munich: Lincom Europa.

Jakobson, R. (1960) "Closing statement: linguistics and poetics," in T. Sebeok (ed.) *Style in Language*, Cambridge, MA: The MIT Press, pp. 350–77.

Labov, W. (1972) *Sociolinguistic Patterns*, Philadelphia, PA: University of Pennsylvania Press.

Lazard, G. (1970) "Persian and Tajik," in T. Sebeok (ed.) *Current Trends in Linguistics*, vol. 6, Paris: Mouton, pp. 64–96.

Meskoob, S. (1992) *Iranian Nationality and the Persian Language*, ed. John Perry, trans. Michael J. Hillmann, Washington, DC: Mage Publishers.

Perry, J. (2005) *A Tajik Persian Reference Grammar*, Leiden: Brill.

Rastorgueva, V. S. (1963) "A Short Sketch of Tajik Grammar." ed. Herbert Paper, *International Journal of American Linguistics*, 29. [Publication Twenty-eight of the Indiana University Research Center in Anthropology, Folklore and Linguistics.]

Rzehak, L. (1999) *Tadschikische Studiengrammatik*, Berlin: Reichert.

——(2001) *Vom Persischen zum Tadschikischen: Sprachliches Handeln und Sprachplannung in Transoxanien zwischen Tradition, Moderne und Sowjetmacht (1900–1956)*, Berlin: Reichert.

Schoeberlein-Engel, J. S. (1994) "Identity in Central Asia: construction and contention in the conceptions of 'Ozbek,' 'Tajik,' 'Muslim,' 'Samarqandi' and other groups," PhD Dissertation. Harvard University.

Spooner, B. (1994) "Are we teaching Persian? or Farsi? or Dari? or Tojiki?," in M. Marashi (ed.) *Persian Studies in America*, Bethesda, MD: Iranbooks (IBEX Publishers), pp. 175–90.

Sprachman, P. (2002) *Language and Culture in Persian*, Los Angeles: Mazda Publishers.

Subtelny, M. E. (1994) "The symbiosis of Turk and Tajik," in B. Manz (ed.) *Central Central Asia in Historical Perspective*, Boulder, CO: Westview Press, pp. 45–61.

Part III

Australasia

14

Sociolinguistics in Australia

Peter Collins

Introduction

In today's Australia, English is, as it has been since the commencement of White settlement in 1788, the dominant language. Accordingly, I shall focus in the first part of this chapter on the mainstream variety of Australian English ('AusE'), rooted in the country's Anglo-Celtic heritage and recognizable as the national language. At the same time Australia ranks as one of the world's most multilingual countries. Appropriately, therefore, the second part of the chapter is devoted to an examination of the migrant and Aboriginal languages that are in use by more than two million speakers, and in particular the varieties that have developed as a result of contact between these languages and AusE.

Australian English

In its origins a variety transported by British convicts and immigrants, AusE is today recognized as a 'major' variety of English (Svartvik 1997). Its distinctive features suggest that it has consolidated its own norms as an independent national standard. On Schneider's (2003) scale for the dynamics of New Englishes, AusE has, I shall argue, moved beyond the stage of 'endonormative stabilization' during which the transplanted English evolves its own standards and its speakers establish a national linguistic identity. As Australians continue to distinguish themselves from speakers of British and American English, there is a good deal of evidence to suggest that AusE has moved to Schneider's final stage of 'differentiation', at which the varieties develop a capacity to support their own kinds of internal diversification and group-specific identification. While earlier scholars often expressed the view that AusE is remarkable for its homogeneity (for example, Mitchell and Delbridge 1965b; Bernard 1969), linguists today are discovering that there is a good deal more, and more highly structured, variation than was at one time thought to exist. Divergent patterns of usage have been identified for Australians of varying background, particularly those of differing socio-economic status, gender, age, regional provenance, and ethnicity. The discussion that follows is organized around the first four of these variables in turn (while recognizing there is typically a co-occurrence of several of these with particular linguistic variables); the fifth, ethnicity, is taken up in the next section.

Socio-economic background

The phonological distinctiveness of AusE with respect to other World Englishes – most clearly marked in its vowel realizations – has long been recognized. Pioneering work by Mitchell and Delbridge (1965a) identified three sociolects of AusE based on vowel-realization ('Broad', 'General', and 'Cultivated'). The validity of Mitchell and Delbridge's tripartite classification has been widely accepted, despite occasional challenges (for example, Leitner 2004, and Kiesling 2006). It is interesting to note, however, that Mitchell and Delbridge themselves candidly acknowledge that they encountered diffi-culties in determining a valid number of groupings: in their original classification, 29 per cent of informants fell into two borderline groups that did not fit into the tripartite system, but were subsequently collapsed with Broad and Cultivated. In one of the most comprehensive sociolinguistic studies in recent decades, Horvath (1985) uses principal components analysis to identify not three but four sociolects in Sydney, each dis-tinguished by a different percentage of the vowel realizations characteristic of Broad, General and Cultivated. Horvath's research provides one possible explanation for a lin-guistic change which her data show to be in progress, a movement away from the Broad end of the accent continuum among teenagers. According to Horvath, the 'ethnic broad' vowel variants that are used by adult migrants represent a low prestige pattern from which their children seek to distance themselves. This suggestion cannot, however, be regarded as a sufficient explanation for the perceived change, given the well-known stigma associated with the Broad variety which has seen it attract criticism and censure for many years (Mitchell and Delbridge 1965b).

Recent research in Australia has documented the sensitivity of a range of types of phonological variation other than vowel realization to socio-economic, and other, fac-tors. For example, Bradley (2005) has identified variation between monophthongs and offglides in sets of /r/-final words such as *near* and *cure*. He claims that the mono-phthongs are used more in casual speech, by lower socio-economic class speakers and by males, and furthermore that they are more frequent in Sydney than Melbourne. Horvath (2005) claims that the palatalization of the phonemes /t d s z/ when they occur before /u/ in words such as *assume* (/əsjum/ → /əʃum/) is more commonly found with those of lower socio-economic status, especially younger males.

The most widely studied case of variation in AusE (for example, Oasa 1989; Bradley 1991, 2005; Horvath and Horvath 2001) is that between the vowels /æ/ and /a/, var-iously noted to be sensitive to formality and socio-economic status (the higher the degree, the greater the likelihood of /a/), as well as to region (see below).

While the major area of interest in the sociolinguistic investigation of AusE has been segmental phonology, there is one prosodic variable that has attracted keen interest, the so-called Australian Questioning Intonation ('AQI'), or High Rising Terminal ('HRT'). This is the use of the rising contour on declarative clauses which, researchers generally agree, is used more by those with lower socio-economic status, more by teenagers than by adults and more by females than males (for example Guy and Vonwiller 1984, 1989; Horvath 1985, 2005). That AQI is a recent development is suggested by its absence from the tapes of the Mitchell and Delbridge survey (McGregor 1980). There is a popular view that AQI expresses deference or uncertainty, a belief presumably deriving from stereotyped social evaluations of the type of speakers who use it and from the meanings systematically associated with intonational rises in English and other languages. However, as Horvath (1985), Guy and Vonwiller (1989), and others have argued, the register distribution of AQI suggests that its linguistic function requires a different kind of explanation. It is found most commonly in descriptions and narratives, registers where its motivation is less likely to be self-effacement than a need to monitor the listener's engagement and comprehension as the discourse unfolds.

Gender

A number of linguistic variables have been found to co-vary with gender in AusE. These include the variable pronunciation of the present participial suffix -*ing* with /ŋ/ as in *running* or /n/ as in *runnin'*. AusE studies date from the 1970s, with Shopen (1978) reporting that women use the standard /ŋ/ variant more than men, a finding confirmed by Shnukal (1982), who also claims that /n/ realizations are less common in AusE than in BrE or AmE. Another morphophonological variable is the pronunciation of -*thing* in the compounds *anything*, *everything*, *nothing* and *something* with a final /ŋ/ or /k/. Here, again, there is co-variation with gender, but according to Shnukal (1982), it is weaker than with -*ing*.

Chevalier (2006) detects gender-sensitive variation in some features of lexical morphology. For instance, the suffixes -/i/ and -*o* exhibit gender-differentiated patterns of use in AusE. According to Chevalier, -/i/ carries associations of 'childishness' (or 'femaleness') when attached to given names, while -*o* — a marker of Australianness — tends to be associated with male names more commonly than with female names. The clipping of names, too, is sensitive to gender in AusE: according to Chevalier, straightforward clipping (e.g. *Jan* < *Janice*; *Zac* < *Zachary*) is considerably more common with male names than female names, while that involving *z*-final forms (e.g. *Gaz* < *Garry* and *Woz* < *Warwick*), has spread from its fairly recently male working-class origins across the gender divide and the socio-economic spectrum.

Age

Various studies of grammatical features of AusE suggest differential practices among younger and older speakers. For instance, Collins and Peters (2005) report a survey of verb morphology involving over 1100 respondents which revealed that it is younger Australians who are more likely to simplify verb paradigms via use of a preterite form which is syncretized with the past participle. For more than two-thirds of the under-25s, *shrunk*, *sunk*, *sprung* were in use as preterite forms, as opposed to about half of those under 45. Age grading was also noted in survey results for irregular past participles such as *gotten*, *sawn*, *striven*, and *woven*, support for which was strongest among the over-45s. Collins (2005), a study of the modals and semi-modals of necessity, finds support for the view that there has been an upsurge in the popularity of *have to* in AusE at the expense of *must* in his finding that *have to* was considerably more popular than *must* in the speech of under-45 speakers, while *must* maintained ascendancy with the over-45s across all age groups in writing.

Phonological changes prompted in recent AusE by American English influence have been discussed by Taylor (1989). Such variation is not systematic but rather associated with the pronunciation of individual words, and tends to be age-related. Thus it is younger Australians who are more likely to pronounce *schedule* as /skedʒul/ rather than /ʃedʒul/, *lieutenant* as /lutenənt/ rather than /leftenənt/, and *anti-* as /æntaɪ/ rather than

/ænti/. American influence would also seem to be behind the preference amongst younger speakers for pronunciations of disyllabic nouns with the stress on the first syllable such as *address* /'ædres/ and defence /'difens/, although Peters (1998) suggests that such changes reflect more general tendencies within English and are not attributable specifically to American influence.

Region

Variation between the vowels /æ/ and /a/ in AusE, discussed above, is sensitive not just to formality and socio-economic status, but also to region (with Adelaide having the strongest preference for /a/ of the capital cities). Bradley (2003) suggests that regional variation here is associated with settlement patterns (with older-established cities such as Sydney and Melbourne having a wider socio-economic spread in their populations and thus more social stratification for /æ/ ~ /a/). Two further instances of regional phonological variation are /l/ vocalization, which in a study by Horvath and Horvath (2002) was found to occur only 7 per cent of the time in Brisbane but 33 per cent in Adelaide, and the prelateral merging of /æ/ and /e/ which occurs predominantly with Melbourne speakers (resulting in some cases in a loss of the distinction between minimal pairs such as *pellet/pallet* and *telly/tally*).

Extensive work on regional lexical variation in AusE has been conducted by Bryant (1989, 1991, 1997), who observes that its largely unobtrusive nature has caused it to go generally unrecognized. Many of the lexical items in question are mundane in nature and may form sets of synonyms for speakers to choose from (for example, *peanut butter* ~ *peanut paste*; *suitcase* ~ *port*; *slippery dip* ~ *slippery slide*). Bryant identifies four areas of lexical usage (North East, South East, South Centre and South West) which account for almost one-third of Australia's landmass, leaving most of the rest yet to be studied. The boundaries of these areas do not correspond exactly with state borders (for instance, the South East includes Victoria and Tasmania along with parts of South Australia and New South Wales) even though when speakers are aware of regionally distinctive words they tend to associate them with interstate differences.

A number of the lexical items studied by Bryant are not true synonyms, or at least not for some speakers. For example, Bryant notes (1989: 310) that the large, smooth, bland sausage with red skin that is usually thinly sliced and eaten cold, and variously named *devon*, *German sausage*, *pork German*, *Strasburg/Stras*, *polony*, *Belgian sausage*, and *fritz*, varies in taste from area to area. Such non-synonymy is also a facet of lexical variation that crosses country lines. Pairs such as *biscuit/cookie*, *lift/elevator*, *trousers/pants* (labelled 'heteronyms' by Görlach 1990) are generally thought of as 'British' or 'American' alternatives, even though the older, more conservative 'British' term may not be exclusively British. The more innovative 'American' terms are associated with community complaints about 'Americanization' and cultural domination (see Taylor 2001), and rarely as a form of lexical enrichment.

LOTEs and ethnic varieties

In Australia today more than 200 languages other than English (LOTEs) are in use, including both migrant languages (whose speakers have increased dramatically in number since the end of World War II), and also a number of surviving Aboriginal languages, used by a rapidly decreasing number of speakers. Between these languages on the one hand, and Standard AusE on the other, we find a diverse set of varieties. Two of these, to which I shall pay particular attention in this section, are identifiably English varieties (with features determined by the ethnicity of their speakers): Aboriginal Australian English and Pan-ethnic Australian English. The first is a relatively stable and homogeneous variety, but the second is not, and its existence is here posited with less confidence.

Aboriginal languages and Aboriginal English

The linguistic context in which the White settlers planted their English language in 1788 was one comprising many different Aboriginal languages, a number of which were typologically related (mainly those along the coastal areas of New South Wales, Western Australia and South Australia). Most of these languages have long since disappeared, and of the hundred or so that survive today, only a few are sufficiently robust to have any chance of surviving into the foreseeable future. Aboriginal languages are inseparably linked to the land and to the identity of their speakers. The arrival of the colonists irreparably damaged this fundamental union, with the Aborigines being progressively dispossessed of their land, then of their languages. The latter were regarded by the colonists as inferior to English and as an obstacle to their learning of English.

It is generally agreed that the development of the indigenized variety of English that is generally referred to in Australia as Aboriginal English ('AbE') was preceded by the pidginization and creolization of English during the early years after colonization (Dixon 1980), a development which undoubtedly followed different paths in different regions. In some areas, such as New South Wales, pidgins and probably creoles existed where only English is now spoken; in others (the Kimberley, the Northern Territory and Cape York Peninsula), varieties of AbE co-exist today with creoles. In other locations, such as southern Western Australia, there may never have been sustained use of a pidgin or creole by a locally-based community.

According to Troy (1993), the first stage of pidgin/creole development began shortly after contact, with Aboriginal people exposed to a range of social and regional varieties of English brought by the colonists, as well as contact varieties from other parts of the Pacific. She suggests that there developed at this stage a jargonized – and stigmatized – variety incorporating many transfers from Aboriginal languages, whose use with other Aboriginal people led within the first half a century to the development of NSW Pidgin English. This localized variety was to be the agent of wide-ranging changes, serving as a lingua franca along traditional trade routes and subsequently permeating a large part of Aboriginal Australia.

The commonality of features displayed today by varieties of AbE across the continent is attributable in part to its inheritance from New South Wales Pidgin, but no doubt also to a process of convergence, or *koinéization*, whereby 'the culturally integrated, increasingly mobile, and nationally-oriented speech community of Aboriginal Australia is expressing its perceived commonality in a reduction of variants, although retaining some degree of stylistic and regional variation' (Malcolm 2001: 214–15). AbE today serves the important role of helping to relate Aboriginal speakers to their shared past and providing some compensation for the rapid extinction of their languages.

What are the distinctive features of contemporary AbE? Most salient, at least for non-Aboriginal observers, is its phonological system. Some recognizable features include such simplifications as the reduction of vowel contrasts and of consonant clusters, blurring of the voiced/voiceless distinction with consonants, non-neutralization of vowels in unstressed positions, and absence of initial unstressed vowels in word like *along*. The phonology of AbE is more variable than that of AusE and, in less restructured (or 'heavy') varieties, may share features with creoles as well as with substrate languages, as in the non-articulation of sibilant, interdental and labiodental consonants, or in their being supplanted by transferred variants (Malcolm 2001: 215). Also distinctive are prosodic features such as stress shifting to the initial syllable as in /'kæŋgəru/ for *kangaroo* (compare AusE /kæŋgə'ru/), and increased use of AQI.

Grammatical differences from AusE include the absence of *be* (both the copula and the auxiliary), variable expression of the past tense, regularization of subject–verb agreement, formation of the future with *gonna*, signalling of questions intonationally rather than syntactically via subject/auxiliary inversion, optional marking of plurality and possession in noun phrases, retention in less structured varieties of the dual vs plural and inclusive vs exclusive distinctions found in creoles, variable occurrence of definite and indefinite articles (and use of the distinctive forms *dat* and *one*).

AbE also displays some distinctive lexical and pragmatic features. While the lexicon comprises mainly English-based lexemes, sometimes with shifted meanings, there are also items transferred from Aboriginal languages. Pragmatic principles are followed which show a continuity with Aboriginal languages, including avoidance of eye contact, long inter-turn pausing, and avoidance of disagreement.

Migrant languages and ethnolects

It is not possible here to provide more than a thumbnail sketch of the transformation of Australia from an essentially British, Anglophone country in the late nineteenth century to a multicultural/multilingual nation whose primary orientation is now towards Asia and the Pacific. Migrant language diversity was insignificant in colonial Australia until the discovery of gold, and political events in Europe, prompted a flood of immigration. Bilingual schools facilitated the maintenance of home languages until the end of the century, when community settlement patterns began to change and changes to education laws made it difficult to retain fee-paying bilingual schools. Nationalistic and xenophobic attitudes in the years leading up to, and following, WWI provoked strong antagonism to community languages. After WWII, immigration was encouraged, with Italy and Greece being the most prolific sources, until the 1980s, when the number of speakers of Arabic and Asian languages began to increase rapidly (and in fact if Cantonese and Mandarin are counted together as 'Chinese', then Italian lost its mantle as the most widely spoken migrant language between the 1996 and 2001 censuses). The success of the various migrant communities in maintaining their languages is dependent upon a range of factors (including numerical strength, cultural similarity, and marriage patterns). The rate of shift to English is consistently greater for second generation than first generation speakers, and for males than females, but differs greatly across communities (very high for German and Dutch speakers, very low for the Greeks and Chinese).

The ethnicity of many second and later generation Australians is marked by their adoption of varieties of English referred to by Clyne, Eisikovits and Tollree (2001: 223) and others as 'ethnolects'. Ethnolects reflect the learning process of their users, and display varying levels of interference from the native language (such as loss of plural inflections on nouns and tense inflections on verbs). They are mainly used in the home domain with parents and grandparents, sometimes in conjunction with a LOTE, and signal their speakers' multiple identities.

Despite the fact that migrants of non-English-speaking background do not constitute a single group, a number of commentators have identified a pan-ethnic variety popularly known as 'Wogspeak' (Warren 1999; Kiesling 2005), used especially by young Australians of second generation Middle Eastern and Mediterranean background. This variety serves as a strong badge of identity enabling its speakers to differentiate themselves from both their parents' values and those of the Anglo host culture. Some of the features of this variety noted by Warren (1999), and Clyne, Eisikovits and Tollfree (2001) are the avoidance of reduced vowels (as in the use of [a] in the final syllable of a word such as *pleasure*), the replacement of /θ/ and ð/ by /t/ and /d/, along with grammatical features such as double negation.

Conclusion

The Australian varieties overviewed in this chapter are continually changing. What does the future hold? There is, I have argued, evidence aplenty that AusE is – as predicted by Schneider's (2003) model – in a period of internal stratification and differentiation. There is no reason to doubt that the formation and intensification of social and regional dialects will continue, particularly in Australia's urban centres. It is furthermore likely that some of these changes will continue to be led by young speakers of ethnic background (Horvath 1985). Aboriginal languages will no doubt continue to disappear and other LOTEs will continue to shift and/or be lost as their speakers are assimilated into the mainstream. Meanwhile, more speculatively, we may foresee an increasing role for AusE as an epicentre in the Asia Pacific region (Leitner 2004).

References

Bernard, J. (1969) 'On the uniformity of spoken Australian English', *Orbis*, 18, 62–73.
Bradley, D. (1991) '/æ/ and /a:/ in Australian English', in J. Cheshire (ed.) *English around the World: Sociolinguistic Perspectives*, Cambridge: Cambridge University Press, pp. 227–34.
——(2003) 'Mixed sources of Australian English', *Australian Journal of Linguistics*, 23, 143–50.
——(2005) 'Regional characteristics of Australian English: phonology', in E. W. Schneider and B. Kortmann (eds) *A Handbook of Varieties of English: A Multimedia Reference Tool*, vol. 1, Berlin: Mouton de Gruyter, pp. 645–55.
Bryant, P. (1989) 'Regional variation in the Australian lexicon', in P. Collins and D. Blair (eds) *Australian English: The Language of a New Society*, St. Lucia, Queensland: University of Queensland Press, pp. 301–14.
——(1991) 'A survey of regional usage in the lexicon of Australian English', in S. Romaine (ed.) *Language in Australia*, Cambridge: Cambridge University Press, pp. 287–303.
——(1997) 'A dialect survey of the lexicon of Australian English', *English World-Wide*, 18, 211–41.
Chevalier, S. (2006) *Ava to Zac: A Sociolinguistic Study of Given Names and Nicknames in Australia*, Tübingen: Francke Verlag.
Clyne, M., Eisikovits, E. and Tollfree, L. (2001) 'Ethnic varieties of Australian English', in D. Blair and P. Collins (eds) *English in Australia*, Amsterdam: John Benjamins, pp. 223–38.
Collins, P. (2005) 'The modals and quasi-modals of obligation and necessity in Australian English and other Englishes', *English World-Wide*, 26, 249–73.
Collins, P. and Peters, P. (2005) 'Australian English morphology and syntax', in E. W. Schneider and B. Kortmann (eds) *A Handbook of Varieties of English: A Multimedia Reference Tool*, vol. 1, Berlin: Mouton de Gruyter.

Dixon, R. M. W. (1980) *The Languages of Australia*, Cambridge: Cambridge University Press.

Görlach, M. (1990) *Studies in the History of the English Language*, Heidelberg: Carl Winter.

Guy, G. and Vonwiller, J. (1984) 'The meaning of an intonation in Australian English', *Australian Journal of Linguistics*, 4, 1–17.

——(1989) 'The high rising tone in Australian English', in P. Collins and D. Blair (eds) *Australian English: The Language of a New Society*, St. Lucia, Queensland: University of Queensland Press, pp. 21–34.

Horvath, B. (1985) *Variation in Australian English: The Sociolects of Sydney*, Cambridge: Cambridge University Press.

——(2005) 'Australian English: Phonology', in E. W. Schneider and B. Kortmann (eds) *A Handbook of Varieties of English: A Multimedia Reference Tool*, vol. 1, Berlin: Mouton de Gruyter, pp. 625–64.

Horvath, B. and Horvath, R. (2001) 'A geolinguistics of short A in Australian English', in D. Blair and P. Collins (eds) *English in Australia*, Amsterdam: John Benjamins, pp. 341–55.

——(2002) 'The geolinguistics of /l/ vocalization in Australia and New Zealand', *Journal of Sociolinguistics*, 6, 319–46.

Kiesling, S. F. (2005) 'Variation, style and stance: word-final -er and ethnicity in Australian English', *English World-Wide*, 26, 1–42.

——(2006) 'English in Australia and new Zealand', in B. Kachru, Y. Kachru and C. L. Nelson (eds) *The Handbook of World Englishes*, Oxford: Blackwell, pp. 74–89.

Leitner, G. (2004) *Australia's Many Voices: Ethnic Englishes, Indigenous and Migrant Languages, Policy and Education*, Berlin: Mouton de Gruyter.

Malcolm, I. G. (2001) 'Aboriginal English: adopted code of a surviving culture', in D. Blair and P. Collins (eds) *English in Australia*, Amsterdam: John Benjamins, pp. 201–22.

McGregor, R. L. (1980) 'The social distribution of an Australian English intonation contour', *Working Papers (Macquarie University Speech and Language Research Centre)*, 2, 1–26.

Mitchell, A. and Delbridge, A. (1965a) *The Speech of Australian Adolescents*, Sydney: Angus and Robertson.

——(1965b) *The Pronunciation of English in Australia*, Sydney: Angus and Robertson.

Oasa, H. (1989) 'Phonology of current Adelaide English', in P. Collins and D. Blair (eds) *Australian English: The Language of a New Society*, St. Lucia, Queensland: University of Queensland Press, pp. 271–87.

Peters, P. (1998) 'Australian English', in P. Bell and R. Bell (eds) *Americanization and Australia*, Sydney: UNSW Press, pp. 32–44.

Schneider, E. W. (2003) 'The dynamics of new Englishes: from identity construction to dialect birth', *Language*, 79, 233–81.

Shnukal, A. (1982) 'You're gettin' somethink for nothing: two phonological variables of Australian English', *Australian Journal of Linguistics*, 2, 197–212.

Shopen, T. (1978) 'Research on the variable (ING) in Canberra, Australia', *Talanya*, 5, 42–52.

Svartvik, J. (1997) 'Varieties of English: major and minor', in H. Lindquist *et al.* (eds) *The Major Varieties of English*, Växjö: Växjö University Press, pp. 15–27.

Taylor, B. (1989) 'American, British and other foreign influences on Australian English since World War II', in P. Collins and D. Blair (eds) *Australian English: The Language of a New Society*, St. Lucia, Queensland: University of Queensland Press, pp. 225–54.

——(2001) 'Australian English in interaction with other Englishes', in D. Blair and P. Collins (eds) *English in Australia*, Amsterdam: John Benjamins, pp. 317–40.

Troy, J. (1993) 'Language contact in early colonial New South Wales 1788 to 1781', in M. Walsh and C. Yallop (eds) *Language and Culture in Aboriginal Australia*, Canberra: Aboriginal Studies Press, pp. 33–50.

Warren, J. (1999) '"Wogspeak": transformations of Australian English', *Journal of Australian Studies*, 62, 86–94.

15

Sociolinguistics in New Zealand

Margaret Maclagan and Jennifer Hay

Introduction

New Zealand consists of three main islands in the southern Pacific Ocean. It is distant from all surrounding countries. Its nearest neighbour, Australia, is 1600 km to the west. The country was first settled by the Maori, who arrived approximately 1000 years ago. Europeans started to arrive in the late eighteenth century. In 1840, the Treaty of Waitangi established British sovereignty in New Zealand and following this, immigration of English-speaking colonists increased greatly (see King 2003, for a general history).

New Zealand has three official languages: English, Maori and New Zealand Sign Language, with English being the most commonly used. Maori make up approximately 14 per cent of the population, and are distributed throughout the country, although concentrated in the north and east of the North Island. Pacific Islanders have been immigrating to New Zealand for some time and now make up 7 per cent of the population. They are concentrated more in the North Island, with Auckland sometimes described as the largest Pacific Island city in the world. Recent immigration from Asia has seen the number of Asians rise to 6 per cent. These immigrants are usually of Chinese descent and their languages can be heard in areas with concentrated Asian populations, such as Christchurch.

Sociolinguistic research in New Zealand

New Zealand is one of the youngest native speaker varieties of English in the world. Its relatively recent origins mean that recordings are available for all of its history (see description of the ONZE project, below). New Zealand English is also one of the most studied varieties of English in the world. Initial studies focused on pronunciation – the most noticeable feature from the perspective of non-New Zealanders. Vocabulary, especially borrowings from Maori, was another early focus. Little work was done on syntax because there were assumed to be few differences between NZE syntax and the syntax of other varieties. The origins of NZE and its relationship with British English and

Australian English have also been a focus of study. A comprehensive bibliography of work on NZE is currently available on line at www.vuw.ac.nz/lals/staff/john-macalister/nzej%20a-zlist.aspx. For a description of earlier work on NZE, see Gordon et al. (2004, Chapter 2) and for an annotated bibliography, see Chapter 7 of Hay, Maclagan and Gordon (2008). *New Zealand Sociology* produced a special issue (16 (1) 2001) on socio-linguistics in New Zealand. A general overview of NZE phonetics and phonology is provided by Bauer and Warren (2004) and of Maori English by Warren and Bauer (2004). An overview of regional and social variation in NZE is given in Gordon and Maclagan (2004).

Major sociolinguistic research projects

Sociolinguistic Research in NZ has been centred in four areas round the country: Auckland (University of Auckland and Auckland University of Technology), Wellington (Victoria University of Wellington), Christchurch (University of Canterbury) and Dunedin (University of Otago).

Auckland

In Auckland, a recent focus has been a project led by Bell and Starks, which examines the Languages of South Auckland. Continuing research focuses on the Pasifika languages within NZ, with particular attention to Tongan, Samoan, Nuiean and Cook Islands Maori. The project has looked at language maintenance within the local communities and also features of the English of the groups (see Taumoefolau et al. 2002; Massam et al. 2006; Starks and Reffell 2006). In his earlier work, Bell also conducted seminal research on style and audience design, including his classic paper (1984) which examined the speech of presenters on Auckland radio stations (see also Bell 2001).

Wellington

Victoria University of Wellington has been the site of much sociolinguistic data gathering and analysis. The Porirua Project was the first large-scale Labovian project conducted in New Zealand, and was started at Victoria University in 1989 under Holmes and Bell. This later developed into the Wellington Social Dialect Survey and involved socio-linguistic interviews of a stratified sample of Maori and Pakeha[1] (see Holmes et al. 1991). Data collection for the Wellington Corpus of Spoken English also started in 1989 (see Bauer 1994; Holmes 1995, 1996; Holmes et al. 1998; Vine 1999). Laurie Bauer directed collection of written material and Holmes directed collection of spoken material for this 3 million-word corpus with three sections: the Wellington Corpus of Written NZE, the Wellington Corpus of Spoken NZE, and the New Zealand component of the International Corpus of English (ICE). Both corpora have been used for numerous analyses of NZE in areas as diverse as features of Maori English (Holmes 1997), /t/-flapping in NZE (Bauer and Holmes 1996) and generic pronouns in NZE (Holmes 1998b). Warren is currently directing collection of material for the third major database at Victoria: the New Zealand Spoken English Database (NZSED). This is based on the Australian National Database of Spoken Language (ANDOSL) and, among other areas, targets phonetic variables of interest to NZE: -ing, t-voicing, final glottals, ear/air diphthongs, the High Rising Terminal intonation pattern, l-vocalization and h-dropping (see www.vuw.ac.nz/lals/staff/paul-warren/nzsed/index.htm).

An area of particular focus at Victoria has been the study of language and gender, which has been much studied by Holmes and her students (Holmes 1998a, 2000). Holmes has recently shifted away from variationist work, focusing more on discourse analysis, though still with a strong language and gender angle. She currently directs the Language in the Workplace (LWP) project which recorded interactions with individuals and team meetings in diverse workplaces. Analysis of this data-set has focused on pragmatic aspects of language: directives (Vine 2004), leadership (Holmes 2005), humour (Holmes 2006), expletives (Daly *et al.* 2004), and women's language (Holmes and Marra 2004). This project has recently been extended to consider the language of leadership in Maori as well as Pakeha organizations.

Ongoing developments in NZE vocabulary are documented in *NZWords* – the Newsletter of the New Zealand Dictionary Centre which is also at Victoria (www.vuw.ac.nz/lals/research/nzdc/). The centre also conducts research on various aspects of language in New Zealand and compiles and publishes dictionaries and related educational materials. Playground vocabulary is a specific area that was studied by Laurie and Winifred Bauer (see Bauer and Bauer 2000, 2003, 2005) who considered names for playground games and found that the country could be divided into three main dialect areas. An interesting finding from this study was that Cook Strait, which divides the North and South Islands, did not usually serve as a dialect boundary.

Also at Victoria is the Deaf Studies Research Unit, which is in the process of completing a Labovian variationist study on New Zealand Sign Language. This project is still in progress, and is led by David and Rachel McKee (McKee 2001; Napier *et al.*, 2006). For details of the project, see www.vuw.ac.nz/lals/research/deafstudies/DSRU%20site/index.aspx.

Christchurch

Sociolinguistic research at the University of Canterbury was initiated by Gordon. Her interest in the history of NZE led her to search written records for clues to the origins and development of the variety (Gordon 1998). She was instrumental in acquiring the Mobile Unit (MU) archive for the University of Canterbury and in setting up the Origins of New Zealand English project (ONZE) (www.ling.canterbury.ac.nz/onze/). After the Second World War, a Mobile Broadcasting Unit of the New Zealand Broadcasting Service travelled round the country recording, among other things, pioneer reminiscences. The recordings are held at the Radio New Zealand Sound Archives, Ngā Taonga Kōrero (www.soundarchives.co.nz). A copy of the Mobile Unit (MU) archive now forms part of the ONZE project.

As well as the MU archive (speakers born between 1851 and 1915), the ONZE corpus contains the Intermediate Archive (IA) (speakers born between 1890 and 1930) and the Canterbury Corpus (CC) (speakers born between 1930 and 1985). The archives cover the whole history of NZE. Data collection is ongoing, with speakers being added to the CC each year by undergraduate students. The ONZE resources have allowed researchers at Canterbury to trace the development of the NZE accent from its origins to the present day (Gordon *et al.* 2004) and to track ongoing changes in NZE (Maclagan 1998; Maclagan *et al.* 1999; Baird 2001). Researchers also use NZE as a test case for exploring wider areas of theoretical interest such as theories of dialect contact and mixing, /r/-sandhi and

161

phonological theory (Hay and Sudbury 2005) and chain shifts and vowel movements (Langstrof 2006a, 2006b).

A major development has been the database management system ONZE Miner (www.ling.canterbury.ac.nz/jen/onzeminer/), a browser-based linguistic research tool that stores audio recordings and associated time-aligned text transcripts and facilitates searches for particular text items or regular expressions. All items of a particular phoneme can be found in the whole data base or in particular speakers, with details saved automatically in a spreadsheet. Hours of scrolling through tapes or CDs are thus saved as the researcher can listen immediately to the relevant sound. It also allows swift retrieval of all examples of a particular grammatical structure.

An ongoing Canterbury-based project that involves change over time is the NEAR/ SQUARE study. The original study used auditory analysis of real-time data to trace the progress of the merger of NEAR and SQUARE in NZE (Gordon and Maclagan 2001). More recent research has related perception and production of NEAR and SQUARE and found that listeners' judgement accuracy is still above chance, even when they are convinced that they are guessing (Hay *et al.* 2006). Perception studies using exemplar theory are currently exploring social factors that influence perception – using the NEAR/SQUARE merger, as well as other vocalic variables in studies by Hay, Nolan and Drager (2006), and Hay, Warren and Drager (2006) (see also Thomas and Hay 2006, Warren *et al.* 2007). The ongoing collaboration between Hay from the University of Canterbury and Warren from Victoria University of Wellington demonstrates that separating research by geographic centre as we have done here is somewhat artificial.

Earlier work in Canterbury considered attitudes to NZE (Gordon 1997). Canterbury-based work in the vocabulary area has primarily focused on register. Kuiper pioneered this work with his studies of horse racing, auctioneering and sports (Hickey and Kuiper 2000, Kuiper 2001). Register study is perhaps most dramatically illustrated by Looser's investigation of 'boob slang', the speech of prison inmates (Looser 2004). Looser's work covers every prison in New Zealand. Deverson (2000) provides a theoretical framework within which NZE vocabulary can be considered.

The MAONZE project (Maori and New Zealand English www.ece.auckland.ac.nz/ ~cwat057/MAONZE/MAONZE.html) is based at Canterbury under Maclagan and King. The other researchers are Harlow (Waikato) and Watson and Keegan (Auckland). This project is tracing sound change over time in both Maori and English using three groups of Maori speakers. Changes have been found in both the quality and the quantity of the long–short Maori vowel pairs and also differences in the speech of young first and second language speakers of Maori (Harlow *et al.* 2009).

Dunedin

Bayard directed sociolinguistic work at the University of Otago in Dunedin. His major area of interest was attitudes. He applied the term 'cultural cringe' to New Zealanders' attitudes towards their own variety of English and used subjective reaction tests to evaluate various speakers (see, e.g. Bayard *et al.* 2001). Recent versions of these attitude surveys have been carried out via the web, where people listen to the speakers and complete the rating on-line, and have extended the study to include comparative international data. The 'Evaluating English Accents Worldwide' website can be found at www.otago.ac.nz/anthropology/Linguistic/Accents.html. The project continues to run, under the leadership of Green. A new area of research into language and medicine is also emerging – being led by Green, based in the School of Pharmacy, and Maria Stubbe, in the School of Medicine and Health Sciences. There has also been some variationist work at Otago. For example, Bartlett carried out a Labovian-style study of the Southland dialect (Bartlett 2003).

Research themes

In this section we highlight some of the main research themes that have been the focus of sociolinguists working in New Zealand. This is necessarily incomplete, and is also biased towards phonetics/phonology. This bias may partially reflect our own research backgrounds, but is appropriate, given that most sociolinguistic work in NZ is sound-system oriented.

The Maori language and Maori English

Description and analysis of Maori have been carried out by Winifred Bauer (1997) and Harlow (2007) building on earlier work by Biggs. Three papers by Harlow, Mutu and Chrisp in issue 172 of the *International Journal of the Sociology of Language* (Harlow 2005; Mutu 2005; Chrisp 2005) illustrate the range of linguistic research that is currently being carried out on the Maori language. Perhaps the most notable recent contribution in the area of Maori language is Boyce's one million-word *Corpus of Spoken Maori* (Boyce 2006). Current research on Maori language focuses mainly on aspects of the revitalization of the language and is spearheaded by three main research groups. The Maori language research unit at Te Puni Kokiri (Ministry of Maori Development) is headed by Chrisp. As a government agency, Te Puni Kokiri is responsible for producing demographic information about the numbers of speakers of Maori and their level of fluency. Reports are available from: www.tpk.govt.nz/publications/subject/default.asp#language

The second research group is based at Massey. *Te Hoe Nuku Roa*, a longitudinal Maori household survey of 550 households, correlates a range of cultural, economic and personal factors, including language use. For linguistic results and analysis based on this research, see Christensen (2003).

The third research group centres on the University of Auckland where nineteenth- and twentieth-century Maori newspapers have been put online at www.nzdl.org. Linguistic analysis from this resource is contained in Curnow, Hopa and McRae (2002). Te Taka Keegan from the University of Waikato, who was involved in aspects of this research, has published a number of papers dealing with the interface between indigenous languages and the internet (see www.cs.waikato.ac.nz/~tetaka/tuhinga.html).

Maori English was first identified as the English variety of speakers for whom Maori was their first and more fluent language. As recently as 1991, Benton (1991) queried whether or not Maori English existed as a distinct variety of NZE. However, Maori English is now acknowledged as the most rapidly developing variety of NZE. Most speakers of Maori English are themselves Maori, but not all Maori speak Maori English, and Pakeha who live and work with Maori also speak it. Researchers from around the country have studied features of Maori English and compared it with Pakeha NZE. The general consensus is that, rather than having unique features, Maori English differs from Pakeha New Zealand English in the degree to which features such as syllable timing are used (see Maclagan *et al.* 2008, for a description and summary). Szakay (2008) investigated

163

the suprasegmental features listeners expected from Maori speakers and the features Maori speakers actually used. A fruitful area of research has been the extent to which Maori words have become accepted into NZE vocabulary (Kennedy 2001; Bartlett 2002; Macalister 2005, 2006; Davies and Maclagan 2006).

Origins of New Zealand English

Researchers at Canterbury used the ONZE archives to trace the development of the NZE accent from its origins to the present day (Gordon *et al.* 2004). Before that, Gordon (1998) had used written records to reconstruct the origins of NZE and Gordon and Trudgill (1999) had found precursors of modern NZE sound changes in early NZ speakers. Bauer (1999) and Trudgill, Maclagan and Lewis (2003) focused on Scottish influences in the development of NZE.

Chain-shifting

The NZE short front vowels KIT, DRESS and TRAP[2] have been involved in a chain shift since the time of the earliest speakers of NZE (Gordon *et al.* 2004). DRESS and TRAP have raised and KIT has centralized and lowered. One question of interest has been whether this shift was a pull-chain led by KIT, or a push chain initiated by TRAP. Initial analysis of written records (Gordon 1998) indicated that KIT had centralized early in the twentieth century, suggesting a pull chain, but later analysis showed that KIT had only centralized in unstressed syllables. Bell (1997) compared Pakeha and Maori speakers and Woods (2000) considered three generations of speakers and suggested that a push chain was more likely. Gordon *et al.* (2004) showed that TRAP was already raised for early NZ speakers in the Mobile Unit. TRAP continued to raise over the time, and DRESS also started to raise. In contrast, there was very little movement for KIT over this period. Langstrof (2006a) traced the centralization and lowering of KIT in speakers born between 1890 and 1930, showing that it was the last of the front vowels to move, and confirming that KIT, DRESS and TRAP have been involved in a push chain-shift. DRESS has continued to raise until, for some speakers, it is higher than FLEECE and FLEECE is showing increased diphthongization in response (Maclagan and Hay 2007).

This push chain-shift is theoretically interesting, because the direction of shifting seems contrary to most other known chain shifts, in which short vowels tend to fall. Recent work on the NZ front vowels has argued that the distinction between short and long vowel sub-systems may have broken down in NZE (Langstrof 2006b).

Vowel merger

There are a number of vowel mergers in NZE. By far the most studied is the merger between the vowels in NEAR and SQUARE (see Gordon and Maclagan 2001). In addition to studying the trajectory of the merger, researchers have investigated whether speakers produce a greater distinction between the diphthongs when the context is ambiguous (Kennedy 2004), whether listeners who make the merger are able to distinguish between the vowels when others make them (Kennedy 2004; Warren *et al.* 2007) and the different ways in which NEAR and SQUARE words prime other words (Rae and Warren 2002). Another merger that has received attention involves vowels before /l/ (Thomas and Hay 2006).

Rhoticity and /r/-sandhi

Modern NZE is a non-rhotic variety of English, so that word final or pre-consonantal /r/ as in *letter* or *bird* is not pronounced except by some speakers in Southland (see the section on dialects below). However, NZE speakers regularly use /r/-sandhi, both linking /r/ as in *car alarm* and intrusive /r/ as in *law-r-and order*. One of the findings of the ONZE project was that there was much more rhoticity than had been expected amongst early New Zealanders. This has been used to argue that rhoticity may have been lost in some dialects of British English later than had previously been thought (Gordon *et al.* 2004: 172–6).

Hay and Sudbury (2005) used the Mobile Unit archive to trace the development from the partial rhoticity of the earliest NZE speakers through to the current NZE /r/-sandhi use of linking and intrusive /r/. Other researchers have investigated /r/ use in modern NZE. Gibson (2005) found that young North Island speakers involved in the hip-hop culture used post-vocalic /r/, though usually only in the NURSE vowel.

Suprasegmentals

Two areas attract particular attention within suprasegmental features: rhythm and the final rising intonation pattern on non-questions, called the High Rising Terminal. Maori English has long been regarded as more syllable-timed than other varieties of NZE. Using auditory analysis, Holmes and Ainsworth (1997) found that Maori speakers used more full vowels in grammatical words in casual conversation than Pakeha speakers while Warren (1998) used acoustic analysis and the Pairwise Vowel Index (PVI, see Grabe and Low 2002) to show that all varieties of broadcast NZE were more syllable-timed than BBC broadcasters, but that speakers on Maori radio stations were even more syllable-timed than other New Zealanders. The relative syllable-timing of Maori English has been confirmed by Szakay (2008), but, in contrast to Warren's (1998) radio broadcasters, Szakay's 12 Pakeha speakers had PVI values similar to those found by Grabe and Low (2002) for British English.

Early work found that High Rising Terminals (HRTs) are more common in NZE than in Australian English and that they have similar functions in both varieties, serving as a feedback mechanism. They are particularly common at the start and end of narratives (Warren and Britain 2000) and in establishing rapport. HRTs are particularly common in Maori English. Warren (2005) found differences in the way men and women produced HRTs and also differences between the formation of HRTs and questions asking for information.

Dialects within NZE

The only dialect area on which linguists have traditionally agreed is Southland in the south of the South Island. This area originally had a higher proportion of Scottish settlers and traces of their influence still linger in some grammatical forms, such as *the cat wants fed* rather than *the cat wants to be fed*, and in traces of post-vocalic /r/ which is now confined to the NURSE vowel as in *girl* or *work* (Bartlett 2003). Ainsworth (2004) found evidence of distinct intonation patterns in Taranaki in the North Island, but other attempts to find regional dialect differences have been unsuccessful. In spite of this, New Zealanders are convinced that there are regional differences around the country, as shown by folk dialectology studies (Gordon 1997; Neilsen and Hay 2006).

Conclusion

Sociolinguistic studies are one of the most fruitful areas in the study of NZE. Socio-linguists have both analysed the variation within NZE and also used NZE as a testing ground to answer questions about variation in general. Both the work that has recently been put into collecting and annotating large corpora, together with a new batch of young scholars working in the field, bode well for the continuing success and vibrancy of sociolinguistic work in New Zealand.

Acknowledgements

We thank Jeanette King and Ray Harlow for information about research on Maori in New Zealand, and Elizabeth Gordon for helpful comments.

Notes

1 *Pakeha* is the term used to indicate a New Zealander of European origin.
2 We use Wells's (1982) KEY WORDS, where each vowel is surrounded by unique consonants to distinguish phonemes, and all words that contain that phoneme. NEAR thus represents the phoneme /ɪə/ and also the set of words such as *here, cheer, beer, fear* that include this phoneme.

References

Ainsworth, H. (2004) 'Regional variation in New Zealand English intonation: Taranaki versus Wellington', unpublished PhD thesis, Victoria University of Wellington.

Baird, S. (2001) 'How "to be like" a Kiwi: verbs of quotation in New Zealand English', *New Zealand English Journal*, 15, 6–19.

Bartlett, C. (2003) 'The Southland variety of English: postvocalic /r/ and the BATH vowel', unpublished PhD thesis, University of Otago.

Bartlett, M. (2002) 'UTU: a bit of give and take?', *NZ Words*, 6, 6–7.

Bauer, L. (1994) 'Introducing the Wellington Corpus of Spoken New Zealand English', *Te Reo*, 37, 21–8.

——(1999) 'The origins of the New Zealand English accent', *English World-Wide*, 20, 287–307.

——(2000) 'The dialectal origins of New Zealand English', in A. Bell and K. Kuiper (eds) *New Zealand English*. Wellington, NZ: Victoria University Press, pp. 40–52.

Bauer, L. and Bauer, W. (2000) 'Nova Zelandia est omnis divisa in partes tres', *New Zealand English Journal*, 14, 7–17.

——(2003) *Playground Talk: Dialects and Change in New Zealand English*, Wellington, NZ: School of Linguistics and Applied Language Studies, Victoria University of Wellington.

——(2005) 'Regional dialects in New Zealand children's playground vocabulary', in A. Bell, R. Harlow and D. Starks (eds) *Languages of New Zealand*, Wellington: Victoria University Press, pp. 194–216.

Bauer, L. and Holmes, J. (1996) 'Getting into a flap! /t/ in New Zealand English', *World Englishes*, 15, 115–24.

Bauer, L. and Warren, P. (2004) 'New Zealand English: phonology', in B. Kortman and E. W. Schneider (eds) *A Handbook of Varieties of English*, Berlin: Mouton de Gruyter, pp. 580–602.

Bauer, W., with Parker, W. and Evans, Te Kareongawai (1997) *The Reed Reference Grammar of Maori*, Auckland, NZ: Reed.

Bayard, D. (2000) 'The cultural cringe revisited: changes through time in Kiwi attitudes towards accents', in A. Bell and K. Kuiper (eds) *New Zealand English*, Wellington, NZ: Victoria University Press, pp. 297–324.

Bayard, D., Weatherall, A., Gallois, C. and Pittam, J. (2001) 'Pax Americana? Accent attitudinal evaluations in New Zealand, Australia and America', *Journal of Sociolinguistics*, 5, 22–49.

Bell, A. (1984) 'Language style as audience design', *Language in Society*, 13, 145–204.

——(1997) 'The phonetics of fish and chips in New Zealand: marking national and ethnic identities', *English World-Wide*, 18, 243–70.

——(2001) 'Back in style: reworking audience design', in P. Eckert and J. R. Rickford (eds) *Style and Sociolinguistic Variation*, Cambridge: Cambridge University Press, pp. 139–69.

Benton, R. (1991) 'Māori English: a New Zealand myth?', in J. Cheshire (ed.) *English Around the World*, Cambridge: Cambridge University Press, pp. 187–99.

Boyce, M. T. (2006) 'A corpus of modern spoken Māori', unpublished PhD thesis. Victoria University of Wellington, Wellington.

Chrisp, S. (2005) 'Māori intergenerational language transmission', *International Journal of the Sociology of Language*, 172, 149–81.

Christensen, I. S. (2003) 'Proficiency, use and transmission, Maori language revitalisation', *New Zealand Studies in Applied Linguistics*, 9, 41–61.

Curnow, J., Hopa, N. and McRae, J. (eds) (2002) *Rere atu, taku manu! Discovering History, Language and Politics in the Maori-Language Newspapers*, Auckland: Auckland University Press.

Daly, N., Holmes, J., Newton, J. and Stubbe, M. (2004) 'Expletives as solidarity signals in FTAs on the factory floor', *Journal of Pragmatics*, 36, 945–64.

Davies, C. and Maclagan, M. (2006) 'Maori words – read all about it: testing the presence of 13 Maori words in four New Zealand newspapers from 1997 to 2004', *Te Reo*, 49, 73–99.

Deverson, T. (2000) 'Handling New Zealand English lexis', in A. Bell and K. Kuiper (eds) *New Zealand English*, Wellington, NZ: Victoria University Press, pp. 23–39.

Gibson, A. (2005) 'Non-prevocalic /r/ in New Zealand hip-hop', *New Zealand English Journal*, 19, 5–12.

Gordon, E. (1997) 'Sex, speech and stereotypes: why women use prestige forms more than men', *Language in Society*, 26, 47–63.

——(1998) 'The origins of New Zealand speech: the limits of recovering historical information from written records', *English World-Wide*, 19, 61–85.

Gordon, E., Campbell, L., Hay, J., Maclagan, M., Sudbury, A. and Trudgill, P. (2004) *New Zealand English: Its Origins and Evolution*, Cambridge: Cambridge University Press.

Gordon, E. and Maclagan, M. A. (2001) '"Capturing a sound change": a real time study over 15 years of the Near/Square diphthong merger in New Zealand English', *Australian Journal of Linguistics*, 21, 215–38.

——(2004) 'Regional and social differences in New Zealand: phonology', in B. Kortman and E. W. Schneider (eds) *A Handbook of Varieties of English*, Berlin: Mouton de Gruyter, pp. 603–13.

Gordon, E. and Trudgill, P. (1999) 'Shades of things to come: embryonic variants in New Zealand English sound changes', *English World-Wide*, 20, 111–24.

Gordon, P. (1997) 'What New Zealanders believe about regional variation in New Zealand English: a folklinguistic investigation', *New Zealand English Journal*, 11, 14–25.

Grabe, E. and Low, E. L. (2002) 'Durational variability in Speech and the rhythm class hypothesis', in C. Gussenhoven and N. Warner (eds) *Laboratory Phonology*, vol. 7, Berlin: Mouton de Gruyter, pp. 515–46.

Harlow, R. (2005) 'Covert attitudes to Māori', *International Journal of the Sociology of Language*, 172, 133–47.

——(2007) *Māori: A Linguistic Introduction*, Cambridge: Cambridge University Press.

Harlow, R., Keegan, P., King, J., Maclagan, M. and Watson, C. (in press) 'The changing sound of the Māori language', in J. N. Stanford and D. R. Preston (eds) *Quantitative Sociolinguistic Studies of Indigenous Minority Languages*, Amsterdam: John Benjamins.

Hay, J. and Maclagan, M. (2008) 'Social and phonetic conditioners on the frequency and degree of "intrusive /r/" in New Zealand English', in D. Preston and N. Niedzielski (eds) *Methods in Socio-phonetics*, Berlin: Mouton de Gruyter.

Hay, J., Maclagan, M. and Gordon, E. (in press) *New Zealand English*, Edinburgh: Edinburgh University Press.

167

Hay, J., Nolan, A. and Drager, K. (2006) 'From fush to feesh: exemplar priming in speech perception', *The Linguistic Review*, 23, 351–79.

Hay, J. and Sudbury, A. (2005) 'How rhoticity became /r/-sandhi', *Language*, 81, 799–823.

Hay, J., Warren, P. and Drager, K. (2006) 'Factors influencing speech perception in the context of a merger-in-progress', *Journal of Phonetics*, 34, 458–84.

Hickey, F. and Kuiper, K. (2000) 'A deep depression covers the South Tasman Sea: New Zealand Meteorological Office weather forecasts', in A. Bell and K. Kuiper (eds) *New Zealand English*, Wellington, NZ: Victoria University Press, pp. 279–96.

Holmes, J. (1990) 'Hedges and boosters in New Zealand women's and men's speech', *Language & Communication*, 10, 185–205.

——(1995) *Women, Men and Politeness*, London: Longman.

——(1996) 'Collecting the Wellington Corpus of Spoken New Zealand English: some methodological challenges', *New Zealand English Journal*, 10, 10–15.

——(1997) 'Maori and Pakeha English: some New Zealand social dialect data', *Language in Society*, 26, 65–101.

——(1998a) 'Apologies in New Zealand English', in P. Trudgill and J. Cheshire (eds) *The Sociolinguistics Reader*, London: Edward Arnold, pp. 201–39.

——(1998b) 'Generic pronouns in the Wellington Corpus of Spoken New Zealand English', *Kotare*, 1, 32–40.

——(ed.) (2000) *Gendered Speech in Social Context: Perspectives from Gown and Town*, Wellington, NZ: Victoria University Press.

——(2005) 'Leadership talk: how do leaders "do mentoring", and is gender relevant?', *Journal of Pragmatics*, 37, 1779–800.

——(2006) 'Sharing a laugh: pragmatic aspects of humor and gender in the workplace', *Journal of Pragmatics*, 38, 26–50.

Holmes, J. and Ainsworth, H. (1997) 'Unpacking the research process: investigating syllable-timing in New Zealand English', *Language Awareness*, 6, 32–47.

Holmes, J., Bell, A. and Boyce, M. (1991) *Variation and Change in New Zealand English: A Social Dialect Investigation. Project Report to the Social Sciences Committee of the Foundation for Research, Science and Technology*, Wellington, NZ: Victoria University of Wellington.

Holmes, J. and Marra, M. (2004) 'Relational practice in the workplace: women's talk or gendered discourse?', *Language in Society*, 33, 377–98.

Holmes, J., Vine, B. and Johnson, G. (1998) *Guide to the Wellington Corpus of Spoken New Zealand English*, Wellington, NZ: Victoria University of Wellington.

Kennedy, G. (2001) 'Lexical borrowing from Maori in New Zealand English', in B. Moore (ed.) *Who's Centric Now? The Present State of Post-Colonial Englishes*, Melbourne: Oxford University Press, pp. 59–81.

Kennedy, M. (2004) 'Prince Charles has two ears/heirs: semantic ambiguity and the merger of NEAR and SQUARE in New Zealand English', *New Zealand English Journal*, 18, 13–23.

King, M. (2003) *The Penguin History of New Zealand*, Auckland: Penguin.

Kuiper, K. (1991) 'Sporting formulae in New Zealand English: two models of male solidarity', in J. Cheshire (ed.) *English around the World: Sociolinguistic Perspectives*, Cambridge: Cambridge University Press.

——(1996) *Smooth Talkers*, Mahwah, NJ: Lawrence Erlbaum.

——(2001) 'Linguistic registers and formulaic performance', *New Zealand Sociology*, 16, 151–64.

Langstrof, C. (2006a) 'Acoustic evidence for a push-chain shift in the intermediate period of New Zealand English', *Language Variation and Change*, 18, 141–64.

——(2006b) 'Vowel change in New Zealand English – patterns and implications', unpublished PhD thesis, University of Canterbury.

Looser, D. (2004) 'Lexicography on the inside: doing time in every New Zealand prison', *International Journal of Lexicography*, 17, 69–87.

Macalister, J. (ed.) (2005) *A Dictionary of Maori Words in New Zealand English*, Melbourne: Oxford University Press.

——(2006) 'The Maori presence in the New Zealand English lexicon, 1850–2000', *English World-Wide*, 27, 1–24.

McKee, R. L. (2001) *People of the Eye: Stories from the Deaf World*, Wellington, NZ: Bridget Williams Books.

McKenzie, J. (2005) '"But he's not supposed to see me in my weeding dress!": the relationship between dress and fleece in modern New Zealand English', *New Zealand English Journal*, 19, 13–25.

Maclagan, M. A. (1998) 'Diphthongisation of /e/ in NZE: a change that went nowhere?', *New Zealand English Journal*, 12, 43–54.

Maclagan, M., Gordon, E. and Lewis, G. (1999) 'Women and sound change: conservative and innovative behaviour by the same speakers', *Language Variation and Change*, 11, 19–41.

Maclagan, M. and Hay, J. (2007) 'Getting *fed* up with our *feet*: contrast maintenance and the New Zealand English "short" front vowel shift', *Language Variation and Change*, 19, 1–25.

Maclagan, M., King, J. and Gillon, G. (2008) 'Maori English', *Clinical Phonetics and Linguistics*, 22, 658–70.

Massam, D., Starks, D. and Ikiua, O. (2006) 'On the edge of grammar: discourse particles in Niuean', *Oceanic Linguistics*, 45, 191–205.

Mutu, M. (2005) 'In search of the missing Māori links: maintaining both ethnic identity and linguistic integrity in the revitalization of the Māori language', *International Journal of the Sociology of Language*, 172, 117–32.

Napier, J., McKee, and Goswell, D. (2006) *Sign Language Interpreting: Theory and Practice in Australia and New Zealand*, Sydney: Federation Press

Nielsen, D. and Hay, J. (2006) 'Perceptions of regional dialects in New Zealand', *Te Reo*, 48, 95–110.

Rae, M. and Warren, P. (2002) 'Goldilocks and the three beers: sound merger and word recognition in NZE', *New Zealand English Journal*, 16, 33–41.

Starks, D. and Reffell, H. (2006) 'Reading "TH": vernacular variants in Pasifika Englishes in South Auckland', *Journal of Sociolinguistics*, 10, 382–92.

Szakay, A. (2008) *Ethnic Dialect Identification in New Zealand: The Role of Prosodic Cues*, Saarbrücken: Vdm Verlag Dr. Muller Aktiengesellschaft & Co.

Taumoefolau, M., Starks, D., Davis, K. and Bell, A. (2002) 'Linguists and language maintenance: Pasifika languages in Manukau, New Zealand', *Oceanic Linguistics*, 41(1): 15–27.

Thomas, B. and Hay, J. (2006) 'A pleasant malady: the Ellen/Allan merger in New Zealand English', *Te Reo*, 48, 69–93.

Trudgill, P., Maclagan M. A. and Lewis, G. (2003) 'Linguistic archaeology: the Scottish input to New Zealand phonology', *Journal of English Linguistics*, 31, 103–24.

Vine, B. (1999) 'A word on the Wellington Corpora', *New Zealand English Journal*, 13, 59–61.

——(2004) *Getting Things Done at Work: The Discourse of Power in Workplace Interaction*, Philadelphia, PA: John Benjamins.

Warren, P. (1998) 'Timing patterns in New Zealand English rhythm', *Te Reo*, 41, 80–93.

——(2005) 'Patterns of late rising in New Zealand: intonational variation or intonational change?', *Language Variation and Change*, 17, 209–30.

Warren, P. and Bauer, L. (2004) 'Maori English: phonology', in B. Kortman and E. W. Schneider (eds) *A Handbook of Varieties of English*, Berlin: Mouton de Gruyter, pp. 614–23.

Warren, P. and Britain, D. (2000) 'Intonation and prosody in New Zealand English', in A. Bell and K. Kuiper (eds) *New Zealand English*, Wellington, NZ: Victoria University Press, pp. 146–72.

Warren, P., Hay, J. and Thomas, B. (2007) 'The loci of sound change effects in recognition and perception', in J. Cole and J. Hualde (eds) *Laboratory Phonology*, vol. 9. Berlin: Mouton de Gruyter, pp. 87–112.

Wells, J. (1982) *Accents of English*, Cambridge: Cambridge University Press.

Woods, N. J. (2000) 'New Zealand English across the generations: an analysis of selected vowel and consonant variables', in A. Bell and K. Kuiper (eds) *New Zealand English*, Wellington, NZ: Victoria University Press, pp. 84–110.

16

Sociolinguistics in the South Pacific

France Mugler and Richard Benton

Introduction

Geographically, the 'South Pacific' covers the island groups occupying a huge area of the Pacific Ocean, and a far smaller area of land, situated south of the Tropic of Cancer and roughly between the 130th West and 130th East degrees of latitude (but also including Easter Island at 109.22 degrees West), that is, the areas often referred to as 'Polynesia', 'Melanesia' and 'Micronesia', and possibly also the continent of Australia. Linguistically at least, Fiji should be grouped with Polynesia, as the Fijian languages, Rotuman and the Polynesian languages share a single common ancestor. The largest land masses in the region, which also have the largest populations – Australia, the island of New Guinea (divided between the Indonesian province of Irian Jaya and Papua New Guinea) and New Zealand, are dealt with in separate chapters in this volume. The State of Hawaii is part of the USA.

This leaves 22 political entities to be covered in this survey, ranging from Pitcairn Island (population about 30), to the Solomon Islands (500,000) and Fiji (almost a million). The others are Vanuatu, New Caledonia, Guam, the Federated States of Micronesia, French Polynesia, Samoa and Tonga, all with populations over 100,000, and Belau, Northern Marianas, the Marshall Islands, Nauru, Kiribati, Tuvalu, Tokelau, American Samoa, Wallis and Futuna, Niue, the Cook Islands, and Easter Island. Our commentary concentrates on specific references to language use and status within some of the larger states south of the equator, but incorporates also works which range over the entire area.

Over 250 'indigenous' languages (i.e. those spoken in or near their current homelands before European exploration of the Pacific began in earnest in the late eighteenth century) are still in use; several major languages of wider communication along with others were brought into the region by colonial administrators, traders, missionaries, settlers and sojourners over the last two centuries, or developed locally for communication with these people and/or among linguistically diverse indigenous groups. Approximately 250 of the local languages are Austronesian, mostly within the Oceanic subgroup of the Eastern Malayo-Polynesian branch, while five are Papuan (all spoken in the Solomon Islands). In Polynesia, Fiji and Micronesia communities within relatively easy access of each other, even when separated by hundreds of kilometres by land or water, generally speak the same language, with minor dialect variation in peripheral areas. The situation is quite different in the Melanesian nations of Solomon Islands, Vanuatu and New Caledonia, where 207 distinct indigenous languages are spoken, many of them in communities which are geographically contiguous and in daily contact with each other. These countries also occupy the bulk of the land area (69,102 of the 108,160 sq km), and show an extraordinary linguistic diversity, compared with the other regions, whether these are substantial land masses like Fiji and Samoa, or the Micronesian atolls spread over several million square kilometres of ocean.[1]

While Melanesian languages spoken in contiguous areas tend to be markedly distinct, within Micronesia apparently distinct languages may be linked by intermediate forms through dialect chains. Similarly, a different analysis of the major Fijian dialects, comprising six of the seven indigenous languages (the other language is Rotuman), could result in a figure of only three languages – Western and Eastern Fijian, and Rotuman. The indigenous people of Guam and the Northern Marianas Islands share Chamorro, like Palauan, a Western Malayo Polynesian language, as their common indigenous language, but with considerable differences in vocabulary because of the long occupation of the Northern Marianas by Japan (1898–1944).

The linguistic diversity and the colonial past of most of these countries are reflected in the legal and educational systems by the hegemony of a small number of languages of wider communication as lingua francas for administrative, educational and commercial purposes and interpersonal communication within each nation, and the formal or *de facto* recognition in the Polynesian and Micronesian states of the official status of a total of 20 indigenous languages and one other for some or all of these same purposes. Vanuatu has Bislama, a Melanesian Pidgin with a lexicon derived substantially from English, as its national language, although the Constitution does provide for the possibility of a local indigenous language being accorded this status in the future. In all, English is designated by Constitutional or statute law as an official language in 12 of the 22 countries, and by convention in 6 others. French has official status in four jurisdictions, and Spanish in one. Fiji Hindi ('Hindustani' in the Constitution) is the only other exotic language with official status in a national Constitution. Seven jurisdictions which have English and one or more others as official languages have explicit constitutional provisions for resolving conflicts between different linguistic versions of laws and legal documents. In five (the Cook Islands, Samoa, Kiribati, the Federated States of Micronesia and Fiji), the English text prevails. However, in the Marshall Islands the Marshallese text prevails, and in Niue the court must determine the original intent by investigating the context and circumstances which gave rise to the conflict.

Most South Pacific countries have explicit legal requirements that interpreters be provided without cost so that persons involved in court cases can participate in their native language, irrespective of its official status or origin. This is an important recognition of linguistic human rights, as in addition to the many local vernaculars, a large number of other languages have been brought by immigrant communities to the region, or been transplanted or developed by people from one jurisdiction within the region who have arrived as immigrants or refugees in another.

Language in the community

The South Pacific is characterized by a great deal of bilingualism and multilingualism, with different patterns prevailing in different parts of the region. In Melanesia, multilingualism has been typical since pre-European contact among speakers of neighbouring indigenous languages (or 'vernaculars', as they are often called both popularly and in some of the literature). It is not unusual for Melanesians belonging to relatively small language groups to speak two, three, or more languages, and passive bilingualism (or 'dual-lingualism') is also common. Since European contact, multilingualism has increased, through the introduction of colonial and other non-indigenous languages, the development of Melanesian Pidgin, and also the spread by missionaries of some local vernaculars for regional evangelization (e.g. Roviana in the West of the Solomons, Mota in the South of the Solomons and the Banks and Torres, in the North of Vanuatu, and Nakanamaga in Central Vanuatu).

The language with the largest number of speakers in the region now is Melanesian Pidgin, an English lexifier pidgin, called Pijin in the Solomons and Bislama in Vanuatu (and Tok Pisin in Papua New Guinea). Melanesian Pidgin, which first emerged in the nineteenth century in New South Wales, was then transplanted to the sugarcane plantations of Queensland, Fiji and Samoa where thousands of Melanesians worked as labourers. Although the pidgin outlived its usefulness in the countries where it developed once the plantation era came to an end, it continued being used among Melanesians when they returned to their homes and functions extensively as a lingua franca in the Solomons and Vanuatu. Indeed, Melanesian Pidgin also has an important role as a transnational, regional lingua franca between Solomon Islanders and ni-Vanuatu in their communication with each other and with Tok Pisin speakers from PNG. The three varieties are mutually intelligible and can be considered regional dialects. Their speakers often communicate by using their own variety, with gradual accommodation to each other's dialect if interaction is more than sporadic. Melanesian Pidgin has also become a creole for a significant proportion of the population in each country, through inter-marriage and increased urbanization. In spite of its widespread use, it continues to suffer from the stigma of its 'mixed' heritage and colonial history, and is often looked down upon, even by some of its speakers, particularly the educated elite. It is often, if not reviled, at best ignored, and is rarely accorded the status or granted the share of the mass media its use as a major language of daily interaction would seem to warrant. The constitution of the Solomon Islands, for instance, makes no mention of Pijin (or of any indigenous language, for that matter). As noted above, in Vanuatu, Bislama has official status alongside French and English. As a powerful symbol of unity in the lead-up to Independence, it was eventually declared the national language. At the same time it is pointedly excluded from among the 'principal languages of education' (Lynch 1996; Early 1999).

Post-contact patterns of multilingualism also involve the use of some of the former colonial languages, essentially now English in most of the region, French in French Polynesia, New Caledonia, Wallis and Futuna, and, alongside English, Vanuatu, and Spanish on Easter Island. In most cases the former colonial language has de jure official status, sometimes alongside the indigenous language, particularly in countries where a single indigenous language predominates and is the de facto national language, a pattern most typical in Polynesia and, to a slightly lesser extent, Micronesia. This official status generally means that the metropolitan language is the major language of record for government documents, can be used in Parliament, and is used extensively in the media and as a medium of instruction in the education system. There is much variation in practice, however; much day-to-day government work is conducted orally rather than in writing, and this is often in an indigenous language or a pidgin, or involves substantial code-switching. The same is often true of parliamentary debates, which can take place in anything from a former colonial language to the national language (either an indigenous language or a pidgin, as in Vanuatu), or the occasional non-standard dialect (in Fiji, for instance, a regional dialect of Fijian). As for education, there is a wide range of different models, from the transitional bilingual systems typical of Polynesia, in which the national language is the main medium of instruction in primary school and continues to be used throughout high school for some subjects (generally in the humanities and social science), to systems in which a metropolitan language is the sole official medium of instruction, either from the very beginning or after the first two or three years of primary school, as in Fiji and Melanesia. No matter what the policy is, however, and in spite of pupils still often being punished for speaking their mother tongue, the reality throughout the region is one of pervasive code-switching at all levels (Lo Bianco 1990; Tamata 1996; Manu 2005). This variation and the 'leaking' of indigenous languages mean that the role of former colonial languages is often less extensive than one would expect from their official status, and in most countries their use in everyday informal conversation is limited, with indigenous languages and pidgins having the lion's share of daily verbal interaction. Among the metropolitan languages, English, for instance, has an important function as a lingua franca only in Fiji, primarily between native speakers of Fijian and of Fiji Hindi, although, as elsewhere in the Pacific, there is also a fair amount of vernacular bilingualism. Most countries of the region have small groups of speakers of minority languages, who typically are conversant with one or more of the major languages of the country they live in (e.g. the Vietnamese in Vanuatu and the French territories, speakers of Kiribati in Fiji, the Solomons and parts of Micronesia, Cantonese- and, increasingly Mandarin-speaking Chinese throughout the Pacific, and many others). As for English, French and Spanish, they are more important as transnational than as national lingua francas.

The linguistic diversity and cultural richness of the South Pacific have always attracted the interest of outsiders and provoked comments of a socio- or ethno-linguistic nature, starting with some of the observations of explorers, sundry beachcombers, missionaries, early settlers and colonial administrators – as witnessed by word lists, for instance. At the same time the sheer number of languages has meant that many are still not described at all, while for others, work is limited to structural descriptions, which are sometimes mere sketches. Thus research is spread unevenly across the region, with some languages or countries attracting more studies than others, reflecting also the vagaries of history and the idiosyncratic interests of researchers. Overall, more work has been done on Polynesian than on Micronesian languages, and even less on Melanesian languages. If the coverage is uneven, the range of topics is quite wide, from comprehensive sociolinguistic histories (e.g. Siegel 1987) to micro-sociolinguistic studies of variation.

There are a number of studies related to general issues of language planning (Baldauf and Luke 1990; Baldauf and Kaplan 2006, Liddicoat and Baldauf 2008), as well as case studies of specific countries (e.g. Early 2003) or discussions of methodological questions (e.g. Crowley 1994). A substantial proportion of work on language planning deals more specifically with vernacular education and literacy (Besnier 1993, 1995b; Mugler and Lynch 1996; Siegel 1996, 1997; Lee Hang and Barker 1997; Crowley 2000, 2005; Gegeo and Watson-Gegeo 2001; Shameem 2002, 2004; Geraghty 2004, 2005; Rehg 2004; Paviour-Smith 2005). Another broad area which has attracted research has to do with various aspects of the distinctive cultures of the region and their relationship with language, from conceptions of space (Hoem 1993, 1995; François 2003), to kinship terminology (Jourdan 2000), to respect vocabulary, speech levels and honorifics (Philips

1991, 2007; Duranti 1992a; Fox 1996; Mayer 2001; Keating and Duranti 2006). There are studies of status, power and language (Keating 2000, 2005) and more generally of political discourse (Brenneis 1984; Duranti 1994; Kempf 2003; Makihara 2007), as well as of discourse and special genres, such as letter writing, sermons, or gossip (Duranti 1992b; Besnier 1994, 1995a, 1995b, 1996; Brenneis 1996; Massam et al. 2006).

The more recent micro-sociolinguistic end of the spectrum is rather less well developed, although some work has been done on gender (e.g. Keating 1998; Besnier 2003) and there are a few variationist studies (Siegel 1991; Tent 2001; Meyerhoff 2003; Mugler 2007). Classic urban dialectology research in the Labovian vein is an area of great potential as urbanization continues, and raises important methodological issues about the extent to which the current framework can be adapted to the different modes of social organization of the region. Western variationist studies of social class, for instance – whose definition itself is contentious – cannot simply be transplanted without adaptation to the urban centres of the region. While one can indeed talk about social class in the contemporary Pacific as it relates to education, occupation, income, and residence, the complex ways in which class interacts with traditional and neo-traditional types of status need to be explored.

The same applies to style, for example, the study of which needs to take into account the many different types of ceremonial styles and other discourse genres specific to the cultures of the region.

Future directions

The past three decades have seen the rise worldwide of concerns about language endangerment, blamed mostly on globalization and the seemingly unstoppable spread of a few large international languages, chief among these English. The South Pacific has not escaped this trend, and indeed many of the early predictions by linguists and others, often based entirely on the demography of individual languages, would mean doom for the vast majority of languages in the region. Others have argued that predictions cannot be based on numbers alone but need to take into account the complex sociolinguistic matrix in which indigenous languages are used, including their functions, status, and interrelations with other languages (Dixon 1991; Mühlhäusler 1992, 1996; Crowley 1995, 1998).

Language death is a concern among speakers themselves, and adults all across the Pacific complain that young people 'don't know their language any more', usually blaming English. While such pronouncements may overstate the seriousness of the problem and reflect in part each generation's disapproval of any change among the young, the anxiety is genuinely felt and not entirely ill-founded. One common perception is of an increase in the use of English, which leads to more frequent code-switching, and eventually a greater use of borrowings. Among some young people, the normal code may indeed become a mixed code, while for others English may be becoming the preferred or most commonly used language. Concerns are particularly strong about the dominance of English over Cook Island Maori and Niuean, due to the two countries' strong ties with New Zealand, which allow for the free flow of people (e.g. Sperlich 1995, 2005), and, perhaps to a slightly lesser extent to countries directly influenced by American English, particularly in Micronesia (e.g. the Marshall Islands and the Northern Marianas), but also in what until recently was known as American Samoa. On Easter Island, the indigenous language had almost stopped being used among young people and for intergenerational communication, having been replaced by a distinctively local dialect of Chilean Spanish (Gómez Macker 1982), but has over the last decade undergone something of a politically and culturally-based revival, and is once more used especially in formal situations to affirm a distinct ethnic identity (Delsing 1998; Makihara 2005b, 2007), and in immersion schools for young children on the model of the New Zealand *kohanga reo* (Makihara 2005a). Perhaps less obvious than wholesale language shift but also worrying is the loss of vocabulary in special registers, in areas in which traditional skills are waning (canoe-building, for example).

While most indigenous languages are probably safe for at least the next few generations – and indeed few have been lost since colonial times – increased popular awareness of the possibility of loss of language and culture in the face of the gathering pace of social change may prompt governments to try strengthening the place of indigenous languages in official spheres of public life, perhaps most of all in education. A number of obstacles remain, however, which could scupper these efforts. Outside of Polynesia, where each national indigenous language tends to have a place throughout the education system both as medium and subject, vernaculars – if they have a place in the school system at all – are often studied only as subjects, and this for only a few hours a week. Moreover, what is taught as the 'vernacular' in schools may be a different variety from the children's first language. In Fiji, for instance, 'vernacular studies' consist of teaching Standard Fijian and Standard Hindi as subjects, even though many Fijians' mother tongue is a different dialect, and Indo-Fijians are nearly all speakers of the local *koiné* Fiji Hindi rather than of what is an external standard. Such confusion can do little to strengthen the children's genuine mother tongues. In most countries of the region, parental pressure to have more English seems stronger at this stage than any pressure in favour of indigenous languages. The wisdom of entrusting language maintenance entirely to the school system is also questionable.

Finally, English and (to a lesser extent) French are not the main threat everywhere. In the Solomon Islands and Vanuatu, the threat to indigenous languages comes much more directly from Melanesian Pidgin than from English. Pidgin has already displaced indigenous languages for a number of young urban speakers for whom it has become the mother tongue – although not all intermarriage results in a loss of vernaculars since many children still grow up with two 'first languages' (their father's language and their mother's language) or even three, in urban areas (with Pijin or Bislama). Similarly, Tahitian has assumed a hegemonic role in French Polynesia, to the possible long-term detriment of the other Polynesian languages in the territory.

Note

1 Based on information in www.ethnologue.com and Crocombe (2001) updated from official sources where available.

References

Baldauf, R. and Kaplan, R. (eds) (2006) *Language Planning and Policy in the Pacific*, vol. 1, Clevedon: Multilingual Matters.

Baldauf, R. and Luke, A. (eds) (1990) *Language Planning and Education in Australasia and the South Pacific*, Clevedon: Multilingual Matters.

Besnier, N. (1993) 'Literacy and feelings: the encoding of affect in Nukulaelae letters', in B. V Sweet (ed.) *Cross-Cultural Approaches to Literacy*, New York: Cambridge University Press, pp. 62–86.

——(1994) 'Christianity, authority, and personhood: sermonic discourse on Nukulaelae atoll', *Journal of the Polynesian Society*, 103, 339–78.

——(1995a) 'The politics of emotion in Nukulaelae gossip', in J. A. Russell *et al.* (eds) *Everyday Conceptions of Emotion*, NATO Advanced Study Institutes D-81, Dordrecht: Kluwer, pp. 221–40.

——(1995b) *Literacy, Emotion and Authority: Reading and Writing on a Polynesian Atoll*, Cambridge: Cambridge University Press.

——(1996) 'Heteroglossic discourse on Nukulaelae spirits', in J. M. Mageo and A. Howard (eds) *Spirits in Culture, History, and Mind*, London: Routledge, pp. 75–97.

——(2003) 'Crossing gender, mixing languages: the linguistic construction of transgenderism in Tonga', in J. Holmes and M. Meyerhoff (eds) *Handbook of Language and Gender*, Oxford: Blackwell, pp. 279–301.

Brenneis, D. (1984) 'Straight talk and sweet talk: political discourse in an occasionally egalitarian society', in D. Brenneis and F. R. Meyers (eds) *Dangerous Words*, New York: New York University Press, pp. 69–84.

——(1996) 'Grog and gossip in Bhatgaon: style and substance in Fiji Indian conversation', in D. Brenneis and R. K. S. Macaulay (eds) *The Matrix of Language*, Boulder, CO: Westview Press, pp. 209–23.

Crocombe, R. (2001) *The South Pacific*, Suva, Fiji: University of the South Pacific.

Crowley, T. (1994) 'Linguistic demography in Vanuatu: interpreting the 1989 census results', *Journal of Multilingual and Multicultural Development*, 15, 1–16.

——(1995) 'Melanesian languages: do they have a future?', *Oceanic Linguistics*, 34, 327–44.

——(1998) 'How many languages will survive in the Pacific?', *Te Reo*, 41, 116–25.

——(2000) 'The consequences of vernacular (il)literacy in the Pacific', *Current Issues in Language Planning*, 1, 368–88.

——(2005) 'Competing agendas in indigenous-language renewal: initial vernacular education in Vanuatu', in H. Lotherington and R. Benton (eds) *International Journal of the Sociology of Language*, 172, 31–50.

Delsing, R. (1998) 'Globalization and cultural identity on Rapa Nui', *Rapa Nui Journal* 12, 99–108.

Dixon, R. M. W. (1991) 'The endangered languages of Australia, Indonesia and Oceania', in R. H. Robins and E. M. Uhlenbeck (eds) *Endangered Languages*, Oxford: Oxford University Press, pp. 229–55.

Duranti, A. (1992a) 'Language in context and language as context: the Samoan respect vocabulary', in A. Duranti and C. Goodwin (eds) *Rethinking Context*, Cambridge: Cambridge University Press, pp. 77–99.

——(1992b) 'Language and bodies in social space: Samoan ceremonial greetings', *American Anthropologist*, 94, 657–91.

——(1994) *From Grammar to Politics: Linguistic Anthropology in a Western Samoan Village*, Berkeley, CA: University of California Press.

Early, R. (1999) 'Double trouble and three is a crowd: languages in education and official languages in Vanuatu', *Journal of Multilingual and Mulicultural Development*, 20, 13–33.

——(2003) 'The status planner's dream come true, or nightmare in paradise', in C. Cabeza *et al.* (eds) *Communidades e individuos bilingüe,* Vigo: Vigo University Press, pp. 998–1010 [CD-ROM edition].

Fox, H. (1996) 'An honorific sub-dialect used among Big Nambas women', in J. Lynch and Fa'afo Pat (eds) *Oceanic Studies*, Canberra: Pacific Linguistics C-133, pp. 367–73.

François, A. (2003) 'Of men, hills, and winds: space directionals in Mwotla', *Oceanic Linguistics*, 42, 407–37.

Gegeo, D. W. and Watson-Gegeo, K. A. (2001) 'The critical villager: transforming language and education in Solomon Islands', in J. W. Tollefson (ed.) *Language Policies in Education*, Mahwah, NJ: Erlbaum, pp. 309–26.

Geraghty, P. (2004) 'Foreigner talk to exonorm: translation and literacy in Fiji', in S. Fenton (ed.) *For Better or for Worse*, Manchester: St Jerome Press, pp. 172–206.

——(2005) 'Literacy and the media in the Fiji Islands', *Pacific Journalism Review*, 11, 48–57.

Gómez Macker, L. (1982). 'El bilingüismo en Isla de Pascua', *Signos* 14, 91–9.

Hoem, I. (1993) 'Space and morality in Tokelau', *Pragmatics*, 3, 137–53.

——(1995) *A Way with Words*, Bangkok, Thailand: White Orchid Press.

Jourdan, C. (2000) 'My nephew is my aunt: features and transformation of kinship terminology in Solomon Islands', in J. Siegel (ed.) *Processes of Language Contact*, Saint-Laurent, Quebec: Fides, pp. 99–121.

Keating, E. (1998) *Power Sharing: Language, Rank, Gender, and Social Space in Pohnpei, Micronesia*, New York: Oxford University Press.

——(2000) 'Moments of hierarchy: constructing social stratification by means of language, food, space, and the body in Pohnpei, Micronesia', *American Anthropologist*, 102, 303–20.

——(2005) 'The sociolinguistics of status in Pohnpei', in H. Lotherington and R. Benton (eds) *International Journal of the Sociology of Language*, 172, 7–30.

Keating, E. and Duranti, A. (2006) 'Honorific resources for the construction of hierarchy', *Journal of the Polynesian Society*, 115, 145–72.

Kempf, W. (2003) '"Songs cannot die": ritual composing and the politics of emplacement among the resettled Banabans on Rabi Island in Fiji', *Journal of the Polynesian Society*, 112, 33–64.

Lee Hang, D. and Barker, M. (1997) 'We need to use both: the place of the indigenous language in science lessons in Western Samoa', *Directions*, 36, 100–121.

Liddicoat, A. J. and Baldauf, R. (2008) *Language Planning and Policy*, Clevedon: Multilingual Matters.

Lo Bianco, J. (1990) 'Language in bilingual classrooms – Samoan as an example', in A. Liddicoat (ed.) *Vernacular Language in South Pacific Education*, Melbourne: National Language Institute of Australia, pp. 45–48.

Lotherington, H. and Benton, R. (eds) (2005) 'Pacific sociolinguistics', *International Journal of the Sociology of Language*, 172, 1–185.

Lynch, J. (1996) 'The banned national language: Bislama and formal education in Vanuatu', in F. Mugler and J. Lynch (eds) *Pacific Languages in Education*, Suva: University of the South Pacific, pp. 245–57.

Makihara, M. (2005a) 'Being Rapa Nui, speaking Spanish: children's voices on Easter Island', *Anthropological Theory*, 5, 117–34.

——(2005b) 'Rapa Nui ways of speaking Spanish: language shift and socialization on Easter Island', *Language in Society*, 34, 727–62.

——(2007) 'Linguistic purism in Rapa Nui political discourse', in M. Makihara and B. B. Schieffelin (eds) *Consequences of Contact*, Oxford: Oxford University Press, pp. 49–69.

Manu, S. S. (2005) 'Language switching and mathematical understanding in Tongan classrooms: an investigation', *Directions*, 27, 47–70

Massam, D., Starks, D. and Ikiua, O. (2006) 'On the edge of grammar: discourse particles in Niuean', *Oceanic Linguistics*, 45, 191–205.

Mayer, J. F. (2001) *Code-Switching in Samoan: t-Style and k-Style*, Ann Arbor, MI: UMI Dissertation Services.

Meyerhoff, M. (2003) 'Formal and cultural constraints on optional objects in Bislama', *Language Variation and Change*, 14, 323–46.

Mugler, F. (2007) ' " ... and the blue bird /flju/ away": yod insertion in Fiji English', in J. Siegel, J. Lynch and D. Eades (eds) *Language Description, History and Development*, Amsterdam: John Benjamins, pp. 183–95.

Mugler, F. and Lynch, J. (eds) (1996) *Pacific Languages in Education*, Suva: University of the South Pacific.

Mühlhäusler, P. (1992) 'Preserving languages or language ecologies? A top-down approach to language survival', *Oceanic Linguistics*, 31, 163–80.

——(1996) *Linguistic Ecology*, London: Routledge.

Paviour-Smith, M. (2005) 'Is it Aulua or education dressed up in Kastom? A report on the ongoing negotiation of literacy and identity in a Ni Vanuatu community', *Current Issues in Language Planning*, 6, 224–38.

Philips, S. U. (1991) 'Tongan speech levels', in R. Blust (ed.) *Currents in Pacific Linguistics*, Canberra: Pacific Linguistics, C117, pp. 369–82.

——(2007) 'Changing scholarly representation of the Tongan honorific lexicon', in M. Makihara and B. B. Schieffelin (eds) *Consequences of Contact*, Oxford: Oxford University Press, pp. 189–215.

Rehg, K. L. (2004) 'Linguists, literacy, and the law of unintended consequences', *Oceanic Linguistics*, 43, 498–518.

Shameem, N. (2002) 'Multilingual proficiency in Fiji primary schools', *Current Issues in Language Planning*, 23, 388–407

——(2004) 'Language attitudes in multilingual primary schools in Fiji', *Language Culture and Curriculum*, 17, 154–72.

Siegel, J. (1987) *Language Contact in a Plantation Environment*, Cambridge: Cambridge University Press.

——(1991) 'Variation in Fiji English', in J. Cheshire (ed.) *English Around the World*, Cambridge: Cambridge University Press, pp. 664–74.

——(1996) *Vernacular Education in the South Pacific*, Boston: University of New England.

——(1997) 'Using a pidgin language in formal education: help or hindrance?', *Applied Linguistics*, 18, 86–100.

Sperlich, W. B. (1995) 'Is Niuean an endangered language species?', *Directions*, 33, 37–55.

——(2005) 'Will cyberforums save endangered languages? A Niuean case study', in H. Lotherington and R. Benton (eds) *International Journal of the Sociology of Language*, 172, 51–78.

Tamata, A. (1996) 'Code-switching in Fiji's schools', in F. Mugler and J. Lynch (eds) *Pacific Languages in Education*, Suva: University of the South Pacific, pp. 92–101.

Tent, J. (2001) 'Yod deletion in Fiji English: phonological shibboleth or L2 English?', *Language Variation and Change*, 13, 161–91.

Tent, J. and Geraghty, P. (eds) (2004) *Borrowing*, Pacific Linguistics vol. 548, Canberra: ANU.

Tent, J. and Mugler, F. (2004) 'The phonology of Fiji English', in B. Kortmann, E. Schneider, K. Burridge, R. Mesthrie and C. Upton (eds) *A Handbook of Varieties of English*, vol. 1, *Phonology*, Amsterdam: Mouton, pp. 193–222.

Tepahae, P. and Lynch, J. (1998) 'The language of family on Aneityum', in A. Piau-Lynch (ed.) *Violence in Paradise*, Canberra: ANU.

Topping, D. M. (2003) 'Saviors of languages', *Oceanic Linguistics* 42, 522–7.

Tryon, D. (2006) 'Language endangerment and globalisation in the Pacific', in D. Cunningham, D. Ingram and K. Sumbuk (eds) *Language Diversity in the Pacific*, Clevedon: Multilingual Matters, pp. 97–111.

Vari-Bogiri, H. (2005) 'A sociolinguistic survey of Araki: a dying language of Vanuatu', *Journal of Multilingual and Mulicultural Development*, 26, 52–66.

Wurm, S. A., Mühlhaüsler, P. and Tryon, D. T. (eds) (1996) *Atlas of Languages of Intercultural Communication in the Pacific, Asia, and the Americas*, Berlin: Mouton.

17

A sociolinguistic sketch of New Guinea

Mark Donohue

Introduction

New Guinea is home to the greatest number, and greatest diversity, of languages in the world. In an area only 2000 km long, over 1,000 languages are regularly spoken, belonging to at least 50 families. The largest language in the area has less than 200,000 speakers; the smallest known stable, non-endangered language situation is Masep, which is not known to be related to any other languages, and has less than 40 speakers (Clouse *et al.* 2002). Politically the region is split into two, with the eastern half the territory of Papua New Guinea independent since 1975, and the western half formerly being a Dutch territory, but Indonesian since annexation in 1961; each half has its own national language(s). In addition to the enormous 'baseline' complexity that such a linguistically diverse environment guarantees, the island has been subject to four different colonial administrations, each with their own official languages (Dutch and Malay in the west, English in the east), and has generated three pidgins/creoles that have achieved widespread use in different areas (local Malay varieties in the west, Tok Pisin in most of the east and Hiri Motu in the south half of the east), as well as the official languages.

Language and identity

Language is very important to the establishment, and maintenance of, identity. Crowther (2001: 4), describing the One linguistic community, summarizes a typical situation:

There is a high degree of linguistic awareness among One speakers, who have a clear (though not always identical) concept of the extent of One, and a recognition of where the borders lie and what lies beyond them (linguistically). All speakers are aware of the linguistic differences between varieties and will cite them enthusiastically. For example, when taking a wordlist in Molmo village, one person who claimed to be married to a Siama woman supplied the Siama equivalents. The forms given were predictable – a substitution of Molmo [l] with [n] (a valid sound correspondence). Upon visiting Siama village, the wordlist was checked and numerous items were found to be completely different. For example, *wala* 'liver' in Molmo was claimed to be *wana* in Siama, but in reality it has an unrelated form kʊnjɔ́. Notwithstanding this awareness of differences, speakers have a very strong sense of membership to the larger One group. They believe they are speaking the same 'language', despite the fact that many of the varieties are unintelligible to one another and a lingua franca (Tok Pisin) is required for communication.

This demonstrates the use, common across New Guinea, of a prescriptive (and frequently variable) interpretation of the linguistic similarities and differences between villages to make political capital.

Despite being touted as a 'sociolinguistic laboratory' (Wurm 1977, 1979), there has been very little detailed research in New Guinea. Numerous sociolinguistic surveys of language use in local language areas, including observations on language use, code-switching and variation, have been carried out by members of SIL International (see the *Ethnologue* website), but little in the way of overall assessment other than Mühlhäusler (1975) and Romaine (1992). Schieffelin (1990) describes language socialization in a southern New Guinea community, making a major contribution to the understanding of the sociolinguistics of children's interaction with language. Kulick (1992) provides an insightful analysis of the form and function of different speech genres in a community with a highly endangered language. A much-needed research topic is the investigation of language use and code-switching between Tok Pisin and (Papua New Guinean) English in Papua New Guinea, and similarly between local Malay varieties and more 'standard' Indonesian in towns and cities in the Indonesian provinces. Work establishing the parameters that define the variation in use and spread of local Malay varieties is ongoing (Kim *et al.* 2007), and appears to be similar to those reported in Grimes (1991).

While national languages are promoted in both countries, the social cohesion of these languages varies. In the west, varieties of Malay, related to Indonesian, have been used for over 100 years along parts of the north coast, and these have developed into locally-influenced creoles (Donohue 2007), which have little or no mutual intelligibility with standard Indonesian. In more isolated areas, Indonesian has only arrived with the formal presence of the government, and so is spoken in a very standard manner, with little regional creolization (though significant first-language phonological interference), and there are reports of a variety of Indonesian or Malay being increasingly used in areas beyond government control where rebel activity is frequent.

Similarly, different dialects of Tok Pisin are found across Papua New Guinea. In addition to an urban/rural divide, with urban Tok Pisin showing considerably more English lexification (for instance, *Yumi i mas diskasim dispela problem*, vs. *Yumi i mas toktok long dispela wari* 'We should discuss these problems'), different areas show different phonologies and/or differences in details of the grammar (e.g. the instantiation of the inclusive/exclusive contrast in the first person plural). In Papua New Guinea the use of Tok Pisin is growing nationally, at the expense of both smaller local languages and other lingue franche. Tok Pisin is still strongest in its homeland along the north coast, where numerous plantations were established in colonial times. The other main lingua franca, Hiri Motu, maintains its position as an important language of interethnic communication in the south, and numerous languages promoted by different missions as the language of religious instruction maintain their functions in restricted areas (e.g. McElhanon 1979).

Pre-contact pidgins were found in numerous areas (e.g. Donohue 1997; Foley 2006), and some are still used as languages of wider communication.

Multilingualism

The populations of New Guinea are overwhelmingly multilingual, traditionally in several local languages (a home or community language, one or more additional local languages, and perhaps a local trade language, if there is one), though in recent years proficiency in national languages, or varieties of national languages, has grown dramatically, replacing the earlier multilingualism with a simple local + national bilingualism in many areas.

At its most extreme, particularly in townships and cities, this tendency has led to the rise of a significant number of people, mostly younger, who do not speak the village-language of their parents, but only the national language of the area they are in, or a variety thereof. In many cases, as is true elsewhere in, for instance, Indonesia, parents are deliberately not transmitting their local languages to children in a deliberate attempt to give their children an advantage in school. Areas in which church-sponsored schooling, in the local language, is prevalent predictably show less of this tendency.

Away from this discussion of loss of varieties, the traditional sociolinguistic environment sponsored not only great bilingualism, but also great variety within the one language, with distinct special speech styles being employed in particular socio-cultural circumstances (e.g. Franklin 1972), or when talking or referring to particular kin relations. The distinction between 'language' and 'dialect', and between 'subgroup' and 'language' is a blurry one at best in the linguistic minds of many New Guineans, with speakers in some cases claiming understanding of what are clearly separate languages on the basis of one or two prominent shibboleths, while in other cases non-comprehension will be reported on the basis of a different (and proscribed) intonation pattern. Crowther (2001) discusses the interaction of social factors that shape the construal of ethnolinguistic identity in the eastern Bewani mountains.

This said, even today, speakers of the Vanimo coast languages often, when they find it advantageous to their argumentation, refer to the different villages from Skou to Vanimo, and Leitre, as speaking the 'same language'. Crowther (2001) documents the use of linguistics terminology by New Guineans to refer not to an individual language, as a linguist would define it, but to a linguistic sub-group, and this appears to be the case for Skou and its relatives as well. When questioned on actual intelligibility, I have found that interviewees usually back-pedal on their claims of linguistic unity, saying that, while they are the same languages, it is true that 'the words are different', 'the sounds are different', or 'the other villages mangle the language'. In the absence of extensive experience of surveying language attitudes in New Guinea, the kinds of information that would be acquired by questioning speakers of languages that one is not familiar with would not be overly helpful in determining language extent.

Language planning and language development

Language policy in Papua New Guinea is enthusiastically supportive of local diversity, but the government basically lacks the skilled workers and the funds to incorporate any languages (other than the main lingue franche, Tok Pisin and Hiri Motu, as well as

English) into the curriculum at school. Local radio in most areas makes only minimal efforts to be linguistically diverse, and television has little, if anything, that is not English.

In western New Guinea, as with other regions inside Indonesia, the official policy that is very supportive of local languages is combined with *de facto* indifference at best, and violent suppression at worst. Various church- or mission-initiated programmes promote local languages, but officialdom obstructs many of the advantages of these initiatives.

Literacy in national languages is developing in cities, but remains minimal in the more numerous rural areas. Literacy in local languages can only be described as being in its infancy. Schieffelin (1995, 2000), and Walker (1987) describe the uptake, and impact, of literacy on traditional societies in New Guinea.

Language in use

Very little work has been done on pragmatics and stylistics in New Guinea. A notable exception is Rumsey's work on the genre of chanted tales (Rumsey 2001, and ongoing work), Goldman (1984) on Huli disputes, and Merlan and Rumsey's ([1991] 2006) work on the role that language, and the manipulation of language, play in a number of conventionalized public, political exchanges in the eastern highlands of New Guinea.

One pervading characteristic of language use in New Guinea is the use of head-tail linkages (as noted by Longacre 1972). This is apparent in examples such as Tok Pisin *em i raunim ol dispela brata, nau ol i raun i kam i stap antap long Wutung. Nau ol i stap long ples Wutung* 'he chased up all the cousins, and they all came to stay in Wutung. So they were all in Wutung ... ', or in Papuan Malay *Dong nae jalan pi sampe di pondok. Sampe di pondok dong duduk isterihat. Selese isterihat dong ambe barang* 'They follow the road to the hut. Arriving at the hut, they sit down and rest. After resting, they take their things ... '. In these examples the end of each clause is repeated as the beginning of the next. That this feature has permeated into the lingue franche of both Indonesian New Guinea and Papua New Guinea is an indication of the prevalence of the construction in numerous local languages.

Language endangerment

As will have been gathered from much of the preceding discussion, language endangerment is a serious issue in New Guinea. Traditional languages are being lost rapidly in the urban context, and also in their more traditional domains. Especially in villages that have increasing contact mediated via a national language, that language creeps into village-internal domains, including use at home. This is most prevalent in coastal villages, but is also true of more interior locations that have regular outside contact. A number of church groups, notably the Seventh Day Adventists, actively campaign against the use of local language. Other churches which are not actively opposed to the use of local languages also provide a domain in which local languages are not thought to be appropriate, thus speeding their endangerment. This is the result of having church workers who do not attempt to learn local languages, or work with translators, either local or overseas.

Mühlhäusler (2003) presents an overview of the issues involved. It should be noted, however, that a quick sociolinguistic survey that shows the failure of children to speak the local language does not necessarily indicate that language loss is imminent. For instance, although children attending school in the Skou villages in north-central New

Guinea do not speak the language, it is apparent that they do understand it, as they are frequently addressed in it by their parents and other elders. Indonesian, while the main language of the school-attending cohort in the village, appears to be, perversely, an 'insider language', actively used in opposition to the language of the village to establish the identity of the teenagers. The fact that Indonesian is also used by the older people who travel to the markets in Abepura and Jayapura seems not to be a problem in its being appropriated by another age group for another purpose. The health of Skou, even when not spoken, can be gauged by the fact that on leaving school these same teenagers are suddenly speakers of Skou, even if only a few months have passed since their final Junior High School exams. This reflects their status now not as wards of the state educational system, immune from prosecution for any violations of village conduct because of their requirement to fulfil governmental requirements, but as members of the village community. As such, in the absence of any significant employment, Papuan school graduates now adopt a more traditional lifestyle, including gardening, hunting, fishing, and speaking the language of their ancestors. This pattern of sociolinguistic comeback in each generation is not unique to the Skou, but has been observed by this writer elsewhere along the North New Guinea coast, on Yapen island (in both Ansus and Saweru), and in Warembori (Donohue 1999). Janet Bateman (pers. comm.) reports a similar sociolinguistic environment among the Iau of the western Lakes Plains, a more traditional society. Amongst the Iau young people below marriageable age (which corresponds roughly to the age that Skou teenagers graduate from Junior High School, roughly 14–15 years old) are not traditionally expected to fit into the highly prescriptive sets of rules and behavioural regulations that characterize society on the Van Daalen river. They are permitted a significant degree of freedom, including that of the language they use, which is denied more 'grown' adults. Youngsters in Korodesi commonly speak in Elopi, a trade language of the lower Tariku river, at least as commonly as they speak Iau, but on reaching societal maturity they make the transition to being mainly Iau speakers, and Iau is no more an endangered language than is English.

On the other hand, different areas show the encroachment of the national language at an alarming rate. Kulick (1992), discussing the situation in Gapun, observes that, despite the remote location, the younger generation are no longer learning the indigenous language Taiap. Furthermore, Taiap and the intrusive Tok Pisin have established different domains of use, all within the bounds of traditional society, even for those people who can speak Taiap.

Conclusion

What work has been carried out in New Guinea reveals that, as a result of having any imaginable combination of factors present in some area or another, it really is a 'sociolinguistics laboratory', waiting to be used as a testing ground for theory, and as a source of empirical data that will change our perception of the issues involved. Despite this potential, almost all aspects of the sociolinguistic ecology of New Guinea are awaiting more detailed investigation.

Acknowledgements

Thanks to Alan Rumsey, for discussion of many of the issues raised here.

References

Clouse, D., Donohue, M. and Ma, F. (2002) 'Survey report of the north coast of Irian Jaya', SIL Electronic Survey Reports 2002–78. Online. Available at: www.sil.org/silesr/abstract.asp?ref=2002–078.

Crowther, M. (2001) 'All the One language(s)', thesis, University of Sydney.

Donohue, M. (1997) 'Some trade languages of insular South-East Asia and Irian Jaya (including Map 78: Precolonial contact languages of Irian Jaya, and Further contact languages of Irian Jaya)', in S. A. Wurm, P. Mühlhäusler and D. T. Tryon (eds) *Atlas of Languages of Intercultural Communication in the Pacific, Asia, and the Americas.* Berlin: Mouton de Gruyter, pp. 713–16.

——(1999) *Warembori*, Languages of the World/Materials 341, München: Lincom Europa.

——(2007) 'Variation in voice in Indonesian/Malay: historical and synchronic perspectives', in Y. Matsumoto, D. Y. Oshima, O. R. Robinson and P. Sells (eds) *Diversity in Language: Perspectives and Implications*, Stanford, CA: CSLI Publications, pp. 71–129.

Ethnologue (nd) Online. Available at: www.ethnologue.org. See also www.pnglanguages.org/pacific/png/index.asp for links to many downloads of material relevant to Papua New Guinea.

Foley, W. A. (2006) 'Universal constraints and local conditions in Pidginization: case studies from New Guinea', *Journal of Pidgin and Creole Languages*, 21, 1–44.

Franklin, K. J. (1972) 'A ritual Pandanus language of New Guinea', *Oceania*, 43, 66–76.

Goldman, L. (1984) *Talk never dies: the language of Huli disputes*, London and New York: Tavistock/Methuen.

Grimes, B. D. (1991) 'The development and use of Ambonese Malay', in H. Steinhauer, (ed.) *Papers in Austronesian Linguistics*, vol. 1, Canberra: Pacific Linguistics A-81, pp. 83–123.

Kim, H., Shon, S., Rumaropen, B., Scott, G. and Scott, E. (2007) 'A description of some linguistic and sociolinguistic features of Papuan Malay', paper presented at the Workshop on the Languages of Papua, Manokwari, 8–10 August, Manokwari, Indonesia.

Kulick, D. (1992) *Language Shift and Cultural Reproduction: Socialization, Self and Syncretism in a Papua New Guinea Village*, Cambridge: Cambridge University Press.

Longacre, R. E. (1972) *Hierarchy and Universality of Discourse Constituents in New Guinea Languages: Discussion*, Washington, DC: Georgetown University Press.

McElhanon, K. A. (1979) 'Some mission lingue franche and their sociolinguistic role', in S. A. Wurm (ed.) *New Guinea and Neighbouring Areas: A Sociolinguistic Laboratory*, The Hague: Mouton, pp. 277–89.

Merlan, F. and Rumsey, A. ([1991] 2006) *Ku Waru: Language and Segmentary Politics in the Western Nebilyer Valley*, Cambridge: Cambridge University Press.

Mühlhäusler, P. (1975) 'Sociolects in New Guinea pidgin', in K. A. McElhanon (ed.) *Tok Pisin i go we? Proceedings of a Conference Held at the University of Papua New Guinea, Port Moresby, P.N.G., 18–21 September 1973.* Kivung special publication, 1, Port Moresby: Linguistic Society of Papua New Guinea, pp. 59–75.

——(2003) 'Language endangerment and language revival', *Journal of Sociolinguistics*, 7, 232–45.

Romaine, S. (1992) *Language, Education and Development: Rural and Urban Tok Pisin in Papua New Guinea*, Oxford: Oxford University Press.

Rumsey, A. (2001) '*Tom Yaya Kange*: a metrical narrative genre from the New Guinea highlands', *Journal of Linguistic Anthropology*, 11, 193–239.

Schieffelin, B. B. (1990) *The Give and Take of Everyday Life: Language Socialization of Kaluli Children*, Cambridge: Cambridge University Press.

——(1995) 'Creating evidence: making sense of written words in Bosavi', *Pragmatics*, 5, 225–44.

——(2000) 'Introducing Kaluli literacy: a chronology of influences', in P. Kroskrity (ed.) *Regimes of Language*, Santa Fe, NM: School of American Research Press, pp. 293–327.

Walker, R. (1987) 'Dani literacy: explorations in the sociolinguistics of literacy', *Irian*, 15, 19–34. Online. Available at: www.papuaweb.org/dlib/irian/index.html.

Wurm, S. A. (1977) *New Guinea Area Languages and Language Study*, vol. 3, *Language, Culture, Society, and the Modern World, Fascicle* 1, Canberra: Pacific Linguistics C-40.

——(ed.) (1979) *New Guinea and Neighboring Areas: A Sociolinguistic Laboratory*, The Hague: Mouton.

Part IV

Africa and the Middle East

18

Sociolinguistics in South Africa

A critical overview of current research

Rajend Mesthrie

Introduction

In this overview, I shall take a broad view of the discipline of Sociolinguistics, assuming it to include variation theory, language contact, dialectology, intercultural communication, sociology of language and sociohistorical linguistics. At the same time I do not exclude certain studies within Applied Linguistics, where the focus is on actual usage and its interface with more normative expectations in domains like education and formal media. For practical purposes pertaining to South Africa, it is also necessary to assess what issues have been prominent in scholarship pertaining to different language groupings: Bantu, Khoe-San, Afrikaans, English, Sign, and languages other than the country's 11 official ones. To fix other parameters: this survey deals with South Africa, rather than Southern Africa and as directed, limits its discussion largely to work undertaken in the decade between 1997 and 2007 (except in reference to earlier foundational works in certain areas). However, chapters in the volume *Language in South Africa* (Mesthrie 2002b) will not generally be cited here, and should be consulted as a baseline for work in the area. An earlier foundational resource is Lanham and Prinsloo (1978).

Sociolinguistic variation

The Labovian paradigm is not as widespread in Africa as in the northern hemisphere. The main reason is that language contact in multilingual settings frequently requires different tools and approaches from situations in which one language dominates in a state. Work on mother-tongue varieties of English was prominent in the 1970s and early 1980s, some of which used Labovian techniques, notably Lanham and Macdonald (1979). Lass (1990, 1995) also produced important work in descriptions of South African L1 English. Although not primarily working in sociolinguistics, his phonetic descriptions are grounded in a social context. Studies of other dialects of South African English tended to focus on individual varieties in isolation, for the main reason that each variety was quite different from the rest, and needed to be described in terms of its own structure, rather than within any kind of diasystem. Prominent among these are the close studies of Black South African English (henceforth BSAE) accents by Van Rooy (2004), Van Rooy and Van Huyssten (2000) and Wissing (2002), all based on laboratory phonetics. The authors confirm acoustically that the basic system for speakers of Tswana background is a five vowel one [i u e o a]. These vowels may vary in length according to position in a word and fluctuate between long, short and intermediate duration. It is not clear who was the first to observe this neutralisation. Hundleby describes the phenomenon in his thesis of 1964, but Lanham was also involved in a study of Black English at that time and published findings concerning length in 1967. Mesthrie (2005a) examines the rarity of schwa in Black English mesolect, whose usual replacements are – in descending order – any of [a i e u o]. He ties his analysis to a critique of an over-emphasis among analysts on the use of spelling forms by speakers. Data from the replacements of schwa show this to be a minor effect; general phonological properties like vowel mappings, analogy and a small degree of vowel harmony account better for the variance. Louw and De Wet (2007) attempted to ascertain whether different subvarieties of BSAE existed according to substrate, especially the broad division between Nguni and Sotho languages, as has sometimes been claimed by speakers. They show via experimental evidence that differential substrate influence cannot in fact be discerned. Other sociophonetic work was done by Bekker and Ely (2007), who provide an acoustic account of the vowels of younger, middle-class, White South Africans. They describe the lowering and backing of the TRAP vowel among high-status, female speakers in Johannesburg. Although not common in their East London data, the feature occurs beyond Johannesburg, and can certainly – in my experience – be heard among younger female speakers in Cape Town. It is not clear to me where the origins of the change lie, but two likely possibilities are: (1) its increase on British television which has an influence on some prominent South African newsreaders; and/or (2) its increase in informal Southern British usage, which influences the many thousands of young South Africans taking a gap year abroad after their high school or university studies. Bekker (2007) also provides the first account of the fronting of /s/ among 'advanced', middle-class, White speakers. This seems to me in fact to be a part of a broader trend among middle-class females of different ethnicities that includes the fronting of alveolars /t d s z n l/, which are (variably) produced as dentals, with some occasional affrication of /t/ and /d/. It is my impression that this trend comes from a global innovation in English, probably beginning in the USA: one can hear it, for example, in Hollywood sitcoms.

Post-apartheid society has brought about rapid social and linguistic changes, especially in creating a new Black middle class, responding to new commercial and educational opportunities. The lifting of restrictions upon residency, travel and work has resulted in new social networks, no longer bounded by the solid barriers of apartheid. A new generation of scholarship is responding to these changes. Much of this work is still in progress and has been reported at conferences, rather than in publications. A PhD thesis by Arista Da Silva (2007) is, to date, the only completed full-length sociolinguistic study of post-apartheid English. The work was based on the Witwatersrand campus, where Da Silva interviewed students from different backgrounds. The thesis focuses on the norms of Black students, to ascertain what changes from what I term 'older Black South African English' were being made in the new non-racial social networks. Da Silva (ibid.: 195) found that while many Black students retain some prototypically older features (like [u] for GOOSE, [ɛ] for NURSE and [a] as one variant for STRUT), they also appear to be adopting some features of the superstrate like [ʌ] in STRUT and [ɪ] or [ë] in KIT. I discuss some of the implications of this work below.

Several other shorter studies report on the role and status of different varieties of English in the repertoires of Black university students. These studies show a particular concern for attitudes and new identity formation. Bangeni and Kapp (2007) report on the new fluidities in identity formation caused by differential multilingual repertoires among students at the University of Cape Town. De Kadt (2005) also provides a richly documented account of attitudes and identities among students on the University of KwaZulu-Natal campus. Makoe (2007) reports on the dilemmas of students at the University of the Witwatersrand in carving out new roles for themselves and avoiding stereotypes that go with different varieties of English. At the centre of these dilemmas are the crucial differences between older BSAE, with its largely five-vowel system and a grammatical system showing a fair deal of substrate influence and second-language processes, and newer varieties current among Black South Africans. Mesthrie (2007a) explores the English of young elites at the University of Cape Town, sometimes labelled 'coconuts', with different degrees of disparagement. The question being studied is whether the new elites of different backgrounds (Black, Coloured, Indian and White) are evolving a new sociolect, or whether they are largely adopting the statusful variety of middle-class Whites in their peer groups. A significant factor in this process is that many of the new elites have been to private schools, where White youth have been in the majority. It appears that the students interviewed (mostly Black, young, female, middle to upper-middle class) show 'crossovers' into the White variety rather than 'crossing' in the sense established by Rampton.

A paper that explicitly draws on early Labovian traditions concerns the stereotyping of *be* + *-ing* among South African Indian English speakers in Natal province by White comic scriptwriters for a radio programme of the 1940s (Mesthrie 2005b). The paper showed how the insights of variationism can be used to illuminate the nature of linguistic stereotyping.

Turning to the Bantu languages, studies of variation have not been a high priority. The *South African Journal of African Languages* carried very few articles that fall into the subfield of language variation in the period 2000 to 2007. Some work on Zulu dialects by S. Ngubane predates this period. Rather more prominent are studies of grammatical structure, literature, folklore and the sociology of language. In the period under review, Mulaudzi (e.g. 2004) has undertaken studies of variation in Venda. Overall, dialect work is very much a desideratum for the country's major Bantu languages. Some of this is likely to be realized via various corpus projects in progress (e.g. Allwood and Hendrickse 2003). More work is being done on African language sociolects, especially on gender and youth languages in the period. Stephanie Rudwick and Magcino Shange (2006) discuss the status of the register *Isihlonipha Sabafazi* ('Women's language of respect'), well known from earlier work by Finlayson (1984) and still used in the modern urban context. They confirm its continuing ambiguity as a cultural resource in traditional and urban Zulu culture, as well as being a socially disempowering speech register for women. Rudwick (2007) discusses work in progress on IsiNgqumo, a little-studied gay Black variety based on Zulu. Youth languages and slang registers in the townships have also been reasonably well-studied, and will be discussed under the effects of language contact below.

Variationist studies in Afrikaans tend to be fewer these days. Deumert (2003) is a full-length study of variation in Afrikaans in the nineteenth century, focusing on the give and take between Dutch and Afrikaans, and the ways in which standardization of the latter occurred. A festschrift to Christo van Rensburg, a prominent scholar of language contact and variation in Afrikaans, edited by Carstens and Grebe (2001), contains articles describing

189

features of Afrikaans dialects. Regional dialectology of Afrikaans is currently being strengthened by collaborative work in progress between local and Dutch scholars on regional
syntactic variation in Continental Dutch and its offshoots abroad, building on Barbiers *et al.*
(2005). Two volumes of the *Journal of Germanic Linguistics* were dedicated to the socio-
historical linguistics of Afrikaans, including still-debated theories of origin (Mesthrie and
Roberge 2001, 2002).

There is a small body of work on South African Sign Language. Penn (e.g. 1992a, 1992b)
and Reagan and Penn (e.g. 1997) have documented lexical variation in the various
communities in the 1980s and 1990s. Aarons and Akach (2002) propose that these lexical
variants do not result in different languages, since the underlying syntax has not been
shown to be different or mutually unintelligible. Aarons and Morgan (1998) discuss some
post-apartheid changes in Sign Language structure. Reagan, Penn and Ogilvy (2006)
discuss ongoing developments in South African Sign Language with regard to education
and government policy.

Dialectological work on languages apart from the country's 11 official languages is rare.
Donnelly (2000) discusses the survival of Phuthi, a Nguni language spoken in the northern
Transkei and (especially) southern Lesotho. Mesthrie (2007b) describes the dialect origins
of South African Tamil, showing it to have strong antecedents in the Northern dialect of
Tamil in India. This makes it different from other diaspora Tamil varieties in Sri Lanka
and Malaysia.

Multilingualism and language contact

More attention to multilingualism can be found in South Africa's sociolinguistic and
applied linguistic literature. Works that are more overtly sociolinguistic will be surveyed
here, i.e. ones that draw on social or sociolinguistic theory and analyse linguistic data.
Two sociohistorical studies of contact in the missionary period of the early nineteenth
century between Xhosa and English and Afrikaans are Mesthrie (1998) and a full-length
study by Gilmour (2006). In the contemporary period, code-switching has been a major
focus of research, given its prominence in people's multilingual repertoires. McCormick
(2002) is a full-length socio-historical study of the intimate bilingualism and code-mixing
found in the Coloured communities of Cape Town, specifically among residents of the
remnants of District Six. The varieties in contact, i.e. non-standard Afrikaans and English,
are close enough structurally to allow a deft weaving of the two codes. McCormick
proposes that the mixed code now has independent status as the informal variety of the
community. Herbert (1997) draws explicitly on Myers-Scotton's work on the social
motivations for code-switching in analysing interactions in African languages and English
on the Witwatersrand campus. The analysis generally bears out Myers-Scotton's account
of speakers being able to use code-switching in response to existing rights and obligations
between interlocutors, as well as to challenge and change them. In addition, Herbert
found a function not mentioned by Myers-Scotton, viz. the use of parallelism in turn
structure. Speakers begin their turn in an African language and then shift to English, the
language of power, status or education. While Herbert (1997) had shown that Myers-
Scotton's 'social motivations' model for switching was generally upheld in a campus
setting, Finlayson and Slabbert (1997) point to significant differences. They raise the
question why some speakers are reluctant to switch and accommodate other speakers (as
was the case with Zulu speakers, for example). They also suggest that code-switching

does not establish multiple, detachable identities so much as a new (singular) identity – albeit a hybrid one that signals urban modernity. Kamwangamalu (1998b) stressed the 'we' versus 'they' orientation in code-switching, in work pursuing Gumperz's interactional account of the phenomenon. He also produced an interesting case study of a 'Coloured' community in Wentworth, Durban, stressing the multiple histories of speakers and their sociolinguistic relations with the rest of the city. However, my current fieldwork in the city suggests that Kamwangamalu (2004) overestimates the amount of code-switching in the community (between English and Afrikaans).

Illuminating work on code-switching in townships of the Witwatersrand has been undertaken by Finlayson and Slabbert (1997), Finlayson *et al.* (1998), and Slabbert and Finlayson (2000). Here all 11 major languages of the country were reputed to enter into code-switching with each other. Closer examination of the data showed that code-switching was more constrained than this. Finlayson, Calteaux and Myers-Scotton (1998) showed that there was structure underneath the apparent randomness of switching, using Myers-Scotton's matrix frame model of the time. Again, the predictions of the model were generally upheld regarding the existence of a matrix language into which elements from one or more languages were embedded. This matrix language is constant within a speaker's turn, except for occasional 'language islands' (also predicted in Myers-Scotton's model). Slabbert and Myers-Scotton (1997) attempted to apply the model to characterize new township codes like Tsotsitaal, a variety associated with youth street culture, gangs and prisons. Whereas previous scholarship had discussed these as independent mixed languages drawing on Afrikaans syntax and lexis from multiple sources for Tsotsitaal, and Zulu syntax and a varied lexis for Iscamtho, subsequent scholarship tended to focus on their more dynamic nature. Slabbert and Myers-Scotton (1997) suggested that these are indeed mixed codes, with Tsotsitaal having Afrikaans as its matrix language and many African languages as the embedded languages. Rudwick (2005) stressed that, in Durban, Tsotsitaal vocabulary was spreading into the home and being accepted by females, leading her to propose a diglossic relation between Tsotsitaal (L) and Zulu (H). It remains to be seen how significant the difference is: whether we are dealing with informal Zulu that accepts some slang terms as informal items and a more formal variety, or whether there really is a discrete Tsotsitaal–Zulu relationship in everyone's code repertoire.

Much work on English tends to discuss the effects of language contact, often of African languages or Afrikaans on different varieties of English. Many of these are grammatical studies based on corpus linguistics methods. The *ICE Corpus of South African English* (see Jeffery 2003) has not yet been completed, but has yielded some studies, e.g. Jeffery and Van Rooy (2004) of the emphasizer *now*. Other important corpora include the Xhosa English corpus developed at Rhodes University (see De Klerk 2006) and the Tswana Learner English corpus at the University of the North West (developed by Van Rooy and Van der Walt). De Klerk (2005) has used the corpus to demonstrate differences between the L2 English of Xhosa speakers and those of L1 varieties like New Zealand English (in adverbials like *actually* and *really*). Van Rooy (2002) has examined phonological aspects like stress placement in the English of Tswana L1 speakers, concluding that stress is attracted to the penultimate syllable, except when the final syllable is superheavy. Makalela (2004) has studied the extent to which the extension of the stative in progressive contexts (a well-known feature of New Englishes) draws on the grammar of the substrates (using Tswana as his exemplar). He concludes that substrate influence is substantial. Van der Walt and Van Rooy (2002) examine the emergence of a norm in Black South African English, with some constructions (like *other … other* for 'some …

others') being more acceptable to educated speakers than others like resumptive pronouns in relative clauses. Mesthrie (2006) studied the mesolectal BSAE speakers to ascertain whether there were general properties in their grammar that went beyond the identification of miscellaneous but unrelated features. He shows that a very large portion of the grammatical variation in his mesolectal data can be attributed to a property that he terms 'anti-deletion'. This is a predilection for retaining surface phrases in their full form, i.e. to spell out the full elements of a syntactic string. He notices the rarity of deletion processes commonly reported in varieties elsewhere, like copula deletion and pro-drop. He also refers to a more specific property within the subset which he terms an 'undeletion', viz. the retention of grammatical elements that tend to be dropped in standard English, e.g. *to* after *make*, *let* and *have* (e.g. BSAE, *He made me to go home*).

Studies in grammatical variation from a sociolinguistic perspective in varieties other than Black South African English are fewer in the period under review. Mesthrie (2002a) described the semi-auxiliary use of *busy* in general South African English (*He was busy crying*) and the use of unstressed *do* in Cape Flats English (Mesthrie 1999). While both constructions appear to involve some convergence with tendencies in Afrikaans grammar, the sociohistorical profile suggests that other factors are at play: the former involves lifting of a stylistic and pragmatic constraint that occurs in other varieties of English in the UK and the USA; the latter shows the importance of looking at the sociohistorical input, in this case, the L2 English of Dutch and German missionaries.

Turning to African languages, Deumert *et al.* (2006) in as yet unpublished work looked at the adoption of discourse markers and logical connectors from English among urban speakers of Xhosa. There is a preponderance of use of connectors like *because*, *if*, *as if*, *so* and of discourse elements like *I mean*, *I think*, etc. These appear to serve symbolic functions of signalling modernity via multilingualism that includes access to English. Conversely – and contradictorily – Makalela's (2007) study of radio conversation in Limpopo Province stresses that speakers who are fluent in English use such connectors and markers from African languages like Tswana. This is clearly a fruitful area for studies of contact and convergence.

An important sociological strand of contact research concerns language maintenance and shift and language survival versus death. The languages most affected in the course of history have been those of the Khoe-San phylum. Languages once spread throughout the region are now close to extinction. The foundational work on this theme comes from the early twentieth century, when Wilhelm Bleek, Dorothea Bleek and Lucy Lloyd pioneered the detailed study of |Xam and other Khoe-San languages, see Traill (1995, 1996) for full references. The field lost an international leader with the passing of Tony Traill in 2006. Apart from Traill's œuvre, other important salvage work on Khoe-San languages can be found in the work of Crawhall (2004), whose thesis dealt with the sociolinguistics of !Ui-Taa languages (especially N|u). Crawhall was able to locate 12 speakers or semi-speakers of N|u, previously believed to be virtually extinct. Crawhall (2005a, 2005b) reports on identity and community issues relating to the language. Close linguistic attention to the variety spoken by these surviving speakers is being undertaken by Güldemann (2006). Historians and linguists at the University of the Free State are involved in a Khoe-San Culture and Memory Project, which is locating speakers of Khoe-San languages like Gri and !Ora, previously thought to be virtually extinct, and working on matters of historical, cultural and linguistic importance with them.

Shift among other groups of speakers involves a greater degree of choice, rather than linguistic devastation. There is some good academic research (De Klerk 2000a, 2000b;

De Kadt 2005; Kamwangamalu 2003a, 2003b; Deumert and Mablanda 2009) on incipient shift among educated, middle-class Black South Africans, from a Bantu language to English. De Klerk (2000a) studied the changing habits of Black pupils and parents in Grahamstown, concluding that pupils were being tilted into a world where English was dominant. De Klerk observed that children were increasingly using English in interactions with friends, even if they shared Xhosa as a home language. More surprisingly, she found that parents were pragmatic about, or even proud of, these children's changing linguistic and cultural norms. This led De Klerk to conclude that the seeds of language shift were in place, and sown first in the minds of parents rather than their children. De Kadt (2005) examines the bifurcation between 'multicultural' and 'traditional' Zulu students at the University of KwaZulu-Natal campus. The first group incorporates English into its code-repertoire to a much greater extent than the second which resists a modernizing identity. These attitudes and bifurcation in identities have implications for both maintenance and shift in the long term. It is necessary to caution that while shift is incipient among younger members of the new elites, on the whole, appeals to language shift in the general Black populace are premature. There have been studies of the ongoing shift from Indian languages to English in South Africa: Prabhakaran (1998) summarizing her previous work on Telugu, Desai (1998) on factors influencing maintenance and shift in Gujarati, and Mesthrie (2007d) examining social conditions and young people's preferences in the crucial decade of the 1960s.

De Klerk and Barkhuizen (2004a) have undertaken some studies of the language attitudes and expectations of Afrikaans-speaking South Africans migrating to New Zealand. They suggest that the predilection for shift occurs even prior to the actual emigration of such middle-class persons. Kotze and Biberauer (2005) examine the status of, and attitudes to, Afrikaans in the UK. Although attitudes to the language remain favourable, speakers appear to decrease the amount of Afrikaans in family conversations than with friends and bilingual outsiders. This is an unexpected reverse pattern that requires further study. Migration into post-apartheid South Africa is a topic of considerable interest, and starting to attract some linguistic research: Vigouroux (2005) on French speakers from West and Central Africa; Reitzes and Crawhall (1998) on the rights of and problems facing refugees; and Kamuangu (2006) on language practices among families from Central Africa in their new environment in Johannesburg. De Kadt and Ige (2005) report on the first generation of migrants from Nigeria in relation to stereotypes about them, their resistance to negative stereotyping and attempts to find an 'identity space' in a new society. Deumert and Mabandla (2009) have undertaken innovative research on internal migration in South Africa, with attention to economics, culture and language as speakers move from the rural Eastern Cape into the Western Cape. They also show that English is starting to make inroads into peer-group interaction in some working-class communities.

The pidgin Fanakalo remains relatively under-studied. In the period under review two articles appeared. Mesthrie (2003) discusses reduplication in the pidgin within the framework of language contact. He shows that the Fanakalo data appear to contradict claims that reduplication is characteristic of expanded pidgins and Creoles, rather than 'non-expanded' pidgins. However, he also finds some substance in the claim, since reduplication is far less common in the pidgin than in the languages of speakers involved in the contact situation. Mesthrie (2007c) explores the differences between pidginization and early second language acquisition of Xhosa and Zulu, closely-related agglutinating languages. He proposes that pidgin and early interlanguage are indeed differentiable, contrary to claims in current creolistics. Wildsmith-Cromarty (2003) provides an engaging social

193

account of her own second-language learning experiences within the socio-pedagogical traditions of Zulu teaching.

Language and culture

This theme has mostly taken a back seat to broader issues of multilingualism and policy. Important collections of essays on language and ethnicity and on multilingualism were edited as guest issues of international journals by Kamwangamalu (1998a, 2000, 2002), McCormick and Mesthrie (1999), Ridge, Makoni and Ridge (1999), and Kamwanga-malu and Reagan (2004). A book of essays on multilingualism and multiculturalism in KwaZulu-Natal province was edited by Extra and Maartens (1998); and one focusing on postcolonial and post-apartheid identities was edited by Finlayson and Slabbert (2005). Differences between clinical and social constructions of identity are covered in Makoni *et al.* (2001). Koopman (2000) is a short book-length treatment of language change and adaptation in Zulu in response to modernization. Full-length book studies of indigenous naming practices can be found in Neethling (2005) on Xhosa and Koopman (2002) on Zulu. Finlayson (2004) discusses language and culture in relation to African languages. Special registers within Venda are treated by Mulaudzi (2001) and Mulaudzi and Poulos (2003): the former on an initiation language for young males, the latter on the special register of the ruling Musanda class. The attitudes and experiences of university-educated Black South Africans in relation to their home languages and English, and tradition and modernity are explored by De Kadt (2005), Bangeni and Kapp (2007), Makoe (2007) and Rudwick (2004). The crux around which these papers revolve is the mock-serious label 'coconut' for youngsters who are allegedly 'dark on the outside, white on the inside'. The label encapsulates new class alignments over the old racial solidities of apartheid, with language forming a key component of this ongoing process (Mesthrie 2007a).

Intercultural communication is a potentially fertile area for research, with early studies in South Africa set by Chick (1995, 2002), Herbert (1985), Kasanga (2001), Kaschula and Anthonissen (1995) and Kaschula (1994). This potential is set to be met in the near future with some graduate programmes now focusing specifically on this area. There was an international conference dedicated to this theme (3rd Symposium on Intercultural Communication and Pragmatics, January 2008) at the University of Stellenbosch, with several papers on South African research. Levin (2005) examines discordant terminology and language use in a children's hospital between mostly English-speaking doctors and Xhosa-speaking patients.

Language, power, planning

Much work in South Africa continues to relate to language policy and planning, with a special emphasis on the role of African languages in education. Only a representative selection of such mostly applied linguistic work is possible here: Alexander (2002), Madiba (2004), Desai (2001), Du Plessis (2006), Heugh (2000), Joseph and Ramani (2004), and Plüddemann *et al.* (2004). Victor Webb's book *Language in South Africa* (2002) is a full-length study of the need for promotion of the African languages. Cautionary counterpoints regarding attitudes and practice can be found in Foley (2004), Ridge (2004), and Wright (2004). The position of Afrikaans in higher education and the efforts at transformation in former Afrikaans universities are treated in Du Plessis (2006). Language choice in specific domains like the prisons is discussed by Barkhuizen and De Klerk (2002), judiciary and security services by Du Plessis (2001), and engineering by Hill and Van Zyl (2002). Deumert (2005) and Webb (2005) assess the state of lexical development and standardization in the country's official African languages. Allwood and Hendrickse (2003) report on a project that is building spoken language corpora for the country's nine official African languages.

Language attitudes, choices and practices are an important underpinning of this area of research and numerous significant articles can be found in the journal, *Southern African Linguistics and Applied Language Studies* in the period 2000–2005. The main focus of these studies is on attitudes and choices of younger Black South Africans at educational institutions, in respect of their roles of English and an African language. There is also a continuing tradition of language activism on behalf of Afrikaans, discussed by Van Rooy and Pienaar (2006: 199–200). Van Rensburg (2000) provides an overview of lost opportunities and subsequent dilemmas surrounding Afrikaans.

Some important work is being undertaken on the notion of linguistic citizenship in a multilingual and multicultural society such as South Africa (Stroud and Heugh 2004). The term was in fact coined by Stroud (2001) in connection with the empowerment of people and their languages and meant to contrast with the more static conception of linguistic rights. Similar interests are evinced by a long-term study of a new township built on non-racial lines in Cape Town, in which Xhosa and English co-exist in equal numbers in a situation of stratification, with English being the dominant language of education and commerce, see Blommaert *et al.* (2005). Finally, two series contain significant papers on sociolinguistic and applied linguistic themes relating to multilingualism and government: (1) the PRAESA working papers series at the University of Cape Town; and (2) *Studies in Language Policy in South Africa*, a book series produced jointly out of a set of conferences run by the University of the Free State and partners from Belgian universities.

Themes from adjacent disciplines

As mentioned earlier, there is of necessity significant overlap between sociolinguistics and studies with a more applied orientation, viz. applied linguistics and discourse analysis. This is too vast an area to cover in detail here and only the most significant trends are mentioned. Translation studies occupy a potentially important place in a multilingual society with gross past and present inequalities. A more applied orientation that sees translation and terminological development as an essential part of empowerment can be seen in the writings of, *inter alia*, Naude (2007), Bedeker and Feinauer (2006), and Beukes (2006, 2007). Another strand examines misinterpretation in courtrooms and other administrative contexts (Kaschula 1995; Moeketsi 1998). The International Association for Translation and Intercultural Studies held its second conference at the University of the Western Cape in 2007, with a focus on intervention in translation, interpreting and intercultural encounters. Several papers dealt with South African issues. A third intercultural dimension is stressed in AIDS research with a linguistic bent (e.g. Clark 2006; Buthelezi, 2007). Here issues of nomenclature, word coinage, taboo, gender and youth language are significant. Discourse and conversation analysis has provided the tools for much work of sociolinguistic interest. Discourse management in gendered

195

groups has been studied by Hunt (2005), De Klerk and Hunt (2000), and Thetela (2002). The analysis of gender, gay language and homophobia can be found in De Kadt (2002), a focus issue of *Southern African Linguistics and Applied Language Studies*. Discourse Analysis has also impacted upon linguistic analyses of South Africa's Truth and Reconciliation Commission which enabled South Africans to bring their stories of oppression under apartheid into the public domain. Here the study of narrative and the linguistic and extra-linguistic aspects of discourse have been significant (Anthonissen 2006; Blommaert *et al.* 2006). An important study of narrative within a sociolinguistic framework is Malan (2000), which analyses the narrative competence of children who are bilingual in Afrikaans and English and who do not always produce 'linear' narratives. Hibbert (2003) studies the lexical and discourse features that BSAE speakers bring from their traditional cultural base to parliamentary discourse.

Conclusion

The period from the 1990s onwards reveals a great deal of interest in the more political aspects of language development, standardization and use in education. Standing up for the rights of minorities and disadvantaged majorities was a priority at the time of political transition. It is important that the linguistic underpinnings of such work should continue to be nurtured, despite the shrinkage of linguistics and language departments nationally. Now, more than ever, there is a need for the scholarly study and research of the wealth of languages still to be found in southern Africa, and their linguistic and sociolinguistic properties.

References

Aarons, D. and Akach, P. (2002) 'South African Sign Language: one language or many?', in R. Mesthrie (ed.) *Language in South Africa*, Cambridge: Cambridge University Press, pp 127–47.

Aarons, D. and Morgan, R. (1998) 'The structure of South African Sign Language after apartheid', paper presented at the Sixth International Conference on Theoretical Issues in Sign Language Research, Gallaudet University, Washington, DC, November.

Alexander, N. (2002) 'Linguistic rights, language planning and democracy in post-apartheid South Africa', in S. J. Baker (ed.) *Language Policy: Lessons from Global Models*, Monterey, CA: Monterey Institute of International Studies.

Allwood, J. and Hendrickse, A. P. (2003) 'Spoken language corpora for the nine official African languages of South Africa', *Southern African Linguistics and Applied Language Studies*, 21, 189–201.

Anthonissen, C. (2006) 'Critical Discourse Analysis as an analytic tool in considering selected, prominent features of TRC testimonies', *Journal of Language and Politics*, 5, 71–96.

Bangeni, B. and Kapp, R. (2007) 'Shifting language attitudes in a linguistically diverse learning environment in South Africa', *Journal of Multilingual and Multicultural Development*, 28, 253–69.

Barbiers, S., Cornips, L. and Kunst, J. P. (2005) *The Syntactic Atlas of the Dutch Dialects: a Corpus of Elicited Speech and Text as On-line Dynamic Atlas*. Online. Available at: www.meertens.nl/sand/zoeken/index.php.

Barkhuizen, G. and de Klerk, V. (2002) 'The role of Xhosa in a South African prison: "The situation is leading you"', *Journal of Multilingual and Multicultural Development*, 23, 160–74.

Bedeker, L. and Feinauer, I. (2006) 'The translator as cultural mediator', *Southern African Linguistics and Applied Language Studies*, 24, 133–41.

Bekker, I. (2007) 'Fronted /s/ in general White South African English', *Language Matters*, 38, 46–74.

Bekker, I. and Ely, G. (2007) 'An acoustic analysis of White South African English monophthongs', *Southern African Linguistics and Applied Language Studies*, 25, 107–14.

Bembe, M. and Beukes, A. M. (2007) 'The use of slang by black youth in Gauteng', *Southern African Linguistics and Applied Language Studies*, 25, 463–72.

Beukes, A. M. (2006) 'Translation in South Africa: the politics of transmission', *Southern African Linguistics and Applied Language Studies*, 24, 1–6.

——(2007) 'Governmentality and the good offices of translation in 20th century South Africa', *Southern African Linguistics and Applied Language Studies*, 25, 115–30.

Blommaert, J., Bock, M. and McCormick, K. (2006) 'Narrative inequality in the TRC hearings: on the hearability of hidden transcripts', *Journal of Language and Politics*, 5, 37–70.

Blommaert, J., Muyllaert, N., Huysmans, M. and Dyers, C. (2005) 'Peripheral normativity: the production of locality in a South African township school', *Linguistics and Education*, 16, 378–403.

Buthelezi, T., Mitchell, C., Moletsane, R., De Lange, N., Taylor, M. and Stuart, J. (2007) 'Youth voices about sex and AIDS!', *International Journal for Inclusive Education*, 11, 445–59.

Carstens, A. and Grebe, H. (eds) (2001) *Taallandskap: huldingsbundel vir Christo van Rensburg*, Pretoria: Van Schaik.

Chick, J. K. (1995) 'Interactional sociolinguistics and intercultural communication in South Africa', in R. Mesthrie (ed.) *Language and Social History: Studies in South African Sociolinguistics*, Cape Town: David Philip, pp. 230–41.

——(2002) 'Intercultural miscommunication in South Africa', in R. Mesthrie (ed.) *Language in South Africa*, Cambridge: Cambridge University Press, pp. 258–78.

Clark, J. (2006) 'The role of language and gender in the naming and framing of HIV/AIDS in the South African context', *Southern African Linguistics and Applied Language Studies*, 24, 461–71.

Crawhall, N. (2004) '!Ui-Taa language shift in Gordonia and Postmasburg Districts, South Africa', PhD dissertation, Dept. of Linguistics, University of Cape Town.

——(2005a) 'The story of !Ui: causality and language shift in Africa', in N. Crawhall and N. Ostler (eds) *Creating Outsiders – Endangered Languages, Migration and Marginalisation, Proceedings of the 9th Conference of the Foundation for Endangered Languages*, Stellenbosch, South Africa, pp. 71–81.

——(2005b) 'Too good to leave behind: the N|u language and the Khomani people of Gordonia district', in R. Finlayson and S. Slabbert (eds) *Languages and Identities in a Postcolony*, Frankfurt: Peter Lang, pp. 67–91.

Da Silva, A. (2007) 'South African English: a sociolinguistic analysis of an emerging variety', PhD thesis, University of the Witwatersrand.

De Kadt, E. (ed.) (2002) 'Focus issue: gender and language', *Southern African Linguistics and Applied Language Studies*, 20, 177–89.

——(2005) 'English, language shift and identities: a comparison between "Zulu-dominant" and "multicultural" students on a South African university campus', *Southern African Linguistics and Applied Language Studies*, 23, 19–37.

De Kadt, E. and Ige, B. O. (2005) 'Finding "space" in South Africa: constructing identity as a Nigerian', in R. Finlayson and S. Slabbert (eds) *Languages and Identities in a Postcolony*, Frankfurt: Peter Lang, pp. 121–45.

De Klerk, V. (2000a) 'Language shift in Grahamstown: a case study of selected Xhosa speakers', *International Journal of the Sociology of Language*, 146, 87–110.

——(2000b) 'To be Xhosa or not to be Xhosa: that is the question', *Journal of Multilingual and Multicultural Development*, 21, 198–215.

——(2005) 'The use of actually in spoken Xhosa English: a corpus study', *World Englishes*, 24, 275–88.

——(2006) *Corpus Linguistics and World Englishes: An Analysis of Xhosa English*, London: Continuum.

De Klerk, V. and Barkhuizen, G. (2004a) 'Pre-emigration reflections: Afrikaans speakers moving to New Zealand', *Southern African Linguistics and Applied Language Studies*, 22, 99–109.

——(2004b) 'English in the prison services: a case of breaking the law?', *World Englishes*, 21, 9–22.

De Klerk, V. and Hunt S. (2000) 'Discourse domination? The role of gender in seminar interaction', *Southern African Linguistics and Applied Language Studies*, 18, 73–88.

197

Desai, U. (1998) 'Investigation of the factors influencing maintenance and shift of the Gujarati language in South Africa', PhD thesis, University of Durban-Westville.

Desai, Z. (2001) 'Multilingualism in South Africa with particular reference to the role of African languages in education', *International Review of Education*, 47, 323–39.

Deumert, A. (2003) *Language Standardization and Language Change: The Dynamics of Cape Dutch*, Amsterdam: Benjamins.

——(2005) 'The shape of the standard: reflections on postcolonial standard languages, with special attention to South Africa', in V. Webb, A. Deumert and B. Lepota (eds) *The Standardisation of African Languages in South Africa*, Report on the Workshop held at the University of Pretoria, 30 June–1 July, pp. 17–34.

Deumert, A., Hurst, E., Masinyana, O. and Mesthrie, R. (2006) 'Urbanization and language change: logical connectors and discourse markers in urban isiXhosa', paper presented at the Linguistics Society of Southern Africa conference, University of KwaZulu-Natal, Durban, July.

Deumert, A. and Mabandla, N. (2009) '*I-Dollar eyi one*! Ethnolinguistic fractionalization, communication networks, and economic participation: lessons from Cape Town, South Africa', *Journal of Development Studies*, 45, 412–20.

Donnelly, S. (2000) 'Southern Tekela Nguni is alive: reintroducing the Phuthi language', *International Journal of the Sociology of Language*, 136, 97–120.

Du Plessis, T. (2001) 'Towards a multilingual policy in the judiciary and security services', in K. Deprez, T. Du Plessis and L. Teck (eds) *Multilingualism, the Judiciary and Security Services*, Pretoria: Van Schaik, pp. 95–105.

——(2006) 'From monolingual to bilingual higher education: the repositioning of historically Afrikaans-medium universities in South Africa', *Language Policy*, 5, 87–113.

Extra, G. and Maartens, J. (eds) (1998) *Multilingualism in a Multicultural Context: Case Studies on South Africa and Western Europe*, Tilburg: Tilburg University Press.

Finlayson, R. (1984) 'The changing nature of Isihlonipho Sabafazi', *African Studies*, 43, 137–46.

——(2004) 'Language and culture in South Africa', in A.W. Oliphant, P. Delius and L. Metzer (eds) *Democracy X: Marking the Present/Re-presenting the Past*, Pretoria: Unisa Press, pp. 219–31.

Finlayson, R., Calteaux, K. and Myers-Scotton, C. (1998) 'Orderly mixing: code-switching and accommodation in South Africa', *Journal of Sociolinguistics*, 2, 395–420.

Finlayson, R. and Slabbert, S. (1997) '"We just mix" – code-switching in a South African township', *International Journal of the Sociology of Language*, 125, 65–98.

——(eds) (2005) *Language and Identities in a Postcolony*, Frankfurt: Peter Lang.

Foley, A. (2004) 'Language policy for higher education in South Africa: implications and complications', *South African Journal of Higher Education*, 18, 57–71.

Gilmour, R. (2006) *Grammars of Colonialism: Representing Languages in Colonial South Africa*, Basingstoke: Palgrave.

Güldemann, T. (2006) 'A forgotten heritage – Southern African Khoisan and importance for modern linguistic research', keynote address at the Linguistics Society of Southern Africa conference, July.

Herbert, R. K. (1985) 'Say "Thank you" or something', *American Speech*, 61, 76–88.

——(1997) 'The meaning of language choices in South Africa', in R. K. Herbert (ed.) *African Linguistics at the Crossroads*, Cologne: Rüdiger Köppe Verlag, pp. 395–415.

Heugh, K. (2000) 'The case against bilingual and multilingual education in South Africa', PRAESA [Project for the Study of Alternative Education in South Africa] Occasional Papers No. 6, University of Cape Town.

Hibbert, L. (2003) 'Changing language practices in parliament, South Africa', *Southern African Linguistics and Applied Language Studies*, 21, 103–18.

Hill, P. and Van Zyl, S. (2002) 'English and multilingualism in the South African engineering workplace', *World Englishes*, 21, 23–36.

Hundleby, C. E. (1964) 'Xhosa-English pronunciation in the South-East Cape', unpublished PhD, Rhodes University.

Hunt, S. (2005) 'Some (more) features of conversation among women friends', *Southern African Linguistics and Applied Language Studies*, 23, 445–57.

Jeffery, C. (2003) 'On compiling a corpus of South African English', *Southern African Linguistics and Applied Language Studies*, 21, 341–4.

Jeffery, C. and Van Rooy, B. (2004) 'Emphasiser *now* in colloquial South African English', *World Englishes*, 23, 269–80.

Joseph, M. and Ramani, E. (2004) 'Academic excellence through language equity: a new bilingual BA degree, (in English and Sesotho sa Leboa)', in H. Griesel (ed.) *Curriculum Responsiveness: Case Studies in Higher Education*, Pretoria: South African Universities Vice-Chancellors Association, pp. 237–61.

Kamuangu, G. (2006) 'Learning and forgetting: the use of languages in the diaspora', *The International Journal of Learning*, 14, 45–52.

Kamwangamalu, N. (ed.) (1998a) 'Aspects of multilingualism in South Africa', Special Issue of *Multilingua*, 17.

——(1998b) ' "We-codes", "they-codes" and "codes in-between": identities of English and code-switching in post-apartheid South Africa', *Multilingua*, 17, 277–96.

——(ed.) (2000) *Language and Ethnicity in the New South Africa*, Special Issue of *International Journal of Sociology of Language*, 144.

——(ed.) (2002) 'Special Issue on *English in South Africa*', *World Englishes*, 28.

——(2003a) 'Globalization of English, and language maintenance and shift in South Africa', *International Journal of the Sociology of Language*, 164, 65–81.

——(2003b) 'Social change and language shift: South Africa', *Annual Review of Applied Linguistics*, 23, 225–42.

——(2004) 'Language, social history, and identity in post-apartheid South Africa: a case study of the "Colored" community of Wentworth', *International Journal of Sociology of Language*, 170, 113–29.

Kamwangamalu, N. and Reagan, T. (eds) (2004) *Special Issue: South Africa. Language Problems and Language Planning*, 28.

Kasanga, L. (2001) 'Intercultural sociolinguistics and communication research in South Africa: its relevance to academic settings and the service industry', *Southern African Linguistics and Applied Language Studies*, 19, 253–75.

Kaschula, R. (1994) 'Cross-cultural communication in a north-eastern Cape farming community', *South African Journal of African Languages*, 9, 100–4.

——(1995) 'Cross-cultural communication in the Eastern Cape with particular reference to law courts', *South African Journal of African Languages*, 15, 9–15.

Kaschula, R. and Anthonissen, C. (1995) *Communicating across Cultures in South Africa*, Johannesburg: Hodder and Stoughton.

Koopman, A. (2000) *Zulu Language Change*, Howick, South Africa: Brevitas.

——(2002) *Zulu Names*, Pietermaritzburg: University of KwaZulu-Natal Press.

Kotze, E. and Biberauer, T. (2005) 'Language and identity: the case of Afrikaans in the United Kingdom', in R. Finlayson and S. Slabbert (eds) *Languages and Identities in a Postcolony*, Frankfurt: Peter Lang, pp. 91–120.

Lanham, L. W. (1967) 'Teaching English in Bantu primary schools', Publication No. 4, Johannesburg: English Academy of South Africa.

Lanham, L. W. and Prinsloo, K. (eds) (1978) *Language and Communication Studies in South Africa*, Cape Town: Oxford University Press.

Lanham, L. W. and Macdonald, C. (1979) *The Standard in South African English and its Social History*, Heidelberg: Julius Groos Verlag.

Lass, R. (1990) 'A "standard" South African vowel system', in S. Ramsaran (ed.) *Studies in the Pronunciation of English: A Commemorative Volume in Honour of A.C. Gimson*, London: Routledge, pp. 272–85.

——(1995) 'South African English', in R. Mesthrie (ed.) *Language and Social History: Studies in South African Sociolinguistics*, Cape Town: David Philip, pp. 89–106.

Levin, M. (2005) 'Discordant definitions of Xhosa medical terminology and their impact on communication between English-speaking doctors and Xhosa-speaking parents at a paediatric hospital', unpublished PhD thesis, Dept. of Linguistics, University of Cape Town.

Louw, P. and De Wet, F. (2007) 'The perception and identification of accent in spoken Black South African English', *Southern African Linguistics and Applied Language Studies*, 25, 91–105.

199

Madiba, M. (2004) ' "Treading where angels fear most": the South African government's New Language Policy for Higher Education and its implications', *Alternation*, 11, 26–43.

Makalela, L. (2004) 'Making sense of BSAE for linguistic democracy in South Africa', *World Englishes*, 23, 355–66.

——(2007) 'Black South African English on the radio: an investigation of oral speech patterns', paper presented at the 13th Annual Conference of the International Association for World Englishes, University of Regensburg, 4–6 October.

Makoe, P. (2007) 'Language, discourses and identity construction in a multilingual South African primary school', *The English Academy Review – Southern African Journal of English Studies*, 24, 55–71.

Makoni, S., Ridge, E. and Ridge, S. (2001) 'Through different lenses: social and clinical constructions of identity', *Southern African Linguistics and Applied Language Studies*, 19, 275–90.

Malan, K. (2000) 'Oral narratives of personal experience: a developmental sociolinguistic study of Cape Flats children', PhD thesis, University of Cape Town.

McCormick, K. (2002) *Language in Cape Town's District Six*, Oxford: Oxford University Press.

McCormick, K. and Mesthrie, R. (eds) (1999) *Post-Apartheid South Africa*, Special Issue of *International Journal of Sociology of Language*, 136.

Mesthrie, R. (1998) 'Words across worlds: aspects of language contact and language learning in the Eastern Cape, 1800–1850,' *African Studies*, 57, 5–26.

——(1999) 'Fifty way to say "I Do": tracing the origins of unstressed *do* in Cape Flats English.' *South African Journal of Linguistics*, 17, 58–71.

——(2002a) 'Endogeny versus contact revisited: aspectual *busy* in South African English', *Language Sciences*, 24, 345–58.

——(ed.) (2002b) *Language in South Africa*, Cambridge: Cambridge University Press.

——(2003) 'Is there reduplication in Fanakalo?', in S. Kouwenberg, (ed.) *Twice as Meaningful: Reduplication in Pidgins, Creoles and Other Contact Languages*, London: Battlebridge, pp. 301–6.

——(2005a) 'Putting back the horse before the cart: the spelling form fallacy in Second Language Acquisition Studies, with special reference to the treatment of schwa in Black South African English', *English World Wide*, 26, 127–51.

——(2005b) 'Assessing representations of South African Indian English in writing: an application of variation theory', *Language Variation and Change*, 17, 303–26.

——(2006) 'Anti-deletions in a second language variety: a study of Black South African English mesolect', *English World Wide*, 27, 111–46.

——(2007a) 'Of coconuts and kings: accelerated linguistic change among young, middle-class females in post-apartheid South Africa', plenary paper at the International Association of World Englishes conference, University of Regensburg, October.

——(2007b) 'The origins of colloquial South African Tamil', *Oriental Anthropologist*, 7, 17–38.

——(2007c) 'Differentiating pidgin from early interlanguage: pidgin Nguni (Fanakalo) versus second language varieties of Xhosa and Zulu', *Southern African Linguistics and Applied Language Studies*, 25, 75–89.

——(2007d) 'Language shift, cultural change and identity retention: Indian South Africans in the 1960s and beyond', *South African Historical Journal*, 57, 134–52.

Mesthrie, R. and Roberge, P. (eds) (2001) *Focus on Afrikaans Sociohistorical Linguistics*, Part I, Special Issue of *Journal of Germanic Linguistics*, 13.

——(2002) *Focus on Afrikaans Sociohistorical Linguistics*, Part I, Special Issue of *Journal of Germanic Linguistics*, 14.

Moeketsi, R. (1998) 'Statements about Sesotho questions used in the South African courtroom', *South African Journal of African Languages*, 18, 72–7.

Mulaudzi, P.A. (2001) 'The Domba variety: an initiation language for adulthood.' *South African Journal of African Languages*, 21, 9–15.

——(2004) 'Chimbedzi variety: a link between the Venda language and the Kalanga cluster', *South African Journal of African Languages*, 24, 132–9.

Mulaudzi, P. A. and Poulos, G. (2003) 'The Musanda variety: the language of the "ruling community" among the Venda people', *South African Journal of African Languages*, 23, 37–45.

Naude, J. (2007) 'Guest editorial: language practice – one profession, multiple applications', *Southern African Linguistics and Applied Language Studies*, 25, iii–vi.

Neethling, B. (2005) *Naming among the Xhosa of South Africa*, London: Edwin Mellen Press.

Penn, C. (1992a) *Dictionary of Southern African Signs*, 5 vols, Pretoria: Human Sciences Research Council.

——(1992b) 'The sociolinguistics of South African Sign Language', in R. K. Herbert (ed.) *Language and Society in Africa*, Johannesburg: Witwatersrand University Press, pp. 277–84.

Plüddemann, P., Braam, D., Broeder, P., Extra, G. and October, M. (2004) 'Language policy implementation and language vitality in Western Cape primary schools', PRAESA Occasional Papers, 15, University of Cape Town.

Prabhakaran, V. (1998) 'Multilingualism and language shift in South Africa: the case of Telugu, an Indian language', *Multilingua*, 17, 297–319.

Reagan, T. and Penn, C. (1997) 'Language policy, South African Sign Language and the deaf: social and educational implications', *South African Journal of Applied Language Studies*, 5, 1–13.

Reagan, T., Penn, C. and Ogilvy, D. (2006) 'From policy to practice: Sign Language studies in post-apartheid South Africa', *Language Policy*, 5, 187–208.

Reitzes, M. and Crawhall, N. (1998) *Silenced by Nation-building: The Exclusion of African Migrants in South Africa*, Occasional Publication, Cape Town: South African Migration Project.

Ridge, E., Makoni, S. and Ridge, S. (eds) (1999) 'Applied Language Studies in Southern Africa', 25th Anniversary Special Issue of *Indian Journal of Applied Linguistics* (also available as Ridge, E., Makoni, S. and Ridge, S. (eds) (2001) *Freedom and Discipline: Essays in Applied Linguistics from Southern Africa*, New Delhi: Bahri.

Ridge, S. (2004) 'Language planning in a rapidly changing multilingual society: the case of English in South Africa', *Language Problems and Language Planning*, 28, 199–215.

Rudwick, S. (2004) ' "Zulu, we need it for our culture": Umlazi adolescents in the post-apartheid state', *Southern African Linguistics and Applied Language Studies*, 22, 159–73.

——(2005) 'Township language dynamics: isiZulu and isiTsotsi in Umlazi', *Southern African Linguistics and Applied Language Studies*, 233, 305–17.

——(2007) 'IsiNgqumo – introducing a gay Black South African linguistic variety', paper presented at the Annual Conference of the Linguistic Society of Southern Africa, University of the North-West, Potchefstroom, 4–6 July.

Rudwick, S. and Shange, M. (2006) 'Sociolinguistic oppression or expression of "Zuluness"? Isihlonipho among isiZulu-speaking females', *Southern African Linguistics and Applied Language Studies*, 24, 473–82.

Slabbert, S. and Finlayson, R. (2000) '"I'm a cleva!": the linguistic make-up of identity in a South African urban environment', *International Journal of Sociology of Language*, 144, 119–35.

Slabbert, S. and Myers-Scotton, C. (1997) 'The structure of Tsotsitaal and Iscamtho: code switching and in-group identity in South African townships', *Linguistics*, 35, 317–42.

Stroud, C. (2001) 'African mother-tongue programmes and the politics of language: linguistic citizenship versus linguistic human rights', *Journal of Multilingual and Multicultural Development*, 22, 339–55.

Stroud, C. and Heugh, K. (2004) 'Linguistic human rights and linguistic citizenship', in D. Patrick and J. Freeland (eds) *Language Rights and Language Survival: A Sociolinguistic Exploration*, Manchester: St. Jerome.

Thetela, P. H. (2002) 'Sex discourses and gender constructions in Southern Sotho: a case study of police interviews of rape/sexual assault victims', *Southern African Linguistics and Applied Language Studies*, 20, 177–89.

Traill, A. (1995) 'The Khoesan languages of South Africa', in R. Mesthrie (ed.) *Language and Social History: Studies in South African Sociolinguistics*, Cape Town: David Philip, pp. 1–18.

——(1996) '!Khwa-Ka Hhoutiten Hhouiten "The rush of the storm" – the linguistic death of |Xam', in P. Skotnes (ed.) *Miscast: Negotiating the Presence of Bushmen*, Cape Town: UCT Press, pp. 161–83.

Van der Walt, J. and Van Rooy, B. (2002) 'Towards a norm in South African Englishes', *World Englishes*, 21, 113–28.

Van Rensburg, C. (2000) 'Afrikaans and apartheid', *International Journal of the Sociology of Language*, 136, 77–96.

Van Rooy, B. (2002) 'Stress placement in Tswana English: the makings of a coherent system', *World Englishes*, 21, 145–60.

——(2004) 'Black South African English', in E. Schneider, K. Burridge, B. Kortmann, R. Mesthrie and C. Upton (eds) *A Handbook of Varieties of English*, vol. 1, *Phonology*, Berlin: Mouton de Gruyter, pp. 943–63.

Van Rooy, B. and Pienaar, M. (2006) 'Trends in recent South African linguistic research', *Southern African Linguistics and Applied Language Studies*, 24, 191–216.

Van Rooy, B. and Van Huyssten, G. (2000) 'The vowels of Black South African English: current knowledge and future prospects', *South African Journal of Linguistics*, 38, 15–35.

Vigouroux, C. B. (2005) ' "There are no Whites in Africa": territoriality, language and identity among Francophone Africans in Cape Town', *Language and Communication*, 25, 237–55.

Webb, V. (2002) *Language in South Africa*, Amsterdam: Benjamins.

——(2005) 'The role of language standardisation in the effective functioning of communities in public life in South Africa', in V. Webb, A. Deumert and B. Lepota (eds) *The Standardisation of African Languages in South Africa*, report on the workshop held at the University of Pretoria, 30 June–1 July 2005, pp. 35–42.

Wildsmith-Cromarty, R. (2003) 'Do learners learn Zulu the way children do? A response to Suzman', *South African Journal of African Languages*, 23, 175–88.

Wissing, D. (2002) 'Black South African English: a new English? – observations from a phonetic viewpoint', *World Englishes*, 21, 129–44.

Wright, L. (2004) 'Language and value: towards accepting a richer linguistic ecology for South Africa', *Language Problems and Language Planning*, 28.

19

Sociolinguistic studies of West and Central Africa

Bruce Connell and David Zeitlyn

Introduction

The regions of West and Central Africa (WCA) may be divided on geographical grounds, with Savannah to the West and Central Africa having most of the remaining rainforest. Within these two regions, however, one also finds considerable geographical and climatic variation. In West Africa – i.e. Mauritania in the west to Cameroon in the east – this runs from north to south as one moves from the Sahara Desert through the Sahel savannahs to forests and coastal plains and swamps. Central Africa is similar, although the region is dominated by rainforest. With respect to political entities, West Africa comprises Mauritania, Mali, Senegal, Gambia, Sierra Leone, Liberia, Ivory Coast, Burkina Faso, Ghana, Togo, Niger, and Nigeria. Central Africa includes Chad, Equatorial Guinea, Gabon, Central African Republic, Republic of Congo and the Democratic Republic of Congo, with Cameroon forming a bridge or transition between these two regions, and sometimes considered part of West and sometimes part of Central Africa.

Linguistic diversity and general characterization of the language situation in WCA

Languages from three of Africa's four major language phyla – Afroasiatic, Nilo-Saharan and Niger-Congo – are found in the region defined here as WCA. Gordon (2005) lists over 1700 languages for WCA, a figure that comprises perhaps 25 per cent of all the world's languages, and some 85 per cent of Africa's languages. Nigeria and Cameroon, the countries that form the meeting ground of West and Central Africa, are home to nearly half (789) of these languages, and their borderland is one of the most linguistically heterogeneous regions in the world. Most parts of WCA are multilingual and constitute rather heterogeneous linguistic settings. A language density map, such as that found in Gordon (2005; available at www.ethnologue.org/show_map.asp?name=Africa&seq=10) reveals the complexity of the linguistic setting of WCA. Even in those countries in WCA which have relatively few languages, e.g. Mauritania, or Niger, where it will be recalled much of their area is desert, multilingualism is the norm. Most of WCA is served by one or more lingua francas or regional languages; individual bi- or multilingualism is high, typically involving at least a home language and a regional lingua franca; it is not uncommon for people to have a repertoire of four or more languages, including the home or village language, one or more other local (or regional) languages, the regional lingua franca, as well as knowledge of a European language – that of the former colonial rulers. There are few areas where monolingualism (i.e. with respect to African languages) predominates; among the Yoruba of western Nigeria, for example, where their sizeable population and political dominance have obliged others to learn their language, rather than the reverse. However, even among such populations, one finds some bilingualism as many people have learned the former colonial language.

Early sociolinguistic research in WCA

The sociolinguistics of WCA is understudied. Indeed, the majority of the languages of this region are understudied from any perspective; for most, the basic descriptive work that must form a foundation for sociolinguistics has yet to be done. One cannot begin a sociophonetic study without first describing the basic phonetic and phonological characteristics of a language; one cannot examine the social correlates of grammatical or lexical variation until a sufficient amount of research has been carried out on the grammar and lexis. This is not to suggest that WCA languages have been totally ignored by sociolinguists. Yet 'traditional' sociolinguistic topics have received relatively little attention among African linguists, in deference to the 'macro' topics of language policy and planning. This is not surprising given the language situation in WCA and the continent generally, where the overwhelming majority of languages remain unwritten and undeveloped, and where in many countries there is public desire to see an African language take on the importance and some of the roles of the dominant European languages.

Early sociolinguistic work in WCA goes back to the immediate post-independence period of the 1960s and 1970s. Much of this work was designed to meet the needs of newly-independent developing nations, and focuses on such issues as language policy with regard to education and choice of national language in settings of massive multilingualism with a dominant non-indigenous, colonial language (e.g. Ansre 1969; Chumbow 1980; Badejo 1989; and contributions to Spencer 1971), with a lesser emphasis on other aspects of multilingualism (e.g. Bokamba 1977), and topics such as language spread (e.g. Greenberg 1971; Samarin 1982), pidgin and creole studies (e.g. Hancock 1971; Lipski 1992). (Work prior to this period does exist: Clements 1989 comments on the popularity of Africa-oriented sociolinguistic topics in American doctoral dissertations dating back to 1933.)

Bokamba (1990), surveying the contribution of African language studies to sociolinguistic theory, draws attention to the paucity of work on bilingualism (and by extension, multilingualism), discourse analysis, ethnography of communication, and language shift, pointing to the great wealth of excellent data available for such work. While work of traditional orientation, especially dealing with language policy and planning predominates, there has recently been an increase in other studies, especially in multilingualism, with growing attention to areas such as language shift and maintenance and linguistic diversity in the context of studies of language endangerment, discourse analysis and pragmatics.

Multilingualism and related issues

Studies of multilingual situations in WCA have mainly focused on urban settings, and especially the interaction between indigenous and former colonial languages. The place and role of English and French, the major colonial languages in WCA, have been examined in depth in early studies such as Alexandre (1963), and Spencer (1971). This continues in more recent work such as the contributions found in Bamgbose, Banjo and Thomas (1995) and Banjo (2000) for English, Chumbow and Bobdo (2000) for French and Mboudjeke (2006) for French and English. Studies on Portuguese (spoken in Capo Verde and Guinée Bissau) and Spanish (Equatorial Guinea) are few.

Recent work on the roles of English and French identify their continuing importance: with some exceptions, they continue to be used at virtually all levels of education (French obligatorily so in all 'francophone' African countries), as the language of government and other official business, and as a general lingua franca, at least among the educated and in certain domains. They have prestige, though indications are that their place in WCA societies is changing. Chumbow and Bobda (2000) point to both the growing respect for and importance of indigenous languages (e.g. most 'francophone' West African countries now have policies promoting indigenous languages) and the increased popularity/importance of English as a world language as factors which may decrease the use of French in the region in the years ahead. Nevertheless, Chumbow and Bobdo see French continuing to be used in official capacities and beyond for the foreseeable future.

Calvet (1999) and Chumbow and Bobda (2000) draw attention to the growth of what might be called 'New Frenches', by analogy with the 'New Englishes'. These include *le français populaire d'Abidjan*, a pidginized form of French (see Hattiger 1983), and Cameroon Pidgin French, although these are nowhere near as widespread or well established as regional varieties of English. Lafage (2003) examines French in Ivory Coast, including discussion of *français populaire ivoirien* (FPI), *nouchi* (an Abidjan variant) and *zouglou*, a variety of Ivorian pidgin French which draws its name from a dance form; see Tschiggfrey (1995). For English, Banjo (2000) suggests that in Nigeria, and possibly in Ghana, there is now an endonormative standard; Calvet (1999) offers evidence that this is also becoming the case for French in countries such as Senegal.

While several studies examine interactions between a colonial language and one or more indigenous languages, only few look at multilingualism exclusively or even primarily in terms of the latter. The former colonial language, or related pidgins and creoles, are not always maintained as a lingua franca. McLaughlin (2001) discusses the role that the Dakar variety of Wolof plays in the development of an overarching urban identity in Senegal's capital. She examines the strong influence French has had on the language, particularly through lexical borrowing. Juillard (1995) describes the language situation of Zuiginchor in the Casamance region of Senegal. Here, a language repertoire of up to five languages is common among much of the population, though Wolof has largely replaced the Portuguese creole as lingua franca. Similarly, Nicolaï's work on Songhay as a regional lingua franca (e.g. Nicolaï 2005) illustrates the importance of not making assumptions about the role of colonial languages.

Oyetade (1995) presents an analysis of the situation of Nupe vis-à-vis Yoruba in the primarily Yoruba-speaking city of Ibadan. Roughly half of interviewees were born in Ibadan, the others having migrated from various Nupe towns or villages. Informants were asked about ability in the two languages, domains where each is used, and attitudes toward each. Oyetade's results suggest that while there is a solid foundation for language shift – Yoruba is the language of the surrounding community, a language of instruction as well as the language of informal communication in school – there is apparently a situation of stable bilingualism. Nupe is used almost exclusively in particular domains, especially the home and, as reported by younger speakers, without coercion from their parents or elders.

Dakubu (2000) examines changing patterns in the multilingual behaviour of Ghanaian migrants, looking first at the situation in the small urban centre of Bawku in the north-east of Ghana, then at how the Bawku community in Accra, Ghana's capital and largest city, responds to a new set of multiple language options. The typical repertoire in Bawku of four or five languages changes as some languages fall into disuse in the new setting, but others are brought in. A similar study reported in Woods (1994) looked at changing patterns of language knowledge and use in Republic of Congo, not among urban immigrants, but comparing urban areas (viz Brazzaville) to towns and villages, and looking at patterning across different age groups, genders and in different domains of use.

One study of multilingualism in a common public domain, the local market, is Calvet (1992). This volume reports language choices made in the markets of several urban centres in WCA. Other studies have also examined market language use, e.g. Ogunsiji (2001), who examines language use in the New Gbagi market in Ibadan. Here choice of language (typically Yoruba, Pidgin or English) is governed by a number of factors, though the overriding one is the desire on the part of both seller and buyer to establish a good rapport. Similar studies of multilingualism in rural settings are practically non-existent, though this should not be taken as an indication that multilingualism in WCA is purely an urban phenomenon. Connell (submitted) explores language choice in a highly mul-tilingual rural market setting, in the Mambila village of Somié in Cameroon. Fourteen languages were observed in use in the market, with six of these accounting for 90 per cent of transactions. Overall, language choice appears to follow a pattern whereby the language of the trader plays a role in determining the language used in a given transac-tion: Mambila speakers use their own language by preference; otherwise either Fulfulde, French or Pidgin is used, determined in part by the language of the trader.

Code-switching

Although based on research in East Africa, Myers-Scotton (1993) sets the theoretical agenda. Studies have looked at code-switching between English and various African lan-guages, e.g. Essien (1995, Ibibio-English), Amuda (1994, Yoruba-English), Amuzu (2005, Ewe-English), and between two or more indigenous languages; Haust (1995) considers Mandinka, Wolof, and English, and Juillard (1995), discussed above, provides examples of four-way code-switching in Ziguinchor between Wolof, Diola, Mandinka and French. Recent work on code-switching between African languages and French has also been collected in, e.g. Queffelec (1998) and the proceedings of the 2004 *Penser la Francophonie* conference in Ouagadougou (see www.ltt.auf.org/IMG/doc/ACTES.doc). These studies document the complex patterns of use which Myers-Scotton's matrix language model describes. Code-switching is a part of language change which may result in language endangerment (considered below). Finally, a conference held in Legon, Ghana, in Novem-ber 2007, promises to provide a series of exemplary studies on code-switching in Ghana and neighbouring countries, including not only interaction between English and African languages but in at least two cases between different African languages (Kabiye-Ewe and Akan-Ewe).

Measures of diversity

Approaching the multilingualism of Cameroon from a different perspective, Robinson (1993) argues for an important shift in emphasis when considering linguistic diversity. Rather than starting with a European model which assumes a majority-minority dynamic, or the Greenbergian measure which looks at the population of each language as a percentage of the total population of the country, Robinson argues that a more appropriate starting point is an elite–non-elite dichotomy, onto which issues of ethnicity may (or may not) be mapped. This helps overcome misleading stereotypes such as that Nigeria has three major/dominant languages (and Democratic Republic of Congo four).[1] His measure of diversity is not based simply on the number of languages spoken or numbers of speakers of different languages. Rather, the country where the largest language group represents the smallest proportion of the population would be deemed as the most linguistically diverse, since all other language groups would represent yet smaller percentages (ibid.: 54). Table 19.1 (Robinson 1993: 55) illustrates the strength of this argument but also its difficulties. As he himself recognizes, the results are highly dependent on how one counts languages (see below); so, for example, Cameroon would be ranked higher if the group of languages here were lumped together as Beti would be split into separate languages, each with far fewer speakers. (On the other hand, the Greenbergian measure as adopted in *Ethnologue* ranks Cameroon eighth in a much differently composed top ten; see Gordon (2005), www.ethnologue.org/ethno_docs/distribution.asp?by=country#6.)

Table 19.1 Language diversity ranking as proposed in Robinson (1993)

Country	Country pop. (millions)	No. of living languages	Largest language group	No. in largest language group	Largest language group as % of pop	Official languages
1. Papua New Guinea	3.6	867	Enga	164 750	5	English Tok Pisin Hiri Motu
2. Vanuatu	0.143	111	Hano	7 000	5	Bislama English French
3. Solomon Islands	0.3	66	Kwara'ae	21 000	7	English
4. Côte d'Ivoire	12.07	75	Baoule	1 620 100	13	French
5. Gabon	1.069	40	Fang	169 650	16	French
6. Uganda	17.593	43	Ganda	2 900 000	16	English
7. Cameroon	11.9	275	Beti	2 000 000	17	French English
8. Kenya	25.393	58	Gikuyu	4 356 000	17	Kiswahili English
9. Namibia	1.372	21	Ndonga	240 000	17	English
10. Zaire	35.33	219	Ciluba	6 300 000	18	Ciluba Kikongo Kiswahili Lingala French

The implications of such radical diversity for the ruling elite (and the formulation of language policy) are that although they retain individual ethnic affiliations, the language of power may well be the former colonial language such as French or English (or in the case of Cameroon, both). These may be preferred locally to the language associated with an ethnic rival.

Language and identity

An association between ethnic (and other identities) and language is commonly assumed. Obeng and Adegbija (1999: 353), for example, begin their overview of this topic by stating, 'There is a strong emotional attachment to language and ethnicity … Each ethnic group expresses and identifies itself by the language it speaks and its cultural paraphernalia is shaped by its language.' The topic, however, remains understudied (partly, we suspect, because it is assumed to be unproblematic), and while such an association may be undeniable at a particular level and in many cases, the connection cannot be assumed to be simple or to run in a single direction. Three examples demonstrate how complex it can be. First, speaking Fulfulde for non-Fulbe is part of the process of Fulbeization. As part of a *shift* of ethnic identity to Pulho (i.e. ethnically Fulbe), speakers are switching from using Fulfulde only as a regional lingua franca to using it as a primary language (in some cases their children are acquiring it exclusively; Burnham 1996). One cannot safely assume that the language is a neutral correlate of ethnicity; in such politicized and dynamic conditions, speaking the language may *precede* acceptance by others of the ethnic affiliation being asserted (see Keen and Zeitlyn 2007). Similar phenomena are found among groups neighbouring Wolof, Mande, and Yoruba speakers, among others (Juillard 1995; Oyetade 1995; McLaughlin 2001; Nicolaï 2005).

Second, in an area in the northern Nigeria–Cameroon borderland, members of the same ethnic group (Chamba) speak different languages: Chamba Leko (classified as Adamawa) and Chamba Daka (Benue-Congo); see Fardon (1988), Boyd (1996/97). Despite speaking languages belonging to different families, they assert common ethnic identity. Similarly, those in the Lower Cross-speaking region of south-eastern Nigeria share a common cultural identity but the population speaks several different (though in this case, related) languages. Dakubu (2000), discussed above, refers to the changing role of Hausa for Bawku settlers in Accra; in speaking Hausa, the language takes on a role of expressing a supra-ethnic identity, without reference to the Hausa ethnic community itself, or assimilation to that ethnicity. It may act as a marker of 'Northern-ness', just as Wolf (1997) argues for the evolving role of English as expressing a supra-ethnic identity in the 'anglophone' region of Cameroon (see also McLaughlin 2001 for a Senegalese parallel which she calls 'de-ethnicized identity').

The complexities of understanding the relationship between language and ethnic identity are illustrated in McLaughlin's (1995) study from Senegal, where the spread of Wolof provokes different responses among different ethnic groups. Among the Pulaar (Fulbe), speaking Wolof is seen as becoming Wolof (or in danger of so being), whereas Seereer people see Wolof now as a necessity, and do not consider it to threaten their ethnic identity. In short, McLaughlin's work shows again that, 'language can sometimes, but not necessarily, serve as an important variable in the construction or reconfiguration of ethnicity' (ibid.: 165).

While these studies focus on language as a marker of identity, Mutaka and Lenaka (1998/99) provide a different perspective on their relationship, looking at how particular aspects of language use are put into play to strengthen group identity and membership. Among the Nso' of the Grassfields region of Cameroon, older women may organize a meeting with a younger woman, for example, one about to marry or one who has given birth out of wedlock, specifically for the purpose of insulting and verbally abusing them. This is not to create or express animosity, but rather to teach appropriate behaviour and it is thereby seen as essentially a means of passing on the culture and reinforcing group identity (which they note is under threat).

Pragmatics, discourse, and conversation analysis

The work undertaken to date has had a considerable emphasis on discourse due in large part to the orientation and perceived needs of Bible translators (e.g. Perrin 1978; Stanley 1982; Aaron 1992). Other topics in pragmatics remain relatively under-researched. Research on discourse has focused on gender (Rasmussen 2003) and media (Adegbite 2005). Building on Irvine's early work (1974) on Wolof, there has been work on greetings in other languages of the region (Youssouf et al. 1976; Akindele 1990) but other speech events remain understudied. Pronominal systems have been examined as part of discourse studies but there remains a paucity of studies on how these are used in different social contexts. Zeitlyn (2005) presents a case study of Mambila, in which he argues that the entire range of possible referring expressions (names, pronouns, kin terms, titles) needs to be examined, and that contexts of use are more complex than captured by the address-reference distinction. Specifically, the types of speech act and the audience for an utterance can affect the choice of person referring term used.

Barber (1991) exemplifies a shift in the study of poetry and oratory from literature studies to sociolinguistics. Her study of Oriki praise poetry in use allows consideration of the influence of performance on the verses produced. We note that she is now studying West African-produced videos, which promises to connect media studies to wider sociolinguistic themes (see e.g. Barber and Waterman 1995). We also note that the study of some key religious texts has not, to date, been so influenced. Yoruba Ifa verses are a case in point, where their study has been dominated by those viewing them from a literary (or theological) viewpoint which leaves out of account the way in which they are used in the performance of divinatory séances. Consequently, the potential impacts of performance on the verses remain unclear. Some of the sociolinguistic studies of Senegalese griots and performance (e.g. Pfeiffer 1997) provide encouraging signs of a shift in emphasis (see also Finnegan 2007). Studies of politeness are few.

Literacy and writing systems is another area where there has been relatively little research. There have been some well-documented cases of indigenous writing systems such as the Vai script in Liberia and the Bamum script in Cameroon (see references below). Within WCA, the norm remains one of restricted and partial literacy but letters have been written for centuries and newspapers have been published in a variety of languages. Here, Blommaert's (1999) pioneering study of writing in Shaba (DRC) provides impetus and resources for future analysis. Nkemleke (2004) looks at discourse strategies (especially verbosity and flattery) in job applications and student complaint letters written in Cameroonian English. He argues that English is being influenced by the conventions of written French. And, as email and text messaging become more widely used, they pose challenges for linguistic analysis which are beginning to be taken up, e.g. Wanjas (2007).

The work of Felix Ameka is a prominent exception to generalizations decrying the lack of broader sociolinguistic research. Ameka has published pioneering research on the interface between linguistics and wider social factors (see e.g. Ameka 2006, and Ameka and Breedveld 2004) in which the notion of cultural scripts is used to explore ways in which cultural factors affect patterns of linguistic behaviour; for example, the avoidance of the use of personal names, a practice common in many African societies. Ameka's earlier work on interjections (Ameka 1992) remains a rare example from our region of work on non-standard parts of speech, and we note the importance of such utterances in the dynamics of conversation. Some interjections are used as back channel signals through which a conversant signals their comprehension and agreement with a speaker at a possible turn transition point, letting them continue speaking.

Language endangerment and language surveys

The linguistic situation in Africa as a whole, but perhaps especially in large parts of WCA, is not stable, as Dakubu (2000) and Woods (1994) point out, due primarily to rapid urbanization.[2] A considerable portion of sociolinguistic work in WCA over the past two or three decades has been based on, or constitutes reports of, surveys to establish 'who speaks what, to whom, and when'; Dakubu and Woods are just two examples of such work. One of the results of such surveys has been the recognition of the endangered status of a great many languages of the region. Woods presents a picture of instability which 'shows an increase in national language (Lingala and Munukutuba) and official language (French) [use] at the expense of the many mother tongues' (1994: 34). Consequently, in the past decade or so, research attention in WCA has begun to focus on the vitality of indigenous languages and the maintenance of linguistic diversity. Linguists have been aiming at the documentation and development of African languages, as well as devoting attention to the broader sociolinguistic questions involved in the assessment of language vitality and understanding the causes of endangerment. Notable among the latter are Schaefer and Egbokhare (1999) and Connell, Ahoua and Gibbon (2001). These studies and others have involved questionnaire-based survey work in endangered language communities which can be characterized as investigations into language knowledge and use (see Vossen 1988, for a model from Southern Africa). Such surveys have typically been undertaken both on a door-to-door basis and administered in school settings. Schaefer and Egbokhare conducted their work in an urban southern Nigerian setting and their results show English to be rapidly becoming dominant. Connell et al.'s work, carried out in rural Côte d'Ivoire (and other as yet unpublished work conducted in rural Cameroon), indicates that in such regions it is not a former colonial language which is threatening smaller, local, languages but rather neighbouring languages, and regional lingua francas. Overviews of language endangerment in WCA can be found in Blench (2007) and Connell (2007).

Future directions

At the outset we made the point that the languages *and* sociolinguistics of WCA are understudied. This suggests a potential for substantial contributions to many areas of sociolinguistics, as work increases. We point here to just a few of these areas. The largest lacuna, and one which African scholars are best placed to resolve, is the paucity of analyses of natural language usage. Corpus linguistic databases contain scarcely any data from any African language, including those of WCA. What is needed are the production and analysis of recordings of African languages as they are used in the street, on the telephone and in different social contexts (see Mutaka and Lenaka 1998/9, and Blommaert 1999, for examples of what is possible). Phone-in programmes broadcast by FM radio stations in large cities actually provide natural laboratories for the development of lingua francas and other variants of languages. To our knowledge, no one is researching them. We have already commented on the way in which market places act as multilingual arenas. The videos and DVDs being produced for sale in local markets also serve as sources for linguistic research without the need to make new recordings (although such recordings are also urgently needed especially if there is to be any possibility of detailed phonetic analysis which low quality commercial recording make all but impossible). Sermons from many different religious affiliations are circulated on cassette and on different radio stations. All of these can provide a basis for the development of linguistic corpora which would have the effect of breaking the Indo-European stranglehold on corpus linguistics and enabling a wide range of different linguistic and sociolinguistic research topics to be undertaken on secure empirical footing.

Another, related, factor is the role of writing. In general terms, a writing system is an important sociolinguistic factor which can have a variety of effects on the way a language develops. The area has long been host to those using different writing systems (Singler 1995). Arab scholars have been established in the Sahel region for more than a millennium and traders and administrators using western scripts were a feature of the slave trade and the subsequent moves to colonialism. A few indigenous writing systems have developed, e.g. Vai (Tuchscherer and Hair 2002) and Bamum (Tardits 1996, for background). Cissé (e.g. 2007) has written on the Arabic influence on scripts and writing systems as used for Wolof and Songhay.

Time-honoured topics in sociolinguistics which appear to have been largely relegated to the realm of textbooks in many parts of the world should regain fresh impetus in the context of African linguistics. These include the debates surrounding concepts such as 'speech community', 'variety', and 'dialect' in opposition to 'language', or more generally how one distinguishes and defines language from a sociolinguistic perspective (cf. Hudson 1996). Such categories, or divisions, in WCA are, at least from one perspective, creations of linguists and administrators rather than of speakers themselves, for whom linguistic boundaries are fluid and where divisions dissolve according to situation.

Maho (2004) asks, 'How many languages are there in Africa, really?' and provides a precise answer (1441) which he contrasts to the more generous answer provided by Gordon (2005), who gives 2058. His discussion illustrates the dilemmas and controversies surrounding the debates between 'splitters' and 'lumpers'. The important thing is to recognize that there is no simple, single definitive answer as to why this should be the case. Such is the difficulty in distinguishing 'language' from 'dialect', especially since in Africa many of the criteria used to 'elevate' a dialect to language status are absent.

In closing, we draw attention to just a couple of areas of study that space constraints have not permitted us to examine properly, but which nevertheless merit mention. First is the study of pidgins and creoles; interesting work has been done, for example, Samarin (1982, 1991), Mufwene (1997) and Pasch (1997), focused on languages in Central Africa. Work on pidgins and creoles in West Africa has tended to be more structural in orientation. Second, space has not permitted examination of work on language attitudes, though the work of Adegbija (e.g. 1994) should be noted. Finally, Arabic should be mentioned, neither an indigenous nor a colonial language in WCA, yet nevertheless has been influential and is part spoken by many speakers in the northerly parts of WCA; the interested reader may see, for example, Owens (1998).

Notes

1 These are arithmetically correct but misleading: they are inaccurate characterizations of the national situations.
2 Woods (1994), for example, cites demographic work in Congo showing urbanization at an astonishing rate, from one-third of the population in 1958, to two-thirds in 1980, and a projected 80 per cent living in cities by 2000.

References

Aaron, U. (1992) 'Reported speech in Obolo narrative discourse', in S. J. Huang and W. R. Merrifield (eds) *Essays in Honor of Robert E. Longacre*, Dallas, TX: Summer Institute of Linguistics, pp. 227–40.

Adegbija, E. (1994) *Language Attitudes in Sub-Saharan Africa: A Sociolinguistic Overview*, Clevedon: Multilingual Matters.

Adegbite, W. (2005) 'Pragmatic tactics in diplomatic communication: a case study of Ola Rotimi's Ovonramwen Nogbaisi', *Journal of Pragmatics*, 37, 1457–80.

Akindele, F. (1990) 'A sociolinguistic analysis of Yoruba greetings', *African Languages and Cultures* 3, 1–14.

Alexandre, P. (1963) 'Aperçu sommaire sur le pidgin à 70 du Cameroun', *Cahiers d'Etudes Africaines*, 3, 577–82.

Ameka, F. (1992) 'Interjections: the universal yet neglected part of speech', *Journal of Pragmatics*, 18, 101–18.

——(2006) '"When I die, don't cry": the ethnopragmatics of "gratitude" in West African languages', in C. Goddard (ed.) *Ethnopragmatics: Understanding Discourse in Cultural Context*, Berlin: Mouton de Gruyter, pp.231–66.

Ameka, F. and Breedveld, A. (2004) 'Areal cultural scripts for social interaction in West African communities', *Intercultural Pragmatics*, 1, 167–88.

Amuda, A. A. (1994) 'Yoruba/English conversational codeswitching', *African Languages and Cultures*, 7, 121–31.

Amuzu, E. K. (2005) 'Revisiting the classic codeswitching-composite codeswitching distinction: a case study of nonverbal predication in Ewe-English codeswitching', *Australian Journal of Linguistics*, 25, 127–51.

Ansre, G. (1969) 'The need for a specific and comprehensive policy on the teaching of Ghanaian languages', in J. R. Birnie and G. Ansre (eds) *Proceedings of the Conference on the Study of Ghanaian Languages*, Legon: Ghana Publishing, pp. 5–11.

Badejo, B. R. (1989) 'Multilingualism in Sub-Saharan Africa', *Africa Media Review*, 3, 40–53.

Bamgbose, A, Banjo, A. and Thomas, A. (eds) (1995) *New Englishes: A West African Perspective*, Ibadan: Moruso Publishers for the British Council.

Banjo, A. (2000) 'English in West Africa', *International Journal of the Sociology of Language*, 141, 27–38.

Barber, K. (1991) *I Could Speak Until Tomorrow: Oriki, Women and the Past in a Yoruba Town*, Edinburgh: University of Edinburgh Press.

Barber, K. and Waterman, C. (1995) 'Traversing the global and the local: Fújì music and praise poetry in the production of contemporary Yorùbá popular culture', in D. Miller. (ed.) *Worlds Apart: Modernity through the Prism of the Local*, London: Routledge, 240–62.

Blench, R. M. (2007) 'Endangered languages in West Africa', in M. Brenzinger (ed.) *Language Diversity Endangered*, Berlin: Mouton de Gruyter, pp. 140–62.

Blommaert, J. (1999) 'Reconstructing the sociolinguistic image of Africa: grassroots writing in Shaba (Congo)', *Text*, 19, 175–200.

Bokamba, E. G. (1977) 'The impact of multilingualism on language structures', *Anthropological Linguistics*, 19, 181–202.

——(1990) 'African languages and sociolinguistic theories', *Studies in the Linguistic Sciences*, 20, 3–34.

Boyd, R. (1996/97) 'Chamba Daka and Bantoid: a further look at Chamba Daka classification', *Journal of West African Languages*, 26, 29–43.

Burnham, P. (1996) *The Politics of Cultural Difference in Northern Cameroon*, International African Library, 17. Edinburgh: Edinburgh University Press for the International African Institute.

Calvet, L.-J. (ed.) (1992) *Les langues des marchés en Afrique*, Paris: Didier Érudition.

——(1999) *Pour une Ecologie des Langues du Monde*, Paris: Plon.

Chumbow, B. S. (1980) 'Language and language policy in Cameroon', in N. K. Kale (ed.) *An Experiment in Nation Building: The Bilingual Republic of Cameroon since Reunification*, Boulder, CO: Westview Press, 281–311.

Chumbow, B. S. and Bobda, A. S. (2000) 'French in West Africa: a sociolinguistic perspective', *International Journal of the Sociology of Language*, 141, 39–60.

Cissé, M. (2007) 'Écrits et Écriture en Afrique de L'Ouest'. Online. Available at: www.editions-harmattan. fr/index.asp?navig=catalogue&obj=article&no=8203&razSqlClone=1 (accessed October 2007).

Clements, G. N. (1989) 'African linguistics and its contributions to linguistic theory', *Studies in the Linguistic Sciences*, 19, 3–42.

Connell, B. (2007) 'Endangered languages in Central Africa', in M. Brenzinger (ed.) *Language Diversity Endangered*, Berlin: Mouton de Gruyter, pp. 163–78.

——(submitted) 'Language diversity and language choice in an African market'.

Connell, B., Ahoua, F. and Gibbon, D. (2001) 'Ega: a preliminary assessment of endangerment', paper presented at ACAL32, Berkeley, CA.

Dakubu, M. E. K. (2000) 'Multiple bilingualisms and urban transitions: coming to Accra', *International Journal of the Sociology of Language*, 141, 9–26.

Essien, O. (1995) 'The English language and code-mixing: a case study of the phenomenon in Ibibio', in A. Bamgbose, A. Banjo and A. Thomas (eds) *New Englishes: A West African Perspective*, Ibadan: Mosuro, 269–83.

Fardon, R. (1988) *Raiders and Refugees: Trends in Chamba Political Development 1750 to 1950*, Washington, DC: Smithsonian Institution Press.

Finnegan, R. (2007) *The Oral and Beyond: Doing Things with Words in Africa*, Oxford: James Currey.

Gordon, R. G. Jr. (2005) *Ethnologue: Languages of the World*, 15th edn, Dallas, TX: SIL International. Online. Available at: www.ethnologue.com.

Greenberg, J. (1971) 'Urbanism, migration, and language', in A. S. Dil (ed.) *Language, Culture, and Communication*, Stanford, CA: Stanford University Press, pp. 198–211.

Hancock, I. (1971) 'A survey of pidgins and creoles of the world', in D. Hymes (ed.) *Pidginization and Creolization of Language*, Cambridge: Cambridge University Press, pp. 509–25.

Hattiger, J.-L. (1983) *Le Français populaire d'Abidjan: Un cas de pidginisation*, Abidjan: Institut de linguistique appliquée.

Haust, D. (1995) 'Codeswitching in Gambia: eine soziolinguistische Untersuchung von Mandinka, Wolof und Englisch in Kontakt', *Language Contact in Africa/Sprachkontakt in Afrika*, vol. 1, Köln: Rüdiger Köppe Verlag.

Hudson, R. (1996) *Sociolinguistics*, Cambridge: Cambridge University Press.

Irvine, J. (1974) 'Strategies of manipulation in the Wolof greeting', in R. Bauman, and J. Sherzer (eds) *Explorations in the Ethnography of Speaking*, Cambridge: Cambridge University Press, pp. 167–91.

Juillard, C. (1995) *Sociolinguistique urbaine. La vie des langues à Ziguinchor (Sénégal)*, Paris: Editions du CNRS.

Keen, A. E. and Zeitlyn, D. (2007) 'Language, diet, and ethnicity in Mayo-Darlé, Adamaoua, Cameroon', *Anthropos*, 102, 213–19.

Lafage, S. (2003) *Le lexique français de Côte d'Ivoire, appropriation et créativité*, vols 1 and 2. Le français en Afrique, Revue du Réseau des Observatoires du Français Contemporain en Afrique Noire, nos 16 and 17, Paris: Institut de Linguistique française – CNRS.

Lipski, J. M. (1992) 'Pidgin English usage in Equatorial Guinea (Fernando Poo)', *English World-Wide*, 113, 33–57.

213

Maho, J. F. (2004) 'How many languages are there in Africa, really?', in K. Bromber and B. Smieja (eds) *Globalisation and African Languages: Risks and Benefits*, Berlin: Mouton de Gruyter, pp. 279–96.

Mboudjeke, J.-G. (2006) 'Bilinguisme, politiques et attitudes linguistiques au Cameroun et au Canada', *Sud Langues 6*. Online. Available at: www.sudlangues.sn (accessed 6 Dec. 2007).

McLaughlin, F. (1995) 'Haalpulaar identity as a response to Wolofization', *African Languages and Cultures*, 8, 153–68.

——(2001) 'Dakar Wolof and the configuration of an urban identity', *Journal of African Cultural Studies*, 14, 153–72.

Mufwene, S. (1997) 'Kitúba', in S. Thomason (ed.) *Contact Languages: A Wider Perspective*, Amsterdam: John Benjamins, pp. 173–208.

Mutaka, N. M. and Lenaka, N. L. (1998/99) 'Group identity strengthening in the Nso culture: the uses of oral abuse by older women', *Journal of West African Languages*, 27, 67–80.

Myers-Scotton, C. (1993) *Social Motivations for Codeswitching: Evidence from Africa*, Oxford: Clarendon Press.

Nicolaï, R. (2005) 'Language processes, theory and description of language change, and building on the past: lessons from Songhay', in Z. Frajzyngier, A. Hodges and D. S. Rood (eds) *Linguistic Diversity and Language Theories*, Amsterdam: John Benjamins, 81–104.

Nkemleke, D. (2004) 'Job applications and students' complaint letters in Cameroon', *World Englishes*, 23, 601–11.

Obeng, S. G. and Adegbija, E. (1999) 'Sub-Saharan Africa', in J. Fishman (ed.) *Handbook of Language and Ethnic Identity*, Oxford: Oxford University Press, pp. 353–68.

Ogunsiji, Y. (2001) 'A sociolinguistic study of the language attitude in market transaction', in H. Igboanusi (ed.) *Language Attitudes and Language Conflict in West Africa*, Ibadan: Enicrownfit Publishers, pp. 68–95.

Owens, J. (1998) *Variation in the Spoken Arabic of Maiduguri, Nigeria*, Amsterdam: John Benjamins.

Oyetade, S. O. (1995) 'Bilingualism and language use in the Nupe settlement in Ibadan', *International Journal of the Sociology of Language*, 116, 61–79.

Pasch, H. (1997) 'Sango', in S. Thomason (ed.) *Contact Languages: A Wider Perspective*, Amsterdam: John Benjamins, pp. 209–70.

Perrin, M. (1978) 'Who's who in Mambila folkstories', in G. E. Grimes (ed.) *Papers on Discourse*, Dallas, TX: SIL, pp. 105–18.

Pfeiffer, K. (1997) *Mandinka Spoken Art: Folk-tales, Griot Accounts and Songs*, Köln: Rüdiger Köppe Verlag.

Queffelec, A. (ed.) (1998) *Alternances codiques et français parlé en Afrique*, Aix-en-Provence: Publications de l'Université de Provence.

Rasmussen, S. J. (2003) 'Gendered discourses and mediated modernities: urban and rural performances of Tuareg smith women', *Journal of Anthropological Research*, 59, 487–509.

Robinson, C. D. W. (1993) 'Where minorities are in the majority: language dynamics amidst high linguistic diversity', in K. de Bot (ed.) *Case Studies in Minority Languages, AILA Review*, 10, 52–70.

Samarin, W. J. (1982) 'Colonization and pidginization on the Ubangi River', *Journal of African Languages and Linguistics*, 4, 1–42.

——(1991) 'The origins of Kituba and Lingala', *Journal of African Languages and Linguistics*, 12, 47–77.

Schaefer, R. P. and Egbokhare, F. O. (1999) 'English and the pace of endangerment in Nigeria', *World Englishes*, 18, 381–91.

Singler, J. (1995) 'Indigenous West African writing systems', in P. T. Daniels and W. Bright (eds) *The World's Writing Systems*, New York: Oxford University Press, pp. 593–8.

Spencer, J. (ed.) (1971) *The English Language in West Africa*, London: Longman.

Stanley, C. (1982) 'Direct and reported speech in Tikar narrative texts', *Studies in African Linguistics*, 13, 31–52.

Tardits, C. (1996) 'Pursue to attain: a royal religion', in I. Fowler and D. Zeitlyn (eds) *African Crossroads: Intersections between History and Anthropology in Cameroon*, Oxford: Berghahn Books, pp. 141–64.

Tschiggfrey, T. (1995) 'Procédés morphologiques de néologie dans un corpus de chansons zouglou en français: situations du français', *Linx*, 33, 71–8.

214

Tuchscherer, K. and Hair, P. E. H. (2002) 'Cherokee in West Africa: examining the origins of the Vai script', *History in Africa*, 29, 427–86.

Vossen, R. (1988) *Patterns of Language Knowledge and Language Use in Ngamiland in Botswana*, Bayreuth: Bayreuth University Press.

Wanjas, E. (2007) 'The sociolinguistics of Cameroonian SMS texts', paper presented at the Signpost Postgraduate Conference, University of Yaounde I, Department of English, 26–28 April.

Wolf, H.-G. (1997) 'Transcendence of ethnic boundaries: the case of the Anglophones in Cameroon', *Journal of Sociolinguistics*, 1, 419–26.

Woods, D. R. (1994) 'Changing patterns of language utilization in the Republic of Congo', *African Languages and Cultures*, 7, 19–35.

Youssouf, I. A., Grimshaw, A. D. and Bird, C. S. (1976) 'Greetings in the desert', *American Ethnologist*, 3, 797–824.

Zeitlyn, D. (2005) *Words and Processes in Mambila Kinship: The Theoretical Importance of the Complexity of Everyday Life*, Lanham, MD: Lexington Books.

20

Sociolinguistics of East Africa

Christina M. Higgins

Introduction

For the purposes of this chapter, East Africa refers to Burundi, Eritrea, Ethiopia, Kenya, Rwanda, Somalia, Tanzania, and Uganda. According to the Ethnologue (www.ethnologue.com), approximately 325 different languages are spoken across these nations, and all four of the language families found in Africa are represented in this region. In small nations like Burundi, only three languages are spoken, but in larger nations such as Tanzania, over 120 languages are still found. Like every country in Africa, these multilingual nations have experienced high degrees of language contact and language shift due to the movements of people from rural regions to urban centers in search of opportunities for education and employment. Moreover, these nations' colonial histories have yielded complex language contact situations that have consequently produced powerful ideologies regarding the symbolic value of indigenous languages vis-à-vis colonial languages.

Although these East African nations do not share a single colonial history, all of them have inherited at least one language of a former colonizer. Kenya, Tanzania, Somalia, and Uganda inherited English directly from the British. In the 1880s, the British occupied Kenya and Uganda and formed the Imperial British East Africa Company to develop trading opportunities for the imperial government in the region, eventually leading to the establishment of a formal colony in Kenya. Originally occupied by the Germans, Tanzania (formerly Tanganyika) was handed over to the British after World War I. After the war, the Allies divided German East Africa into League of Nations mandates. Great Britain was given most of the area (now Tanzania), while Belgium received Rwanda and Burundi. Zanzibar became a protectorate of the British in 1890 and eventually became part of Tanzania in 1964. Somalia has a more complex history, as it was sliced up at the Berlin Conference of 1884 into British Somaliland, Italian Somaliland, and French Somaliland. Somali is the official language next to Arabic and English, and Somali serves as the medium of instruction (MOI) in primary schools, while English is the medium for most secondary education.

Several nations that comprise the Horn of Africa also share an English legacy. Though never officially colonized by any nation, Ethiopia was occupied by Italy from 1936–41 under Mussolini. The British helped to liberate the Ethiopians from Italian occupation, thereby giving Emperor Haile Selassie power to impose Amharic, the language of the dominant political group, as Ethiopia's official language. In the 1950s, English was also given a dominant position in schooling as the MOI in secondary schools due to the Amhara's elite status and political ties with western governments (Hameso 1997). Formerly colonized by the Italians, Eritrea was handed over to Ethiopia by the United Nations in 1952. In spite of tremendous resistance from Eritrea, the nation was officially annexed by Ethiopia ten years later, thus sparking a 30-year struggle for independence. Under Ethiopian rule, Eritrea's co-official languages of Arabic and Tigrigna were replaced by the official language of Ethiopia, Amharic, and English became the language of schooling. After independence in 1993, no official languages were selected, though Tigrigna, Arabic, and English function as *de facto* working languages.

Rwanda and Burundi were governed as one nation by Belgium from 1923 to 1961, when they were split into two separate nations in preparation for independence. These small nations are those with the least linguistic and ethnic diversity among the nations to be discussed in this chapter. In Burundi, Kirundi, French, and Kiswahili are used, and in Rwanda, Kinyarwanda, French, Kiswahili are spoken. English is also an official language in Rwanda and is used by a small number of elites, particularly those who have been educated in Uganda.

Sociolinguistic research on East Africa

Current sociolinguistic research on languages in East Africa largely focuses on *the sociology of language* (Fishman 1972), a field of study that investigates the effects that languages have on society. The dominance of this perspective makes sense given these nations' concerns with the role of language in improving education, creating national stability, and developing and sustaining economic partnerships both within and beyond East Africa. Sociolinguistic research on how gender, age, class, and ethnicity shape language use is rather scarce, and studies on discourse and social interaction are still few in number. As Musau notes in his discussion of indigenous language rights in Kenya, "At the moment there appears to be a tendency for university research to treat these [unstandardised African] languages as sources of data for testing linguistic theories" (2004: 63) rather than as data for understanding the relationships between language and society. A promising sign of new lines of research is the increased number of publications on the very contemporary study of language in domains of popular culture and the media in East Africa.

In the pages that follow, I focus on the areas of sociolinguistic inquiry that have garnered the most attention from researchers, namely language policy and planning, language in education, bi/multilingualism, and the recent focus on language and popular culture. Due to restrictions on space, I will not be able to review the sociolinguistically relevant topics of language shift and language loss, topics which in themselves have merited book-length treatments elsewhere (e.g. Brenzinger 1992; Batibo 2005).

Language planning

Language planning in East Africa has been identified as a means of increasing democracy and economic opportunity, building regional unity within and between nations, and

217

advocating for linguistic human rights. One of the most important developments in language planning work on East Africa in the past ten years was the Asmara Declaration on African Languages and Literatures, formed at a conference on African languages and literatures in Eritrea in 2000. The ten principles of the Declaration include the recognition of African languages as the basis for decolonization, as sources of empowerment, as the medium of instruction in schooling, as instruments of African unity, and as resources for democracy. Following these principles, Mazrui (2004) argues that the most promising way to strengthen democratic participation among more citizens of each nation is to rely on African lingua francas, rather than western languages which tend to produce horizontal socio-economic divisions.

As a case in point, the Somalian government led one of the most effective campaigns among East African nations to reinstate an indigenous language after independence. The government supported the development of a writing system and then led national literacy campaigns. The Somali example has been examined in detail by Laitin (1977), in which he argues that the government's support for Somali significantly affected the course of the country's political development. More recently, Warsame (2001) has summarized the Somali experience in a historical overview that discusses theories of development and decolonization.

Beyond offering theoretical perspectives on language planning, researchers have engaged in and described language planning efforts to expand African languages' domains of use. Much has been written about Kiswahili, a language which has its own national planning council (BAKITA), Institute of Kiswahili Research (TUKI), and the Institute of Kiswahili and Foreign Languages (TAKILUKI) in Tanzania (see Kishe 2004). Legère (2006) describes the success that these institutions have had, but he highlights the more utilitarian successes achieved through efforts made by institutions in private enterprise, such as Microsoft's decision to produce MS Office software in Kiswahili. In a parallel manner, Kihore (2004) shows how the informal sector of Kiswahili newspapers has increased the pace of the adoption of new words and has made street language increasingly acceptable for a wider number of domains, thereby expanding the various registers of the language. In comparison, the Kenyan context reveals many obstacles to Kiswahili language planning, most of which are due to vague language policy and the lack of a cohesive effort by the government (Onyango 2005). Unlike Tanzania, no language council or Kiswahili institute exists in Kenya, and the development of technical terms in Kiswahili is due to volunteer efforts by scholars who do not always have the opportunity to work together to agree upon terms. Moreover, Kiswahili planning in Kenya suffers from a lack of dissemination routes and the lack of any mechanism for the assessment of any language planning that is carried out.

Mukuthuria (2006) examines Uganda's recent efforts to expand the use of Kiswahili as well, offering an analysis of political and institutional changes that have led to the renewed interest in the language. Mukuthuria cites the recognition of Kiswahili as an official language of the African Union, developments by the Inter-university Council of East Africa to promote student exchange and joint research projects across borders, and the resurgence of the East African Community, the regional intergovernmental organization that allows Kenya, Tanzania, Uganda, Rwanda, and Burundi to develop political and economic ties.

Language planning is intricately bound up with the ideologies that people have towards languages and people's access to linguistic resources. Blommaert's (1999, 2005) research on language ideologies in Tanzania examines how the legacies of colonization and globalization have impacted the value of Kiswahili, English, and varieties of both languages. Using ethnography and discourse analysis, he has analyzed varieties such as Campus Kiswahili, Public English, and *Kihuni* (Swahili-English street language) to demonstrate how access to linguistic resources invariably creates social and linguistic divisions. His scholarship offers both theory and methodology for the study of language ideology, language planning, and linguistic human rights in the age of globalization. Rather than focusing on the social values attributed to languages, his work encourages sociolinguists to shift their attention to the distribution of linguistic resources among speakers.

In Kenya, researchers have also undertaken the study of language ideologies, but the majority of the research in the past decade has surveyed people's views towards varieties of English. Buregeya (2006) devised a judgment task in which university students were asked to decide whether sentences containing lexical and grammatical aspects of Kenyan English were acceptable. He found that approximately half of the features he tested were considered acceptable by the majority of participants. Kembo-Sure (2004) analyzed several examples of Kenyan English in search of a model of Educated Kenyan English. He settled on a text that exhibited use of Kenyan cultural references, Kenyan English grammar, and codeswitching into local languages. Using questionnaires, Kioko and Muthwii (2004) surveyed Kenyans' attitudes towards varieties of English and found that most were in favor of an English that differed from British English and which was also free of any ethnically marked features.

Research on language planning in Eritrea, Ethiopia, Rwanda, and Burundi is not available, and research on Somalia is rather scant. There has been one dissertation (Noor 1999) on the Somali people's attitudes towards Arabic language and script that investigated how Somalis view Arabic alongside European languages and Somali. The study found that in spite of the historical preference for Somali, which was due to the result of a vast Somali literacy project sponsored by the Somali government in the 1970s, loyalty has now shifted toward European languages.

Language policy and planning in schools

Perhaps the most research on East Africa published in the past decade has been on language policy and planning as it relates to education. The predominance of this topic is not surprising given the importance of education in economic development, a concern shared by all of the nations surveyed here. In countries where English is the MOI for primary and/or secondary education, research has focused on both the attitudes towards English as well as empirical studies investigating classroom practices. Most publications offer descriptive overviews of the historical events that have led to current language policy in education (e.g,. for Eritrea, see Hallemariam *et al.* 1999; for Ethiopia compared with Tanzania and Kenya, see Hameso 1997; for Uganda, see Tembe 2006). Survey and questionnaire research has shown that in spite of the many challenges involved in teaching through the medium of English, teachers, students, and parents are in favor of maintaining this policy rather than considering mother-tongue instruction or bilingual education (e.g. Sprenger-Tasch 2003).

Among all East African countries, research on MOI issues in Kenya and Tanzania is the most abundant. In Kenya, policy allows for indigenous languages to be used in the first three years of primary school, with English taking over in the fourth year. In Tanzania, Kiswahili is the MOI in primary school, and English is introduced as a subject at grade 5. When children move on to secondary school, however, the medium is English.

In Uganda, the MOI is English for all urban students, while students in rural areas may be taught in their home languages during the first four years of primary school. Researchers have asserted that low achievement among students is directly related to students' and teachers' poor command of English, particularly in rural areas (Roy-Campbell and Qorro 1997; Brock-Utne 2005; Bunyi 2005; Tembe 2006). Lack of proficiency has been shown to relate to little exposure to English, poor teacher education, a lack of materials and resources, and underdeveloped literacy skills in the first language (Parry 2000). In Tanzania, fluency and literacy in Kiswahili also contribute to the achievement gap. Wedin (2005) provides a study on literacy practices in Karagwe, Tanzania, that shows how unequal access to Kiswahili leads to inequality in pupils' chances in education and to a low level of achievement in academic content in schools.

Ethnographic classroom research reveals the limitations of English as a MOI. In her research on Kenyan primary schools, Bunyi (2005) found that rigid, drill-based, rather tedious teaching practices dominated the classroom. She found high degrees of initiation-response-feedback (IRF), choral responses, and strongly teacher-fronted lessons in both Gikuyu and English that yielded little opportunity for literacy development. Research on private English medium primary schools in Tanzania by Rubagumya (2003) found very similar teaching methods to characterize much of the learning that takes place. Experimental research comparing Tanzanian secondary school students who were taught science in Kiswahili with students who were taught in English showed that students leaarnt more in Kiswahili (Mwinsheikhe 2003). Despite these facts, many teachers, students, and parents prefer that English remain as the MOI, citing the prestige of the language, their desire to move upward socio-economically and the need for English as a language of development (Vavrus 2002; Muthwii 2004).

Research on French MOI educational practices is scarce. Ndayipfukamiye (1996) reveals how language practices in Burundi mirror those in Tanzania and Kenya in that French is valued much more highly than Kirundi in spite of students' lack of fluency in the language. In a close analysis of talk in two French-medium classrooms, Ndayipfukamiye shows that the teachers' use of code-switches into Kirundi served to bridge gaps in both cultural and linguistic knowledge, and in the process, constructs Kirundi as symbolic of local knowledge and French as symbolic of worldly knowledge.

Bilingualism, multilingualism, and hybrid languages

A prominent area of research on all African contexts is the study of language alternation, or code-switching. In East Africa, research on this topic has tended to focus on language alternation between local African languages and previously colonial languages, so it is no surprise that a fair amount of code-switching research has been carried out in educational contexts. Much of this research describes how code-switching is used as a means by which teachers create order, provide scaffolding for learning new concepts, mitigate low proficiency in the MOI, and encourage student participation. Bunyi (2005), Brock-Utne (2005), and Rubagumya (2003) have explored the functions of language switching in Kenya and Tanzania. Their research focuses largely on switches among teachers, and it shows that switches are used to check understanding, to translate difficult vocabulary, and to keep students on task.

Myers-Scotton's research on code-switching is the best known for this region and beyond, as her publications have been central in establishing explanatory frameworks for the study of bilingual conversation. Her widely cited (1993) monograph includes data from Kenya and other African contexts to demonstrate her Markedness Model, a framework which uses rational choice theory to postulate that speakers operate in a world of rights and obligations (ROs). In choosing marked or unmarked codes, speakers index various RO sets; they may consciously choose to violate RO sets in order to achieve a desired outcome, or they may conform to the expected RO set to produce unmarked language.

Other research on code-switching has theorized language alternation as acts of identity construction, drawing upon critical and social theory and making use of interpretive discourse analysis and ethnographic methodologies. This research explores how speakers identify as belonging to social groups through language choice. Blommaert's (1999, 2005) research on varieties of Kiswahili and English is relevant for its investigation of how speakers use their various linguistic resources to establish spheres of belonging and social divisions. Similarly, Higgins (2007a, 2007b) makes use of membership categorization analysis, interactional sociolinguistics and ethnography to demonstrate how Tanzanians establish and maintain social boundaries of in-groups and out-groups through language alternation. This research shows how Kiswahili-English language alternation offers speakers a linguistic resource through which they can manage identities produced in interaction. In contrast, McIntosh (2005) reports that the Giriama in Kenya code-switch between Kigiriama, Kiswahili, Arabic, and English to discursively construct essentialized religious identities that are tied directly to language choice.

Other researchers who have examined bilingual speech have been interested in describing new forms of language mixing and establishing how to distinguish among borrowings, code-switches, and other more hybrid language forms. Sheng, an urban mixed language spoken in Kenya, has received a fair amount of description (e.g. Abdulaziz and Osinde 1997; Kang'ethe-Iraki 2004) including the publication of a Sheng-English dictionary (Mbaabu and Nzuga 2003), but little research shows how it is used in everyday talk. A much more comprehensive linguistic and sociolinguistic description for the street language of Tanzania, *Lugha ya Mitaani* (Reuster-Jahn and Kießling 2006), is now available. This impressive publication describes the street language of Tanzania from historical and current sociolinguistic perspectives, and it provides a dictionary of 1100 words and phrases with etymologies and sample usages that are based on fieldwork in Tanzania.

More descriptive and grammar-oriented research on code-switching includes Ntahonkiriye's (2000) examination of Kirundi-French bilingual speech, a study that offers evidence for a new categorization of lexical items that are not easily classified as borrowings or code-switches. Similarly, Bernsten (1998) offers a description and sociolinguistic analysis of Runyakitara, a new language that has developed in Western Uganda as a result of language contact. According to Bernsten, Runyakitara has developed increased ethnolinguistic vitality due to political shifts in the country that altered the value of the Luganda speakers, the largest ethnic group in Uganda that had previously dominated the political and economic spheres of life.

Language in popular culture

As the field of sociolinguistics continues to become more interdisciplinary, scholarship in linguistic anthropology and cultural studies has taken a more central role in the field. This research has enriched sociolinguistics by bringing new theories and methodological approaches to the study of language contact and cultural change, introducing the analysis of globalization to the analysis of language, and theorizing the relationship between local and global language and cultural practices.

A prolific strand of research within this area is the study of language and popular music, with most attention paid to Tanzanian rap and hip hop. Remes (1998) examines how youth in Mwanza, Tanzania, act as cultural brokers between street life, imagined realities, and the promises of development and opportunity in their production of rap. He discusses how Tanzanian youth protest their categorization as hooligans, and how they appropriate and localize themes of American hip hop. In a similar manner, Higgins (2009) and Perullo and Fenn (2003) examine Tanzanian hip hop lyrics, illustrating the ways in which Tanzanian artists have localized both the content and form of hip hop. They show how artists have moved away from the early days of imitation and have developed their own cultural and linguistic forms of artistic expression. Connections between street language and hip hop are also the subject of Reuster-Jahn's (2007) analysis of a popular rap song by Tanzanian artist Ngwair. She uses discourse analysis to explore how youth identities are dialogically performed through the use of street language, boasting, and derogatory remarks about women.

Rap and hip hop have also garnered attention in Kenya, and it is no surprise that Sheng and other street language forms are central to this research. Samper (2004) focuses on Kenyan rap lyrics performed in Sheng, Luo, and Kiswahili to illustrate how rappers lament the loss of African traditions due to Western modernity. He shows how the use of ethnic languages can index a desire to return to one's African roots, and how Sheng symbolically functions as the expression of youth culture.

Billings (2006) explores beauty pageants, another aspect of popular culture and performance that is prevalent in much of East Africa. She examines expressions of language ideologies towards English, Kiswahili, and mixed varieties of these languages at beauty contests across Tanzania. While mixed varieties of language and street Swahili are used by many of the pageant performers and emcees, beauty contestants are obligated to produce "pure" languages in their on-stage performances; their inability to do so is a target of loud vocal audience criticism. Billings also found that in spite of the strong relationship between Kiswahili and Tanzanian national identity, the beauty queens who had the most fluent English are typically judged more positively, particularly at the highest levels of competition.

Finally, Mechthild (2004) examines the use of multiple languages and hybrid forms in a study of multilingual advertising in Lira Town, Uganda. Mechthild explains that the layering of language in advertising offers a way to assess the communicative, social, and emotional functions of language in this part of Uganda, and it provides evidence for challenges to English as the sole language of the marketplace.

Research on the diaspora of displaced East Africans

Any reader of this chapter will see that much more research is available on Kenya, Tanzania, and Uganda, relative to Burundi, Rwanda, Somalia, Ethiopia, and Eritrea. It is worth pointing out that a fair amount of research has been carried out on the acquisition of new literacy practices as well as language shift among displaced Somalis and Eritreans (e.g. Clyne and Kipp 1997; Masny and Ghahremani-Ghajar 1999; Arthur 2004). Most of this research is situated in the United Kingdom, North America, and Australia and addresses the challenges that these populations face in adapting to western cultures and

English-medium educational environments. Other research studies on diaspora populations include Gafaranga's (2007) research on conversational code-switching practices
among Rwandan speakers in Belgium, using the tools of conversation analysis.

Future directions

While this survey of East Africa shows that language policy and educational contexts
have been widely researched, there is still a paucity of research that illustrates how languages are used in public and private domains of social life. Little has been published
regarding diglossia, register use, pragmatics, and gendered and ethnic forms of language.
Future research that examines these topics is needed in order to both deepen and widen
the scope of sociolinguistic research on East Africa. Of course, research will always
remain tied to the availability of funding and publishing opportunities, both of which
present daunting challenges for African scholars.

Another problem is that much of the existing research remains rather descriptive,
rather than making use of available sociolinguistic theories or recognized methodological
approaches to advance our understandings of the relationship between language and
society. It seems clear that economic disparities in the world have led to an imbalance in
the amount of research produced in and about developing nations, and the result seems
to be that most sociolinguistic research is based on largely monolingual societies and western
languages. Future research on the East African context is needed to address this disparity,
not only to more fully represent the social aspects of the world's languages, but also to provide space for African-based theories of language use. For example, it has been pointed
out that much sociolinguistic research is borne on the premise that monolingualism is the
starting point for building linguistic and sociolinguistic theory (e.g. Romaine 1995).
However, in East Africa, bilingualism, and more often, multilingualism, are the norm. It
will be very interesting to see how a shift in perspective that takes bi-/multilingualism as
a baseline could expand sociolinguistic theory in new ways, and how such developments
might positively impact the fields of language policy and planning as well.

References

Abdulaziz, M. and Osinde, K. (1997) "Sheng and English: development of mixed codes among the
urban youth in Kenya," *International Journal of the Sociology of Language*, 125, 43–63.
Arthur, J. (2004) "Language at the margins: the case of Somali in Liverpool," *Language Problems and
Language Planning*, 28, 217–40.
Batibo, H. (2005) *Language Decline and Death in Africa: Causes, Consequences and Challenges*, Clevedon:
Multilingual Matters.
Bernsten, J. (1998) "Runyakitara: Uganda's 'new' language," *Journal of Multilingual and Multicultural
Development*, 19, 93–107.
Billings, S. (2006) "Speaking beauties: language use and linguistic ideologies in Tanzanian beauty
pageants," unpublished doctoral dissertation, the University of Chicago.
Blommaert, J. (1999) *State Ideology and Language in Tanzania*, Köln: Koppe.
——(2005) "Situating language rights: English and Swahili in Tanzania revisited," *Journal of Socio-
linguistics*, 9, 390–417.
Brenzinger, M. (ed.) (1992) *Language Death: Factual and Theoretical Explorations with Special Reference to
East Africa*, Berlin: Mouton de Gruyter.

Brock-Utne, B. (2005) "Language-in-education policies and practices in Africa with a special focus on Tanzania and South Africa – insights from research in progress," in A. Lin and P. Martin (eds.) *Decolonisation, Globalisation: Language-in-education Policy and Practice*, Clevedon: Multilingual Matters, pp. 173–93.

Bunyi, G. (2005) "Language classroom practices in Kenya," in A. Lin and P. Martin (eds.) *Decolonisation, Globalisation: Language-in-education Policy and Practice*, Clevedon: Multilingual Matters, pp. 131–52.

Buregeya, A. (2006) "Grammatical features of Kenyan English and the extent of their acceptability," *English World-wide*, 27, 199–216.

Clyne, M. and Kipp, S. (1997) "Trends and changes in home language use and shift in Australia, 1986–96," *Journal of Multilingual and Multicultural Development*, 18, 451–73.

Fishman, J. (1972) "The relationship between micro- and macro-sociolinguistics in the study of who speaks what language to whom and when," in J. B. Pride and J. Holmes (eds.) *Sociolinguistics: Selected Readings*, Harmondsworth: Penguin Books, pp. 15–32.

Gafaranga, J. (2007) *Talk in Two Languages*, Basingstoke: Palgrave Macmillan.

Hallemariam, C., Kroon, S., and Walters, J. (1999) "Multilingualism and nation building: Language and education in Eritrea," *Journal of Multilingual and Multicultural Development*, 20, 475–93.

Hameso, S. (1997) "The language of education in Africa: the key issues," *Language, Culture, and Curriculum*, 10, 1–13.

Higgins, C. (2007a) "Shifting tactics of intersubjectivity to align indexicalities: a case of joking around in Swahinglish," *Language in Society*, 36, 1–24.

——(2007b) "Constructing membership in the in-group: affiliation and resistance among urban Tanzanians," *Pragmatics*, 17, 49–70.

——(2009). "From 'da bomb' to bomba: Global Hip Hop nation language in Tanzania," in A. Ibrahim, H. S. Alim, and A. Pennycook (eds.) *Global Linguistic Flows: Hip Hop Cultures, Youth Identities, and the Politics of Language*, Mahwah, NJ: Erlbaum, pp. 95–112.

Kang'ethe-Iraki, F. (2004) "Cognitive efficiency: the Sheng phenomenon in Kenya," *Pragmatics*, 14, 55–68.

Kembo-Sure (2004) "Establishing a national standard and English language curriculum change in Kenya," in M. Muthwii and A. Kioko (eds.) *New Language Bearings in Africa: A Fresh Quest*, Clevedon: Multilingual Matters, pp. 101–15.

Kihore, Y. (2004) "Masuala ya kisarufi katika magazeti ya mitaani ya Kiswahili-Tanzania," [Issues of grammar in popular Swahili magazines in Tanzania], *Swahili Forum*, 11, 107–19.

Kioko, A. and Muthwii, M. (2004) "English variety for the public domain in Kenya: speakers' attitudes and views," in M. Muthwii and A. Kioko (eds.) *New Language Bearings in Africa: A Fresh Quest*, Clevedon: Multilingual Matters, pp. 34–49.

Kishe, A. (2004) "Kiswahili as vehicle of unity and development in the Great Lakes region," in M. Muthwii and A. Kioko (eds.) *New Language Bearings in Africa: A Fresh Quest*, Clevedon: Multilingual Matters, pp. 122–34.

Laitin, D. (1977) *Politics, Language and Thought: The Somali Experience*, Chicago: University of Chicago Press.

Legère, K. (2006) "Formal and informal development of the Swahili language: focus on Tanzania," in O. F. Arasanyin and M. A. Pemberton (eds.) *Selected Proceedings of the 36th Annual Conference on African Linguistics*, Somerville, MA: Cascadilla Press, pp. 176–84.

Masny, D. and Ghahremani-Ghajar, S. (1999) "Weaving multiple literacies: Somali children and their teachers in the context of school culture," *Language, Culture and Curriculum*, 12, 72–93.

Mazrui, A. (2004) *English in Africa after the Cold War*, Clevedon: Multilingual Matters.

Mbaabu, I. and Nzuga, K. (2003) *Sheng-English Dictionary: Deciphering East Africa's Underworld Language*, Dar es Salaam: Institute of Kiswahili Research.

McIntosh, J. (2005) "Baptismal essentialisms," *Journal of Linguistic Anthropology*, 15, 151–70.

Mechthild, R. (2004) "Multilingual writing: a reader-oriented typology – with examples from Lira Municipality (Uganda)," *International Journal of the Sociology of Language*, 170, 1–41.

Mukuthuria, M. (2006) "Kiswahili and its expanding roles of development in East African cooperation: a case of Uganda," *Nordic Journal of African Studies*, 15, 154–65.

224

Musau, P. (2004) "Linguistic human rights in Africa: challenges and prospects for indigenous languages in Kenya," in M. Muthwii and A. Kioko (eds.) *New Language Bearings in Africa: A Fresh Quest*, Clevedon: Multilingual Matters, pp. 59–68.

Muthwii, M. (2004) "Language of instruction: a qualitative analysis of the perceptions of parents, pupils and teachers among the Kalenjin in Kenya," *Language, Culture and Curriculum*, 17, 15–32.

Mwinsheikhe, H. M. (2003) "Science and the language barrier: using Kiswahili as a medium of instruction in Tanzania secondary schools as a strategy of improving student participation and performance in science," in B. Brock-Utne, Z. Desai and M. Qorro (eds.) *The Language of Instruction in Tanzania and South Africa*, Dar es Salaam: E & D Publishers, pp. 129–49.

Myers-Scotton, C. (1993) *Social Motivations for Codeswitching: Evidence from Africa*, Oxford: Oxford University Press.

Ndayipfukamiye, L. (1996) "The contradictions of teaching bilingually in post-colonial Burundi: from nyakatsi to maisons de étage," *Linguistics and Education*, 8, 35–47.

Noor, A. A. (1999) "Arabic language and script in Somalia: history, attitudes, and prospects," unpublished doctoral dissertation, Georgetown University.

Ntahonkiriye, M. (2000) "Code-mixing among French-Kirundi bilinguals: interference, code-switching, or linguistic borrowing? Analysis of a few lexical items," *Langues et Linguistique* 26, 49–72.

Onyango, J. (2005) "Issues in national language terminology development in Kenya," *Swahili Forum*, 12, 219–34.

Parry, K. (ed.) (2000) *Language and Literacy in Uganda: Towards a Sustainable Reading Culture*, Kampala, Uganda: Fountain Publishers.

Perullo, A. and Fenn, J. (2003) "Language ideologies, choices, and practices in Eastern African hip hop," in H. M. Berger and M. T. Carroll (eds.) *Global Pop, Local Language*, Mississippi: University of Mississippi Press, pp. 19–52.

Remes, P. (1998) "Karibu geto langu/welcome to my ghetto: urban youth, popular language and culture in 1990s Tanzania," unpublished doctoral dissertation, Northwestern University.

Reuster-Jahn, U. (2007) "Let's go party! Discourse and self-portrayal in the Bongo Fleva song 'Mikasi'," *Swahili Forum*, 14, 225–44.

Reuster-Jahn, U. and Kießling, R. (2006) "Lugha ya mitaani in Tanzania: the poetics and sociology of a young urban style of speaking with a dictionary comprising 1100 words and phrases," *Swahili Forum*, 13, 1–200.

Romaine, S. (1995) *Bilingualism*, Malden, MA: Blackwell.

Roy-Campbell, Z. and Qorro, M. (1997) *Language Crisis in Tanzania: The Myth of English versus Education*, Dar es Salaam: Mkuki na Nyota Publishers.

Rubagumya, C. (2003) "English-medium primary schools in Tanzania: a new 'linguistic market' in education?" in B. Brock-Utne, Z. Desai and M. Qorro (eds.) *The Language of Instruction in Tanzania and South Africa*, Dar es Salaam: E & D Publishers, pp. 149–70.

Samper, D. (2004) "Africa is still our mama: Kenyan rappers, youth identity, and the revitalization of traditional values," *African Identities*, 2, 37–51.

Sprenger-Tasch, M. (2003) "Attitudes towards Luganda, Kiswahili, English, and mother tongue as media of instruction in Uganda," in H. Cuyckens, T. Berg, R. Dirven, and K. Panther (eds.) *Motivation in Language: Studies in Honor of Gunter Radden*, Amsterdam: Benjamins, pp. 347–65.

Tembe, J. (2006) "Teacher training and the English language in Uganda," *TESOL Quarterly*, 40, 857–60.

Vavrus, F. (2002) "Postcoloniality and English: exploring language policy and the politics of development in Tanzania," *TESOL Quarterly*, 36, 373–97.

Warsame, A. (2001) "How a strong government backed an African language: the lessons of Somalia," *International Review of Education*, 47, 341–60.

Wedin, A. (2005) "Language ideologies and schooled education in rural Tanzania: the case of Karagwe," *International Journal of Bilingual Education and Bilingualism*, 8, 568–87.

21

Israeli sociolinguistics

From Hebrew hegemony to Israeli plurilingualism

Zhanna Burstein-Feldman, Alek D. Epstein,
Nina Kheimets, Shulamith Kopeliovich,
Dafna Yitzhaki and Joel Walters

Introduction

Israel's geographical position as a land bridge connecting Europe, Asia and Africa, its history of repeated conquest, and its centrality for three major religions have assured a long tradition of multilingualism. Two thousand years ago triglossia reigned, with Hebrew, Judeo-Aramaic and Greek playing meaningful roles. Multilingualism was the norm for the Jewish people during most of the Dispersion, with separate functions: Hebrew and Talmudic Aramaic for religious and literacy purposes, Jewish languages like Yiddish, Ladino or Judeo-Arabic for community and home functions (Rabin 1981), and one or more "co-territorial vernaculars" for communication with Gentiles.

Current Israeli multilingualism began to take shape with the return of Jews to Palestine in the latter part of the nineteenth century. Subsequent revitalization of Hebrew (Fellman 1973; Myhill 2004) was central to nation-building, providing a common vernacular for the integration of a steady stream of immigrants (Bachi 1956), and guaranteed linguistic diversity (Cooper 1984).

The close of the nineteenth century brought changes in the pattern of multilingualism. Turkish was the language of Ottoman soldiers and government officials. Village and town-dwellers spoke local dialects of Arabic. Classical Arabic was the written language of the educated elite. Indigenous Sephardic Jews spoke Arabic, too, but inside the community the language was Judezmo. French, German and English were encouraged by missionary churches and foreign consuls (Spolsky and Cooper 1991). Ashkenazi Jews arriving from Eastern Europe spoke Yiddish, also bringing with them co-territorial vernaculars like Russian, Polish and Hungarian.

The late nineteenth century also brought a different kind of immigrant – ideological Jewish nationalists committed to the revival of Hebrew and its intimate connection to identity in their homeland. Jewish nationalism took two distinct paths: a non-territorial cultural nationalism that chose standardized and secularized Yiddish as its language, and a territorialist socialist movement that aimed to develop a "new Hebrew man," speaking

Hebrew in the newly-redeemed land. The battle between these two ideologies and languages was fought in Europe and in Palestine, with Hebrew the victor in the Holy Land (Harshav 1993; Kuzar 2001; Myhill 2004). The brief successes of Yiddish in Europe were weakened by migration and all but wiped out by the Holocaust.

Revitalization of Hebrew, from the early teaching of Hebrew in the schools in the 1890s, to its use as the main language by Zionist socialists who founded the communal settlements, and ideological monolingualism in the new "Hebrew" city of Tel Aviv, facilitated the spread of Hebrew. In 1913, its supporters were able to succeed in a bitter argument over the language of instruction to be used at the first university, naming it "The *Hebrew* University of Jerusalem" (Landau 1996). By the 1920s, Hebrew was a native language for many and the public language of the Jewish community of Palestine (Bachi 1956), although many leading academic and literary figures were still far from speaking it comfortably.

The British Mandatory government bolstered the standing of Hebrew in several ways. First, when General Allenby occupied the country in 1918, German was banned in schools and teachers interned. Even before the Mandate was formally proclaimed, Hebrew was an official language alongside Arabic and English. Second, to minimize its financial commitment to the mandated territory, the British allowed the Jewish community to conduct its own educational system. As the language of instruction in Jewish schools and in the university, Hebrew adapted to modern life and technology with the help of a Language Committee, which was renamed The Hebrew Language Academy after independence in 1948.

Under British Mandatory rule (1923–48), English was the main language of government, and Jewish and Arab communities remained distinct, with separate school systems. Contact bilingualism developed, English serving both communities as a potential language of wider communication. And yet, new Jewish immigrants who wished to integrate needed to acquire Hebrew, the language of work, education and public cultural life. When the State of Israel was established, Hebrew was the principal language of the bulk of the Jewish population of 650,000 (Bachi 1956). In the next decade, large numbers of new immigrants arrived, and their linguistic heterogeneity (Arabic, German, Romanian, Yiddish) contributed to the acceptance of Hebrew. Cooper (1984) enumerated other factors contributing to the spread of Hebrew, including: age on arrival (the younger, the faster), linguistic proximity (Arabic speakers learned more quickly than speakers of other languages), formal education and managerial, clerical, or professional employment.

Revitalization of Modern Israeli Hebrew was central in the nation-building process. Over three generations, this language succeeded in replacing the native language of most immigrants as the language of wider communication. Nevertheless, today it is still the native language of a minority of Israel's 7.2 million citizens. In addition to Arabic (1,000,000 Muslims, 500,000 Jews from North Africa, Iraq and Yemen, 150,000 Christians, and 120,000 Druze) and Russian (1,000,000 native speakers), there are more than 200,000 native speakers each of English, Romanian, and Yiddish. Another half million native speakers of ten different languages (Amharic, Bukharic, Georgian, Dzidi/Judeo-Persian, French, German, Hungarian, Juhuri/Judeo-Tat, Ladino, Spanish and Polish) and many other languages with 5–50,000 native speakers (Armenian, Bulgarian, Chinese, Czech, Dutch, Greek, Israeli Sign Language, Italian, Portuguese, Tagalog, Thai, Tigrigna, Turkish) give Israel multilingual vitality and make Hebrew, in a strange sense, a minority language in its own borders.

Brief history of sociolinguistic research in Israel

In Israel, as elsewhere, sociolinguistic research cuts across the disciplines of linguistics, anthropology, sociology, social psychology, history, cultural studies and education. While the field has no exact starting point, the joint presence of Fishman, Cooper and Spolsky (each in the prime of his career) in Jerusalem from 1969–72 promised a strong foundation for research and training. This period generated empirical research on the spread of English (Fishman *et al.* 1977) and later a volume on the languages of Jerusalem (Spolsky and Cooper 1991). Cooper's interests turned to theoretical issues in language spread and later to his seminal monograph on language policy (Cooper 1990). Fishman left Israel. Spolsky also left but re-immigrated in 1980 to Bar-Ilan University, where he established the Language Policy Research Center with Elana Shohamy, initially with a Ministry of Education-funded project on language and education. Later he conducted a study of language use in Bethlehem (with Amara and Tushiyeh) and a study of language and integration among Russian immigrants in Israel and Germany (with Dittmar and Walters). His prolific writings include books on testing, second language learning, sociolinguistics, and language policy. In pragmatics, discourse and social interaction, Shoshana Blum-Kulka's depth and productivity and mentoring of a large number of scholars have left an indelible mark on Israeli sociolinguistics. Her work on cross-cultural speech acts is grounded in the philosophy of language, her studies of dinner conversation in discourse analysis, and her research on children's talk in a merger of sociolinguistics, discourse analysis and developmental psychology.

Two international conferences at Bar-Ilan University in the late 1990s led to the founding of the Israeli Association for Language and Society (IALS), which holds a one-day meeting annually with papers and symposia primarily in Hebrew. Two other regular national meetings are: ILASH (Israel Applied Linguistics Association), an AILA affiliate, and SCRIPT (Israel Association for Literacy) (www.scriptil.org). Finally, the Jewish languages website (www.jewish-languages.org) has been a source of discussion for a wide range of sociolinguistic topics.

Language variation

Since Yaeger-Dror left Israel in 1992, there is no classical Labovian variationist research going on in the country. Her notions of hypercorrection and cognitive salience in the use of Hebrew *resh* by Israeli singers drew from social psychology (attitudes/ethnicity) and sociolinguistics. Variation is, however, treated from a range of other perspectives, focusing especially on gender and ethnicity. Bogoch's (1999) studies of "gendered courtroom discourse" in Israel, grounded in legal semiotics, feminist theory, and pragmatics, examine address terms, interruptions, and the content and pragmatics of courtroom proceedings in 656 segments from civil and criminal cases involving interaction primarily among legal professionals. Women attorneys were addressed less deferentially and were interrupted more often, which Bogoch concluded "undermined their professional status." Other work on legal discourse is found in Morris's (1998) studies of the Demjanjuk trial and Shlesinger's (1991) papers on multilingual court proceedings. Other papers on gender include Ariel and Giora (1993) and Muchnik (2007).

The untimely death of Rafi Talmon in 2004 struck a severe blow to research on Arabic dialectology. But Henkin (1998) has continued this project with work on Bedouin

Arabic dialects; and Galilean Arabic has been investigated by Geva-Kleinberger (2005) and Rosenhouse (1984). Among ethnic distinctions Moroccan Hebrew and Arabic has been documented by, for example, Bentolila (1994).

Bilingualism

Research on bilingualism has focused on the acquisition and use of English, Arabic, Russian and Hebrew. Dittmar, Spolsky and Walters (2001) showed how advanced adult Russian immigrant learners' attitudes were grounded in language preferences, proficiency and code-switching as well as lexical, syntactic and phonetic variation. Burstein-Feldman (2008) extended this project, looking at cross-generational differences in attitudes and identities through the use of reference terms (names of people/places) and pronouns (we/they, us/them). Her study paints an integrated picture of multiple factors involved in convergence toward and divergence from the immigrants' native cultures and languages. Amara (1999) showed how identity is reflected in the pronunciation of linguistic variables such as [q] in the speech of Arab-Hebrew-English multilingual communities in Palestinian border villages.

Walters' (2005) model of bilingualism integrates socio-pragmatic and psycholinguistic information in a single framework to account for language choice decisions (e.g. code-switching). The primary sociolinguistic information included in this model is social identity, context (setting, topic, participants), and genre (conversation/scripted speech), drawing on literature from sociology, ethnography, discourse analysis and social cognition. Altman (2007) applied the sociopragmatic-psycholinguistic distinction to show how different motivations account for code-switching in three groups of mature (ages 60–90) immigrant bilinguals (English-Hebrew, Russian-Hebrew and Georgian-Hebrew) across the lifespan.

Early bilingual acquisition and social integration is currently under investigation by Armon-Lotem and Walters and colleagues (2008), funded by the Israel Science Foundation and the German Ministry of Education. These projects examine morphosyntactic, narrative, lexical and pragmatic abilities along with measures of identity and attitudes in English-Hebrew and Russian-Hebrew pre-school children. Saiegh-Haddad (2003a, 2003b) has explored biliteracy acquisition among native speakers of Arabic and Russian, her studies challenging anglo-centered research with data on Arabic diglossia and Russian-Hebrew and Arabic-English bilingualism. From an ethnographic perspective, Kopeliovich (2006) investigated child–parent interaction in Russian-Hebrew bilingual families using a "Communities of Practice" framework, identifying four structurally distinct contact varieties with Russian and Hebrew elements in family discourse.

Studies of code-switching in Israel include: Maschler's (2002) work on bilingual discourse; Regev's (2004) dissertation on academic service encounters during university course registration; Baumel's (2002) study of ultra-orthodox use of Hebrew, English and Yiddish; Altman's (2007) investigations of code-switching and crossover memories in maturing adults; and Raichlin's (2009) multi-task (spontaneous speech, elicited imitation, retelling) study of socio-pragmatic and psycholinguistic motivations and directionality of code-switching among Russian-Hebrew pre-school children.

Multilingualism in Israeli higher education

Influenced by European nationalism, the leaders of the Zionist movement gave priority to the revitalization of Hebrew as a national language. However, in contrast to European national movements, the universities played a relatively marginal role in the nation-building process, and the cultural revolution took place outside of academia (Shapira 1996). Scholars of modern Hebrew appeared only later and were not particularly involved in revitalization.

Israel's seven research universities and 50 colleges today have over 200,000 students, more than double the number in 1980. A large portion of this increase resulted from a government decision to allow degree-granting status to more than 35 public and private colleges. By 2005, more than 60 percent of bachelor's degrees were conferred by colleges, not universities.

Although founded as "The *Hebrew* University," this institution has never been monolingual. Early on, European languages/literatures were recognized as essential for its students. Since many, if not most, faculty members were themselves graduates of German universities, German scholarship played an important role at the Hebrew University (Kheimets and Epstein 2005a). While Hebrew was the language of instruction, students were required to be able to read in English, French, or another modern European language. In 1949, the Yiddish department was founded as well.

Nevertheless, language study has never been popular among Israeli students; the numbers who major in language or literature has been decreasing. In 1969, 12 percent of university students majored in languages/literatures, while by 2000 this proportion had dropped to 8.6 percent. Although English is compulsory at all universities and colleges, only 1.5 percent of university students major in this field, and the level of English achieved by most has been described as less than optimal. In contrast, the number of students in Asia Studies and Spanish almost doubled during the 1990s (Kheimets and Epstein, 2005b).

Israeli universities' language policy is quite clear: English is the dominant language with regard to promotion opportunities and preferred language for publication (a perennial joke being that God would not have received tenure since the Bible was not written in English). However, virtually all instruction, examinations, seminar papers and most M.A. theses and Ph.D. dissertations are still written in Hebrew (ibid.). This appears to be changing somewhat in the sciences, where successful employment requires higher levels of English. Furthermore, most scientific conferences in Israel are conducted in English and journals in law, medicine and natural sciences are published in English. Finally, even Hebrew language journals tend to include abstracts in English.

Israeli higher education has become increasingly multilingual and multicultural, partly due to a relatively liberal policy of admissions for Arabic-speaking minority students as well as Russian and Ethiopian immigrants. This is especially true at colleges in Galilee and Negev, some of which have up to 50 percent language minority students in student bodies ranging from 1,000–1,003,000. These students are the first generation of their families in higher education and come to college as speakers of Hebrew as a second or third language and English as a third or fourth language, putting them at a severe disadvantage in comparison to native Hebrew speakers. The liberal admissions policy has not been accompanied by serious thinking as to how to deal with academic limitations and dropout rates among these populations.

Language and culture, power and language policy

Israel's social cleavages are almost as numerous as its political parties and as deep as the Syrian-African rift. Jews and Arabs, Muslims, Druze and Christians, immigrants and *sabras* (native-born Israelis), Ashkenazim and Sefardim, religious and secular confront each other in battles which play themselves out everywhere from the Knesset (Parliament) to the soccer field, with the mass media eagerly fanning the fires. In these conflicts, where words are weapons and symbolic identity is more important than legal rights, language is the maker of collective identity and ideology.

Arabic among Arabs and Jews in Israel

One point of conflict between Jews and Arabs in Israel revolves around the issue of *nationality*. Israel was established as a Jewish state with Arabs (both Muslims and Christians) and other minorities (Druze, Circassians, Maronites, Copts, Armenians) acknowledged to have equal rights. The conflict is complicated by the notion of "national minority" according to which Arabs are entitled to citizenship rights while maintaining their own "national" identity. Although both Hebrew and Arabic have official status since 1948, *de jure* rights do not always find expression in practice. While Hebrew is used in all public contexts (Parliament, courts, academia, government documents, commerce) and in most television and radio programs, Arabic is used for most local matters in Arab villages and towns (Spolsky and Shohamy 1999). Hebrew's actual strength is derived not from its legal status but rather from its position as a symbol of a Jewish-Zionist national identity. This unique status has been constantly and actively promoted from the early days of statehood (Harshav 1993; Kuzar 2001).

Arabic has been seen as both a reflection of the ongoing *political conflict* and a link between political and linguistic dimensions of the conflict. Shohamy and Donitsa-Schmidt (1998) showed how negative attitudes of Israeli Jews towards peace in the Middle East were correlated with negative stereotypes of Arabic and low motivation to study the language. Suleiman (2004), writing from Edinburgh, sees the relation between Hebrew and Arabic in Israel as "linguistic conflict," where language is used as a "loaded weapon" (ibid.: 218). He states that the opposition of members of the Language Council (forerunner of the Hebrew Language Academy) to borrow lexical items from Arabic (ibid.: 140) shaped negative perceptions of the Arabic language and its users. Spolsky and Cooper (1991) and Ben-Rafael *et al.* (2006) examined the use of languages on public and private signs, showing that a Hebrew-Arabic pattern is very rare in Jewish environments, whereas Hebrew was found in Arabic areas mainly for commerce. Ben-Rafael's (1994) interviews with Israeli Arabs indicate that despite general proficiency of Arabs in Hebrew, the desire to retain Arabic as a symbol of national identity has impeded a shift to Hebrew dominance.

Language and multilingual identity of the Russian Jewish intelligentsia

The mass immigration from the former Soviet Union in the 1990s created a rich ethno-linguistic community with its own economic, social and political networks based on Russian language and culture and identity choices ranging from assimilation to separatism.

Since Soviet language policy aimed at suppressing minority languages in favor of Russian, the contemporary cultural world of former Soviet Jews has been mediated mostly in Russian. The ethnolinguistic vitality of Russian has been assessed as very high for former Soviet immigrants in Israel (e.g. Olshtain and Kotik 2000). Such "exaggerated loyalty" towards Russian was attributed by Yelenevskaya and Fialkova (2002: 207) to the fact that "upon immigration [people] tend to emphasize the significance of their past." It is further argued that the Soviet "attitude to minority languages and speakers of minority languages" has been transferred by the immigrants to the linguistic situation in Israel, giving a minority language (Russian) more cultural and educational potential than the majority language (Hebrew) (Yelenevskaya and Fialkova 2003: 45).

Using sociolinguistic surveys and interviews with Russian-speaking community leaders in several towns in Israel, Ben-Rafael et al. (2006) report a strong desire to maintain Russian language/culture, which is perceived by immigrants as a source of collective pride. Remennick (2003) interprets use of Russian in public realms and high self-esteem among bearers of a Russian accent as indicative of the rising sociolinguistic status of Russian speakers in Israel. Kopeliovich (2006) claims that the Russian-immigrant intelligentsia retains Russian cultural values, even when these values are expressed in Hebrew or English. Russian language and cultural maintenance in Israel, against the background of Hebrew-English bilingualism, has resulted in the creation of *triglossia* in this population (Kheimets and Epstein 2001). Specifically, Russian is used within the family and community framework, Hebrew is employed for social and civil integration, while English is required for academic and professional advancement.

In studies of younger generation immigrants, Kopeliovich (2006) reports a rapid shift away from Russian language use among adolescents and children together with positive attitudes to their parents' cultural heritage. Similarly, adolescents examined by Burstein-Feldman (2008) reported language and behavior patterns typical of their Israeli-born peers, while at the same time expressing satisfaction with their being "different" as a result of exposure to the "more cultured" Russian values fostered by their families. This complex interplay of two interacting identities exhibited by immigrant children may be problematic for the future of the Russian maintenance in Israel.

English: everybody's third language

With some foundation from the nineteenth century, English grew after the conquest of Palestine by the British and the subsequent British Mandate. Under Mandatory rule English was the language of government, but contact bilingualism developed, and English served both Jews and Arabs as a "neutral" albeit imperial language of wider communication.

English is one of the four compulsory subjects on secondary school matriculation exams; university students must satisfy an English-proficiency requirement at both B.A. and M.A. levels. English is a requirement for a substantial proportion of jobs; it is a vehicle for international pop culture; and it is the language most likely to be used between an Israeli and someone from abroad, whether the foreigner is a supplier, a customer, a tourist, or a relative. Cooper (1985) maintains that English, as a marker of educational status, is a key determinant of socio-economic status. The high status of English in Israel has been claimed to be one of the reasons North American immigrants do not attain the same level of Hebrew as former Soviet citizens (Beenstock 1996).

By the early 1970s, the effects of globalization were obvious to the Israeli public, and English grew in status and competence (Spolsky and Shohamy 1999: 156–86). The teaching of English moved from pre-1960 concern for literature and culture to a focus on English as an international language of communication. That change has brought increased emphasis on oral ability. Besides access to business, science, education, and travel, English is the language of some major Jewish diasporas (e.g. Canada, the UK, the US, South Africa). There has also been significant influence of English-speaking immigrants who arrived after 1967. This group was the first to speak a language which could compete with Hebrew in standing, and they provided a stock of native speakers of the language, many of whom became English teachers. About 40 percent of teachers of English in Jewish high schools are native speakers of the language, a figure probably not matched anywhere else (Spolsky 1997).

Language policy

There is no single comprehensive document which regulates government policy towards the languages spoken in Israel. Two relevant documents are the Declaration of Independence (1948) and Article 82 of the Palestinian Order in Council (1922). The former establishes the character of Israel as a Jewish state and Hebrew as its national symbol and at the same time grants equal status to all citizens. The latter is the document which recognizes Hebrew and Arabic as the official languages in Israel. Nevertheless, the Declaration of Independence does not have legal authority and Article 82 concerns only official governmental and municipal publications. Over the years, a number of Parliamentary laws have been passed, most concerned with use of Arabic, a few regarding Russian and Amharic (see Deutsch 2005, for a review). Nonetheless, the social dynamics of Israeli society dictate a different reality. Arabic is a *de facto* minority language while the public usage of Russian is prevalent despite the scarcity of legislation.

An educational language policy was proffered by the Israeli Ministry of Education in 1995 and 1996. The policy reaffirms the importance of Hebrew and Arabic as mother tongues and as languages of instruction in the two educational systems as well as the need for members of each community to learn the other language. In addition, English is designated as the first foreign language and immigrants are encouraged to maintain their home languages while acquiring Hebrew (see Spolsky and Shohamy 1999).

A question has recently been asked whether a distinction should be made between different types of linguistic minorities with relation to the state's legal obligation towards their speakers. More specifically, it is claimed that the state has a stronger obligation to the languages of national and indigenous minorities than to immigrant languages on sociological and moral grounds (Kymlicka 1995: 76–8). Applied to the Israeli context, this question would distinguish between Arabic, the language of a national minority, and Russian, an immigrant language. Up to now, this issue had been discussed in the Israeli public discourse and by Israeli legal scholars (Saban 2004) but it certainly requires sociolinguistic examination as well.

Pragmatics, discourse, and conversation

Israel has been richly fertile for this branch of sociolinguistics, producing work grounded in philosophy/linguistics (Ariel 2002; Dascal 1989; Kasher 1998), poetics/semiotics (Giora 2003), in developmental psycholinguistics (e.g. Ravid and Berman 2006) and discourse and socialization (Blum-Kulka 1997).

Blum-Kulka's lab has been most prolific. It was she who initiated the cross-cultural pragmatics project (CCSARP) in the early 1980s, looking at speech acts such as requests, hints, compliments, apologies with other Israeli (Weizmann, Olshtain) and German scholars (House, Kasper). From this lab, Weizmann's early work was grounded in the philosophy of language (speech acts), focusing on indirect speech acts (Weizman 1993), on indirectness in journalistic/literary language and more recently on political and journalistic writing (Weizman 2008). Blum-Kulka's research moved later to family discourse

(Blum-Kulka 1997), and most recently to children's pragmatic development. This level of activity gave Israeli sociolinguists an important voice in IPrA, but alas, politics and the academic boycott of Israel soon after led to a rift which made many Israeli scholars feel unwelcome at these conferences.

In her peer talk research, Blum-Kulka argues that "certain questions about social development can only be fully addressed with recourse to discourse analysis of peer interactions." She goes on to indicate that these questions include issues as broad as gender identity, social relationships, empathy/perspective taking, race, ethnic and cultural differences. Despite the wide net she has cast, each one of these questions is grounded in theoretical terms a sociolinguist will readily understand.

From structural, functional and developmental perspectives, Berman, Ravid and their students have examined background information, temporality, verb tense and semantics in narrative discourse; and topic introduction, generality, nominal structure and content in expository texts. Among the most innovative aspects of this work is the notion of information density (Ravid and Berman 2006).

Finally, discourse markers, little words and phrases used almost exclusively in spoken language (and numbering 50–100 in most languages), have been shown to convey a variety of *structural* purposes to mark changes in topic, to connect clauses, and to frame conversation; *sociopragmatically* to create relationships between speaker and listener, to convey affect and emotion; and *psycholinguistically* to allow a speaker time for planning and maintaining fluency in production. Israel has been a center for work in this area, beginning with Jucker and Ziv's (1998) volume, where four of the ten articles dealt with Hebrew.

From a sociopragmatic perspective, Weizman (2003, Weizman *et al.* 2007) has studied positioning in news interviews on Israeli television. She argues for the relevance of implicit challenge strategies to the co-construction and dynamic negotiations of interactional and social roles, focusing on discursive practices such as address terms and irony. Her cross-cultural interests include a comparative analysis of news interviews on Israeli television and Al Jazeera (Weizman *et al.* 2007). Livnat has applied a discourse-analytic approach to political speeches, bumper stickers, the daily press, legal discourse and scientific writing (e.g. Livnat 2005). This work focuses on the relations between addressee and audience, and examines the social role played by the text in the discourse community.

Conclusion

Multilingualism was not necessarily envisioned by the founders of the state when they legislated both Arabic and Hebrew as the official languages of the country in 1948. Nor did Jewish refugees who came from Europe, North Africa and the Middle East think they were coming to a place known for its pluralism. But the years since perestroika have been paralleled in Israel by unsurpassed demographic changes from immigration and natural birth rates among Muslims and religious Jews far beyond those of the secular population – to a point that Israel can be seen today as a nation in a struggle to clarify a very complex collective identity. Multilingualism is strong among languages like Arabic, English and Russian, where vitality comes from demographics and/or a long literary tradition. Endangered languages such as Yiddish and Syriac (among Maronite Christians) hope to earn a place in the Israeli mosaic. Israeli sociolinguistics cries for more intensive study of the country's major social cleavages, between Arabs and Jews, Ashkenazim and

Sefardim, young and old, and between elites and the disenfranchised. This kind of research is labor-intensive in data gathering, transcription, coding and interpretation. Tough issues are often treated by descriptive, media-oriented approaches, some of them imbued more with ideology than science. It is too bad that despite the large number of dissertations cited in this chapter, very few young scholars have found a place in academia. Fortunately, the diversity of languages, language users, and language issues in polyphonic Israel offers fertile ground for many more devoted sociolinguists.

References

Altman, C. (2007) "Bilingual autobiographical memory across the lifespan," PhD dissertation, Bar-Ilan University.

Amara, M. H. (1999) *Politics and Sociolinguistic Reflexes: Palestinian Border Villages*, Amsterdam: John Benjamins.

Ariel, M. (2002) "The demise of a unique concept of literal meaning," *Journal of Pragmatics*, 34, 361–402.

Ariel, M. and Giora, R. (1993) "The role of women in linguistic and social change: a study of pre-state literature," *Journal of Narrative and Life History*, 2, 309–32.

Armon-Lotem, S., Gagarina, N., Altman, C., Burstein-Feldman, Z., Gordishevsky, G., Gupol, O. and Walters, J. (2008) "Language acquisition as a window to social integration among Russian language minority children in Israel," *Israel Studies in Language and Society*, 1, 155–77.

Bachi, R. (1956) "A statistical analysis of the revival of Hebrew in Israel," *Scripta Hierosolymitana*, 2, 179–247.

Baumel, S. D. (2002) "Language policies of ethnic minorities as influenced by social, economic, religious and political constraints: an examination of Israeli Haredim," PhD dissertation, Bar-Ilan University.

Beenstock, M. (1996) "The acquisition of language skills by immigrants: the case of Hebrew in Israel," *International Migration*, 34, 3–29.

Ben-Rafael, E. (1994) *Language, Identity, and Social Division: The Case of Israel*, Oxford: Oxford University Press.

Ben-Rafael, E., Lyubansky, M., Gluckner, O., Harris, P., Israel, Y., Jasper, W. and Schoeps, J. (2006) *Building a Diaspora: Russian Jews in Israel, Germany and the USA*, Leiden: Brill.

Bentolila, Y. (1994) "Bilingualism in a Moroccan settlement in the South of Israel," *Israel Social Science Research*, 9, 89–108.

Blum-Kulka, S. (1997) *Dinner-Talk: Cultural Patterns of Sociability and Socialization in Family Discourse*, Mahwah, NJ: Lawrence Erlbaum.

Bogoch, B. (1999) "Courtroom discourse and the gendered construction of professional identity," *Law and Social Inquiry*, 24, 601–47.

Burstein-Feldman, Z. (2008) "Language and Identity of Russian-speaking Immigrants in Israel: An Intergenerational Study," PhD dissertation, Bar-Ilan University.

Cooper, R. (1984) "A framework for the description of language spread: the case of modern Hebrew," *International Social Science Journal*, 36, 87–112.

——(1985) "Language and social stratification among the Jewish population of Israel," in J.A. Fishman (ed.) *Readings in the Sociology of Jewish Languages*, Leiden: E.J. Brill, pp. 65–81.

——(1990) *Language Planning and Social Change*, Cambridge: Cambridge University Press.

Dascal, M. (1989) "On the roles of context and literal meaning in understanding," *Cognitive Science*, 13, 253–7.

Deutsch, Y. (2005) "Language law in Israel," *Language Policy*, 4, 261–85.

Dittmar, N., Spolsky, B. and Walters, J. (2001) *Convergence and Divergence in Second Language Acquisition and Use: An Examination of Immigrant Identities*, Final Project Report, Jerusalem: German Israeli Foundation for Scientific Research and Development.

Donitsa-Schmidt, S. (1999) "Language maintenance or shift: Determinants of language choice among Soviet immigrants in Israel," PhD thesis, Ontario Institute for Studies in Education.

Fellman, J. (1973) *The Revival of a Classical Tongue: Eliezer Ben Yehuda and the Modern Hebrew Language*, The Hague: Mouton.

Fishman, J. A., Cooper, R. L. and Conrad, A. W. (1977) *The Spread of English: a Sociology of English as a Second Language*, Rowley, MA: Newbury House.

Geva-Kleinberger, A. (2005) "The last informant: a text in the Jewish-Arabic dialect of Peqiin," in G. Procházka-Eisl (ed.) *Wiener Zeitschrift für Kund des Morgenlandes*, Vienna: Institute for Oriental Studies.

Giora, R. (2003) *On Our Mind: Salience, Context, and Figurative Language*, New York: Oxford University Press.

Harshav, B. (1993) *Language in Time of Revolution*, Berkeley, CA: University of California Press.

Henkin, R. (1998) "Narrative styles of Palestinian Bedouin adults and children," *Pragmatics*, 8, 47–78.

Jucker, A. H. and Ziv, Y. (eds.) (1998) *Discourse Markers: Description and Theory*, Amsterdam: John Benjamins.

Kasher, A. (1998) "Pragmatics: critical concepts," in *Communication, Interaction and Discourse*, vol. 5, London: Routledge.

Kheimets, N. and Epstein, A. (2001) "The role of English as a central component of success in the professional and social integration of scientists from the Former Soviet Union in Israel," *Language in Society*, 30, 187–215.

——(2005a) "Languages of science in the era of nation-state-formation: the Israeli universities and their (non)participation in the revival of Hebrew," *Journal of Multilingual and Multicultural Development*, 26, 12–36.

——(2005b) "Languages of higher education in contemporary Israel," *Journal of Educational Administration and History*, 37, 55–70.

Kopeliovich, S. (2006) "Reversing language shift in the immigrant family: a case-study of a Russian-speaking community in Israel," PhD dissertation, Bar-Ilan University.

Kuzar, R. (2001) *Hebrew and Zionism: A Discourse Analytic Cultural Study*, Berlin: Mouton de Gruyter.

Kymlicka, W. (1995) *Multicultural Citizenship*, New York: Oxford University Press.

Landau, J. (1996) "Culture, religion and language in Middle Eastern universities," *Judaism: A Quarterly Journal of Jewish Life and Thought*, 45, 163–9.

Livnat, Z. (2005) "Argumentation in a complex action game: a court judgement as a dialogic suasive text," *Studies in Communication Sciences*, Special Issue, 203–14.

Maschler, Y. (2002) "On the grammaticization of *ke'ilu* ('like', lit. 'as if') in Hebrew talk-in-interaction," *Language in Society*, 31, 243–76.

Morris, R. (1998) "Justice in Jerusalem: interpreting in Israeli legal proceedings," *Meta*, XLIII, 1–10.

Muchnik, M. (2007) "Gender differences in slang expressions as social communications" [in Hebrew], *Social Issues in Israel*, 3, 5–20.

Myhill, J. (2004) *Language in Jewish Society*, Clevedon: Multilingual Matters

Olshtain, E. and Kotik, B. (2000) "The development of bilingualism in an immigrant community," in E. Olshtain and G. Horenczyk (eds.) *Language, Identity and Immigration*, Jerusalem: Magnes Press pp. 201–17.

Rabin, C. (1981) "What constitutes a Jewish language?," *International Journal of the Sociology of Language*, 30, 19–28.

Raichlin, R. (2009) "Codeswitching among sequential bilingual children: structural, psycholinguistic and sociopragmatic dimensions," PhD dissertation. Bar-Ilan University.

Ravid, D. and Berman, R. A. (2006) "Information density in the development of spoken and written narratives in English and Hebrew," *Discourse Processes*, 41, 117–49.

Regev, I. (2004) "Social-pragmatic and psycholinguistic-cognitive aspects of bilingual code-switching," PhD dissertation, Bar-Ilan University.

Remennick, L. (2003) "Language acquisition as the main vehicle of social integration: Russian immigrants of the 1990s in Israel," *International Journal of the Sociology of Language*, 164, 83–105.

Rosenhouse, J. (1984) *The Bedouin Arabic Dialects: General Characteristics and a Detailed Study of North Israel Bedouin Dialects*, Wiesbaden: Harrassowitz.

Saban, I. (2004) "Minority rights in deeply divided societies: a framework for analysis and the case of the Arab-Palestinian minority in Israel," *New York University Journal of International Law and Politics*, 36, 885–1003.

Saiegh-Haddad, E. (2003a) "Linguistic distance and initial reading acquisition: the case of Arabic diglossia," *Applied Psycholinguistics*, 24, 431–51.

——(2003b) "Bilingual oral reading fluency and reading comprehension: the case of Arabic/Hebrew (L1) – English (FL) readers," *Reading and Writing: An Interdisciplinary Journal*, 16, 717–36.

Shapira, A. (1996) "The Zionist labor movement and the Hebrew University," *Judaism: A Quarterly Journal of Jewish Life and Thought*, 45, 183–98.

Shlesinger, M. (1991) "Interpreter latitude vs. due process: simultaneous and consecutive interpretation in multilingual trials," in S. Tirkkonen-Condit (ed.) *Empirical Research in Translation and Intercultural Studies*, Tübingen: Narr, pp. 147–55.

Shohamy, E. and Donitsa-Schmidt, S. (1998) *Jews vs. Arabs: Language Attitudes and Stereotypes*, The Tami Steinmets Center for Peace Research, Research Report Series, 9, Tel Aviv University.

Spolsky, B. (1997) "Multilingualism in Israel," *Annual Review of Applied Linguistics*, 17, 138–50.

Spolsky, B. and Cooper, R. (1991) *The Languages of Jerusalem*, Oxford: Oxford University Press.

Spolsky, B. and Shohamy, E. (1999) *The Languages of Israel: Policy, Ideology and Practice*, Clevedon: Multilingual Matters.

Suleiman, Y. (2004) *A War of Words: Language and Conflict in the Middle East*, New York: Cambridge University Press.

Walters, J. (2005) *Bilingualism: The Sociopragmatic-Psycholinguistic Interface*, Mahwah, NJ: Erlbaum.

Weizman, E. (1993) "Interlanguage requestive hints," in S. Blum-Kulka and G. Kasper (eds.) *Interlanguage Pragmatics*, Oxford: Oxford University Press, pp. 123–37.

——(2003) "News interviews on Israeli television: normative expectations and discourse norms," in S. Stati and M. Bondi (eds.) *Dialogue Analysis 2000*, Tübingen: Niemeyer, pp. 383–94.

——(2008) *Positioning in Media Dialogue: Negotiating Roles in the News Interview*, Amsterdam: John Benjamins.

Weizman, E., Levi, I. and Schneebaum, I. (2007) "Variation in interviewing styles: challenge and support in Al-Jazeera and on Israeli television," in A. Fetzer and G. Lauerbach (eds.) *Political Discourse in the Media*, Amsterdam: John Benjamins, pp. 197–223.

Yelenevskaya, M. and Fialkova, L. (2002) "When time and space are no longer the same: stories about immigration," *Studia Mythologica Slavica*, 5, 207–30.

——(2003) "From 'muteness' to eloquence: immigrants' narratives about languages," *Language Awareness*, 12, 30–48.

22

Arabic sociolinguistics in the Middle East and North Africa (MENA)

Catherine Miller and Dominique Caubet

Introduction

Arabic is one of the major language bundles of the world, in terms of native speakers (estimated between 250 to 350 millions), geographical expansion, and role as language of religion (Islam). However, both Arab and non-Arab linguists have tended to focus on Classical Arabic (known as *fushaa* in Arabic) and its modern variant known as Modern Standard Arabic (hence MSA). But one can also point to a rather long history of linguistic descriptions that take into account the sociological diversity of the Arabic-speaking world.

When and where can we consider that Arabic sociolinguistics proper emerged as a semi-autonomous discipline? It is extremely difficult to make clear-cut distinctions between sociolinguistics, dialectology and more general Arabic linguistics. If we consider that any description of the language, which draws some correlates with sociological categories, may be included in sociolinguistics, then we can find very early ancestors, among the Medieval Arab grammarians, then among European and Arab dialectologists of the nineteenth and twentieth centuries, who always associated certain features with certain social groups.

However, if we narrow the field to studies dealing primarily with description of variation, contact and change and their correlation with social categories, then the starting point of Arabic sociolinguistics as a recognized or self-claimed autonomous discipline, comes back to the early 1960s, following the emergence of sociolinguistics in the USA. Among the American founders of sociolinguistics, the work of Charles Ferguson had a particular impact on Arabic sociolinguistics, as some of his papers were to have a very strong influence and led to numerous research studies (Ferguson 1959a, 1959b and 1987, in particular). In France and among French-speaking researchers working on the MENA area, Marcel Cohen and David Cohen played an important role. Marcel Cohen was the founder of the field with his book *Pour une sociologie du langage* (1956) and his early study of the Jewish speech in Algiers (Cohen 1912). His student, David Cohen, Professor of Semitic Studies at the University Paris III in the 1970s, set up a CNRS research team, thus raising Arabic dialectology and sociolinguistics to an object worthy of research in

France, but also in the countries of origin of the students who went back and took up university positions in the 1980s and 1990s in their respective countries.

As we shall see, most of the works presenting themselves as Arabic sociolinguistic studies were first concerned with the famous issue of diglossia, or followed Labov's variationist approach, particularly within English-speaking publications, while the French-speaking publications developed a historical dialectal and sociolinguistic approach (Caubet 2004a). For the past two decades the focus has been on code-switching, language shift, dialect accommodation, language attitudes, studies on the diasporas in Europe or in America, interaction, and ethno-methodological approaches. Like everywhere else, Arabic sociolinguistics has operated a progressive shift from using pre-existing categories to those based on the practices of the interactants.

Previous states of the art on Arabic sociolinguistics have been provided by Daher (1987), Haeri (2000) and Owens (2001). A new, major reference is Bassiouney (2009).

The ancestors: Medieval Arab grammarians and modern dialectologists

While standard Western grammars of Classical Arabic tend to present a rather standardized and homogenous language, a close look at the Medieval Arab grammarian tradition indicates that early Arab grammarians were aware of the heterogeneity of the Arabic language and were discussing a number of variants. Studies on Medieval Arab grammarians (Owens 1990; Versteegh 1993) have shown that this early acknowledgement of variation among grammarians busy fixing the norm of Classical Arabic was due to their wish to select the best and purest variants, with the idea that variants associated with the most isolated Bedouin groups were more correct and closer to Classical Arabic.

In the tenth century, following the final fixing of the Classical Arabic language, Arab grammarians rarely paid attention to social variants and the few valuable remarks are provided by geographers or historians like Ibn Khaldoun in the fourteenth century (Larcher 2006). After Ibn Khaldoun, we find almost no source in the Arab world describing social or areal variation until the first dialect descriptions started to appear from the seventeenth century onwards such as a lexicon of Egyptian Arabic written by Al-Maghribi in the seventeenth century (Zack, in Haak et al. 2003).

The European colonial conquests of the nineteenth and early twentieth centuries provided the first important dialect descriptions and dictionaries. Some of these works are still invaluable references for the dialects and provide interesting data when investigating variation. Among the founders of Arabic dialectology one may quote A. Barthélemy, L. Bauer, G. Bergstrasser, L. Brunot, J. Cantineau, M. Cohen, G.S. Colin, M. Feghali, G. Kampffmeyer, Landberg, W. Marçais, P. Marçais, W. Spitta-Bey, etc. Most of these dialect descriptions tended to describe stable systems and emphasized homogeneity rather than social variation and diversity.[1] However, they paid careful attention to areal (Western versus Eastern) and group distinction. They applied Ibn Khaldoun's categorization, distinguishing between sedentary versus bedouin dialects and within the sedentary between rural versus urban dialects (Marçais and Guiga 1925).[2] They also highlighted communal, religious or sectarian variation (between Jewish, Christian, Muslim Shi'i, Muslim Sunni etc.) as well as gender variation (men/women).

Their work developed the bases for comparative and historical dialectology that would be developed further by linguists such as H. Blanc, D. Cohen, W. Diem, O. Jastrow,

D. Rabin, etc. Particularly important was the attention paid to the history of settlements of the various Arab groups that led to different types of Arabic dialects (*qeltu* and *geltu* dialects in Mesopotamia, pre-Hilali (rural, Jbâla and city dialects) and Hilali dialects in North Africa) as well as attention paid to phenomena of dialect mixing and interference with the local non-Arab languages (Aramaic, Berber, Coptic, etc.). It is in the writings of these founders that we find mention of two concepts taken from the Greek-Latin tradition of linguistics and imported into Arabic linguistics, *diglossia* and *koiné* that became extremely popular in Arabic sociolinguistics and studies on dialect contact.

Since the late nineteenth century, a number of Arab linguists had worked as collaborators/informants for Western dialectologists. Since then, many have published dialect works either in Arabic such as I. Anis (1967), or in 'Western' languages such as M. Feghali (1919), and many others since. But Arabic dialectology was quickly associated with colonialism among the circles of Arab nationalists, who were acting for the revival and modernization of the Arabic classical language to oppose the influence of the European languages. Arab nationalists were looking for national linguistic homogeneity and were opposed to any type of linguistic diversity (Suleiman 2003).

Diglossia, mixed styles and the issue of standard and prestige

The coming of independence in the mid-twentieth century, and the dominance of pan-Arab nationalism in most MENA countries both conspired in the stigmatization of Arabic dialectology. Interest in Arabic dialects was considered to be a means of weakening Arab unity. All Arab states chose Classical Arabic (*fushaa*) as the official language of the country and those who were acting for the promotion of the local Arabic vernaculars became politically marginalized. Therefore, in most Arab countries, description of Arabic vernaculars was restricted to folkloric domains such as oral literature, proverbs, songs, etc. and was not considered proper linguistics. It was thought that Modern Classical Arabic would and should act as a common language among all Arab speakers and that, thanks to education and mass media, it would and should replace the local dialects.

It is in this general political context, that the concept of diglossia imported from Greek linguistics to Arabic by W. Marçais (Marçais 1930) was discussed and widely popularized by Ferguson (Ferguson 1959a, and its revised version, Ferguson 1991). In this idealized model, one linguistic variety has a high status while the other has a lower status. They have different and complementary functions and are distinguished by clear structural differences. High functions are associated with the written and oral official domains while low functions are mainly associated with the oral informal domains. In Ferguson's classical model of diglossia, the high and the low varieties belong to the same language, even if they are distinguished by structural differences (Classical/Standard Modern Arabic versus Arabic dialects). In Fishman's functional model of diglossia (1968), different languages may fill different functional niches.

Ferguson's paper on diglossia represents a crucial step that marks the beginning of Arabic sociolinguistics as an academic entity in its own right (Owens 2001), particularly in the Middle East, where the concept of the Fergusonian diglossia was compatible with the pan-Arabic ideology and was therefore used widely by both Westerners and Arabs, although it led to several refinements or adjustments (see below). But for a number of authors (particularly those working on North Africa), diglossia is perceived as an ideologically biased concept which implies that the vernacular language (being Arabic or whatever vernaculars) is treated as an inferior language due to its status of 'low variety' (Drettas 1981; Messaoudi 2003; Tabouret-Keller 2006).

Ferguson's paper led to numerous studies investigating the use of the high/low varieties in contemporary Arab societies. Observation revealed that native speakers of Arabic who had access to both the standard language and the dialect rarely used purely one or the other variant. A number of alternative or refined models were proposed. The first model using terms such a tri-, quadri-, multi or pluriglossia, positions a series of discrete levels on the scale between the ideal standard versus dialect poles (Badawi 1973; Meiseles 1980; Dichy 1994; Youssi 1995; Hary 1996; Ennaji 2001). These discrete levels are supposed to be characterized by linguistic traits and are often associated with the speakers' degree of education (cf. Badawi's illiterate colloquial as opposed to educated colloquial). But as Mejdell comments: 'Attempts to construct models tend to be flawed by lack of, or only minimal, empirical support, and turn out to be difficult to apply to natural data' (Mejdell 2006: 47). Moreover matched guise experiments reveal that there is no consensus among the speakers and the hearers as to where the boundaries of standard and dialect stand (Parkinson 1991).

Related to this first model, another alternative model which appeared in the 1970s (known as the Leeds Project),[3] considered that the intermediate variety between standard and dialect is a separate new entity, known as Educated Spoken Arabic (Mitchell 1986, and several other publications) in English and *arabe conceptuél* or *arabe médian* or *moyen arabe* in French (Taine-Cheikh 1978; Youssi 1986). ESA is defined as 'informal educated speech', consisting of elements from both standard Arabic and the dialect and possessing hybrid forms unique to the ESA level.

Another approach within this general diglossic framework describes the situation in terms of code-switching (Eid 1988; Bassiouney 2006; Boussofora-Omar 2006) or mixed-styles (Blanc 1960; Diem 1974; Mazraani 1997; Mejdell 2006). Instead of discrete levels, the relationship between the two idealized poles is conceptualized as a continuum with various patterns of mixing (Kaye 1994). Studies on code-switching and mixed-styles followed the development of the field, from an approach in terms of structural constraints (Schmidt 1974; Eid 1988) to the discussion of the Matrix Language Frame of Myers-Scotton or to Auer's model and the difference between borrowings and code-switching (Heath 1989; Bassiouney 2006; and a number of papers in Rouchdy 2002). Mejdell (2006) reviews and analyses all the previous literature on the subject and provides a deep syntactic and semantic analysis of mixed styles in Egyptian Arabic. She does not limit her analysis to the syntactic surface level but goes deep into the semantic and functional levels.

The use of linguistic corpora for defining Educated Spoken Arabic and stylistic variation led to several quantitatively-based variationist studies, looking at the realization of a particular feature and trying to link the variant with various extra-linguistic categories such as age, education, gender, ethnic or communal origin as well as with contextual uses, with particular attention to Egypt and the Levant (El-Hassan 1978; Beni Yassin and Owens 1987; Parkinson 1985, and numerous theses) and few works on North Africa (Talmoudi 1984). The point that emerged from the study of spoken corpora drawn from a cross-section of speakers is that the classification of variants according to a pre-set scale ranging between standard and dialect was problematic. Very often the number of variables cross-examined is not sufficient and gives an impression of superficiality, leading to conclusions too hurriedly made.

A problematic assumption of some of the works investigating variation among the various levels or within ESA was to postulate that the closer the variant is to *fushaa*, the higher its prestige, while the stigmatized forms are always associated with the dialect. This postulate of Modern Standard Arabic (MSA) as the prestigious language came to be challenged by those linguists working in an urban environment like Abdel Jawad (1987), Ibrahim (1986) and many others whose studies reveal that urban dialect variants can be selected over standard variants in a number of contexts and that direction of change is not uni-directionally from dialects toward MSA.

Correlation between standard variants, education and gender gave birth to passionate discussion. Studies dealing with the realization of the variable *q indicate that men tend toward greater usage of standard /q/ whereas women tended toward urban /ʔ/ (glottal stop) (Bakir 1986; Abdel Jawad 1987; Haeri 1995; Daher 1999). This difference between men and women was the reason that led Ibrahim (1986) to differentiate between standard and prestige and to highlight the influence of urban speech even among educated speakers (see also Ferguson 1987; Palva 1982; Walters 1991; Al-Wer 2002). Al-Wer (2002) shows that education, *per se*, is not a decisive factor but often leads to a widening of the individual's network and mobility and, in the case of Jordanian women, leads to higher use of urban variables. However, other studies such as Abu-Haidar (1987) found precisely the opposite, i.e. women used a greater percentage of SA forms than men in Baghdad. Walters (2003) and Mejdell (2006) indicate also a tendency among educated women to use many standard variants in formal speech.

Urban Arabic sociolinguistics emerged at the cross-roads of dialect and diglossia studies. Research on dialect accommodation in urban environments pointed out that an important caveat of diglossia studies was to treat the dialect as a single homogeneous entity, without taking into account the actual internal dialect variation.

Dialect contact, variation and change

From the 1960s onwards, dialect studies were carried out in many countries with important development in the 1970s, 1980s and 1990s. Numerous descriptions, questionnaires as well as Atlases on Egypt, Syria, Tunisia, Yemen, etc.,[4] gave a better picture of the dialect situation in the Arabic-speaking world, including its marginal or peripheral areas such as Malta, Sub-Saharan Africa, Central Asia, as well as Arabic varieties spoken by Arab minorities in Europe, Turkey, Iran, Africa, the USA, South America, etc. This development of dialect studies was particularly strong in Europe, centring around figures like D. Cohen and his students in France and the Arab world; J. Fischer, O. Jastrow, K. Versteegh, M. Woidich and P. Behnstedt in Germany and the Netherlands; T. H. Johnstone, C. Holes and B. Ingham in England, F. Corriente and his students in Spain, H. Palva in Finland and Sweden, J. Retsö in Norway, J. Grand'Henry in Belgium, T. Prochazka and A. Ambros in Austria, B. Zaborski in Poland, without forgetting Israel (H. Blanc, Piamenta, etc.) and some American scholars such as P. Abboud, J. Heath, A. Kaye, D. Parkinson and J. Owens. A number of Arab scholars who described Arabic vernaculars were to become leading linguists in their country such as H. Bakalla in Saudi Arabia; Beni Yassin, M. Ibrahim and H. Abdel Jawad in Jordan; S. Badawi and A. Elgibali in Egypt, A.A. Matar and M. Yassin in Kuwait; Boukous, M. Ennaji, L. Messaoudi and A. Youssi in Morocco, and T. Baccouche in Tunisia.

This mushrooming of dialect/sociolinguistic studies led to the creation of an International Association of Arabic Dialectology (AIDA) in Paris in 1993, as it was felt necessary to build a network that would help the recognition of the field and its independence from general Arabic linguistics, very much dominated at that time by generative linguistics and Classical Arabic. AIDA is one of the rare arenas where dialectology and socio-linguistics meet.[5] Many of the dialect studies stick to structural description and provide a rather homogeneous picture of each variety (examples of such descriptions can be found in the numerous lemmas of the recent *Encyclopaedia of Arabic Language and Linguistics* Versteegh (2006–8). However, the growing amount of data contributes to a better understanding of the social history of spoken Arabic and dialect contact phenomena. Dialect studies describe the phonological and morphosyntactic features that characterized each dialect and pave the way for a sociolinguistic analysis of their uses by different speakers in various contexts, particularly within urban centres.

Within this general development of dialect studies, two trends emerged as major directions of research: historical sociolinguistics and variationist sociolinguistics.

Historical sociolinguistics

One trend can be described as historically oriented, investigating present variation in order to understand historical and present-day changes, particularly regarding the process of dialect mixing and koineization, following population movements and settlement processes. Special attention is given to communal varieties (either regionally-based, ethnic-based or religious-based communities) to understand when, how, where and why they emerged and evolved. This trend is well represented in studies about North Africa on the one hand and Iraq on the other, in areas where contact between Bedouin dialects and old-city dialects led to several processes of dialect shift and koineization.

Blanc's seminal study of communal dialects in Baghdad (Blanc 1964) is a pioneer illustration of how contemporary variation can explain historical development. Three communal varieties were recorded in Baghdad (Jewish, Christian and Muslim, see also Abu-Haidar 1991), characterized by specific linguistic traits. Blanc's study showed that this communal distinction did not exist in the fourteenth and fifteenth centuries when Muslims and non-Muslims alike were speaking the same variety similar to the sedentary *qeltu* dialects of northern Iraq. It was the subsequent migration of Bedouin groups coming from the Arabic peninsula and progressively settling and taking over political power in the nineteenth century that led to a dialect shift among the Muslim groups adopting a *geltu* dialect while Jewish and Christians kept the former city dialect. Another example of Bedouinization of a former city dialect is the Jordanian city of Salt (Palva 1994, and further papers). Holes (1987, and many other publications) investigated sectarian differences in Bahrain. His work showed that the sedentary Shia Baharna are the older settlers while the Bedouin Sunni Arab arrived in the eighteenth century and took over power. Isolating 19 variables for comparison between the two groups, Holes' work on Bahrain is among the few research programmes that articulate an historical reflection with contemporary quantitative corpus data-based work.

Concerning North Africa, dialect studies link linguistic data with historical research and investigate the various strata of Arabization as well as the different actors of the Arabization process (Bedouin groups, Berber speakers, families from Andalousian or Kairouanese origin, Jewish groups, etc., see Cohen 1975; Stillman 1988; Lévy 1990; Aguadé and El Yaaccoubi 1995; Aguadé *et al.* 1998; Vicente 2000; Heath 2002). As in Iraq, they point to many cases of koineization and a process of re-bedouinization of old-city dialects, a process that continues up to the present day. Put in very general terms, rural-urban migration led to the marginalization of the old-city dialects and the

243

dominance of new urban *koiné* very much influenced by the rural/Bedouin varieties brought by the migrants. The old city dialect tended to become restricted to religious minorities (Jewish) and women, while Muslim men tend to keep (if they are migrants) or acquire (if they belong to the old-city groups), at least in public spaces, the variants of the new *koiné* characterized by a mixture of sedentary/Bedouin features (see various papers in Aguadé *et al.* 1998; and Cohen 1981; Jabeur 1987; Trabelsi 1988; Messaoudi 2003; Miller *et al.* 2007). An interesting consequence of these changes is that old-city dialects came to be considered as effeminate compared to the new urban speech forms (Miller 2003). Apart from those authors writing in English, most of the studies dealing with dialect contact in North Africa do not follow a quantitative-base variationist approach but rely on ethnographic observation or recording of a few selected speakers (see, for example, Boucherit 2002b, for Algiers).[6]

Three edited collections developed a social historical approach (with the collaboration of historians and linguists) that described the long-term evolution of the sociolinguistic situation and highlighted the historical depth of linguistic diversity: Miller and Doss 1997, for Egypt, Aguadé *et al.* 1998, for Morocco, Dakhlia 2004, for North Africa. They represent the first attempts of a still awaited social history of languages in the Middle East.

Variationist sociolinguistics

The second trend of research is more contemporary-oriented and applies the methodology of western variationist sociolinguistics. Investigating the realization of a few selected features among a sample of urban speakers of various ages, sex, social groups, etc., it looks at orientation of change and tries to postulate some regular correlations. This trend of research has particularly been applied to Jordan (Abdel Jawad 1986, 1987; Sawaie 1994; Al-Wer 2007), Palestine and Israel (Amara 2005), Bahrain (Holes 1987), Egypt (Haeri 1996; Miller 2005), Syria (Ismail 2007), Tunisia (Jabeur 1987; Walters 1989), and Morocco (Gibson 2002; Hachimi 2007).

A number of variationist studies have focused on processes of dialect accommodation among migrant population within urban centres, investigating the role of ethnicity, religion, age and sex. These studies found that migrant women used urban variants more than men (Abdel Jawad 1986; Benrabah 1994; Sawaie 1994). In Palestine (City of Bethlehem), Christians, and above all Christian women, tend to use more urban variables than Muslims (Amara 2005). Among men, it was found that some variables associated with Bedouin speech show strong resistance, particularly in Jordan with the development of a national discourse built on Bedouin heritage, which led some urban Palestinian men to use these Bedouin variables in the public space (Al-Wer 2007). Studies on dialect contact and processes of accommodation are now developing in most MENA countries, with the emergence of a new generation of researchers, like students from the Gulf, no longer inhibited by Classical Arabic (see a number of theses presently in preparation under the direction of Enam Al-Wer at Essex University). All these research studies on dialect accommodation and processes of koineization in Arab urban centres point to the fact that rural–urban migration has been a major factor of change, but that the impact of migration varies greatly according to the historical and social setting of the city and the country. In many cities, accommodation processes are rather low. Miller *et al.* (2007) provide a comparison between 13 Arab cities and highlight large discrepancies concerning trends of koineization, dialect focusing, and the emergence of 'new urban lects'. It appears that it is almost impossible to generalize models of change and development, and we have to be sceptical about studies that aim to generalize laws and rules from the analysis of only a few features. It is clear that in the case of dialect contact, not all levels of the language change in the same direction. Another important point is that, so far, social class is not the strongest factor of difference within Arab societies, as 'ethnic' and 'communal' affiliations have an important impact on language choice.

Another trend of variationist research is concerned with intra-vernacular variation, investigating the influence of social class, gender and age on language uses and language change. One of the findings for the Middle East was that urban middle-upper class women tended to use less emphatic consonants than their male counterparts (Naim-Sambar 1985; Royal 1985; Haeri 1996; Wahba 1996). A few studies tried to investigate the actors of the change in progress (Haeri 1996; Ismail 2007; Al Wer 2007), but results still seem too scanty or too 'fresh' to come out with any kind of regular laws. For example, Haeri (1996) found out that young middle class women were initiating a sound change (palatalization) in Cairo, while Ismail (2007) postulates that in Damascus, young middle-aged men initiate a phonological change from [r] to [ɹ].

While the studies developed in the 1980s associated variants with more or less fixed categories (e.g. either gender or age or ethnic/religious groups), more recent research insists on the importance of networks and on the variability of practices according to context and interaction (a focus on the speech act). Speakers' representations and attitudes are also more and more taken into account (Bennis 2001; Hachimi 2007), following the general evolution of sociolinguistics. Research on language attitudes and value judgements is not new and a number of studies based on questionnaires or matched guise tests evaluate the judgement of the speakers towards different Arabic varieties (MSA and various Arabic vernaculars) such as Herbolich (1979), Sawaie (1994) and Hussein and El-Ali (1989). But these studies were investigating value judgements on reported usage while recent research such as Hachimi (2007) correlates reported language usage with observed corpus-based usage.

Language contact, multilingualism, language shift and language policies

Many MENA countries are *de facto* multilingual countries. They host a number of important non-Arabic speaking groups (Berbers and Kurds, in particular) and had numerous former colonial languages such as Ottoman-Turkish, Italian, Spanish, English and French. English and French still occupy important niches and functions.

It is in North Africa, due to the strong presence of French, Spanish and Berber, that we find the largest number of references to the language situation, the state of multilingualism and the reality of code-switching (CS), either by linguists who did their research in the US (Abbassi 1977; El-Biad 1985; Ennaji 1991, 1995, 2005; Sadiqi 2003), or in France in the Bourdieu and L.-J. Calvet spheres of influence (Boukous 1995; Laroussi 1991; Morsly 1983, 1986) and more recently in the Netherlands (de Ruiter 2001). Abbassi's work is the pioneer reference, when he undertook a sociolinguistic analysis of multilingualism in Morocco for his PhD at Austin as early as 1977. He was the first to study code-switching in detail. He remained in the US, but nonetheless his work was an inspiration for many sociolinguists to come. Fishman further opened the gates to North Africa when he decided to devote special issues of the *International Journal of the Sociology of Language* (1991, 1995, 1997), the first two of these under the direction of M. Ennaji.

The language situation in North Africa has been mainly described in terms of conflicts at various levels: Arabic versus French at the official level, Arabic versus Berber at the informal level. The Arabization policy, particularly in Morocco and Algeria has been and still is extremely controversial and led to completely divergent interpretations of its success and failure (Benrabah 1999; Boukous 1996; Boucherit 2002a; Ennaji 1988; Grand-guillaume 1983). Numerous studies on language attitudes have explored the complex and ambivalent attitudes towards French, Arabic and Berber (Bentahila 1983; Chebchoub 1985; Lawson-Sako and Sachdev 1996; Ennaji 2005; de Ruiter 2006). What most studies and surveys indicate is that French is still considered the most important language for social and economic promotion and the preferred language of scientific discourse and modern culture. Standard Arabic (i.e. *fushaa*) is highly respected as the language of religious and historic heritage, but is not considered a real 'modern' language. But the use of French has expanded from the academic and scientific domains and is encroaching on daily speech, not only of the educated population but more and more of the young urban population. Sadiqi's work (2003 and many other publications) is particularly innovative in looking at the gendered dimension of language in Morocco and making a parallel between dominated languages (such as Berber and Vernacular Arabic) and dominated social groups (women).

Following on from Abbassi's (1977) work, code-switching (CS) soon became an object of research, but until the early 1990s there was no real scientific framework and linguists made up their own tools. Studies on code-switching indicated the deep interpenetration of the various languages and, moreover, the fact that code-switching was a means of expression and a way of refusing the monolithic ideology of the state (Caubet 2002). While early studies on French-Arabic code-switching (Bentahila and Davies 1983) approached it as a sign of an incomplete mastering of both codes, more recent research has indicated the opposite (Lahlou 1991; Ziamari 2008): the more the speakers are at ease with the different languages, the more they may switch and develop new processes of switching that push back the constraints and the limits of switching.

A number of studies on CS have focused on the Arab and Berber diaspora in Western countries (Boumans 1998, on Dutch-Arabic CS in the Netherlands; Caubet 2001, on French-Arabic CS in France; Nortier 1990, on Berber-Dutch CS in the Netherlands; Vicente 2005 on Arabic-Spanish CS in Ceuta). While studies devoted to testing the language skills and competence in the mother tongue show evidence of language attrition (El-Aissati 2002; Boumans and de Ruiter 2002), it appears that Arabic and Berber vernaculars play important symbolic and creative roles, particularly in the artistic sphere (see Caubet 2004b, and many other publications for France).

Studies on Berber-Arabic CS are still few, as are reliable surveys or description of language use among urban Berber population (Ennaji 1995; El-Kirat 2001).

In the Arabic-speaking Middle East, studies on multilingualism, language contact and code-switching are scarcer (but see Spolsky and Cooper 1991),[7] although the Middle Eastern educated elite has used multilingualism as a sign of social distinction for a very long time. In Lebanon, French-Arabic bilingualism is particularly associated with the Maronite (educated) community, even if in actual use the gap is not that much (Abou *et al.* 1996; Al-Battal 2002; Joseph 2004). It seems that use of French was more important in the 1960s than now, particularly among the Muslim populations and that English is taking over from French. Joseph (2004) indicates that the relationship between French and Christians changes according to the political situation. In periods of communal tensions, Christians tend to emphasize a specific Lebanese Christian identity, different from the dominant surrounding Muslim Arab identity (see also Kallas 1999). A few papers have been dedicated to the study of code-switching among Lebanese youth in both Lebanon and the diaspora (Al-Khatib 2003; Edwards and Dewaele 2007).

Arabization policies in the Middle East, and particularly literacy policies, are a sphere of controversy, but not at the same level as in North Africa. Studies on contact between Arabic and local vernaculars in Middle Eastern countries where Arabic is the dominant language are even more scarce, apart from Rouchdy's study on Nubian-Arabic contact in Upper Egypt (Rouchdy 1991). An exception is Sudan, due to the high degree of language diversity and the political conflict regarding language issues. Apart from many papers and theses discussing language policies, numerous language surveys undertaken since the 1970s in various areas of Sudan have shown the spread of Arabic as a second or first language and have analysed the language use and attitudes of non-Arab Sudanese speakers.[8] Most of these studies remain at a questionnaire level and do not describe the reality of language use apart from Miller and Abu Manga (1992), which includes a linguistic description of the processes of accommodation among non-Arab migrants in Khartoum. Structural investigations of language contact between Arabic and the main local vernaculars are to be found in many linguistic descriptions of both Sudanese Arabic and other Sudanese languages but yet more remains to be done in this domain due to the high number of Sudanese languages and long history of interaction with Arabic.

Moving away from the central field of Arabic dialectology, an expanding field of research since the 1980s has been the study of Arabic as a minority language in countries like Afghanistan, Iran, Nigeria and Turkey (Arnold 1998; Owens 2000; Prochazka 2002) and the study of Arabic as a lingua franca, or Arabic-based Pidgin-Creoles in a number of Sub-Saharan countries (Chad, Djibouti, Eritrea, Kenya, Uganda and Southern Sudan) and in the Gulf (Owens 1997). Still little described, although highly mixed, is the language situation of the Gulf countries, where the local Arabic-speaking population is demographically a minority compared to the high number of migrants. In Chad, Arabic, which was spoken by less than 10 per cent of the population, is now the first lingua franca of the country (Jullien de Pommerol 1997). The South Sudanese basin was the location, in the nineteenth century, of the emergence of Arabic-based contact languages such as Juba-Arabic and Ki-Nubi (see Owens 1997; Luffin 2005; Wellens 2005, for detailed bibliographies). While Ki-Nubi is a mother tongue and has developed regional varieties, Juba-Arabic is spoken either as a lingua franca or a mother tongue and is therefore spoken with a very high degree of variation according to speaker and context.

New trends in research: the linguistic impact of new technologies, youth languages and the new urban cultures

While urbanization and spread of education have been among the major social changes of the Arab world in the twentieth century, it appears that globalization and the development of new technologies led to important language changes in the MENA area at the beginning of the twenty-first century. One of the most important changes is the spread of code-mixing in both writing and oral use and the weakening of language boundaries as well as oral–written boundaries. This change is particularly strong at the written level. Until the 1980s, the writing of Arabic vernaculars was rather limited: private correspondences, pieces of dialogue in novels, scripts of theatre productions or movies, and vernacular poetry, for example. Most of this writing used Arabic script.

Authors who willingly wrote in plain vernaculars were a minority, as well as Arab intellectuals advocating the written use of Arabic vernaculars either in Latin or Arabic scripts, like H. Salame (Doss 1995) and more recently M. Safouan in Egypt[9] or Said Aql in Lebanon (Plonka 2004). It may be noted, however, that in Egypt, writing in dialect is a rather old tradition (Rosenbaum 2004) while it is far more recent and still less developed in Morocco (Aguadé 2006).

The explosion of the market for mobile phones and the internet during the last five years has opened the door to a completely new way of writing in vernacular Arabic, either in Latin or in Arabic script. In Latin script, numbers have been used to represent specific Arabic letters in an iconic way: 7 for the pharyngeal ح and 3 for the pharyngeal ع. In many chat sites, one finds mixing of different languages (English–standard Arabic and vernacular Arabic (*'aamiyya*) for the Middle East, French–standard Arabic and vernacular Arabic (*dariija*) for North Africa) as well as an integration of icons, etc. We are witnessing a move towards a freer written expression, which was not available before and which may have important repercussions on the relationship between writing and language norms more generally.

At the oral level, one of the emerging trends is the public visibility of 'youth speech', i.e. specific kinds of speech used by groups of youngsters, with specific discourse devices such as mixing, truncation, over-use of metaphor, epentheses etc. (Caubet *et al.* 2004). Secret languages or slang speech have always been recorded but they were more confined and less visible. Today, youth languages (speech) are popularized through songs and movies and become social phenomena. Arabic-based youth speech forms appear to be at the crossing of various influences: popular vernacular means of joking and teasing, interaction with French youth speech in the cases of young North Africans, the influence of Black American style through hip-hop for all, etc. In this sense, youth speech, as well as the emergence of a 'youth' social category associated with mobile phones, leisure, music, commercials, etc., represent the quintessence of a new globalized category.

Together with the internet and youth speech, MENA cities are witnessing new urban cultures, highly influenced by new world trends (hip-hop, fusion and rock musics; graphics; video, etc.). New websites such as *YouTube* and *Myspace* are the new support for these musical and graphic expressions and foster a quick world-wide circulation. As in other places in the world, the development of these new urban cultures did not lead to an exclusive use of English, but to a shift from English to the local vernaculars in order to root the new musical trend in the national arena. By doing so, a number of young musicians are taking inspiration from traditional local music and are interacting with older forms of the languages. A new trend of anthropological research (research projects and conferences) is developing to study the cultural scene in its modern and traditional forms (Puig and Mermier 2008, for Lebanon; Miliani 2004, for Algeria; Caubet 2007, and many other publications and films for Morocco; Holes 2001, for the Gulf and Jordan; Ritt-Benmimoun 2007, for Tunisia, etc.). Since independence, the artistic scenes have played an important role in the expression of local nationalism (Stone 2008) and have accompanied the development of urban cultures. But this field of research was often confined to the circles of ethnomusicologists or cultural anthropologists and was not considered a central issue by sociolinguists. The development of a political anthropology, which highlights the interplay between cultural representations and nationalist constructions shows that sociolinguistics cannot disregard the importance of artistic expressions in the evolution of the language. In Morocco, for example, following the public success of the 'new urban music', the media have started using *dariija* (Moroccan

Arabic) more often for the news (*Hit radio*), in discussions on TV and radio, and in magazines (like *Nichane*), combined with Standard Arabic (see Caubet 2007). In the Middle East the oral use of vernacular Arabic in all these domains is not recent but is expanding, particularly in writing.

Conclusion

This concise state-of-the-art chapter shows the diversity of research, and we can consider whether the MENA area forms a specific sociolinguistic field. It is evident that North Africa and the Middle East do not share the same dynamics. In North Africa (particularly Morocco and Algeria) the interaction with France and Spain is crucial to understanding the present dynamics, particularly regarding the development of youth urban speech and urban cultures. However, globalization contributes to bridge the gap between North Africa and Middle East. In both areas, satellite TV stations and the internet participate in the spread of Arabic vernaculars, French, English and all other languages (Berber, Kurdish, etc.). And besides their differences, North Africa and Middle East share some common characteristics. A common finding, after more than 30 years of research, is that Modern Standard Arabic is not threatening Arabic vernaculars but that, on the contrary, Arabic vernaculars are more and more used in official settings.

Arabic sociolinguistics in the MENA follows the main theoretical developments of Western sociolinguistics. However, the Arabic-speaking world presents a number of situations which do not fit with the dominant models of western sociolinguistics, at least those that dominated the field in the 1960s–1980s. First, western sociolinguistics has to a great degree been established on the basis of a class-based variation whereas variation in the Arab world is defined either by 'diglossia' or by ethnic or communal variation. Second, the Arab world does not have a single standard-prestige language, and therefore it is extremely difficult to predict linear direction of changes. Classical Arabic, urban varieties, Bedouin varieties when available, as well as international languages (such as French and English) have all a certain degree of prestige, in their respective fields. Therefore, Arabic sociolinguistics is certainly benefiting from a shift from linear developmental interpretations to contextual and situational interpretation.

Arabic sociolinguistics could not and cannot have developed without the contribution of dialect and historical linguistic studies. Due to the complexity of the field, it might be extremely hazardous to postulate, on the basis of a sample of speakers, that a given feature is expanding or is borrowed or is dying out without deep comparative research. The most important achievement of the last decades is, without doubt, the fact that several types of data (from Atlases, monographs, questionnaires, etc.) could be compared and cross-checked, which helped us to rethink traditional language categories (Lentin 2002).

While dialect studies were mainly written by Western non-native speakers, Arabic sociolinguistics, through the window of diglossia has been investigated more by Arab linguists. Jordanian linguists in particular (Abdel Jawad, Ibrahim, Sawai) were among the first scholars to contest the idea that Modern Standard Arabic was the sole prestigious variety in the Middle East. Therefore, the issue of diglossia has been a means to progressively, and still very cautiously, introduce the local vernaculars as legitimate objects of research. However, the situation is still delicate in many countries. First, the focus on diglossia has for years shadowed other fields of research and nationalistic ideology is still prevalent in the ruling and academic spheres. Autonomous linguistics departments are still rare or non-existent.

Arabic departments focus on classical Arabic and linguistic studies take place in departments of foreign languages (English, French, Spanish, German, and so on), where research on Arabic vernaculars cannot occupy a dominant position. Therefore, even if we notice a growing number of sociolinguistic PhD theses on Arabic vernaculars presented by MENA students, most of these theses are still undertaken in western universities. However, a very recent development is taking place due to the restrictions on visas in most European countries. In Morocco, for example, a number of PhD dissertations are prepared and submitted in the local universities but this research lacks international dissemination.

Many issues remain extremely ideological and polemical: are standard Arabic and Arabic vernaculars different languages or varieties of the same language? Can Arabic be at the same time a 'sacred language' and a modern daily language? What is Modern Arabic? Is it important to write Arabic vernaculars? Can Arabic vernaculars become national languages if not official ones? Can the national languages be named in the definition of new national independent identities (i.e. not supranational, not pan-Arabic)? Is the teaching of Classical Arabic one of the causes of the Arab world's problems particularly regarding access to literacy? These types of on-going debate are often polluted by ideological stands which have little to do with scientific research and flourish in the columns of newspapers. However, they pave the way for further research investigating the linguistic dimension of modernity, such as Haeri (2003) who analyzes the difference between vernacular and classical languages and discusses the issue of the rights of the speakers towards the language they speak and write. The question remains to be investigated as to how far the vernacularization process is related to the emergence and constitution of modernity. The role and place of the vernaculars (either Arabic or non-Arabic vernaculars) will certainly be one of the crucial points of the twenty-first century with the development of many national, regional movements asking for more linguistic rights and the contestation of the monolithic linguistic policies that characterized most of the Arab states during the second part of the twentieth century.

Notes

1 The trend towards homogeneous dialect description was further reinforced in the 1960s and 1970s, due to the influence of structural and functional linguistics, particularly within the Arabic Research Program of Georgetown University led by Richard S. Harrell, which published Reference Grammars of Moroccan, Syrian and Iraqi Arabic by Harrell, Cowell and Erwin respectively.

2 William Marçais was the first to introduce in 1925 the distinction among sedentary dialects in North Africa between what he called "parlers citadins" (old city dialects) and "parlers villageois" (village dialects).

3 The Leeds Project is based on a comprehensive corpus of oral data recorded in 1976. It produced several publications by Mitchell and El-Hassan around the notion of Educated Spoken Arabic.

4 See in particular the Atlases directed by P. Behnsted and M. Woidich.

5 The AIDA network is at the origin of more specialized informal networks working on oral literature, Middle Arabic (Lentin and Grand'Henry 2008), urban sociolinguistics (Miller et al. 2007), etc. and contributed indirectly to collective publications on Arabic dialectology such as Haak et al. (2003).

6 French authors working on Middle Eastern cities tend also to stick to an ethnographic approach rather than a quantitative variationist approach, see Lentin (1981).

7 It is interesting to note that studies on contact and code-switching in the Middle East are mainly orientated towards the MSA/vernacular Arabic contact while in North Africa most studies on contact and code-switching deal with French-Arabic CS. This difference between Middle East and North Africa reflects the dominant position of French in North Africa, which overshadows the Standard Arabic/Vernacular Arabic dichotomy.

8 Most of these surveys were done for Master's or PhD degrees in the Institute of Afro-Asian studies in Khartoum (IAAS); some have been published in the form of documents (Bell 1979–80) and others as books such as Mahmud (1983), Miller and Abu Manga (1992); and Jahallah (2005)

9 Mustafa Safouan, an Egyptian psychoanalyst, is among the recent defenders of the use of Egyptian Arabic instead of standard Arabic.

References

Abbassi, A. (1977) 'A sociolinguistic analysis of multilingualism in Morocco', PhD dissertation, the University of Texas.

Abdel Jawad, H. R. (1986) 'The emergence of an urban dialect in the Jordanian urban centres', *International Journal of the Sociology of Language*, 61, 53–63.

——(1987) 'Cross-dialectal variation in Arabic: competing prestigious forms', *Language in Society*, 16, 359–68.

Abou, S., Haddad, K. and Kasparian, C. (1996) *Anatomie de la francophonie libanaise*, Montréal: AUPEL-UREF.

Abu-Haidar, F. (1987) 'The treatment of the Reflexe of /q/ and /k/ in the Muslim dialect of Baghdad', *Zeitschrift für Arabische Linguistik*, 17, 41–57.

——(1991) *Christian Arabic of Baghdad*, Wiesbaden: Otto Harrassowitz.

Aguadé, J. (2006) 'Writing dialect in Morocco', *EDNA*, 10, 253–74.

Aguadé, J., Cressier, P. and Vicente, A. (eds) (1998) *Peuplement et Arabisation au Maghreb Occidental*, Madrid-Zaragoza: Casa de Velazquez-Universidad de Zaragoza.

Aguadé, J. and El Yaacoubi, M. (1995) *El dialecto árabe de Skūra (Marruecos)*, Madrid: CSIC.

Al-Battal, A. (2002) 'Identity and language tensions in Lebanon: the Arabic of local news at LBCI', in A. Rouchdy (ed.) *Language Contact and Language Conflict Phenomena in Arabic*, New York: Routledge-Curzon, pp. 91–115.

Al-Khatib, H. (2003) 'Language alternation among Arabic and English youth bilinguals: reflecting or constructing social realities?', *Bilingual Education and Bilingualism*, 6, 409–22.

Al-Wer, E. (2002) 'Education as a speaker variable', in A. Rouchdy (ed.) *Language Contact and Language Conflict Phenomena in Arabic*, New York: RoutledgeCurzon, pp. 41–53.

——(2007) 'The formation of the dialect of Amman: from chaos to order', in C. Miller *et al.* (eds) *Arabic in the City: Issues in Dialect Contact and Language Variation*, London: Routledge, pp. 55–76.

Amara, M. (2005) 'Language, migration and urbanization: the case of Bethlehem', *Linguistics*, 43, 883–902.

Anis, I. (1967) *The Arabic Dialects* [in Arabic], Cairo: Dâr Al Fikr al-Arabî.

Arnold, W. (1998) *Die arabischen Dialekte Antiochens*, Wiesbaden: Semitica Viva 19.

Badawi, A. S. M. (1973) *Levels of contemporary Arabic in Egypt* [in Arabic Mustawayyât al 'arabiyya al mu'âsira fi Misr], Cairo: Dâr al Ma'ârif.

Bakir, M. (1986) 'Sex difference in the approximation to Standard Arabic: a case study', *Anthropological Linguistics*, 28, 3–9.

Bassiouney, R. (2006) *Functions of Code Switching in Egypt: Evidence from the Monologues*, Leiden: Brill.

——(2009) *Arabic Sociolinguistics*, Edinburgh: Edinburgh University Press.

Bell, H. (ed.) (1979–80) *Language Survey of the Sudan: Sample of Locality*, vols. 1–29, Khartoum: Institute of Afro-Asian Studies.

Beni Yasin, R. and Owens, J. (1987) *Variation in Rural Northern Jordanian Arabic*, Yarmuk: Yarmuk University Press.

Bennis, S. (2001) 'Normes fictives et identités au Maroc. Rapport des sujets ruraux aux lectes de la ville', in T. Bulot, C. Bauvois, and P. Blanchet (eds) *Sociolinguistique urbaine. Variations linguistiques, images urbaines et sociales*, Rennes: Presses de l'Université de Rennes, pp. 75–86.

Benrabah, M. (1994) 'Attitudinal reactions to language change in an urban setting', in Y. Suleiman (ed.) *Arabic Sociolinguistic: Issues and Perspectives*, Richmond: Curzon, pp. 213–26.

——(1999) *Langues et pouvoir en Algérie. Histoire d'un traumatisme linguistique*, Paris: Séguier.

Bentahila, A. (1983) *Language Attitudes among Arabic-French Bilinguals in Morocco*, Clevedon: Multilingual Matters.

Bentahila, A. and Davies, E. (1983) 'The syntax of Arabic-French code-switching', *Lingua*, 59, 331–43.

Blanc, H. (1960) 'Stylistic [style] variations in spoken Arabic: a sample of interdialectal educated conversation', in C. Ferguson (ed.) *Contributions to Arabic Linguistics*, Cambridge, MA: Center for Middle Eastern Studies, pp. 81–161.

——(1964) *Communal Dialects in Baghdad*, Cambridge, MA: Harvard University Press.

Boucherit, A. (2002a) 'Algérie: de l'Arabe à l'Arabisation', in A. Rouchdy (ed.) *Language Contact and Language Conflict Phenomena in Arabic*, New York: RoutledgeCurzon, pp. 54–69.

——(2002b) *L'arabe parlé à Alger. Aspects sociolinguistiques et énonciatifs*, Paris-Louvain: Peeters.

Boukous, A. (1995) *Société, langues et cultures au Maroc. Enjeux symboliques*, Rabat: Faculté des LSH de Rabat.

——(1996) 'La politique linguistique au Maroc: enjeux et ambivalences', in C. Juillard and L.-J. Calvet (eds) *Les Politiques linguistiques. Mythes et réalités*, Paris, pp. 73–82.

Boumans, L. (1998) *The Syntax of Codeswitching: Analyzing Moroccan Arabic/Dutch Conversations*, Tilburg: Tilburg University Press.

Boumans, L. and de Ruiter, J. J. (2002) 'Moroccan Arabic in the European diaspora', in A. Rouchdy (ed.) *Language Contact and Language Conflict Phenomena in Arabic*, New York: Routledge-Curzon, pp. 259–85.

Boussofara-Omar, N. (2006) 'Diglossia', in K. Versteegh *et al.* (eds.) *EALL*, vol 1, Leiden: Brill, pp. 629–36.

Caubet, D. (2001) 'Maghrebine Arabic in France', in G. Extra and D. Gorter (eds) *The Other Languages of Europe: Demographic, Sociolinguistic, and Educational Perspectives*, Clevedon: Multilingual Matters, pp. 261–77.

——(2002) 'Jeux de langues: humor and codeswitching in the Maghreb', in A. Rouchdy (ed.) *Language Contact and Language Conflict Phenomena in Arabic*, New York: RoutledgeCurzon, pp. 233–58.

——(2004a) 'Dialectologie et histoire au Maghreb: pour une sociolinguistique historique', in J. Dakhlia (ed.) *Trames de langues. Usages et métissages linguistiques dans l'histoire du Maghreb*, Paris: Maisonneuve et Larose, pp. 59–70.

——(2004b) 'La *darja*, langue de culture en France', *Hommes et Migrations*, 1252, 34–44.

——(2007) 'Génération *darija!*', *EDNA (estudios de dialectología norteafricana y andalusí)*, 9, 233–43.

Caubet, D., Billiez, J. Bulot, T., Léglise, I. and Miller, C. (2004) *Parlers Jeunes ici et là-bas*, Paris: L'Harmattan.

Chebchoub, Z. (1985) 'A sociolinguistic study of the use of Arabic and French in Algiers', PhD thesis, Edinburgh University.

Cohen, D. (1975) *Le parler arabe des Juifs de Tunis*, vol. II, *Etude linguistique*, La Haye: Mouton de Gruyer.

——(1981) 'Remarques historiques et sociolinguistiques sur les parlers des juifs maghrébins', *International Journal of the Sociology of Language*, 30, 91–106.

Cohen, M. (1912) *Le parler arabe des Juifs d'Alger*, Paris: Champion.

——(1956) *Pour une sociologie du langage*, Paris: Albin Michel [reprinted in 1971 as *Matériaux pour une sociologie du langage*, Paris, Maspero].

Daher, J. (1999) 'Gender in linguistic variation: the variable (q) in Damascus', *Perspectives on Arabic Linguistics*, XI, 183–206.

Daher, N. (1987) 'Arabic sociolinguistics: State of the Arts', *Al-Arabiyya*, 20, 125–59.

Dakhlia, J. (ed.) (2004) *Trames de langues, Usages et métissages linguistiques dans l'histoire du Maghreb*. Paris: Maisonneuve et Larose.

De Ruiter, J. J. (ed.) (2001) *Plurilinguisme au Maroc et dans les communautés marocaines en Europe*, Fès (Langues et Linguistiques 8).

——(2006) *Les jeunes marocains et leurs langues*, Paris: L'Harmattan.

Dichy, J. (1994) 'La pluriglossie de l'arabe', *Bulletin d'Etudes Orientales*, XLVI, 19–42.

Diem, W. (1974) *Hochsprache und Dialekt im Arabischen. Untersuchungen zur heutigen arabischen Zweisprachigkeit*, Wiesbaden: Franz Steiner.

Doss, M. (1995) 'Discours de réforme', in A. Roussillon (ed.) *Entre réforme sociale et mouvement national*, Le Caire: Cedej, pp. 235–46.

Drettas, G. (1981) 'La *Diglossie*: un pèlerinage aux sources', *Bulletin de la Société de Linguistique*, 76, 61–98.

Edwards, M. and Dewaele, J.-M. (2007) 'Trilingual conversations: a window into multicompetence', *International Journal of Bilingualism*, 11, 221–42.

Eid, M. (1988) 'Principles for code switching between Standard and Egyptian Arabic', *Al Arabiyya*, 21, 51–79.

——(2007) 'Arabic on the media: hybridity and styles', in E. Ditters and H. Motzki (eds) *Approaches to Arabic Linguistics Presented to Kees Versteegh on the Occasion of his Sixtieth Birthday*, Leiden: Brill, pp. 403–34.

El-Aissati, A. (2002) 'Moroccan languages and identity in a multicultural neighborhood', in A. Hvenekilde and J. Nortier (eds) *Meetings at the Crossroads: Studies of Multilingualism and Multiculturalism in Oslo and Utrecht*, Novus: Forlag, pp. 249–59.

El-Biad, M. (1985) 'A sociolinguistic study of the Arabization process and its conditioning factors in Morocco', PhD thesis, State University of New York at Buffalo.

El-Hassan, S. (1978) 'Variation in the demonstrative system in educated spoken Arabic', *Archivum linguisticum*, 9, 32–57.

El-Kirat, Y. (2001) 'The current status and future of the Amazigh language', *Langues et Linguistique*, 8 Fès (*Multilingualism in Morocco and Moroccan Communities in Europe*, J.J. de Ruiter ed.), pp. 81–96.

Ennaji, M. (1988) 'Language planning in Morocco and changes in Arabic', *International Journal of the Sociology of Language*, 74, 9–39.

——(1991) 'Aspects of multilingualism in the Maghreb', *International Journal of the Sociology of Language*, 87, 7–26.

——(1995) 'Sociolinguistics in Morocco', *International Journal of the Sociology of Language*, 9, 112.

——(2001) 'De la diglossie à la quadriglossie', in J. J. de Ruiter (ed.) *Plurilinguisme au Maroc et dans les communautés marocaines en Europe*, Fès (Langues et Linguistiques 8), pp. 49–64.

——(2005) *Multilingualism, Cultural Identity, and Education in Morocco*, New York: Springer.

Feghali, M. (1919) *Parler arabe de Kfar 'Abida*, (Liban). Paris: Imprimerie nationale.

Ferguson, C. (1959a) 'Diglossia', *Word*, 15, 325–40.

——(1959b) 'The Arabic koine', *Language*, 35, 616–30.

——(1987) 'Standardization as a form of language spread', in *Georgetown University Round Table in Language and Linguistics*, pp. 119–32 (reprinted in K. Belnap, and N. Haeri, 1997, *Structural Studies in Arabic Linguistics: Charles A. Ferguson's Papers 1954–1994*, Leiden: Brill, pp. 69–80).

——(1991) 'Diglossia revisited', *South West Journal of Linguistics*, 10, 214–34.

Fishman, J. A. (1968) 'Bilingualism with and without diglossia; diglossia with and without bilingualism', *Journal of Social Issues*, 23, 29–38.

Gibson, M. (2002). 'Dialect levelling in Tunisian Arabic: towards a new spoken standard', in A. Rouchdy (ed.) *Language Contact and Language Conflict Phenomena in Arabic*, New York: Routledge Curzon, pp. 24–40.

Grandguillaume, G. (1983) *Arabisation et politique linguistique au Maghreb*, Paris: MaisonNeuve & Larosse.

Haak, M., De Jong, R. and Versteegh, K. (eds) (2003) *Approaches to Arabic Dialects*, Leiden: Brill.

Hachimi, A. (2007) 'Becoming Casablancan: Fessi in Casablanca as a case study', in C. Miller *et al.* (eds) *Arabic in the City: Issues in Dialect Contact and Language Variation*, London: Routledge, pp. 97–122.

Haeri, N. (1995) 'Language and gender in the Arab world: analysis, explanation, and ideology', *Nimeye Digar (The Other Half)*, Special Issue on Language and Gender, 2, 25–45.

——(1996) *The Sociolinguistic Market of Cairo: Gender, Class and Education*, New York: Kegan Paul International.

——(2000) 'Form and ideology: Arabic sociolinguistics and beyond', *Annual Reviews of Anthropology*, 29, 61–87.

——(2003) *Sacred Language, Ordinary People: Dilemmas of Culture and Politics in Egypt*, New York: Palgrave.

Hary, B. (1996) 'The importance of the language continuum in Arabic multiglossia', in A. Elgibali (ed.) *Understanding Arabic*, Cairo: The American University in Cairo Press, pp. 69–90.

253

Heath, J. (1989) *From Code Switching to Borrowing: Foreign and Diglossic Mixing in Moroccan Arabic*, New York: Kegan Paul International.

——(2002) *Jewish and Muslim Dialects of Moroccan Arabic*, London: Curzon Press.

Herbolich, J. (1979) 'Attitudes of Egyptians towards various Arabic vernaculars', *Lingua*, 47, 301–21.

Holes, C. (1987) *Language Variation and Change in a Modernising Arab State: The Case of Bahrain*, London: Kegan Paul International.

——(1995) *Modern Arabic, Structures, Functions and Varieties*, London: Longman.

——(2001) *Dialect, Culture, and Society in Eastern Arabia*, Leiden: Brill.

Hussein, R. and El-Ali, N. (1989) 'Subjective reactions of rural university students towards different varieties of Arabic', *Al 'Arabiyya*, 22, 37–54.

Ibrahim, M. (1986) 'Standard and prestige language: a problem in Arabic sociolinguistics', *Anthropological Linguistics*, 28, 115–26.

Ismail, H. (2007) 'The urban and suburban modes: patterns of linguistic variation and change in Damascus', in Miller, C. *et al.* (eds) *Arabic in the City: Issues in Dialect Contact and Language Variation*, London: Routledge, pp. 188–212.

Jabeur, M. (1987) 'A sociolinguistic study in Tunisia: Rades', PhD, University of Reading, Reading.

Jahallah, K. M. (2005) *The Linguistic Situation of the Nuba Mountains* [in Arabic], Khartoum: International African University, Center for African Studies.

Joseph, J. E. (2004) *Language and Identity: National, Ethnic, Religious*, New York: Palgrave Macmillan.

Jullien de Pommerol, P. (1997) *L'arabe tchadien. L'émergence d'une langue véhiculaire*, Paris: Karthala.

Kallas, E. (1999) *Qui est arabophone?* Gorizia: Istituto di Sociologia Internazionale di Gorizia.

Kaye, A. (1994) 'Formal vs informal Arabic. diglossia, triglossia, tetraglossia etc., multiglossia viewed as a continuum', *Zeitschrift für Arabische Linguistik*, 27, 47–66.

Lahlou, M. (1991) 'A morpho-syntactic study of code switching between Moroccan Arabic and French', unpublished PhD dissertation, University of Texas at Austin.

Larcher, P. (2006) 'Sociolinguistique et histoire de l'arabe selon la Muqaddima d'Ibn Khaldûn (VIII/XIV siècle)', in P. G. Borbone, A. Mengozzi, and M. Tosco (eds) *Loquentes Linguis. Studi linguistici e orientali in onore di F. A. Pennacchietti*, Wiesbaden: Harrassowitz, pp. 431–41.

Laroussi, F. (1991) *L'alternance de code arabe dialectal-français, étude de quelques situations dans la ville de Sfax (Tunisie)*, thèse de doctorat nouveau régime, Université de Rouen.

Lawson-Sako, S. and Sachdev, I. (1996) 'Ethnolinguistic communication in Tunisian streets: convergence and divergence', in Y. Suleiman (ed.) *Language and Identity in the Middle East and North Africa*, Richmond: Curzon, pp. 61–79.

Lentin, J. (1981) 'Remarques sociolinguistiques sur l'arabe parlé à Damas', thèse de 3ème cycle, Université Paris III-Sorbonne Nouvelle.

——(2002) 'Variantes dialectales objectives et subjectives: l'écart entre différences de formes et différences de statut sociolinguistique, et ses implications pour l'enquête dialectologique', in A. Youssi *et al.* (eds) *Aspects of the Dialects of Arabic Today*, Rabat: Amapatril, pp. 43–54.

Lentin, J. and Grand'Henry, J. (eds) (2008) *Moyen Arabe et variétés mixtes de l'arabe à travers l'histoire*, Louvain-La-Neuve: Institut Orientaliste de Louvain.

Lévy, S. (1990) 'Parlers arabes des Juifs du Maroc: particularités et emprunts – Histoire, sociolinguistique et géographie dialectale', thèse d'état, Paris VIII.

Levy-Provencal, E. (1922) *Textes arabes de l'Ouargha, dialecte des Jbala (Maroc septentrional)*, Paris: Ernest Leroux.

Luffin, X. (2005) *Un créole arabe: le Kinubi de Mombasa, Kenya*, München: Lincolm.

Mahmud, U. (1983) *Arabic in the Southern Sudan*, Khartoum: FAL.

Marçais, W. (1930) 'La diglossie arabe', *L'enseignement public*, 14, 401–9.

Marçais, W. and Guiga, A. (1925) *Textes arabes de Takroûna*, (Textes, Transcription et Traduction annotée), Paris.

Mazraani, N. (1997) *Aspects of Language Variation in Arabic Political Speech-Making*, Richmond: Curzon.

Meiseles, G. (1980) 'Educated spoken Arabic and the Arabic language continuum', *Archivum Linguisticum*, 11, 118–43.

Mejdell, G. (2006) *Mixed Styles in Spoken Arabic in Egypt*, Leiden: Brill.

Messaoudi, A. (2003) 'Genèse d'une frontière vécue: un retour historique sur la diglossie de l'arabe au Maghreb', in T. Kondratieva and D. Terrier (eds) *Territoires, frontières, identités: concordances et discordances*, actes du colloque de l'Université de Valenciennes, 15–17 Nov. 2001, Revue du Nord, hors-série no. 18, 2003.

Messaoudi, L. (2003) *Etudes sociolinguistiques*, Kenitra: Faculté des Lettres et Sciences Humaines.

Miliani, H. (2004) 'Variations linguistiques et statuts thématiques dans la chanson algérienne au cours du XXème siècle', in J. Dakhlia (ed.) *Trames de langues. Usages et métissages linguistiques dans l'histoire du Maghreb*, Paris: Maisonneuve et Larose, pp. 423–38.

Miller, C. (2003) 'Variation and changes in Arabic urban vernaculars', in M. Haak, R. De Jong and K. Versteegh (eds) *Approaches to Arabic Dialects*, Leiden: Brill, pp. 177–206.

——(2005) 'Between accommodation and resistance: Upper Egyptian migrants in Cairo', *Linguistics*, 43, 903–56.

Miller, C., and Abu Manga, A.-A. (1992) *Language Change and National Integration, Rural Migrants in Khartoum*, Readings-Khartoum: Garnett-Khartoum University Press.

Miller, C., Al-Wer, E., Caubet, D. and Watson, J. (eds) (2007) *Arabic in the City: Issues in Dialect Contact and Language Variation*, London: Routledge.

Miller, C. and Doss, M. (eds) (1997) *Les langues en Egypte (Egypte-Monde Arabe 27–28)*, Le Caire: Cedej.

Mitchell, T. F. (1986) 'What is educated spoken Arabic?', *International Journal of the Sociology of Language*, 61, 7–32.

Morsly, D. (1983) 'Sociolinguistique de l'Algérie: du discours institutionnel à la réalité des pratiques linguistiques', in L.-J. Calvet (ed.) *Sociolinguistique du Maghreb*, 5, 135–42.

——(1986) 'Multilingualism in Algeria', in J. Fishman, A. Tabouret-Keller, M. Klein, B. Krishnamurti and A. Abdulaziz (eds) *The Fergusonian Impact: In Honor of Charles A. Ferguson on the Occasion of his 65th Birthday*, Berlin: Mouton de Gruyter, vol. II, pp. 253–63.

Naim-Sambar, S. (1985) *Le parler arabe de Ras Beyrouth*, Paris: Geuthner.

Nortier, J. (1990) *Dutch-Moroccan Arabic Code Switching among Young Moroccans in the Netherlands*, Dordrecht: Kluwer.

Owens, J. (1990) *Early Arabic Grammatical Theory: Heterogeneity and Standardization*, Amsterdam: John Benjamins.

——(1997) 'Arabic-based pidgins and creole', in S. G. Thomason (ed.) *Contact Languages: A Wider Perspective*, Amsterdam: John Benjamins, pp. 125–72.

——(ed.) (2000) *Arabic as a Minority Language*, Berlin: Mouton de Gruyter.

——(2001) 'Arabic sociolinguistics', *Arabica*, XLVIII, 419–69.

Palva, H. (1982) 'Patterns of koineization in Modern colloquial Arabic', *Acta Orientalia*, XLIII, 13–32.

——(1994) 'Bedouin and sedentary elements in the dialect of Es Salt: diachronic notes on the socio-linguistic development', in D. Caubet and M. Vanhove (eds) *Actes des Premières Journées Internationales de Dialectologie Arabe*, Paris: Inalco, pp. 459–69.

Parkinson, D. (1985) *Constructing the Social Context of Communication: Terms of Address in Egyptian Arabic*, Berlin: Mouton de Gruyter.

——(1991) 'Searching for modern Fusha: real life formal Arabic', *Al Arabiyya*, 26, 61–111.

Plonka, A. (2004) *L'idée de la langue libanaise d'après Sa'îd 'Aql*, Paris: Gueuthner

Prochazka, S. (2002) *Die arabischen Dialekte der Cukurova (Südtürkei)*, Wiesbaden: Harrassowitz.

Puig, N. and Mermier, F. (2008) *Itinéraires esthétiques et scènes culturelles*, Damas: IFPO.

Ritt-Benmimoun, V. (2007) 'The gap between tradition and modernity as mirrored in the Bedouin poetry of Southern Tunisia', *Quaderni di Studi Arabi*, n.s. 2, 53–70.

Rosenbaum, G. (2004) 'Egyptian Arabic as a written language', *Jerusalem Studies in Arabic and Islam*, 29, 281–340.

Rouchdy, A. (1991) *Nubians and the Nubian Language in Contemporary Egypt: A Case of Cultural and Linguistic Contact*, Leiden: Brill.

——(ed.) (2002) *Language Contact and Language Conflict Phenomena in Arabic*, New York: Routledge-Curzon.

Royal, A.-M. (1985) 'Male/female pharyngealization patterns in Cairo Arabic: a sociolinguistic study of two neighborhoods', *Texas Linguistic Forum*, 27.

Sadiqi, F. (2003) *Women, Gender and Language in Morocco*, Leiden: Brill.

Sawaie, M. (1994) *Linguistic Variation and Speakers' Attitudes*, Damas: Al Jaffar & Al Jabi Publisher.

Schmidt, R. W. (1974) 'Sociolinguistic variation in Spoken Egyptian Arabic: a re-examination of the concept of diglossia', PhD dissertation, Georgetown University, Washington, DC.

Spolsky, B. and Cooper, R. (1991) *The Languages of Jerusalem*, Oxford: Oxford University Press.

Stillman, N. (1988) *The Language and Culture of the Jews of Sefrou, Morocco*, JSS Monograph II, University of Manchester.

Stone, C. (2008) *Popular Culture and Nationalism in Lebanon*, London: Routledge.

Suleiman, Y. (2003) *The Arabic Language and National Identity: A Study in Ideology*, Edinburgh: Edinburgh University Press.

Tabouret-Keller, A. (2006) 'A propos de la notion de diglossie. La malencontreuse opposition entre 171 haute 187 et 171 basse 187: ses sources et ses effets', *Langage & Société*, 118, 109–28.

Taine-Cheikh, C. (1978) 'L'arabe médian parlé par les arabophones de Mauritanie – Etude morpho-syntaxique', thèse de 3ème cycle, Paris V-Descartes.

Talmoudi, F. (1984) *The Diglossic Situation in North Africa*, Gothenburg: Acta Universitatis Gothoburgensis.

Trabelsi, C. (1988) 'Les usages linguistiques des femmes de Tunis', thèse de 3ème cycle, Université de Paris III, Paris.

Versteegh, K. (1993) *Arabic Grammar and Qur'ânic Exegesis in Early Islam*, Leiden: Brill.

——(ed.) (2006–8) *Encyclopedia of Arabic Language and Linguistics (EALL)*, 4 vols, Leiden: Brill.

Vicente, A. (2000) *El dialecto árabe de Anjra (Norte de Marruecos), estudio lingüístico y textos*, Zaragoza: Universidad de Zaragoza, Área de Estudios Árabes e Islámicos, 6.

——(2005) *Ceuta: une ville entre deux langues (Une étude sociolinguistique de sa communauté musulmane)*, Collection Espaces Discursifs, Paris: L'Harmattan.

Wahba, K. (1996) 'Linguistic variation in Alexandrian Arabic', in A. Elgibali (ed.) *Understanding Arabic: Essays in Contemporary Arabic Linguistics in Honor of El-Said Badawi*, Cairo: AUC Press, pp. 103–28.

Walters, K. (1989) 'Social change and linguistic variation in Korba, a small Tunisian town', PhD dissertation, University of Texas, Austin.

——(1991) 'Women, men and linguistic variation in the Arab world', *Perspectives on Arabic Linguistics*, III, 199–229.

——(2003) 'Fergie's prescience: the changing nature of diglossia in Tunisia', *International Journal of the Sociology of Language*, 163, 77–110.

Wellens, I. (2005) *The Nubi Language of Uganda: An Arabic Creole in Africa*, Leiden: Brill.

Youssi, A. (1986) 'L'arabe marocain médian. Annalyse fonctionaliste des rapports syntaxiques', Doctorat d'Etat, Université de Paris III.

——(1995) 'The Moroccan triglossia: facts and implications', *International Journal of the Sociology of Language*, 112, 29–44.

Zaidane, E. K. (1981) 'Emprunt et mélange. Produits d'une situation de contact de langues au Maroc', thèse de 3ème cycle, Université de Paris III.

Ziamari, K. (2008) *Le code switching au Maroc: l'arabe marocain au contact du français*, Collection Espaces Discursifs, Paris: L'Harmattan.

Part V

Europe

23

Sociolinguistics of the German-speaking area

Winifred V. Davies

Introduction

German is spoken as a mother tongue by over 100 million speakers in a number of different countries, mainly in Europe. It has official status at the national level in Austria, Germany, Luxembourg, Liechtenstein and Switzerland, regional official status in Belgium and Italy, and is spoken by ethnic minorities in Hungary, Romania, parts of the Russian Federation and immigrant countries like the USA. This chapter will focus on work produced in those countries where German is a national official language, and on research into German rather than into the other languages spoken in those countries (e.g. Frisian, Romani, Turkish). Even then, I cannot hope to do full justice to the wide range of sociolinguistic work produced in this active research community.

Variation in the German-speaking area has been studied for many years, with an eminent tradition of dialect geography going back to Georg Wenker and the Marburg school in the late nineteenth century. Marburg University still produces dialect atlases, although nowadays in digital form (web.uni-marburg.de/dsa/). The influence of dialectology is also seen in the tendency to concentrate on 'authentic' or 'traditional' dialect, which meant that, up until about the mid-1990s, there were few studies of non-standard urban speech in German-speaking countries. Moreover, unlike in the US and the UK, the reception of William Labov's work did not spawn many empirical studies of variation within the quantitative and correlative paradigm (for an overview of sociolinguistic trends in the old FRG, see Stevenson 1995). While Labov's notion of style was criticized as too static and deterministic, there was more openness to the interactional and interpretive approach to variation as propounded by, for example, John Gumperz.

Dialectology

Dialectology is still important in the German-speaking countries, but most current research be described as modern or new dialectology. Such research investigates not only traditional dialects, but the whole spectrum of variation from local dialect to regionally coloured forms of spoken standard German (SG). Since few (if any) German-speakers, especially south of the River Main, speak or even aim to speak SG as prescribed in the codex, and few habitually speak traditional dialect, studies of the rest of the variety space are welcome. A few are presented below.

Möller (2006) investigates the continuum between traditional dialect and codified standard in the Rhineland. He analyses co-occurrence restrictions to see how stable this variety space is and to what extent recognizable varieties have emerged. He finds that there is a clear break between the 'pure' dialectal space, in which only dialect variants appear, and a space where certain dialect features can co-occur with standard variants. This latter space is more like a continuum and there is no clear break between it and the (spoken) standard. Lenz (2004) uses a range of different methods to analyse the variety space in a central German region. In addition to quantitative analyses of phonological variables she uses cluster analysis and phonetic measurements to describe the space objectively before studying links with subjective attitudes and perceptions. She shows that the 'objective' boundaries are reflected in speaker perceptions.

New methods of data collection, analysis and presentation of results are constantly being developed, e.g. internet databases, digital corpora and online dialect maps. The new media not only provide data (e.g. Siebenhaar 2005 studies intra- and inter-language variation in internet chat rooms), but also facilitate data collection via email and/or web-based questionnaires. Elspaß and Möller (2006) use the latter in their study of regionally coloured everyday language. Their longitudinal study uses an atlas of colloquial German from the 1970s as a point of reference. They use a similar sample, from the same locations, and ask the same questions. Email and internet allow them to ask more people per location and to repeat the data collection annually, in order to track changes in real time. They have covered every German-speaking area and asked questions about phonology, lexis and word order. Php-script then transfers the data into a text document on the server that is like a database. This document is then changed into a second database in which the answers of all the informants from a particular location are gathered together and sorted according to majority and minority responses. Maps are drawn on the basis of this database.

Perceptual dialectology is taking root in Germany: researchers at Kiel University have launched a pilot project in six German cities and have questioned 1200 informants about their knowledge of dialects (cf. germa.germsem.uni-kiel.de/hundt/forsch-dialekt.shtml) and perceptions of linguistic boundaries. Such studies acknowledge the importance of language attitudes and subjective perceptions and reflect a growing trend to accept that linguists should engage with lay people's conceptualizations and evaluations of language if they are to understand, for example, why communication between specialists and lay people is often unsuccessful. Such studies may also help us to better understand linguistic change, which is indubitably influenced by speakers' subjective language awareness.

Standard German

In recent years, much attention has been devoted to SG, e.g. the annual conference of the Institute for German Language (IGL) in 2004 had the theme 'How much variation can standard German tolerate?' Topics discussed included the emergence of regional standard varieties, regional and situative variation in intonation, the effect of the new media on SG, the nature of spoken SG and the effects of contact between youth registers and SG (cf. Eichinger and Kallmeyer 2005). The acceptance that SG is internally variable is a welcome move away from the earlier tendency to define it narrowly and to label anything that did not correspond to the codified norm (the German of Germany has a full codex) as non- or sub-standard. The relatively late emergence of SG, its importance as a symbol of national identity (in Germany), and the fact that it came into being as a written variety, have all contributed to a tendency to regard it as a cultural artefact in need of strict gate-keeping. Nowadays, there is a much greater willingness to re-examine the concept of SG and to define it more pragmatically (e.g. as a variety that is considered appropriate in formal situations), accepting that spoken SG cannot be as uniform as written SG.

Even if the phonology of spoken SG does not agree with the codex, new studies (e.g. Lenz 2004) have shown that there is a large degree of agreement among communities regarding what counts as spoken SG, and the presence of regional variants is not in principle ruled out. It seems that, as long as the number and quality of the regionalisms remain below a certain threshold, speakers are unaware of them. These studies appear to support Berend (2005)'s arguments that one can identify regional standard varieties of German, which are not identical with the codified standard variety, but which are used over wide geographical areas, enjoy prestige in those areas, and are considered appropriate and accepted in formal and informal situations.

Spiekermann (2006) confirms that SG is not a homogeneous variety. His investigation, based on data from interviews with teachers and trainee teachers from 11 towns in south-western Germany uncovers a form of regional standardization which involves suppressing those features perceived as most locally restricted, stabilizing more regional features and adopting heteronymous variants from other areas. On the basis of a comparison with a corpus from the early 1960s, Spiekermann suggests that some regional variants can now be considered characteristic of regional standard in south-western Germany, thus helping to open up the notion of what qualifies as SG (the regional features are not considered standard in the codex).

The project 'Variation in spoken standard German' at the IGL (www.ids-mannheim. de/prag/AusVar) aims to describe and analyse variation in spoken SG to help foreign learners as well as native speakers. It addresses questions such as: Is SG still regionally coloured or is there nowadays a supraregional uniform standard variety? Is SG the same in each country where German is an official language? To what extent is the variety described in dictionaries and grammar books the same as that used everyday? How much situative variation is there in SG? Since the last comprehensive survey of spoken SG was 30 years ago and only covered the old FRG, new data are being collected in 160 towns and cities throughout German-speaking Europe.

Recent studies of standardization processes often employ new data produced by social groups whose usage has not traditionally been considered worthy of study (or whose literary products were not particularly accessible), e.g. letters written by German emigrants to the US (Elspaß 2005). Such data have led to a re-interpretation of the linguistic situation in the nineteenth century and the level of uniformity achieved by then, even in writing. It also means that the use of labels like destandardization to refer to the ousting of standard variants by non-standard (regional) variants is not necessarily accurate because non-standard variants have co-existed with standard variants for centuries, even in written German. The historiography of the language needs to focus on a range of registers when investigating language use in the eighteenth and nineteenth centuries, not only that taught to the middle classes and used by them in formal, mainly written contexts.

261

Today there is also a greater acceptance of the pluricentric nature of German and a willingness to accept national varieties of SG rather than one homogeneous SG; however, many writers still use SG synonymously with German standard German (GSG), thus implying that GSG is the norm from which other national varieties deviate. Much recent work on pluricentricity has been carried out by Ulrich Ammon (e.g. Ammon 1995). He tries to encourage a more critical approach to lexicography, showing that many variants in conventional dictionaries which have no national label (e.g. A or CH) are in fact limited to Germany and should be marked as such, rather than being recorded as neutral, pan-German forms. Recently a group based at Duisburg, Innsbruck and Basle produced a dictionary of national and regional variants of SG (Ammon et al. 2004), and although the methodology has been criticized, this is still a useful attempt to highlight the variation which exists at national level and an admirable attempt to promote the notion of pluricentricity among Germans as well as Austrians and German-speaking Swiss. Ammon's work deals not only with the taxonomy of standard but also with the question of who decides what counts as standard. Pöll (2006) criticizes the fact that the corpus is not based on a systematic user survey and that no serious quantitative analysis was carried out. He also criticizes the labelling, claiming that it does not correspond to the perceptions of speakers, who tend to see one national variety as being better than others. He is also concerned that situative variation is not given enough consideration.

Anne Betten (Betten and Graßl 1995) studies the SG spoken by emigrants to Israel in the 1930s (recorded in the 1980s and 1990s), using qualitative and quantitative methods, and argues that there is a clear break between the norms of the educated middle class of the 1930s and those of comparable social groups today. The Jewish emigrants brought their language and culture with them to Palestine and, isolated from the linguistic and cultural developments in post-war Germany, appear to have conserved linguistic attitudes and behaviour which now rarely exist outside this social group. Betten describes the form of German used by almost all of her informants as 'Weimar German', which refers to the inter-war Weimar Republic as well as to the Weimar Classicism represented by writers like Goethe and Schiller. Her syntactic and morphological analyses show that this 'Weimar German' is characterized by an orientation towards written norms, even in speech.

New media

In German-speaking Switzerland, studies of language choice in chat rooms have illuminated the shifting relationship between Swiss Standard German (SSG) and the Swiss German dialects. Siebenhaar (2005) confirms the trend from diglossia by medium to active/passive diglossia, since dialect is now used in writing as well as in speech, at least in informal or familiar situations. However, there is no evidence of the emergence of a standardized or even regional orthography/ies for writing dialect, which implies that the dialect is not in the process of evolving (or being made) into an autonomous language.

Several studies of computer-mediated communication (CMC) have been carried out, e.g. Ziegler (2005) examines regional variation in chat rooms using participant observation, i.e. she enters chat rooms in order to investigate the usage of a particular online community. Her quantitative and qualitative analysis of interactional sequences shows how regional features are used to convey different modalities, e.g. teasing or serious. What emerges clearly is that there is no one-to-one link between form and content and regional forms assume new roles as markers of informality even in areas where the variants are not indigenous. They co-occur with other features of spoken language but other dialect features are not as common and she interprets this as destandardization. Regional features function as contextualization cues, indicating shifts in structure or the modality of the interaction or contributing to the construction of social stereotypes. The genre 'social chat' in online chat rooms thus allows one to see what happens when the written medium is combined with conceptual orality.

Young people

Young people's usage has been the object of research since the end of the 1970s, when researchers started producing empirical work to test lay-linguistic assumptions about how young people used or (more frequently) abused German (Neuland 2003). The first studies consisted mainly of word lists. Now the methodology and theoretical approaches are more sophisticated and researchers no longer use just questionnaires and collections of words, but participant observation, interactional analyses and corpora. Today, too, researchers are far less likely to talk of *the* language of young people, acknowledging its heterogeneity and the importance of factors like age, gender, education, regional background and migration history.

Some of the most interesting work on young people's language has been done in the context of research with multilingual youngsters in urban centres. Hinnenkamp (2000) examines what he calls the 'mixed talking' (*gemischt sprechen*) and code-switching of young people whose parents and grandparents immigrated to Germany. He deliberately uses the terms 'mixed talking' and 'language mixing' to show that this is not something bad or impure. By looking in detail at conversational excerpts he shows how young people deliberately use bilingual speech to negotiate social meanings: 'mixed talking' is a resource which they employ with other resources like regional/local variants and different registers. Hinnenkamp believes that one has to talk of one (mixed) code rather than of two separate codes being mixed in an utterance.

He goes on to criticize the traditional discourse about immigrants which tends to be essentialist and assumes one fixed identity, interpreting the use of two languages as an identity conflict, with speakers torn between two languages and cultures. This is perhaps especially true in Germany where German has traditionally been a potent symbol of national identity. There is strong resistance to accepting Germany as a multicultural and multilingual state although a fifth of the population has a foreign mother tongue.

Hinnenkamp argues that we should see 'mixed talking' as an expression of an autonomous identity, not as a symbol of conflicting identities, of not belonging to one society or the other. These young people's linguistic skills show how misguided is the deficit view of bilingualism summed up in the term semilingualism (*Halbsprachigkeit*), which used to be applied frequently to the children of immigrants. Such a re-evaluation of the mixed codes of bilingual youngsters is very important but as a consequence of the strong lay-linguistic tendency to insist on the 'purity' of what are conceived of as autonomous languages, it is doubtful if such studies will make much of an impact on public opinion.

Multilingualism

As mentioned above, there continues to be strong public resistance to accepting the fact that Germany is a multilingual state despite the fact that six indigenous minority languages

263

are spoken in Germany: Low German, Danish, North Frisian, Sater Frisian, Sorbian and Romani. Multilingualism tends to be seen as a problem rather than a resource. However as we also saw above, some interesting work is currently being done on the multilingual repertoires of young people. Furthermore, there are some studies of multilingual primary schools e.g. Oomen-Welke (1999): she investigates the language awareness and knowledge about language of monolingual and bilingual children, with the aim of helping teachers make better use of resources in multilingual classes.

East and West

During 1949 to 1989, much was written about the real and perceived differences between language in the GDR and FRG, and since 1989 much has again been written on East-West communication. It was only after unification that linguists could test their hypotheses, which ranged from the assumption that two separate varieties had developed to the assumption that the only differences were in the lexis of the official register. Much of what is written here is based on Achtnich (2000), a comprehensive overview in German. Stevenson (2002) provides an excellent overview in English. Studies produced since 1989 have used a variety of approaches and methods, ranging from studies of lexical differences to more qualitative studies based on ethnographic interviews. Many studies recognize that an interdisciplinary approach is necessary. Among the topics that have been investigated are: What has changed in the East and the West since unification? How do East and West Germans talk to each other? How does their communicative behaviour differ? It became increasingly clear that German–German communication was and has continued to be more problematic than expected: the differences may have been exaggerated before 1989, but they were certainly underestimated afterwards.

Many studies of East–West communication deal with identity and the question of who adapts or accommodates to whom in the context of East–West interaction. For example Auer, Barden and Großkopf (2000) studied how East Germans who had moved to the West accommodated to their new linguistic environments over time, showing correlations between linguistic behaviour and network structures and attitudes. Other studies investigated language use in particular situations, e.g. job interviews. For example Auer (1998) established, via role plays, that East Germans tended to use language reminiscent of the official register of the old GDR. However, it has been pointed out that the participants in the study were untypical – they had all belonged to the elite in the GDR so it was unsurprising that they should have recourse to that particular, familiar register in what was for them a novel and unfamiliar speech event.

Two criticisms of work on East–West communication are the assumption of the homogeneity of the eastern speech community (before and after unification), and a tendency to equate the public official register with *the* language of the GDR or East Germany now. Another problem is the tendency to view the communication skills of East Germans as deficient, because they are often considered inappropriate by West Germans in situations like job interviews (see above). Furthermore, there is often a naïve tendency to assume that use of GDR-specific language signals the survival of eastern-specific totalitarian ways of thinking. An important future research area is the issue of the influence of the researcher on the research being undertaken – to what extent is the researcher's identity as East or West German relevant? This does not seem to have been reflected upon sufficiently in the work carried out so far.

Gender

According to the introduction to Schoenthal (1998), most studies of women's and men's communicative behaviour are quantitative rather than interactional and make little use of Conversation Analysis (CA). The data often come from TV discussions and the educational domain, sometimes with the focus on teachers, at other times on pupils or students. Some studies of workplace communication have now appeared and of communication in all-women groups. According to Schoenthal, there is a need for larger-scale projects. Research now tends to investigate differences between the sexes in specific contexts and in specific roles, i.e. gender is no longer seen as *the* variable that overshadows all others. Kowal *et al.*'s (1998) study of interruptions in media interviews responds to criticism of earlier works by using clearer definitions, a larger sample, and avoiding experimental situations. This study shows that it is not gender as such that is relevant, but the role of the interlocutor: interviewers of either sex interrupt more than politicians who are being interviewed.

German in Switzerland: pluricentricity and diglossia

In German-speaking Switzerland all native-born Swiss speak a Swiss German dialect and acquire Swiss SG (SSG) at school. It is the dialect that is important as a symbol of national identity, not SSG. I shall concentrate on three research issues which are currently salient in German-speaking Switzerland. The first is diglossia: is the model still relevant to contemporary German-speaking Switzerland as the situation no longer seems to fulfil the original criteria listed by Ferguson (1959)? For example, it is debatable if SSG is regarded as a High variety by dialect-speakers, and the dialects are no longer restricted to speech and informal situations. Berthele (2004) suggests that the privileging of the diglossia model is ideologically driven: certain social groupings are afraid that describing the situation as bilingualism might encourage (even) greater alienation from the rest of the German-speaking area and an even greater lack of enthusiasm for learning SG. But Berthele suggests that the bilingualism model would better reflect the perceptions of most lay speakers and outsiders.

The second issue is the validity of pluricentricity: is there a Swiss variety of SG? Hove (2002) is an empirical study of the phonology of SSG, i.e. does the pluricentric model have validity in real life? Her data come from young educated German-speaking Swiss in relatively formal situations. Many of the variants which are different from GSG (as prescribed by the codex) also occur in Austria or parts of Germany but some, like geminate consonants, appear only in Switzerland. She finds few variants that are peculiar to SSG *and* are used consistently by Swiss speakers. But others are typically Swiss in the sense that they do occur only in Switzerland. However, SSG also contains variants that occur in other German-speaking areas, and some of the features that occur only in Switzerland do not occur in the speech of all informants. With other variants, what is typically Swiss is the frequency with which they occur rather than the fact that they occur. Hove claims that phonology alone is rather a weak basis for postulating SSG as a separate national variety but suggests that if one were to look also at prosody, vocabulary, idioms and syntax the claim would be stronger. Attitudes towards SSG are positive – almost two-thirds of her informants are in favour of SSG as a norm, and reject accommodation to the GSG norm.

The third issue concerns the acquisition of SSG in the classroom. Ostermai (2000) found that younger children were more orientated towards GSG (a result of familiarity with German TV programmes, etc.) whereas one year later they were already more orientated towards SSG. Häcki Buhofer and Burger (1998) found that attitudes changed too: children were more negative towards GSG in the second year of primary than in the first year. The researchers found that the children had quite a good active competence in spoken SG when they came to school, but the teachers did not exploit this: SG was introduced and taught as a FL (cf. Berthele above), and acquisition of SG was firmly linked to the acquisition of literacy and the norms of written language. The authors describe this as an unnecessary and contra-productive new start at school and call for changes in didactic methods.

Austrian German

Whereas in Switzerland, there is a lively debate concerning the relative status of SSG and the Swiss German dialects, in Austria, research tends to focus on the nature of Austrian SG (ASG). Many academics as well as lay people are concerned to raise the status of ASG and to ensure it has more legitimacy and prestige both within and outside Austria, but they are hampered by a lack of knowledge about what counts as SG in Austria since there is no full codex and many speakers refer to exonormative works produced in Germany. A contribution to the creation of an endonormative codex is the corpus of ASG pronunciation compiled at Graz University. There is a database comprising 13,000 phonetically rich words spoken by six model speakers (i.e. trained speakers from radio or TV stations) from Austria, Germany and Switzerland, as well as 24 realizations of four texts from different genres (cf. www.iem.at/projekte/dsp/varietaeten/view).

Ransmayr (2006) reports on a survey of German teachers and students at 23 universities in four countries (France, the Czech Republic, Hungary and the UK) and shows that the status of ASG is lower than that of GSG, since it is often seen as a dialect, rather than as a national variety with equal status. However, she also shows that attitudes are more positive in central and eastern European countries. So the pluricentricity concept as preached by experts is not yet realized by the practitioners of German as a Foreign Language, but this may change with more codification and more knowledge about what is ASG, and therefore acceptable in the classroom.

Luxembourg

Three languages are spoken in Luxembourg, in what is usually labelled a triglossic situation. Since 1984, Luxembourgish has legally been a national language, and French, German and Luxembourgish are all recognized as administrative and judicial languages. Horner and Weber (2008) critically examine many of the assumptions on which language and education policies in Luxembourg are based (e.g. French is the prestige language, Luxembourgish is a minority language). Horner (2005) analyses the discourse of linguistic purism, demonstrating how it is used to construct a link between language and national identity. A new university has just been established in Luxembourg and one of its remits is to carry out research into the linguistic situation (cf. www.lux.ipse.uni.lu). Questions that will be addressed are, for example, the historical development of the present triglossic situation (one research project is investigating private literacies in the twentieth century in order to analyse language choice from a historical perspective), and to what extent the dialects are converging to form a new *koiné*.

Low German

Low German (LG) is spoken in eight federal states in northern Germany. Although it is recognized as a regional language in the European Charter for Regional or Minority Languages, its status (autonomous language or dialect of German?) is still the subject of debate among linguists, and that is why I shall discuss it briefly here although space restrictions do not allow me to deal with the other minority languages spoken in Germany. LG is a collective term since there is no one standard spoken or written variety. Structurally it is quite distinct from GSG and from the Central and Upper German dialects on which GSG is based. Those who argue that it is a dialect point to its sociolinguistic status: many of its speakers seem to regard it as a dialect of GSG, e.g. they borrow words from the latter, and switch to the latter in formal situations.

Elmentaler *et al.* (2006) describe a new project which aims to describe the whole repertoire of varieties used in northern Germany, including LG but also varieties of German, including GSG and non-standard varieties, and investigate their use and attitudes towards them. While waiting for funding, the researchers have started collecting data in Schleswig-Holstein and Niederrhein but have not yet been able to launch the comparative study of all the different locations (Michael Elmentaler, pers. comm.). They intend to use quantitative and qualitative methods for analysis, since they will be collecting and analysing objective and subjective data. Other research desiderata are up-to-date figures for the numbers of speakers and information on their competence and use of LG. Young speakers are not always included in surveys so we know little about the group which is essential for the survival of LG. Furthermore, it would be interesting to know to what extent the signing of the Charter has affected the use of LG, and another research question is the extent to which the relatively new *Niederdeutsche Grammatik* (LG Grammar = Lindow *et al.* 1998) is contributing to the standardization of LG.

Language planning: ideology, orthography, identity

One topic that has to be mentioned is the recent reform of German spelling, which was extremely controversial. Johnson (2005) explores, in English, the linguistic, cultural and political issues underpinning the public disputes surrounding the reform. Her analysis of the public debates throws light on language ideologies and how they are constructed and maintained. It also illuminates the relationship between language and cultural/national identity which, as we mentioned above, is extremely important in Germany (the reform was not nearly so controversial in Austria and Switzerland). In this context, one should also mention the large body of research into purism in modern Germany, e.g. Spitzmüller (2007), who examines how debates about the influence of English on German are deeply embedded in the current socio-political discourse concerning socio-political changes following German unification. More and more studies are being devoted to the role of German in Europe, especially in the EU (cf. the special issue of the journal *Muttersprache* 117/2 (2007), devoted entirely to the subject).

Conclusion

It will be clear from the above that the sociolinguistic research landscape in Germany is rich and diverse and can offer much of interest to sociolinguists in other countries, e.g.

the division and subsequent (re)unification of Germany allow one to study the effects of different economic and political conditions on the development of what was originally one speech community, while work on pluricentricity allows one to gauge the relevance of state borders for the emergence or consolidation of linguistic boundaries. The debate about orthography shows the extent of the gap between expert and lay opinion and the importance of improved communication between the two groups: for the former, spelling was a relatively unimportant level of language, which, in any case, had only been codified in the late nineteenth century, but many lay people perceived even relatively minor changes as an act of unwarranted interference in German culture and identity. I would expect topics like language and national identity and multilingualism to remain on the research agenda since the debate about the role of English and the extent of its influence on German is likely to continue, as is the debate about language requirements for citizenship.

Websites

web.uni-marburg.de/dsa
www.germa.germsem.uni-kiel.de/hundt/forsch-dialekt.shtml (accessed 18 April 2007).
www.ids-mannheim.de/prag/AusVar/ (accessed 6 June 2007).
www.iem.at/projekte/dsp/varietaeten/view (accessed 14 September 2007).
www.lux.ipse.uni.lu (accessed 14 September 2007).

References

Achtnich, U. (2000) 'Kommunikation und Sprache in Deutschland nach 1989, dargestellt an ausgewählten Forschungsprojekten', Master's dissertation, University of Frankfurt am Main. Online. Available at: www.uni-frankfurt.de/fb/fb10/inst_ii/histSprw/ehemalige/Schlosser/dateien/Achtnich.pdf (accessed 23 June 2007).

Ammon, U. von (1995) *Die deutsche Sprache in Deutschland, Österreich und der Schweiz*, Berlin: de Gruyter.

Ammon, U. von, Bichel, H., Ebner, J., Esterhammer, R., Games, M., *et al.* (2004) *Variantenwörterbuch des Deutschen. Die deutsche Sprache in Österreich, der Schweiz und Deutschland sowie in Liechtenstein, Luxemburg, Ostbelgien und Südtirol*, Berlin: de Gruyter.

Auer, P. (1998) 'Learning how to play the game: an investigation of role-played job interviews in East Germany', *TEXT*, 18, 7–38.

Auer, P., Barden, B. and Großkopf, B. (2000) 'Long-term linguistic accommodation and its sociolinguistic interpretation: evidence from the inner-German migration after the *Wende*', in K. Mattheier (ed.) *Dialect and Migration in a Changing Europe*, Frankfurt: Peter Lang, pp. 79–98.

Berend, N. (2005) 'Regionale Gebrauchsstandards – Gibt es sie und wie kann man sie beschreiben?', in L. Eichinger and W. Kallmeyer (eds) *Standardvariation. Wieviel Variation verträgt die deutsche Sprache?* Berlin: de Gruyter, pp. 143–70.

Berthele, R. (2004) 'Vor lauter Linguisten die Sprache nicht mehr sehen. Diglossie und Ideologie in der deutschen Schweiz', in H. Christen (ed.) *Dialekt, Regiolekt und Standardsprache im sozialen und zeitlichen Raum*, Vienna: Praesens, pp. 111–36.

Betten, A. with S. Graßl (1995) *Sprachbewahrung nach der Emigration. Das Deutsch der 20er Jahre in Israel, Teil 1: Transkripte und Tondokumente*, Tübingen: Niemeyer.

Eichinger, J. and Kallmeyer, W. (eds) (2005) *Standardvariation. Wieviel Variation verträgt die deutsche Sprache?*, Berlin: de Gruyter.

Elmentaler, M., Gessinger, J., Macha, J., Rosenberg. P., Schröder, I. and Wirrer, J. (2006) 'Sprachvariation in Norddeutschland, in Projekt zur Analyse des sprachlichen Wandels in Norddeutschland', in

A. Voeste and J. Gessinger (eds) *Dialekt im Wandel. Perspektiven einer neuen Dialektologie* (= *Osnabrücker Beiträge zur Sprachtheorie* 71), Duisburg: Gilles & Francke, pp. 159–78.

Elspaß, S. (2005) *Sprachgeschichte von unten. Untersuchungen zum geschriebenen Alltagsdeutsch im 19. Jahrhundert*, Tübingen: Niemeyer.

Elspaß, S. and Möller, R. (2006) 'Internet-Exploration: zu den Chancen, die eine Online-Erhebung regional gefärbter Alltagssprache bietet', in A. Voeste and J. Gessinger (eds) *Dialekt im Wandel. Perspektiven einer neuen Dialektologie* (= *Osnabrücker Beiträge zur Sprachtheorie* 71), Duisburg: Gilles & Francke, pp. 143–58.

Ferguson, C. A. (1959) 'Diglossia', *Word*, 15, 324–40.

Häcki Buhofer, A. and Burger, H. (1998) *Wie deutschschweizer Kinder Hochdeutsch lernen*, Stuttgart: Franz Steiner.

Hinnenkamp, V. (2000) '"Gemischt sprechen" von Migrantenjugendlichen als Ausdruck ihrer Identität', *Der Deutschunterricht*, 52, 1–12.

Horner, K. (2005) 'Reimagining the nation: discourses of language purism in Luxembourg', in N. Langer and W. V. Davies (eds) *Purism in the Germanic Languages*, Berlin: de Gruyter, pp. 166–85.

Horner, K. and Weber, J. J. (2008) 'The language situation in Luxembourg', *Current Issues in Language Planning*, 9, 69–128.

Hove, I. (2002) *Die Aussprache der Standardsprache in der deutschen Schweiz*, Tübingen: Niemeyer.

Johnson, S. (2005) *Spelling Trouble: Language, Ideology and the Reform of German Orthography*, Clevedon: Multilingual Matters.

Johnson, S. and Stenschke, O. (eds) (2004) 'Special number on the German spelling reform', *German Life and Letters*, 58.

Kowal, S., Barth, H.-C., Egemann, H., Galusic, G., Kögel, C., Lippold, N., Pfeil, A. and O'Connel, D. C. (1998) 'Unterbrechungen in Medieninterviews, Geschlechtstypisches Gesprächsverhalten', in G. Schoenthal (ed.) *Germanistische Linguistik 139–140: Feministische Linguistik – Linguistische Geschlechterforschung*. Hildesheim: Olms, pp. 279–99.

Lenz, A. (2004) 'Verdichtungsbereiche und Varietätengrenzen im Methodenvergleich', in H. Christen (ed.) *Dialekt, Regiolekt und Standardsprache im sozialen und zeitlichen Raum*, Vienna: Praesens, pp. 199–220.

Lindow, W., Möhn, D., Niebaum, H., Stellmacher, D., Taubken, H. and Wirrer, J. (1998) *Niederdeutsche Grammatik*, Leer: Schuster.

Möller, R. (2006) 'Mögliches und Unmögliches zwischen Dialekt und Standard, Konkurrenzrestriktionen als Zugang zur Struktur regionaler Umgangssprache im Rheinland', in A. Voeste and J. Gessinger (eds) *Dialekt im Wandel. Perspektiven einer neuen Dialektologie* (= *Osnabrücker Beiträge zur Sprachtheorie* 71), Duisburg: Gilles & Francke, pp. 101–17.

Neuland, E. (2003) 'Entwicklungen und Perspektiven der Jugendsprachforschung. Zur Einführung', in E. Neuland (ed.) *Jugendsprachen – Spiegel der Zeit*, Frankfurt am Main: Peter Lang, pp. 9–18.

Oomen-Welke, I. (1999) 'Sprachen in der Klasse', *Der Deutschunterricht*, 157, 14–23.

Ostermai, G. (2000) *Sprachvariation im Grenzbereich: eine Untersuchung zur Standardsprache nordwestschweizerischer und südbadischer PrimarschülerInnen*, Aarau: Sauerländer.

Pöll, B. (2006) 'Das "Variantenwörterbuch des Deutschen" aus romanistischer Sicht', in R. Muhr and M. B. Sellner (eds) *Zehn Jahre Forschung zum Österreichischen Deutsch: 1995–2005. Eine Bilanz*, Frankfurt am Main: Peter Lang, pp. 79–94.

Ransmayr, J. (2006) 'Der Status des österreichischen Deutsch an Auslandsuniversitäten', in R. Muhr and M. B. Sellner (eds) *Zehn Jahre Forschung zum österreichischen Deutsch: 1995–2005. Eine Bilanz*, Frankfurt am Main: Peter Lang, pp. 39–48.

Schoenthal, G. (ed.) (1998) *Germanistische Linguistik 139–140: Feministische Linguistik – Linguistische Geschlechterforschung*, Hildesheim: Olms.

Siebenhaar, B. (2005) 'Die dialektale Verankerung regionaler Chats in der deutschsprachigen Schweiz', in E. Eggers, J. E. Schmidt and D. Stellmacher (eds) *Moderne Dialekte – Neue Dialektologie*, Stuttgart: Franz Steiner, pp. 691–717.

Spiekermann, H. (2006) 'Standardsprache als regionale Varietät. Regionale Standardvarietäten', in A. Voeste and J. Gessinger (eds) *Dialekt im Wandel. Perspektiven einer neuen Dialektologie* (= *Osnabrücker Beiträge zur Sprachtheorie* 71), Duisburg: Gilles & Francke, pp. 81–99.

Spitzmüller, J. (2007) 'Staking the claims of identity: purism, linguistics and the media in post-1990 Germany', *Journal of Sociolinguistics*, 11, 261–85.

Stevenson, P. (1995) 'The study of real language: observing the observers', in P. Stevenson (ed.) *The German Language and the Real World*, Oxford: Clarendon Press, pp. 1–23.

——(2002) *Language and German Disunity: A Sociolinguistic History of East and West in Germany, 1945–2000*, Oxford: Oxford University Press.

Ziegler, E. (2005) 'Die Bedeutung von Interaktionsstatus und Interaktionsmodus für die Dialekt-Standard–Variation in der Chatkommunikation', in E. Eggers, J. E. Schmidt and D. Stellmacher (eds) *Moderne Dialekte – Neue Dialektologie*. Stuttgart: Franz Steiner, pp. 719–45.

24

Sociolinguistics in the
Dutch language area in Europe

Jeroen Darquennes

Introduction

Quite a number of publications have already been devoted to the state of the art of sociolinguistics in the Dutch language area in Europe. In 1984, for example, Roeland Van Hout's article on 'Sociolinguistics in the Netherlandic language area' appeared in *Sociolinguistics in the Low Countries* (Van Hout 1984). Four years later, Judith Stalpers and Florian Coulmas devoted an issue of the *International Journal of the Sociology of Language* to the *Sociolinguistics of Dutch* (Stalpers and Coulmas 1988). And after having published a volume on aspects of sociolinguistics in The Netherlands in 1980, the Dutch Association of Applied Linguistics (Anéla) in 1991 published the first of currently five volumes on *Themes and Trends in Sociolinguistics*. As part of the series *Toegepaste Taalwetenschap in Artikelen* (*Articles on Applied Linguistics*), each of these five volumes contains a selection of papers presented at Anéla's Sociolinguistics Conference in the Dutch town of Lunteren in 1991, 1995, 1999, 2003 and 2006 respectively. One of the strengths of the volumes is that, unlike the regular conference proceedings (also published by Anéla), they each offer the reader an introductory article on the state of the art of sociolinguistics in the Dutch language area. The present overview on sociolinguistics in the Dutch language area builds on these five introductory articles as well as on Roland Willemyns' article 'Sociolinguïstiek' (1999) and Durk Gorter's account of 'Sociolinguistics in The Netherlands' (2003). The overview starts with a very brief description of the Dutch language area. After a short sketch of the introduction and emancipation of sociolinguistics as a research discipline in the Dutch language area, it turns to the problem of defining sociolinguistics. What follows then is an account of present trends in sociolinguistic research in Flanders and The Netherlands. The overview ends with a brief outlook. Although the picture that emerges of sociolinguistics in the Dutch language area in Europe might on some points be too general, it is hoped that the present chapter will arouse interest in a vibrant part of linguistic research in a small geographic area.

The Dutch language area

On a world scale, approximately 22 million people regularly use varieties of Dutch. Some of them live in The Netherlands Antilles, Aruba or in Surinam. The heartland of the Dutch language area is, however, situated in Europe. There, approximately 15 million persons in The Netherlands (the northern part of the language area) and approximately 6 million in the Flemish part of Belgium (the southern part) use Dutch. Approximately 90,000 persons in that part of France that borders the West of Flanders also use varieties of Dutch. These people, however, tend to use their variety of Dutch mainly in private domains of language use. Recent studies show that their number is gradually diminishing.

The pluricentric nature of the Dutch language inside and outside of Europe encouraged the Dutch and the Belgian governments to establish the Nederlandse Taalunie (Dutch Language Union) in 1980. The Dutch Language Union started off as an organization in which initially only The Netherlands and the Flemish Community of Belgium officially cooperated, with the aim of facilitating the joint development of the Dutch standard language, on the one hand, and the promotion of the spread and study of the Dutch language and literature abroad, on the other. In 2004, Surinam – i.e. the former Dutch colony known as Dutch-Guyana where Dutch still has official status – became an associated member of the Language Union. And in 2007, a framework agreement was established with Aruba and The Netherlands Antilles that, together with The Netherlands, build the Kingdom of The Netherlands and where Dutch has official status too.

With respect to the aim of the Dutch Language Union to jointly develop the Dutch standard language, it needs to be noted that in order to adapt their linguistic performance to the historically grown exocentric northern norm, the Flemish standard language learners/speakers long before 1980 tried to come to grips with pronunciation, lexical aspects and morphological and syntactic issues. The tendency to adapt to the northern norm was strongly influenced by the language debates surrounding the emancipation of the Flemish population in the late nineteenth and the first half of the twentieth century (see Willemyns et al. 2002 and Willemyns 2003, for details). On the one hand, the process of South-to-North convergence is ongoing. On the other hand, studies reveal that centripetal evolutions co-occur with centrifugal evolutions that, e.g., show themselves in the emergence of new diatopic varieties of Dutch that are used by (larger) parts of the Flemish or Dutch population to underline a separate (often regional) Flemish or Dutch identity. Such new developments ensure the continuation of traditional sociolinguistic research on language variation and standardization.

Introduction and emancipation of sociolinguistics in the Dutch language area

Sociolinguistic approaches to diatopic/diastratic variation and standardization were often more than marginally present in (scientific) documents long before the emergence of sociolinguistics as a discipline. The awareness of and the long-standing occupation with aspects of standardization and variation not only positively influenced the development of dialectology in Flanders and The Netherlands. Combined with the active involvement of Flemish and Dutch linguists in international networks, it most certainly also contributed to the rapid introduction of sociolinguistics and the sociology of language.

Shortly after the alleged birth of sociolinguistics and the sociology of language in 1964, the Dutch dialectologist Jo Daan, with a combination of healthy suspicion and a genuine interest, had already by 1967, in a volume entitled *Taalsociologie* (*Sociology of Language*), devoted an article to the – at that time – rather revolutionary (research) ideas on language variation as proposed by a number of 'hyphenated linguists' residing in North America (Daan 1967). In 1969, Martin Van de Ven published the first sociolinguistic study in The Netherlands on language in the Noordoostpolder (Van de Ven 1969). It was, however, during the 1970s that sociolinguistic research really took off. Anton Hagen, Sjef Stijnen and Ton Vallen started a large-scale empirical study on dialect and education in Kerkrade and published the results in 1975 (Hagen *et al.* 1975). In 1976, René Appel, Gerard Hubers and Guus Meijer published the first monograph on sociolinguistics that was written in Dutch (Appel *et al.* 1976). In the same year, Lieuwe Pietersen published a Dutch monograph on the sociology of language (Pietersen 1969). (Cf. Van Hout 1984 and Gorter 2003, for a more detailed account and a description of the developments since then.) Next to the rapidly detected and consulted anglophone, francophone and German sociolinguistic literature, both monographs clearly influenced sociolinguistic research in the Dutch language area.

'Coming to terms' with sociolinguistics

In his 'A Brief History of American Sociolinguistics', published in Paulston and Tucker's *The Early Days of Sociolinguistics*, Roger Shuy (1997: 29) presents the widely accepted statement that sociolinguistics is a term that 'conjures up different things to different people' for the simple reason that 'sociolinguistics means many things to many different people'. Like most scientists active in any other research field, sociolinguists are fully aware of the open-ended semantics of their field's name. This awareness does not, however, prevent them from coming up with rather broad working definitions of their discipline. In their monograph entitled *Sociolinguïstiek*, Appel *et al.* (1976: 10), for example, define sociolinguistics as a discipline that deals with the study of language and language use in a socio-cultural context. This definition is repeated in the *Inleiding in de Sociolinguïstiek* (Introduction to Sociolinguistics) written by Boves and Gerritsen (1995: 35). Van Hout *et al.* (1992: 7) in their introductory article to the first Anéla volume on 'Themes and Trends in Sociolinguistics' propose a somewhat different working definition of sociolinguistics as 'a shared perspective in combination with a heterogeneous interest in the relation between language and the social context of language and language behaviour'. Van Hout *et al.* picked up the idea of a 'shared perspective' in an article written by Dell Hymes in 1984 (Hymes 1984). The problem with the notion of a 'shared perspective', however, is, that without any further interpretation, it tends to appeal more to our intuition than to facts and thus holds the danger of increasing rather than reducing the vagueness that already surrounds the term sociolinguistics. This probably explains why Van Hout *et al.*'s working definition is accompanied by a descriptive account of actual research topics. As such, Van Hout *et al.* find themselves on the same wavelength as Trudgill (2006: 1) who – together with his fellow editors of the international handbooks *Sociolinguistics/Soziolinguistik* – aims for an elucidation of the notoriously broad and slippery field of sociolinguistics by covering the field 'in terms of what sociolinguists actually *do*, and *why* they do it'. As soon as the full picture of sociolinguistic praxis becomes apparent, it (albeit rather intuitively) becomes easier to imagine what is meant by a 'shared perspective' or to grasp what Peter Trudgill (2006: 5) envisages when he – as part of a justification of the fact that 'sociolinguistics is a unitary subject in its own right' – writes that 'all of us who work in sociolinguistics share a common preoccupation with human beings as speaking, thinking, communicating, social animals'.

Current trends in sociolinguistics

Rather than starting a more philosophical discussion on the characteristics of sociolinguistics and sociolinguists, the following sections aim at an elucidation of the praxis of socio-linguistics in the Dutch language area both in a tabular and in a more descriptive way.

Tabular overview

In 1984, Pieter Muysken published a rather polemical article on the scientific evolution during 20 years of sociolinguistics (Muysken 1984). In his article, Muysken lamented the theoretical and methodological standstill of a horizontally rather than vertically expand-ing 'discipline'. He also presented a table in which he thematically listed the content of a number of journals including *Language in Society*. Van Hout *et al.* (1992) took Muysken's tabular overview as a point of departure for categorizing those papers read at the 1991 Sociolinguistics Conference in Lunteren that were published in the conference pro-ceedings. This exercise was repeated after the Sociolinguistics conferences in 1995, 1999, 2003 and 2006 and resulted in Table 24.1.

For the sake of clarity, two remarks need to be made with respect to Table 24.1. First of all, Table 24.1 contains some minor changes compared to Muysken's original classifica-tion: 'language variation and change' covers Muysken's original categories 'grammatical variation and change' and 'social aspects of variation', and 'multilingualism' has replaced 'bilingualism' (cf. Huls *et al.* 1999: 10). Second, the way in which the table is compiled contains a few weaknesses. Apart from being a 'snapshot' of the sociolinguistic contributions

Table 24.1 Thematic ordering of papers published in the proceedings of the Sociolinguistics Conferences in Lunteren in 1991, 1995, 1999, 2003 and 2006

		1991	1995	1999	2003	2006
1	Multilingualism and language contact	7	5	4	2	7
2	Ethnography of speaking	0	2	0	0	0
3	Taxonomies and terminology	0	1	0	0	0
4	Surveys and the sociology of language	0	3	0	0	0
5	Language acquisition and socialization	4	15	11	24	19
6	Language variation and change	4	5	10	10	7
7	Socio-psychological approaches	1	3	1	0	0
8	Methodology	1	1	3	0	0
9	Pragmatics, interaction, conversation–analysis	13	10	9	11	11
10	Language planning	1	1	1	4	1
11	Language and gender	3	2	4	2	1
12	Creoles	1	1	1	0	0
13	Language and ideology	0	0	0	0	2
	Total	35	49	43	53	48

Source: Adapted from Koole and Nortier (2006: 10).

Table 24.2 Research topics featuring in the papers published in the proceedings of the Sociolinguistics Conferences in Lunteren in 2003 and 2006

	2003	*2006*
Total number of articles	53	48
Education	23	21
Multilingual and multicultural society	26	17
Language variation	10	6
Language development	4	4
Language and gender	2	1
Interethnic communication	2	–
Language policy	2	2
Food and health	3	–
Institutional communication	2	3
Minority languages	2	–
Sign languages	2	–
Survey interviews	1	–
Political language use	1	1
International communication	–	3
Other	–	4

Source: Adapted from Koole and Nortier (2006: 11).

to a single series of conferences, the table follows the principle that each article published in the conference proceedings can only be allotted to one single theme. Since some articles obviously cover more than one theme, the table indisputably reflects arbitrary choices and should be interpreted with care. Next to this, the categories of the table combine research domains (e.g. language acquisition and socialization) and empirical approaches (e.g. the ethnography of speaking) and thus show some lack of coherence. To allow a better overview of research topics, Koole and Nortier (2003) in their summary article introduced a complementary table. Table 24.2 presents the result of the updated version presented by Koole and Nortier in 2006.

Despite a few shortcomings of Table 24.2 (each article was, e.g., again allotted to one single research topic), it certainly provides in combination with Table 24.1 a picture of research trends in sociolinguistics over the past 17 years. To expand the scope of Table 24.1 and Table 24.2 beyond the contributions to the Sociolinguistics Conferences in Lunteren one could – as a first step – try to complete both tables on the basis of the data presented in the sociolinguistic bibliographies for Belgium and The Netherlands as listed in *Sociolinguistica: The Annual Yearbook of European Sociolinguistics* over the past 21 years (1987–2008). For this overview, however, the choice was made to omit this time-consuming exercise and to concentrate instead on a descriptive review of current research in sociolinguistics.

A descriptive account of contemporary research trends

The introductory articles to the Anéla volumes on Themes and Trends in Socio-linguistics as well as Gorter (2003) make it clear that sociolinguistics in the Dutch language area mainly covers four lines of research: (1) language acquisition and socialization in educational settings; (2) multilingualism and language contact; (3) language variation and change; and (4) interaction and conversation analysis. The following paragraphs will concentrate on research directions in Flanders and The Netherlands that correspond to these lines of research. Three preliminary remarks need to be made in this respect: (1) the description is necessarily limited to what the author of this article based on accessible information perceives as the sociolinguistic core business of the university faculties, departments, institutions or research centres mentioned; (2) the author is aware that the description might not cover the full picture of research in the selected research areas; and (3) to prevent an accumulation of personal names, the description contains names of university faculties, departments, institutions or research centres rather than the names of individual researchers. One way of getting acquainted with the names of the persons active in the field of sociolinguistics is to follow the links provided in the body of the text below. Another possibility is to browse through the contents of *Taal & Tongval*, a journal specializing in research on variation in Dutch (available at www.meertens.knaw.nl/taalentongval/) and/or to consult the contents of the already mentioned series *Toegepaste Taalwetenschap in Artikelen* on the website of Anéla (www.anela.nl).

Language acquisition and socialization in educational settings

In Flanders, quite a number of research institutes are active in the field of language acquisition and socialization in educational settings. At the Free University of Brussels, individual researchers within the Centre for Linguistics (www.vub.ac.be/TALK/clin.html) and especially within the research group on the acquisition of languages, ACQUILANG (www.vub.ac.be/TALK/acquilan.html), focus on the investigation of sociolinguistic, sociopsychological and psycholinguistic factors in instructed second language learning. ACQUILANG's research is characterized by a strong focus on theory. The same is true for FLAE (Foreign Language Acquisition and Education) at KU Leuven. FLAE (www.ling.arts.kuleuven.be/flae/) mainly investigates the effectiveness of different types of second/foreign language instruction. The research of FLAE is influenced by cognitive psychological instruction theories, yet it also addresses contextual and societal factors which may affect language acquisition and, in particular, teacher perception of the acquisition of intercultural competence in multilingual settings. The investigation of the consequences of social and cultural diversity in present society for and within education is one of the main activities of the Centre for Diversity and Learning at Ghent University (www.steunpuntico.be). Fundamental and applied research into the relation between language, education and migration is the core business of the Centre for Language and Education at KU Leuven (www.nt2.be). From a sociolinguistic point of view, this centre among other things studies the language behaviour in social interaction in classroom settings and conducts research on ethnographic research into teachers' and pupils' compliance with, and reactions to, language norms in multilingual settings.

In The Netherlands, research in the field of language acquisition and socialization in educational settings is one of the themes on which Babylon, the Centre for Studies of the Multicultural Society at the University of Tilburg (www.tilburguniversity.nl/babylon/) concentrates. Babylon is especially interested in the way in which the acquisition of language and literacy is influenced by globalization processes. Located in the bilingual (Frisian/Dutch) Province of Fryslân/Friesland (Frisia), the Mercator European Research Centre on Multilingualism and Language Learning (www.mercator-education.org/) conducts and/or coordinates Europe-wide research on various aspects of bilingual and trilingual education, such as interaction in multilingual classrooms, language proficiency in different languages, and teachers' qualifications for the multilingual classroom. Mercator mainly focuses on educational settings in the context of the Frisian and other indigenous European minority language communities. Many other Dutch researchers interested in sociolinguistic aspects of multilingual education and working at various universities in The Netherlands cooperate within the Network on Research into Second Language Acquisition, i.e. one of the two active working groups of Anéla (www.anela.nl).

Multilingualism and language contact

The broad theme of multilingualism and language contact that, e.g., deals with intra-linguistic aspects of language contact at the individual level as well as with the issue of language policies related to the management of linguistic diversity on a societal level, is covered by a number of research centres in Flanders with clearly different interests. The research group Language Media and Socialization at the University of Antwerp (www. ua.ac.be/tames) studies the interaction between language, media and socialization from a broad communicative and developmental perspective and covers topics such as the role of language in the social development of young children, social identities of youngsters and the use of home languages in Flanders. Members of the Antwerp Centre for Pragmatics (www.ipra.ua.ac.be/) study various features of social multilingualism from a sociolinguistic point of view. Located at the Free University of Brussels, BRIO, i.e. the interdisciplinary Centre for Information, Documentation and Research on Brussels (www.briobrussel.be), specializes among other things in the sociological study of language use and language attitudes in the Greater Brussels Region. The study of societal multilingualism in the context of indigenous European minority language communities with an emphasis on language conflict, language shift, language maintenance, language revitalization, language planning and language policy was the central topic in the research carried out by the Research Centre on Multilingualism (RCM) as it existed from 1977–2007 at the Catholic University of Brussels (www.kubrussel.ac.be/ovm). The research tradition of the RCM is continued within the department of Germanic languages of the Faculty of Arts at the University of Namur in the francophone part of Belgium (www.fundp.ac.be). Within the department of African languages and cultures at Ghent University (www.africana. ugent.be), researchers (sometimes collaborating with colleagues in the department of Dutch at the University of Antwerp) focus on language contact, language policy and ideology related to endangered African languages. Individual members of the research unit, French, Italian and Comparative Linguistics at KU Leuven, study (historical) socio-linguistic aspects of French and Italian in Belgium (www.kuleuven.be/researchteam/ 50518146.htm). A research group within the Centre for Linguistics at the Free University of Brussels (www.vub.ac.be/TALK/clin.html) has specialized in historical socio-linguistic research on nineteenth-century Flanders (especially the period of the United Kingdom of The Netherlands, 1814–30). Within HiSoN, the Historical Sociolinguistics Network (www.philhist.uni-augsburg.de/hison/), this group largely contributes to the methodological and theoretical development of historical sociolinguistics.

In The Netherlands, historical sociolinguistic topics are covered by members of the department of English language and culture at the University of Leiden (www.letteren. leidenuniv.nl/engels/organisatie/staf-filologie.jsp). Contemporary aspects of language identity, language shift, language ideology and linguistic landscaping are studied by the members of the research group 'Sociolinguistic Aspects of Multilingualism' within the Center for Language and Communication of the University of Amsterdam (www.hum. uva.nl/aclc/). In the department of Applied Linguistics at the University of Groningen (www.rug.nl/let/appliedlinguistics), researchers focus on language integration. The department runs a project entitled 'Language, multilingualism and integration: Linguistic, sociolinguistic, social and sociodemographic factors of bilingual development among migrants'. Various aspects related to language contact among the migrant population in The Netherlands (e.g. code-switching, the link between language and identity) feature in the work of individual researchers affiliated to the department of Dutch in the Utrecht Institute of Linguistics at Utrecht University (www.uilots.let.uu.nl/). The Babylon research centre at Tilburg University (www.tilburguniversity.nl/babylon/) covers a whole spectrum of research on multilingualism and language contact. It investigates processes of language mixing, code-switching, language change and the emergence of new varieties, registers or hybrid codes as well as questions concerning the relationship between language, culture and identity in the age of globalization, and how these questions are also discursively shaped in media, policy and popular culture. Babylon shares the interest in the 'sociolinguistics of globalization' (to be understood as the study of social and linguistic processes in contexts of heightened multilingualism as a result of immigration and diaspora) with linguists in the English department at Ghent University (www.english.ugent.be) – a department known for its contributions to discourse analysis on the one hand and sign languages on the other hand. In cooperation with researchers at the Meertens Instituut (www.meertens.knaw.nl), the Centre for Language Studies at the University of Nijmegen (www.ru.nl/cls/) within the programme on Language Acquisition and Multilingualism of the NWO runs a project on 'The Roots of Ethnolects', an experimental comparative study that aims to explore the roots of ethnolects, which result from the interaction between second language acquisition, multilingual language use, and ingroup/outgroup dynamics in urban settings. This project finds itself on the verge between language contact and language variation and change.

Language variation and change

The Centre for Language Studies at the University of Nijmegen is a stronghold for the study of variation and change in Dutch on the phonetic, phonological, lexical, morphological and syntactic level (www.ru.nl/cls/research_programmes_0/language_in_time_and/). Individual researchers active in the Utrecht Institute of Linguistics and affiliated to the linguistics department at Utrecht University (www–uilots.let.uu.nl/) also concentrate on phonetic and phonological aspects of Dutch; as also do researchers within the Centre for Language Technology at the University of Leiden (www.let.leidenuniv.nl/ulcl/). Language variation and change are also part of the research in the Centre for Language and Cognition at the University of Groningen (www.rug.nl/let/onderzoek/onderzoekinstituten/clcg/index), the Fryske Akademy (www.fa.knaw.nl/fa) and the Meertens Instituut (www.meertens.knaw.nl). The Meertens Instituut was, for example, in charge of a project on syntactic variation in Dutch dialects to which the Universities of Leiden, Amsterdam, Ghent and Antwerp contributed.

At Ghent University the linguists within the department of Dutch linguistics (www.nederlandsetaalkunde.ugent.be) devote a great deal of their research to variation and change in standard Dutch and Dutch dialects. This subject is equally tackled within the linguistics department of the University of Antwerp and especially within the Centrum voor Nederlandse Taal en Spraak (www.cnts.ua.ac.be). At the Free University of Brussels, the already mentioned research group on historical sociolinguistics also studies aspects of variation related to nineteenth-century Dutch (www.vub.ac.be/TALK/clin.html). The research unit Quantitative Lexicology and Variational Linguistics at KU Leuven (www.ling.arts.kuleuven.be/qlvl/) among other things concentrates on sociolexicology, i.e. onomasiological variation as determined by traditional sociolinguistic factors (such as geographical or stylistic variation) with a specific focus on the synchronic and diachronic relationship between Belgian and Netherlandic Dutch.

Interaction and conversation analysis

Research on interaction and conversation analysis in different settings (hospitals, courtrooms, companies, classrooms, centres for asylum seekers, etc.) is conducted by many individuals in various research centres and departments of universities in Flanders and The Netherlands, e.g. the Utrecht Institute in Linguistics and the department of Dutch at Utrecht University (www.uilots.let.uu.nl/), the Faculty of Social and Behavioural Sciences at the University of Amsterdam (www2.fmg.uva.nl/#researchinstitutes), the Faculty of Arts at the Free University of Amsterdam (www.let.vu.nl), the group of Communication Sciences at Wageningen University (www.com.wur.nl/UK/), the group of Communication and Information Sciences at the University of Tilburg (www.uvt.nl/faculteiten/fgw/dci/), the Centre for Language and Cognition at the University of Groningen (www.rug.nl/let/onderzoek/clcg/index), the Department of English Language and Culture at the University of Groningen (www.rug.nl/let/onderwijs/talenenculturen/engelsetaalcultuur/index), the research unit Dutch, German and Computational Linguistics at KU Leuven (www.kuleuven.be/research/50518147.htm), the Antwerp Centre for Pragmatics at the University of Antwerp (www.ipra.ua.ac.be/), the English department at Ghent University (www.english.ugent.be) and the Department of Language and Communication at Ghent University (www.taalcom.ugent.be). In The Netherlands, many of the researchers in the field of interaction and conversation cooperate within the thematic group of Anéla called AWIA (the Anéla Working Group on Interaction Analysis).

Future directions

Although it faces competition from functional, cognitive, generative and other schools, sociolinguistics finds a – sometimes marginal, sometimes more prominent – place in the research landscape within the Dutch language area. In recent years, the organization of the Sociolinguistics Symposium in Ghent (2002) and Amsterdam (2008) has certainly added to the lustre of sociolinguistics in the Low Countries. The momentum caused by these events as well as the fact that the retired or retiring generation of those who introduced sociolinguistics in the Low Countries was or is being successfully replaced by young researchers who consider sociolinguistics to be their core business promises to have a positive impact on sociolinguistic research in the decades to come. For future students of sociolinguistics in Flanders and The Netherlands it would be a welcome initiative to either update the last monograph on sociolinguistics in Dutch published by Boves and Gerritsen in 1995 and/or to complement that monograph by a new introduction that manages to place contemporary sociolinguistic research in the Dutch language area in an international setting and to translate recent international theoretical and methodological developments and research findings to a Dutch audience. A particular challenge for those in charge of sociolinguistic research will be the maintenance of cooperation between Flanders and The Netherlands now that the structural funding lines for cross-border (socio)linguistic cooperation provided by the Flemish-Dutch Committee for Dutch Language and Culture (a joint venture between the Dutch Organization for Scientific Research and its counterpart in Flanders, the Flemish Fund for Scientific Research) are no longer open.

References

Appel, R., Hubers, G. and Meijer, G. (1976) *Sociolinguïstiek*, Utrecht: Het Spectrum.

Boves, T. and Gerritsen, M. (1995) *Inleiding in de sociolinguïstiek*, Utrecht: Het Spectrum.

Daan, J. (1967) 'Communicatie-taalkunde', in J. Daan and A. Weijnen (eds) *Taalsociologie* (*Bijdragen en Mededelingen van de Dialectencommissie*, 32), Amsterdam: Noord-Hollandsche Uitgeversmaatschappij, pp. 3–15.

Deprez, K. (ed.) (1984) *Sociolinguistics in the Low Countries*, Amsterdam: Benjamins.

Gorter, D. (2003) 'Sociolinguistics in The Netherlands', *Sociolinguistica: Yearbook of European Sociolinguistics*, 17, 168–80.

Hagen, A., Stijnen, S. and Vallen, T. (1975) *Dialekt en onderwijs in Kerkrade*, Nijmegen: NCDN/Nivor.

Hymes, D. (1984) 'Sociolinguistics: stability and consolidation', *International Journal of the Sociology of Language*, 45, 39–45.

Huls, E., Meijers, G. and Van de Velde, H. (1999) 'De sociolinguïstiek in het Nederlandse taalgebied anno 1999: centrale thema's en theorieën', *Toegepaste Taalwetenschap in Artikelen*, 52, 9–24.

Koole, T. and Nortier, J. (2003) 'De sociolinguïstiek in het Nederlandse taalgebied anno 2003', *Toegepaste Taalwetenschap in Artikelen*, 70, 9–14.

——(2006) 'De sociolinguïstiek in het Nederlandse taalgebied anno 2006', *Toegepaste Taalwetenschap in Artikelen*, 76, 9–12.

Muysken, P. (1984) '20 jaar sociolinguïstiek?', *TTT: Interdisciplinair Tijdschrift voor Taal-en Tekstwetenschap*, 4, 259–68.

Pietersen, L. (1969) *Taalsociologie (minderheden, tweetaligheid, taalachterstand)*, Groningen: Tjeenk Willink.

Shuy, R. (1997) 'A brief history of American sociolinguistics', in C. Bratt Paulston and G. R. Tucker (eds) *The Early Days of Sociolinguistics: Memories and Reflections*, Dallas, TX: Summer Institute of Linguistics, pp. 11–32.

Stalpers, J. and Coulmas, F. (eds) (1988) *The Sociolinguistics of Dutch* (*International Journal of the Sociology of Language*, vol. 73), Berlin: Mouton de Gruyter.

Trudgill, P. (2006) 'Sociolinguistics: An Overview', in U. Ammon, N. Dittmar, K.J. Mattheier and P. Trudgill (eds) *Sociolinguistics/Soziolinguistik: An International Handbook of the Science of Language and Society/Ein internationales Handbuch zur Wissenschaft von Sprache und Gesellschaft*, 2nd edn/2. Auflage, Berlin: Walter de Gruyter, pp. 1–5.

Van de Ven, M. (1969) *Taal in Noordoostpolder: een sociolinguïstisch onderzoek*, Amsterdam: Swets & Zeitlinger.

Van Hout, R. (1984) 'Sociolinguistics in the Netherlandic language area', in K. Deprez (ed.) *Socio-linguistics in the Low Countries*, Amsterdam: Benjamins, pp. 1–41.

Van Hout, R., Huls, E. and Verhallen, M. (1992) 'De sociolinguïstiek in het Nederlandse taalgebied anno 1991', *Toegepaste Taalwetenschap in Artikelen*, 42, 7–16.

Willemyns, R. (1999) 'Sociolinguïstiek', in W. Smedts and P. C. Paardekoper (eds) *De Nederlandse taalkunde in kaart*, Leuven: Acco, pp. 197–203.

——(2003) 'Dutch', in A. Deumert and W. Vandenbussche (eds) *Germanic Standardizations: Past to Present*, Amsterdam: Benjamins, pp. 93–125.

Willemyns, R., De Groof, J. and Vandenbussche, W. (2002) 'Die Standardisierungsgeschichte des Niederländischen im 18, und 19. Jahrhundert. Einige Ergebnisse und Forschungsdesiderate', in J. Androutsopoulos and E. Ziegler (eds) *Standardfragen. Soziolinguistische Perspektiven auf Sprachgeschichte, Sprachkontakt und Sprachvariation*, Frankfurt am Main: Peter Lang, pp. 27–38.

25

Sociolinguistics in the Nordic region

Sally Boyd

Introduction

This chapter presents an overview of sociolinguistic research in the Nordic region,[1] that is to say in Denmark, Finland, Iceland, Norway and Sweden. My aim is to show how American and British-style sociolinguistics became established in the region and how it has developed, mainly in the four largest Nordic countries.

The chapter is divided into several sections. The introduction gives some background to the sociolinguistic situation in the Nordic region: its geography, its languages and the role of English. The next sections present short overviews of sociolinguistic research in the four largest Nordic countries, country by country, based largely on overviews previously published (e.g. Nordberg 1976, 1999, 2003; Maehlum 1996; Kristensen and Jørgensen 1998; Lainio 2000). At the end of each section, I present some results of a bibliographic study of recently published PhD dissertations in the areas of variationism, language contact, language policy and conversation analysis. A final section sums up my conclusions and some possible future trends.

Obviously, sociolinguists all have slightly different ideas of the scope of the term *sociolinguistics*. This chapter reflects my own view, which is rather broad, but excludes most historical studies and studies within the social sciences which do not have a clear linguistic aim.

The Nordic region as a sociolinguistic region

The Nordic region consists of five sovereign countries: Denmark, Finland, Iceland, Norway and Sweden, as well as Greenland and the Faroe Islands, which are self-governing provinces of Denmark. Table 25.1 presents the population and area of the five Nordic countries. While there are small universities in Greenland and the Faroes, where advanced studies of Greenlandic and Faroese are conducted, I have not found any evidence of sociolinguistic research conducted at these universities. Nor does Iceland yet have a tradition of sociolinguistic research in the Anglo-Saxon sense (Friðriksson 2008), so the remainder of this chapter will focus on the four remaining Nordic countries.

Table 25.1 Population and area of the five Nordic countries

Country	Population in millions	Area in thousand km^2
Denmark	5.5	43
Finland	5.3	338
Iceland	0.3	103
Norway	4.8	324
Sweden	9.1	450

Norway, Sweden and Denmark are often mentioned in introductions to linguistics as comprising a region where the majority languages of these countries: Danish, Norwegian and Swedish are to varying degrees mutually comprehensible. Furthermore, Finland has a sizeable Swedish-speaking minority, so even there a Scandinavian language is spoken natively and (in principle) learned in school by its Finnish-speaking majority. The linguistic situation contributes to the strong sense of linguistic and cultural unity in the Nordic region, which is further increased by a number of common institutions, such as the Nordic Language Secretariat (Wiggen 1995: 65). Universities co-operate to a high extent over national boundaries; there are summer courses, scholarships, conferences and journals that are common to the Nordic region as a whole. There is even a common Nordic Research Council, which supports co-operative projects involving researchers in different countries in the region. There are a few Nordic journals of linguistics or of Scandinavian languages, which publish sociolinguistic articles. Because of mutual intelligibility among the Scandinavian languages, the Nordic region functions in many ways as a single area for linguistic science, even if there are also many activities which are organized on a national basis, and Nordic researchers participate in European and international conferences and projects and publish their work in international journals.

Multilingualism in the Nordic region

The four major Nordic countries have official (historical) minority languages. Finland is officially bilingual. Finnish, the majority language and Swedish the largest minority language, have equal legal status. Finnish, which has a relatively large number of speakers in Sweden, due both to the common history of the two nations and to recent immigration, recently achieved official minority status in Sweden. Other official minority languages in the Nordic countries include Sami (official in Sweden, Finland and Norway), Meänkieli and Kven. The latter two languages are both closely related to Finnish, but regarded as languages in their own right, and are spoken in northernmost Sweden and Norway respectively. In Denmark, German, Faroese and Greenlandic have official status.

Another important aspect of linguistic diversity in the Nordic region is the over 150 languages which are spoken natively in the region as a result of post-war migration. In Sweden, Norway and Denmark, migration on a large scale has led to marked linguistic diversity. As we will see below, the integration of migrants into these three countries has had a major impact on sociolinguistic research in the Nordic region. Finland and Iceland have received relatively few immigrants. Finnish research on multilingualism continues to focus on language contact between Swedish, Finnish and, to some extent, Sami.

Communication within the Nordic region and the role of English

As mentioned above, it is true that some degree of mutual intelligibility is enjoyed by speakers of Swedish, Danish and Norwegian, but perhaps not to the degree introductory linguistic textbooks portray. English is becoming a more important lingua franca, while communication in "common Scandinavian" is decreasing even among academics. The practice of speaking "common Scandinavian" involves each person speaking his/her main Scandinavian language, avoiding problematic expressions and false friends, in order to maximize comprehensibility.

English has been claimed to have acquired the role not only of a new lingua franca but of a superposed language in the region (Hyltenstam 1999). Its role in higher education has been hotly debated and certain universities have formulated a language policy regulating its use in teaching and publication. At most universities, the majority language is the medium of instruction at the undergraduate level, where English is common in course literature and guest lectures. At higher levels, English has begun to be used also as a medium of instruction, particularly in the natural sciences, medicine and technology. Publications in these subjects are almost always in English, while in the humanities and social sciences, publications are in the majority languages, English, and to a limited extent in other languages. There has been a widespread debate about whether the Scandinavian languages are threatened as languages of science, due to the expansion of English. In part, in light of this debate, I will comment briefly below on the language in which dissertations in sociolinguistics have been published in the region since 1995.

Sociolinguistics in Denmark

Kristensen and Jørgensen (1998) describe sociolinguistics in Denmark as being both hard to find and pervasive. They claim that it is hard to find in the form of chairs, obligatory courses or special centers of sociolinguistic research, but it is pervasive in that "few Danish linguists really have committed themselves to 'pure formalism' of any kind" (ibid.: 230). This means that many, perhaps most Danish linguists have a sociolinguistic perspective in the broad sense, even if only a handful would call themselves primarily sociolinguists.

American-style sociolinguistics was introduced in Denmark in 1967, when Mogens Baumann Larsen returned from his visit to the Center for Applied Linguistics in Washington, DC, and held a lecture in Copenhagen entitled "Renewal in American dialectology" (Pedersen 2000: 18). At the time, Denmark, like Sweden and Norway, had a strong tradition of dialectological research. The main channel of publications within this tradition was the journal *Dansk Folkemål/Dansk Talesprog* [*Danish Popular Language/Danish Spoken Language*]. According to I. L. Pedersen (2000), the journal started out as a forum for both amateur and professional dialectologists to publish dialectological material and descriptions in the Wörter und Sachen tradition and later within the structuralist paradigm. After 1970, the journal began to publish increasingly for a professional academic readership. From about 1980 it was dominated by sociolinguistics. In the 1990s, articles on discourse and conversation analysis began to appear there also. Pedersen describes the current theoretical orientation of publications in the journal as "eclectic" and the contents as including articles on attitudes, variation and dialectology as well as discourse analysis.

The sociolinguistics that was introduced by Baumann Larsen in the late 1960s has developed into four main sub-fields. The first is the one which most directly represents a continuation of Denmark's dialectological tradition, i.e. language variation and change. This tradition includes a major urban sociolinguistic project from the late 1980s, carried out in Copenhagen (Gregersen and Pedersen 1991). The project studied the socio-phonetics of the Copenhagen dialect, as exemplified in one neighborhood of the city. This was clearly the largest and broadest sociolinguistic study (in the narrow sense) in Denmark.

A second body of research is that of studies of language use. These began mainly as studies within the school context, and were inspired by the work of Basil Bernstein (1971). Later on, they re-emerged as conversation analysis or discourse analysis, and broadened to include many fields of study. For several years in succession in the late 1990s and early 2000s, summer schools were held in Odense at the University of Southern Denmark in conversation and discourse analysis, which featured well-known teachers and researchers from other parts of the world and attracted graduate students from the entire Nordic region and parts of Northern Europe. Summer schools in discourse analysis have also been arranged in Aalborg.

A third strand of research has been that of bi- and multilingualism. In Copenhagen, a group first at the School of Education, later at the University of Copenhagen, carried out a longitudinal project on the language of children with Turkish background in the town of Køge. The children were studied throughout their nine years of compulsory school-ing. This project, in addition to studies of second language acquisition, included studies of code-switching, school-related language policy and bilingual pedagogy (Jørgensen 2003). Another example of this strand of research is the work of K. M. Pedersen (e.g. 2000). She has carried out extensive and long-term research on language contact among the Danish-speaking minority in South Schleswig (Germany).

A final strand of research is that of language policy in relation to multilingualism and language contact. This includes the work of Skutnabb-Kangas, which centers around the concept of linguistic human rights (e.g. Jernudd et al. 1994; García et al. 2006). Some of this work has been carried out with Phillipson, who has also published extensively (e.g. Phillipson 2003) on the question of the spread of English in Europe and in other parts of the world.

My search for sociolinguistic dissertations published from 1995–2007 in Denmark only succeeded in locating 18. This may be due to the fact that the PhD in Denmark is by

Table 25.2 Keywords in Danish dissertations in sociolinguistics since 1995 and in the Nordic database as a whole

	Danish dissertations (total 18)		Dissertations from entire region (total 192)	
	Number	(%)	Number	(%)
Conversation	4	20	69	32
Sociolinguistics	6	30	52	24
Language contact	0	0	19	9
Language policy	1	10	12	5
Sex/gender	0	0	3	1
Bi-/multilingualism	9	45	63	29
Total keywords	20	100	218	100

tradition a more advanced degree than, for example, in the US or in Sweden. The 18 dissertations come from all the major universities and include several from the School of Education, recently incorporated into Aarhus University. The dissertations are not only in the discipline of Scandinavian languages, but also quite a few in pedagogy and one in Romance languages.

As can be seen from Table 25.2, the proportion of dissertations which can be found with the keywords "conversation," "sociolinguistics," "language policy" and "bi-/multilingualism" follow fairly closely the proportions in my database of Nordic dissertations as a whole. It is difficult to draw any firm conclusions based on this small number of dissertations, but there seems to be a larger proportion of dissertations in bi-/multilingualism than in the Nordic region as a whole. The reason for this relative domination may be due to the fact that integration of persons with foreign background has been a research topic given high priority in Denmark in recent years.

Sociolinguistics in Finland[2]

As mentioned above, Finland is officially a bilingual country, where 5.5 percent of the population are native speakers of Swedish. Despite this seemingly rather low percentage, the Swedish-speaking minority has an unusually strong position as a historical minority. This position can be traced to the historical relationship between the two language groups. The region that is at present Sweden and Finland was once a single country, dominated by Swedish-speakers, for over 700 years. Bilingualism in Finnish and Swedish is still required for certain official posts in Finland. There are Swedish medium schools in the bilingual parts of the country (certain coastal areas including the capital) and there is a university (Åbo Akademi) where the primary language is Swedish. The other major universities have departments of Scandinavian languages.

Finland's bilingual status has led to a lively debate in the media about the role of the two languages in official life. In parallel with Trudgill's tongue-in-cheek claim that "every Norwegian is a sociolinguist" (see below), one could equally well claim that "every Finn" is an expert on bi-/multilingualism, language contact or language policy. These topics are also addressed by professional linguists in many disciplines.

Finnish research on bilingualism is quite varied. Research at the Center for Immersion and Multilingualism in Vasa, which is in the bilingual area, has been carried out with immersion education (i.e. Swedish medium for Finnish-speaking children) as one of its major points of departure. This is only one recent example of a long tradition of research into language contact, bilingualism and language pedagogy in Finland, conducted primarily in the bilingual cities of Helsinki, Åbo and Vasa, but also elsewhere. Saukkonen (1994) reviews briefly quantitative work on language contact, such as work on Sami by Aikio in the mid-1980s (e.g. 1984) and by Tandefelt, whose dissertation on the survival of Swedish in kinship groups in Helsinki was presented in Uppsala (Sweden) in 1988.

Finnish researchers have also devoted themselves to studies of language variation and change. Since 2006, a Centre of Excellence for the study of variation and change in English has been established at the Universities of Helsinki and Jyväskylä, headed by Terttu Nevalainen. Research within this joint center is focused on historical variation and change in English as well as phenomena which arise in contact situations between English and the languages of Finland. Their publications are in English and available in full-text online (Varieng: www.helsinki.fi/varieng/journal/index.html).

Table 25.3 Keywords in dissertations from Finland in sociolinguistics since 1995 and in the database as a whole

	Finnish dissertations (total 35)		Dissertations from entire region (total 192)	
	Number	(%)	Number	(%)
Conversation	14	36	69	32
Sociolinguistics	9	23	52	24
Language contact	2	5	19	9
Language policy	2	5	12	5
Sex/gender	1	3	3	1
Bi-/multilingualism	11	28	63	29
Total keywords	39	100	218	100

Saukkonen's (1994) overview of quantitative linguistics in Finland through the early 1990s includes a description of Paunonen's work in Helsinki in the 1970s and that of Suojanen in Turku/Åbo in the mid-1980s. Paunonen carried out a sociolinguistic survey of south-west Finland in the 1970s as well as some more "anthropological" work, according to Nordberg (1976).

The website of the project Grammar in conversation (www.liu.se/isk/research/gris/bibliografi.html) provides a source of information about research on this topic in Finland, at least some of which is sociolinguistic. For example, some of the work on Finnish by Hakulinen at the University of Helsinki (e.g. 1998) is clearly sociolinguistic, insomuch as it is based on recordings of spontaneous conversation. Similarly, the work of Helasvuo (e.g. 1997) on noun phrases in conversational discourse in Finnish and the work of Lehti-Eklund on discourse particles both in Finnish and in Swedish.

My search for Finnish PhD dissertations succeeded in locating 35 published from 1995–2007 (see Table 25.3). All the major universities in Finland are represented. Among the Finnish dissertations, the proportions of the various major keywords follow quite closely that of the database as a whole. The surprising fact that bi-/multilingualism doesn't dominate sociolinguistic research may be more an indication that the importance of this research theme is declining, as compared to the theme of interaction and conversation.

Sociolinguistics in Norway

In his overview of Norwegian sociolinguistic research, Trudgill (1995: 7) repeats the tongue-in-cheek stereotype that "all Norwegians are sociolinguists," due to the interesting and unusual linguistic developments that have taken place there. The fact that Norway has two written standards, Bokmål and Nynorsk, is widely known, but perhaps not the fact that dialects are legally protected in Norway, i.e. schools are explicitly prohibited from trying to change the way children speak their native language (Wiggen 1995). The controversies that naturally arise from these two facts lead to sociolinguistic questions having a relatively high profile in Norwegian society. Among the Nordic countries, Norway has the reputation for having a high tolerance for linguistic variation, at least as regards native speakers, and a relatively good record for protecting the Sami minority's language rights.

Like their Danish counterparts, Norwegian surveys mark the beginning of modern sociolinguistics in Norway to the early 1970s and the visits of Mogens Baumann Larsen, a Dane, and Bengt Loman, a Swede, to Washington, DC, in the late 1960s. Maehlum (1996: 188) credits Loman with introducing sociolinguistics to Norway, as well as to Sweden. Another important early landmark was the publication of an anthology of translations of several sociolinguistic articles from English into Norwegian by linguists at the University of Oslo (Engh 1972), used widely in the region as course literature. Later, course literature in English replaced it, as well as original articles and textbooks in the Scandinavian languages.

Variation

The new initiatives in the area of sociolinguistics landed also in Norway on the "fertile soil" of a strong tradition of dialectology, as they had in Denmark. The political climate of the early 1970s also provided a suitable context for the introduction of sociolinguistics, both in Norway and elsewhere in the Nordic region. Maehlum (1996: 199) writes that Labovian sociolinguistics has been the dominant tradition within Norway, and my survey of recent doctoral dissertations confirms that this is still the case (see Table 25.4). Other strands of sociolinguistics have also been taken up in Norway, although work on variation and change has dominated here probably more than elsewhere in the region.

Urban sociolinguistic projects have been carried out in Oslo (see below), Bergen, Trondheim and Stavanger. The project in Trondheim included a statistically sophisticated analysis of 14 mainly phonological variables. Other important work in this area has been carried out in the form of *hovedoppgaver* (approx. MA theses) at the Nordic Institute at the University of Oslo (Trudgill 1995: 12).

The results of increasing mobility within Norway have also been an important theme of quantitative sociolinguistic studies, such as Kerswill (1993). Maehlum's doctoral dissertation (1992) addresses the question of what happens sociolinguistically in Longyearbyn, Svalbard, a community where virtually all the residents are new in-migrants, and where there is no "historical dialect."

Wiggen (1995) describes Norwegian sociolinguistic studies with a gender perspective as mainly having to do with address terms, terminology (e.g. occupational terms) and wording. He refers to his own research on men's and women's use of Bokmål and Nynorsk (ibid.: 61).

Table 25.4 Keywords in dissertations from Norway in sociolinguistics since 1995 and in the database as a whole

	Norwegian dissertations (total 33)		Dissertations from entire region (total 192)	
	Number	(%)	Number	(%)
Conversation	8	20	69	32
Sociolinguistics	13	32	52	24
Language contact	6	15	19	9
Language policy	4	10	12	5
Sex/gender	0	0	3	1
Bi-/multilingualism	10	24	63	29
Total keywords	41	100	218	100

Bi-/multilingualism

Two main centers of research into language contact and bi-/multilingualism are currently found in Norway: Tromsø and Oslo. Tromsø, located in the far north of Norway, is a center for the study of contact between Sami, Kven and Norwegian, which is concentrated in the polar region. Language shift has been a major topic. Notable examples of the research in this area include that carried out by Aikio (e.g. 1984), Bull (e.g. 1993) and more recently by Lane (2006). Bull's (1993) and Aikio's research (e.g. 1992) have taken an innovative gender perspective on language planning and policy. A good deal of research co-operation on minority languages and language contact takes place in the North Kalotte region as a whole.

In Oslo, recently a number of projects have been undertaken to study language contact due to recent migration from different parts of the world. These projects have in some cases looked at language contact or multilingualism regarding specific languages (Türker 2000; Aarsether 2004; Svendsen 2004) or second language acquisition (Glahn et al. 2001). As in Sweden and Denmark, some of this research has directly or indirectly addressed issues of school instruction for children with foreign background. Research into bi-/multilingualism has also been carried out in Bergen and Trondheim. A large-scale project has recently been launched to study the language of young people in multilingual urban settings in Oslo and other Norwegian cities (Svendsen and Quist, forthcoming).

Interaction

As in Denmark and Sweden, Bernstein's work had its impact in Norway as well. Maehlum indicates that the first major urban sociolinguistic project, the TAUS project in Oslo (e.g. Wiggen 1980), worked with "categories of error" such as interruptions, self-corrections, anacolutha, omissions, etc. In other words, spoken language was analyzed with reference to written language norms.

An early study of spoken language interaction in Norway was Blom and Gumperz's (1971) classic article on language use in Hemnes. Interestingly, this article seems to have had a bigger impact outside of Norway than within it. The reason for this may be that local linguists immediately recognized that there were factual errors in the paper (Maehlum 1990). Compared at least with the development in Sweden and Finland, research in interaction has not been as strong in Norway (Maehlum 1996: note 45). One recent exception is Svennevig whose dissertation (1997) treated ways of introducing oneself, making contact, etc. in Norwegian, using a conversation analytical framework.

Interest in and knowledge about Norwegian sociolinguistics outside of Norway may be relatively great due to the work of Einar Haugen (e.g. 1966), the paper by Blom and Gumperz (1971), and Peter Trudgill's research in Norway (e.g. Trudgill 1974; Jahr and Trudgill 1993).

My search for dissertations in sociolinguistics since 1995 from Norway located a total of 33 (see Table 25.4). As in Denmark and Sweden, the clear majority of these were published in 2002–07, indicating that the number is increasing steadily. This collection includes almost one-third with the keyword "sociolinguistics." This is clearly higher than in the other Nordic countries and indicates that variationism is stronger in Norway than in the other countries surveyed. While the proportion of dissertations in bi-/multi-lingualism is on the same level as for the region as a whole, the proportion of dissertations with "conversation" as a keyword is clearly smaller here, indicating that the trend toward conversation research is not as strong in Norway as in other Nordic countries.

Sociolinguistics in Sweden

In comparison to Norway, Sweden has an image of relative linguistic homogeneity (Nordberg 1976). This image might lead the naïve outsider to assume that sociolinguistic research is not strong here. That is not the case, perhaps in part due to the enthusiasm for sociolinguistics in the 1970s and the continued interest in it not only within the discipline of Scandinavian languages, but in other disciplines as well. Its early success depended on factors which also apply in other parts of the Nordic region: the dialectological tradition and the socially conscious political climate of the 1970s, which provided a favorable context for the establishment of sociolinguistics. When linguistic heterogeneity increased noticeably, as a result of immigration during the 1970s and onwards, bi-/multilingualism also became a major topic of sociolinguistic research.

Sociolinguistics in Sweden can be said to have been introduced by not only Bengt Loman, mentioned above but also Bengt Nordberg, whose sociolinguistic study of the town of Eskilstuna (1976) was in the style of Labovian sociolinguistics. Nordberg became Sweden's first professor of sociolinguistics in Uppsala in the late 1970s. Throughout his career, he was the head of a center for research on modern Swedish (FUMS) in Uppsala, which played a leading role in sociolinguistically oriented research on Swedish.

In Sweden, there are three major centers of sociolinguistic research, each with a different profile. In addition to FUMS in Uppsala, there is the Department of Culture and Communication in Linköping, which has provided a center for studies of interaction and conversation under the leadership of Per Linell and Karin Aronsson and the Center for the Study of Bilingualism at Stockholm University, under the leadership of Kenneth Hyltenstam. The related subject of second language research has more recently established a center in Göteborg, due to the funding of a chair there.

In contrast to what Kristensen and Jørgensen (1998) write about Denmark, there are many compulsory or optional courses on sociolinguistics, discourse analysis and bi- or multilingualism at many universities in Sweden. There is also an annual national conference, OFTI, with the theme of spoken language and interaction.

Variation and change

In Sweden, as in other parts of the Nordic region, there were two early strands of sociolinguistic research, one Bernsteinian and one Labovian. The Labovian strand of research was taken up primarily at FUMS in Uppsala. In addition to Eskilstuna, Uppsala has been studied using sociolinguistic methods (Widmark and Trost 1971). The language of Stockholm has also been studied from somewhat different perspectives by Janson (1973) and Kotsinas (2000).

An interesting Nordic project was carried out in the 1980s and 1990s looking at the effects of urbanization on language variation. This project was led by Nordberg in Uppsala, but included researchers in Norway, Denmark and Finland as well (see Nordberg 1994). In some areas, Swedish can best be described as a single system with quantitative variation (e.g. Aniansson 1996), while in some peripheral areas, language use tends to be described in terms of code-switching between standard and dialect (Helgander 1996). Since 2000, an excellent resource, SWEDIA, a database with recordings of informants from 100 different locations in Sweden (and Swedish-speakers in Finland) is available on the web at www.swedia.ling.gu.se. These digital resources complement the traditional analogue collections in the dialect archives in Uppsala, Göteborg and Lund.

289

Studies with a gender perspective have been carried out in many different sub-fields of sociolinguistics in Sweden. There are studies of interaction and socialization, such as the study of teachers' talk with male and female pupils by Einarsson and Hultmann (1984). Nordenstam (1998) and Adelswärd (1991) have studied gossip from a gender perspective, emphasizing its empathetic rather than slanderous nature. When sociodialectal variation has been studied, a gender variable is always present; Grönberg (2004) has attempted to combine gender and life style in an interesting analysis of young people's language in Alingsås. Kotsinas's (1994) studies of young people's language in Stockholm has a clear gender perspective also.

Interactional sociolinguistics

The Bernsteinian strand of research was taken up in Loman's early project Talsyntax (the syntax of speech) in Lund (Loman 1972). Like the TAUS project in Oslo, this project analyzed recorded conversations in Swedish, but analyzed them in terms of deviations from a written language norm. Very few qualitative differences were found between middle-class and working-class speakers. The conclusion in educational circles was that little if any compensatory education was needed in the country, at least not among native speakers. We could consider later research into the differing access to public language to be a continuation of this strand of research, e.g. Gunnarsson's (1982) research on the comprehensibility of law texts. This strand of research has continued to be pursued by educational scientists, at the University of Gothenburg (e.g. Säljö 1997).

Interactional studies of a more clearly sociolinguistic nature got a somewhat later start than other sociolinguistics, but now seem to be the dominant area of sociolinguistics in Sweden, together with studies of bi-/multilingualism, although not all of these are sociolinguistic. There is no single theory which has hegemony; some researchers employ CA more or less strictly (e.g. A. Lindström 1999), others use pragmatically-inspired theories and methods; some analyze with the help of systemic functional linguistics. Linell and his associates in Linköping developed the initiative-response model for analysis in the late 1980s and Linell later developed his theory of dialogical grammar (Linell 2002).

An important recent research project in this field has been the project "Grammar in Conversation," a study of Swedish, which was led from Linköping but involved researchers in Göteborg, Helsinki and Uppsala. (See "Grammar in conversation." Available at: www.liu.se/isk/research/gris/texter.html, for a list of publications.)

Multilingualism and language contact

A publication by Hansegård (1968) can be regarded as the starting point for socio-linguistic studies of multilingualism in Sweden. In that book, the concept of semi-lingualism (non-native competence in two languages) was launched. This concept, was soon popularized in large part by Skutnabb-Kangas, who used it to describe the situation of children with immigrant background in southern Sweden (Skutnabb-Kangas 1981). The concept, which has also been strongly criticized, was used as an argument to start supplementary education in the mother tongue both of children with immigrant background and children with minority language background.

Research into multilingualism and Swedish as a second language gained a higher profile when the Center for Bilingualism Research was established in the early 1980s at Stockholm university. The former has been the site of research on multilingualism, both

Table 25.5 Keywords in dissertations from Sweden in sociolinguistics since 1995 and in the database as a whole

	Swedish dissertations (total 106)		Dissertations from entire region (total 192)	
	Number	(%)	Number	(%)
Conversation	43	36	69	32
Sociolinguistics	24	20	52	24
Language contact	11	9	19	9
Language policy	5	4	12	5
Sex/gender	2	2	3	1
Bi-/multilingualism	33	28	63	29
Total keywords	118	100	218	100

in Sweden and abroad (Stroud 1991), much of it related to the acquisition of Swedish by children (Axelsson 1994) and adults (Lindberg 1995), inside and outside the classroom. Research in Finnish-Swedish language contact has been undertaken in Uppsala by Lainio (1989), Huss (1991) and Bijvoet (1998), but also in Stockholm. Research in various aspects of multilingualism and language contact from a sociolinguistic perspective has been carried out in Göteborg (e.g. Boyd *et al.* 1997).

Research by Kotsinas (e.g. 1998) in Stockholm led to a series of recent or ongoing research projects on the language of young people in the multilingual outskirts of the major cities of Sweden (Boyd and Fraurud forthcoming), Norway (Svendsen and Quist forthcoming) and Denmark (Quist 1998, 2005).

Studies of language planning and policy in Sweden have been carried out by Wingstedt (1998) and in other parts of the world by Jahani (1989) and by Janson and Tsonope (1991).

The Swedish dissertations in my database total 106 (see Table 25.5). This relatively high figure is probably partly due to the fact that the Swedish doctoral degree has been "modernized" to be more like the North American doctorate.

Among the Swedish dissertations from 1995–2007, there is a slightly higher proportion with the keyword "conversation" than in the database as a whole. The proportion of dissertations with the keyword "sociolinguistics" is proportionally less, while the proportion with bi/multilingualism is close to the figure for the entire database. My conclusion is that the focus in sociolinguistic research in Sweden has shifted from variationism to conversation research, as is the case in Finland.

Conclusion

What sociolinguistics in the Nordic region has in common is its heritage in dialectology. This is evident at least for Norway, Sweden and Denmark. This heritage explains at least in part the fact that a large proportion of sociolinguistic research is carried out at departments of the national languages of the country. My survey of sociolinguistic dissertations indicates that at least more recently, sociolinguistic research has been carried out in other disciplines as well, particularly in pedagogy and in the Romance languages.

Looking at the development of the field historically, from the 1970s onwards, it seems clear that research on variationism and Bernsteinian interaction analyses has given way at least in part to studies of multilingualism and conversation or discourse analysis. This trend is somewhat less pronounced in Norway than in the other Nordic countries. The interest in bi-/multilingualism has grown as the Nordic countries have become to a greater degree multilingual societies.

Interestingly, it turned out that the proportion of dissertations written in English had actually declined slightly from 1995 until 2007, when the beginning of the 12-year period was compared with the end of it. There may be several reasons for this development. One might be the debate referred to above about the use of the Nordic languages in science. Another might be the increasing pressure on graduate students to complete their degrees in a relatively short period of time. This is easier to accomplish if the dissertation is in the student's stronger language

Whatever the trend is in the language of Nordic dissertations, it seems clear that more sociolinguistics is being disseminated in English, more researchers are attending international conferences, spending time abroad, and co-operating with others internationally. These developments are in line with efforts in all four Nordic countries to allocate research resources in relation to quality, usually measured in part in terms of international, refereed publications. A new system for resource allocation has already been implemented in Norway, and a new one is partially implemented in Sweden. This will certainly lead to a greater number of publications which are accessible to non-speakers of Scandinavian languages. Another trend is that both old and new publications in the Scandinavian languages are using referee systems, which makes at least the abstracts of their publications available in international databases. Hopefully, these trends will further break down the isolation that has partly characterized Nordic sociolinguistics in the past.

Notes

1 The Nordic Council of Ministers recommends use of the term *Nordic* for these countries, rather than the term *Scandinavian*. The latter term is sometimes used about the entire region, and sometimes only the countries Denmark, Norway and Sweden. The term *Scandinavian* can be used unambiguously about the languages Danish, Icelandic, Faroese, Norwegian and Swedish.
2 Unfortunately my lack of language skills has made the coverage of Finland more scanty than that of the other Scandinavia countries. It has made existing survey articles inaccessible to me. Even a "Nordic" overview like Maehlums (1996) doesn't mention Finnish research at all. My lack of Finnish also made it surprisingly difficult to use the national bibliographic data base. My review will thus be slanted toward work which is available or reviewed in Swedish (e.g. Nordberg 1976) or English.

References

Aarsether, F. (2004) "To språk i en tekst: kodeveksling i samtaler mellom pakistansk-norske tiåringar" [Two languages in a text: code-switching in conversations between Pakistani-Norwegian ten-year-olds], dissertation, University of Oslo.

Adelswärd, V. (1991) *Prat, skratt, skvaller och gräl och annat vi gör när vi samtalar* [Chat, Laughter, Gossip and Arguments and Other Things We Do When We Have a Conversation], Stockholm: Bromberg.

Aikio, M. (1984) "The position and use of the Sami language: historical, contemporary and future perspectives," *Journal of Multilingual and Multicultural Development*, 5, 3–4.

——(1992) "Are women innovators in the shift to a second language? A case study of reindeer Sami women and men," *International Journal of the Sociology of Language*, 94, 43–61.

Aniansson, E. (1996) "Språklig och social identifikation hos barn i grundskoleåldern" [Linguistic and social identification among children of school-age], dissertation, Uppsala University.

Axelsson, M. (1994) "Noun phrase development in Swedish as a second language: a study of adult learners acquiring definiteness and the semantics and morphology of adjectives," dissertation, Stockholm University.

Bernstein, B. (1971) *Class, Codes and Control*, vol. 1, *Theoretical Studies towards a Sociology of Language*, London: Routledge.

Bijvoet, E. (1998) "Sverigefinnar tycker och talar: om språkattityder och stilistisk känslighet hos två generationer sverigefinnar," [Sweden Finns speak out: on language attitudes and stylistic perception among two generations of Sweden Finns], dissertation, Uppsala University.

Blom, J.-P. and Gumperz, J. (1971) "Social meaning in linguistic structures: code-switching in Norway," in A. S. Dil (ed.) *Language in Social Groups: Essays by John J. Gumperz*, Stanford, CA: Stanford University Press, pp. 274–310.

Boyd, S., Andersson, P. and Thornell, C. (1997) "Patterns of incorporation in language contact: language typology or sociolinguistics?," in G. Guy, C. Feagin, D. Schiffrin and J. Baugh (eds.) *Towards a Social Science of Language: Papers in Honor of William Labov*, Amsterdam: Benjamins, pp. 259–84.

Boyd, S. and Fraurud, K. (forthcoming) "Challenging the homogeneity assumption in language variation analysis. Findings from a study of multilingual urban spaces," in P. Auer and H-J. Schmidt (eds.) *Language and Space: An International Handbook of Linguistic Variation*, vol. 1, Berlin: Mouton de Gruyter.

Bull, T. (1993) "Språkskifte hos kvinner og menn i ei nordnorsk fjordsamebygd" [Language shift among women and men in a northern Norwegian Sami community], in G. Bjørhovde, and Å. H. Lervik (eds.) *Gå mot vinden: festskrift till Åse Hiorth Lervik på 60-årsdagen 2. juli 1993*, Oslo: Emilia, pp. 190–211.

Einarsson, J. and Hultman, T. G. (1984) *Godmorgon pojkar och flickor: om språk och kön i skolan* [Good Morning, Boys and Girls: On Language and Sex in School], Malmö: LiberFörlag.

Engh, J. (ed.) (1972) *Språksosiologi* [Sociolinguistics], Oslo: Univforlaget.

Friðriksson, F. (2008) "Language change vs. stability in conservative language communities: a case study of Iceland," dissertation, University of Gothenburg. Available at: www.gupea.ub.gu.se/dspace/handle/2077/18713.

García, O., Skutnabb-Kangas, T. and Torres-Guzmán, M. E. (eds.) (2006) *Imagining Multilingual School: Languages in Education and Globalization*, Clevedon: Multilingual Matters.

Glahn, E. (2001) "Processability in Scandinavian second language acquisition," *Studies in Second Language Acquisition*, 23, 389–416.

Gregersen, F. and Pedersen, I. L. (eds.) (1991) *The Copenhagen Study in Urban Sociolinguistics*, Copenhagen: Reitzel.

Grönberg, A. (2004) "Ungdomar och dialekt i Alingsås" [Young people and dialect in Alingsås], dissertation, University of Gothenburg.

Gunnarsson, B. (1982) "Lagtexters begriplighet: en språkfunktionell studie av medbestämmandelagen" [The comprehensibility of law-texts: a pragmatic study of the Act on the Joint Regulation of Working Life], dissertation, Uppsala University.

Hakulinen, A. (1998) "The use of Finnish *nyt* as a discourse particle," in A. H. Jucker and Y. Ziv (eds.) *Discourse Markers: Descriptions and Theory*, Amsterdam: John Benjamins, pp. 83–96.

Hansegård, N. E. (1968) *Tvåspråkighet eller halvspråkighet?* [Bilingualism or Semilingualism?], Stockholm: Aldus/Bonnier.

Haugen, E. (1966) *Language Conflict and Language Planning: The Case of Modern Norwegian*, Cambridge, MA: Harvard University Press.

Helasvuo, M.-L. (1997) "When discourse becomes syntax: noun phrases and clauses as emergent syntactic units in Finnish conversational discourse," unpublished dissertation, Department of Linguistics, University of California, Santa Barbara.

Helgander, J. (1996) *Mobilitet och språkförändring: exemplet Övre Dalarna och det vidare perspektivet* [Mobility and Language Change: The Example of Upper Dalecarlia], Falun: Högskolan Dalarna.

Huss, L. (1991) "Simultan tvåspråkighet i svensk-finsk kontext" [Simultaneous bilingualism in a Swedish-Finnish context], dissertation, Uppsala University.

Hyltenstam, K. (1999) "Introduction" and "Chapter 5," in *Sveriges sju inhemska språk* [Sweden's Seven Indigenous Languages], Lund: Studentlitteratur.

Jahani, C. (1989) "Standardization and orthography in the Balochi language," dissertation, Uppsala University.

Jahr, E. H. and Trudgill, P. (1993) "Parallels and difference in the linguistic development of modern Greece and modern Norway," in E. H. Jahr (ed.) *Language Conflict and Language Planning*, Berlin: Mouton, pp. 83–98.

Janson, T. (1973) *Reversed Lexical Diffusion and Lexical Split: Loss of –d in Stockholm*, Stockholm: Stockholm University.

Janson, T. and Tsonope, J. (1991) *Birth of a National Language: The History of Setswana*, Gaborone: Heinemann Botswana, National Institute of Development, Research and Documentation (NIR University of Botswana).

Jernudd, B. H., Rannut, M., Phillipson, R. and Skutnabb-Kangas, T. (eds.) (1994) *Linguistic Human Rights: Overcoming Linguistic Discrimination*, Berlin: Mouton de Gruyter.

Jørgensen, J. N. (2003) "Bilingualism in the Køge project," *International Journal of Bilingualism*, 7, 333–52.

Kerswill, P. (1993) "Rural dialect speakers in an urban speech community: the role of dialect contact in defining a sociolinguistic concept," *International Journal of Applied Linguistics*, 3, 33–56.

Kotsinas, U. (1994) *Ungdomsspråk* [Young People's Language], Uppsala: Hallgren and Fallgren.

——(1998) "Rinkebysvenska – en dialekt?" [Rinkeby Swedish – a dialect?], in P. Linell *et al.* (eds.) *Svenskans beskrivning*, 16, Linköping: Linköping University, Tema Kommunikation.

——(2000) *Kontakt, variation och förändring: studier i Stockholmsspråk : ett urval uppsatser* [Contact, Variation and Change: Studies in the Language of Stockholm], Stockholm: Almqvist and Wiksell International.

Kristensen, T. and Jørgensen, J. N. (1998) "Sociolinguistics in Denmark," *Sociolinguistica*, 12, 230–50.

Lainio, J. (1989) "Spoken Finnish in urban Sweden," dissertation, Uppsala University.

——(2000) "Sweden, its social splits and language studies at the turn of the millennium," *Sociolinguistica*, 14, 183–91.

Lane, P. (2006) "A tale of two towns: a comparative study of language and culture contact," dissertation, University of Oslo.

Lindberg, I. (1995) "Second language discourse in and out of classrooms: studies of learner discourse in the acquisition of Swedish as a second language in educational contexts," dissertation, Stockholm University.

Lindström, A. (1999) "Language as social action: grammar, prosody, and interaction in Swedish conversation," dissertation, Uppsala University.

Linell, P. (2002) *What Is Dialogism? Aspects and Elements of a Dialogical Approach to Language, Communication and Cognition*, Linköping: Linköping University, Tema Kommunikation.

Loman, B. (ed.) (1972) *Språk och samhälle* [Language and Society], Lund: LiberLäromedel.

Maehlum, B. (1990) "Codeswitching in Hemnesberget – Myth or reality? Tromsø Linguistics in the Eighties," *Tromsø Studies in Linguistics*, 11, 338–55.

——(1992) *Dialektal sosialisering: en studie av barn og ungdoms språklige strategier i Longyearbyen på Svalbard* [Dialectal Socialization: A Study of Children's and Young People's Linguistic Strategies in Longyearbyen in Swalbard], Oslo: Novus forlag.

——(1996) "Norsk og nordisk sosiolingvistikk: en historisk oversikt" [Norwegian and Nordic sociolinguistics: an historical survey], in C. Henriksen, E. Hovdhaugen, F. Karlsson and B. Sigurd (eds.) *Studies in the Development of Linguistics in Denmark, Finland, Iceland, Norway and Sweden*, Oslo: Novus forlag.

Nordberg, B. (1976) "Sociolinguistic research in Sweden and Finland: Introduction," *Linguistics*, 183.

——(ed.) (1994) *The Sociolinguistics of Urbanization: The Case of the Nordic Countries*, Berlin: de Gruyter.

——(1999) "Sociolinguistic research in Europe: Sweden part I," *Sociolinguistica*, 13, 261–71.

——(2003) "Sociolinguistic research in Europe: Sweden part II," *Sociolinguistica*, 17, 141–67.

Nordenstam, K. (1998) *Skvaller: om samtalsstrategier hos kvinnor och män* [Gossip: On Conversational Strategies Among Women and Men], Uppsala: Hallgren and Fallgren.

Pedersen, I. L. (2000) "Fra folkemål til multietnolekt: Kontinuitet eller brud?" [From folk language to multiethnolect; continuity or abrupt change?] *Dansk talesprog*, 1, 5–29.

Pedersen, I. L. and Gregersen, F. (eds.) (1991) *The Copenhagen Study in Urban Sociolinguistics*, Copenhagen: Reitzel.

Pedersen, K.M. (2000) *Dansk sprog i Sydslesvig: det danske sprogs status inden for det danska mindretal i Sydslesvig* [Danish Language in South Schleswig: The Status of the Danish Language within the Danish Minority], Aabenraa: Institutet for Graenseforskning.

Phillipson, R. (2003) *English-only Europe? Challenging Language Policy*, London: Routledge.

Quist, P. (1998) *Ind i gruppen, ind i sproget* [Into the Group, Into the Language], Copenhagen: Royal Danish School of Education.

——(2005) "Stilistiske praksisser i storbyens heterogene skole: en etnografisk og sociolingvistik under-søgelse af sproglig variation," [Stylistic practices in urban heterogeneous schools: an ethnographic and sociolinguistic study of language variation], dissertation, University of Copenhagen.

Säljö, R. (1997) *Learning and Discourse: A Sociocultural Perspective*, London: British Psychological Society.

Saukkonen, P. (1994) "Main trends and results of quantitative linguistics in Finland," *Journal of Quantitative Linguistics*, 1, 2–15.

Skutnabb-Kangas, T. (1981) *Tvåspråkighet* [Bilingualism], Lund: LiberLäromedel.

Stroud, C. (1991) "Language, literacy and code-switching in a Papua New Guinean village," dissertation, Stockholm University.

Svendsen, B. A. (2004) *Så lenge vi forstår hverandre: språkvalg, flerspråklige ferdigheter og språklig sosialisering hos norsk-fillipinske barn i Oslo* [As long as we understand each other: language choice, multilingual proficiencies and language socialization among Norwegian-Filippino children in Oslo], dissertation, University of Oslo.

Svendsen, B. A. and Quist, P. (eds.) (forthcoming) *Linguistic Practices in Multilingual Urban Scandinavia*, Clevedon: Multilingual Matters.

Svennevig, J. (1997) "Getting acquainted in conversation: a study of initial interactions," dissertation, University of Oslo.

Tandefelt, M. (1996) *På vinst och förlust. Om tvåspråkighet och språkförlust i Helsingforsregionen* [For Better or Worse: On Bilingualism and Language Loss in the Helsinki Region], Forskningsrapporter no. 35, Helsinki: Svenska handelshögskolan.

Trudgill, P. (1974) "Linguistic change and diffusion: description and explanation in sociolinguistic dialect geography," *Language in Society*, 3, 215–46.

——(1995) "Sociolinguistic studies in Norway 1970–91: a critical overview," *International Journal of the Sociology of Language*, 115, 7–23.

Türker, E. (2000) "Turkish-Norwegian codeswitching: evidence from intermediate and second generation Turkish immigrants in Norway," dissertation, University of Oslo.

Widmark, G. and Trost, J. (1971) *Språk i förändring: studier i Uppsalaspråk, 1* [Language Change: Studies in the Language of Uppsala, I], Uppsala: Uppsala University.

Wiggen, G. (1980) "Dialektal samvariasjon i Oslomål: en statistisk beskrivelse" [Dialectal variation in the language of Oslo: a statistical description], dissertation, University of Oslo.

——(1995) "Norway in the 1990s: a sociolinguistic profile," *International Journal of the Sociology of Language*, 115, 47–83.

Wingstedt, M. (1998) "Language ideologies and minority language policies in Sweden: historical and contemporary perspectives," dissertation, Stockholm University.

26

Sociolinguistics in the British Isles

Jane Stuart-Smith and Bill Haddican

Introduction

In the space afforded us for this chapter, it is impossible to do justice to the wealth of sociolinguistic research on the British Isles over the past ten years. The UK has been a major centre for research in different areas of sociolinguistics over the last half-century, and the volume and breadth of work focusing on sociolinguistic issues in the British Isles only approaches that for the USA. This chapter is therefore intended as a summary and guide to a small portion of the widely expanding themes within British sociolinguistics. Omission reflects the practical constraints of the chapter, and the inevitable bias of the authors. Here we focus on sociolinguistic research which we gather under two main headings – though they are not, of course, mutually exclusive: *quantitative sociolinguistics*, mainly variationist analyses of regional and urban dialects, particularly within a dialect contact framework; and *bilingualism, ethnicity and code choice* including work ranging from investigations into ethnic accents, to research focusing on the linguistic consequences of languages in contact.

Geography and demography

The British Isles are an archipelago off the north-west coast of continental Europe divided between two states – the Republic of Ireland and the United Kingdom of Great Britain and Northern Ireland (UK). The latter of these consist of four constituent countries: England, Northern Ireland, Scotland, and Wales.

The archipelago is made up of over 6000 islands, covering 315,134 square kilometres. The 2006 population of the Republic of Ireland was 4,239,848 (Central Statistics Office of Ireland 2008). The 2006 UK population was 60,597,300: 50,762,900 in England; 1,741,900 in Northern Ireland; 5,116,900 in Scotland and 2,965,900 in Wales (UK Census 2008).

The changing demographics of the British Isles can be linked with current and/or developing themes within sociolinguistic research:

1 The population of the British Isles is increasingly urban. Nearly 80 per cent of the UK population and just over 60 per cent of the Republic of Ireland population now live in urban areas. The population is particularly concentrated in large and increasing urban conurbations such as those surrounding London, Birmingham and the West Midlands, and the sprawling interconnecting cities of Yorkshire. Much recent quantitative sociolinguistic research has looked at urban accents, and at the consequences of migration for linguistic variation and change (e.g. Williams and Kerswill 1999; Watt 2002). There is also a counter-tendency to start thinking about language variation in ultra rural communities (e.g. Smith 2007–8; Corrigan in press).

2 The proportion of the English and Welsh populations reported as 'minority ethnic' has increased by 53 per cent since the 1991 UK Census, from 3 million in 1991 to 4.6 million in 2001 (similar data were not collected for Northern Ireland in 1991). It is difficult to assess the actual implications of the increase of the 'minority ethnic' population for minority ethnic language speaking and/or survival (and the number is inflated by the introduction of the novel category 'mixed'), but we might expect ethnicity and language to become increasingly important for British sociolinguistics – and this is also reflected in what is presented here.

3 Recent census data on proficiency in, and use of, indigenous minority languages in the British Isles (Welsh, Irish, Scottish Gaelic) indicates substantial variation in patterns of change across contexts. On the one hand, Welsh speakers are increasing. In 2001 census data, 21 per cent of Welsh residents aged 3 and over were reported to be able to speak Welsh, an increase from 19 per cent in 1981 and 1991 census data (UK Census 2008). The situation of Irish is stable. In 2006 Republic of Ireland census data, 1,656,790 Irish respondents (40 per cent of all respondents) reported knowing Irish, a slight increase from 1,430,205 in 1996 data. The outlook is less encouraging for Scots Gaelic. In 2001 census data, 58,652 respondents aged 3 and over were reported able to speak Gaelic, an 11 per cent decrease from 1991 census data (General Register Office for Scotland 2005). Reversing language shift in these languages, along with trying to understand better the position of these languages for contemporary speakers, is an issue for British sociolinguistic research, though not one which can be pursued further here.

Previous sociolinguistic work

The research that we present in this schematic survey has its roots in a long-standing tradition of sociolinguistics in Britain. The methods of quantitative sociolinguistics formulated and established in America by Labov, e.g. (1966, 1972), were quickly transposed into a British context. The first variationist studies appear to be Houck's (1968) study of language variation in Leeds, and the Tyneside Linguistic Survey (Strang 1968; Allen et al. 2007) of Newcastle; in southern England we have Trudgill's seminal study of Norwich (e.g. 1974), and shortly afterwards, in Scotland, Macaulay's important contribution for Glasgow (e.g. 1977). Research in other locations and with other communities, mainly urban, quickly followed, some also extending the focus from phonological to morpho-syntactic variation (e.g. Cheshire 1982). This is represented in the useful collections gathered by e.g. Trudgill (1978), Romaine (1982), Trudgill (1984), among others.

Quantitative sociolinguistics

Dialect change and contact

The study of British accents received a new focus in Foulkes and Docherty's (1999) important summary of recent descriptions of urban accents, *Urban Voices*, updating and extending Wells' (1982) invaluable, *Accents of English*. Key themes identified in their introduction included the influence of non-standard varieties on variation and change, for example, in the rapid emergence of features such as TH-fronting (using [f] for [θ] in e.g. *think*) across the UK, and the processes underlying such changes, such as dialect levelling (subject to many definitions, and well discussed alongside 'diffusion' by Kerswill 2003).

The modelling and explanation of variation and change starting from the kind of dialect contact model set out by Trudgill (1986) are at the core of much variationist sociolinguistic work of the past decade. A good illustration is provided by the special issue of the *Journal of Sociolinguistics* (2002), with Lesley Milroy's introduction laying out the theoretical context, and noting three recurring themes (Milroy 2002: 4): (1) the linguistic consequences of mobility; (2) the impact of language attitudes and ideologies; (3) and the cognitive constraints on the possible outcomes of dialect contact.

Much interesting research has been conducted within this framework, see, e.g. Watt and Milroy (1999) who discuss levelling in Newcastle vowels and argue for the importance of recognizing local vs supra-local as more relevant sociolinguistic distinctions for speakers than 'standard'/'non-standard'; or Dyer's (2002) study of the West Midlands town of Corby, whose population was swelled by the influx of Scottish steelworkers, and whose young male speakers have now reallocated former Scottish variants like [o] in the GOAT vowel to 'Corby' speech, as opposed to that of nearby Kettering; or more recently, Llamas' (2007) discussion of sociolinguistic identity and phonetic variation in speakers from the north-eastern town of Middlesborough, which concludes that linguistic variation is best interpreted in the context of speakers' own 'local knowledge, orientation, and language variation' (ibid.: 602). In connection with work on language and identity, we can also note that the 'third wave' has now broken on British shores, notably in Moore's study of Bolton adolescents (2006), and Lawson's ongoing research into language and violence in young Glaswegian males (e.g. Lawson 2008).

Important in developing theoretical perspectives for dealing with data from British dialect contact situations have been three large UK-government-funded projects:

1   The first (Kerswill and Williams 1994) looked at the formation of an urban *koiné*, in the new town, Milton Keynes, in the speech of 48 children, aged 4, 8, and 12, and their caregivers, and some elderly locally-born residents. Kerswill and Williams (2000) set out a series of eight principles for koineization in progress; noteworthy are the roles of age and social networks, with the oldest children, young adolescents, showing most focusing.

2   The second project (Williams *et al.* 1998) intensified interest on adolescents, looking hard at potential social and demographic factors which might have an impact on dialect levelling in three towns with differing profiles: Milton Keynes and Reading, both in the south-east of England but one a new town, the other well-established, and Hull on the north-east coast of Yorkshire, suffering from the blight of a declining industrial base. A further dimension was achieved by working across linguistic levels: phonology, morphosyntax, syntax and discourse. Cheshire

et al. (2005) provide a nice summary: evidence was found for phonological and morphosyntactic convergence, especially towards more typically non-standard variation (e.g. TH-fronting; negative concord, 'we haven't got no diseases') in working-class adolescents (gender appears to be less important); but divergence is also observed (e.g. in Hull phonology). Apart from the discourse marker *like*, as in 'we were like rushing home', which occurred across the three towns, variation in syntax and discourse forms proved more difficult to analyse; interactional context appears to be crucial for understanding the extent to which a feature might be converging or diverging for a specific community of speakers.

3 The third study (Kerswill and Cheshire 2007) turned to the often-named source of accent innovations, London. The sample was composed of older and younger speakers in both an inner and outer London borough (Hackney and Havering respectively), also taking account of ethnicity and social network relationships. Interestingly, the findings for vowels (e.g. Torgersen *et al.* 2006) reveal innovation and divergence in the speech of young inner-city Londoners, not dialect levelling, with contact with non-native forms of English, as well as specific ethnolects seeming to play an important role in such patterning.

Overall, these studies demonstrate that British urban dialect changes currently in progress are characterized by both dialect levelling (or 'supralocalization', Torgersen *et al.* 2006) and dialect divergence; the challenge is how to deal theoretically with such complexity, and the motivating factors underlying it.

Sociophonetics

At times, an integral part of recent work on accent change, intensive scrutiny has been applied to the nature of phonological variation. Good summaries of recent sociophonetic research in the British Isles may be found in Foulkes and Docherty (2006, 2007), at least in part grounded in the important results of an earlier ESRC-funded project, *Phonological Variation and Change in Contemporary Spoken British English* (see Docherty *et al.* 1997). Most research has concentrated on sound segments, though see the cross-dialectal work on intonation based on the *IViE* corpus (e.g. Grabe 2004), or Stuart-Smith's (1999) analysis of voice quality in Glaswegian.

Acoustic analysis is generally used (with normalization procedures) for vowel description in sociolinguistics. Instrumental phonetic analysis of consonants has typically been less common, but close examination of, for example, the variability in glottal stops in Newcastle and Derby, or final released /t/ in the same cities (e.g. Docherty and Foulkes 1999), reveals far more complexity than auditory transcriptions such as [ʔ] or [t] for /t/, might imply. Moreover, fine-grained phonetic variation patterns significantly with social factors, showing that speakers have very subtle sociophonetic control over their speech production.

The gradient nature of such variation also requires us to acknowledge the same in our auditory categories; for example, a recent study of phonetic variation of eight consonant variables in Glasgow revealed phonetically 'intermediate' variant categories for five variables, including (x), in e.g. *loch* whose final consonant is merging with /k/ (*lock*) in working-class adolescents (cf. Lawson and Stuart-Smith 1999). Auditorily and acoustically we find: [x], voiceless guttural fricatives; [k], voiceless velar plosives; *and* what we represent with the label '[kx]', reflecting the identification of variants showing features of plosives and fricatives together. Such research clearly deepens our sociolinguistic descriptions, and refines our accounts of phonetic change, but it also enriches and challenges phonetic and phonological theory, and in particular how speakers acquire, store, access and abstract across such variability (e.g. Foulkes and Docherty 2006).

Language acquisition

Fundamental to our understanding of patterns of sociolinguistic variation is how and when they are acquired by children. Kerswill (1996) observes that key factors in the acquisition of dialect features seem to be: linguistic level, complexity of the linguistic feature, and age; his own data from Milton Keynes show clearly that young (= 4 years old) children's variation is more closely related to that of their caregivers, while older children orient more to their peers. This decade has seen an important shift to working with much younger children, in two partly complementary studies.

The study of the *emergence of structured variation*, reported in e.g. Docherty *et al.* (2005), Foulkes and Docherty (2006) and carried out in Newcastle, looked at fine-grained phonetic variation in 40 children aged 2;0–4;0 and their caregivers. Even such young children show variation in their speech production (e.g. in the realization of /t/ in e.g. *water*) which correlates with that of their mothers. At the same time, mothers provide their children with socio-indexical input relevant for their community: the speech directed to their children is quantitatively and qualitatively different from that to their adult contemporaries. Less vernacular variants are addressed to their children, but within that, young girls receive more standard variants, boys more vernacular ones, with this pattern clearest for the youngest children.

Smith *et al.*'s (2007) study of acquisition in the Scottish north-eastern town of Buckie, from 11 children aged 2;10–13;6 and their caregivers, also found that speech addressed to children is more standard than that towards adults; there was also close linguistic and stylistic matching between children's and caregivers' variation. But interestingly this pattern was found only for the phonological/lexical variable *hoose* (use of /u/ in a restricted set of words in place of /ʌu/), but not for the morpho–syntactic variable *–s* in 3rd person plural contexts (e.g. 'my trousers is fa'in doon'). An additional factor in the acquisition of sociolinguistic variation may also be the level of social awareness carried by particular features.

The influence of television

Another possible factor for dialect change in the UK, which has been frequently mentioned in the literature over the past decade, is the role of the broadcast media, and especially television (e.g. Stuart-Smith 2006). Empirical support for engagement with television as a factor in language change has now emerged from Glasgow (e.g. Stuart-Smith 2005; Stuart-Smith *et al.*, in progress). But it is important to note that the statistical evidence, based on a large-scale multifactorial model, also argues for the integration of theoretical approaches. Amongst others, factors representing dialect contact, social practices and identity construction, and engagement with the television are all required *together* to explain the variation satisfactorily.

Comparative sociolinguistics

Several different groups of researchers in British sociolinguistics over the past decade have used innovative comparative techniques in approaching problems in current sociolinguistics literature. In particular, since the late 1990s, Tagliamonte, Smith and colleagues have reported on a series of studies addressing different problems in the language variation and change literature by comparing the effect of internal constraints on variation within and across corpora from different varieties.

Particularly influential in this line of research has been work on the history of African American English (AAE) and its kinship to British English dialects. Based on comparisons of constraint effects across different African American and White dialectal English corpora, Poplack and Tagliamonte have proposed that many distinctive features of contemporary African American English (AAE) are not attributable to creolization or contact with creoles contrary to much previous literature (Singler 1991; Rickford 1998), but rather are traceable to English dialects (Tagliamonte and Smith 2000b; Poplack and Tagliamonte 2001; Tagliamonte 2001). Using similar comparative techniques, Tagliamonte, Smith and collaborators have explored grammaticalization and other kinds of language change in several features of contemporary British and Irish Englishes including variation in deontic modality marking (*have to* vs. *have got to* vs. *must*) (Tagliamonte and Smith 2006), complementizer deletion (Tagliamonte and Smith 2005), aux/neg contraction (Tagliamonte and Smith 2000a), quotatives (Tagliamonte and Hudson 1999), and relative clause markers (*that* vs. *wh-* vs. zero) (Tagliamonte *et al.* 2005).

Also influential in recent literature has been Milroy's (2000) comparison of ideologies of standard language in the United States and Britain. Milroy describes how the different sociolinguistic histories of these two societies have produced different ideologies of non-standard speech: non-standard language is understood primarily as a class 'problem' in Britain but a race/ethnicity 'problem' in the United States.

In a similar vein, Buchstaller (2006b) compares perceptions of quotative use in the UK with results from a similar US study by Dailey-O'Cain (2000). Using an innovative written matched guise methodology, Buchstaller collected data on perceptions of *be like* and *go* as verbs for introducing direct speech, see examples (1) and (2).

1 *I'm like* 'urgh' you know 'Indian candy is not very good.' (Buchstaller 2006a).
2 and she'll *go* 'get me a cup of tea I've been at work all day.' (ibid.).

Buchstaller's results suggest that while many attitudes toward quotative use are similar in the UK and the US, others vary. On the one hand, Buchstaller notes that both *be like* and *go* use are similar in the US and UK studies: both of these quotatives are associated with young speakers and women. However, while *be like* use is associated with middle-class speakers in the US, it is also associated with working-class speech in the UK. Similarly, in Dailey-O'Cain's US data, *be like* use is consistently evaluated positively across solidarity attributes, while in the UK *be like* is evaluated positively for some attributes (trendiness, animated) and negatively for others (unpleasant). As Buchstaller notes, these results are instructive for current understanding of diffusion, in that they suggest that as innovative features spread, the social meaning of the innovation may be re-evaluated in local context (Buchstaller and D'Arcy 2007).

Regional variation

Walking in the footsteps of English dialectologists of the nineteenth and twentieth centuries (Wright 1892), much recent sociolinguistic work continues to describe variation across and within local and regional varieties. The touchstone for much of this research since the 1970s has been Trudgill's variationist work.

Of particular note among recent regional studies are Watson's (2006) and Sangster's (2001) careful studies of variable lenition of /p,t,k/ in Liverpool, a feature of Irish English brought by Irish immigrants to Liverpool in the nineteenth and twentieth centuries (cf. Kallen 2004). As Watson (2006) notes, an intriguing question with a view towards the future of Liverpool English is whether t-lenition, an emblematic feature of local speech, will be displaced in the short term by t-glottalling, which is diffusing into many northern English dialects (Foulkes and Docherty 1999). Richards' (2008) thesis describes patterns of variation and change in Leeds, a major Northern urban centre that, like Liverpool, has received little attention in the sociolinguistic literature. Richards reports a rich pattern of variation in apparent time data for eight different variables from different parts of the grammar. On the one hand, a handful of features which recent literature reports to be diffusing quite rapidly in other UK dialects – be like quotatives, t-glottalling, TH-fronting – likewise appear to be entering Leeds English. At the same time, however, many localized emblematic features of the dialect including 'secondary contraction' – [dǫt] don't, [kạt] can't – are being retained. The pervasiveness of such uneven patterns of diffusion and retention across variables in a single community underscores the need for more perceptual work and a more refined model of social and linguistic constraints on borrowing in processes of dialect contact (Trudgill 1986; Bailey et al. 1993; Kerswill and Williams 2002).

The literature focusing on regional variation in the Irish Republic is relatively small compared to that for the UK, for reasons perhaps related to the symbolic importance of Irish and the process of shift from Irish to English in Irish national life (Hogan 1927; Kallen 1997; Corrigan 2003b). However, in recent years, Kallen (1997) and Hickey (2002, 2004, 2005, 2007a, 2007b) have contributed important descriptive work in this area.

Northern Ireland is much better represented in the literature and has been the focus of seminal research. Milroy's (1987) careful examination of different aspects of phonological variation in Belfast is a landmark study of the relationship between social network structure and language use. More recently, McCafferty (1999, 2001) has examined the way religious and ethnic identity shape language use in Derry.

Henry's (1995, 2002) study of morphosyntactic variation in Belfast has been influential in both variationist and comparative syntax literature. In a similar vein, Corrigan (2000, 2003a, in press) has studied syntactic variation and language contact in the Northern Irish dialect South Armagh from a perspective that draws on both generative and variationist traditions. In particular, Corrigan's (2003a) study of for to infinitives in South Armagh, is a good example of ways that formal syntactic analyses may be enhanced by experimental and variationist data collection techniques.

Related to these regional studies have been efforts to disseminate corpora of regional speech for research and teaching purposes. Most notably, a Newcastle-based team of researchers led by Corrigan have recently produced the NECTE corpus, a digital collection of dialect speech from Tyneside in north-east England (Allen et al. 2007, www. ncl.ac.uk/necte/). Similarly the IViE corpus, produced by researchers based at Oxford contains recordings of nine urban dialects from the British isles: Belfast, Bradford, Cambridge, Cardiff, Dublin, Leeds, Liverpool, London and Newcastle. Two other online corpora have appeared during this period: the SCOTS corpus offering a substantial number of written texts and speech recordings for varieties of Scottish English (www. scottishcorpus.ac.uk), and BBC Voices website (see also Coupland and Bishop 2007).

Bilingualism, ethnicity and code choice

Code choice and language use in Celtic-speaking areas

A considerable amount of literature has focused on bilingualism and code choice among speakers of the British Isles' surviving Celtic languages, Scottish Gaelic, Irish and Welsh. In the following brief discussion, we highlight some key recent literature in this area, setting aside extensive recent work on language policy and planning in these communities.[1]

Work by Deuchar and collaborators on Welsh-English bilingual speech has been influential in recent code-mixing literature. In a series of recent papers, Deuchar and colleagues have used Welsh-English data to test and inform different models of code-switching in adult grammars including the Matrix-Language Frame model (Deuchar and Vihman 2005; Deuchar 2006) and Muysken's (2000) typology of mixed bilingual speech (Deuchar *et al.* 2007), as well as models of acquisition of code-switching in developing bilinguals (Deuchar and Quay 2001; Deuchar and Vihman 2005). Since Stenson's (1990) approach to Irish-English code-switching within government and binding theory, relatively little work has focused on Irish-English and Gaelic-English switching, with the notable exception of O'Malley-Madec's (2007) study of borrowing in Irish-English bilingual speech.

Much other literature has examined consequences of language contact between English and Celtic for change in these languages. In particular, many properties of Irish English, especially perfect constructions, have been attributed to substrate influence from Irish, however, the extent and nature of this influence remain debated. A useful overview of this debate is provided in Hickey (2007b).

The language(s) of Britain's Anglo-Caribbean, Asian and Chinese communities – developing ethnolects

In the mid-twentieth century, during the UK's post-war economic expansion, workers from several different parts of Britain's shrinking empire – principally present-day India, Pakistan, Bangladesh, Hong Kong and the Caribbean – began immigrating in large numbers to the UK to work in England's industrial centres. Until fairly recently, the speech of these groups had received relatively little attention in the sociolinguistic literature, compared to that for 'indigenous' varieties. In recent years, however, more sociolinguistic work has focused on these communities.

Hewitt's (1986) ethnographic study of language use and code choice in South London's Jamaican and Anglo communities has been seminal for studies of language use among Britain's 'new' ethnic groups. Sebba (1993) and Rampton (1995, 1998) have subsequently drawn on this work in studying use of Jamaican Creole and Asian features not only among Afro-Caribbeans and south Asians but among whites as well.

Similarly, since the mid-1990s, Li Wei and collaborators have published a series of papers on code-switching between Chinese and English in Newcastle (Li 1994; Li and Milroy 1995; Raschka *et al.* 2002) which have been influential in the development of conversational analytic approaches to code-switching, as has Sebba and Wootton's (1998) work on Creole-English code-switching. More recently Pert and Letts (2006) have focused on code-switching and code-choice among Mirpuri heritage speakers.

Increasingly, sociophonetic literature has focused on these communities as well. Thus, we note Heselwood and McChrystal's study on Bradford Asian (e.g. Heselwood and

McChrystal 2000) who find evidence of retroflexion in Asian English speakers, Hirson and Nabiah (2007) on rhoticity and expressed Asian identity in London Asians, and the recent (and ongoing work) trying to unpick the characteristics of 'Glaswasian' (i.e. Glaswegian Asian) accent, such as postalveolar place of articulation for /t d/ and clear syllable-initial /l/ (e.g. Lambert *et al.* 2007). Ethnicity and local accent are also a feature of Straw and Patrick's work (e.g. 2007) on Barbadians in Ipswich.

Finally, a further vein of sociolinguistic research which we felt should be included here, is represented in the recent interesting studies which have emerged from linguistic ethnography (cf. Rampton 2007). The chosen sites of ethnography, mainly (greater) London secondary schools, with catchments comprising communities with a range of ethnic backgrounds, mean that such research either has a focus on ethnicity and language, such as Harris (2006), which considers the construction of new ethnicities and language use in hybrid sociolinguistic identities such as 'Brasian' (as opposed to 'British Asian'), or includes ethnicity as a key element in linguistic interaction (Rampton 1995), or for which ethnicity is a pervasive or underlying issue (Rampton 2006).

Future directions

British sociolinguistic research – within the themes noted here – continues apace, as is indicated by the wealth of projects either just starting, or ongoing at the time of writing. In particular, identity, place, and language will be explored along the Scottish-English border in Llamas and Watt's project *Linguistic variation and national identities on the Scottish/English border*. Kerswill and Cheshire's current project *Multicultural London English* focuses on ethnicity and its potential impact on mainstream varieties of English. Finally, Sharma, Rampton and Harris are employing an innovative combination of quantitative and qualitative/interactional sociolinguistic approaches in their study of dialect development in families of Indian origin in London, *Dialect development and style in a diasporic community*.

Innovative experimental work currently in progress includes Scobbie and Stuart-Smith's efforts to develop new articulatory methods for analysing sociolinguistic variation (using ultrasound tongue imaging to investigate derhoticization in Scottish English in the first instance (Lawson *et al.* 2008)). Foulkes *et al.* (forthcoming) are carrying out much-needed work on the perception of sociophonetic variation; and Stuart-Smith and Smith are starting to tackle experimentally the challenging issues of what and how we learn about accents from mediated speech (Stuart-Smith and Smith 2008).

Finally, we have said nothing about the wealth of sociolinguistic research relating to education, institutional talk, language and globalization, different emerging forms of textual communication, or even the explosion of interest in internet language; but even a cursory glance at the list of contributors to the recent *Encyclopedia of Language and Linguistics: Sociolinguistics*, underscores the significant contribution of British and Irish sociolinguists to these areas.

Note

1 We refer interested readers to Williams and Morris (2000) and Jones (1998) for recent discussions of revitalization efforts on behalf of Welsh, and to McLeod (2006) for Scottish Gaelic.

References

Allen, W., Beal, J. C., Corrigan, K. P., Moisl, H. and Maguire, W. (2007) 'The Newcastle Electronic Corpus of Tyneside English', in J. C. Beal, K. P. Corrigan and H. Moisl (eds) *Creating and Digitizing Language Corpora*, vol. 2, *Diachronic Databases*, Basingstoke: Palgrave, pp. 16–48.

Bailey, G., Wikle, T., Tillery, J. and Sand, L. (1993) 'Some patterns of linguistic diffusion', *Language Variation and Change*, 3, 359–90.

Buchstaller, I. (2006a) 'Diagnostics of age-graded linguistic behavior: the case of the quotative system', *Journal of Sociolinguistics*, 10, 3–30.

——(2006b) 'Social stereotypes, personality traits and regional perception displaced: attitudes towards the "new" quotatives in the U.K.', *Journal of Sociolinguistics*, 10, 362–81.

Buchstaller, I. and D'Arcy, A. (2007) 'Localized globalization: a multi-local, multivariate investigation of quotative like', paper presented at New Ways of Analysing Variation 36, University of Pennsylvania, Philadelphia, November.

Central Statistics Office of Ireland (2008) Statistical data. Online. Available at: www.cso.ie. (accessed 18 March 2008).

Cheshire, J. (1982) *Variation in an English Dialect: A Sociolinguistic Study*, Cambridge: Cambridge University Press.

Cheshire, J., Kerswill, P. and Williams, A. (2005) 'Phonology, grammar and discourse in dialect convergence', in P. Auer, F. Hinskens and P. Kerswill (eds) *Dialect Change: Convergence and Divergence in European Languages*, Cambridge: Cambridge University Press.

Corrigan, K. P. (2000) '"*What bees to be maun be:*" aspects of deontic and epistemic modality in a northern dialect of Irish-English', *English World-Wide*, 21, 25–62.

——(2003a) 'For-to infinitives and beyond: Interdisciplinary approaches to non-finite complementation in a rural Celtic English', in H. L. C. Tristram (ed.) *Celtic Englishes*, vol. III, Heidelberg: Carl Winter Verlag.

——(2003b) 'The ideology of nationalism and its impact on accounts of language shift in nineteenth century Ireland', in C. Mair (ed.) *Acts of Identity*, Special Issue of *Arbeiten aus Anglistik und Amerikanistik*, 28, 201–30.

——(in press) 'Irish daughters of Northern British relatives: internal and external constraints on the system of relativization in South Armagh English', in M. Filppula, J. Klemola and H. Paulasto (eds) *Vernacular Universals vs. Contact-Induced Language Change*, London: Routledge.

Coupland, N. and Bishop, H. (2007) 'Ideologised values for British accents', *Journal of Sociolinguistics*, 11, 74–93.

Dailey-O'Cain, J. (2000) 'The sociolinguistic distribution and attitudes towards focuser like and quotative like', *Journal of Sociolinguistics*, 4, 60–80.

Deuchar, M. (2005) 'Congruence and code-switching in Welsh', *Bilingualism: Language and Cognition*, 8, 1–15.

——(2006) 'Welsh-English code-switching and the Matrix Language Frame model', *Lingua*, 116, 1986–2011.

Deuchar, M., Muysken, P. and Wang, S. (2007) 'Structured variation in code-switching; towards an empirically based typology of bilingual speech patterns', *International Journal of Bilingual Education and Bilingualism*, 10, 298–340.

Deuchar, M. and Quay, S. (2001) *Bilingual Acquisition: Theoretical Implications of a Case Study*, Oxford: Oxford University Press.

Deuchar, M. and Vihman, M. (2005) 'A radical approach to early mixed utterances', *International Journal of Bilingualism*, 9, 137–57.

Docherty, G. J. and Foulkes, P. (1999) 'Newcastle upon Tyne and Derby: instrumental phonetics and variationist studies', in P. Foulkes and G. J. Docherty (eds) *Urban Voices: Accent Studies in the British Isles*, London: Arnold.

——(2005) 'Glottal variants of (t) in the Tyneside variety of English: an acoustic profiling study', in W. Hardcastle and J. Mackenzie Beck (eds) *A Figure of Speech: A Festschrift for John Laver*, London: Lawrence Erlbaum.

Docherty, G., Foulkes, P., Milroy, J., Milroy, L. and Walshaw, D. (1997) 'Descriptive adequacy in phonology: a variationist perspective', *Journal of Linguistics*, 33, 275–310.

Docherty, G., Foulkes, P., Tillotson, J. and Watt, D. (2005) 'On the scope of phonological learning: issues arising from socially-structured variation', in C. Best, L. Goldstein, and D. Whalen (eds) *Papers in Laboratory Phonology 8*, Berlin: Mouton de Gruyter, pp. 393–421.

Dyer, J. (2002) '"We all speak the same round here": dialect levelling in a Scottish-English community', *Journal of Sociolinguistics*, 6, 99–116.

Foulkes, P. and Docherty, G. J. (eds) (1999) *Urban Voices*, London: Arnold.

——(2006) 'The social life of phonetics and phonology', *Journal of Phonetics*, 34, 409–38.

——(2007) 'Phonological and prosodic variation in the English of England', in D. Britain (ed.) *Language in the British Isles*, 2nd edn, Cambridge: Cambridge University Press.

Foulkes, P., Docherty, G. J., Khattab, G. and Yaeger-Dror, M. (forthcoming) 'Sound judgements: perception of indexical features in children's speech', in D. Preston (ed.) *Handbook of Sociophonetics*, Oxford: Blackwell.

Foulkes, P., Docherty, G. J. and Watt, D. J. L. (2005) 'Phonological variation in child directed speech', *Language*, 81, 177–206.

General Register Office for Scotland (2005) Statistical data. Online. Available at: www.gro-scotland.gov.uk (accessed 18 March 2008).

Grabe, E. (2004) 'Intonational variation in urban dialects of English spoken in the British Isles', in P. Gilles and J. Peters (eds) *Regional Variation in Intonation*, Linguistische Arbeiten, Tübingen: Niemeyer.

Harris, R. (2006) *New Ethnicities and Language Use*, Basingstoke: Palgrave Macmillan.

Henry, A. (1995) *Belfast English and Standard English Dialect Variation and Parameter Setting*, Oxford: Oxford University Press.

——(2002) 'Variation and syntactic theory', in J. Chambers, P. Trudgill, and N. Schilling-Estes (eds) *Handbook of Language Variation and Change*, Oxford: Blackwell.

Heselwood, B. and McChrystal, L. (2000) 'Gender, accent features and voicing', *Leeds Working Papers in Linguistics and Phonetics*, 8, 45–69.

Hewitt, R. (1986) *White Talk Black Talk: Inter-racial Friendship and Communication amongst Adolescents*, Cambridge: Cambridge University Press.

Hickey, R. (2002) *A Source Book for Irish English*, Amsterdam: Benjamins.

——(2004) *A Sound Atlas of Irish English*, Berlin: Mouton de Gruyter.

——(2005) *Dublin English: Evolution and Change*, Amsterdam: Benjamins.

——(2007a) *Irish English: History and Present Day Forms*, Cambridge: Cambridge University Press.

——(2007b) 'Southern Irish English', in D. Britain (ed.) *Language in the British Isles*, Cambridge: Cambridge University Press.

Hirson, A. and Nabiah, S. (2007) 'Variability of rhotics in Punjabi-English Bilinguals', *Proceedings of ICPhS XVI*, Saarbrücken, pp. 1501–4.

Hogan, J. (1927) *The English Language in Ireland*, Dublin: Educational Company of Ireland.

Houck, C. L. (1968) 'Methodology of an Urban Speech Survey', *Leeds Studies in English*, 2, 115–28.

Jones, M. C. (1998) *Language Obsolescence and Revitalization*, Oxford: Clarendon Press.

Kallen, J. (ed.) (1997) *Focus on Ireland*, Amsterdam: Benjamins.

——(2004) 'The influence of the languages of Ireland and Scotland on linguistic varieties in Northern England', MS, University of Aberdeen.

Kerswill, P. (1996) 'Children, adolescents and language change', *Language Variation and Change*, 8, 177–202.

——(2003) 'Dialect levelling and geographical diffusion in British English', in D. Britain and J. Cheshire (eds) *Social Dialectology: In Honour of Peter Trudgill*, Amsterdam: Benjamins.

Kerswill, P. and Cheshire, J. (2007) *Linguistic Innovators: The English of Adolescents in London*, Final Report on ESRC Grant No. 000230680.

Kerswill, P. and Williams, A. (1994) *A New Dialect in a New City*, Final Report on ESRC Grant No. 000232376.

——(2000) 'Creating a new town koine: children and language change in Milton Keynes', *Language in Society*, 29, 65–115.

——(2002) '"Salience" as an explanatory factor in language change: evidence from dialect levelling in urban England', in M. C. Jones and E. Esch (eds) *Language Change: The Interplay of Internal, External and Extra-linguistic Factors*, Berlin: Mouton de Gruyter.

Labov, W. (1966) *The Social Stratification of English in New York City*, Washington, DC: Center for Applied Linguistics.

——(1972) *Sociolinguistic Patterns*, Philadelphia, PA: University of Pennsylvania Press.

Lambert, K., Alam, F. and Stuart-Smith, J. (2007) 'Investigating British Asian accents: studies from Glasgow', *Proceedings of the XVIth International Congress of Phonetic Sciences*, Saarbrücken, pp. 1509–11.

Lawson, E. and Stuart-Smith, J. (1999) 'A sociophonetic investigation of the "Scottish" consonants (/x/ and /hw/) in the speech of Glaswegian children', in *Proceedings of the XIVth International Congress of Phonetic Sciences*, Saarbrücken, pp. 2541–4.

Lawson, E., Stuart-Smith, J. and Scobbie, J. (2008) 'Articulatory insights into language variation and change: preliminary findings from an ultrasound study of derhoticisation in Scottish English', *University of Pennsylvania Working Papers in Linguistics*, Philadelphia: University of Pennsylvania.

Lawson, R. (2008) 'Sociolinguistic constructions of identity in a Glasgow high school', paper presented at the Linguistics Society of America annual meeting. Chicago, Illinois, January.

Li Wei (1994) *Three Generations Two Language One Family: Language Choice and Language Shift in a Chinese Community in Britain*, Clevedon: Multilingual Matters.

Li Wei and Milroy, L. (1995) 'Conversational codeswitching in a Chinese community in Britain: a sequential analysis', *Journal of Pragmatics* 23, 281–99.

Llamas, C. (2007) 'A place between places: language and identities in a border town', *Language in Society*, 36, 579–604.

Macaulay, R. (1977) *Language, Social Class and Education: A Glasgow Study*, Edinburgh: University of Edinburgh Press.

McCafferty, K. (1999) '(London)Derry: between Ulster and local speech – class, ethnicity and language change', in P. Foulkes and G. Docherty (eds) *Urban Voices: Accent Studies in the British Isles*, London: Arnold.

——(2001) *Ethnicity and Language Change: English in (London)Derry, Northern Ireland*, Amsterdam: Benjamins.

McLeod, W. (ed.) (2006) *Revitalising Gaelic in Scotland*, Edinburgh: Dunedin Academic Press.

Milroy, L. (1987) *Language and Social Networks*, Oxford: Blackwell.

——(2000) 'Two nations divided by the same language (and different language ideologies)', *Journal of Linguistic Anthropology*, 10, 1–34.

——(2002) 'Introduction: mobility, contact and language change – working with contemporary speech communities', *Journal of Sociolinguistics*, 6, 3–15.

Moore, E. (2006) '"You tell all the stories": using narrative to understand hierarchy in a community of practice', *Journal of Sociolinguistics*, 10, 611–40.

Muysken, P. (2000) *Bilingual Speech: A Typology of Code-mixing*, Cambridge: Cambridge University Press.

O'Malley-Madec, M. (2007) 'How one word borrows another: the process of language-contact in two Irish-speaking communities', *International Journal of Bilingual Education and Bilingualism*, 10, 494–509.

Pert, S. and Letts, C. (2006) 'Codeswitching in Mirpuri speaking Pakistani heritage preschool children: bilingual language acquisition', *International Journal of Bilingualism*, 10, 349–74.

Poplack, S. and Tagliamonte, S. A. (2001) *African American English in the Diaspora: Tense and Aspect*, Oxford: Blackwell.

Rampton, B. (1995) *Crossing: Language and Ethnicity among Adolescents*, London: Longman.

——(1998) 'Language crossing and the redefinition of reality', in P. Auer (ed.) *Code-switching in Conversation*, London: Routledge.

——(2006) *Language in Late Modernity*, Cambridge: Cambridge University Press.

——(2007) 'Neo-Hymesian linguistic ethnography in the UK', *Journal of Sociolinguistics*, 11, 584–608.

Raschka, C., Li Wei and Lee, S. (2002) 'Bilingual development and social networks of British-born Chinese children', *International Journal of the Sociology of Language*, 153, 9–25

Richards, H. (2008) 'Mechanisms, motivations and outcomes of change in Morley (Leeds) English', unpublished PhD thesis, University of York.

Rickford, J. (1998) 'The Creole origins of African American vernacular English: evidence from copula absence', in S. S. Mufwene, J. R. Rickford, G. Bailey and J. Baugh (eds) *African American English*, London: Routledge.

Romaine, S. (ed.) (1982) *Sociolinguistic Variation in Speech Communities*, London: Arnold.

Sangster, C. (2001) 'Lenition of alveolar stops in Liverpool English', *Journal of Sociolinguistics*, 5, 401–12.

Sebba, M. (1993) *Jamaican English: Language Systems in Interaction*, London: Longman.

Sebba, M. and Wootton, T. (1998) 'We, they and identity: sequential versus identity-related explanation in code-switching', in P. Auer (ed.) *Code-switching in Conversation: Language, Interaction, and Identity*, London: Routledge.

Singler, J. (1991) 'Copula variation in Liberian Settler English and American Black English', in W. F. Edwards and D. Winford (eds) *Verb Phrase Patterns in Black English and Creoles*, Detroit: Wayne State University Press.

Smith, J. (2007–8) *Obsolescence vs. Stability in a Shetland Dialect: Evidence from Three Generations of Speakers*, ESRC funded project no. RES-000-22-2052.

Smith, J., Durham, M. and Fortune, L. (2007) 'Community, caregiver and child in the acquisition of variation in a Scottish dialect', *Language Variation and Change*, 19, 63–99.

Stenson, N. (1990) 'Phrase structure congruence, government, and Irish-English code-switching', in R. Hendrick (ed.) *Syntax and Semantics*, vol. 23, *The Syntax of the Modern Celtic Languages*, San Diego: Academic Press.

Strang, B. M. H. (1968) 'The Tyneside Linguistic Survey', *Zeitschrift für Mundartforschung*, NF 4 (Verhandlungen des Zweiten Internationalen Dialektenkongresses), Wiesbaden: Franz Steiner Verlag.

Straw, M. and Patrick, P. (2007) 'Dialect acquisition of glottal variation in /t/: Barbadians in Ipswich', *Language Sciences*, 29, 385–407.

Stuart-Smith, J. (1999) 'Glasgow: accent and voice quality', in P. Foulkes and G. Doherty (eds) *Urban Voices: Accent Studies in the British Isles*, London: Arnold, pp. 201–22.

——(2005) *Is TV a Contributory Factor in Accent Change in Adolescents?* Final Report on ESRC Grant No. R000239757.

——(2006) 'The influence of media on language', in C. Llamas, P. Stockwell and L. Mullany (eds) *The Routledge Companion to Sociolinguistics*, London: Routledge, pp. 140–48.

Stuart-Smith, J. and Smith, R. (2008) 'Phonological learning based on interactive and mediated speech', paper presented at Laboratory Phonology, 11, University of Wellington, New Zealand.

Stuart-Smith, J., Timmins, C., Pryce, G. and Gunter, B. (in progress) 'Television is a factor in language variation and change: evidence from Glasgow'.

Stuart-Smith, J., Timmins, C. and Tweedie, F. (2007) 'Talkin' Jockney: accent change in Glaswegian', *Journal of Sociolinguistics*, 11, 221–61.

Tagliamonte, S. (2001) 'Comparative sociolinguistics', in J. Chambers, P. Trudgill, and N. Schilling-Estes (eds) *Handbook of Language Variation and Change*, Oxford: Blackwell.

Tagliamonte, S. and Hudson. R. (1999) 'Be like et al. beyond America: the quotative system in British and Canadian youth', *Journal of Sociolinguistics*, 3, 147–72.

Tagliamonte, S. and Smith, J. (2000a) 'Either it isn't or it's not: NEG/AUX contraction in British dialects', *English World Wide*, 23, 251–81.

——(2000b) 'Old ways; new ecology: viewing English through the sociolinguistic filter', in S. Poplack (ed.) *The English History of African American English*, Oxford: Blackwell.

——(2005) 'No momentary fancy! The zero complementizer in English dialects', *English Language and Linguistics*, 9, 1–12.

——(2006) 'Layering, competition and a twist of fate: Deontic modality in dialects of English', *Diachronica*, 23, 341–80.

Tagliamonte, S., Smith, J. and Lawrence, H. (2005) 'No taming the vernacular! Insights from the relatives in northern Britain', *Language Variation and Change*, 17, 75–112.

Torgersen, E., Kerswill, P. and Fox, S. (2006) 'Ethnicity as a source of changes in the London vowel system', in F. Hinskens (ed.) *Language Variation – European Perspectives: Selected Papers from the Third International Conference on Language Variation in Europe (ICLaVE3)*, Amsterdam, June 2005, Amsterdam: Benjamins.

Trudgill, P. (1974) *The Social Differentiation of English in Norwich*, Cambridge: Cambridge University Press.

——(ed.) (1978) *Sociolinguistic Patterns in British English*, London: Edward Arnold Ltd.

——(ed.) (1984) *Language in the British Isles*, Cambridge: Cambridge University Press.

——(1986) *Dialects in Contact*, Oxford: Blackwell.

UK Census (2008) Statistical data. Online. Available at: www.statistics.gov.uk/census2001 (accessed 18 March 2008).

Watson, K. (2006) 'Phonological resistance and innovation in the North-West of England', *English Today*, 22, 55–61.

Watt, D. (2002) '"I don't speak with a Geordie accent, I speak, like, the Northern accent": contact-induced levelling in the Tyneside vowel system', *Journal of Sociolinguistics*, 6, 44–63.

Watt D. J. L. and Milroy, L. (1999) 'Patterns of variation and change in three Tyneside vowels: is this dialect levelling?', in P. Foulkes and G. J. Docherty (eds) *Urban Voices,* London: Arnold, pp. 25–46.

Wells, J. C. (1982) *Accents of English*, Cambridge: Cambridge University Press.

Williams, A. and Kerswill, P. (1999) 'Dialect levelling: change and continuity in Milton Keynes Reading and Hull', in P. Foulkes and G. Docherty (eds) *Urban Voices: Accent Studies in the British Isles*, London: Arnold, pp. 141–62.

Williams, A., Kerswill, P. and Cheshire, J. (1998) *The Role of Adolescents in Dialect Levelling*, Final Report on ESRC Grant 000236180.

Williams, G. and Morris, D. (2000) *Language Planning and Language Use: Welsh in a Global Age*, Cardiff: University of Wales Press.

Wright, J. (1892) *A Grammar of the Dialect of Windhill*, London: Paul, Trench, Trübner & Co.

309

27

Sociolinguistics in France

Nadine Di Vito

Introduction

For hundreds of years merely one of many competing language varieties, at the end of the eighteenth century French was spoken by only a third of the population (Chaurand 1999). In the nineteenth century its use spread to the upper classes in northern urban areas, and similar enough to local varieties for those users to be considered French-speaking, it acquired the valuable social perception of being widespread (Lodge 1993). French continued to establish itself throughout rural Gallo-Romance areas and in major cities, first in the upper classes as a vehicle for sociopolitical advancement, and then, with increasing mobility and access to educational institutions, in the middle and lower classes. As the French language was founded in sociocultural and sociolinguistic diversity, so today it remains a vibrant reflection of the multifaceted life of its speakers.

Lexicon

Perhaps the most visible domain of the social life of the French language is its borrowings. It is common knowledge that borrowings are the result of intercultural contact, of which France has been the site of many over the years, from conflictual to collaborative. Gallic terms related to rural life (e.g. 'alouette' – lark) and Frankish military terms (e.g. 'guerre' – war) came into the language in the twelfth century, followed in the thirteenth century (through cultural contact during the Crusades) by Arabic terms in the areas of commercial life and mathematics, such as 'orange' and 'chiffre' (number). Beginning with the first wars with Italy in the late fifteenth century and continuing through the Renaissance period, numerous Italian terms entered the French lexicon (e.g. 'capitaine'), including '–o', '–i', '–on', and '–esse' words (e.g. 'piano', 'spaghetti', 'violon', 'politesse'). Spanish contributed military and literary terms (e.g. 'adjudant'), and German added hundreds of terms related to military life (e.g. 'boulevard' ← 'Bollwerk' – bulwark), commodities (e.g. 'nouilles' – noodles), nature (e.g. 'bois' – wood), wildlife (e.g. 'chouette' – owl), and science (e.g. 'quartz'). By the early nineteenth century, enthusiasm for

310

British commerce, politics, daily life, sports, and industry resulted in borrowings in all those domains (e.g. 'importer', ' budget', 'bifteck', 'football', 'ballast'). Interactions in commercial and maritime affairs added hundreds of terms with Dutch and Flemish origins (e.g. 'boulanger' – baker), and French also embraced terms from languages of central and eastern Europe (e.g. Russian: 'cosaque'; Hungarian: 'sabre'; Czech: 'pistolet'; Polish: 'meringue'; Turkish: 'gilet' – waistcoat) and a handful of words from northern European languages (e.g. Norwegian: 'ski'; Icelandic: 'geyser'; Finnish: 'sauna'; Danish: 'lump' – lumpfish).

In addition to sociocultural influences from outside the mainland, the influence of non-Capetian language varieties within France is noteworthy. A land-based language, French developed a maritime vocabulary with help from Picard (e.g. 'bateau' – boat), Normand (e.g. 'matelot' – sailor), and Provençal (e.g. 'cigale' – swan), from which more than 700 words can be attributed, including many '–ade' words (e.g. 'ballade'). Finally, terms related to specific regions of France were adopted from local language varieties, such as Breton ('dolmen'), Franco-Provençal ('avalanche'), Walloon ('houille' – coal), Alsatian ('quiche'), Béarnais ('béret'), Gascon ('barrique' – barrel), and Cevennes ('airelle' – blueberry). During this same time, a rise in the symbolic value of intellectual pursuits resulted in a new wave of borrowings from Latin and Greek. Often an existing Latin-based term was re-borrowed, resulting in doublets. French has thus been consistently open to lexical enrichment, having taken words from more than 150 languages and dialects (Walter 2000).

Here, then, is the linguistic backdrop against which to interpret the efforts of French institutions to prevent borrowings from English. As noted by Wise (1997), French and English have added to each other's lexicon since the twelfth century, with borrowings into French comparatively modest until the mid-seventeenth century. It is only in the 1930s, however, that French borrowings from English first exceeded its contributions. Spikes of American influence are evident in the overall flow of lexical borrowings, such as the number of cinema-related terms borrowed in the 1920s (e.g. 'spot', 'screengirl') and economics-related terms in the 1960s (e.g. 'businessman', 'marketing'). By then the French government had decided to aggressively promote French and curb English borrowings. Key interventionist efforts, discussed in Judge (1993), can be summarized as follows:

1966   de Gaulle establishes the Haut Comité de défense et d'expansion de la langue française, whose goal, like that of the Académie française, is to establish the terminological purity of French.

1971   The Banque des Mots, a review published by the Conseil international de la langue française, is inaugurated to disseminate research and recommendations regarding technical and scientific terminology.

1975   (May) The Association française de terminologie (AFTERM), replaced eventually by FRANTERM (Recherche et application de terminologie française), is created to help administrative and commercial enterprises work together on terminological issues.

1975   (December) The Bas-Lauriol law is enacted to enforce government decrees regarding terminology. French is compulsory in all government, commercial, and educational spheres. Use of a non-French word when a French equivalent exists can result in fines.

1983   The Minister of Communication publishes a list of approximately 100 terms to replace Anglo-Saxon terms in advertising and technology.

1984   The Haut Comité is replaced by two groups: (1) Comité consultatif de la langue française, a group advising the prime minister on language matters that produces a

311

circular on approved feminization of profession names (1986); and (2) Commissariat général de la langue française, whose goal is to protect French from outside linguistic influence and to oversee the development of specialized lexicons and neologisms. The first *Dictionnaire des néologismes officiels* is published by FRANTERM.

1986 All government ministries (approximately 20) have their own commissions responsible for controlling domain-specific terminology.

1987 A technology decree is issued whose terminological position must be followed in all government-sponsored publications.

1988 Commissions ministérielles de terminologie (CMT) have by now issued approximately 30 decrees regulating terminology in numerous domains (e.g. tourism, sports, geographical names, telecommunications).

1989 The two 1984 groups are replaced by groups with a more directive quality: (1) Délégation générale à la langue française, created to actively promote the French language; and (2) Conseil supérieur de la langue française, with permanent representation by the Académie française, charged with designating 'le bon usage'. The promotion of regional languages is no longer explicitly indicated.

1994 The Loi Toubon (Toubon Act) is enacted, requiring French in all commercial materials.

Given these numerous efforts to stem the influence of English on French, one might assume that English words represent a significant percentage of the French lexicon. However, examination of the 650 words considered core French vocabulary shows them all to be French-based (Rolland and Laffitte 1995). Why, therefore, such a frenzy to stem recent borrowings from English? Perhaps, as suggested by Noreiko (1993), the issue is primarily one of control. In the past, the court and then the intellectual elite controlled French language use. Now, however, despite online access to officially sponsored words in the FRANTERM and La Banque des mots databases and the use of academic, professional, and legal sanctions as leverage, institutional control over French lexical norms is questionable.

Despite some victories (e.g. 'ordinateur' over 'computer'), French efforts to replace Anglo-Saxon words with French-based terms have been impeded at times by the semantic opacity of the recommended form (e.g. 'sonal' to replace 'jingle'), the widespread distribution of trademarks (e.g. 'Walkman' over 'baladeur'), and the relative user-friendliness of English-based technology. In some cases, the derivational success of English-based suffixes is dependent on disparate processes. The '–ing' suffix, used in the sixteenth century with currency (Walter 1983), gained productivity more recently (with 150 new words) with the brevity and semantic clarity of English '–ing' words over French-based equivalents (e.g. 'le casting' over 'la distribution artistique'). This expansion spread to place names, sometimes resulting in semantic meanings unfamiliar to an Anglophone (e.g. 'un bowling' – bowling or a bowling alley, 'un pressing' – steam pressing or a dry cleaner, 'le zapping' – channel surfing). Some French '–ing' neologisms are merely English-sounding (e.g. 'un lifting' – a face-lift, 'un smoking' – a tuxedo, 'un brushing' – a blow-dry). There are, however, also productive French-based suffixes. One successful French-based neologism was 'logiciel' (software), using the semantic base '–iel' from 'matériel', and expanding to 'logiciel intégré' (integrated software) and 'logiciel de navigation' (browser), with the suffix spreading with varying success to technical words (e.g. 'progiciel' – software package, 'didacticiel' – educational software, 'ludiciel' – video game). The French-based 'informatique' has won over 'computer science', with the '–tique' suffix indicating system computerization (e.g. 'documentique'). Other productive suffixes include

'–thèque' (e.g. 'vidéothèque' – video library) and '–man', evoking an Anglo-Saxon feel (e.g. 'tennisman' – tennis player).

Certain lexical and morphological borrowings are more prevalent in particular sectors. Borrowings from English are especially widespread in youth-centred domains such as music (e.g. 'hip hop'), fashion (e.g. 'baskets' – sneakers), and drugs (e.g. 'shit' – hashish) (George 1993). Also found are pseudo-English words (e.g. 'off' – off the record), words with new semantic meanings (e.g. 'golden boy' – financially successful), and English-based words with French morphology (e.g. 'jamer' – to jam, 'scoopant' – newsworthy, 'punkette' – female punk) or in French-based syntactic expressions (e.g. 'faire son coming out' – come out, 'un reporting hebdomadaire' – weekly report). The use of verlan (reversing the order of phonemes or syllables) among French youth has been studied extensively, especially since its rise as an identity marker for Parisian youth in the 1970s (Lefkowitz 1991). Among suffixes marking contemporary youth discourse are '–os' (e.g. 'tristos' – sad) and '–oche' (e.g. 'sac en plastoche' – plastic bag). Other characteristics of youth discourse include:

1   word reductions through apocope (e.g. 'petit-déj' ← 'petit-déjeuner' – breakfast), especially in academia (e.g. 'ordi' ← 'ordinateur' – computer);
2   hyperbole (e.g. 'hypersensass' – really sensational);
3   litotes (e.g. 'pas triste' – not sad = fun);
4   acronyms and initialisms, also markers of identity in academic circles (e.g. 'CAPES' /kapɛs/ – Certificat d'aptitude au professorat de l'enseignement du second degré).

Recent borrowings from English are typically pronounced, regardless of one's social status, with the English phoneme as opposed to the French phoneme of earlier borrowings, such as the /ʒ/ of 'jockey' but the /ʤ/ of the more recent borrowing 'job', and the French nasal vowel of 'punch' /pɔ̃ʃ/ meaning 'fruit drink' compared with the English-sounding vowel and nasal consonant of 'punch' /pœnʃ/ re-borrowed as a boxing term (Wise 1997).

Lexical variants in French urban speech are more likely to be associated with different registers and stylistic choices while dialectal forms in northern rural France have become socioeconomic markers (Armstrong and Boughton 1998; Armstrong 2001; Armstrong and Blanchet 2006). In southern France, regional variants remain markers of sociocultural identity, even if they also symbolize a more rural, traditional lifestyle and lower socio-economic status and, as such, are sources of linguistic insecurity and shame (Blanchet 1997). The 1999 census indicated a general population shift of urban French speakers to rural areas, which will likely stimulate further decline of local dialectal forms.

Gender

Although gender marking in French may, in fact, correspond to biological gender, there are many instances where it does not (e.g. 'un éléphant femelle' – a female elephant, 'une souris mâle' – a male mouse). Some words in French have no feminine form (e.g. 'un gourmet'), some have no masculine form (e.g. 'une victime'), and others have gained or lost one or the other gender marking over the years (e.g. 'papesse' [f.] – female pope, existed in the fifteenth century even in the absence of the reality) (Trudeau 1988). Trudeau traces the sociohistorical evolution of French gender marking for professions, noting that for centuries it was possible to mark profession names for both female and male gender even if women were not actively engaged in those professions (e.g. 'jugesse' [f.] – female judge). During the Renaissance and Classical periods, the feminization of profession names flourished (e.g. 'sacristaine' [f.] – female sacristan). As gender-based job specialization developed, certain gender markings died out or gained the meaning 'wife of' (e.g. 'ambassadrice' [f.] – wife of the ambassador). This practice extended to the adjectivization of proper nouns, as in Zola's mention of 'la Maheude' (the wife of Maheu). As more women entered historically male professions in the early twentieth century, feminine gender marking proliferated (e.g. 'avocate' [f.] – female lawyer, 'artisane' [f.] – craftswoman, 'pharmacienne' [f.] – female pharmacist). With the first wave of feminism in France (1920–60), however, came the notion that the male form was more progressive. Feminists challenged the traditional notion of 'femininity' in rejecting terms such as 'poétesse' [f.] (female poet) and 'docteresse' [f.] (female doctor). Public controversy over gender assignment rules continued, with feminist opinion swinging back toward feminine marking. With the passage of the equal rights law in 1983 came a renewed consciousness of the relationship between gender marking and social perception. Yvette Roudy, Ministre des Droits de la Femme (Minister of Women's Rights), argued that women were impeded from accessing positions where only masculine marking existed (e.g. 'un ingénieur' [m.] – an engineer [m./f.]) and spearheaded efforts to eliminate gender-based inequalities. The Roudy Commission, comprising representatives of various governmental ministries, sociologists, linguists, and a representative from the Académie française, conducted public opinion surveys which showed resistance to feminization especially noteworthy in professions that had excluded women until recently (e.g. medicine, law, military, business). The commission rejected gender marking by use of 'femme' + noun (e.g. 'femme médecin' – woman doctor), Madame le + noun (e.g. 'Madame le professeur' [m.] – Madam Professor, or the '–esse'/'–oresse' suffix (ambiguous because of its possible meaning 'wife of'), recommending instead the use of minimal phonetic and morphological mechanisms already productive in the French language:

1 –ier → –ière   (pompière [f.] – female firefighter);
2 –ien → –ienne   (chirurgienne [f.] – female surgeon);
3 –eur → –euse   (chercheuse [f.] – female researcher);
4 final consonant → –e (sculpteure [f.] – female sculptor).

Despite the critical response to these recommendations by the Académie française (claiming that such changes contradicted the tradition of 'le bon usage'), the parliament, and even the media, the official resurgence of feminization of profession names was launched, with some terms (e.g. institutrice [f.] – female elementary school teacher) meeting with greater acceptance than others (e.g. auteure [f.] – female author) (Gervais 1993). French women intellectuals and politicians have also promoted feminization of the French language, with early feminist writers rejecting traditional syntax as being repressive (Leclerc 1974; Cardinal 1975; Aebischer 1983) and some even advocating the creation of a 'parler femme' (women's discourse). Others have experimented with unconventional discursive forms, such as Monique Wittig in her use of 'on' (one) instead of 'il' (he) in *L'Opoponax* (1964) and 'elles' (they [f.] plural) instead of 'il' (he) as the narrator in *Les Guérillères* (1969). In 1997, female ministers of Jospin's cabinet refused to be called 'Madame le ministre' (Madam Minister [m.]), resulting in a joint meeting of the more conservative COGETER (commission générale de terminologie et de néologie – General commission of terminology and neologism) and the more progressive INALF (Institut national de la langue française – National Institute of the French Language). The

INALF sponsored an official feminization guide in 1999. Not all women professionals have supported feminization efforts, however, with some objecting to the potential ambiguity of certain feminine markers (e.g. 'rédactrice' – either a woman editor or the editor of a women's magazine) and others arguing that some profession names are nouns and not adjectives (Fleischman 1997; Gervais-le Garff 2002).

Grammar

'Ne' deletion

In negative constructions, French speakers, regardless of social class, delete 'ne' more than 75 per cent of the time (Gadet 1989). Deletion increases when the speech is fast, speaker engagement is high, and formality low. Younger speakers delete 'ne' significantly more than older speakers. Even highly educated speakers delete 'ne' (Gadet 1989; Di Vito 1997), although some research shows greater 'ne' retention by women and when the clause is emphatic (Malécot 1972). 'Ne' may also be retained to repair miscomprehension (Coveney 1996) or to provide a solemn, compassionate nuance to the discourse (Armstrong 2001). Blanche-Benveniste (1997) notes that age-correlated 'ne' deletion dates from at least the seventeenth century; this has led Blanche-Benveniste and Jeanjean (1987) and Coveney (1991) to suggest that 'ne' deletion is not a change in progress but rather an age-graded phenomenon, with increased 'ne' use cultivated in educational settings. Another possibility is that the factors promoting 'ne' retention (e.g. formal relationship between the participants, social contexts where speech is monitored) are more common after adolescence.

Interrogative syntax

Most studies of French interrogatives have focused on informal spoken discourse, with notable exceptions being Behnstedt's (1973) study of middle-class formal interrogatives and Di Vito's (1997) analysis of educated native speaker spoken and written interrogatives. In all spoken corpora, regardless of socioeconomic status or discourse formality, the preferred syntax is Subject–Verb. Nevertheless, the more spontaneous and casual the context, the more likely speakers will use Subject–Verb syntax, with a higher probability of Subject–Verb syntax in conversational speech than in news broadcasts (Di Vito 1997). Certain Verb–Subject expressions (e.g. 'Qu'y a-t-il?' – What's the matter?) mark a higher socioeconomic class and more formal speech (Armstrong 2001). The 'est-ce que' Subject–Verb construction is frequently used in the construction 'qu'est-ce que', in less interactive contexts (e.g. news broadcasts and conference speech), and in rhetorical or lengthy questions (Di Vito 1997; Coveney 2000), possibly as an overt interrogative cue (Maury 1973). The evolution towards Subject–Verb syntax can be seen in written French interrogatives in both literary and nonliterary genres, with narrative prose at the forefront of this change (Di Vito 1997). However, 'est-ce que' is rare in all written corpora, reinforcing the idea that its functions are linked to the constraints of real-time speech events and speaker-listener needs.

'Que'

The widespread use of 'que' as an all-purpose relative, infringing most notably on the domains of 'dont', has been noted since the beginning of the twentieth century. Some researchers have suggested that unconventional 'que' use carries negative social judgement and functions to stereotype working-class speakers (Deulofeu 1981; Gadet 1989). However, such use of 'que' and hypercorrect use of 'dont' in formal contexts are also widespread among the intellectual elite (Gadet 1989), and conventional use of 'dont' and the 'lequel' relative series is declining in both educated spoken and written French (Di Vito 1997). While Gadet argues that unconventional 'que' use can provide semantic nuances that standard relatives cannot, she also notes that their social import depends at least in part on the perceived social status of the speaker, with unconventional 'que' excused as a lapsus more often when used by academics than by other categories of speakers.

Other unconventional structures

Other unconventional French structures, outlined in Blanche-Benveniste (1997), include:

1 use of 'on' instead of 'nous' by both working-class (Boutet 1986) and highly educated speakers (Di Vito 1997), with a higher frequency among younger speakers (Ashby 1992);
2 lack of past participle agreement in the passé composé with 'avoir', even by educated speakers (Audibert-Gibier 1992);
3 left dislocation correlated with pronoun–verb combinations (e.g. 'Moi, je pense' – Me, I think), discourse emphasis, and other presentative structures ('C'est X qui … ' – It's X who …) (Blasco-Dulbecco 2004; Cappeau 2004; Di Vito 1997);
4 'qu'est-ce que' instead of 'ce que' even among educated speakers;
5 hanging prepositions (Durand 1993; Roberge and Vinet 1989);
6 article + Noun + Que instead of Quel + Noun in indirect questions;
7 'c'est' instead of 'ce sont' to refer to plural nouns;
8 'Pour pas que' instead of 'pour que … ne … pas'.

Unconventional elements with negative social value include the use of the indicative in obligatory subjunctive contexts, the use of 'avoir' in the passé composé with 'être' verbs, and the use of 'au' instead of 'chez' in expressions such as 'aller au docteur' (Gadet 1989). However, use of the passé simple, at one time associated with meridional speech, is now more a stylistic feature of academic or solemn discourse concomitant with the use of particular lexical items (e.g. 'lorsque' – when) (Blanche-Benveniste 1997).

Regionalisms

Perhaps one of the most salient syntactic features of meridional speech, geographically charted by Walter (1988), is use of the surcomposed past (e.g. Gea 1995). Other salient characteristics of meridional speech, discussed by Blanche-Benveniste (1997), include the use of:

1 'beaucoup' (much, many), 'tant' (so much), and 'autant' (so many) with adjectives;
2 quantifiers with 'du', 'des', 'de la' instead of 'de';
3 the pluperfect in principal clauses;
4 'comme' (as, like) instead of 'comment' (how);
5 adverbs before present participles;
6 both negative particles before present participles and other unconventional or archaic negative structures (e.g. 'pas rien', 'point').

Discourse studies

Other recent discourse studies include a corpus-based examination of discourse markers (e.g. Chanet 2004), an analysis of the contextual meanings of phonetic strings (Wioland 2005), a study of adverb use to signal turn-taking (Bilger 2004) and of personal pronoun use in French political speeches (Gaffney 1993), and a cross-cultural discussion of French conversational norms (Kerbrat-Orrechioni 1994). Recent speech act research has examined French norms for making requests (Kerbrat-Orrechioni 1994; Izaki 2000) and giving thanks (Held 1989), giving and responding to compliments (Kerbrat-Orrechioni 1994; Wieland 1995; Traverso 1996), and complaining (Kraft and Geluykens 2002).

'Tu/Vous'

In addition to regional variation, factors relevant to 'tu'/'vous' use include the age and relationship of the participants, the type of interaction, and the formality of the situation (Béal 1989; Kerbrat-Orrechioni 1992). Current usage norms, summarized in Clyne *et al.* (2003), indicate that symmetry ('tu'–'tu' or 'vous'–'vous') is still preferred and has been shown to be indexed both to the interlocutors and to the setting (Morford 1997). For example, people who have a 'tu' relationship may address each other using 'vous' in a meeting. In general, 'tu' is still the norm with close family and friends, regardless of age (Hughson 2001; Coffen 2002), and is commonly used between people with the same social status who have known each other for a long time, even in the workplace, suggesting a general trend towards more informal speech norms (Coffen 2002).

Pronunciation

Variationist studies have challenged long-standing beliefs regarding French pronunciation, from Martinet's (1945) analysis of the speech of 409 military officers, which shattered the myth of a single norm and showed that Parisian speech was a melting pot of regional variants, to Walter's (1982) regionally diverse sociolinguistic analysis of native speech through which she identified 34 phonologically distinct regions. In these and other studies, Parisian speech is at the crossroads of patterned variation and change, a battlefield between tradition and innovation.

Vowels

Deletion of schwa (/ə/)

While the maintenance and even the insertion of schwa have become emblematic of southern French speech, its deletion in non-meridional France dates from as early as the fourteenth century (Bourciez 1967), was widespread in both medial ('batt(e)rie' – drum) and word-final ('une seul(e)' – a single) position by the nineteenth century, and appears on its way to categorical deletion in word-final position (Walter 1982, 1990). Although education, social class, and character traits appear insignificant to schwa deletion, frequently occurring lexical items and idiomatic chunks increase the probability of deletion (e.g. 's(e)maine' – week), with men favouring deletion more than women, and younger speakers more than older speakers. There is, nevertheless, increased probability of schwa retention in initial syllables receiving emphatic stress and in formal contexts favouring monitored speech (Léon and Tennant 1990).

Mid-vowel contrasts

Studies have found considerable variation and reductions in mid-vowel contrasts (Martinet 1990; Armstrong and Unsworth 1999). In fact, some researchers maintain that all mid-vowels (/e/, /ɛ/, /o/, /ɔ/, /ə/, /œ/, /ø/) can be neutralized (/E/, /OE/, /O/) in unaccented position (Armstrong 2001; Wioland 2005), with working- and middle-class Parisian speech reduced to only three mid-vowels (Landick 1995).

/u/ or /o/?   'chouse' or 'chose'

Exposure to rural speech added an /u/ (e.g. 'chouse' – thing) variant to the pronunciation of 'o' /o/ (e.g. 'chose') in Parisian speech, which became firmly associated with lower-class speech by the sixteenth century (Blanche-Benveniste and Jeanjean 1987). The /u/ variant in these contexts has henceforth become associated with rurality and illiteracy (Ayres-Bennett 1990).

/u/ or /y/?   'soumettre' or 'sumettre'

Here, as well, the /u/ pronunciation of the popular classes prevailed for some words (e.g. 'soumettre' – submit) while the academic value of the /y/ pronunciation claimed others (e.g. 'suffire' – to suffice) (Pasques and Baddeley 1989).

/y/ or /œ/?   'abruver' or 'abreuver'

During the seventeenth century, the regional variant /y/ (e.g. 'abruver' – to water) competed with the Parisian variant /œ/ ('abreuver'), with the regional form again associated with the popular classes (Pasques and Baddeley 1989). The Parisian variant won this battle, even sometimes with words whose etymology should have given /y/ ('augurium' → heureux /œrœ/ – happy), with the /y/ variant becoming a marker of rural speech (Ayres-Bennett 1990).

/ɑ/ and /a/

While a difference in vowel length in certain words containing (a) and (â) (e.g. 'tache' /a/ – stain, and 'tâche' /a:/ – task) has been a feature of northern provincial speech since the eighteenth century (Léon 1971), vowel backing (/a/ – /ɑ/) replaced vowel length in Parisian speech in the early twentieth century (Martinet 1990). By the end of World War II, this distinction had become associated with the bourgeois speech of the sixteenth arrondissement of Paris, with the back variant /ɑ/ now associated with highly monitored speech.

Nasal vowels

Although the maintenance of four, five, and even six nasal vowels can still be heard in some regions of France, the merger of (in) /ɛ̃/ and (un) /œ̃/, which began in Paris and has spread outward toward the east (Champagne) and to the west (Maine-Orléans), is largely complete in Parisian speech (Walter 1982). There is also indication that /ã/ is assimilating to /ɔ̃/, despite the potential for communicative misunderstandings (Hansen 1998). In addition to nasal vowel mergers, diphthongized and denasalized vowels are characteristic of rural, meridional speech communities (Léon 1993; Armstrong 2001).

Consonants

From palatalized /l/ to yod

By the seventeenth century and despite strong opposition by grammarians, the evolution from /ʎ/ to /l/ to /j/ (e.g. 'fiye' = 'fille' – girl) was fairly complete in Parisian French and widespread in popular writings (Chaurand 1989). Settling on an orthographic convention for the depalatalized 'l' was a battle among numerous notations, however, including 'lh' (Peletier du Mans 1550) and 'l' with a hook (Meigret 1542). Meigret's recommendation proved too costly to print, and Peletier's recommendation was used mostly in rural areas where printers were less accessible. The forms 'il' and 'ill' better represented variations in pronunciation and were the general practice in bigger towns where printers allowed for a wider distribution, facilitating their establishment as a general orthographic norm (Baddeley 1989).

/ŋ/, /ɲ/, and /nj/

Many descriptivists now consider /ŋ/ to be a standard feature of French rather than a phonological borrowing. The combination /n+j/ is increasingly replacing /ɲ/, even in the speech of young children (e.g. 'gagne' /ganj/ – win) (Martinet 1990).

'i(l)' (he, it) and 'e(lle)' (she)

The deletion of /l/ in pronouns is significant for both men and women across all social classes (Ashby 1991). The probability of /l/ deletion increases when:

1   The pronoun is impersonal ('i(l) faut' – it is necessary).
2   The pronoun is part of a common collocation ('i(l) y a' – there is/are).
3   The speaker is male (although the importance of gender decreases with age).
4   The speaker is under 30 years old.

(r)

The pronunciation of (r) in French has marked social identity since at least the sixteenth century, with particular realizations symbolic of popular speech and others reflecting aristocratic pronunciation (Catach 1989). Although seventeenth-century grammarians encouraged voicing final (r), especially in formal contexts (e.g. poetry reading), the unvoiced final (r) of popular speech was adopted for some words and the voiced final (r) promoted by grammarians for others (Ayres-Bennett 1990). Another feature of popular speech was the substitution of intervocalic (r) with (z) (e.g. 'Pazis' instead of 'Paris'). Seventeenth-century grammarians successfully battled against this practice in Paris, although it has remained a regional feature. The current pronunciation standard is the voiced uvular fricative /ʁ/, a change from the trilled /r/ initiated by seventeenth-century aristocracy (Pasques and Baddeley 1989), with the uvular trill /ʀ/ reflective of formal or emphatic speech and the trilled /r/ considered provincial or old-fashioned (Ager 1990).

The deletion of postconsonantal (r) (e.g. 'gen(re)') is attested as early as the fifteenth century (Wüest 1985). With the frequent loss of word-final mute (e), words such as 'capre' (caper) were reduced often enough to create doublets ('cape' – cloak) (Ayres-Bennett 1990). Such reductions became characterized as popular Parisian speech, and are associated in some communities with a more problematic socioeconomic path (e.g. lower education level, lower job status, higher criminal profile) (Laks 1983). Nevertheless, age, gender, linguistic context, lexical frequency, speech rate, and situational formality have a stronger effect on postconsonantal (r) and (l) deletion than social class, education, or character (Ayres-Bennett 1990; Armstrong 2001).

Liaison

Studies of liaison (i.e. the pronunciation of typically silent word-final consonants across larger discourse units) have covered a wide range of socioeconomic profiles, geographical areas, time periods, and contexts. Collectively, these studies point to a steady decrease in liaison even as its association with formal speech contexts continues to be strong. Most studies confirm the maintenance of obligatory liaison, although Green and Hintze (1990) suggest that the number of obligatory liaison contexts is shrinking.

The importance of sociolinguistic and stylistic factors is most evident in optional liaison contexts. Younger speakers (male and female) make fewer liaisons than older ones (Léon and Tennant 1990). All speakers make fewer liaisons in casual contexts than in formal contexts. Lower-class adolescent Parisians make virtually no optional liaisons (Laks 1983) and upper-middle-class 20- to 29-year-old Parisians, the age group for whom joining mainstream society is most professionally relevant, make more liaisons than older Parisians (Malécot 1975). While older, middle-class women tend to be more conservative, highly educated women are surprisingly perceived more positively when they make fewer liaisons while highly educated men are perceived more positively when they make more liaisons, pointing to different linguistic criteria by which men and women are socially judged (Léon and Tennant 1990).

Trends in pronunciation

According to Lodge (1993), increasing mobility, universal conscription, a tightly controlled national education system, centralized access to many domains of professional advancement, and relatively recent urbanization and industrialization are factors conducive to pronunciation levelling in northern France. Many researchers agree that dialect features are becoming less marked, and Hawkins (1993) has posited that it is impossible to tell the origin of a standard speaker of French with a standard accent. The dialect levelling hypothesis was tested by Armstrong (2001), who examined French speakers' ability to distinguish the social and regional features of the discourse of speakers in two comparable northern French cities (Rennes and Nancy), distinctly different from each other in terms of regional characteristics. Overall, informants showed some ability to identify the speakers' social class, with working-class men perceived as having the most salient accent and middle-class women perceived as having the least noticeable accent. Perceived accents, however, were associated more with rurality in general than with any particular region, leading Armstrong to claim (following the model proposed by Labov 1972) that recent expansion of Parisian French and the need for mutual accommodations had provoked dialect levelling, with regional traits associated more with class and rurality than with geography.

Northern (Oïl) and Southern (Oc) French varieties

The sociolinguistic situation of regional varieties of French is examined by Blanchet and Armstrong (2006), who suggest that dialectal forms in northern France have become primarily social markers while those in southern France are perceived as markers of regional identity. Alongside northern French varieties associated with entire regions (e.g. Picard, Normand) are ones linked more closely with specific cities (e.g. Poitevin, spoken in Poitiers). The many supra-regional and local speech forms have given rise to numerous studies and publications, among them a series of regional dictionaries, numbering more than 30 to date. Some varieties show evidence of vitality, with newly-arrived immigrant youths acquiring Picard (Eloy 2003) and the dialectal French spoken in Lille and Vannes (Blanchet 2001). There are, however, numerous indicators that local dialects are on the decline, such as the decreased use of vowel duration among university students in Normandy (Lepelley 1996) and decreased code-switching among the younger population (Auzanneau 1998). While new morphological and syntactic dialectal structures can be found in local varieties of French in Picardy (Carton 1998), highly-marked dialectal traits are consistently correlated with lower-class, old-fashioned speech (Blanchet 1997) and, as such, are subject to a greater decline than socially unmarked dialectal forms (Blanchet and Walter 1999).

Occitan

Occitan refers to the group of speech varieties spoken in Provençal France, originating with the language of the twelfth-century troubadours and later encompassing numerous dialects. With Occitan's rich literary tradition and sociocultural history, its vitality is evident even in its lexical productivity (e.g. 'Occitanique', 'Occitaniste', 'Occitanisme'). French was not widespread in urban Occitan areas until the nineteenth century and in some rural areas until the early twentieth century. Even with the arrival of French, the maintenance of Occitan dialects has been helped by a substantial educational infrastructure, extensive radio and television programming easily accessible through the internet (www. oc-tv.net), and initiatives of the Félibrige and the Institut d'études occitanes (IEO), both promoting Occitan language, literature, and culture. Even so, establishing a common standard Occitan norm has been difficult (Gasquet-Cyrus 2004), with some speech communities rejecting the Occitan appelation (Soupel 2004). Signs of dialect decline can be seen in the decrease in speakers from 10 million in 1920 to 2 million in 1999 (Sibille 2005) and the association of Occitan with lack of education, old age, and the rural world (Maurand 1981).

Breton

While 31 per cent of all Bretons in a 1997 survey claimed to understand Breton and 20 per cent to speak it well or very well, two-thirds of those respondents were over 60 years old (Broudic 2003), with the younger generation speaking Breton less frequently, whether at home or at work. Even if nearly 90 per cent of all Bretons support the preservation of Breton as a regional language, its social and functional decline portends its eventual linguistic demise.

Alsatian

Consistently spoken by 85 per cent of the population until the 1960s, by 1990 Alsatian had decreased in number of speakers by 25 per cent (Bothorel–Witz and Huck 2003), with a steeper decline among 25- to 34-year-olds (Veltman 1982). Social contexts favouring use of Alsatian have steadily decreased, with its primary sphere limited to family life. Only 19 per cent of 18- to 24-year-old speakers of Alsatian intend to teach it to their children, giving as reasons functional impracticality and their own linguistic insecurity (Bothorel–Witz and Huck 2003).

Basque

The social life of north Basque (in France) has been tied to that of south Basque (in Spain), despite their different sociocultural origins and linguistic particularities. With the promotion of south Basque to the status of an official language in 1980 came a revival of interest in north Basque, which benefited from the development of Basque media, technological resources, and a significant educational infrastructure. According to a 1996 sociolinguistic survey reported by Oyharçabal (2003), about one-quarter of the population in the French Basque region are fluent Basque speakers, of which 85 per cent were taught Basque by their parents as a native language. Although the functional usefulness of north Basque for everyday life has decreased, there is evidence of linguistic and sociocultural vitality, seen in a rise in popularity of Basque rock music and poetry, and in the possibility of specializing in Basque studies up through the doctoral level.

Conclusion

Patterned variation within and across numerous domains of the French language in time and space, together with increased geographical and social mobility, indicates noteworthy sociolinguistic trends. As French continues to expand linguistically and spatially, employing old and new mechanisms to assimilate borrowings and spreading steadily to more rural areas, dialectal traits are becoming less socially marked and regional languages less functionally relevant. And as public domains of informal French language use continue to spread, we can anticipate the progressive weakening of linguistically-marked class distinctions to give rise to an increasing importance of stylistic indicators as well as new domains of sociolinguistic differentiation.

References

Aebischer, V. (1983) 'Bavardages: sens commun et linguistiques', in V. Aebischer and C. Forel (eds) *Parlers masculins, parlers féminins?* Paris: Delachaux et Niestlé, pp. 173–88.
Ager, D. (1990) *Sociolinguistics and Contemporary French*, Cambridge: Cambridge University Press.

Armstrong, N. (2001) *Social and Stylistic Variation in Spoken French: A Comparative Approach*, Philadelphia, PA: John Benjamins.

Armstrong, N. and Blanchet, P. (2006) 'The dynamics of levelling and diversity in French', *Journal of French Language Studies*, 16, 247–50.

Armstrong, N. and Boughton, Z. (1998) 'Identification and evaluation responses to a French accent: some results and issues of methodology', *Revue Parole*, 5, 27–60.

Armstrong, N. and Unsworth, S. (1999) 'Sociolinguistic variation in southern French schwa', *Linguistics*, 37, 127–56.

Ashby, W. (1991) 'When does variation indicate linguistic change in progress?', *Journal of French Language Studies*, 1, 119–37.

——(1992) 'The variable use of on versus tu/vous for indefinite reference in spoken French', *Journal of French Language Studies*, 2, 135–57.

Audibert-Gibier, M. (1992) 'Etude de l'accord du participe passé sur des corpus de français parlé', *Langage et société*, 61, 8–27.

Auzanneau, M. (1998) *La parole vive du Poitou. Une étude sociolinguistique en milieu rural*, Paris: L'Harmattan.

Ayres-Bennett, W. (1990) 'Variation and change in the pronunciation of French in the seventeenth century', in J. N. Green and W. Ayres-Bennett (eds) *Variation and Change in French*, New York: Routledge, pp. 151–79.

Baddeley, S. (1989) 'Le traitement de *L* mouillé au XVI siècle', in W. Ayres-Bennett (ed.) *La variation dans la langue en France du XVIe au XIXe siècle*, Paris: CNRS, pp. 105–21.

Béal, C. (1989) '"On se tutoie": second person pronominal usage and terms of address in contemporary French', *Australian Review of Applied Linguistics*, 12, 61–82.

Behnstedt, P. (1973) *Viens-tu, est-ce que tu viens? Formen und Strukturen des direkten Fragessatzes im Französischen*, Tübingen: Narr.

Bilger, M. (2004) 'Quelques données sur les adverbes en *ment* dans le corpus de référence de français parlé', *Recherches sur le français parlé*, 18, 63–81.

Blanche-Benveniste, C. (1997) *Approches de la langue parlée en français*, Paris: Ophrys.

Blanche-Benveniste, C. and Jeanjean, C. (1987) *Le français parlé: transcription et édition*, Paris: Didier Erudition.

Blanchet, B. (1997) 'Pratiques linguistiques et sentiments d'appartenance dans le pays de Retz (Loire-Atlantique). Résultats d'enquêtes', in F. Manzano (ed.) *Vitalité des parlers de l'Ouest et du Canada francophone*, Rennes: Presses Universitaires de Rennes, pp. 15–45.

——(2001) 'Enquêtes sur les évolutions générationnelles du français dans le pays vannetais (Bretagne)', *Le français moderne*, 69, 58–76.

Blanchet, B. and Armstrong, N. (2006) 'The sociolinguistic situation of contemporary dialects of French in France today: an overview of recent contributions on the dialectalisation of standard French', *French Language Studies*, 16, 251–75.

Blanchet, B. and Walter, H. (1999) *Dictionnaire du français régional de Haute-Bretagne*, Paris: Bonneton.

Blasco-Dulbecco, M. (2004) 'Quelques éclairages sur le sujet de type *moi je* à l'oral', *Recherches sur le français parlé*, 18, 127–44.

Bothorel-Witz, A. and Huck, D. (2003) 'Alsace et Moselle', in B. Cerquiglini (ed.) *Les langues de France*, Paris: Presses Universitaires de France, pp. 23–45.

Bourciez, E. J. (1967) *Phonétique française*, Paris: Klincksieck.

Boutet, J. (1986) 'La référence à la personne en français parlé: le cas de *on*', *Langage et société*, 38, 19–50.

Broudic, F. (2003) 'Le breton', in B. Cerquiglini (ed.) *Les langues de France*, Paris: Presses Universitaires de France, pp. 69–78.

Cappeau, P. (2004) 'Les formes disjointes des pronoms sujets', *Recherches sur le français parlé*, 18, 107–25.

Cardinal, M. (1975) *Les mots pour le dire*, Paris: B. Grasset.

Carton, F. (1998) 'Evaluation de la vitalité du français régional par tranches d'âge (domaine picard)', in J.-M. Eloy (ed.) *Evaluer la vitalité des variétés d'oïl et autres langues*, Amiens: Centre d'Etudes Picardes de l'Université d'Amiens, pp. 141–58.

Catach, N. (1989) 'La variation dans la langue en France du XVIe au XIXe siècle', in W. Ayres-Bennett (ed.) *La variation dans la langue en France du XVIe au XIXe siècle*, Paris: CNRS, pp. 45–59.

Chanet, C. (2004) 'Fréquence des marqueurs discursifs en français parlé: quelques problèmes de méthodologie', *Recherches sur le français parlé*, 18, 83–106.

Chaurand, J. (1989) '*L* mouillé: Quelques aspects des variantes graphiques médiévales et régionales', in W. Ayres-Bennett (ed.) *La variation dans la langue en France du XVIe au XIXe siècle*, Paris: CNRS, pp. 87–103.

——(ed.) (1999) *Nouvelle histoire de la langue française*, Paris: Seuil.

Clyne, M., Kretzenbacher, H., Catrin, N. and Warren, J. (2003) 'Address in some Western European languages', *Proceedings of the 2003 Conference of the Australian Linguistic Society*, 1–10.

Coffen, B. (2002) *Histoire culturelle des pronoms d'adresse. Vers une typologie des systèmes allocutoires dans les langues romanes*, Paris: Honoré Champion.

Coveney, A. B. (1991) 'Contemporary variation in the omission of *ne*', paper presented at a Workshop on Historical Linguistics, University of Oxford.

——(1996) *Variability in Spoken French: A Sociolinguistic Study of Interrogation and Negation*, Exeter: Elm Bank.

——(2000) 'Variation in interrogatives in spoken French: a preliminary report', in J. N. Green and W. Ayres-Bennett (eds) *Variation and Change in French*, New York: Routledge, pp. 116–33.

Deulofeu, J. (1981) 'Perspective linguistique et sociolinguistique dans l'étude des relatives en français', *Recherches sur le français parlé*, 3, 135–93.

Di Vito, N. O. (1997) *Patterns Across Spoken and Written French: Empirical Research on the Interaction among Forms, Functions, and Genres*, New York: Houghton Mifflin.

Durand, J. (1993) 'Sociolinguistic variation and the linguist', in C. Sanders (ed.) *French Today: Language in Its Social Context*, Cambridge: Cambridge University Press, pp. 257–85.

Eloy, J.-M. (2003) 'Immigrations et langue régionale: les acteurs du contact des langues', in J. Billiez and M. Rispail (eds) *Contacts de langues*, Paris: L'Harmattan, pp. 111–26.

Fleischman, S. (1997) 'The battle of feminism and bon usage: instituting nonsexist usage in French', *The French Review*, 70, 834–44.

Gadet, F. (1989) *Le français ordinaire*, Paris: Armand Colin.

Gaffney, J. (1993) 'Language and style in politics', in C. Sanders (ed.) *French Today: Language in its Social Context*, Cambridge: Cambridge University Press, pp. 185–98.

Gasquet-Cyrus, M. (2004) 'The sociolinguistics of Marseilles: the sociolinguistics of Southern Occitan France, revisited', *International Journal of the Sociology of Language*, 169, 107–23.

Gea, J.-M. (1995) 'Entre norme et usage: quelques formes surcomposées dans les lettres de deux soldats', *Langage et société*, 71, 65–85.

George, K. (1993) 'Alternative French', in C. Sanders (ed.) *French Today: Language in Its Social Context*, Cambridge: Cambridge University Press, pp. 155–70.

Gervais, M.-M. (1993) 'Gender and language in French', in C. Sanders (ed.) *French Today: Language in Its Social Context*, Cambridge: Cambridge University Press, pp. 121–38.

Gervais-le Garff, M.-M. (2002) 'Liberté, égalité, sororité: a new linguistic order in France?', *Women and Language*, 22 September, 1–7.

Green, J. A. and Hintze, M.-A. (1990) 'Variation and change in French linking phenomenon', in J. N. Green and W. Ayres-Bennett (eds) *Variation and Change in French*, London: Routledge.

Hansen, A. B. (1998) *Les voyelles nasales du français parisien moderne. Aspects linguistiques, sociolinguistiques et perceptuels des changements en cours*, Copenhagen: Museum Tusculanum.

Hawkins, R. (1993) 'Regional variation in France', in C. Sanders (ed.) *French Today: Language in Its Social Context*, Cambridge: Cambridge University Press, pp. 55–84.

Held, G. (1989) 'On the role of maximization in verbal politeness', *Multilingua*, 8, 167–206.

Hughson, J. (2001) 'Le tu et le vous: étude sociolinguistique dans la banlieue parisienne', unpublished Diplôme d'études approfondies, Université Paris-X Nanterre.

Izaki, Y. (2000) 'Cultural differences of preference and deviations from expectations in requesting: a study of Japanese and French learners of Japanese in contact situations', *Journal of Japanese Language Teaching*, 104, 79–88.

Judge, A. (1993) 'French: a planned language?', in C. Sanders (ed.) *French Today: Language in Its Social Context*, Cambridge: Cambridge University Press, pp. 7–26.

Kerbrat-Orrechioni, C. (1992) *Les interactions verbales*, vol. II, Paris: Armand Colin.

——(1994) *Les interactions verbales*, vol. III, Paris: Armand Colin.

Kraft, B. and Geluykens, R. (2002) 'Complaining in French L1 and L2: a cross-linguistic investigation', in S. Foster-Cohen, T. Ruthenberg, and M.-L. Poschen (eds) *Eurosla Yearbook*, vol. *2*, pp. 227–42.

Labov, W. (1972) *Sociolinguistic Patterns*, Philadelphia, PA: University of Pennsylvania Press.

Laks, B. (1983) 'Langage et pratiques sociales. Etude sociolinguistique d'un groupe d'adolescents', *Actes de la recherche en sciences sociales*, 46, 73–97.

Landick, M. (1995) 'The mid-vowels in figures: hard facts', *The French Review*, 69, 88–103.

Leclerc, A. (1974) *Parole de femme*, Paris: Grasset.

Lefkowitz, N. (1991) *Talking Backwards, Looking Forwards: The French Language Game Verlan*, Tübingen: Gunter Narr Verlag.

Léon, P. (1971) 'Aspects phonostylistiques des niveaux de langue', in A. Rigault (ed.) *La grammaire du français parlé*, Paris: Hachette, pp. 149–59.

——(1993) *Précis de phonostylistique*, Paris: Nathan.

Léon, P. and Tennant, J. (1990) 'Bad French and nice guys: a morphophonemic study', *The French Review*, 63, 763–78.

Lepelley, R. (1996) 'Les marques du genre et du nombre dans les adjectifs à finale vocalique en Basse Normandie', in F. Manzano (ed.) *Vitalité des parlers de l'Ouest et du Canada francophone*, Rennes: Presses Universitaires de Rennes, pp. 89–101.

Lodge, R. A. (1993) *French: From Dialect to Standard*, London: Routledge.

Malécot, H. (1972) 'New procedures for descriptive phonetics', in *Papers in Linguistics and Phonetics to the Memory of Pierre Delattre*, The Hague: Mouton.

——(1975) 'French liaison as a function of grammatical, phonetic and paralinguistic variables', *Phonetica*, 32, 161–79.

Martinet, A. (1945) *La prononciation du français contemporain, Témoignages recueillis en 1941 dans un camp d'officiers prisonniers*, Genève: Librairie Droz.

——(1990) 'Remarques sur la variété des usages dans la phonie du français', in J. N. Green and W. Ayres-Bennett (eds) *Variation and Change in French*, New York: Routledge, pp. 13–26.

Maurand, G. (1981) 'Situation linguistique d'une communauté rurale en domaine occitan', *International Journal of the Sociology of Language*, 29, 99–119.

Maury, N. (1973) 'Observations sur les formes syntaxiques et mélodiques de l'interrogation dite totale', *The French Review*, 47, 302–11.

Meigret, L. (1542) 'Traité touchant le commun usage de l'escriture françoise', Paris: D. Janot, reprinted (1972) Genève: Slatkine.

Morford, J. (1997) 'Social indexicality in French pronominal address', *Journal of Linguistic Anthropology*, 7, 3–37.

Noreiko, S. (1993) 'New words for new technologies', in C. Sanders (ed.) *French Today: Language in Its Social Context*, Cambridge: Cambridge University Press, pp. 171–84.

Oyharçabal, B. (2003) 'Le basque', in B. Cerquiglini (ed.) *Les langues de France*, Paris: Presses Universitaires de France, pp. 59–68.

Pasques, L. and Baddeley, S. (1989) 'Alternances vocaliques de type sociolinguistique aux XVIe et XVIIe siècles', in W. Ayres-Bennett (ed.) *La variation dans la langue en France du XVIe au XIXe siècle*, Paris: CNRS, pp. 61–71.

Peletier du Mans, J. (1550) *Dialogue de l'ortografe et prononciation françoese*, Poitiers: Marnef, reprinted (1964) Geneva: Slatkine.

Roberge, Y. and Vinet, M.-T. (1989) *La variation dialectale en grammaire universelle*, Montréal: Presses Universitaires de Montréal.

Rolland, J.-C. and Laffitte, J.-D. (1995) *Dicofle*, Sèvres: Centre international d'études pédagogiques.

Sibille, J. (2005) 'L'occitan ou langue d'oc', in B. Cerquiglini (ed.) *Les langues de France*, Paris: Presses Universitaires de France, pp. 173–90.

Soupel, S. (2004) 'The special position of Auvergnat: the sociolinguistics of Southern Occitan France', *International Journal of the Sociology of Language*, 169, 91–106.

Traverso, V. (1996) 'La conversation familière: analyse pragmatique des interactions', Lyon: Presses Universitaires de Lyon.

Trudeau, D. (1988) 'Changement social et changement linguistique. La question du féminin', *The French Review*, 62, 77–87.

Veltman, C. (1982) 'La régression du dialecte', *Chiffres pour l'Alsace*, 3, 39–62.

Walter, H. (1982) *Enquête phonologique et variétés régionales du français*, Paris: Presses Universitaires de France.

——(1983) 'La nasale vélaire, un phonème du français?', in H. Walter (ed.) *Phonologie des usages du français*, Paris: Larousse, pp. 14–29.

——(1988) *Le français dans tous les sens*, Paris: Robert Laffont.

——(1990) 'Une voyelle qui ne veut pas mourir', in J. N. Green and W. Ayres-Bennett (eds) *Variation and Change in French*, New York: Routledge, pp. 27–36.

——(2000) 'An accommodating language: the chronology, typology, and dynamics of borrowing', in S. Wright (ed.) *French: An Accommodating Language?* New York: Multilingual Matters Ltd, pp. 195–220.

Wieland, M. (1995) 'Complimenting behavior in French/American cross-cultural dinner conversations', *The French Review*, 68, 796–812.

Wioland, F. (2005) *La vie sociale des sons du français*, Paris: L'Harmattan.

Wise, H. (1997) *The Vocabulary of Modern French*, New York: Routledge.

Wüest, J. (1985) 'Le patois de Paris et l'histoire du français', *Vox Romanica*, 44, 234–58.

28

Sociolinguistics in Italy

Mair Parry

Introduction

Only in recent decades has Italian come to replace regional dialects as the main language of the home and, although monoglot dialect speakers are now increasingly rare in Italy, approximately half the population still speaks both dialect and Italian (ISTAT 2007), with passive competence even more widespread. A perceptive overview of the current complex sociolinguistic situation, based on innovative research, is found in D'Agostino (2007), and an English survey in Tosi (2001). The major demographic and linguistic changes that Italy witnessed during the past century presented fertile ground for the development of a linguistic approach that, rather than offering a totally new vision, reinforced trends inherent in the vigorous tradition of dialectology by providing a more formal framework supported by quantitative methodology (for details, see Berruto 1995, and Sornicola 2002). Revitalized by advances in general sociolinguistic theory and methodology over the past 60 years, Italian dialectology continues to thrive, given the still significant vitality of the traditional dialects, which are not varieties of Italian but parallel developments from Latin (Muljačić 1997) and which can differ more from Florentine/Tuscan-based Italian than Spanish (for structural, as well as brief sociolinguistic overviews, see Maiden and Parry 1997).

Sociolinguistic research in Italy is flourishing and wide-ranging, but space restrictions limit discussion to work on language variation and use within Italy and the Italo-Romance area of Switzerland, while bibliographical references have had to be drastically reduced. Recent publications include large-scale studies of correlations between linguistic and social variables (urban dialectology and linguistic atlases) and, in particular, detailed analyses of language use in context (register variation, code alternation/code-switching / code-mixing), as well as typologies of repertoires and studies of the status and vitality of the many codes (Italian, dialects, minority languages, immigrant languages), together with issues related to language planning, standardization, identity and education. They thus mirror the profoundly multilingual nature of a country which was unified barely a century and a half ago and which, since then, has witnessed mass internal migration into the cities from rural areas, and from the impoverished south to the more industrial north (especially to the north-west), followed by significant recent immigration. The accompanying major advances in literacy, education, technology and communication have revolutionized the linguistic behaviour of Italy's inhabitants. Tullio De Mauro, *Storia linguistica dell'Italia unita* (1963), offered a ground-breaking socio-linguistic analysis of the factors that brought about the major language shift whereby the mainly written code of a small elite became in the space of a century a widely spoken language. The boost it gave to the new discipline is celebrated in Lo Piparo and Ruffino (2005).

The impressive spread of Italian (e.g. 78 per cent of respondents to the 2006 ISTAT survey claimed to use Italian in the family, either exclusively or alternating with dialect) and the corresponding steady decline in dialect use, correlate with a notable increase in bilingual usage. This has produced a rich area of interference and variation between the two poles of standard Italian and local dialect, a *continuum* which has been subjected to division on the basis of clusters of features into various *gradata* (e.g. 'regional' Italian, 'popular' Italian, dialect *koinè*). While the changing relationship between Italian, on the one hand, and indigenous dialects or 'historical' minority languages (see below), on the other, continues to be a major topic of study, the advent of many typologically very different immigrant languages into a country more used to emigration, has also recently attracted much attention: for a typology of repertoires, see Mioni (1989). The establishment of a research centre in 2000 at Siena's Università per Stranieri, *Osservatorio linguistico permanente dell'italiano diffuso fra stranieri e delle lingue immigrate in Italia*, reflects a resolve to undertake detailed descriptive and applied studies of all types of language use in Italy, in the hope of promoting greater linguistic awareness among native and immigrant communities and better social integration (Bagna *et al.* 2003).

After briefly mentioning useful reference sources for the wealth of publications, I shall consider key aspects of those areas considered more strictly sociolinguistic, such as variationist and contact phenomena, together with broader topics pertaining to the sociology of language: linguistic repertoires (diglossia, bilingualism, etc.); language planning and the minority language issue; questions of identity and perception. For strictly pragmatic and conversational studies, see Caffi and Hölker (2002), and for Italo-Romance varieties outside Italy, the general bibliography in Vedovelli and Villarini (1998).

Journals and overviews

Italian sociolinguistic research deserves to be better represented in international journals, although publication in English has increased since the useful introductions to the Italian scene in Berruto (1989), Zuanelli Sonino (1989) and Trumper (1993). G. Berruto's annual bibliographies in *Sociolinguistica: International Yearbook of European Sociolinguistics*, are essential reference tools, as are his manuals (1987a, 1995), which include theoretical and methodological discussion. Sociolinguistic research features prominently in the activities of Italy's linguistic societies, in particular the Società di Linguistica italiana, which publishes regular critical surveys of this and other disciplines (Còveri 1977; Mioni 1992; Berruto 2002a). The Sappada/Plodn dialectology conferences promote a socio-linguistic approach (see Marcato and Tiozzo 2007), as does the journal, *Rivista italiana di dialettologia*. Two recent periodicals dedicated to minority languages and multilingualism in general are *Plurilinguismo* (1994–) and *Lingue e Idiomi d'Italia* (2006).

Sociolinguistic variation

The description and classification of varieties identified within the Italian–dialect continuum have spawned many models, the most influential being the attempt by Berruto (1987a) to capture the dynamism inherent in the 'architecture' of Italian through the use of three intersecting axes representing the diastratic, diaphasic and diamesic continua of variation. It has long been held that an oral Italian standard is a myth and that it is essential to distinguish between written and spoken Italian: regardless of educational level or social background the latter inevitably betrays some degree of regional provenance, at least in intonation and pronunciation. Aside from this pervasive regional variation (see below), key issues have included the concept of 'restandardization', which affects both written and spoken Italian, for example, it is often pointed out that today's Italian (i.e. *l'italiano dell'uso medio*; Sabatini 1985) involves the resurfacing of linguistic traits long suppressed by the prescriptive norms of the literary canon and the educational system. The elucidation of the concepts of 'popular Italian' and 'standard/substandard Italian' has commanded much attention, e.g. Lepschy (1990), Sobrero (1993), but focus is now shifting to the analysis of variation in the language of the media, e.g. Maraschio (1997) for radio, and for television (Spina 2005), and to the relaxed writing practices of new channels of communication provided by computers and mobile phones, e.g. Ursini (2001). The new technology has also given a boost to the dialects, whose use in websites, chat-rooms and texts invites sociolinguistic analysis, as in Fiorentino (2005). A major new resource for research into the Italian spoken in different contexts (dialogue, the media, telephone, etc.) and recorded in 15 Italian cities in different regions is the CLIPS (*Corpora e Lessici di Italiano Parlato e Scritto*) electronic archive (www.clips.unina.it; directed by F. Albano Leoni).

According to Sobrero (1997), the range of varieties of Italian is now narrowing, in the sense that there is a lowering process affecting the upper half, while varieties in the lower half are tending to become less sub-standard and the dialects become more Italianized, often by-passing a regional dialect-*koiné* stage, since small communities are now less regionally and more nationally oriented, due to technological advances and improved transport. As elsewhere, the diminishing relevance of social status has encouraged more flexible sociolinguistic norms (Grassi 2001), to the extent that colloquial and non-standard features occur in the speech of educated people and even politicians, whose language used to be notoriously formal and abstruse. Syntactic variation is shown by Trumper (1995) to correlate directly with the level of education of Calabrian speakers only for some non-standard features, e.g. lack of the infinitive and auxiliary selection, whereas relative clause formation and use of the subjunctive are similar, regardless of educational background. Alfonzetti (2002) also takes issue with too facile a distinction between 'colloquial' Italian, on the one hand, and substandard *italiano popolare*, on the other, demonstrating through a rigorous sociolinguistic and statistical study of Sicilian regional Italian, both spontaneous and questionnaire-based, that features which may be totally stigmatized in writing often pass unremarked in speech: non-standard relative clauses (using the simple complementizer instead of a case-marked relative pronoun) are not rare in educated speech, and cannot therefore be used as a diagnostic for *italiano popolare*.

Regional Italian and dialects

The regular statistical surveys performed by Doxa (1974–) and ISTAT (1989–) reveal significant differences in the amount of Italian/dialect used in the various regions (see

Bruni 1992, for the diverse social histories of Italian in the regions). As noted, spoken Italian is intrinsically regional, so that diatopic variation interacts with all other socio-logical variables, e.g. Bentley (1997) prefaces her description of the regional Italian of Sicily by identifying the main variables affecting choice of code: as elsewhere, education and age are key factors. The situation obtaining in Tuscany and Rome is particularly complex, due to their dialects' close structural affinity with Italian (Bernhard 1999). Quantitative analyses showing correlations between sociological variables and linguistic features include contributions to Cortelazzo and Mioni (1990), while Amenta and Cas-tiglione (2003) draws on speakers' self-evaluation regarding use and perceptions of acceptability to re-examine the distinction between *italiano regionale* and *italiano popolare*. Variationist dialect studies, such as Parry (1991), Cravens and Giannelli (1995), Tufi (2005), highlight widespread structural changes that reveal koinization tendencies in the direction of Italian, especially among younger speakers. Theoretical considerations may emerge from formal studies of dialect variation, e.g. Sornicola (2001) argues that pervasive vocalic variation in the Neapolitan area admits different sociolinguistic inter-pretations, while the analysis of an intricate morphosyntactic change in progress involving the distribution of perfective auxiliaries (Cennamo 2001) relies not only on syntactic and semantic variables but also on sociolinguistic ones, such as age, class and register.

Gender

This variable's effect on language performance and choice is often considered alongside other variables in many of the investigations mentioned (its impact being generally less significant), see Marcato (1995), Marcato and Thüne (2002); studies on forensic socio-linguistics, e.g. Bellucci *et al.* (1998). The issue of sexism in language is critically examined in Lepschy (1987) and Cirillo (2002).

Age

The linguistic behaviour of young people continues to attract attention, e.g. Còveri (1988), Radtke (1993), Cortelazzo (1994), Marcato (2006). Studies of regional variation often focus on lexis, e.g. Binazzi (1997), and the response to new electronic forms of communication, e.g. Fusco and Marcato (2005). Following Klein (1995), recent research also prioritizes attitudes and choices (Italian/dialect, code-switching, etc.) in urban environments, e.g. Turin (Ruggiero 2004), Naples (De Blasi and Montuori 2006). Breaking new ground (in the context of Italian sociolinguistics) is Taddei Gheiler's (2005) in-depth study of the language of older people in the Ticino.

Large-scale projects and linguistic atlases

The flourishing state of Italian dialectology owes much to innovative research under-taken for regional atlases based on sociolinguistic principles, using digital technology for the collection, analysis and on-going presentation of large amounts of data relating not only to the traditional Italo-Romance dialects but also to the new regional varieties of Italian. Among the most productive projects are: NADIR (Nuovo Atlante dei Dialetti e dell'Italiano Regionale), based at Lecce (see Sobrero *et al.* 1991), and the ALS (Atlante Linguistico della Sicilia), based at Palermo, whose impressive series of publications starting with Ruffino (1995) continues the important sociolinguistic research undertaken by the *Osservatorio linguistico della Sicilia* (Lo Piparo *et al.* 1990). D'Agostino and Pennisi (1995) explain the theoretical and methodological framework for the ALS surveys, stressing the importance of sensitivity to sociological detail and variability, both in the collection of data and their interpretation. Interesting points to emerge from their statistical analyses include clear indications that the variables of age and level of education have greater impact on performance in Italian than in the dialect: the young and the more educated have less regionally-marked Italian than older and less educated speakers, while retaining their local pronunciations in dialect. Topographical considerations, in the sense of social space and the 'mobility' of informants, remain crucial to the explanation of variation in use, with the innovative atlas framework permitting constant refinement, e.g. language choice is found to depend not only on whether the towns in which speakers live are dynamic or not (Ruffino 1990), but also on whether the towns themselves are located within a forward-looking area (D'Agostino and Pennisi 1995: 203).

An oral dialect archive (Archivio dei dialetti campani) is under way in the Neapolitan area (Sornicola 1999), where detailed analyses of dialect variation, e.g. Sornicola (2006), query the universal applicability of traditional sociolinguistic concepts and methodology. Given the diversity of individual situations, Sornicola argues that a more appropriate model than 'social network' could be in some cases a 'sociolinguistic habitat' model that takes due account of specific geographical and historical contexts.

Urban language

Unlike traditional dialectology, the new atlas projects devote particular attention to the intricate patterns of language behaviour in urban contexts. Although slow to attract the attention it deserved, this is now a key concern of Italian sociolinguists, whose use of social network analysis is producing a much more nuanced picture to complement correlational studies, as evidenced by contributions to Klein (1989). Investigations in Puglia (Tempesta 2000) reveal how the size of towns, as well as the strength of network ties and social class, influences the ratio of Italian, dialect and use of both (i.e. code-switching and code-mixing). D'Agostino (1996) highlights the influence of mental maps on language choice in Palermo, where the city's dialect projects a particularly negative image. An analysis of the spontaneous speech of youngsters in Palermo (Christoffersen 2003), stresses the importance of speakers' attitudes and the need to supplement data derived through elicitation with small-scale qualitative studies of authentic use, since the lack of stigmatized features registered by the ALS among the educated can be traced to their ability to adapt their language to an interview situation.

Radtke (2000) analyses sociolinguistic data to reveal how a metropolis such as Naples encourages koineization of surrounding dialects, while the effects of social degradation and neglect are explored in a sociolinguistic/psycholinguistic study of adolescents by Giuliano (2004). A major collaborative project targets Naples, Trieste, Venice, Udine and their hinterlands, using both correlational and interpretative approaches to examine language attitudes and use, including *koiné* formation, as well as educational issues and policy (De Blasi and Marcato 2006). Indeed, an urban perspective informs many investigations of multilingualism (as in Bombi and Fusco 2004).

331

Multilingualism and diglossia

A major concern of Italian sociolinguists has been the study of bi-/multilingual repertoires and their linguistic consequences, especially code-switching and code-mixing.
Discussion of the relevance of the concept of diglossia to contemporary Italy has exercised many linguists, the increasing lack of a clear-cut functional differentiation in certain
domains (e.g. the home) leading to a distinction between *macro-* and *micro-diglossic* regions
by John Trumper (see Trumper 1993) and the coining of a new term, *dilalia* (Berruto
1987b), to describe a situation in which the high language is also used in informal contexts, often interchangeably with the 'low' language(s). The result of functional overlapping is widespread interference and the development of the continuum mentioned
above, with code-switching and code-mixing the norm, in both urban and rural (e.g.
Maturi 2001) contexts. In addition to functional analyses of convergence, important
theoretical considerations are raised by Berruto (1997, 2005), Franceschini (1998) and
Alfonzetti (1998), all of whom call into question the validity of various constraints on
code-switching proposed in the literature. Alfonzetti follows Peter Auer in highlighting
the contribution of an extra dimension, in addition to the structural and macro-
sociolinguistic ones, which may be exploited by bilingual speakers: that of discourse or
conversational organization. Franceschini proposes a dual-focus model of language production to account for non-functional code-switching, while Berruto rejects Myers-
Scotton's Matrix Language Frame model in favour of a more flexible language-contact
model based on a double continuum that correlates patterns of language use with their
structural consequences.

Minority languages and language planning

Descriptions abound of multilingual repertoires involving the 12 'historical' minority
language groups legally but not uncontroversially recognized by the state in 1999
(Albanian, Catalan, Croatian, Franco-Provençal, French, Friulian, German, Greek, Ladin,
Occitan, Sardinian, Slovene). The northern Italian border areas are well served, e.g.
Bauer (1999), while Francescato and Solari Francescato (1994) present an exemplary
investigation of a trilingual Germanic enclave in Friuli. Picco (2001) describes a sociolinguistic survey carried out in Friuli in 1998–99: as with the dialects, numbers claiming
to use both Italian and Friulian with family members are on the increase and, interestingly, more Friulian is used outside than inside the family. Contact between old (Arbëresh)
and new Albanian immigrants opens up a promising direction of research (Maddalon and
Belluscio 2002).

In Friuli, where Friulian and Venetan dialects are spoken alongside Slovene and new
immigrant languages, a major research centre to investigate multilingualism in both
written and oral communication was established in 1993. The *Centro Internazionale sul
Plurilinguismo* supports an ethnographic archive of recorded speech and informal written
texts, promoting both contemporary and historical research, including study of the literary
exploitation of multilingualism (see Petronio and Orioles 2004).

The 1999 law (Law 482), whereby the Italian state belatedly recognized and offered
limited financial support for the protection and promotion of minority languages (previously only a few varieties in certain Special Statute Regions enjoyed protection) has
generated much discussion. Savoia (2002) reviews negative reactions deriving from fears

that it poses a threat to national unity or to levels of proficiency in Italian, while many linguists take issue with some of the linguistic and sociolinguistic assumptions it incorporates, e.g. Orioles (2003) and Telmon (2006). Particularly controversial are the inclusion of some erstwhile traditional 'dialects', such as Friulian and Sardinian, but not others, and the exclusion of isolated Italo-Romance communities such as Tabarchino (Ligurian) speakers in Sardinia. The implementation of the law, which raises the thorny issue of standardization, is also seen as problematic, given the widespread dialectal diversity of these communities. Language policy in general (e.g. Guardiano *et al.* 2005) and regarding minorities specifically, receives increasing academic attention, e.g. Dal Negro (2005). Coluzzi (2007) examines the relationship between minority language planning and micro-nationalism in a comparative context (with Spain).

The more liberal attitude of the EU towards regional and minority languages has encouraged greater tolerance and a certain revitalization of the indigenous Italian varieties, so that dialects are making a relative come-back, though not necessarily in traditional domains: among the new functions we find commercial exploitation in advertising to evoke traditional, authentic produce or life-styles, and new expressive uses even among youngsters raised in Italian (see Sobrero and Miglietta 2006). On the other hand, the precariousness of many minority varieties has stimulated discussion of language decline, as in Dal Negro (2004) and Perta (2004).

New immigrant minorities

Internal migration, especially northwards from southern regions, such as Calabria, Campania and Sicily, as well as emigration abroad continue to shape Italian demographic patterns, but immigration, especially from eastern Europe and Africa, is now a major phenomenon that increasingly brings families seeking permanent stability as well as temporary migrants who see Italy as a staging post on the way to their ultimate goal, such as Australia or Canada. Much sociolinguistic research in Italy has been devoted to the changing repertoires of different areas and to the linguistic integration of immigrants, e.g. Vedovelli (2002). Giacalone Ramat (2003) contains detailed studies by the Pavia group of the gradual acquisition of Italian as a second language, while the social, linguistic, and discourse patterns of interaction relating to both old and new minorities, e.g. Peruvians and Ghanaians in northern Italy, are analysed in Dal Negro and Molinelli (2002). D'Agostino (2005) draws on research based on the social network concept to compare the behaviour of earlier immigrants from the Sicilian hinterland with that of new immigrants to Palermo. The different cultural backgrounds of overseas immigrants also produce different attitudes to the local dialect, some more positive than others (Amoruso and Scarpello 2005). Immigrants to northern cities, however, reveal a tendency to shun the rarely encountered local dialect.

Italo-Romance varieties in Switzerland

In Switzerland, descriptive and theoretical research into linguistic and sociolinguistic aspects of situations of multilingualism involving Italian and Italo-Romance dialects is flourishing, supported by the *Osservatorio linguistico della Svizzera italiana* (OLSI, founded in 1991), e.g. Moretti's (1999) detailed study of declining dialect use, countered by its adaptation to new functions; Moretti and Antonini's (2000) statistical analysis of language use in bilingual families in the Ticino (the fact that Italian is eclipsing German, contrary to alarmist predictions, indicates that the children of immigrants are becoming fully integrated into the local communities); Pandolfi's (2006) investigation of spoken Swiss Italian.

Questions of identity and perception

Much of the research mentioned above engages in varying degrees with the way in which issues of personal identity and the perception of linguistic varieties affect linguistic choice. In Italy, current interest builds on a tradition going back to the 1970s (e.g. Marcato et al. 1974). Since Galli De' Paratesi's investigation into the impact of attitudes towards regional varieties of Italian on standardization trends (Galli De' Paratesi 1984), elicitation strategies have been perfected, notably using the matched-guise technique, e.g. the analysis in Volkart-Rey (1990) of teachers' responses in Catania and Rome confirms traditional stereotypical associations whereby, for example, heavily marked regional Italian is viewed negatively, whereas a light regional colouring is judged more favourably on certain parameters than a standard accent. The study of language attitudes is seen as an integral part of urban and immigrant research (Vedovelli et al. 2004), while the recent atlas projects also embrace new developments in perceptual dialectology, e.g. Romanello (2002). This approach is stimulating much publication and methodological discussion, e.g. Canobbio and Iannàccaro (2000), Telmon (2002), but a cautious note is sounded by Berruto (2002b) regarding its centrality within the discipline of sociolinguistics.

Education

Applied research into the teaching of Italian continues to thrive, e.g. Lo Duca (2003), fuelled in particular by anxiety about the sociolinguistic integration of immigrants, which now tends to eclipse previous concern about linguistic inequality among native Italians (but see Colombo and Romani 1996). The numerous studies insist on the importance of sociolinguistic research for educational policy, e.g. GISCEL (2007).

Historical sociolinguistics

The best diachronic studies of language use and repertoires rely extensively on socio-linguistic principles, e.g. Bianconi (1989) and De Blasi (2002). Toso (2004) considers within a European context of emergent national identities (and languages) the varied linguistic scene of sixteenth-century Genoa, where the local vernacular, with its strong tradition of literary and political use, did not yield meekly to Tuscan (Italian). Even more prestigious and still the most flourishing of Italy's dialects is Venetian, whose complex structural and social history is reconstructed by Ferguson (2007). While the scrutiny of non-literary texts has a long tradition in Italy, especially the correspondence of less educated emigrants and soldiers, innovatory interdisciplinary research by Trumper and Chiodo (2000) into the far-reaching effects of earthquakes on dialect distribution and evolution in southern Italy reveals how different social factors led to regional linguistic influence in opposite directions. Despite discussion on the feasibility of detailed sociolinguistic analysis of the past (Dardano 1999), Loporcaro (2000) rightly insists that the debate on the respective merits of external and internal explanations of language change cannot be settled once and for all and that for each individual case the relevance of structural and sociolinguistic factors needs to be taken into account.

Conclusion

The impact of recent technological innovations on language use, together with the widespread bi-/plurilingualism that major social change has produced among both native and immigrant population in Italy, offer an incomparably rich area of variation for sociolinguists to research. Investigation of the dynamic relationship between Italian and the dialects or other languages will continue to be a major focus of research, in terms both of functional distribution in the various regions, especially in urban communities, and of the linguistic reflexes of language contact. Although it seems that automatic generational transmission of the dialects is largely a thing of the past, there is evidence of new uses and some acquisition at a later stage by a significant number of youngsters brought up in Italian (D'Agostino 2007: 178–9). In certain regions the dialects are proving particularly tenacious and for many speakers the level of competence in Italian is far from assured (see Sornicola 2006). While the growing immigrant population will ensure that issues of linguistic identity and the contact between immigrant languages and the indigenous varieties will command increasing attention, the setting up of large-scale collaborative projects, which also support detailed micro-sociolinguistic analyses of particular situations and all types of discourse, promises well for the future of the discipline in Italy.

Acknowledgments

I am grateful to Gaetano Berruto for additional bibliographical assistance.

References

Alfonzetti, G. (1998) 'The conversational dimension in code-switching between Italian and dialect in Sicily', in P. Auer (ed.) *Code-switching in Conversation: Language, Interaction and Identity*, London: Routledge, pp. 180–211.

——(2002) *La relativa non standard: italiano popolare o italiano parlato?*, Palermo: Centro di Studi Filologici e Linguistici Siciliani.

Amenta, L. and Castiglione, M. (2003) 'Convergenza linguistica fra conoscenza, uso e percezione: l'italiano regionale di Sicilia', in N. Maraschio and T. Poggi Salani (eds) *Italia linguistica anno mille, Italia linguistica anno duemila: Atti del XXXIV congresso internazionale di studi della Società di linguistica italiana* (SLI), Firenze, 19–21 ottobre 2000, Rome: Bulzoni, pp. 287–301.

Amoruso, C. and Scarpello, I. (2005) 'Dialetto, integrazione, esclusione. Percorsi immigratori urbani a Palermo', in G. Marcato (ed.) *Dialetti in città*, Padua: Unipress, pp. 171–84.

Bagna, C., Machetti, S. and Vedovelli, M. (2003) 'Italiano e lingue immigrate: verso un plurilinguismo consapevole o verso varietà di contatto?', in A. Valentini, P. Molinelli, P. Cuzzolin, and G. Bernini (eds) *Ecologia Linguistica, Atti del XXXVI Congresso internazionale di studi della Società di Linguistica Italiana (SLI)*, Bergamo, 26–28 settembre 2002, Rome: Bulzoni, pp. 201–22.

Bauer, R. (1999) *Sprachsoziologische Studien zur Mehrsprachigkeit im Aostatal. Mit besonderer Berücksichtigung der externen Sprachgeschichte*, Tübingen: Niemeyer.

Bellucci, P., Antognoli, S., Carmignani, B. and Grimaldi, M. (1998) 'Studi di sociolinguistica giudiziaria italiana', in G. Alfieri and A. Cassola (eds) *La "lingua d'Italia". Usi pubblici e istituzionali, Atti del XXIX Congresso della Società Linguistica Italiana, Malta, 3–5 novembre, 1995*, Rome: Bulzoni, pp. 226–68.

Bentley, D. (1997) 'Language and dialect in modern Sicily', *The Italianist*, 17, 204–30.

Bernhard, G. (1999) *Das Romanesco des ausgehenden 20. Jahrhunderts*, Tübingen: Niemeyer.

Berruto, G. (1987a) *Sociolinguistica dell'italiano contemporaneo*, Florence: La Nuova Italia Scientifica.

——(1987b) 'Lingua, dialetto, diglossia, dilalia', in G. Holtus and J. Kramer (eds) *Romania et Slavia adriatica. Festschrift für Žarko Muljačić*, Hamburg: Buske, pp. 57–81.

——(1989) 'Main topics and findings in Italian sociolinguistics', *International Journal of the Sociology of Language*, 76, 7–30.

——(1995) *Fondamenti di sociolinguistica*, Bari: Laterza.

——(1997) 'Code-switching and code-mixing', in M. Maiden and M. Parry (eds) *The Dialects of Italy*, London: Routledge, pp. 394–400.

——(2002a) 'Sociolinguistica', in C. Lavinio (ed.) *La linguistica italiana alle soglie del 2000 (1987–97 e oltre)*, Rome: Bulzoni, pp. 471–503.

——(2002b) 'Sul significato della dialettologia percettiva per la linguistica e la sociolinguistica', in M. Cini and R. Regis (eds) *Che cosa ne pensa oggi Chiaffredo Roux? Percorsi della dialettologia percezionale all'alba del nuovo millennio*, Alessandria: Dell'Orso pp. 341–60.

——(2005) 'Dialect/standard convergence, mixing, and models of language contact: the case of Italy', in P. Auer, F. Hinskens and P. Kerswill (eds) *Dialect Change: Convergence and Divergence in European Languages*, Cambridge: Cambridge University Press, pp. 81–95.

Bianconi, S. (1989) *I due linguaggi. Storia linguistica della Lombardia svizzera dal '400 ai giorni nostri*, Bellinzona: Casagrande.

Binazzi, N. (1997) *Le parole dei giovani fiorentini. Variazione linguistica e variazione sociale*, Rome: Bulzoni.

Bombi, R. and Fusco, F. (eds) (2004) *Città plurilingui. Lingue e culture a confronto in situazioni urbane*, Udine: Forum.

Bruni, F. (ed.) (1992) *L'italiano nelle regioni. Lingua nazionale e identità regionali*, Turin: UTET.

Caffi, C. and Hölker, K. (2002) 'Pragmatica linguistica e analisi della conversazione', in C. Lavinio (ed.) *La linguistica italiana alle soglie del 2000 (1987–1997 e oltre)*, Rome: Bulzoni, pp. 505–31.

Canobbio, S. and Iannàccaro, G. (2000) *Contributo per una bibliografia sulla dialettologia percettiva*, Alessandria: Dell'Orso.

Cavalli, M. and Coletta, D. (eds) (2003) *Langues, Bilinguisme et Représentations sociales au Val d'Aoste*, Aosta: Institut Régional de Recherche Educative de la Vallée d'Aoste.

Cennamo, M. (2001) 'L'inaccusatività in alcune varietà campane: teorie e dati a confronto', in F. Albano Leoni, R. Sornicola, E. S. Krossbakken, and C. Stromboli (eds) *Dati empirici e teorie linguistiche. Atti del XXXIII Congresso Internazionale di Studi, Napoli 28–30 ottobre 1999*, Rome: Bulzoni, pp. 427–53.

Christoffersen, A. W. (2003) 'Lingua, società ed ideologia: le condizioni personali che influenzano le scelte linguistiche – Giovani a Palermo', in A. Valentini, P. Molinelli, P. Cuzzolin, and G. Bernini (eds) *Ecologia Linguistica*, Atti del XXXVI Congresso Internazionale di Studi della SLI, Rome: Bulzoni, pp. 96–104.

Cirillo, C. (2002) 'Sexism and gender issues in the Italian language', in A. L. Lepschy and A. Tosi (eds) *Multilingualism in Italy: Past and Present*, Oxford: Legenda, pp. 141–49.

Colombo, A. and Romani, W. (eds) (1996) *"E' la lingua che ci fa uguali". Lo svantaggio linguistico: problemi di definizione e di intervento*, Scandicci (FI): La Nuova Italia.

Coluzzi, P. (2007) *Minority Language Planning and Micronationalism in Italy: An Analysis of the Situation of Friulian, Cimbrian and Western Lombard with Reference to Spanish Minority Languages*, Frankfurt: Lang.

Cortelazzo, M. A. (1994) 'Il parlato giovanile', in L. Serianni and P. Trifone (eds) *Storia della lingua italiana*, II, *Scritto e parlato*, Turin: Einaudi, pp. 290–317.

Cortelazzo, M. A. and Mioni A. M. (1990) *L'italiano regionale, Atti del XVIII Congresso internazionale di Studi, Padova-Vicenza, 14–16 settembre 1984*, Rome: Bulzoni.

Còveri, L. (1977) 'Sociolinguistica e pragmatica', in D. Gambarara and P. Ramat (eds) *Dieci anni di linguistica italiana (1965–75)*, Rome: Bulzoni, pp. 247–71.

——(1988) 'Lingua e età', in G. Holtus, M. Metzeltin, and C. Schmidt, *Lexikon der romanistischen Linguistik*, IV, *Italiano, Corso, Sardo*, Tübingen: Niemeyer, pp. 231–36.

Cravens, T. D. and Giannelli, L. (1995) 'Relative salience of gender and class in a situation of multiple competing norms', *Linguistic Variation and Change*, 7, 261–85.

D'Agostino, M. (1996) 'Spazio, città, lingue. Ragionando su Palermo', *Rivista italiana di dialettologia*, 20, 35–87.

——(2005) 'Nuove condizioni linguistiche, Gli effetti dell'immigrazione', in F. Lo Piparo and G. Ruffino (eds) *Gli italiani e la lingua*, Palermo: Sellerio, pp. 70–92.

——(2007) *Sociolinguistica dell'Italia contemporanea*, Bologna: Il Mulino.

D'Agostino, M. and Pennisi, A. (1995) *Per una linguistica spaziale. Modelli e rappresentazioni della variabilità linguistica nell'esperienza dell'ALS*, Palermo: Centro di Studi Filologici e Linguistici Siciliani.

Dal Negro, S.(2004) *The Decay of a Language: The Case of a German Dialect in the Italian Alps*, Bern: Lang.

——(2005) 'Minority languages between nationalism and new localism: the case of Italy', *International Journal of the Sociology of Language*, 174, 113–24.

Dal Negro, S. and Molinelli, P. (eds) (2002) *Comunicare nella torre di Babele. Repertori plurilingui in Italia oggi*, Rome: Carocci.

Dardano, M. (1999) 'Ist eine Historische Soziolinguistik des Altitalienischen möglich?', *Sociolinguistica: International Yearbook of European Sociolinguistics*, 13, 4–16.

De Blasi, N. (2002) 'Notizie sulla variazione diastratica a Napoli tra il 1500 e il 2000', *Bollettino Linguistico Campano*, 1, 89–129.

De Blasi, N. and Marcato, C. (eds) (2006) *La città e le sue lingue. Repertori linguistici urbani*, Atti del Convegno Repertori linguistici urbani, (Udine 14–15 aprile 2005), Naples: Liguori, pp. 293–310.

De Blasi, N. and Montuori, F. (2006) 'I giovani a Napoli e il dialetto tra continuità e risorgenza', in G. Marcato (ed.) *Giovani, lingua e dialetto. Atti del Convegno di Sappada/Plodn, Belluno, 29 giugno– 3 luglio 2005*, Padua: Unipress, pp. 117–28.

De Mauro, T. (1963) *Storia linguistica dell'Italia unita*, Bari: Laterza.

Ferguson, R. (2007) *A Linguistic History of Venice*, Florence: Olschki.

Fiorentino, G. (2005) 'Dialetti in rete', *Rivista italiana di dialettologia*, 29, 111–47.

Francescato, G. and Solari Francescato, P. (1994) *Timau. Tre lingue per un paese*, Galatina: Congedo.

Franceschini, R. (1998) 'Code-switching and the notion of code in linguistics: proposals for a dual focus model', in P. Auer (ed.) *Code-Switching in Conversation: Language, Interaction and Identity*, London: Routledge, pp. 51–74.

Fusco, F. and Marcato, C. (eds) (2005) *Forme della comunicazione giovanile*, Rome: Il Calamo.

Galli De' Paratesi, N. (1984) 'Attitudes and standardization trends in contemporary Italian: An enquiry', in N. Dittmar and B. Schlieben Lange (eds) *Die Soziolinguistik in romanischsprachigen Ländern*, Tübingen: Narr, pp. 237–48.

Giacalone Ramat, A. (ed.) (2003) *Verso l'italiano. Percorsi e strategie di acquisizione*, Rome: Carocci.

GISCEL (2007) *Educazione linguistica democratica. A trent'anni dalle Dieci tesi*, Milan: Franco Angeli.

Giuliano, P. (2004) *Abilità narrativa ed emarginazione sociale*, Naples: Liguori.

Grassi, C. (2001) 'Dialetto, quasi dialetto, non più dialetto, … ', in G. Marcato (ed.) *I confini del dialetto*, Padua: Unipress, pp. 35–9.

Guardiano, C., Calaresu, E., Robustelli, C. and Carli, A. (eds) (2005) *Lingue, Istituzioni, Territori. Riflessioni teoriche, proposte metodologiche ed esperienze di politica linguistica. Atti del XXXVIII Congresso Internazionale di Studi della Società di Linguistica Italiana*, (Modena, 23–25 settembre 2004), Rome: Bulzoni.

ISTAT (2007) 'La lingua italiana, i dialetti e le lingue straniere. Anno 2006. Istituto nazionale di statistica. Online. Available at: www.culturaincifre.istat.it/sito/Pubblicazioni/LALINGUAITALIANA.pdf (accessed 28 October 2007).

Klein, G. (ed.) (1989) *Parlare in città. Studi di sociolinguistica urbana*, Galatina: Congedo.

——(1995) *La città nei discorsi e nell'immaginario giovanile. Una ricerca socio-linguistica a Napoli*, Galatina: Congedo.

337

Lepschy, G. (1987) 'Sexism and the Italian language', *The Italianist*, 7, 158–69.

——(1990) 'How popular is Italian?', in Z. G. Baranski and R. Lumley (eds) *Culture and Conflict in Postwar Italy: Essays on Mass and Popular Culture*, London: Macmillan, pp. 63–75.

Lo Duca, M. G. (2003) *Lingua italiana ed educazione linguistica: tra storia, ricerca e didattica*, Rome: Carocci.

Lo Piparo, F., D'Agostino, M., Ferreri, S., Pennisi, A., Ruffino, G. and Vecchio, S. (1990) *La Sicilia linguistica oggi*, Palermo: Centro di Studi Filologici e Linguistici Siciliani.

Lo Piparo, F. and Ruffino, G. (eds) (2005) *Gli italiani e la lingua*, Palermo: Sellerio.

Loporcaro, M. (2000) 'Dialect variation across time and space and the explanation of language change', *Sprachwissenschaft*, 25, 387–418.

Maddalon, M. and Belluscio, G. M. (2002) 'Italo-Albanians and Albanians: a problematic case of (socio-) linguistic contact', in R. Rapp (ed.) *Sprachwissenschaft auf dem Weg in das dritte Jahrtausend. Akten des 34. Linguistischen Kolloquiums in Germersheim 1999*, vol. 2: *Sprache, Computer, Gesellschaft*, Frankfurt: Lang, pp. 193–202.

Maiden, M. and Parry, M. (1997) *The Dialects of Italy*, London: Routledge.

Maraschio, N. (ed.) (1997) *Gli italiani trasmessi: la radio*, Florence: Accademia della Crusca.

Marcato, G. (ed.) (1995) *Donna e linguaggio*, Padua: CLEUP.

——(ed.) (2006) *Giovani, lingua e dialetto. Atti del Convegno di Sappada/Plodn, Belluno, 29 giugno–3 luglio 2005*, Padua: Unipress.

Marcato, G. and Thüne, E. M. (2002) 'Gender and female visibility in Italian', in M. Hellinger and H. Bussmann (eds) *Gender Across Languages*, Amsterdam: Benjamins, pp. 187–217.

Marcato, G. and Tiozzo, P. G. (2007) *Dialettologia in Veneto. Indici degli atti dei Convegni Internazionali di studi di Sappada/Plodn (Belluno), 1995–2007*, Padua: Unipress.

Marcato, G., Ursini, F. and Politi, A. (1974) *Dialetto e italiano. Status socioeconomico e percezione sociale del fenomeno linguistico*, Pisa: Pacini.

Maturi, P. (2001) *Dialetti e substandardizzazione nel Sannio Beneventano*, Frankfurt: Lang.

Mioni, A. M. (1989) 'Osservazioni sui repertori linguistici in Italia', in G. L. Borgato and A. Zamboni (eds) *Dialettologia e varia linguistica per M. Cortelazzo*, Padua: Unipress.

——(1992) 'Sociolinguistica', in A. M. Mioni and M. A. Cortelazzo (eds) *La linguistica italiana degli anni 1976–1986*, Rome: Bulzoni, pp. 507–36.

Moretti, B. (1999) *Ai margini del dialetto*, Locarno: Osservatorio linguistico della Svizzera italiana, Dadò.

Moretti, B. and Antonini, F. (2000) *Famiglie bilingui. Modelli e dinamiche di mantenimento e perdita di lingua in famiglia*, Locarno: Osservatorio linguistico della Svizzera italiana, Dadò.

Muljačić, Ž. (1997) 'The relationship between the dialects and the standard language', in M. Maiden and M. Parry (eds) *The Dialects of Italy*, London: Routledge, pp. 387–93.

Orioles, V. (2003) *Le minoranze sociolinguistiche. Profili sociolinguistici e quadro dei documenti di tutela*, Rome: Il Calamo.

Pandolfi, E. M. (2006) *Misurare la regionalità*, Locarno: Osservatorio linguistico della Svizzera italiana, Dadò.

Parry, M. M. (1991) 'Evoluzione di un dialetto', *Rivista italiana di dialettologia*, 14, 7–39.

Perta, C. (2004) *Language Decline and Death in Three Arbëresh Communities in Italy: A Sociolinguistic Study*, Alessandria: Dell'Orso.

Petronio, F. F. and Orioles V. (eds) (2004) *Intersezioni plurilingui nella letteratura medioevale e moderna*, Rome: Il Calamo.

Picco, L. (2001) *Ricercje su la condizion sociolenghistiche dal furlan/Ricerca sulla condizione sociolinguistica del friulano*, Udine: Forum Editrice Universitaria Udinese.

Radtke, E. (1993) *La lingua dei giovani*, Tübingen: Narr.

——(2000) 'The migration factor and the convergence and divergence of Southern Italian dialects', in K. Mattheier (ed.) *Dialect and Migration in a Changing Europe*, Frankfurt: Lang, pp. 15–23.

Romanello, M. T. (2002) 'The perception of urban varieties: preliminary studies from the south of Italy', in D. Long and D. R. Preston (eds) *Handbook of Perceptual Dialectology*, vol. 2, Tokyo: Tokyo Metropolitan University/Michigan State University, pp. 331–50.

Ruffino, G. (1990) 'Dinamiche socioeconomiche e variazione linguistica', in F. Lo Piparo *et al.* (eds) *La Sicilia linguistica oggi*, Palermo: Centro di Studi Filologici e Linguistici Siciliani, pp. 179–205.

——(1995) *Percorsi di geografia linguistica. Idee per un atlante siciliano della cultura dialettale e dell'italiano regionale*, Palermo: Centro di Studi Filologici e Linguistici Siciliani.

Ruggiero, R. S. (2004) 'Il dialetto tra i giovani a Torino', *Rivista italiana di dialettologia*, 28, 11–43.

Sabatini, F. (1985) '"L'italiano dell'uso medio": una realtà tra le varietà linguistiche italiane', in G. Holtus and E. Radke (eds) *Gesprochenes Italienisch in Geschichte und Gegenwart*, Tübingen: Narr, pp. 154–84.

Savoia, L. M. (2002) 'La legge 482 sulle minoranze linguistiche storiche. Le lingue di minoranza e le varietà non standard in Italia', *Rivista italiana di dialettologia*, 25, 7–50.

Sobrero, A. A. (ed.) (1993) *Introduzione all'italiano contemporaneo*, vol. 1, *Le Strutture*, vol. 2, *La variazione e gli usi*, Bari: Laterza.

——(1997) 'Varietà in tumulto nel repertorio linguistico italiano', in K. J. Mattheier and E. Radtke (eds) *Standardisierung und Destandardisierung europäischer Nationalsprachen*, Frankfurt: Lang, pp. 41–59.

Sobrero, A. A. and Miglietta, A. (eds) (2006) *Lingua e dialetto nell'Italia del duemila*, Galatina: Congedo.

Sobrero, A. A., Romanello, M. T. and Tempesta, I. (eds) (1991) *Lavorando al Nadir. Un'idea per un atlante linguistico*, Galatina: Congedo.

Sornicola, R. (1999) 'La variazione dialettale dell'area costiera napoletana. Il progetto di un archivio di testi dialettali parlati', in G. Marcato (ed.) *Dialetti oggi, Atti del convegno, "Tra lingua, cultura, società. Dialettologia sociologica" (Sappada-Plodn 1–4 luglio 1999)*, Padua: Unipress, pp. 103–22.

——(2001) 'Alcune recenti ricerche sul parlato: le dinamiche vocaliche di (e) nell'area flegrea e le loro implicazioni per una teoria della variazione', in M. Dardano, A. Pelo and A. Stefinlongo (eds) *Scritto e parlato. Metodi, testi e contesti*, Rome: Aracne, pp. 239–64.

——(2002) 'Sulla dialettologia sociologica', *Revue de linguistique romane*, 66, 79–117.

——(2006) 'Dialetto e processi d'italianizzazione in un habitat del Sud d'Italia', in A. A. Sobrero and A. Miglietta (eds) *Lingua e dialetto nell'Italia del duemila*, Galatina: Congedo, pp. 195–242.

Spina, S. (2005) *Il Corpus di Italiano Televisivo (CiT): struttura e annotazione*, in E. Burr (ed.) *Tradizione e Innovazione. Il parlato: teoria – corpora – linguistica dei corpora. Atti del VI Convegno internazionale della SILFI (28 Giugno– 2 Luglio 2000, Duisburg)*, Florence: Franco Cesati, pp. 413–26.

Stehl, T. (1995) 'La dinamica diacronica fra dialetto e lingua: per un'analisi funzionale della convergenza linguistica', in M. T. Romanello and I. Tempesta (eds) *Dialetti e lingue nazionali. Atti del XXVII Congresso Internazionale di Studi. Lecce 28–30 ottobre 1993*, Rome: Bulzoni, pp. 55–73.

Taddei Gheiler, F. (2005) *La lingua degli anziani. Stereotipi sociali e competenze linguistiche in un gruppo di anziani ticinesi*, Locarno: Osservatorio linguistico della Svizzera italiana, Dadò.

Telmon, T. (2002) 'Questioni di metodo in dialettologia percezionale', in M. D'Agostino (ed.) *Percezione dello spazio, spazio della percezione. La variazione linguistica fra nuovi e vecchi strumenti di analisi*, Palermo: Centro di Studi Filologici e Linguistici Siciliani, pp. 39–58.

——(2006) 'La sociolinguistica e le leggi di tutela delle minoranze linguistiche', *LIDI – Lingue e Idiomi d'Italia*, 1, 38–52.

Tempesta, I. (2000) *Varietà della lingua e rete sociale*, Milan: Franco Angeli.

Terracini, B. (1937) 'Minima. Saggio di ricostruzione di un focolare linguistico (Susa)', *Zeitschrift für romanische Philologie*, 57, 673–726.

Tosi, A. (2001) *Language and Society in a Changing Italy*, Clevedon: Multilingual Matters.

Toso, F. (2004) 'Un modello di plurilinguismo urbano rinascimentale. Presupposti ideologici e risvolti culturali delle polemiche linguistiche nella Genova cinquecentesca', in R. Bombi and F. Fusco (eds) *Città plurilingui. Lingue e culture a confronto in situazioni urbane*, Udine: Forum, pp. 491–530.

Trumper, J. B. (1993) 'Italian and Italian dialects: an overview of recent studies', in R. Posner and J. N. Green (eds) *Trends in Romance*, vol. V, Berlin: Mouton de Gruyter, pp. 295–325.

——(1995) 'Riflessioni pragmo-sintattiche su alcuni gruppi meridionali: italiano "popolare,"' in P. Benincà *et al.*, *Italiano e dialetti nel tempo. Saggi di grammatica per Giulio C. Lepschy*, Rome: Bulzoni, pp. 351–67.

Trumper, J. B. and Chiodo, G. (2000) 'A changing Europe: the presence versus absence of drastic events provoking or blocking internal migration and their possible contribution to linguistic change or conservation. Part 1: Reggio Calabria', in K. Mattheier (ed.) *Dialect and Migration in a Changing Europe*, Frankfurt: Lang, pp. 195–244.

Tufi, S. (2005) 'I dialetti dei castelli romani: ausiliari perfettivi e accordo participiale', *Rivista italiana di dialettologia*, 28, 237–87.

Ursini, F. (2001) 'Multimodalità nella scrittura? Gli SMS tra telefoni cellulari', in E. Magno Caldognetto and P. Cosi (eds) *Multimodalità e Multimedialità nella Comunicazione*, Padua: Unipress, pp. 75–80.

Vedovelli, M. (2002) *L'italiano degli stranieri*, Roma: Carocci.

Vedovelli, M., Massara, S. and Giacalone Ramat, A. (eds) (2004) *Lingue e culture in contatto. L'italiano come L2 per gli arabofoni*, Milan: Franco Angeli.

Vedovelli, M. and Villarini, A. (eds) (1998) 'La diffusione dell'italiano nel mondo. Lingua, scuola ed emigrazione. Bibliografia generale (1970–99)', *Studi Emigrazione*, 35, 132.

Volkart-Rey, R. (1990) *Atteggiamenti linguistici e stratificazione sociale: la percezione dello status sociale attraverso la pronuncia: indagine empirica a Catania e a Roma*, Rome: Bonacci.

Zuanelli Sonino, E. (ed.) (1989) 'Italian sociolinguistics: trends and issues', *International Journal of the Sociology of Language*, 76, 87–107.

29

Sociolinguistics in Spain and Portugal

David Atkinson, Mercedes Bengoechea and
Sandi Michele de Oliveira

Introduction

Given the differences in the linguistic situations and sociolinguistic research traditions of Spain and Portugal, the two countries are addressed separately in this chapter. Spain's complex geolinguistic situation is reflected in the structure of the section, which distinguishes between the historically 'bilingual' areas and officially 'monolingual' areas of the country. Portugal's geolinguistic complexity is of another type altogether; the focus in this section is on the methodological traditions which have shaped sociolinguistic research in that country.

Spain

The 'bilingual' areas

There are three 'bilingual areas' (Moreno-Fernández 2007) partly or wholly within the Spanish state: (1) the Catalan-speaking areas (*els Països Catalans* or *àrea lingüística catalana*); (2) the Basque Country (*Euskal Herria* or *Euskadi*); and (3) Galicia: the first, located at the eastern end of the Pyrenees and in the Mediterranean; the second, on the Atlantic coast at the western end of the Pyrenees; and the third, in the north-west of Iberia. Historically, the *Països Catalans* comprise primarily the regions of Catalonia, Valencia and the Balearics (currently constituting three separate 'autonomous communities' in Spain's quasi-federal structure) and part of the French state north of the Pyrenees. *Euskal Herria* straddles the western end of the Pyrenees, comprising four provinces in Spain (three forming the 'autonomous community' of *Euskadi;* the other, a separate 'autonomous community', Navarre) and three *départements* in France. The 'autonomous community' of Galicia borders the Atlantic Ocean, with Portugal to the south and two other areas of Spain to the east.

The historical link between these areas is that all have sizeable communities of speakers of autochthonous languages, respectively, Catalan, Basque and Galician. Although numbers of speakers are notoriously difficult to estimate accurately, linguistic census and other data suggest around nine million Catalan speakers, three million Galician speakers and one million Basque speakers (for recent work on demographic projections, see Casesnoves et al. 2006). Currently, many see Galician as faring worst in the struggle for survival (e.g. Ramallo 2007) and Catalan in Catalonia as the best example of successful 'normalization' in Spain, if not Europe (e.g. Vila-Pujol 2007). For further background, see Turell (2001), Mar-Molinero (2000), Azurmendi and Martínez de Luna (2006) or Ramallo (2007).

Catalan is usually considered to have received the most attention of the three languages, followed by Basque and then Galician (e.g. Moreno-Fernández 2007). Perhaps most important is the sheer wealth of research accumulated over the past 50 years, underrepresented in the international English-language sociolinguistic literature (e.g. Boix-Fuster 2006; Branchadell 2006). For example, very few sociolinguists from Spain are mentioned (and none are profiled in the section on 'The Profession') in the 1,031-page Elsevier *Concise Encyclopedia of Sociolinguistics* (Mesthrie 2001).

Background

Sociolinguistic enquiry in these regions goes back at least a century, one conspicuous example being the sociolinguistic dimension of the *Primer Congreso Vasco* of 1918. However, interest in sociolinguistic questions grew rapidly in the decades following the Spanish Civil War (1936–39); see the Basque publication *Jakin* (www.jakingunea.com), launched in the 1950s and still in existence. Early on, work was rooted in a linguistic conflict approach to language and society (e.g. Ninyoles 1969, SIADECO's 1977a, 1977b landmark publications in the Basque Country, Aracil 1982). This orientation was inextricably linked with systematic linguistic repression under Franco's dictatorship (1939–75). As Badia i Margarit, one of the founders of Catalan sociolinguistics, recently stated, his own interest in sociolinguistics was indelibly marked by his personal experiences as a speaker of an 'oppressed language' (2006: 18), a background intimately connected to a commitment to ensuring that Catalan would be able to 'recover its lost normality' (ibid.: 14). The related notion of normalization (*normalització*), coined to lexicalize this process of 'recovering normality' (i.e. achieving the 'default' status of, say, Portuguese in Portugal or Spanish in Argentina), remains at the centre of much sociolinguistic activity in these areas.

Consequently, research in these regions has often emphasized the sociolinguistics of *society* rather than of *language*, as Boix-Fuster puts it, paraphrasing Fasold (2006: 86). This entailed foregrounding macrosociolinguistics, with some notable 'micro' exceptions (e.g. code-switching). Much of the relevant work can be summarized as focusing on overlapping categories: corpus; status; acquisition, maintenance and use. This often took place through a localized application of 'classic' language planning theory (e.g. Haugen 1972). Linking much of the work is a shared interest in establishing the reality of language maintenance/shift up to the late 1970s and determining how best to facilitate successful 'normalization' of the languages (e.g. Mendiguren and Iñigo 2006).

Corpus

Standardization and dialectal and stylistic variation have been major concerns. In addition to issues such as technology and 'modernization' (e.g. Urkizu 2006), some work has focused on investigating the degree of Castilianization of the lexis, phonology, syntax, pragmatics, etc., of the three languages and the extent to which this influence, and/or the inverse influence of these languages on Spanish, continues to take place (e.g. Moreno-Fernández 2007). Also relevant is the unusually great distance between literary and colloquial varieties which developed in these languages due to their virtual absence from the education system in the period 1939–75 (e.g. Vallverdú 2006). In Catalan, the corpus variation issue generating most popular and academic interest in the post-Franco period is the distinction between 'dialect' and 'language', specifically whether Balearic Catalan and especially the variety spoken in the *País Valencià* (i.e. *valencià* or 'Valencian') should be viewed as separate languages from Catalan. The academic consensus is that viewing Valencian as a different language is historically and linguistically untenable (e.g. Stewart 1996; Kremnitz 2006).

Status

Language planning, policy, rights and duties have been a central focus as regards status. The dynamic legislative and judicial situation since the late 1970s (when the first post-Franco statutes of autonomy were ratified) has attracted considerable academic debate, as the Spanish Constitution of 1978 neither makes any of the three languages in question official throughout the Spanish state nor gives them exclusive official status within the relevant 'autonomous communities' (where they are 'co-official' with Spanish); see e.g. Strubell (1998), Mateo (2005), Tuson (2004).

Due to Spain's recent history, (im)migration research and debate have often been key in the area of status, particularly in Catalonia, where for many years there was much emphasis on the sociolinguistic effects of the migration to Catalonia of around 2 million people from southern Spain between the 1950s and the 1970s, starting with Badia i Margarit's pioneering study of language use (1969). In recent years focus has begun to shift towards the 'new' immigration since the 1990s from, principally, Latin America, Eastern Europe and North Africa (e.g. Vila i Moreno 2005, or Turell 2001 for an overview of 'new' as well as autochthonous language groups throughout Spain).

As in many other post-prohibition contexts, education has also been a major focus, not least in the Basque Country, where secondary education has played a central role in the 'normalization' process (e.g. Maruny and Domínguez 2001; Bouzada Fernández *et al.* 2002; Lasagabaster 2003; Unamuno 2005; Fernández Paz *et al.* 2007).

Acquisition, maintenance and use

Paralleling the focus on language status, a wide gamut of activity has occurred in the study of acquisition, maintenance and use, again emphasizing the languages' situations and making a commitment to language survival and 'normalization'. The following are represented in this gamut: intergenerational transmission and language shift (e.g. Montoya 2000; O'Donnell 2001; Rodríguez-Neira 2002/2003; Real Academia Galega 2007); ethnolinguistic vitality, diglossia and bilingualism (e.g. Herrero-Valeiro 2003); attitudes, interaction and code-switching (e.g. Woolard 1989); knowledge versus use (e.g. Flaquer 1996; Reixach 1997; Solà 2005; see also the Catalan government's extensive data on language use, available at www6.gencat.net/llengcat/socio/estadistica.htm); second language acquisition (e.g. Azkue and Perales 2005); linguistic landscapes, technology and the media (e.g. Cenoz and Gorter 2005; Atkinson and Kelly-Holmes 2006; Moriarty 2007); linguistic capital, identity and ideology (Domínguez-Seco 2002/2003; Iglesias-Álvarez and Ramalo 2002/2003; Prego-Vázquez 2002/2003, Marshall 2006; Woolard 2008); survival prospects, linguistic sustainability and globalization (e.g. Querol 2002; Bastardas 2007).

Furthermore, Argenter *et al.* (2003) delineate examples of research, particularly in universities as opposed to government-funded activity (see below), focusing increasingly on issues such as the implications of the increasing linguistic diversity of Catalan society within the context of globalization, and employing methods such as ethnography, citing various groups and publications:

1 *GrEPAD* www.upf.edu/dtf/recerca/grups/xarxa/xarxa/grepad/
2 *GELA* www.ub.es/ling/gela.htm
3 Codó 2003, the *UVAL* www.iula.upf.es/uval/upresuk.htm
4 MERCATOR: www.mercator-central.org/
5 See also the xarxa cruscat: www.demolinguistica.cat/web/.

Local government infrastructures

A long tradition exists of 'grassroots' support for these languages, e.g. in the Basque Country, there were approximately 50 support groups in 2000 (Azurmendi, personal communication). Additionally, local administrations have been proactive in promoting sociolinguistic research into Catalan, Basque and Galician. Infrastructures have been developed over the past 30 years designed to actively further 'normalization' of the language and to promote research into the situations of the languages. Argenter *et al.* (2003: 1296) indicate the significance of this infrastructure by noting that in Catalonia in recent years sociolinguistic research in universities has received only around a third as much as that provided by Catalan government (see also Branchadell 2006).

The infrastructure in Catalonia is located within the *Secretaria de Política Lingüística*: www6.gencat.net/llengcat/dgpl/. For information on its counterparts in Valencia, the Balearics, the Basque Country and Galicia, see respectively: www.avl.gva.es/, www.caib.es/govern/organigrama/area.do?lang=en&coduo=34, www.kultura.ejgv.euskadi.net/r46–17893/es/ and www.xunta.es/linguagalega/.

Gibraltar

A British overseas territory at the southernmost tip of the Iberian Peninsula, Gibraltar shares a border with Spain to the north. Its 28,000-speaker community can be defined as bilingual with diglossia – the H and official language English, and the vernacular L *llanito* (or *yanito*), a dialect of Andalusian Spanish strongly influenced by English. After the earliest studies on Gibraltar, the focus was intra-sentential code-switching (Moyer 1998) and more recently intercultural aspects of language contact, lexical availability and domains of usage (Díaz-Hormigo 2001; Wienhold 2003; Escoriza-Morera 2006; Levey 2008).

The officially 'monolingual' territories

Spain's rich cultural and linguistic diversity is not confined to the officially bilingual territories. Although Castilian political dominance of the Iberian Peninsula at the end of the fifteenth century led to the emergence of a hegemonic standard of Castilian, six other main dialects can be distinguished within 'monolingual' Spain: Asturian-Leonese, Aragonese, Andalusian, Extremaduran and Murcian, all deriving from Latin and part of the Romance languages continuum. Spanish (or Castilian) is the language of education, public life, the media and status, and the only official language in the territories where those dialects are spoken. However, at least one region of 'monolingual' Spain has attempted to have its variety recognized as a separate language – Asturias (for the pro-Asturian movement and diglossia in Asturias: see González-Quevedo 2001; Boyer and Lagarde 2002; De Andrés-Díaz 2007).

According to Gimeno-Menéndez's history of Spanish sociolinguistics (2003), the second half of the twentieth century witnessed simultaneously traditional dialectal studies of most of the vernacular peculiarities of rural and urban Spain (collected in Alvar 1996) and studies framed within variationist sociolinguistics. The latter are summarized, in Spanish, in the excellent volume by Blas-Arroyo (2005), and, in English, in Moreno-Fernández (2008), a monographic issue on *The Sociolinguistics of Spanish* with the significant subtitle *Social History, Norm, Variation and Change*, synthesizing the most relevant findings of correlational investigations into geo-social varieties of Spanish in officially non-bilingual regions of Spain, the process of standardization of non-standard areas, maintenance or change of the sociolinguistic situation, the outcome of internal migratory movements, and convergent and divergent tendencies in language contact and sociolinguistic identities.

Language attitude studies reveal a pattern of overt prestige of the national standard variety, Castilian, in officially monolingual communities (e.g. Blanco-Canales 2004). However, other investigations into attitudes towards non-standard varieties have proved revealing concerning language loyalty. For example, Hernández-Campoy and Jiménez-Cano (2003) document the gradual yet consistent spread of standard Castilian features across the Murcian social substrata of the officially monolingual Murcian region to the detriment of local features, and the stigmatization (but covert prestige) of Murcian among local speakers (Hernández-Campoy 2003; Jiménez-Cano 2003). Other studies on speakers' attitudes towards low prestige varieties have been applied to educational policies in officially monolingual but actually bilingual communities (e.g. Asturias: Huguet-Canalís and González-Riaño 2004) or trilingual (e.g. areas of Aragon: Huguet and Lapresta 2006).

Language contact on the borders of speech communities

Language contact on the borders of two or more speech communities has been investigated as a site of construction of hybrid identities and resistance to normativization, e.g. ambivalent attitudes in the Valencian territory close to the frontier with Castile characterized by a Spanish-based variety, *churro*, highly influenced by Catalan/Valencian; the small towns in Alicante characterized by use of Majorcan (Gargallo-Gil 2002); the community of Benasquese/Patués, an Aragonese variety with Catalan and French elements; the Aran Valley, a Pyrenean region where Occitan, Aragonese and Catalan meet in a 3,000-speaker variety, Aranese (Suïls and Huguet 2001; Fort-Cañellas 2007); the 6,000-speaker community of *fala*, a dialect of Portuguese close to the frontier between Extremadure and Portugal, whose sociolinguistic reality and 'enviable' vitality are the focus of Salvador-Plans *et al.* (2000) and Gargallo-Gil (1999). Most of these studies are concerned with policies of normalization of the vernacular and with language attitudes (Gargallo-Gil 2001).

Migrants and ethnic minorities

Immigrants are estimated to be 10 per cent of the total population and to account for an even higher percentage of the birth-rate in Spain. Research into their linguistic situation has focused on diglossia, linguistic conflict, linguistic rights of minority groups, inter-cultural matters and language policy. García-Marcos (2005) exemplifies this trend, claiming that the south-eastern Andalusian province of Almeria, with a very high per-centage of immigrants working in agriculture, should be considered the 'multilingual laboratory of Southern Europe' for language policies. Turell (2001) explored several of the speech communities of the new migrants (Brazilian, Cape-Verdean, Chinese and Maghrebi), and Turell (2007) investigates the most important challenges involved in the integration of the Pakistani and five Sub-Saharan communities. For research on migra-tion and educational matters, specifically the distribution of symbolic capital and the construction of social difference and inequality, see e.g. Martín-Rojo (2003, 2007), Martín-Rojo *et al.* (2004), Martín-Rojo and Moyer (2007) and Pujolar (2007).

More settled compared to some *gitanos* in other countries in Europe, Spanish *gitanos*, an ethnic minority community numbering approximately 400,000, have Spanish or Catalan as their own language. Some 100,000 also speak Caló, the Spanish-based variety of Romani used in restricted domains. Marzo and Turell (2001) described *gitanos'* socio-demographic profile, patterns of language use and cultural identity. Taking as a starting point the high school drop-out rate among *gitanos*, Poveda (2001) and Poveda *et al.* (Poveda and Martín 2003; Poveda *et al.* 2006) focus on issues of language and education.

Language and gender

Although most variationist studies consider sex as one of their variables, few have taken a gender perspective in their assumptions or in the interpretation of their findings, and sex has been associated principally with language change or resistance to change (e.g. López-Morales 1992; Calero-Fernández 1993; Molina 1998).

There has been empirical research into lexical genderlects, summarized by García-Mouton (1999, 2003) and Blas-Arroyo (2005), e.g. vocatives (Azorín *et al.* 1999), taboo words (González-Martínez 1997), lexical availability (Blas-Arroyo and Casanova-Ávalos 2001/2002), lexical preferences, prefixes, suffixes, and euphemisms (López-García and Morant 1992). As for gendered conversation, Cestero (2000, 2006) studied cooperative strategies, and Páramo (2002) showed how boys and girls support each other's statements, con-structing the other's and one's own face. Blanco-Canales (1999) focused on left dislocation of topicalized first person pronoun at the beginning of women's turns, while others have studied discourse markers (Serrano 1995), interpreted in terms of female linguistic mitigation and insecurity, or male factual and self-positioning support. Álvarez-López (2002/03) explored male strategies of humour; Acuña-Ferreira (2002/03) the gendered display of emotion in complaints; and Martín-Rojo (1997, 1998), Martín-Rojo and Garí (2002), Martín-Rojo and Gómez-Esteban (2003, 2005) how female bosses and executives have to negotiate their gendered professional identities at work. Gendered paralinguistic features have also been studied by López-García and Morant (1992) and by Cestero (1996), who showed how laughter contributes to engendering female solidarity plaiting but to the manifestation of male disagreement. Calero-Fernández (2007) analysed social attitudes towards genderlects.

In the 1990s, research was also concerned with sexist language usage (Calero-Fernández 1991, 1992; Bengoechea 2003), and standard reference works of official languages. The sexist representation of women in the 21st and 22nd editions of the highly influential normative *Dictionary of the Spanish Academy* (RAE 1992, 2001) has been exposed in Vargas *et al.* (1998), Lledó *et al.* (2004) or Bengoechea (2008). Lledó (2005) analysed the sexist bias of two major Catalan reference works and Marco (1991) did the same with Galician school dictionaries.

Language and youth culture

Given the connection between gender and age as regards language change and a concern with descriptive studies of lineal stratification, most variationist research has taken both variables together, documented by Blas-Arroyo (2005) and Moreno-Fernández (2008). Thus, most variationist investigations of age have been interpreted with a view to detecting future directions and prospects rather than analyzing in depth the construction of youth identities, a task taken on by others. For instance, Boix-Fuster (1993) linked language production, code-switching and the construction of youth identity in Barcelona, a study followed by others in bilingual areas (e.g. Pujolar 2000, on gender identity and language choice among Catalan peer-groups). Rodríguez-Fernández (2002) dealt with juvenile speech varieties.

Complementary perspectives of sociolinguistic research

A number of oral Spanish corpora have been elaborated (López-Morales 1996): e.g. ALFAL (Samper-Padilla *et al.* 1998); COLA; *Corpus del habla en Almería* (Cortés-Rodríguez *et al.* 2006); *Corpus oral de referencia del español contemporáneo*; COSER; ALCORE/COVJA (Azorín and Jiménez 1997); PRESEEA (Moreno-Fernández 2005a, 2005b, 2005c); Val. Es.Co (Briz and grupo Val.Es.Co 2002). The oral corpus of the Spanish Academy (CREA), a mere 10 per cent of its macro-corpus, includes some of those corpora. Additionally, many corpora-based studies examining perspectives of conversation analysis and pragmatics exist.

A final point needs to be made: relevant as it is, the development of sociolinguistics in Spain has been quantitatively inferior to other concerns within linguistics (Monroy-Casas and Hernández-Campoy 1994–95; Gimeno-Menéndez 2003). Here we have restricted ourselves to mentioning the main studies of 'traditional' sociolinguistics, as space limitations do not permit addressing the enormous number of investigations in complementary disciplines, such as discourse analysis or pragmatics.

Portugal

The changing face of Portugal

Despite historical similarities, Portugal's sociolinguistic situation is very different from Spain's. Today Portugal encompasses its continental regions and the archipelagos of Madeira and the Azores. However, as recently as 1974, Portugal administered five African colonies, Macau and Timor-Leste. The African colonies gained independence in 1974–75, Macau was 'returned' to China in 1999, and in 2002 Timor-Leste gained its independence from Indonesia and designated Portuguese an official language.

Under Portuguese law (1975), citizens were those born or naturalized in any territory under Portuguese rule. Accordingly during decolonialization people from the former colonies could (re)locate to Portugal, irrespective of their colour, ethnic or religious origin, native language or previous residence. Rocha-Trindade (2001) estimates that in the mid-1970s alone, 500,000 to 800,000 *retornados* located in Portugal, a large, heterogeneous group requiring assimilation.

Political oppression and desire to avoid military service in Africa led to the emigration of approximately 1.5 million Portuguese in the 1960s and 1970s (see Royo 2005). Not only did this represent more than 10 per cent of the population, but the demographic structure of certain regions was dramatically altered in light of different emigration patterns: (1) the male guest worker (wife and children left behind); (2) the couple (children left with family); and (3) the entire family. The diaspora is currently estimated at 4.5 million, equivalent to nearly half of Portugal's resident population, according to the Presidency of the European Union (2007).

With entry into the European Union (1985) and greater economic and political stability in the early 1990s, Portugal became attractive to immigrants; Cape Verde, Brazil and the Ukraine currently provide the largest numbers of registered foreigners (Instituto Nacional de Estatística 2006). Marques and Góis note that between 2001 and 2004 alone, the Government gave residence permits to more than 100,000 Eastern Europeans (2007: 1), equivalent to 1 per cent of Portugal's population. This new pattern brings an additional challenge, as, for the first time, large numbers of immigrants do not speak Portuguese.

The linguistic situation

Portuguese is the only official language nationally, its norm being loosely defined as the speech of educated speakers along the Lisbon–Coimbra corridor (e.g. Inês Duarte 2004: 53). Minority language status has been recognized for Mirandese (in Miranda do Douro), a variety of Astur-Leonese mixed with Portuguese, an official language in that region since 1998. Attempts to recognize a second variety, Barranquenho, spoken in the border town of Barrancos and combining features of Portuguese with Extremaduran and Andalusian Spanish, have been unsuccessful.

Brief description of sociolinguistic research

The influx of *retornados* and immigrants over the past three decades has changed the face of Portugal irrevocably. Its population is more diverse than one would expect, given its political isolation for much of the twentieth century, providing a rich sociolinguistic environment for study. Nevertheless, research in sociolinguistics is scant. The Portuguese National Library database (PORBASE) lists only eight doctoral dissertations under 'sociolinguistics', three presented at foreign universities. Topics include classroom talk (Pedro 1992), socio-semantic variation (Faria 1983), address forms (Medeiros 1985; Hammermüller 1993), sociolinguistic aspects of verb complementation (M.E.R. Marques 1988), urban studies of Lisbon (Navas Sánchez-Elez 1983) and Aveiro (Matias 1993), and two contrastive studies: power in the Portuguese and French media (Capucho 2000) and Portuguese-English language contact in the United Kingdom (Cardoso 2004). This concentration of studies in the 1980s could have led to the development of a strong sociolinguistics research tradition; however, the three researchers residing in Portugal at that time soon followed an academic path outside Portuguese sociolinguistics.

Studies of language variation

The few sociolinguistic studies involving dialectal variation are not a cohesive group, but are nevertheless interesting. Cardoso's study (1999) is innovative, adding to Labov's methodology a modified dialectological interview and evaluation of alternate pronunciations. D.J. Silva's studies of Azorean Portuguese (e.g. 2005) use variable rule analysis to examine changes in vowel quality and lenition; his work brings precision to features often ignored or poorly described. Moutinho's study of Oporto speech (2001) has led to work developing synthetic voices able to mimic dialect, particularly useful for giving authentic-sounding voices to people with special needs (e.g. Paiva et al. 2005). Language contact on the Portuguese-Spanish border (particularly Galicia's) has been researched, but studies generally initiate in Spain (e.g. Álvarez Cáccamo 2000; Beswick 2005).

One area receiving sustained attention during the last 25 years is the complex system of Portuguese address. Carreira (e.g. 2001) focuses on socio-pragmatic and semantic aspects of address and politeness, demonstrating how, by identifying the addressee, the speaker engages in self-identification and proxemic play or attenuates the mood of the exchange. Hammermüller (e.g. 2003) considers semantic implications of the selection and omission of address forms (particularly *você*). S.M. Oliveira has developed theoretical models of increasing complexity to demonstrate how speakers construct identities for themselves and others through address (cf. Medeiros 1985 and S.M. Oliveira 1993, 1995, 1996, 2006, in press); replicating her original fieldwork study at intervals over 20 years, her data provides real-time comparisons (e.g. 1995, 2005).

Discourse analysis

Discourse analysis has been a productive research area in Portugal. Theses produced since 1994 number 31 (7 PhDs, 24 MAs), so the critical mass for developing a strong research tradition appears to exist. Among the issues analysed: drugs (e.g. Alves 2000), abortion (e.g. Estrada 1998), homosexuality and the construction of gender (e.g. Figueiredo 2004), emigration (e.g. V. Santos 2004), the environment (e.g. Carvalho et al. 2005) and rising racism (e.g. Cunha et al. 2003). Analyses of politics and the media often focus on ways discourse strategies of the powerful differ from those of the powerless (e.g. Dias 1994). Isabel Duarte (2004) considers the discourse of journalists, demonstrating how they simultaneously appear to be objective yet reveal their subjectivity through the way they quote sources, while J.R. dos Santos considers the power of language to transmit and transform reality in war reporting (2001). M.A. Marques (2006) presents the current state of pragmatics- and semantics-based discourse analysis research in Portugal – its history, conferences, journals and academic courses, complementing this chapter in which social issues are in focus.

For many reasons, including the above-mentioned massive emigration of males, the percentage of women in the workforce doubled (to 50 per cent) between 1960 and 1995 (Barreto 2002). Nevertheless, the glass ceiling and gender stereotypes remain. Nogueira (2006) describes competing discourses of women in power: *essentialist-individualist* thinking in denying sex discrimination, while *experience-acquired competence* discourse providing an outlet for acknowledging it. These women neither challenge the stereotypes nor see themselves as facilitators of change (ibid.: 71). Analyses of anti-drug campaign literature reveal stereotypical images of women's roles. Men are portrayed as capable problem-solvers, both at work and home, while career women create 'disharmony': Pinto Coelho describes the brochure image of a woman professionally dressed, facing away from her family as she leaves home for her job (2004). See Oliveira and Amâncio's (2006) excellent overview on the importance of discourse analysis and feminist theories to social psychology.

Identity construction research is another emerging field, with varying attention to the role that language plays (e.g. Figueiredo 2004). However, not generally addressed is the commodification of prestige or status via discourse strategies. Gomes and Freitas (2002) discuss metaphors of national identity and pride deriving from the connection between Portugal's Euro 2000 team's achievements and the nation; S.M. Oliveira (2002) reviews coverage of the announcement of Saramago, controversial recipient of the 1998 Nobel Prize in Literature. In both examples, prestige is a commodity to be bought (attributed), sold (denied) or even borrowed (represented by the sale of more newspapers).

Additional resources

Few Portuguese articles are indexed in full-text databases, so university research centers provide a good assessment of ongoing research:

Universidade Nova de Lisboa	www.fcsh.unl.pt/clunl/
University of Aveiro	www2.ii.ua.pt/cidlc/gcl/Publicacoes.htm
University of Coimbra	www.uc.pt/celga/eng/home.htm and www.ces.fe.uc.pt/
University of Évora	www.cidehus.uevora.pt/index.htm
University of Lisbon	www.clul.ul.pt
University of Minho	www.cecs.uminho.pt
University of Oporto	www.clup-porto.com/

Additionally, the Universities of Minho and Beira Interior disseminate their staff's publications online; see www.repositorium.sdum.uminho.pt and www.bocc.ubi.pt/, respectively.

Final considerations and suggestions for future research

Given Portugal's cultural and linguistic diversity and continued ties to its former colonies, more researchers are needed to investigate issues of sociolinguistic interest. Avenues for investigation not (widely) addressed include sociolinguistic correlates of social integration to provide linguistic counterpoint to sociological studies, such as Cabecinhas' of racial stereotypes (2003), social trajectories, language attitude studies, issues in cross-cultural politeness, bilingualism/multilingualism, code-switching, nationalism and language use and urban dialectology.

References

Acuña-Ferreira, V. (2002/2003) 'Gendered emotive displays in complaint discourse', *Estudios de Socio-lingüística*, 3/2 and 4/1, 139–72.

Alvar, M. (ed.) (1996) *Manual de Dialectología Hispánica. El español de España*, Barcelona: Ariel.

Álvarez Cáccamo, C. (2000) 'Para um modelo do "code-switching" e a alternância de variedades como fenómenos distintos: dados do discurso galego-português/espanhol na Galiza', *Estudios de Socio-lingüística* ed. by Xoán Paulo Rodríguez Yáñez, Anxo Lorenzo Suárez and María Carmen Cabeza Pereiro, 1(1), 111–28. Online. Available at: www.udc.es/dep/lx/cac/publ.htm.

Álvarez-López, S. (2002/2003) 'Functions and strategies of male humour in cross-gender interactions', *Estudios de Sociolingüística*, 3/2 and 4/1, 173–205.

Alves, A. F. R. (2000) 'Abordagem narrativa da dependência da heroína: estrutura, processo e conteúdo das narrativas de dependentes de heroína', PhD dissertation, University of Minho.

Aracil, L. V. (1982) *Papers de sociolingüística*, Barcelona: La Magrana.

Argenter, J. A., Marti, J. and Massanell, M. (2003) 'Lingüística i ciències dl llenguatge', *Reports de la Recerca a Catalunya 1996–2002*, Barcelona: Institut d'Estudis Catalans.

Atkinson, D. and Kelly-Holmes, H. (2006) 'Linguistic normalisation and the market: advertising and linguistic choice in El Periódico de Catalunya', *Journal of Language Problems and Language Planning*, 30, 3, 239–60.

Azkue, J. and Perales, J. (2005) 'The teaching of Basque to adults', in M. J. Azurmendi and I. Martínez de Luna (eds) *The Case of Basque: From the Past toward the Future. International Journal of the Sociology of Language*, 174, 73–85.

Azorín, D. and Jiménez, J. L. (1997) *Corpus oral de la variedad juvenil universitaria del español hablado en Alicante*, Alicante: Instituto de Cultura Juan Gil-Albert.

Azorín, D., Martínez, M. A. and Santamaría, M. I. (1999) 'Léxico y creación léxica en un corpus oral de lenguaje juveni', in J. Fernández González, C. Fernández Juncal, M. Marcos Sánchez, E. Prieto de los Mozos and L. Santos Río (eds) *Lingüística para el siglo XXI*, Salamanca: Universidad de Salamanca, vol. I, pp. 217–27.

Azurmendi, M.-J. and Martínez de Luna, I. (eds) (2006) *The Case of Basque: Past, Present and Future*, Donostia/San Sebastián: Soziolinguistika Klusterra.

Badia i Margarit, A. M. (1969) *La llengua dels barcelonins: resultats d'una enquesta sociològico-lingüística*, Barcelona: Edicions 62.

——(2006) 'Sociolingüística homogènia i comportaments idiomàtics varis', in F. Vallverdú (ed.) *Cap on va la sociolingüística? II Jornada de l'Associació d'Amics del Professor Antoni M. Badia i Margarit (Barcelona 20 d'octubre de 2005)*, Barcelona: Institut d'Estudis Catalans, pp. 13–49.

Barreto, A. (2002) 'Mudança social em Portugal, 1960/2000', *Working Paper* 6–02. Lisbon: Instituto de Ciências Sociais, University of Lisbon.

Bastardas, A. (2007) 'Linguistic sustainability for a multilingual humanity', *Glossa: An Ambilingual Interdisciplinary Journal*, 2, Catalans.

Bengoechea, M. (2003) 'La representación de la agencia femenina en las secciones políticas de cuatro diarios españoles', *Estudios de Sociolingüística*, 4, 2, 563–88.

——(2008) 'Textualización de una identidad genérica femenina homogeneizada: Rasgos esencialistas en el Diccionario de la RAE', in A. Davies, P. Kumaraswami and C. Williams (eds) *Making Waves*, Cambridge: Cambridge Scholar Press, pp. 71–89.

Beswick, J. (2005) 'Linguistic homogeneity in Galician and Portuguese borderland communities', *Estudios de Sociolingüística: Linguas, Sociedades e Culturas*, 6, 1, 39–64.

Blanco-Canales, A. (1999) 'Presencia/ausencia de sujeto pronominal de primera persona en español', *Español Actual*, 72, 31–9.

——(2004) *Estudio sociolingüístico de Alcalá de Henares*, Alcalá de Henares: Universidad de Alcalá.

Blas-Arroyo, J. L. (2005) *Sociolingüística del Español*, Madrid: Cátedra.

Blas-Arroyo, J. L. and Casanova-Ávalos, M. (2001/2002) 'Factores sociales y de adscripción lingüística en el léxico disponible de una comunidad bilingüe española', *Lenguas Modernas*, 28/29, 24–43.

Boix-Fuster, E. (1993) *Tria no és trair. Identitat i llengua en els joves de Barcelona*, Barcelona: Edicions 62.

——(2006) 'La sociolingüística catalana', in F. Vallverdú (ed.) *Cap on va la sociolingüística? II Jornada de l'Associació d'Amics del Professor Antoni M. Badia i Margarit (Barcelona 20 d'octubre de 2005)*, Barcelona: Institut d'Estudis Catalans, pp. 81–90.

Bouzada Fernández, X., Fernández Paz, A. and Lorenzo Suárez, A. (2002) *O Proceso de Normalización do Idioma Galego (1980–2000)*, vol. II: *Educación*, Santiago: Consello da Cultura Galega.

Boyer, H. and Lagarde, C. (eds) (2002) *L'Espagne et ses langues. Un modèle écolinguistique?*, Paris: L'Harmattan.

Branchadell, A. (2006) 'Ser competitius, i fins i tot capdavanters, a nivell europeu i internacional', in F. Vallverdú (ed.) *Cap on va la sociolingüística? II Jornada de l'Associació d'Amics del Professor Antoni M. Badia i Margarit (Barcelona 20 d'octubre de 2005)*, Barcelona: Institut d'Estudis, pp. 91–100.

Briz, A. (ed.) (1995) 'La conversación coloquial (Materiales para su estudio)', *Cuadernos de Filología*, Anejo XVI, València: Universitat de València.

——(2001) 'Corpus de conversaciones coloquiales', *Oralia*, Anejo 1. Madrid: Arco.

Briz, A. and grupo Val.Es.Co. (2002) *Corpus de conversaciones coloquiales*, Madrid: Arco.

Cabecinhas, R. (2003) 'Categorização e diferenciação: a percepção do estatuto social de diferentes grupos étnicos em Portugal', *Cadernos do Noroeste. Sociedade e Cultura*, 5, 69–91.

Calero-Fernández, M. A. (1991) *La imagen de la mujer a través de la tradición paremiológica española (lengua y cultura)*, Barcelona: Publicacions Universitat de Barcelona.

——(1992) 'Términos y expresiones sexistas en español: los "duales aparentes" y los tacos', in R. Lorenzo Vázquez (ed.) *Actas do XIX Congreso Internacional de Lingüística e Filoloxia Romanicas*, Santiago de Compostela: Fundación Pedro Barrie de la Maza, 3, 371–80.

——(1993) *Estudio sociolingüístico del habla de Toledo*, Lérida: Pagés.

——(2007) *Percepción social de los sexolectos*, Cádiz: Universidad de Cádiz.

Capucho, M. F. D. (2000) 'Je voudrais dire un petit mot langage et pouvoir: analyse du(-es) discours en télévision', PhD dissertation, Catholic University of Portugal.

Cardoso, J. N. P. C. (1999) *Sociolinguística rural: A freguesia de Almalaguês*, Coimbra: Edições Colibri.

——(2004) 'Sociolinguística urbana de contacto. O português falado e escrito no Reino Unido', PhD dissertation, University of Coimbra.

Carreira, M. H. A. (2001) 'Formas de tratamento de Português como designação do outro e de si: Perspectivas de investigação e de transposição didáctica', *Cadernos de PLE (Português Língua Estrangeira)* 1, University of Aveiro.

Carvalho, A., Lázaro, A., Cabecinhas, R. and Ramos, R. (2005) 'Discursos e representações ambientais: processos comunicativos entre actores sociais, media e cidadãos', paper presented at the Portuguese Association of Communication Sciences, Aveiro. Online. Available at: www.repositorium.sdum.uminho.pt/bitstream/1822/3210/1/acarvalho_Com.SOPCOM_2005.pdf (accessed 1 May 2007).

Casesnoves, R., Sankoff, D. and Turell, M. T. (2006) 'Linguistic shift and community language: the effect of demographic factors in the Valencian region, Balearic islands and Catalonia', in C. Mar-Molinero and M. Stewart (eds) *Globalization and Language in the Spanish Speaking World: Macro and Micro Perspectives*, Basingstoke: Palgrave Macmillan, pp. 197–219.

Cenoz, J. and Gorter, D. (2005) 'Linguistic landscape and minority languages', *International Journal of Multilingualism*, 3, 67–80.

Cestero, A. M. (1996) 'Funciones de la risa en la conversación en lengua española', *LEA, Lingüística Española Actual*, 18, 2, 279–98.

——(2000) 'La influencia de la edad y el sexo en la producción y duración de los turnos de apoyo en la conversación en español', in A. Englebert, M. Pierrard, L. Rosier and D. Van Raemdonck (eds) *Actes du XXIIe Congrès International de Linguistique et de Philologie Romanes*, VII, Tübingen: Max Niemeyer, pp. 102–7.

——(2006) 'Cooperación en la conversación: estrategias estructurales características de las mujeres', *Lingüística en la Red*. Online. Available at: www.linred.com/articulos_pdf/LR_articulo_24042007.pdf.

Codó Olsina, E. (2003) 'The struggle for meaning: immigration and multilingual talk in an institutional setting', unpublished PhD thesis, Universitat Autònoma de Barcelona.

Cortés-Rodríguez, L., Carbonero, P. and Bañón, A. (2006) 'Corpus para el estudio de las hablas andaluzas I. El corpus del habla de Sevilla y el corpus del habla en Almería', *Oralia*, 8, 161–88.

Cunha, I. F., Policarpo, V., Monteiro, T. L. and Figueiras, R. (2003) 'Media and discrimination: an exploratory study of the Portuguese case'. Online. Available at: www.bocc.ubi.pt/pag/ferin-isabel-media-and-discrimination.pdf (accessed 28 July 2009).

De Andrés-Díaz, R. (2007) 'Linguistic borders of the Western Peninsula', *International Journal of the Sociology of Language*, 184, 121–38.

Dias, I. (1994) 'Família e discurso político: algumas pistas de análise', *Sociologia* 4, 97–171. Faculty of Letras do Porto. Online. Available at: www.ler.letras.up.pt/uploads/ficheiros/1319.pdf (accessed 7 August 2007).

Díaz-Hormigo, M. T. (2001) 'La situación intercultural e interlingüística de Gibraltar', in J. Calvo Pérez (ed.) *Contacto interlingüístico e intercultural en el mundo hispano. Valencia, 8–12 de noviembre 1999*, vol. 1, Valencia: Universitat de València, pp. 91–112.

Domínguez-Seco, L. (2002/2003) 'Social prestige and linguistic identity: on the ideological conditions behind the standardisation of Galician', *Estudios de Sociolingüística*, 3/2 and 4/1, 207–28.

Duarte, I. (2004) 'Gramática descritiva, língua padrão e variação', in R. Álvarez Blanco and H. Monteagudo (eds) *Norma Lingüística e variación*, Santiago de Compostela: Consello da Cultura Galega: Instituto da Língua Galega, pp. 43–59.

Duarte, I. M. (2004) 'A citação no discurso de imprensa: uma "Amostra" do Caso Moderna', in I. M. Duarte and F. Oliveira (eds) *Da Língua e do Discurso*, Porto: Campo das Letras, pp. 311–21.

Escoriza-Morera, L. (2006) 'Disponibilidad léxica y multilingüismo. El contacto entre inglés y español en Gibraltar', *Actas del VI Congreso de Lingüística General*, Madrid: Arco, pp. 756–62.

Estrada, M. R. N. G. (1998) 'A despenalização do aborto: textos/discursos, argumentos e imagens', MA thesis, University of Oporto.

Faria, I. H. (1983) 'Para a análise da variação sócio-semântica: Estrato sócio-profissional, sexo e local de produção enquanto factores reguladores, em Português contemporâneo, das formas de auto-referência e de orientação para o significado', PhD dissertation, University of Lisbon.

Fernández Paz, A., Lorenzo Suárez, A. M. and Ramallo, F. (2007) *A planificación lingüística nos centros educativos*, Santiago: Xunta de Galicia.

Figueiredo, S. A. M. da S. de. (2004) 'Eles e elas: a construção identitária do género: uma análise em sociolinguística', MA thesis, Catholic University, Viseu.

Flaquer, L. (1996) *El català, llengua pública o privada?*, Barcelona: Empúries.

Fort-Cañellas, M. R. (2007) 'Sociolinguistics on the Aragon-Catalonia border', *International Journal of the Sociology of Language*, 184, 109–20.

García-Marcos, F. J. (2005) 'Contacto y planificación lingüística en Almería', *Language Design*, 7, 85–104.

García-Mouton, P. (1999) *Cómo hablan las mujeres*, Madrid: Arco.

——(2003) *Así hablan las mujeres*, Madrid: La esfera de los libros.

Gargallo-Gil, J. E. (1999) *Las hablas de San Martín de Trevejo, Eljas y Valverde del Fresno*, Mérida: Junta de Extremadura.

——(2001) 'Aranés, mirandés, ¿valego? Tres enclaves romances de fronteira, tres retos de supervivencia e da identidade na Europa do novo milenio', *A Trabe de Ouro*, 47, 349–63.

——(2002) 'Dues menes de frontera (lingüística i administrativa), diversos models de parlars (i de parlants) xurros fronterers', *Caplletra*, 32, 127–41.

Gimeno-Menéndez, F. (2003) 'Historia de la dialectología y sociolingüística españolas', in J. C. Rovira Soler (ed.) *Con Alonso Zamora Vicente*, vol. I, Alicante: Universidad de Alicante, pp. 67–84.

Gomes, R. and Freitas, M. (2002) 'A construção da identidade nacional na imprensa desportiva portuguesa: análise do discurso jornalístico durante o Euro 2000 de futebol', *Revista Digital* 8 (48). Online. Available at: www.efdeportes.com/efd48/jurnal.htm (accessed 28 August 2007).

González-Martínez, A. (1997) 'Disponibilidad léxica de Cádiz,' PhD dissertation, Universidad de Cádiz.

González-Quevedo, R. (2001) 'The Asturian speech community', in M.T. Turell (ed.) *Multilingualism in Spain*, Clevedon: Multilingual Matters, pp. 165–82.

Hammermüller, G. (1993) *Die Anrede im Portugiesischen: Eine soziolinguistische Untersuchung zu Anredekonvention und Anredeformen des gegenwärtigen europäischen Portugiesisch*, Chemnitz: Nov neuer Verlag.

——(2003) 'Adresser ou éviter, c'est la question … – comment s'adresser à quelqu'un en portugais sans avoir recours à un pronom ou à une autre forme équivalente', paper presented at the 'Second person pronouns and forms of address in the European languages' conference, organized by the Cervantes Institute, Paris. Online. Available at: www.cvc.cervantes.es/obref/coloquio_paris/ponencias/pdf/cvc_hammermueller.pdf (accessed: 1 May 2007).

Haugen, E. (1972) *The Ecology of Language*, Stanford, CA: Stanford University Press.

Hernández-Campoy, J. M. (2003) 'Geolinguistic patterns of diffusion in a Spanish region: the case of the dialect of Murcia', *Estudios de Sociolingüística*, 4, 2, 613–52.

Hernández-Campoy, J. M. and Jiménez-Cano, J. M. (2003) 'Broadcasting standardisation: An analysis of the linguistic normalisation process in Murcian Spanish', *Journal of Sociolinguistics*, 7, 3, 321–47.

Herrero-Valeiro, M. J. (2003) 'The discourse of language in Galiza: normalisation, diglossia, and conflict', *Estudios de Sociolingüística*, 3/2 and 4/1, 289–320.

Huguet, A. and Lapresta, C. (2006) 'Las actitudes lingüísticas en Aragón. Una visión desde la escuela', *Estudios de Sociolingüística*, 7, 2, 265–88.

Huguet-Canalís, A. and González-Riaño, X. A. (2004) *Actitudes lingüísticas, lengua familiar y enseñanza de la lengua minoritari*, Barcelona: Horsori.

Iglesias-Álvarez, A. and Ramallo, F. (2002/2003) 'Language as a diacritical in terms of cultural and resistance identities in Galicia', *Estudios de Sociolingüística*, 3/2 and 4/1, 255–88.

Instituto Nacional da Estatística [INE] (2006) 'Foreign population in Portugal 2005'. Online. Available at: www.ine.pt/portal/page/portal/PORTAL_INE/Destaques?DESTAQUESdest_boui=5453867& DESTAQUESmodo=2 (accessed 27 August 2007).

Jiménez-Cano, J. M. (ed.) (2003) *Estudios sociolingüísticos del dialecto murciano*, Murcia: Universidad de Murcia.

Kremnitz, G. (2006) 'Català, valencià, balear: despostes científiques a qüestions polítiques? Reflexions sobre la unitat i la diversitat de l'espai lingüístic català', in F. Vallverdú (ed.) *Cap on va la sociolingüística? II Jornada de l'Associació d'Amics del Professor Antoni M. Badia i Margarit (Barcelona 20 d'octubre de 2005)*, Barcelona: Institut d'Estudis Catalans, pp. 63–76.

Lasagabaster, D. (2003) *Trilingüismo en la Enseñanza: Actitudes hacia la Lengua Minoritaria y la Extranjera*, Lleida: Milenio.

Levey, D. (2008) *Language Change and Variation in Gibraltar*, Amsterdam: John Benjamins.

Lledó, E. (2005) *L'espai de les dones als diccionaris: silencis i presències*, Barcelona: Eumo.

Lledó, E., Calero-Fernández, M. A. and Forgas-Berdet, E. (2004) *De mujeres y diccionarios. Evolución de lo femenino en la 22 edición del DRAE*, Madrid: Instituto de la Mujer.

López-García, Á. and Morant, R. (1992) *Gramática femenina*, Madrid: Cátedra.

López-Morales, H. (1992) 'Style variation, sex and linguistic consciousness', *LynX*, 3, 43–54.

——(1996) '*Corpora* orales hispánicos', in A. Briz, J. Gómez, M. I. Martínez and grupo Val.Es.Co. (eds) *Pragmática y gramática del español hablado*, Valencia: Universidad de Valencia, pp. 137–45.

Marco, A. (1991) 'Estereotipos sexistas em dicionários escolares', *Agália*, 28, 433–43.

Mar-Molinero, C. (2000) *The Politics of Language in the Spanish-speaking World: From Colonisation to Globalisation*, London: Routledge.

Marques, J. C. and Góis, P. (2007) 'Ukrainian migration to Portugal: from non-existence to the top three immigrant groups', *Migration Online. Focus on Central and Eastern Europe*. Online. Available at: www.aa.ecn.cz/img_upload/3bfc4ddc48d13ae0415c78ceae108bf5/JCMarquesPGois_UkraniansinPortugal.pdf (accessed 1 September 2007).

Marques, M. A. (2006) 'El análisis del discurso en Portugal: estado de la cuestión', in M. Villayandre Llamazares (ed.) *Actas del XXXV Simposio Internacional de la Sociedad Española de Lingüística*, León: University of León, pp. 1177–95.

Marques, M. E. R. (1988) 'Complementação verbal: estudo sociolinguístico', PhD dissertation, Universidade Nova de Lisboa.

Marshall, S. (2006) 'Spanish-speaking Latin Americans in Catalonia: reflexivity and knowledgeability in constructions of Catalan', in C. Mar-Molinero and M. Stewart (eds) *Globalization and Language in the Spanish Speaking World: Macro and Micro Perspectives*, Basingstoke: Palgrave Macmillan, pp. 158–77.

Martín-Rojo, L. (1997) 'The politics of gender: agency and self-reference in women's discourse', *Belgian Journal of Linguistics*, 11, 231–54.

——(1998) 'Intertextuality and the construction of a new female identity', in M. Bengoechea and R. Sola (eds) *Intertextuality/Intertextualidad*, Alcalá de Henares: Universidad de Alcalá, pp. 81–98.

——(2003) 'Ideological dilemmas in language and cultural policies in Madrid schools', in D. R. Patrick and J. Freeland (eds) *Language Rights and Language 'Survival': A Sociolinguistic Exploration*, Manchester: St Jerome, pp. 243–72.

——(2007) *Constructing Inequality in Multilingual Classrooms*, Berlin: Mouton.

Martín-Rojo, L. and Garí, A. (2002) 'El obstáculo de ser mujer. Prácticas comunicativas en el trabajo', *Quaderns de Filologia*, 7, 129–44.

Martín-Rojo, L. and Gómez-Esteban, C. (2003) 'Discourse at work: when women take on the role of manager', in G. Weiss and R. Wodak (eds) *Critical Discourse Analysis: Theory and Interdisciplinarity*, New York: Palgrave Macmillan, pp. 241–71.

——(2005) 'The gender of power: the female style in labour organizations', in M. Lazar (eds) *Feminist Critical Discourse Analysis*, London: Palgrave, pp. 61–89.

Martín-Rojo, L. and Moyer, M. (2007) 'Language, migration and citizenship: new challenges in the regulation of bilingualism', in M. Heller (ed.) *Bilingualism: A Social Approach*, London: Palgrave, pp. 137–60.

Martín-Rojo, L., Nussbaun, L. and Unamuno, V. (eds) (2004) *Estudios de Sociolingüística*, 5, 2, Special Issue, *Escuela e inmigración: dilemas de las políticas lingüística*.

Maruny, C. L. and Domínguez, M. M. (2001) 'L'adquisició del català en alumnes d'origen marroquí a l'ensenyament obligatori', Noves de SL: estiu.

Marzo, A. and Turell, M. T. (2001) 'The Gitano communities', in M. T. Turell (ed.) *Multilingualism in Spain*, Clevedon: Multilingual Matters, pp. 215–34.

Mateo, M. (2005) 'Language policy and planning of the status of Basque, I: the Basque Autonomous Community (BAC)', in M.-J. Azurmendi and I. Martínez de Luna (eds) *The Case of Basque: From the Past toward the Future. International Journal of the Sociology of Language*, 174, 9–24.

Matias, M. de F. de R. F. (1993) 'Aspectos da estrutura sociolinguística da cidade de Aveiro', PhD dissertation. University of Coimbra.

Medeiros, S. M. de. (1985) 'A model of address from negotiation: a sociolinguistic study of continental Portuguese', PhD dissertation, University of Texas at Austin (University Microfilms, Ann Arbor, Michigan).

Mendiguren, X. and Iñigo, J. I. (2006) 'The social movement in favour of the normalization of the Basque language', in M.-J. Azurmendi and I. Martinez de Luna (eds) *The Case of Basque: Past, Present and Future*, Donostia/San Sebastián: Soziolinguistika Klusterra, pp. 53–66.

Mesthrie, R. (ed.) (2001) *Concise Encyclopedia of Sociolinguistics*, Oxford: Elsevier.

Molina, I. (1998) *La fonética de Toledo. Contexto geográfico y social*, Alcalá de Henares: Universidad de Alcalá.

Monroy-Casas, R. and Hernández-Campoy, J. M. (1994–95) 'La sociolingüística aplicada en la lingüística aplicada española (1983–93)', *Revista Española de Lingüística Aplicada*, 10, 177–204.

Montoya, B. (2000) *Els Alacantins catalanoparlants: una generació interrompuda*, Barcelona: Institut d'Estudis Catalans.

Moreno-Fernández, F. (2005a) 'Corpus para el estudio del español en su variación geográfica y social', El corpus PRESEEA, *Oralia*, 8, 123–39.

——(2005b) 'Project for the Sociolinguistic Study of Spanish from Spain and America (PRESEEA): a corpus with a grammar and discourse bias', in T. Takagaki, S. Zaima, Y. Tsuruga, F. Moreno Fernández and Y. Kawaguchi (eds) *Corpus-Based Approaches to Sentence Structures*, Amsterdam, John Benjamins, pp. 265–88.

——(2005c) 'Corpora of spoken Spanish language: the representativeness issue', in Y. Kawaguchi, S. Zaima, T. Takagaki, K. Shibano and M. Usami (eds) *Linguistic Informatics: State of the Art and the Future*, Amsterdam: John Benjamins, pp. 120–44.

——(ed.) (2007) 'Spanish in Spain: the sociolinguistics of bilingual areas', *International Journal of the Sociology of Language*, 184.

——(2008) 'The sociolinguistics of Spanish. Social history, norm, variation and change', *International Journal of the Sociology of Language*, 193/194.

Moriarty, M. (2007) 'Minority language television as a mechanism of language policy: a comparative study of the Irish and Basque sociolinguistic contexts', unpublished PhD thesis, University of Limerick.

Moutinho, L. de C. (2001) *Falar do Porto com todos os bês – um estudo sociolinguístico*, Oporto: Campo das Letras.

Moyer, M. (1998) 'Bilingual conversational strategies in Gibraltar', in P. Auer (ed.) *Code-Switching in Conversation: Language, Interaction and Identity*, London: Routledge, pp. 215–34.

Navas Sánchez-Élez, M. V. (1983) 'Niveles sociolingüísticos en el habla popular de Lisboa, Aplicación de una encuesta sociolingüística en Lisboa,' PhD dissertation, Universidad Complutense de Madrid.

355

Ninyoles, R. L. (1969) *Conflicto lingüístic valencià*, Valencia: Tres i Quatre.

Nogueira, M. da C. de O. C. (2006) 'Os discursos das mulheres em posições de poder', *Caderno de Psicologia Social do Trabalho*, 9, 2, 57–72.

O'Donnell, P. (2001) *Mother Language, Father Language, Nanny Language: Who Learns What from Whom in Catalonia*, Noves de SL: hivern/primavera.

Oliveira, S. M. de. (1993) 'Um modelo psico-sociolinguístico de formas de tratamento', *Actas do VIII Encontro da Associação Portuguesa de Linguística*, Lisbon: University of Lisbon, pp. 330–42.

——(1995) 'Mudança e continuidade nas formas de tratamento em Évora', in *Actas do 4 Congresso da Associação Internacional de Lusitanistas, University of Hamburgo, 6 a 11 de Setembro de 1993*, Lisbon: Lidel, pp. 203–14.

——(1996) 'A theoretical construct for examining social and personal identity', in *The Linguistic Construction of Social and Personal Identity: First International Conference on Sociolinguistics in Portugal*, Évora: University of Évora, pp. 19–24.

——(2002) 'Press coverage of the 1999 Nobel Prize-Winner for Literature: whose prize is it anyway?', in J. Cannon, P. A. O. de Baubeta and R. Warner (eds) *Advertising and Identity in Europe: The I of the Beholder*, Bristol: Intellect, pp. 102–12.

——(2005) 'A retrospective on address in Portugal (1982–2002): rethinking power and solidarity', *Journal of Historical Pragmatics*, 6, 2, 307–23.

——(2006) 'Identidade pessoal e a relevância da análise de "frames" (molduras) para um modelo da negociação de tratamento', in M. Olsen and E. H. Swiatek (eds) *XVI Congreso de Romanistas Escandinavos*, Roskilde: Roskilde University. Online. Available at: www.ruc.dk/cuid/publikationer/publikationer/XVI-SRK-Pub/SMO/ (accessed 7 September 2007).

——(in press) 'La integración de la teoría y la metodología como desencadenante de un nuevo modelo de formas y fórmulas del tratamiento', in M. Hummel, B. Kluge and M. E. Vázquez Laslop (eds) *Formas y fórmulas de tratamiento en el mundo hispánico*, Mexico City: El Colegio de México and Vervuert/Iberoamericana.

Oliveira, M. de and Amâncio, L. (2006) 'Teorias feministas e representações sociais: desafios dos conhecimentos situados para a psicologia social', *Revista Etudos Feminista*, 14, 597–615.

Paiva, S. M. P., Moutinho, L. de C. and Teixeira, A. (2005) 'Síntese por concatenação em variantes regionais – o falar do Porto', in I. Duarte and I. Leiria (eds) *Actas do XX Encontro da Associação Portuguesa de Linguística*, Lisbon: APL/Colibri, pp. 777–88.

Páramo, M. L. (2002) 'Uso de estrategias comunicativas de género en adolescentes', in A. M. Vigara Tauste and R. M. Jiménez Catalán (eds) *'Género', sexo, discurso*, Madrid: Laberinto, pp. 311–76.

Pedro, E. R. (1992) *O discurso na aula: uma análise sociolinguística da prática escolar em Portugal*, 2nd edn, Lisbon: Caminho.

Pinto Coelho, Z. (2004) 'Género no discurso das campanhas anti-droga', Centro de Estudos de Comunicação e Sociedade. Online. Available at: www.repositorium.sdum.uminho.pt/bitstream/1822/1012/1/zpcoelho_GeneroPub_2003.pdf (accessed 1 August 2007).

Portugal (1975) 'Decreto-Lei n. 308-A/75 de 24 de Junho', Article 1.

Poveda, D. (2001) 'La educación de las minorías étnicas desde el marco de las continuidades-discontinuidades familia-escuela', *Gazeta de Antropología*, 17, 31. Online. Available at: www.ugr.es/~pwlac.

Poveda, D. and Martín, B. (2003) 'Marcos de participación y género en las conversaciones narrativas de los niños y las niñas gitanas', *Estudios de Sociolingüística*, 4, 2, 455–84.

Poveda, D., Palomares-Valera, M. and Cano, A. (2006) 'Literacy mediations and mediators in the escuela dominical of a Gitano Evangelist church', *Ethnography and Education Journal*, 1, 2, 256–83.

Prego-Vázquez, G. (2002/2003) ¿De onde es? ¿De quen es? Local identities, discursive circulation, and manipulation of traditional Galician naming patterns', *Estudios de Sociolingüística*, 3/2 and 4/1, 229–54.

Presidency of the European Union (2007) 'Portuguese communities'. Online. Available at: www.eu2007.pt/UE/vEN/Bem_Vindo_Portugal/Mundo/Comunidades+Portuguesas.htm (accessed 13 September 2007).

Pujolar, J. (2000) *Gender, Heteroglossia and Power: a Sociolinguistic Study of Youth Culture*, Berlin: Mouton de Gruyter.

——(2007) 'African Women in Catalan Language Courses: Struggles over Class, Gender and Ethnicity in Advanced Liberalism', in B. McElhinny (ed.) *Words, Worlds and Material Girls: Language, Gender, Global Economies*, Berlin: Mouton de Gruyter, pp. 305–49.

Querol, E. (2002) 'A new model to the evaluation of language planning. a case study: Catalonia (1993–2000)', *Sociolinguistica*, 16, 129–42.

RAE (Real Academia Española) (1992) *Diccionario de la lengua española*, 21st edn, Madrid: Espasa Calpe.

——(2001) *Diccionario de la lengua española*, 22nd edn, Madrid: Espasa Calpe.

Ramallo, F. (2007) 'Sociolinguistics of Spanish in Galicia', *International Journal of the Sociology of Language*, 184, 21–36.

Real Academia Galega (2007) MAPA sociolingüístico de Galicia 2004, vol. I, Lingua inicial e competencia lingüística en Galicia, A Coruña: RAG.

Reixach, M. (ed.). (1997) *El coneixement del català. Anàlisi de les dades lingüístiques del cens lingüístic de 1991 de Catalunya, Illes Balears i País Valencià*, Barcelona: Generalitat de Catalunya, Departament de Cultura.

Rocha-Trindade, M. B. (2001) 'História da imigração em Portugal (1)', *Janus Online*. Available at: www.janusonline.pt/2001/2001_3_3_2.html (accessed 1 September 2007).

Rodríguez-Fernández, F. (ed.) (2002) *El lenguaje de los jóvenes*, Barcelona: Ariel.

Rodríguez-Neira, M. (2002/2003) 'Language shift in Galicia from a sociolinguistic point of view', *Estudios de Sociolingüística*, 3/2 and 4/1, 75–112.

Royo, S. (2005) 'Portugal's migration experience: redefined boundaries and uneasy transformations', *Mediterranean Quarterly*, 16, 4, 112–39.

Salvador-Plans, A., García-Oliva, M. and Carrasco-González, J. (eds) (2000) *Actas del I Congreso sobre A Fala*, Mérida: Publicaciones de la Junta de Extremadura.

Samper-Padilla, J. A., Hernández-Cabrera, C. E. and Troya-Déniz, M. (1998) *Macrocorpus de la norma lingüística culta de las principales ciudades del mundo hispánico (MC-NLCH)* (edición en CD-ROM), Las Palmas de Gran Canaria: Universidad de Las Palmas de Gran Canaria.

Santos, J. R. dos. (2001) 'O correspondente de guerra, o discurso jornalístico e a história. Para uma análise da reportagem de guerra em Portugal no século XX', PhD dissertation, Universidade Nova de Lisboa.

Santos, V. (2004) *O discurso oficial do Estado sobre a emigração dos anos 60 a 80 e emigração dos anos 90 à actualidade*, Observatório da Imigração: 8. Online. Available at: www.oi.acime.gov.pt/docs/pdf/EstudoOI%208.pdf (accessed 27 August 2007).

Serrano, M. J. (1995) 'El uso de "la verdad" y "pues" como marcadores discursivos de respuesta', *Español Actual*, 64, 5–16.

SIADECO (ed.) (1977a) *Conflicto Lingüístico en Euskadi*, Bilbao: Euskaltzaindia.

——(1977b) *Planificación Lingüística del Euskara*, Bilbao: Euskaltzaindia.

Silva, D. F. M. B. M. da. (2004) 'Estratégias de argumentação e construção da imagem pessoal no debate político televisivo', MA thesis, University of Minho.

Silva, D. J. (2005) 'Vowel shifting as a marker of social identity in the Portuguese dialect of Nordeste, São Miguel (Azores)', *Luso-Brazilian Review*, 42, 1, 1–22.

Solà, D. (2005) 'El repte dels Plans pilots per a l'impuls del coneixement i l'ús de la llengua catalana: del coneixement a l'ús social', *Noves de SL*: primavera/estiu.

Stewart, M. (1996) 'Name wars; the case of Valenciano', *International Journal of Iberian Studies*, 9, 3, 180–90.

Strubell, M. (1998) 'Language, democracy and devolution in Catalonia', *Current Issues in Language and Society*, 5, 3, 146–80.

Suïls, J. and Huguet, A. (2001) 'The Occitan speech community of the Aran Valley', in M. T. Turell (ed.) *Multilingualism in Spain*, Clevedon: Multilingual Matters, pp. 141–64.

Turell, M. T. (ed.) (2001) *Multilingualism in Spain*, Clevedon: Multilingual Matters.

——(2007) *El plurilingüismo en España*, Barcelona: Institut Universitari de Lingüística Aplicada.

Tuson, J. (2004) *Patrimoni natural: Elogi i defensa de la diversitat lingüística*, Barcelona: Empúries.

Unamuno, V. (2005) 'L'entorn sociolingüístic i la construcció dels repertoris lingüístics de l'alumnat immigrat a Catalunya', *Noves de SL*: primavera/estiu.

Urkizu, K. (2006). 'Basque language corpus planning', in M.-J. Azurmendi and I. Martinez de Luna (eds) *The Case of Basque: Past, Present and Future*, Donostia/San Sebastián: Soziolinguistika Klusterra, pp. 43–52.

Vallverdú, F. (2006) 'Reptes de la sociolingüística: una perspectiva catalana', in F. Vallverdú (ed.) *Cap on va la sociolingüística? II Jornada de l'Associació d'Amics del Professor Antoni M. Badia i Margarit (Barcelona 20 d'octubre de 2005)*, Barcelona: Institut d'Estudis Catalans, pp. 51–62.

Vargas, A., Lledó, E., Bengoechea, M., Mediavilla, M., Rubio, I., Marco, A. and Alario, C. (1998) *Lo femenino y lo masculino en el Diccionario de la Real Academia Española*, Madrid: Instituto de la Mujer.

Vila i Moreno, F. X. (2005) 'Barcelona (Catalonia): Language, Education and Ideology in an Integrationist Society', in E. Witte, L. van Mensel, M. Pierrard, L. Mettewie, A. Housen and R. DeGroof. *Language, Attitudes and Education in Multilingual Cities*, Brussels: Contactforum – Koninklijke Vlaamse Academie van België voor Wetenschappen en Kunsten, pp. 53–86.

Vila-Pujol, M. R. (2007) 'Sociolinguistics of Spanish in Catalonia', *International Journal of the Sociology of Language*, 184, 59–78.

Wienhold, D. (2003) *Spanisch-englische Kontaktsituationen auf der Welt und die daraus entstehenden Mischtexte*, München: Grin Verlag.

Woolard, K. (1989) *Double Talk: Bilingualism and the Politics of Ethnicity in Catalonia*, Stanford, CA: Stanford University Press.

——(in press) 'Language and identity choice in Catalonia: the interplay of contrasting ideologies of linguistic authority', in K. Süselbeck, U. Mühlschlegel, and P. Masson (eds) *Lengua, nación e identidad. La regulación del plurilingüismo en España y América Latina*, Berlin: Ibero-Amerikanisches Institut P.K.

Some corpora of oral Spanish

- *ALCORE/ COVJA, Corpus oral de la variedad juvenil universitaria del español hablado en Alicante* – 800-minute interview discussions of 63 university students in Alicante (www.ua.es/dfelg/lengua/inicio.html)/ALFAL, 84-hour recording corresponding to 14 interviews with educated standard speakers in the main cities of the Hispanic world.
- *Corpus del habla en Almería* – www.nevada.ual.es/otri/ilse/corpus/.
- *Corpus oral de referencia del español contemporáneo* – www.lllf.uam.es/~fmarcos/informes/corpus/corpulee.html.
- *COSER (Corpus Oral y Sonoro del Español Rural)* – sociolinguistic interviews to informants of rural areas of Spain collected regularly from the year 1990 until 2005 – www.pidweb.ii.uam.es/coser/contenido.php/es.
- *CREA* A most comprehensive collection of oral and written corpora, Spanish Academy (REA) – www.corpus.rae.es/creanet.html.
- *PRESEEA, Proyecto para el Estudio Sociolingüístico del Español de España y América* – www.linguas.net/preseea.
- *Project COLA (Corpus oral del lenguaje adolescente)* A corpus with speech of youths between 13 and 19 years from Madrid and several Latin American capitals, still in the making at the University of Bergen, Norway – www.hf.uib.no/i/Romansk/spansk/colam/.
- *Val.Es.Co.* Colloquial Spanish (conversations, interviews and some samples of telephone, radio and television material) spoken in the city of Valencia – www.uv.es/valesco/.

30

Sociolinguistics in Hungary, the Czech Republic and Poland

*Miklós Kontra, Jiří Nekvapil and
Agnieszka Kiełkiewicz-Janowiak*

Introduction

All three countries in the title of this chapter belong to the geographical area usually called Central Europe or East Central Europe in English. The authors of this chapter agree that Central Europe is a concept of shared history, in opposition to the East (the Ottoman Empire and Imperial Russia, Eastern Orthodoxy and Islam) and the West (France and Great Britain).

Sociolinguistics in the post-1960 Anglo–American sense did not have an easy ride into the Soviet satellite countries of Central Europe (see Harlig and Pléh 1995). Nevertheless, Peter Trudgill (2000: 190) in his review of sociolinguistics in the former socialist bloc recognized 'a number of thriving indigenous eastern European sociolinguistic traditions prior to 1989'. Some of this work is also available in English, e.g. Chloupek and Nekvapil (1987).

Janicki (1989), Kontra and Pléh (1995) and Nekvapil and Čmejrková (2003) edited volumes of the *International Journal of the Sociology of Language* on Polish, Hungarian and Czech sociolinguistic research. At the turn of the millennium, a special issue of *Multi-lingua* (Kontra 2000) was devoted to language contact in East Central Europe. Also, Central Europe loomed large at a conference on Linguistic Human Rights held in Budapest in 1997 (see Kontra *et al.* 1999) and in another issue of *IJSL* (see Marti and Nekvapil 2007). In 2009, Peter Lang Publishing launched a new series, *Prague Papers on Language, Society and Interaction*.

This chapter concentrates on sociolinguistics in the three Central European countries Hungary, the Czech Republic and Poland, with occasional side-glances into other countries of the region. Kontra wrote the piece on Hungarian, Nekvapil wrote on the Czech Republic and Kiełkiewicz-Janowiak on Poland.

Hungarian inside and outside Hungary

At the turn of the twenty-first century at least one in four, possibly one in three native speakers of Hungarian lived outside the Hungarian Republic. Genetically a Uralic language, Hungarian is unrelated to German, Rumanian and the Slavic languages it has been in contact with since the Hungarian Conquest of the Carpathian Basin in 895. For a millennium prior to World War I, historic Hungary extended over the entire central Danubian Basin, with a largely multilingual and multiethnic population. Following the dissolution of the Austro-Hungarian Empire and the Peace Treaty of Trianon in 1920, Hungary lost about two-thirds of her territory and more than half of her population to Czechoslovakia, Rumania, Yugoslavia and Austria, and millions of ethnic Hungarians became citizens of another state overnight. According to the census of 2001, Hungarian is the mother tongue of all but 1.5 per cent of Hungary's total population of 10,198,000. Among L1 speakers of Hungarian must be counted the indigenous Hungarian national minorities in Slovakia (521,000), Ukraine (157,000), Rumania (1,434,000), Serbia (290,000), Croatia (17,000), Slovenia (6,200), and Burgenland, Austria (4,700). Thus indigenous Hungarians belong to one cultural nation and eight political nations. In 2001, L2 speakers of Hungarian in Hungary included 48,685 people who claimed Gypsy or Boyash (an archaic dialect of Rumanian) as their mother tongue, 33,792 who claimed German, 14,345 who claimed Croatian, 11,817 who claimed Slovak, 8,482 who claimed Rumanian, 3,388 who claimed Serbian, and 3,187 who claimed Slovene.

Sociolinguistic stratification and intralingual linguicism

The first serious study of the social stratification of Hungarian in Hungary was carried out at the fall of the communist regime in 1988 by M. Kontra, C. Pléh and T. Terestyéni. This study elicited grammaticality judgements, oral sentence completion data, and written correction data from a random stratified sample of adult literate Hungarians (N = 832), see Cseresnyési (2005) for a review in English. One remarkable finding of the study is that Hungarian language cultivators and school teachers promulgate a set of rules adhered to by only 8 per cent of the country's population, even when they are on their best linguistic behaviour, as they are when answering questions on linguistic correctness posed by a social scientist. In other words, the correctness judgements of 92 per cent of the adult population of Hungary differ from those prescribed by the language cultivators (good usage mavens). The oral sentence completion data reveal that Hungarian language cultivators and school teachers are striving to change the speechways of two-thirds of the country's adult population.

The stated aim of many educational systems across the globe is to teach the standard variety of language X, which is believed by many to be the linguistic means to social empowerment. After World War II, education in Hungary became much more socially widespread and educational mobility increased a great deal. Thus it was possible to test the following hypothesis (Kontra 2006b: 114):

> Language use becomes more standard not as a result of speakers' higher educational levels, but as a result of educatedness accumulated through several generations of being part of the intelligentsia.

The obvious null hypothesis will then be: In a group of people with the same level of education, there will be no linguistic differences correlated to educational mobility. This null hypothesis has been refuted several times, e.g. the stigmatized nonstandard form *elhalasszák* 'they postpone (it)' (vs. standard *elhalasztják*) was judged 'grammatically correct' by 48 per cent of the educationally immobile group (those whose educational level equalled that of their fathers), but by 73 per cent of the upwardly mobile group (those whose educational level was higher than that of their fathers). Similar statistically significant differences have been found in oral sentence completions. Thus this country-wide representative study shows that the educationally upwardly mobile are less standard than the immobile, meaning that a greater proportion of the upwardly mobile group have nonstandard features in their speech than the immobile group.

Our study also furnishes quantitative evidence for Myhill's (2004) proposition that linguistic discrimination causes most damage when prestige-based correctness reinforces textual and prescriptive correctness. Analysis of grammaticality judgements by social class (upper level managers vs. unskilled workers) shows, for instance, that 30 per cent of the highest social class but 66 per cent of the lowest class respondents judged a nonstandard verb-form like *elhalasszák* correct. Many other variables show the same pattern (see Kontra 2006b).

Analyses of the Hungarian data from the viewpoints of the learnability of second-dialect features coupled with age show that the requirement of standard speakers that others also should speak like them is wholly unrealistic (ibid.).

Hungarian language contact outside Hungary

Despite the fact that millions of indigenous Hungarians have lived in daily contact with Slovak, Rumanian, Serbian and other languages in the neighbouring countries since 1920, Hungarian contact linguistics in the modern sense of the word began only around the fall of the communist regime in the late 1980s. (The only exception to this generalization is Gal 1979.) In the mid-1990s the Sociolinguistics of Hungarian Outside Hungary project was launched by linguists in Hungary and the neighbouring countries. A quota sample was used (N = 739) with a control group in Hungary (N = 107). Questionnaire data were systematically gathered in a replicable fashion to answer such questions as:

- In what domains are Hungarian and the majority languages used?
- What is the *de jure* and *de facto* situation of Hungarian in the neighbouring countries?
- What are the attitudes to Hungarian used in Hungary, to Hungarian used in the neighbouring countries, and to the majority languages therein?
- What roles do Hungarian and the majority languages play in education and in government?
- Are the contact varieties diverging from the Hungarian of Hungary?
- How could L1 teaching for minority Hungarians be improved?
- In order to help minority Hungarians to maintain their mother tongue, what should and what should not be done with regard to language policy, linguistic ideology, etc.?
- What is the social and geographic distribution of important linguistic variables, i.e. what makes the contact varieties of Hungarian similar to and different from Hungarian in Hungary?

Before this project, most of these questions were not even asked by linguists, let alone answered.

In a recent book edited by Fenyvesi (2005), seven chapters detail the contact varieties in the neighbouring states, one each on Hungarian in the USA and Australia, and two

361

chapters (by Sarah Grey Thomason and Casper de Groot) summarize the typological and theoretical aspects of contact-induced change in Hungarian. De Groot concludes when considering the type of changes from Hungarian spoken in Hungary to the varieties of Hungarian spoken outside Hungary:

> The study of language change through language contact offers new insights in linguistic typology. In this chapter, it appears that in all cases but one linguistic hierarchies and universals established on synchronic descriptions of a sample of languages also account for the type of changes.
>
> (2005: 369)

Hungarian language contact inside Hungary

Bartha and Borbély (2006) conducted truly pioneering research on six linguistic minorities in Hungary: Boyash, German, Romani, Rumanian, Serbian and Slovak. In their description of the situation in present-day Hungary, a new EU member state, the authors identify the 'double standards with respect to the way in which the claims of Hungarian minorities living outside Hungary and linguistic communities within the country are actually recognised' (ibid.: 345). A total of 420 respondents were surveyed (70 from each of the six communities studied) 'in order to develop powerful multidisciplinary comparative research methodologies and tools, which would have predictive power with respect to future linguistic assimilation processes' (ibid.: 347). Respondents were asked 142 questions concerning general information, language use and language choice, knowledge of languages, and stereotypes and prejudices. In this 'sociolinguistic language shift survey' of Hungary, the authors convincingly demonstrate that the language–identity link is by no means self-evident (for similar findings, see also Nekvapil 2000). One interesting hypothesis that the authors found to be wrong was that the Orthodox Church affected both the Serbian and Rumanian communities in Hungary similarly in experiencing their identity. The Rumanians in Hungary express their Rumanian identity 'by preference through their association with the Romanian mother tongue, while the Serbians are likely to express their identity by their connection to the Serbian nationality' (ibid.: 356). As a result, the authors hypothesize that 'if a Serbian person in Hungary loses his/her native language, he/she will not lose the Serbian identity as rapidly as a Romanian, because of his/her strong experience of belonging to the Serbian community' (ibid.: 358).

Universal language rights

In Rumania, the current Law on Education and language-in-education policies legitimize linguicism[1] and ethnic discrimination (see Benő and Szilágyi 2005: 138–40, 142–4). Szilágyi (2003), an ethnic Hungarian professor of linguistics in Rumania, has published a Bill of Rights Concerning Ethnic and Linguistic Identity, and the Fair and Harmonious Coexistence of Ethnic and Linguistic Communities, which is emphatically not a bill on minority language rights but one on universal language rights. Based on the principle of civil coexistence of all citizens of a state, rather than on the principle of the superiority of the dominant nation, the bill explicitly legislates for the language rights of all the citizens of Rumania.

(One crucial problem of most if not all minority language laws is that they formulate the language rights of minorities explicitly, but the same rights remain implicit for dominant majorities. Hence mother-tongue-medium education or use of the L1 in govern-ment, public administration, courts, health care, etc. is a 'natural' right for Rumanians in Rumania, but a 'privilege' for Hungarians, which the Rumanian state may grant to Hungarians if it chooses to be 'nice' to them.)

Szilágyi's Bill is based on the principle of equality before the law. While it is clearly impossible to review here the preamble and the 148 paragraphs of the Bill, I will select a few important features to illustrate its strengths:

- If at least 8 per cent of the population of a local/regional administrative district belongs to an ethnic/linguistic minority, that minority has the right (legal capacity) to use its language as a co-official language in the local/regional administrative district. (As the language of the national ethnic/linguistic majority, Rumanian is the official language throughout the state.)
- This will automatically guarantee the same language rights for most Hungarians (who are an ethnic/linguistic minority in Rumania) and for those Rumanians who are a local minority in the predominantly Hungarian-populated counties in Rumanian Transylvania.
- Equality before the law for all members of all ethnic/linguistic communities (i.e. majority and minorities alike, provided they constitute at least 8 per cent of the local population) is regulated in detail for public signage in bi- or multilingual towns/regions, public administration, communication with government offices, administration of justice, economic and social life, health-care, public education, mass media, church matters, etc.
- Among other things, the Bill offers a principled and practical solution to the pro-blem of setting limits on mother-tongue-medium higher education in a multi-lingual state, i.e. how to prevent a state from granting equal rights *and* funds to a large minority (e.g. 1.5 million Hungarians, who constitute about 7 per cent of the citizens of Rumania, and 30 per cent of the population in Northern Transyl-vania) and a tiny one (e.g. 1,780 Armenians out of a total population of 21.7 million): for details, see Kontra (2006a).
- Equality before the law in mother-tongue-medium higher education could reduce the educational discrimination (undereducation) of national minorities such as Hungarians in Rumania, Slovakia, Serbia and Ukraine. For instance, in 1992, Hungarians constituted 7.12 per cent of the citizens of Rumania, but only 5.18 per cent of its university students. In 2002, 7.34 per cent of the Rumanians held a higher educational degree, but only 4.92 per cent of the Hungarians. Similar pat-terns of educational discrimination of minority Hungarians in (Czecho)Slovakia and Yugoslavia/Serbia have been documented for several decades.

Szilágyi's bill is an excellent illustration of a human rights-based approach to ensuring that the language rights of minority-language speakers are respected.[2]

The Czech Republic

According to the 2001 census, the Czech Republic (CR) has a population of 10,230,060. Czech was declared their mother tongue by 9,707,397 people (94.9 per cent), Slovak by 208,723 (2.0 per cent), Polish by 50,740 (0.5 per cent), German by

41,328 (0.4 per cent), Romani by 23,209 (0.2 per cent), other languages by 121,795 (1.2 per cent), and 76,868 (0.8 per cent) did not declare any language as their mother tongue. Any sociolinguistic description of the language situation in the CR has to take into consideration the geographical division of the country into the larger western part traditionally called Bohemia (Čechy) with the capital Prague, and the smaller eastern part Moravia (and the even smaller northeastern part of Silesia).

Research traditions

Czech sociolinguistics has been grounded on the linguistic tradition of the Prague School. Due to this tradition it has been oriented primarily towards the standard language and its cultivation, with relevant theories being formulated and elaborated on (see the works of B. Havránek, V. Mathesius, partly R. Jakobson, and more recently F. Daneš; these theories were further developed and made well known abroad especially by the Czech emigrants P. Garvin and J.V. Neustupný. For a summary of this development, see Nekvapil (2008). Understandably, the strong internationally accepted domestic tradition has hindered the reception of foreign sociolinguistic trends; some of them, such as variationist sociolinguistics, have never taken root in the CR. Since the 1960s, the specific linguistic situation in the CR (see below), and the orientation towards the study of standard language and corpus language planning have led to the publication of a comprehensive literature on 'diglossia' in the CR and on the ways of overcoming it. Since the 1970s, works of foreign scholars dealing with the analysis of various types of discourse started to be more widely recognized. Consequently, Czech sociolinguistics became more discourse-oriented, both with respect to variation in Czech and to the use of several languages. Bilingualism could be studied in terms of the specific relationship between Czech and Slovak, which coexisted within a single state – the former Czechoslovakia. Serious sociolinguistic research, however, started only recently. The linguistic behaviour of certain minorities (Polish and German in particular) has received some attention since the 1960s, but it has only been studied systematically since the late 1990s.

Since the 1960s, there have been disputes over the form and function of the standard language in Czech linguistics. The disputes arise out of the generally observed fact that spoken discourse often displays phonological and morphological features different from those codified as standard. Importantly, these alternative non-standard features are not restricted to a particular territory, but they are used actively in the whole of Bohemia, expanding also to parts of Moravia. Therefore, they are often referred to as Common Czech (CC) although, from the point of view of Moravians, they could be called Common Bohemian. To a certain extent, the relationship between this variety and the standard language is reminiscent of diglossia (as used by Ferguson 1959). Some linguists suggest that this situation of 'diglossia' can be amended by assigning the status of Standard Czech (SC) to a number of features of CC. Surprisingly, despite the heated discussions, there have been few empirical studies concerning either the way speakers of Czech actually use SC and CC, or their attitudes towards these varieties. The empirical description of Czech 'diglossia', characteristically, has been provided by foreign rather than Czech linguists.

Current research

Bayer's comprehensive book (2003) plays an important role in the Czech context because, apart from giving a description of the variation in spoken Czech in formal and informal situations taking place in west Bohemia and in Prague, it introduces a systematic analysis of language attitudes to Czech sociolinguistics. The author conducted formal and informal interviews with 105 informants, after which she studied their attitudes towards variation in Czech. She followed the socio-psychological theory, which distinguishes among cognitive, evaluative and conative dimensions of attitudes. Comparing the actual speech of the informants and their attitudes towards variation in the spoken language (particularly in terms of the conative dimension), she concluded that although speakers declare that they are prepared to use SC both in formal and informal situations, in the interviews they use mostly CC. The extent of the discrepancy depends not on the informants' regional background (west Bohemia vs. Prague) or on their sex, but primarily on their education (the discrepancy decreases with higher education). For the sake of corpus planning of Czech, it is also worth mentioning that all the 105 informants responded negatively to the question 'Would you approve of a reform of SC, whereby features of the spoken language would be recognized as Standard so that the differences between Standard and spoken Czech would quickly disappear?' Note the way the question is formulated: the author does not ask about the elements of CC but rather about spoken features – this is because CC is an 'etic' rather than an 'emic' concept.

While Bayer focuses on speakers from Bohemia, Wilson (2009) analyzes the linguistic behaviour of speakers from Moravia living in Prague. Using a sample of 37 respondents, he tests a hypothesis that was formulated by some Czech linguists who support a more extensive inclusion of the features of CC into the standard language, according to which Moravian migrants in Bohemia accommodate to CC rather than to SC. The author's methodology is unusual in the Czech context: he uses a quantitative analysis of several linguistic variables; however, his fieldwork is based also on ethnographic and qualitative methods. The author correlated the acquisition of six features of CC with four independent social variables (gender, region of origin, length of residence, level of network integration). The results support the above-mentioned hypothesis, demonstrating that the acquisition of CC features follows marked patterns. A significant finding is that a high level of network integration correlates with a high level of accommodation in the direction of CC, while the other social variables affect the acquisition of CC variants to a much lesser extent.

While Wilson's study is based primarily on the quantitative paradigm, Hoffmannová and Müllerová (2007) carry out their research by using a qualitative approach. The authors focus on autobiographical narratives of speakers over 75 years old, originating in interactions with much younger interlocutors. Since the analysis concerns various aspects of the narratives, the methodology is varied: it includes the methods of narratology, conversation analysis, sociolinguistics, stylistics, discourse analysis and others. The (generational) variation in Czech does not constitute the main focus of the book; nevertheless, it is dealt with in an original way – as an aspect correlating with the organization of turns and speakers in the conversation. One of the chapters concentrates on repetition sequences consisting of the initial turn and the following one in which a certain expression is repeated (the expression often varies in terms of its association with CC or SC). The fact that each of the turns is produced by another speaker makes it possible to observe the extent to which speakers of different generations accommodate to the 'code' that is used by their interlocutors in natural conversation. As is usually the case in qualitative research, the most important results of the study consist in revealing interesting connections that have been neglected in the investigation of variation in Czech. The formulation and testing of hypotheses in more extensive quantitatively oriented research have been left to other investigators.

365

Recently, Czech sociolinguistics has been inspired by the Language Management Theory (LMT), originally associated with J.V. Neustupný and B.H. Jernudd (see, for example, Jernudd and Neustupný 1987, and Nekvapil 2006). Through Neustupný the LMT continued the Prague School cultivation theory, while, thanks to Jernudd, it gained historical links to the classical theory of language planning, at the same time being inspired also by the ethnography of speaking and conversation analysis. Due to its wide scope – it deals not only with macro-phenomena at the level of states, but also with micro-phenomena at the level of particular interactions – it can be used to analyse various aspects of communicative situations, in which language becomes the focus of attention, in particular for the analysis of language problems. The theory has been used mostly in Australia and Japan (the places of Neustupný's activity), and since the 1990s also in the CR (and in Slovakia and elsewhere in Central Europe). Neustupný and Nekvapil (2003) offer a comprehensive analysis of linguistic, communicative and socio-cultural problems in the CR based not only on their empirical research but also on the sociolinguistic, ethnographic, historical and demographic research that has been carried out so far in the CR. The study provides a specific synthesis presented from the point of view of one theory (some foreign universities use it as an introduction to the Czech linguistic and socio-cultural situation). The core of the monograph comprises a description of the linguistic behaviour of ethnic communities, including the Czech community. It is therefore logical that the LMT became the theoretical basis for the Czech team taking part in the European project Dimensions of Linguistic Otherness – Prospects of Maintenance and Revitalization of Minority Languages (Sixth Framework Programme). Another area in which the LMT has been applied recently is the analysis of the problems in multinational companies in the CR (Nekvapil and Nekula 2006). This research has been also carried out within the framework of the European project Languages in a Network of European Excellence (Sixth Framework Programme) and the Czech team's approach is again grounded in the LMT. It is worth mentioning that Neustupný and Nekvapil (2003: 233–7) also constitutes an analysis of the problems which derive from the coexistence of Standard and CC – nevertheless, systematic research into this coexistence from the point of view of the LMT (making extensive use of the method of follow-up interviews) is still to be carried out. On the most recent usage of LMT, see Nekvapil and Sherman (2009).

Poland

Poland may be described as a relatively large country in Central Europe which has a particularly homogeneous national/ethnic and linguistic constitution. In the 2002 National Census, 96 per cent of the population declared Polish nationality. Other national identities most frequently claimed were: Silesian (173,153), German (152,897), Belarusian (48,737), Ukrainian (30,957), and Romani (12,855).

In the same census, people were asked about their language use in the home. In the population of 38.2 million, 97.8 per cent declared speaking Polish at home (including 96.5 per cent exclusively Polish-speaking). Other languages declared to be spoken in Polish homes are German (204,573), English (89,874), Kashubian (52,665), Silesian (56,643), Ukrainian (22,698).[3]

Polish work in sociolinguistics was first presented to an international audience in 1989, when Janicki (1989) edited a special issue of the *International Journal of the Sociology of Language* entitled 'Sociolinguistics in Poland'. In his more recent account, Janicki (1995) considered the period from 1970 to 1995, during which the sociolinguistic work focused on urban dialectology, sociolects and situational varieties. Janicki also appreciated the theoretical strength and empirical orientation of the work of Polish sociologists in the area of the sociology of language. Finally, linguists working on other European languages (notably English, German and French) contributed their contrastively oriented studies to the sociolinguistic picture of Polish.

The present report concerns the latest developments in Polish sociolinguistic research, which both encompass new topics and elaborate on traditional ones.

Over the decades, Polish language studies were predominantly guided by the normative ideology of the one 'correct' (standard) variety. On the other hand, communist ideology was – according to Janicki (1995: 169) – only marginally relevant to Polish sociolinguistic research. It may have, however, implicitly affected the area of linguistic minority problems, which were considered politically sensitive and were barely discussed in the sociolinguistic literature.

Minority language issues

Even though dialect geography was very well established in Poland, for years it focused on the dialects of Polish and did not really address issues of national and ethnic identity as naturally related to language use. The implicit suggestion of the communist regime had been that Poland had no minority language problems, let alone social conflicts related to linguistic minorities. After the 1989 political transition, (socio)linguists felt free to explore the topics of linguistic minorities more openly (e.g. Adamczuk and Łodziński 2006). The attempts were gradually facilitated by a growing body of relevant legislation (including Article 27 of the new Constitution passed in 1997 and the 1999 Law on the Polish Language).

The debate about the status of Polish dialects (such as Kashubian and Silesian)[4] and national/ethnic minority languages, in view of regionalization in European culture, was concluded by the Act on National and Ethnic Minorities and the Regional Language of 6 January 2005, which spelled out the rights of minority members and recognized the official status of Kashubian as a regional language variety.[5]

Language variation and the normative tradition

The socio-political changes following 1980 and 1989 called for a different approach to the description and explanation of social communication and the resulting sociolinguistic patterns. Polish society could no longer be represented as stable and its language use as (mainly unidirectionally) normatively regulated. The multidimensionality and diversity of the linguistic picture came to be acknowledged. This brought to the fore several themes related to linguistic diversification. Also, some new tendencies were recognized.

One of them is the apparent rapid expansion of informal styles in (especially public) communication (cf. Lubaś 2003). The volume edited by Gajda et al. (2002)[6] includes, in its pragmalinguistic section, several articles devoted to this very process, which has possibly been triggered by the economic changes following 1989 and the elimination of censorship. In sociolinguistic terms, the colloquialization of Polish is described as related to speaker age but also to speakers' individual need for self-expression.

It seems that the traditional linguistic norm, until recently considered the property of the educated elite, is in fact not being appropriated by the less educated. Rather, in the

367

process of democratization, it is becoming redefined and expanded to serve the purposes of individual expression and to provide a more vigorous appeal to the 'general public'.

The above suggests a major reformulation of the norm in the minds of speakers. In the context of Poland's new participation in the socio-cultural developments of a United Europe, this phenomenon may be called the *glocalization of the norm*: it results in the presence, in public domains, of *locally* defined language use patterns which are made *globally* available and spread through the mass media. In this definition 'local' may be understood – in geographical as well as social terms – as anything from territorially restricted to individual and idiosyncratic. One aspect of glocalization, the expanding use of informal styles, is being additionally strengthened by the new tendency to promote individualism in linguistic expression.

The increased frequency of colloquial vocabulary has also found its reflection in lexicographic work. The sociolinguistic branch of the Polish Academy of Sciences in Cracow has been editing a multi-volume *Dictionary of Polish Informal Lexemes* (Lubaś 2001–5).

Finally, prescriptive lexicographers have responded to the changes by accepting the greater variability of the norm in that they now distinguish between a so-called usage norm (Polish: *norma użytkowa*) and a model norm (Polish: *norma wzorcowa*).

Polish in the context of other languages

The processes of globalization have added a new perspective to the study of the Polish language as influenced by globally significant languages, notably English. For one thing, the English language has been considered a threat to Polish by many non-linguists. The strong impact of English has also received much attention from linguists. In particular, studies have documented the influx of borrowings from English into Polish (e.g. Mańczak-Wohlfeld 2002). The adaptation of Anglicisms has been the main point of interest, but their social motivation and distribution have also been examined (e.g. Okulska 2006).

Corpus studies

As for research methodology, Polish (socio)linguistics has increasingly relied on empirical work (with emphasis on methods of data collection and on working with authentic language data). Several major corpora have been created (e.g. the PWN Corpus of Polish; the IPI PAN Corpus – see Przepiórkowski 2006) and have become available for linguists, which has resulted in various corpus-based studies and applications. In a country with a long-standing normative tradition, guided by the belief in a single (superior) language variety, exploring language variation through corpora has been a really mind-broadening change.

Research topics

Sociolinguists in Poland have continued work in dialectology in an attempt to uncover the dynamic processes of the rise of (new) urban dialects. The renewed interest in the stylistic differentiation of language has resulted in researching mostly informal styles, especially as they have found their way into media discourse.

Many new topics have been taken up by Polish sociolinguists to relate the findings about the local (Polish) communities to those of sociolinguistic and pragmatic research about foreign (and global) contexts. Research into generational sociolects focused on the language of children and adolescents. Language and gender studies – rather acutely under-developed – have now received some attention (e.g. Anusiewicz and Handke 1994). Stereotypes in language use proved an important topic in times of social transition (Anusiewicz and Bartmiński 1998; Kiełkiewicz-Janowiak and Pawelczyk 2006). The language of advertising has attracted the attention of linguists as an area of linguistic novelty and socio-psychological manipulation (e.g. Mosiołek-Kłosińska and Zgółka 2003). Studies of political discourse have compared the language of new political propaganda with communist Newspeak. Finally, linguistic investigations have recently been extended to the specialized discourses of disciplines such as medicine or the law.

Conclusion

In the past decade Polish linguistics has shown a steadily growing interest and appreciation for studies of language in (social) context. Consequently, more and more linguists have practised the study of discourse(s). With the increased understanding of language variation, the traditional prescriptive approach to language use has been evolving towards more liberal attitudes. The sociolinguistic study of the Polish language is becoming integrated with investigations of other languages. Also apparent in Polish sociolinguistic research has been the tendency to rely on empirical work and a socially representative body of language data.

Acknowledgements

The authors wish to acknowledge gratefully the comments and suggestions offered by Prof. Władysław Lubaś, Dr Anna Fenyvesi and Prof. Sarah G. Thomason.

Notes

1 The term *linguicism*, first introduced by Tove Skutnabb-Kangas, describes the processes and policies of linguistic discrimination or social discrimination between groups of people defined on the basis of language. Linguicism refers to the stigmatization and (social, economic and political) marginalization of speakers of non-standard varieties and minority languages, see Swann *et al.* (2004: 184).
2 Unfortunately, the Democratic Alliance of Hungarians in Rumania (RMDSZ), which first became part of the coalition government of Rumania in 1996 and is part of it again at the time of this writing in October 2007, has not supported Szilágyi's Bill. Linguists, educators and some lawyers recognize the great merits of the Bill, but Hungarian politicians in Rumania don't.
3 The fact that English is rated as the second (non-Polish) language most frequently used in the home environment (*Narodowe Spisy Powszechne* 2006) is difficult to interpret: this result may be due to the high prestige of English in Poland and perhaps a misunderstanding of the census questions.
4 For the moment, speakers who use these dialects (or the dialects of Ukrainian and Belarusian) at the local level, typically choose standard Polish for supralocal communication, and of the local dialects only Kashubian has made concrete steps to develop a fully-fledged standard (also written) variety (Hentschel 2002).
5 Cf. Wicherkiewicz (2004) on the status of the Kashubian language in education in Poland.
6 The volume was published as a festschrift dedicated to Władysław Lubaś, an outstanding Polish sociolinguist and Slavist.

References

Adamczuk, L. and Łodziński, S. (eds) (2006) *Mniejszości narodowe w Polsce w świetle Narodowego Spisu Powszechnego z 2002 roku* [National minorities in Poland in View of the 2002 National Census Results], Warszawa: SCHOLAR.

Anusiewicz, J. and Bartmiński, J. (eds) (1998) *Język a Kultura* Vol. 12: *Stereotyp jako przedmiot lingwistyki. Teoria, metodologia, analizy empiryczne* [Language and Culture, vol 12, Stereotype as a Topic in Linguistics: Theory, Methodology, Empirical Analyses], Wrocław: Towarzystwo Przyjaciół Polonistyki Wrocławskiej.

Anusiewicz, J. and Handke, K. (eds) (1994) *Język a kultura*, vol. 9, *Płeć w języku i kulturze* [Language and Culture, vol. 9, Sex/Gender in Language and Culture], Wrocław: Wiedza o Kulturze.

Bartha, C. and Borbély, A. (2006) 'Dimensions of linguistic otherness: prospects of minority language maintenance in Hungary', *Language Policy*, 5, 335–63.

Bayer, L. (2003) *Sprachgebrauch vs. Spracheinstellung im Tschechischen*, München: Otto Sagner.

Benő, A. and Szilágyi, N. S. (2005) 'Hungarian in Romania', in A. Fenyvesi (ed.) *Hungarian Language Contact Outside Hungary: Studies on Hungarian as a Minority Language*, Amsterdam: John Benjamins, pp. 133–62.

Chloupek, J. and Nekvapil, J. (1987) *Reader in Czech Sociolinguistics*, Amsterdam: John Benjamins.

Cseresnyési, L. (2005) 'Review of Miklós Kontra (ed.), *Nyelv és társadalom a rendszerváltáskori Magyarországon* [Language and society in Hungary at the fall of communism], Budapest: Osiris Kiadó, 2003', *Journal of Sociolinguistics*, 9, 307–13.

De Groot, C. (2005) 'The grammars of Hungarian outside Hungary from a linguistic-typological perspective', in A. Fenyvesi (ed.), *Hungarian Language Contact Outside Hungary: Studies on Hungarian as a Minority Language*, Amsterdam: John Benjamins, pp. 351–70.

Fenyvesi, A. (ed.) (2005) *Hungarian Language Contact Outside Hungary: Studies on Hungarian as a Minority Language*, Amsterdam: John Benjamins.

Ferguson, C. (1959) 'Diglossia', *Word*, 15, 325–37.

Gajda, S., Rymut, K. and Żydek-Bednarczuk, U. (eds) (2002) *Język w przestrzeni społecznej* [Language in Social Space], Opole: Uniwersytet Opolski.

Gal, S. (1979) *Language Shift: Social Determinants of Linguistic Change in Bilingual Austria*, New York: Academic Press.

Harlig, J. and Pléh, C. (eds) (1995) *When East Met West: Sociolinguistics in the Former Socialist Bloc*, Berlin: Mouton de Gruyter.

Hentschel, G. (2002) 'Czy mogą powstać śląski, kaszubski albo góralski język nieliteracki?' [Can Silesian, Kashubian and Podhalean arise as non-literary languages?], in S. Gajda, K. Rymut and U. Żydek-Bednarczuk (eds) *Język w przestrzeni społecznej* [Language in Social Space], Opole: Uniwersytet Opolski, pp. 83–91.

Hoffmannová, J. and Müllerová, O. (eds) (2007) *Čeština v dialogu generací* [Inter-Generational Discourse in Czech], Praha: Academia.

Janicki, K. (ed.) (1989) 'Sociolinguistics in Poland', *International Journal of the Sociology of Language*, 78, 165–84.

——(1995) 'Sociolinguistics in Poland: history and prospects', in J. Harlig and C. Pléh, (eds) *When East Met West: Sociolinguistics in the Former Socialist Bloc*, Berlin: Mouton de Gruyter, pp. 165–84.

Jernudd, B. H. and Neustupný, J.V. (1987) 'Language plannning: for whom?', in L. Laforge (ed.) *Proceedings of the International Colloquium on Language Planning*. Québec: Les Presses de l'Université Laval, pp. 69–84.

Kiełkiewicz-Janowiak, A. and Pawelczyk, J. (2006) 'Gender stereotypes in language use: Polish and English', in K. Dziubalska Kołaczyk (ed.), *IFAtuation: A Life in IFA. A Festschrift for Professor Jacek Fisiak on the Occasion of His 70th Birthday*, Poznań: Wydawnictwo Naukowe UAM, pp. 349–83.

Kontra, M. (ed.) (2000) 'Language contact in East-Central Europe', *Multilingua*, 19, 1/2.

——(2006a) 'Your right to your language', in K. Dietz (ed.) *My Fulbright Experience*. Budapest: Hungarian-American Commission for Educational Exchange, pp. 39–54.

——(2006b) 'Sustainable linguicism', in F. Hinskens (ed.) *Language Variation – European Perspectives*, Amsterdam: John Benjamins, pp. 97–126.

Kontra, M., Phillipson, R., Skutnabb-Kangas, T. and Várady, T. (eds) (1999) *Language: A Right and a Resource: Approaching Linguistic Human Rights*, Budapest: Central European University Press.

Kontra, M. and Pléh, C. (eds) (1995) *Hungarian Sociolinguistics* (*International Journal of the Sociology of Language*, No. 111).

Lubaś, W. (ed.) (2001–5) *Słownik polskich leksemów potocznych* [Dictionary of Polish Colloquialisms], vols 1–3, Kraków: Wydawnictwo Naukowe DWN/Wydawnictwo LEXIS.

——(2003) *Polskie gadanie. Podstawowe cechy i funkcje potocznej odmiany polszczyzny*, [Polish Talk: Major Characteristics and Functions of Colloquial Polish], Opole: Wydawnictwo Uniwersytetu Opolskiego.

Magocsi, P. R. (1993) *Historical Atlas of East Central Europe*, Seattle: University of Washington Press.

Mańczak-Wohlfeld, E. (2002) 'Polish', in M. Görlach (ed.) *English in Europe*, Oxford: Oxford University Press, pp. 213–28.

Marti, R. and Nekvapil, J. (eds) (2007) 'Small and large Slavic languages in contact', *International Journal of the Sociology of Language*, 183.

Mosiołek-Kłosińska, K. and Zgółka, T. (eds) (2003) *Język perswazji publicznej* [Language of Public Persuasion], Poznań: Wydawnictwo Poznańskie.

Myhill, J. (2004) 'A parameterized view of the concept of "correctness"', *Multilingua*, 23, 389–416.

Narodowe Spisy Powszechne (2006) *Główny Urząd Statystyczny w Warszawie*. Online. Available at: www. stat.gov.pl/gus/nsp_PLK_HTML.htm (accessed 15 July 2007).

Nekvapil, J. (2000) 'On non-self-evident relationships between language and ethnicity: how Germans do not speak German, and Czechs do not speak Czech', *Multilingua*, 19, 1/2, 37–53.

——(2006) 'From language planning to language management', *Sociolinguistica*, 20, 92–104.

——(2008) 'Language cultivation in developed contexts', in B. Spolsky and F.M. Hult (eds) *The Handbook of Educational Linguistics*, Oxford: Blackwell Publishing, pp. 251–65.

Nekvapil, J. and Čmejrková, S. (eds) (2003) 'Languages and language communities in the Czech Republic', *International Journal of the Sociology of Language*, 162.

Nekvapil, J. and Nekula, M. (2006) 'On language management in multinational companies in the Czech Republic', *Current Issues in Language Planning*, 7, 307–27.

Nekvapil, J. and Sherman, T. (eds) (2009) *Language Management in Contact Situations. Perspectives from three Continents*. Frankfurt am Main: Peter Lang.

Neustupný, J.V. and Nekvapil, J. (2003) 'Language management in the Czech Republic', *Current Issues in Language Planning*, 4, 181–366.

Okulska, U. (2006) 'English borrowings in the Polish media: assimilation processes and gender', *Kwartalnik Neofilologiczny*, LIII, 3, 208–31.

Przepiórkowski, A. (2006) 'The potential of the IPI PAN Corpus', *Poznań Studies in Contemporary Linguistics*, 41, 31–48.

Szilágyi, N. S. (2003) 'Törvény az etnikai és nyelvi identitással kapcsolatos jogokról, valamint az etnikai és nyelvi közösségek méltányos és harmonikus együttéléséről [Bill of Rights Concerning Ethnic and Linguistic Identity, and the Fair and Harmonious Coexistence of Ethnic and Linguistic Communities], in *Mi egy más: Közéleti írások*. Kolozsvár: Kalota Könyvkiadó, pp. 576–664.

Swann, J., Deumert, A., Lillis, T. and Mesthrie, R. (2004) *A Dictionary of Sociolinguistics*, Edinburgh: Edinburgh University Press.

Trudgill, P. (2000) 'Review of Jeffrey Harlig and Csaba Pléh (eds), *When East Met West: Sociolinguistics in the Former Socialist Bloc*. Berlin: Mouton de Gruyter, 1995', *Multilingua*, 19, 1/2, 190–5.

Wicherkiewicz, T. (2004) *The Kashubian Language in Education in Poland*. Regional Dossiers SeriesLjouwert/ Leeuwarden: Mercator-Education, Fryske Akademy.

Wilson, J. (2009) *Moravians in Prague: a sociolinguistic study of dialect in the Czech Republic*. Frankfurt am Main: Peter Lang.

31

Sociolinguistics in the Balkans

Robert D. Greenberg

Introduction

Any discussion of sociolinguistic issues in a region such as the Balkans must include a set of understandings regarding a definition of the Balkans and some historical perspectives on languages, peoples, nations, and states that have emerged in this often volatile region of Europe.

In the fields of linguistics and sociolinguistics, the term "Balkan" has been used regularly in connection with the Balkan speech territory or *Sprachbund*. This speech territory includes prominent Balkan languages and is cited as an example of areal linguistic phenomena, where speakers of diverse languages came into contact with each other, thus facilitating the development of common linguistic features. These features are called "Balkanisms," and are typically found in Albanian, Arumanian, Bulgarian, Greek, Macedonian, Romanian, Serbian dialects, and Turkish. Numerous Balkan features spread north into contiguous areas including northern and central Serbia, Bosnia-Herzegovina, Croatia, and Montenegro. While many scholars have focused on the phonological, morphological, syntactic, and lexical commonalities of the Balkan languages, few have studied comparative sociolinguistic evidence. Such a study would expose broader Balkan commonalities or differences in the areas of language policy, language planning, and the attitudes towards linguistic minorities. My survey fills this gap by comparing and contrasting the sociolinguistic trends across the Balkan region. The last decades of the twentieth century and the early 2000s were marked by the demise of the multiethnic Yugoslav state and the emergence of seven less diverse successor states. Such nationalist-inspired Balkanization resulted in the emergence of states that have embraced mono-ethnicity and the supremacy of a single language. This move was an antithesis to multicultural, multi-ethnic, and multilingual models of the past. Several of the new polities have embraced a nation-state model, where a primary ethnic group embodies the national identity. This group holds an advantageous position in society in relation to the state's minorities. The primary ethnic group determines the official state language, religion, and cultural identity. This nation-state model had been much the norm outside of the former Yugoslavia, especially in Albania, Bulgaria, Greece, Romania, and Turkey. The new post-1991 national boundaries inadequately correspond to the ethnic and linguistic boundaries, so that in the former Yugoslav territories old majority populations have become new minorities in the new states. The policies of the new and old Balkan states toward minorities lack consistency when it comes to providing official communication in minority languages or allowing primary and secondary school education in the mother tongue. I argue that while there has been some pressure from outside of the Balkans to conform to European models on linguistic minorities, local resistance to change has prevented significant progress in this direction. This lack of progress has been prevalent, no matter the history, past political system, or ethnic configuration of the Balkan states examined. While much of my effort will be focused on ex-Yugoslavia, I will draw upon data and scholarship from the other Balkan states as well.

Language policy models

When considering language policy models, Schmidt (1998) proposed four language policy approaches typically used by states to manage potential language conflicts. These models are:

- *Domination/exclusion*: the dominant ethnic group maintains power over minority ethnic groups by preserving the supremacy of the dominant language and not providing minorities with the means to learn the "language of power" or to use their own languages to move up the social/economic/political ladder.
- *Assimilation*: the state seeks to assimilate its minority populations by encouraging them to learn and use the national language.
- *Pluralism*: the state promotes tolerance towards minority languages, encourages multilingualism, and preserves the rights of speakers of less widely spoken languages within the polity.
- *Linguistic confederation*: languages within a polity are territorially-based, and each language is identified with specific regions, municipalities, or towns/villages.

These models are not mutually exclusive; a given policy may combine elements from some of the models, and policies may shift from one model to the next over time. The four models represent a continuum from the most restrictive language policies (domination/exclusion) to the most tolerant ones (linguistic confederation). For instance, the United States may be viewed as a country with largely assimilationist language policies, especially on the state and local level. Thus, while North Carolina and Georgia are among 30 U.S. states with official English laws, primarily designed to promote linguistic assimilation of immigrant communities, other states, such as Connecticut or New York have no such laws and may be viewed as more pluralistic in their approach. On the federal level, the United States has refrained from official English legislation, so, as a whole, U.S. policy lies somewhere between the assimilationist approach and the pluralistic one.

In Europe, the language model most frequently promoted is that of pluralism. The Council of Europe has played an important role in advancing this model through its 1992 European Charter on Regional and Minority Languages (ECRML). The ECRML attempted to create a protective mechanism for regional and minority languages traditionally spoken on the continent, while simultaneously protecting the status of a given country's majority (official) language(s). The Charter defined a regional or minority language as follows:

> [A language] traditionally used within a given territory of a State by nationals of that State who form a group numerically smaller than the rest of the State's population; and is different from the official language(s) of that State; it does not include either dialects of the official language(s) of the State or the languages of migrants.[1]

A regional language is spoken in a defined region within the state. The minority language is spoken in the state, but not confined to a specific geographic region. The Charter emphasizes that the only regional or minority languages worthy of protective measures are those "traditionally spoken" within the territory of a state. No protective measures, therefore, would be afforded to the languages of migrants. Each signatory to the Charter declares which of the regional and minority languages it recognizes, and determines a minimum number of measures to protect and preserve the country's minority languages. These determinations could be arbitrary. The Council of Europe has no enforcement powers, and acceptance and ratification of the Charter are optional. The ECRML is designed to promote multiculturalism and multilingualism. Moreover, the Charter allows for "Each contracting State … [to] specify in its instrument of ratification, acceptance or approval, each regional or minority language, or official language which is less widely used on the whole or part of its territory, to which the paragraphs chosen … shall apply."[2] Signatory countries are required to implement at least 35 paragraphs and sub-paragraphs of the Charter, in the areas of education/cultural activities, judicial authority, administrative authorities/public services, media, and economic/social life. The signatory countries are expected to produce periodic reports to the Council of Europe on the status of ECRML implementation, outlining the country's progress in ensuring that the Charter's provisions are followed.

The Balkan states have had a mixed record of compliance with the ECRML. Only Slovenia, Croatia, Serbia and Montenegro have signed, ratified, and begun implementing the Charter. Macedonia and Romania have signed but not ratified the ECRML, while Albania, Bosnia-Herzegovina, Bulgaria, and Greece have not even signed it.[3] The reasons for the divergent approaches to the ECRML among the Balkan states are complex. To further their political agenda individual governments in the region either refrained from signing or supported the adoption of the Charter. Three scenarios evolved: (1) countries in which the Charter represents a continuation of past language policy practices; (2) countries where language policy is in stark contrast to the pluralistic model espoused through the ECRML; and (3) countries where language and minority rights issues remain a constant source of internal tension. In the latter countries these tensions are unlikely to dissipate enough to allow for the Charter's implementation. In determining the likelihood of additional Balkan countries adopting the Charter, I propose evaluating the relative strength of two fundamental principles: (1) the nation-state principle; and (2) the accommodationist principle.

I consider the nation-state principle to be strong in a state formed by a dominant national or ethnic group. Often strong nation-states espouse a narrative of the centuries-old aspirations of a specific ethnic or national group to gain freedom and independence. The nation-state principle may also be strong in a country with a well-developed shared nation-state narrative. Such states are formed by two or more main ethnic groups, sometimes unified by an over-arching state identity. Shared nation-states could be unitary or federal in their structure. The accommodationist principle is strong in states that have shown high degrees of tolerance towards their minority populations. Such states tend to embrace the pluralistic or linguistic confederation language policy models. States exhibiting a weak accommodationist principle adhere to a dominant/exclusion or strongly assimilationist language policy, and are less likely to be signatories to the ECRML.

In a country such as Belgium, there have been very strong accommodationist tendencies, a form of linguistic confederation, but these tendencies have greatly weakened the concept of a Belgian identity and the notion of a strong shared nation-state. Rather, regionalism and the powers of the Walloon and Flemish communities have served to create federalization of the state and the potential of the Belgian state splitting along community lines.[4] With its weak nation-state and tension between its main communities, Belgium has thus far not signed the ECRML. By contrast, multilingual Switzerland has proven to be an example of a strong shared nation-state that has accommodated its various communities. It also still boasts a relatively strong sense of an over-arching Swiss identity. Switzerland signed and ratified the ECRML in the 1990s; its adherence to the principles of the ECRML derives from its history of accommodation and the strong belief in Swiss national unity despite the linguistic, religious, and cultural differences among its various peoples.

The nation-state principle and accommodationist principle evolve over time. Some states have long traditions as strong nation-states, while others may have contentious relations between majority and minority populations. These principles may be fluid and depend upon divergent ideologies of governments, political parties, or change in conjunction with broader pan-European movements or policies. In the table overleaf, I apply the nation-state principle and the accommodationist principle to the Balkans.

In countries with a strong nation-state principle, the Constitution often is explicit with regard to the nation-forming role of the primary ethnic/national group of the state, and declares that this group's language is the country's official language. For instance, Article 8 of the Albanian Constitution of 1998 stipulates that the Republic of Albania protects "the national rights of the Albanian people who live outside its borders."[5] While there is no Article in the "Basic Principles" section explicitly declaring ethnic Albanians to be the primary group within the state, Article 8 implies that Albania feels a responsibility to protect ethnic Albanians wherever they reside. The Constitution is also unequivocal in the designation of Albanian as the country's sole official language.[6] The Greek Constitution from 1975 includes no official language designation, but makes it clear that "all Greeks" are equal under the Constitution, and the assumption is that all citizens of Greece belong to the Greek nation. In several former Yugoslav republics, including Croatia, Serbia, and Slovenia, the nation-state principle is explicit; these states continue the Yugoslav tradition of "constitutional nationalism" (Hayden 1992). The ethnic conflicts of post-Yugoslav succession and the 2006 breakup of a joint Serbian-Montenegrin state have yielded several contested or unresolved nation-states in the post-Yugoslav areas, especially in Bosnia-Herzegovina, Macedonia, Kosovo, and Montenegro. Thus, in Montenegro, a separate Montenegrin language and identity are still evolving, and the linguistic differences between Montenegrin and Serbian remain unclear. The Dayton Accords of 1995 created the republic of Bosnia Herzegovina as a shared nation state for Bosniaks, Croats, and Serbs. This state consists of two political entities, a Serb Republic and a Federation of Bosnia-Herzegovina. All three state-forming ethnic/national groups of Bosnia-Herzegovina theoretically share equal rights in the two entities. Tensions among the three groups have persisted, and the future structure and nature of the

Table 31.1 The Balkan countries: summary of state-forming principles

Country	Nation-state principle	Accommodationist principle
Albania	strong	weak
Bosnia-Herzegovina	weak/contested	enforced by post-conflict agreements
Bulgaria	strong	weak
Croatia	strong	strong
Greece	strong	weak
Macedonia	weak	enforced by post-conflict agreements
Montenegro	contested	strong
Romania	strong	weak
Serbia	strong	strong
Slovenia	strong	strong

Republic of Bosnia-Herzegovina remain uncertain. In such a contested nation–state where the accommodationist principle has been imposed by the international community, adoption and implementation of the ECRML have not yet been achieved. The international community played a pivotal role in resolving Macedonia's ethnic conflict in 2001, and the revised Macedonian Constitution institutes a non–nation-state. According to the Preamble of the 2001 Constitution, the citizens of the Republic of Macedonia include "the Macedonian people, as well as citizens living within its borders who are part of the Albanian people, the Turkish people, the Vlac people, the Serbian people, the Romany people, the Bosniac people and others."[7]

The various peoples are referred to in later paragraphs as the country's "communities," and terms such as "nationality," "national minority," or "minority" are avoided throughout the text. In Table 31.1, I have called the accommodationist principle "enforced" in Macedonia, since the compromises between ethnic Macedonians and ethnic Albanians were achieved as a means of defusing a 2001 ethnic conflict that had erupted between these two communities. The Albanian minority was seeking enhanced rights and hoped to elevate its status from a "minority" to a "co-national" group within the state. The constitutional compromises provided for enhanced language rights for the Albanian community, as will be discussed below. The Macedonian government had successfully integrated other, smaller ethnic communities such as the Turks and the Vlahs, but international intervention was required to better accommodate the Albanian minority's linguistic needs.

The application or non-application of the ECRML will be the focus of the remainder of this chapter. The analysis will reveal a broad spectrum of language policies among the Balkan states, and uncover several significant inconsistencies in language policy that are symptoms of continuing intra-Balkan tensions. Ultimately, without harmonization of these divergent language policies, relations among the Balkan states and their constituent ethnic groups are unlikely to improve.

The Balkans and the ECRML

The ECRML sets up a mechanism for improving the lot of speakers of regional and minority languages within Europe. For the Balkans, where ethnic and linguistic diversity is so pronounced, the recent nationalist-inspired destruction of Yugoslavia has proven to be a challenge to those espousing an accommodationist policy towards minority groups.

Nevertheless, four former Yugoslav republics have signed and ratified the ECRML, including Croatia, Montenegro, Serbia, and Slovenia. Ironically, two of the most virulently nationalistic states in the 1990s—Croatia and Serbia—have adopted the ECRML. Conversely, in Greece, a nation that did not experience Communist rule and was the first Balkan country to join the EEC, the ECRML has been neither signed nor ratified. In the following sections, I consider: (1) the nations that have signed and ratified the ECRML; (2) the nations that have signed but not ratified the ECRML; and (3) the nations that have not signed the ECRML. I attempt to draw conclusions based on contrasts and comparisons among the three groups of Balkan nations. I suggest that historical context and a desire for European integration have motivated some Balkan nations to adopt the ECRML, while others have remained stubbornly entrenched nation-states that continue to suppress and exclude their minority populations. Without overt pressure from European institutions, the ECRML has had only a limited moderating effect on language policies across the Balkans.

Adoption of the ECRML: Croatia, Montenegro, Serbia, and Slovenia

Croatia was the first state in the region to ratify the ECRML in 1997, followed by Slovenia in 2000, and Serbia and Montenegro in 2006. Serbia and Montenegro ratified the Charter a mere three months before Montenegro declared independence. These four states represent four of the five original "nations" of Tito's Yugoslavia, and include the three "founding nations" of the first joint South Slavic state established after World War I, known in its first decade as the Kingdom of Serbs, Croats, and Slovenes. The Croats, Serbs, and Slovenes have what Bellamy (2003) called a tradition of strong "historical statehood narratives." Hence, the Croats claim to have an uninterrupted sense of statehood and national identity not dampened by almost nine centuries of foreign rule, beginning with the independent Croatian state that had lasted until 1102 and continued until Croatia regained full independence in 1991. Similarly, the Serbs could look back to their medieval Serbian Kingdom that had fallen to the Ottoman Turks in the fourteenth and fifteenth centuries—events that did not extinguish the Serbian sense of national identity. The Slovenes could look back to their linguistic tradition during the time of the Reformation and to a centuries-long evolution of a distinct Slovene language and identity. Even the Montenegrins, the dominant national group in the last of the former Yugoslav republics to become independent, have made claims back to the independent Kingdom of Montenegro of the nineteenth and early twentieth century, and the historical fact that some regions of contemporary Montenegro had never fallen under Ottoman rule (particularly those around the Bay of Kotor).

These four former Yugoslav republics have continued to follow the spirit of the language policies outlined in the Yugoslav Constitution of 1974. As I have discussed elsewhere (Greenberg 1996, 2004), this Constitution provided for enhanced language rights for the country's "nationalities" (narodnosti) and "national minorities" (nacionalne manjine). This complex system included constitutive nations of Yugoslavia, each of which had a home republic, nationalities consisting of ethnic groups whose ancestral state was outside of the former Yugoslavia, and national minorities consisting of ethnic groups with no ancestral homeland. The new states that emerged after Yugoslavia's breakup simplified this three-tier system by conflating nationalities and national minorities. The resulting system is that of a leading ethnic/national group and minorities who enjoy constitutional protections. Such a reconfiguring of the Yugoslav system has not been possible in

Bosnia-Herzegovina and Macedonia because the majority/minority relations are either contested or not equally applied across regions.

Croatia, Slovenia, and Serbia recognized through the ECRML many of the same languages and minority groups that had already enjoyed protected status under Yugoslavia. Thus, Slovenia declared as regional/minority languages Italian, Hungarian, and Romani. Croatia declared its protected languages to be Hungarian, Serbian, Rusyn, Ukrainian, Italian, Czech, and Slovak, while Serbia acknowledged Albanian, Bosniak,[8] Bulgarian, Croatian, Hungarian, Romani, Romanian, Rusyn, Slovak, and Ukrainian as its regional and minority languages.

One of the challenges language planners face in the four former Yugoslav republics has been accommodating the national/ethnic groups that had previously enjoyed elevated status in the Yugoslav system as members of Socialist Yugoslavia's six constitutive "nations," i.e., Croats, Macedonians, Montenegrins, Muslims (now known as Bosniaks), Serbs, and Slovenes. During the Yugoslav era, Serbo-Croatian had been declared the joint language of Croats, Montenegrins, Muslims, and Serbs, and it served as a language of broader communication across the territory of Socialist Yugoslavia (Naylor 1978). As I have discussed elsewhere, the breakup of Yugoslavia caused this joint language to splinter into Bosnian, Croatian, Montenegrin, and Serbian (Greenberg 2004), resulting in a new sociolinguistic situation in the emergent independent states. As the above list of officially recognized regional and minority languages in Croatia, Serbia, and Slovenia reveals, "Serbian" has become a minority language of Croatia, while "Croatian" and "Bosniak" have become minority languages of Serbia. Slovenia has not provided for protective measures to a single successor language to Serbo-Croatian, and Croatia, Serbia, and Slovenia have not officially acknowledged a separate Montenegrin language. Thus, the signing and ratification of the ECRML in these states have not removed the following hurdles: (1) the exclusion of certain minority languages (with the justification that these languages are not autochthonous to the territory and represent the languages of migrant communities); and (2) the exclusion of recently declared languages resulting from the breakup of Serbo-Croatian.

The Slovenes justified the exclusion of the languages of nearly all of the ethnic/ national groups from the former Yugoslavia, claiming that these groups were not autochthonous within Slovenia's borders. While this claim may be applicable to Bosniaks or Macedonians, the notion that Croats are not autochthonous to the territory of Slovenia or that Slovenes are not autochthonous in Croatia is dubious. The Slovenian/Croatian political boundary does not correspond to the ethnic boundary; this scenario is typical of most of the states in the region. The north-western Croatian dialects share many features with Slovene dialects, and here, too, Croats and Slovenes have frequently argued about the boundary between north-western Croatian and eastern Slovene dialects.[9] The 2002 Slovenian census revealed that there are more Croats in Slovenia than Italians or Hungarians. Similarly, Croatian census figures from 2001 include 13,173 citizens declaring themselves to be Slovene or 0.3 percent of the total population. This number is only slightly lower than the number of Hungarians, but higher than that of Czechs, Slovenes, and Rusyns, all of whom enjoy protections under the ECRML in Croatia.[10] Nevertheless, Slovenia did not grant recognition to speakers of Croatian, and Croatia did not extend protections to Slovene speakers.

The Slovene exclusion of all peoples from the other republics of the former Yugoslavia is even more problematic when considering that the Slovenes granted protection to Romani, a language whose autochthonous roots in Slovenia may also be questionable. In the periodic report that Slovenia submitted to the Council of Europe in 2002 on the implementation of the ECRML, the Roma are referred to as residing on the fringes of the Republic (north-eastern and southern regions along the Croatian border) and that Roma migrants have also moved to the cities. Their numbers, however, are relatively small, totaling a population of 3246 in 2002. By contrast, other groups from the other former Yugoslav republics are listed in the census pages as residing in Slovenia continuously since at least 1953, the first year for which statistics are provided. Thus, Croats numbered 17,978 in 1953 and 35,642 in 2002, while Serbs numbered 11,225 in 1953 and 38,964 in 2002. Both Serbs and Croats outnumber Italians, Hungarians, and Roma in the 2002 census.[11]

Similar exclusions of prominent linguistic minorities within signatory states to the ECRML are not limited to Slovenia. Typically these exclusions are politically motivated. Slovenia was keen to break with its Yugoslav past and move rapidly towards the European Union and NATO. The speakers of the Slovene language had felt threatened by the spread of Serbo-Croatian during the many years of joint South Slavic/Yugoslav states, and as an independent country may have preferred a policy of assimilation towards its former Yugoslav cousins, rather than a tolerant pluralistic model which would have granted protections to Croatian, Serbian, Bosnian, or Macedonian. Serbia faced a similar dilemma in February 2006 when the joint state of Serbia-Montenegro did not extend protection to its Macedonian community through the ECRML. This omission caused consternation in Macedonia, a country which had only five years earlier reaffirmed protection to its citizens that were defined as "part of the Serbian people."[12]

The signing and ratifying of the ECRML in the four former Yugoslav republics may have had positive ramifications for the public image of these states within Europe and among members of the Council of Europe. However, the Charter has done little to contribute to better relations among the former Yugoslav republics. This absence of positive influence is manifest in the lack of reciprocity among the signatory Balkan nations. Since the new political boundaries do not correspond to the ethnic ones, new majority/minority relations have evolved in the four republics. The Charter provided an opportunity for reciprocity with regard to treatment of minorities across the region. Had Slovenia recognized a Croat or Serb minority, perhaps Croatia and Serbia would have reciprocated and protected a Slovene minority. Croatia recognized the Serbian language as a minority language, but as of 2003 did not make provisions for government-funded Serbian-language schools, as seen in Croatia's report to the Council of Europe: "The Serbian national minority realize this right in pre-school education, but their right to elementary school education in a separate institution has not yet been realized."[13] Meanwhile, in 2007, Serbia reported that several Croatian-language elementary schools were functioning in the country, especially in the Vojvodinian city of Subotica.[14] Thus, at least on the basis of the self-reported compliance with the Charter, Croatia and Serbia have not displayed reciprocity regarding the providing of elementary school education in Serbian and Croatian in the regions of mixed Serb/Croat populations. Similar inconsistencies can be seen in the lack of reciprocity between Serbia and Montenegro. In October 2007, over a year after seceding from the joint state of Serbia and Montenegro, Montenegro adopted a new Constitution in which Montenegrin was declared the official language, alongside Bosnian, Croatian, Serbian, and Albanian. However, Serbia has not recognized the separateness of the Montenegrin language and has not made any provisions through the ECRML to protect the rights of Montenegrin speakers on its territory. Thus, while Serbian is a recognized language in Montenegro, there are few chances Montenegrin would gain official status within Serbia. This non-recognition of a language has precedence in the Balkans. The Bulgarians have not recognized the separateness of the Macedonian language, and Serbia provides recognition to a Bosniak language, even though the Bosniaks prefer calling their own language "Bosnian." These language debates represent unresolved issues, and may in themselves be impediments to normalization of majority/minority relations among the Balkan peoples.

Signed but not ratified: Macedonia and Romania

Macedonia and Romania have signed the ECRML but have still not ratified the Charter. Both countries signed within the first four years subsequent to the Charter's drafting, Romania in 1995 and Macedonia in 1996. Given the long period of inaction towards ratification, it seems unlikely that the Charter will be implemented in either country in the near future. Romania and Macedonia have had to make accommodations for the largest ethnic minorities in their respective countries, namely the Hungarian community in Romania and the Albanian community in Macedonia. Since both of these communities have fielded powerful ethnic parties in national elections, they have enhanced power as minority communities. The states that have ratified the Charter may have an easier task in accommodating minorities, since the minorities do not wield the same level of political power that their counterparts in Romania and Macedonia have gained.

According to Romania's 1991 Constitution, which was amended in 2003, the sole official language of Romania is Romanian (Article 13). The Constitution also declares Romania to be an indivisible national state, which some commentators have called an implication that Romania is a nation-state formed by the Romanian people.[15] Article 6 protects the rights of Romania's citizens to embrace their identity, stating that the "State recognizes and guarantees the right of persons belonging to national minorities to the preservation, development and expression of their ethnic, cultural, linguistic and religious identity." The Constitution is vague regarding specific provisions designed to guarantee the linguistic rights of the country's national minorities. Thus, Article 32, par. 3 guarantees members of national minorities the right to learn their mother tongue and to be educated in their native language, and that this guarantee will be regulated by additional laws. Paragraph 2, however, contradicts this statement, stipulating that "education at all levels" will be carried out in Romanian, and that education could also be carried out in "a foreign language in international use." This statement suggests that English or French may be allowed for educational purposes, but not necessarily smaller or less internationally-used languages. Controversies about the use of Hungarian in Romanian institutions of higher education have occasionally erupted since the fall of Communism in Romania in 1989. Hungarians in Romania have long been dissatisfied with what they view as their marginalization at the Babes-Bolyai University of Cluj.

In the 1990s, the Hungarians had campaigned for a division of the institution into a Romanian-language university and a Hungarian-language university. Their campaign was unsuccessful; rather, the decision was to allow for degree programs in both Romanian and Hungarian. This compromise provided for some courses of study in the Hungarian language and instituted official equality of the two languages at the University. However, many of the Hungarian faculty felt disenfranchised by this arrangement, complaining that they had no autonomy within the University. The tensions reached a climax in 2006 when two ethnic Hungarian professors were dismissed by the University administration for putting up signs in Hungarian at the University.[16] The Hungarian linguistic minority in Romania would probably welcome the protections of the

ECRML; however, the Romanian-speaking majority has thus far resisted greater accommodations for the Hungarian population. If a single pan-Balkan similarity could be drawn from the Romanian situation, it would be that certain language controversies have remained entrenched or frozen, and little progress has been made to resolve them.

In Macedonia, the country's two largest ethnic groups were on the verge of a full-scale ethnic conflict in 2001. Under pressure from international mediators, both sides signed the Ohrid Framework Agreement, and this agreement served as a mechanism for enhancing the linguistic rights of Albanians in the country. Unlike the surrounding nation-states, the new Macedonian Constitution of 2001 allows for languages spoken by at least 20 percent of the country's population to be co-official with Macedonian. The only group for which this provision applies is the country's ethnic Albanian community. Would Macedonia's ratification of the ECRML in the 1990s have forestalled the rising discontent of its Albanians? Now that Albanian has gained a co-official status with Macedonian, however, it seems unlikely that Macedonia will pursue further consideration of the ECRML. This document would require reopening the debate on whether Albanian is an official, regional or minority language of Macedonia, and what should be the status of other regional/minority languages in a state that recognizes its diverse "communities" but no longer allows for "national" majority or "national" minorities. Macedonia is the one Balkan state to move, albeit unwillingly, towards a model of linguistic confederation. The Macedonian language seems to be on the decline in predominantly Albanian areas of Western Macedonia.[17] Linguistic confederation in Macedonia violates a key tenet of the ECRML, namely that the promotion of regional/minority languages should not occur at the expense of the official language(s). And when the status of official languages is still contested or controversial, as with Albanian in Macedonia, the ECRML becomes irrelevant since it does not address criteria for determining whether a language should have official status.

Lack of accommodation to minority languages: Albania, Bosnia-Herzegovina, Bulgaria, and Greece

In Albania, Bulgaria, and Greece, official monolingualism has been a norm that successive governments and Constitutions have embraced. Minority groups in these states have been either too weak, too poorly organized, or too heavily persecuted. Their linguistic rights have been largely ignored, as the states they live in have strongly adhered to the nation-state and non-accommodationist principles. The one exception is Bosnia-Herzegovina, where the international community has been enforcing accommodationist policies in a nation-state shared by Bosniaks, Croats, and Serbs.[18]

Bulgaria's record on languages other than Bulgarian on its territory has been assimilationist. From the notorious campaigns of the Communists in the 1980s to Bulgarianize all Turkish names to the country's official stance of not recognizing a Macedonian language (both within its own borders and across the border in the Republic of Macedonia), Bulgaria has attempted to impress a Bulgarian identity and language on its citizens. While compromises with the country's Turkish minority have been made since the fall of Communism, the Bulgarian majority has not yet garnered the political will to enshrine any of these rights through the ECRML.

Similarly, Albania has been lukewarm about accommodating its linguistic minorities. According to the Macedonian news agency MIA, the Macedonian ambassador to Albania requested that Macedonian language schools be established in Albania to serve the Macedonian-speaking population. According to the report, the Albanians rejected this demand, and claimed that the Macedonians were copying the Greeks of southern Albania who had made a similar demand. MIA reported that the ambassador had indicated that since Macedonia has supported Albanian-language schools, Albania should reciprocate and Macedonia would help finance the enterprise.[19]

Greece has perhaps been the most entrenched nation-state of the Balkans. The Greek state has long held a domination/exclusion language policy. The speakers of minority languages in Greece have had few rights to use their language in official capacities, and in the 1930s under General Metaxis had been banned from speaking their native languages altogether. The intractable policy on minorities has affected Greek relations with neighboring states, especially Albania and Macedonia. The latter has repeatedly attempted to advocate for the Macedonians in northern Greece, including through a 2007 proposed resolution in the Council of Europe. However, Greece has not suffered politically or economically because of its non-compromising attitudes towards its minority populations. Like France, it remains an anomalous example of the philosophy of "one nation, one flag, one language."

Conclusion

While some Balkan states have tried to harmonize their language policies with those of other European states, other Balkan states have been mired in assimilationist or domination/exclusion language policies that often continue earlier language policies or perpetuate or even exacerbate the grievances of disenfranchised minority groups. The broad comparisons of language policies across the contemporary Balkan states recall Friedman's (1998) categorization of language controversies as "recurring, remissive, resolved, or new issues." Many of the issues discussed above are recurring, such as the status of the Hungarian language in Romania, the status of Macedonian speakers in Greece, or the status of Albanian within Macedonia. Few of the issues seem resolved, although some progress has been made among the successor states in ex-Yugoslavia to recognize the new linguistic realities resulting from the breakup of Serbo-Croatian. In addition, it is clear that the signing and ratification of the ECRML do not automatically result in resolving all language policy issues regarding minority groups. The new issues to arise include the status of the Montenegrin language, whether the Bosnian language should be known as Bosnian or Bosniak, and whether higher education should be provided to significantly large linguistic communities in places where these languages typically had no such status in the past.

The integration of Slovenia, Romania and Bulgaria into the European Union has not necessarily changed existing policy towards linguistic minorities in these countries. Slovenia signed and ratified the ECRML several years before acceding to the EU, and Bulgaria and Romania have not been more accommodationist toward their own linguistic minorities since joining the EU in 2007. While Europe has attempted to push for more inclusionist language policies, the Council of Europe has no enforcement mechanism, and states are free to choose the languages and provisions of the Charter they intend to implement.

The notion of a multilingual Europe has not truly trickled down to the Balkans. Multilingual Yugoslavia was replaced by smaller less linguistically diverse nation-states, and the other Balkan states have remained strong nation-states with a largely monolingual character. Nationalist ideologies remain strong in the Balkan countries, and this ideology has not been conducive to tolerance of linguistic minorities. Nevertheless, the Balkan countries are not monolithic in their language policies. The countries that have signed and ratified the ECRML have moved towards a pluralistic model, while those that have not adopted the Charter embrace domination/exclusion or assimilation as their policy paradigms. What the Balkan states lack is reciprocity on minority issues, and this lack of reciprocity allows for mutual resentments to simmer and for relations among the Balkan states to stagnate. As the post-Communist states complete their democratic transitions, perhaps they will begin to celebrate the cultural wealth of their many diverse linguistic minorities.

Notes

1 The text of the Charter is available at: www.conventions.coe.int/Treaty/EN/Treaties/Html/148.htm.
2 Ibid.
3 I do not consider language policies in Kosovo since at the time of this writing not enough time had elapsed since Kosovo's declaration of independence in February 2008 and Kosovo is not a member of the Council of Europe.
4 In 2007–8, Belgium endured a prolonged period of political paralysis as its politicians had great difficulties in forming a coalition government. See also "Seams of Belgium's Quilt Threaten to Burst," *New York Times*, May 14, 2008.
5 The text of the Albanian Constitution is available at: www.ipls.org/services/kusht/cp1.html
6 Ibid., Article 14, Para. 1 which states that "[t]he official language in the Republic of Albania is Albanian."
7 The text was taken from: www.minelres.lv/NationalLegislation/Macedonia/Macedonia_Const2001 _excerpts_English.htm.
8 This language is usually called Bosnian. See below and compare with Greenberg (2004: 139ff.).
9 The debate was particularly acrimonious in the 1930s as revealed in the work of the Croat linguist Stjepan Ivšić (1936).
10 These data are found in Croatia's second periodic report on the implementation of the ECRML, downloaded from the Council of Europe website listed in Note 1 above.
11 See www.stat.si/popis2002/en/rezultati/rezultati_red.asp?ter=SLO&st=7 for the Slovenian census data.
12 The Macedonian reaction to the decision of Serbia and Montenegro not to include Macedonian as a protected minority language was published in the daily newspaper *Dnevnik* on April 7, 2006. The headline for the article read: "After Belgrade's Decision on Minorities: Macedonians in a Struggle for Recognition in Serbia and Montenegro" (*Po odlukata na Belgrad za malcinstvata: Makedoncite vo bitja za priznavanje vo SCG*).
13 See the Croatian report to the Council of Europe on implementation of the Charter from 2003, available from the website listed in Note 1.
14 See the Serbian report on implementation of the Charter, downloaded from the website listed in Note 1.
15 See www.coe.ro/pdf/CDL-AD(2003)004-e.pdf for an opinion from the Council of Europe on a proposed draft of the amended Romanian Constitution.
16 See "Hungary asks Romania to reinstate 2 ethnic Hungarian professors," *International Herald Tribune*, December 6, 2006. The text is available at: www.iht.com/articles/ap/2006/12/06/europe/ EU_GEN_Hungary_Romania_Minority.php.
17 Admittedly, this observation is subjective and based on anecdotal evidence I gathered during a stay in the Tetovo region of Western Macedonia in the summer of 2006.
18 For further discussion of language policies in Bosnia-Herzegovina, see Greenberg (2004).
19 See "Macedonia wants Macedonian language schools in Albania" from October 10, 2008. The text is available at: www.macedoniaonline.eu/content/view/3905/2.

References

Bellamy, A. (2003) *The Formation of Croatian National Identity: A Centuries-Old Dream?*, Manchester: Manchester University Press.
Friedman, V. A. (1998) "The implementation of standard Macedonian: problems and results," *International Journal of the Sociology of Language*, 131, 31–57.

Greenberg, R. (1996) "The politics of dialects among Serbs, Croats, and Muslims in the Former Yugoslavia," *East European Politics and Societies*, 10/3, 393–415.

——(2004) *Language and Identity in the Balkans: Serbo-Croatian and Its Disintegration*, Oxford: Oxford University Press.

Hayden, R. (1992) "Constitutional nationalism in the formerly Yugoslav Republics," *Slavic Review*, 51/4, 654–73.

Ivšić, S. (1936) "Jezik Hrvata kajkavaca," *Ljetopis Jugoslavenske akademije znanosti i umjetnosti*, 48, 47–88.

Naylor, K. (1978) "The eastern variant of Serbo-Croatian as the lingua communis of Yugoslavia," in W. Schmalstieg and T. Magner (eds.) *Sociolinguistic Problems in Czechoslovakia, Hungary, Romania and Yugoslavia*, Columbus, OH: Slavica Publishers, pp. 456–68.

Schmidt, R. (1998) "The politics of language in Canada and the United States: explaining the differences," in T. Ricento and B. Burnaby (eds.) *Language and Politics in the United States and Canada*, Mahwah, NJ: Lawrence Erlbaum Associates, pp. 37–70.

384

32

Sociolinguistics in the Russian Federation, Ukraine, Belarus and Moldova

Victoria Gulida

Introduction

The four countries discussed in this chapter are all, to varying degrees, multiethnic and multilingual: Russia, with its 122 ethnic languages and a population of 150 million, Ukraine – 8 languages and 53 million people, 4 million-strong Belarus with its 4 languages; and Moldova, with a population of 4 million speaking 8 languages between them. Like the other countries in the post-Soviet space, they have experienced dramatic social changes in the past 15 years.

Among many other things, the break-up of the Soviet Union into 15 independent states in 1991 signalled the end of Soviet Union control over language planning and policy (LPP) and set the task of devising the countries' own LPP. Another major transformation was the conversion from planned economies to the free market system, which led to significant societal shifts in interpersonal relations, values and patterns of behaviour, including speech.

Among the factors that greatly contributed to shaping the sociolinguistic agenda was the task, faced by the new independent states (and members of the Russian Federation), of ensuring that their national languages are effective at the state level, which involved redistributing the domains of use between them and the previously dominant Russian, as well as regulating the new relationship between the national and minority languages on their territory. The way this was carried out, both at the policy level and with respect to ordinary people's real lives, was of immediate concern for sociolinguists. Other important changes included the lifting of restrictions on language use, and the innovative tendencies which were set in motion by the end of political censorship, yet which also developed as a way of adapting to the changing communicative needs of the free market society.

Apart from these new challenges, sociolinguists continued to pursue their traditional interests in language variation and change, communication and speech genres, language shift, pidgin and creoles.

Background

Post-Soviet sociolinguistics builds on a century-long tradition dating back to Baudouin de Courtenay, in which three stages can be identified: (1) the early Soviet sociolinguistics of the 1920 and 1930s; (2) the sociolinguistics of the 1960s and 1970s; and (3) the latest period.

1 The early Soviet sociolinguistics pioneered the social study of language by doing the following:

(a) proclaiming urban speech as the third major area of linguistic research (after standard languages and traditional dialects);
(b) viewing the history of standard languages as the result of continuous interaction between standard and non-standard varieties, instrumental in structuring a national language;
(c) pioneering the idea of speaking as a situated activity, which has now evolved into interactional sociolinguistics;
(d) specifying the role of social factors in language evolution.

At the time, sociolinguists were also effectively implementing large-scale LPP projects of promoting minority cultures and languages and eradicating illiteracy in the largely illiterate country. The academic standard of their work and the originality of their ideas, together with the desire to give them due recognition, continue to inspire sociolinguistic research (Brandist 2003; Sociological Theories 2006).

2 After Stalin's repressions, resulting in the physical or intellectual death of many brilliant academics and the collapse of the discipline, Soviet sociolinguistics gained a new lease of life in the 1960s by resuming research on the following:

(a) urban dialectology;
(b) sociolects;
(c) language change and the interaction between the standard and non-standard language varieties (Panov 1968; Russkiy jazyk 1974; Bondaletov 1987). With the fall of the Iron Curtain, some of the rest of the world's research in the field became available (Schweitser 1976).

3 In the past 15 years, sociolinguistics in this part of the world seems to be experiencing another regeneration, this time overcoming the ideological constraints on research material (Krysin 2003: 77) and its conceptualization (Dolinin 2004). It is now on its way to joining the world academic community after decades of restrictions on contact and access to state-of-the-art research (Gulida 1999, in press; Vakhtin and Golovko 2004). It is also a period of critical re-evaluation of the implementation and long-term effects of Soviet language policies of the 1930–1970s and of the methods employed in sociolinguistics at the time (Belikov 1997).

Growth in sociolinguistic inquiry will be brought about by its increasing presence in academic life. The European University in St. Petersburg has organized a three-year Summer School to promote the knowledge of modern theory and latest research methods among academics from post-Soviet countries (University 2006–7). The first university course books have been published, informed by studies carried out here and abroad (Belikov and Krysin 2001; Vakhtin and Golovko 2004). Social typology has been included in a general course on language typology (Mechkovskaya 2006).

Language policies and planning (LPP)

Having standardized their ethnic national languages, Ukraine, Belarus and Moldova started the implementation of language status policy, promoting the use of Ukrainian, Belarusian and Moldovan in official and public domains.

Their common problem was the Soviet legacy of Russian being firmly established in administrative, legal, political and cultural areas as well as in the media and urban communication. Its associations with world culture, great literature and advanced technology made it highly prestigious and advantageous for social mobility. Indeed, Russian constituted an important personality aspect for individuals with social aspirations (Pogorelaya 2003).

In response to the widespread criticism of the 'Russification' policy of the 1930s–1970s, V. Alpatov (2005a) warns against oversimplifying the situation: Russian was the only available lingua franca for the multilingual empire not only during, but also long before the Soviet period, and its power is largely a logical outcome of this role. One unfortunate result of this policy, however, was that the ethnic languages suffered reduction in certain communicatively important functions, hence some linguistic deterioration and, more importantly, a loss of prestige.

LPP in Ukraine

Historically divided into the Ukrainian-speaking west and the mostly Russian-speaking east and south, with ethnic Ukrainians making up 73 per cent (40 per cent of this number in favour of using Ukrainian and 33 per cent of Russian) and ethnic Russians 20 per cent of the population (all in favour of Russian) (Martyniuk 2000, quoted in Bilanyuk 2002), Ukraine proved to be linguistically problematic from the very outset. There is also a divide in terms of culture, political affiliations (the west is pro-European and the east pro-Russian) and economic development. The ideal of linguistically homogeneous polity favoured by the current state authorities is not shared by all Ukrainian citizens; neither are their negative attitudes to the massive Russian language presence. The multilingual Crimea has other language controversies as well.

By the Language Law of 1991, Ukrainian became the state national language. However, the wording of the law concerning the use of Ukrainian in the official domain was vague (Vakhtin et al. 2006) and allowed the use of Russian if preferred. Parents were free to choose Russian or Ukrainian schools for their children, though Russian as a subject was now grouped with other foreign languages.

The clash between language professionals and activists in favour of one as opposed to two national languages has by now developed into fully-fledged ideological discourse, voicing calls for 'de-colonizing' Ukraine by doing away with 'the imperialist Russian language policy' and the 'fifth column' of the ethnic Ukrainians advocating Russian as the second national language. The 'anti-colonial' rhetoric in the public sphere is belied by the resistance to change in everyday language use (why make the effort to speak

Ukrainian in local council meetings when everybody is comfortable speaking Russian?), protests about 'infringed rights' and legally dubious actions (such as several eastern city councils citing the Council of Europe charter for regional and minority languages in their attempt to grant Russian regional status in 2006–7). Crimean academics see little use for the charter in their region even if applied (Chulkova 2004). Highly politicized, the language issue is now a trick played by every political party in their election games.

Much of the ideological discourse has been informed by sociolinguistic accounts of the past and present Ukrainian language situation (Masenko 2004). Language ideologies are subjected to critical discourse analysis in Kulyk (2007).

Meanwhile, a much-needed non-partisan sociolinguistic analysis of the first decade of the language reforms shows some change in Ukrainian-Russian domain distribution (Zaliznjak and Masenko 2001). This questionnaire survey examined the speech patterns, language attitudes and views on the future of Ukrainian-Russian distribution of 1,000 Kiev residents (two-thirds university students and one-third academics). Together with data on the use of Ukrainian in Kiev educational institutions and the media, it reveals considerable progress in promoting Ukrainian in the classroom, state TV and some of the press. It is true that Russian remains the language of informal communication among students, in the street, the entertainment industry, cable and satellite TV, on the Internet and is dominant in book and newspaper publishing. Apart from its associations with having fun, news and technology, Russian is the source of the latest slang (Stavizka 2003), which is seen as worrying because slang as innovative material indicates trends in future use. And yet the attitudes of the young towards Ukrainian are positive, indeed enthusiastic; they tend to want to see its prestige grow, with Kiev becoming a Ukrainian-speaking city. At odds with their speech behaviour, this is accounted for as a contradiction between their 'ideological stance and historical-cultural habits' (Vakhtin et al. 2006).

Further professional assessment of the language situation can be found in interview studies in Kiev and Kharkov (Zhironkina 2007). Performed on smaller samples, these indicate a growing acceptance of change: the interviewed Russian speakers are comfortable with the present situation, reporting their intention of placing their (grand)children into Ukrainian language schools. The authors' other important contribution is identifying *surzhyk* (a low-prestige dialect mixing Ukrainian pronunciation and grammar with Russian vocabulary) as the third element of the language situation. Considered by linguists of the prescriptive orientation as a threat to both Russian and Ukrainian (Stebunova 2004), it has recently been recognized in wider academic discourse on mixed varieties (Trasjanka 2007).

While both 'language parties' blame the government for lack of progress in the language situation irrespective of what outcome they see as desirable, language specialists feel that the government would benefit from professional advice on how to make their LPP more effective (Kiyak 2004).

LPP in Belarus

Belarus, which is politically closer to Russia, went through two distinct stages. A short period of actively implementing the 1991 language legislation prescribing the use of Belarusian, the national language, in official and education domains at all levels saw its increased presence on state television, and the number of Belarusian-instructed schools grow from 20 per cent in 1989 to 75 per cent in 1994. City-dwelling parents were not happy about the changes, and an attempt to introduce Belarusian in the beginner year of universities failed (Korjakov 2002: 46).

In 1994, under President Lukashenka, who referred to Belarusian as 'a poor language incapable of expressing great things' (Furman and Bukhovets 1996: 57), and with the 83 per cent referendum vote for Russian as the second national language, the policy of active promotion of Belarusian was relaxed. The requirement for public section employees to speak Belarusian was dropped, university tuition provided in Russian only (except for Belarusian language and literature), and the small group of pro-Belarusian activist intelligentsia denied public presence. Yet the government did make efforts to urge the use of Belarusian in education, culture and the media – a 'contradictory policy', says Korjakov (2002: 63).

Ten years later, the situation is not far from where it started: parents prefer Russian schools for their 7-year-olds (a dramatic drop from 75 per cent of school starters in Belarusian in 1994 to 4.7 per cent in 1999), Russian is used in the workplace and in the streets, broadcasting and book publishing. While the press is largely bilingual, the capital city of Minsk has 3 per cent of its population speaking Belarusian. In small towns and villages, however, Belarusian dialects are spoken by one-third of the population, and schools remain largely Belarusian.

This seems to suggest that whatever attempts at reforms, the process of shifting to Russian in urban settings has been too powerful to be reversed quickly. A number of researchers maintain that the language situation here is more accurately described as a language continuum with standard Belarusian and Russian at its extremes, incorporating strongly interfered varieties of both as well as *trasianka*, considered by some researchers (e.g. Mechkovskaya 1994) to be a transitional, individually variable short-lived variety acquired by village/country speakers of Belarusian settling in urban areas to be eventually substituted by Russian. A recent study by Liskovec (2006) reports data on the social stratification of the continuum, its varieties' perceived status and prestige, with Russian (both standard and Belarusian accented) as high, *trasianka* as low, associated with the lack of education (at least in Minsk), and Belarusian as special, prestigious or hated, depending on the perceivers' ideology.

Given – as is often the case with genetically close languages – the mutual intelligibility of Russian and Belarusian, the speakers of mixed varieties are unlikely to have an accurate idea of their command in either language. In this context, some linguists' concern about the future survival of Belarusian seems justifiable. Korjakov (2002: 73–4) identifies the factors in favour of revitalization of Belarusian (Belarusians' distinct ethnic and linguistic identity, their sovereign state and the continuing use of its dialects) and against it (the language continuum, the genetic and typological closeness of Belarusian and Russian, the lower prestige of Belarusian), singling out effective language policy as the crucial factor.

LPP in Moldova

Moldovan, already the national language in 1989, with Latin script having replaced Cyrillic, was re-named Romanian[1] in 1991, along with the abolition of the Soviet flag, hymn, monuments, national holidays, re-naming of streets and a prescription to write personal names and toponyms in Romanian phonetic form (Mlechko 2006).

The language of parliament and government, official domains, of jobs in public communication was to be Romanian. Centrally located urban schools became Romanian, with Russian-instructed schools moving out and parents rallying against the 'discrimination against Russian language schools'. A number of national healthcare and education professionals lost their jobs on the grounds of poor language performance, although this did not allow for the gap between the bilingual competence of ethnic Russians (with 2 per cent speaking fluent Moldovan in the capital) and ethnic Moldovans (85 per cent speaking fluent Russian) (Ostapenko and Subbotina 2003). Moldovan language courses, so popular among non-Moldovans during the times of 'Our National Language' demonstrations, lost 80 per cent of their clients. In the words of V. Sennik, Head of the Parliamentary Commission on science, culture, education and the media, people 'refused to learn' the language.

In the 1994 Constitution, the language regime was liberalized to grant Russian a special status, to specify language competence requirements for those seeking jobs in the public domain and to allow more Russian language groups in universities. The Gagauz autonomous group obtained the right to use Russian as its official language. The name 'Moldovan' was brought back to continue public discourse on 'Moldovan-Romanian' identity (Digol 2005).

Further attempts at raising the status of Russian by the 2001 Communist government failed: the parliamentary draft law on Russian as a second state language was banned by the Constitutional Court and the instructions by educational authorities to start Russian in Year 2 (rather than Year 5) at school met with opposition from the Moldovan 'People's Front'; yet the law on national minorities was adopted, compelled by European legislation.

Despite a familiar forward–backward pattern of LPP in Moldova the implementation of the national language has been completed in official and education domains, and promoted in the workplace, with Russians and Moldovans jointly acquiring new Moldovan-based specialist terminologies. Still greater change was brought about by the first generation of young monolingual Moldovans raised in Moldovan families no longer feeling the urge to speak Russian to their children and supported by the growing number of Moldovan-based schools. Yet in everyday communication Russian continues functioning as a lingua franca for all speakers, and urban bilingualism is still asymmetrical in favour of Russian. People prefer to watch the latest news, popular TV programmes and latest films in Russian, although over 65 per cent of television time is in Moldovan. A popular newspaper *Independent Moldova* is also published in Russian.

Russian still enjoys prestige among adults and older people and is valued by younger people for its association with business and advanced technologies. Ethnosociological surveys of the last decade demonstrate little change in the language competence of both Moldovans (in Russian) and Russians (in Moldovan) but the awareness of the need and readiness to become bilingual is growing in ethnic Russians (Ostapenko and Subbotina 2003).

The authorities of Pridnestrovye, a separatist part of Moldova, recognize three national languages: Cyrillic-written Moldovan, Ukrainian and Russian. A recent conflict over the closure of six new Latin alphabet-using Moldovan schools demonstrates that the language policy pursued there does not reflect the views of the Moldovan community, which accounts for 40 per cent of the population (Shaffire 2007). Interestingly, Tiraspol academics are working on the 'Slavonic Educational Unity' – a joint language and cultural project aimed at creating common education space for Russian-speaking post-Soviet regions (Slavyanskij 2002).

Nikoglo (2006) voices an offer by Moldovan academics to participate in state LPP (like their Ukrainian colleagues) to make it more effective for all parties concerned.

LPP in the Russian Federation

With Russian being the native tongue of 85 per cent of its population and serving as a lingua franca for speakers of all other languages, the choice of the national language for multiethnic and multilingual Russia (122 languages: 1989 census) was a straightforward task (Alpatov 2000: 146). As part of the national policy of protecting peoples' and individuals' language rights, the 1991 language legislation granted the non-Russian member states of the Russian Federation the right to establish their titular languages in their territories (with Russian recognized as the state language at the federal level). The challenge of ensuring their use in official and public domains called for effective language planning.

As elsewhere, the language policy in the member states followed an 'attack–retreat' pattern. At the early stage, the authorities strove to implement their ambitious LPP of speedy promotion of their title languages into all relevant domains, including the full education cycle. This was halted by the apparent gap between their idea of people's command of their mother tongue and reality. It turned out that quite often school starters, expected to use new programmes and textbooks, could speak little or no ethnic language, especially in urban areas. For instance, the Kalmyk education authorities had to abandon their plan of an immediate start of schooling in Kalmyk in 1991; and, similarly, the Khakassian educators (Alpatov 2000: 155–6; 2005a: 3). In fact, the younger generation in quite a few minority communities speak Russian as their first language and learn their ethnic language at school. Many of the members of ethnic minorities (up to half of the Karels, over one-third of Bashkir, Komi, Mordva, Udmurt, almost one-quarter of Mari and Chuvash) consider Russian their mother tongue (Jazykovye 1994: 34), a sign of low prestige of their ethnic language. Even when some state support is given to ethnic minorities, they may be indifferent to their languages and reluctant to speak them. 'Ethnic erosion' as stated by Shabaev (1994: 232) for speakers of Komi, makes the extreme case for some languages of the North. The publication of a reference book (Jazyki 2002) on endangered languages came as a belated recognition of the language shift in progress in many areas of Russia.

This suggests that, for some of the minority languages, LPP needs to be re-oriented towards revitalization, while others should be able to proceed with their plans, if less ambitious ones. Comparing intentions and achievements, Alpatov (2000: 161) finds that language regulations administered by the authorities, such as introducing bilingual road signs and official place names, translating legal documents and taking up more time on state television, have proved to be the easier part; yet it is much harder to ensure the use of a language in everyday communication in all, including official, domains. This is not true, however, of three of the non-Russian minority language communities: replacing Russian, the Saha-Yakut, Tuva and partly, Tatar languages have been increasingly used in all relevant domains, including informal communication.

Language shift

It has to be said that the massive shift in minority languages cannot be accounted for entirely by the Soviet policy of Russification, although its negative impact is undeniable. Neither is it a specifically Soviet problem. At present any minority culture and language in contact with a major one is at risk of perishing, not necessarily under coercion, but quite often without any resistance. The process is worldwide and, with linguistic diversity at stake, is of huge concern for sociolinguists and one of the most thoroughly investigated areas of sociolinguistic study.

What makes some communities part with their languages (sometimes over as few as two generations), while others stay loyal to theirs? Nikolay Vakhtin, the author of *The Languages of the Peoples of the North in the XX Century* (2001), believes that it is, to an extent, a 'mystery', since external factors conducive to language shift do not constitute its immediate cause, and the ultimate community choice between giving up their native tongue or staying loyal to it comes down to whether individuals commit 'to speaking the language or not' (ibid.: 230).

The book is a large-scale study of language shift in 26 language minorities, widely varying in terms of their demographics, culture and traditional activities, which are spread over a huge territory between the Kola Peninsula in the west and the Commander islands in the east, bordering with China along the Amur River in the south (with the 'North' used as an administrative and ethnographic, rather than a geographic, term). The study conceptualizes a wealth of field data collected over the past 50 years, including the author's own field materials, within the contemporary sociolinguistic paradigm, which makes it a remarkable academic achievement as well as an influential manual for newcomers in the field.

According to the author, had the Soviet language policy not changed drastically in the 1950 and 1960s, setting the catastrophic shift in motion, minority languages would have had a chance of developing from the monolingual phase of the 1920s into a stable bilingualism that started to emerge in the 1940s. While quite a few languages may by now have passed the point of no return, Vakhtin maintains that the issue of language death is open to discussion. Unlike its biological counterpart, language death can go on for years (in fact, a hundred years in the case of the Yukaghir language), when upon proclaiming a language 'almost dead', every subsequent fieldwork team expecting to register its final death finds a small group of speakers still 'in office'. These will be representatives of a generation that has replaced those who were seen as the 'last' by the previous expedition. Under the guise of what looks a 'dying language', there seems to be evolving an age-related system of language competence, capable of prolonging the process considerably, if not indefinitely. Thus, the linguist's view and the community of speakers' view of language death, indeed, of language itself, may differ drastically.

A similar pattern of an age-related system of language competence, together with features of language attrition is registered for Rumei, a dialect of Greek, spoken by minority communities living by the Azov Sea (Viktorova 2006). With its Greek, Albanian and Bulgarian communities brought here in the eighteenth century by order of Catherine II, this part of Ukraine is of great interest to sociolinguistics. Thus, a study of Urum, a Crimean Tatar dialect, spoken by ethnic Greeks who are orthodox Christians (similar to Rumeians), presents an intricate relation between the linguistic and ethnic aspects of identity (Baranova 2005). Issues of ethnic identity studied in social constructivist terms are taken up in the Vakhtin, Golovko, and Schweitzer (2004) study of ethnically mixed groups of Russians and local indigenous peoples of the Far North formed during the colonization of Siberia in the eighteenth century.

Kleiner and Svetozarova (2006) describe the remains of Yiddish, once active on the St Petersburg linguistic scene, as no longer a means of communication but a clear symbol of identity.

Dobrushina (2007) reports an inspiring case of Archin, a Daghestan minority language in the Caucasus. This unwritten language of 1200 people living in a remote mountain village has proved capable of carrying enough prestige for its speakers to stay loyal to it despite their proficiency in the national language and a couple of others. Children speak Archin only for the first seven years of their life, adding another 2–3 languages to it at school. Neither the command of dominant languages, nor leaving their village for a city makes them give up their native tongue. The old rule still holds: 'It is disrespectful to answer in Russian when you are addressed in Archin, especially by an elderly person.'

Pidgin and creole languages

The sociolinguistic study of Russian-based pidgins and creoles (as well as other types of contact languages) has the potential to make a significant contribution to language contact theory, since in this way the regularities established for the typical case – a Western European language providing lexis and a substrate African or Asian language, grammar – can be tested on typologically different source languages in socially different contact situations.

Extinct but well-documented, Russenorsk, a Russian-Norwegian pidgin, has been investigated from various angles. Lexically sourced by both languages, it proves distinct from conventional pidgins, and the difference is accounted for by symmetrical social relations between communicators. Klonova (2007) attempts to verify the hypothesis about foreigner talk as a lexical source of pidgins by experimentally simulating an extreme language contact situation between Russians and Norwegians and comparing the resulting linguistic forms to the pidgin in question.

Perekhvalskaja (2006) describes a dialect of the Chinese-Russian Siberian pidgin, the 'Far East pidgin', whose other dialects are Kyakhta and Maymachin. It completes the list of nearly extinct varieties of a proto-pidgin, presumably a product of Russian traders' foreigner talk and the substrate Ural-Altaic languages, going back to the start of colonizing the Urals and Siberia. An adept of the monogenetic theory, she also insists that the 'pragmatic code' phase is essential for a variety to be classified as a pidgin.

Mednij Aleut, an Aleut-Russian mixed language is, like pidgins, a product of extreme contact situation, yet structurally it is a unique combination of 'ready-made' parts from both source languages. In his inquiry into the emergence of this type of structure, Evgeniy Golovko (1997, 2003) offers an interesting explanation: the Mednij community members, initially bilingual in Russian and Aleut, were likely to switch and mix codes, at a subconscious level. The need to establish themselves as a distinct community may have prompted them to consciously employ this play-like spontaneous language mixing as a strategy for creating their own code. The resultant patterns of mixing were already specific to this particular language.

Romani languages are a rich test field for investigating language contact, and the North Russian Romani dialect (NRRd), investigated by Alexander Rusakov (2004), is a typical sample of interrelated contact-induced features and processes manifested by any language of this group. Like all Romani languages, the NRRd shows remarkable linguistic vitality and its community's strong sense of linguo–ethnic identity. Notwithstanding its long history of code-switching and mixing, and strong interference from Russian, it has retained its Romani core. Although the elements of the original Romani system continue to be replaced by Russian borrowings, threatening it with language death, it is helped to survive, paradoxically, by the very presence of the dominant Russian as the source of as many borrowings as the limited Romani might need to incorporate to stay functional. The author believes that code-switching and mixing as partly controllable processes may perform the language maintenance function while interference is likely to speed up language shift.

Sociolects

As elsewhere, language varieties produced by the latest technologies, such as computer lects, mobile text message codes (in Latin and Cyrillic scripts), the languages of internet communities, (e.g. Olbanskiy), a Russian Live Journal product of orthographic language play (Kostomarov 2007), role-player and hiker sociolects as well as other social group jargons have been registered in Russia, Ukraine and Belarus (Sotsialnye 2003–5; Jakhontova 2004). Dictionaries of jargons and obscene language are compiled in large numbers, though sometimes produced below professional standards (Nikolaeva 2004). No wonder this language attracts interest: the Russian Gulag language, a taboo before perestroika, is now open to study.

Two register studies should be mentioned of those examining more traditional topics: Gavrilova (2002) on baby talk and Fedorova (2002) on foreigner talk.

Communication and culture

Concerned with investigating speech genres and related concepts of socio-communicative interaction, genrology builds on a sound tradition started by Bakhtin (1979). Recognized worldwide (Alpatov 2005b), his ideas on speech genre are elaborated at home, both in Russia (mostly the Saratov group) and Ukraine. Some recent research develops Bakhtin's suggestion that the infinite diversity of speech genre forms should be categorized by domains of use, with a basic division into primary and secondary ones (Sedov 2001); or Jakubinskiy's context of communication, e.g. urban communication (Kitaygorodskaya and Rozanova 2003). A lot of sociolinguistic fieldwork has gone into establishing the nomenclature and linguistic description of individual speech genres (e.g. Fedosyuk 1997; Baykulova 2001; Milekhina 2001; Kushnir 2003), their pragmatics (Ratmayer 2003), particular typology types (Sedov 1998; Dementyev 2000; Romanenko 2002; Shmeleva 2003). Batsevich (2005) is a comprehensive volume on the issues of the theory, including several case studies from Ukrainian.

For a communicator, all communication is strategic, and speech genres and speech acts are just tactical moves in the strategies employed by communicators to achieve their goals in discourse. Issers (2006) uses a strategic approach to discourse analysis to identify the Russian repertoire of strategies and tactical moves in the domains of interpersonal communication, political rhetoric and advertising. Thoroughly rooted in the basics of communication theory Karasik's (2002) discussion of social status and language makes it a widely quoted academic source.

Gender linguistics is a particularly popular area of investigation in the post-Soviet space, with record numbers of publications and large conferences. As Kirilina and Tomskaya (2005) suggest in their survey, the early 1990s studies of the differences in male–female lexicon and verbal behaviour (Zemskaya et al. 1993) laid the foundation for the mid-1990s gender linguistics, in which they identify three strands: (1) diagnostically relevant features of female and male speech identified by Goroshko (1999) for forensic purposes, belong to the first, psychosociolinguistic line of research; (2) studies of Russian stereotypes vs reality of femininity and masculinity (Sternin 1999; Timofeev 2001; Uzina 2002; Kirilina 2003) are examples of cultural anthropological research; (3) the discursive strand is represented by Grizenko (2003), who analyses gender as a factor in the electoral discourse.

The feminist orientation is not common in academic literature in the field, while application-oriented research is, as some topics above indicate. Another typical feature of gender studies here is an appreciation by the authors of the social nature of the link between gender and language – perhaps, the legacy of our Marxist background.

Language attitudes

The sensitive matter of jargonization and excessive borrowing into Russian was examined in a survey in which 1200 respondents – St Petersburg university students, young working-class people, journalists and mature professionals – were asked about their attitudes towards these issues. The survey reveals that, in contrast to older people's disapproval, young people have relaxed attitudes towards English borrowings and the use of substandard language in informal situations; both age groups are united, however, in their demand for a 'proper' language from media professionals (Semenov and Jurkov 2004).

Another study on language attitudes uses the classical method of the matched guise technique for sound vs video stimuli and sociolinguistic interviewing to study St Petersburg teachers' attitudes to schoolchildren of non-Russian ethnic origin (Panova 2006). Teachers working with ethnically mixed classes were found to have positive attitudes, both academic and personal, towards their students while teaching and assessing them. Even so, their conversations in non-school contexts were not free from negative stereotyping of non-Russians.

Variation studies

Of the large-scale stratification studies of Russian, E. Erofeeva's (2005) 'On the Probabilistic Structure of Idioms' follows the closest approximation of the established variation paradigm. It shows the sociolinguistic system of Russian in the Perm region to be a statistically structured stratified distribution of 16 phonetic variables across several social strata in quantitatively varying combinations. Every variable is correlated with a social or psychosocial factor (age, gender, education level, place of origin, extrovert/introvert type), and the relevance of each of the factors for the recurrence of particular variables is calculated. Statistically significant differences in variable frequencies reveal a discrete organization of what appears to be a linguistic continuum of basic (dialects, prostorechie, spoken standard) and intermediary (semi-dialects, the regiolect) varieties of modern Russian.

The quantitative approach to investigating language stratification has been employed in the Perm sociolinguistic school since the early 1990s when A. Shtern (2006) and T. Erofeeva (1999) started their social dialectology project in the linguistically rich Perm region. Their work links back to early Soviet sociolinguistics and the 1960s period (see Introduction) and, while informed by W. Labov's work, has evolved independently.

Kochetov's (2007) study of language change in progress applies a strictly Labovian research paradigm to the study of Russian in two cases of sound change in a small rural community of Pokcha (the Urals), and the role played in it by age, sex, education and mobility. By employing the apparent time technique, the author can tell that local features will be replaced by the regional ones in just two generations.

An intermediary variety such as the Perm regiolect, produced by the interaction of the standard, dialects and prostorechie, is one example of koinization which continues among national language varieties elsewhere. The emerging Russian 'city jargon', a hybrid of spoken standard, prostorechie and professional, criminal and youth jargons, discussed by sociolinguists in Moscow (Jermakova *et al.* 1999), Perm (Khorosheva 2001) and Kiev (Kudrjavzeva 2006), is another. Apparently unrelated to social class or education, and serving as an expressive colloquial way of sharing one's emotions or opinions, this jargon is a style rather than a stratificational variety. In terms of sociolinguistic description, these novel 'mixed' varieties indicate that Russian is undergoing a sociolinguistic restructuring, although whether they are independent varieties is currently under discussion.

Conclusion

This chapter reflects the wide scope of sociolinguistic research carried out in the four post-Soviet countries, its new challenges and the substantial tradition it builds on. The following seem to be promising areas for sociolinguistic study in the future:

- ways of further promoting national languages in all domains in Ukraine, Belarus, Moldova and the non-Russian member states of the Russian Federation, since the task is by no means completed;
- both stratificational and stylistic sociolinguistic variation, to address the deepening social class stratification in each country and the new standards of verbal behaviour that are emerging, especially in commerce-associated domains;
- the use of Russian in diasporas (25 million speakers) as areas of contact-induced language change, the human factor in language loyalty, and Russia's new LPP area.

Note

1 Genetically, Moldovan is a northern Romanian dialect.

References

Alpatov, V. (2000) *150 jazykov i politika: 1917–2000* [150 languages and Politics: 1917–2000], Moskva: KRAFT + IV RAN.
——(2005a) 'Jazykovaya situatsiya v regionax Rossii' [Language situation in the regions of Russia], *Otechestvennye zapiski*, 2 (23), Moskva. Online. Available at: www.strana-oz.ru (accessed 13 May 2007).
——(2005b) *Voloshinov, Bakhtin i lingvistika* [Voloshinov, Bakhtin and Linguistics], Moskva: Jazyki slavjanskix kultur
Bakhtin M. (1979) 'Problema rechevyx zhanrov' [The problem of speech genres], in M. Bakhtin (ed.) *Estetika slovesnogo tvorchestva*, Moskva.
Baranova, V. (2005) Greki Priazovja: etnicheskoe samosoznanie i jazyk [The Azov Greeks: Ethnic Identity and the Language], Candidate of Philology dissertation, St Petersburg.

Batsevich, F. (2005) *Lingvistichna genologiya: problemi i perspektuvu* [Linguistic genealogy: Problems and Perspectives], Lviv: Pais.

Baykulova, A. (2001) 'Semejnaya beseda' [Family conversation], in M. Kormilitsyna and O. Sirotinina (eds) *Xoroshaya rech*, Saratov State University, pp. 151–63.

Belikov, V. (1997) 'Nadezhnost sovetskix etnographicheskix dannyx' [The reliability of Soviet ethno-demographic data], in *Malye jazyki Evrazii: sotsiolingvisticheskiy aspect*, Moskva, pp. 12–43.

Belikov, V. and Krysin, L. (2001) *Sotsiolingvistik* [Sociolinguistics], Moskva.

Bilanyuk, L. (2002) 'Gender, language attitudes, and language status in Ukraine', *Language in Society* 32, 47–78.

Bondaletov, V. (1987) *Sotsialnaya lingvistika* [Social Linguistics], Moskva: Public Education.

Brandist, C. (2003) 'The origins of Soviet sociolinguistics', *Journal of Sociolinguistics*, 2, 7, 213–32.

Chulkova, L. (2004) 'Russkiy jazyk v Krymu I Evropejskaya khartiya o regionalnyx jazykax I jazykax menshinstv' [Russian in Crimea and the European Charter for Regional or minority languages, Simferopol, Ukraine], in *Russkiy jazyk: Istoricheskiye sudby i sovremennost. II Mezhdunarodny Congress rusistov-issledovateley*, Moskva, MGU, Filologichskiy fakultet. Sekziya XXI 'Russkiy jzyk v novyx geopoliticheskix usloviyax'. Online. Available at: www.philol.msu.ru/~rlc2004/ru/abstracts/?id=21&type =doc (accessed 02 June 2007).

Dementyev, V. (2000) *Neprjamaya kommunikaziya i ee zhanry* [Indirect Communication and its Genres], Saratov: izd. Saratovskogo universiteta.

Digol, S. (2005) 'Paradigmy i paradoxy konzepzii nazionalnogo gosudarstva v postsovetskoy Moldavii: jazyk, gosudarstvennost i narod' [Paradigms and paradoxes of the national state concept in post-Soviet Moldova: the language, statehood and people], in *Ab Imperio*, 2, *History of Romania and Moldova*. Online. Available at: www.dacoromania.org/index.php?nma=catalog&fla=stat&cat_id=8&nums=157 (accessed 20 May 2007).

Dobrushina, N. (2007) 'Mnogojazychiye v Dagestane, ili zachem cheloveku tri jazyka' [Multilingualism in Dagestan, or who needs three languages?], *Sotsiologicheskij zhurnal*, 1, Moskva.

Dolinin, K. (2004) 'Socialisticheskiy realism v lingistike (k istorii funkzionalnoy stilistiki v SSSR)' [Socialist realism in linguistics (On the history of functional stylistics in the USSR)], in *Teoreticheskiye problemy jazykoznaniya*, a volume dedicated to the 140th anniversary of the Department of General Linguistics, St. Petersburg University, pp. 596–607.

Erofeeva, E. (2005) *Veroyatnostnye struktury idiomov. Sociolinvisticheskiy aspect* [The Probability Structure of Idioms: A Sociolinguistic Approach], Perm: izd. Permskogo universiteta.

——(1999) 'Lingvisticheskiye portrety gorodov Permskoy oblasti (stratifikazionnoe opisaniye)' [Linguistic portraits of Perm region towns (a stratification study)], in T. Erofeeva (ed.) *Lingvisticheskaya retrospektiva, sovremennost I perspektiva goroda I derevni*, Proceedings of the International meeting, Perm University, pp. 75–80.

Fedorova, K. (2002) 'Lingvopovedencheskie strategii v situatsii obscheniya s inostrantsem (na materiale russkogo jazyka)' [Linguo-behavioural strategies of communication with a foreigner (in the Russian language)], Candidate of Philology dissertation, St Petersburg.

Fedosyuk, M. (1997) 'Kompleksnye zhanry razgovornoy rechi: utesheniye, ubezhdeniye, ugovory' [The complex genres of spoken language: comforting, urging, persuading], in *Russkaya razgovornaya rech kak javleniye gorodskoy kultury*, Ekaterinburg.

Furman, D. and Bukhovets, O. (1996) 'Belorusskoye samosoznanie I belorusskaya politika' [Belorussian self-identification and Belorussian politics], in *Svobodnaya mysl* N1, 108. Online. Available at: www. library.by/shpargalka/belarus/belorus/001/bel-033.htm (accessed 16 June 2007).

Gavrilova, T. (2002) 'Registr obscheniya s detmi: strukturny i sociolingvisticheskiy aspekty' [Baby talk: structural and sociolinguistic aspects)], Candidate of Philology dissertation, St Petersburg.

Golovko, E. (1997) 'Jazyk mednovskikh aleutov' [The language of the Mednij Aleut], *Jazyki mira: Paleoaziatskiye jazyki*, 117–25.

——(2003) 'Language contact and group identity: the role of "folk" linguistic engineering', in Y. Matras and P. Bakker (eds) *The Mixed Language Debate*, Berlin: Mouton de Gruyter, pp. 177–209.

Goroshko, E. (1999) 'Osobennosti muzhskogo i zhenskogo stilja pisma' [The distinctive features of male and female writing styles], in *Genderny factor v jazyke i kommunikazii*, Proceedings of Moscow State Linguistic University, vyp 446: 44–60.

Grizenko, E. (2003) 'Gendernye aspekty nazionalnoy identichnosti v rossijskom predvybornom diskurse' [Gender aspects of national identity in Russian electoral discourse], *Journal of Eurasian Research*, 3, 3, 71–9.

Gulida,V. (1999) 'Anglojazychnaya sotsiolingvistika segodnja: obzor. Part I [Contemporary English-speaking sociolinguistics: a review: Part I], *Jazyk I rechevaya dejatelnost* [Language and Speech Activity], SPb. 2, 305–26.

——(in press) 'Anglojazychnaya sotsiolingvistika segodnja. Discourse: obzor. Part II' [Contemporary English-speaking sociolinguistics. Discourse: a review; Part II], *Jazyk I rechevaya dejatelnost* [Language and Speech Activity], SPb.

Issers, O. (2006) *Kommunikativnye strategii i taktiki russkoj rechi* (Communicative Strategies and Tactical Moves of Russian Speech], Moskva: Komkniga.

Jakhontova, T. (2004) 'Elektronna grupova diskussiya jak zhanr miznarodnogo naukovogo spilkuvannja' [Electronic group discussion as a genre of international academic communication], *Movni i kulturni kartyny svitu*, 10, Kyiv.

Jazyki (2002) *Jazyki narodov Rossii. Krasnaya kniga: Entsiklopedicheskiy slovar-spravochnik* [The Languages of the Peoples of Russia. The Red Book: The Encyclopedic Reference Book], Moskva.

Jazykovaya (1992) *Jazykovaya situatsiya v Rossijskoy Federatsii* [Language Situation in the Russian Federation], Moskva.

Jazykovye (1994) *Jazykovye problemy Rossijskoy Federatsii i zakony o jazykax* [Language Problems of the Russian Federation and Language Laws], Moskva.

Jermakova, O., Zemskaya, E., and Rozina, R. (1999) *Slova, s kotorymi my vse vstrechalis:tolkovy slovar russkogo obschego zhargona* [Words, We All Have Come across: Russian-Russian Dictionary of Common Jargon], Moskva.

Krasik, V. (2002) *Jazyk socialnogo statusa* [The Language of Social Status], Moskva: Gnozis.

Khorosheva, N. (2001) 'Russkiy obschiy zhargon: k opredeleniyu ponjatiya' [On the definition of common jargon in Russian], in *Izmenjayuschjisa jazykovoy mir* [The Changing Linguistic World], International Linguistic Conference, Perm. Online. Available at: www.language.psu.ru/bin/view.cgi?art=0079&lang=rus%20 (accessed 2 Sept. 2007).

Kirilina, A. (2003) 'Gender: lingvisticheskie aspekty' [Gender: the linguistic aspects], Candidate of Philology dissertation, Moskva.

Kirilina, A. and Tomskaya, M. (2005) 'Lingvisticheskie gendernye issledovaniya' [Linguistic gender studies], in *Otechestvennye zapiski*, 2 (23). Online. Available at: www.strana-oz.ru (accessed 10 April 2007).

Kitaygorodskaya, M. and Rozanova, N. (2003) 'Sovremennoe gorodskoe obschenie: tipy kommunikativnyx situaziy i ix zhanrovaya realizatsiya' [Contemporary urban communication: types of communicative situation and their genre realizations], in L. Krysin (ed.) *Sovremenny russkij jazyk. Sotsialnya I funktsionalnaya differentsiatsiya* [Social and Stylistic Differentiation of Modern Russian], Part II, Chapter 3; Part II Chapter 1, Moskva: Jazyki slavjanskoy kultury.

Kiyak, T. (2004) 'How to do away with the "paper" status of the language', *Zerkalo nedeli*, 31 (506), 7–13 August.

Kleiner, Ju. and Svetozarova, N. (2006) 'Maly jazyk v bolshom gorode: idish v Peterburge nashix dney' [A minority language in a city: Yiddish in St Petersburg today], in *Vtoroy mezhdunarodny symposium po polevoy lingvistike. Materialy*, Moskva, pp. 69–72.

Klonova, O. (2007) Uproschennye jazykovye sistemy i formirovanie pidjina (na materiale russko-norvezhskix jazykovyx kontaktov) [Simplified language systems and the formation of pidgins (Russian-Norwegian language contacts)], Candidate of Philology dissertation, St Petersburg.

Kochetov, A. (2007) 'The role of social factors in the dynamics of sound change: a case study of Russian dialect', *Language Variation and Change*, 18, 99–119.

Krjakov, Ju. (2002) 'Jazykovaya situatsiya v Belorussii i tipologiya jazykovyx situatsiy' [Language situation in Belorussia and a typology of language situations], Candidate of Philology dissertation, Moskva, MGU.

Kostomarov, V. (2007) 'Zachem nam 'olbanskiy' jazyk?' [Why should we need the 'Olbanskiy' language?]. Online. Available at: www.rian.ru/society/20070402/62962803.html (accessed 04 August 2007).

Krysin, L. (2003) 'Formy suschestvovaniya (podsistemy) russkogo nazionalnogo jazyka' [The subsystems of the Russian national language], in *Social and Stylistic Differentiation in Modern Russian*, part I, chapter 1.

Kudrjavzeva, L. (2006) 'Kyiv National University, Ukraine. Jazyk goroda: obschiy sleng' [Urban language: common slang], in *Philologiya. Russkiy jazyk. Obrazovanie: A Collection of Articles in Honour of Professor L.A. Verbitskaya*, St Petersburg, pp. 158–67.

Kulyk, V. (2007) 'Jazykovye ideologii v ukrainskom politicheskom i intellektualnom diskursax' [Language ideologies in Ukrainian political and intellectual discourses], in *Otechestvennye zapiski*, 1(34), Moskva. Online. Available at: www.strana-oz.ru/?ozid=34&oznumber=1 (accessed 06 June 2007).

Kushnir, N. (2003) 'Osoblivosti vzhivannja neprjamyx movnix aktiv u kommunikativniy situazii 'osvodchennja u koxannji' (na materiali suchasnoy rossijskoy prozi)' [The use of indirect speech acts in the situation of 'declaring love' (in Russian contemporary prose)], in *Movni i konzeptualni kartyny svitu*, Kyiv, vyp.9.

Liskovec, I. (2006) 'Russkiy i belorusskiy jazyki v Minske: problemy dvuyazychiya i otnosheniya k jazyku' [Russian and Belorussian in Minsk: problems of bilingualism and language attitude], Candidate of Philology dissertation, St Petersburg.

Masenko, L. (2004) 'Ukrainska mova u sociolingvostichnomu aspekti' [A sociolinguistic approach to the Ukrainian language], in *Studii z ukrainistiki: Zb. nauk. pr*, Kyiv Nationalny Univ. im. T. Shevchenka. Institut filologii, vyp.6, 130–47.

Mechkovskaya, N. (1994) 'Jazykovaya situatsya v Belrusi: Eticheskie kollizii dvujazychiya' [Language situation in Belarus: ethical collisions of bilingualism], *Russian Linguistics*, 18, 312.

Mechkovskaya, N. (2006) *Obschee jazykoznaniye. Strukturnaya I sociolingvisticheskaya tipologiya jazykov* [General Linguistics. Structural and Sociolinguistic Typology of Languages], Moskva: Flinta Nauka.

Milekhina T. (2001) 'Svetskiy razgovor' [Mundane talk], in M. Kormilitsyna and O. Sirotinina (eds) *Khoroshaya rech*, Saratov State University, pp. 131–51.

Mlechko, T. (2006) 'Tiraspol State University, Pridnestrovje Russkiy jazyk kak sociokulturnaya peremennaya' [The Russian language as a social variable], in *Philologiya. Russkiy jazyk. Obrazovanie: A Collection of Articles in Honour of Professor L.A. Verbitskaya*, St Petersburg, pp. 252–65.

Nikoglo, D. (2006) 'Jazykovaya situaziya v Gagauzii: problemy i perspektivy' [Language situation in Gagauziya: problems and perspectives], Moldova Noastra, Russian Information Agency 'Novy region'. Online. Available at: www.mdn.md/ru/print.php?id=2464&lang=ru (accessed 28 May 2007).

Nikolaeva, T. (2004) 'Boduen de Courtenay, the editor of V.F.Trakhtenberg's 'Thieves' cant' ('Prison jargon')', in *Russkaya i sopostavitelnaya philologiya: lingvokulturologicheskiy aspect*, Kazan, pp. 176–81.

Ostapenko, L. and Subbotina, I. (2003) 'Russkiy jazyk v sovremennoy Moldove' [Russian in Moldova today], in *Politcheskoye prosveschenie*, 1(3). Online. Available at: webknow.ru/kultura_02040.html (accessed 30 March 2007).

Panov, M. (1968) 'Prinzipy sociologicheskogo izucheniya russkogo jazyka' [The principles of sociological study of Russian], in *Russkiy jazyk I sovetskoye obschestvo*, Moskva.

Panova, E. (2006) 'Inoetnihny uchenik v peterburgskoy shkole: sociolingvisticheskiy aspect' [Ethnic students of St Petersburg schools: a sociolinguistic approach], Candidate of Philology dissertation, St Petersburg.

Perekhvalskaja, E. (2006) 'Sibirskiy pidjin (Dalnevostochny variant). Formirovaniye. Istoriya. Struktura' [Siberian pidgin (the Far East variety): formation, history. structure], Doctor of Philology dissertation, St Petersburg.

Pogorelaya, E. (2003) 'Jazykovaya situaziya i jazykovaya politika (russkiy jazyk v Pridnestrovje)' [Language situation and language policies (Russian in Pridnestrovje)], Doctor of Philology dissertation, Moskva: Nauka, RGB.

Ratmayer, R. (2003) *Pragmatika izvineniya. Sravnitelnoye issledovaniye na materiale russkogo jazyka I russkoy kultury* [The Pragmatics of Apology. A Comparative Study of Apology in the Russian Language and Russian Culture], Moskva.

Romanenko, A. and Sandji-Girjaeva, Z. (2002) Obschephilologicheskiye issledovaniya sovetskoy zhanrovoy sistemy' [A general philological study of the Soviet genre system], in *Genres of speech*, Saratov, vyp.3.

Rusakov, A. (2004) 'Interferenziya I pereklucheniye kodov (severnorusskiy dialect tsyganskogo jazyka v kontaktologicheskoy perspective' [Interference and code-switching (North Russian Romani dialect in language contact perspective)], Doctor of Philology dissertation, St Petersburg.

Russkiy jazyk (1974) *Russkiy jazyk po dannym massovogo obsledovaniya: opyt socialno-lingvisticheskogo izuche-niya* [The Russian language by the data of mass examination: a sociolinguistic study], Moskva: Nauka.

Schweitser, A. (1976) *Sovremennaya sotsiolingvistika. Teoriya, problemy, metody* [Contemporary Sociolinguistics. Theory, Problems, Methods], Moskva: Nauka.

Sedov, K. (2001) 'Zhanr i kommunikativnaya kompetenziya' [Genre and communicative competence], in M. Kormilitsyna and O. Sirotinina (eds) *Khoroshaya rech*, Saratov State University, pp. 107–31.

Sedov, K. (1998) 'Anatomiya zhanrov bytovogo obscheniya' [The anatomy of everyday communication genres], in *Issues of Stylistics*, Saratov, vyp.27.

Semenov, V. and Jurkov, E. (2004) *Russkaya rech v sovremennoy Rossii: tendenzii razvitiya (po rezultatam sociologicheskogo issledovaniya)* [Russian Speech in Contemporary Russia: Tendencies of Change (According to the Data of Sociological Investigation], St Petersburg: Politechnika.

Shabaev, Ju. (1994) 'Jazykovaya situatsiya i etnojazychnye problemy v Komi-Permjatskom Avto-nomnom okruge' [The language situation and ethnolinguistic problems in Komi-Perm Autonomous Region], in *Jazykovye problemy Rossijskoy Federazii i zakony o jazykax* [Language Problems of the Russian Federation and Language Laws], Moskva.

Shaffire, M. (2007) 'Pridnestrovje, Rossiya i disput vokrug shkol' [Pridnestrovje, Russia and the school disputes], Inopressa, Radio Liberty. Online. Available at: www.inopresa.ru/radio/2004/08/06/14:44:00/tiraspol (accessed 02 Sept. 2007).

Shmeleva, T. (2003) 'Imperativnye rechevye zhanry (Imperative speech genres)', in M. Ivanov, L. Ivanov, A. Skovopodnikov and E. Shirokova (eds) *Kultura russkoy rechi. Entsiklopedicheskiy slovar-spravochnik*. Moskva.

Shtern, A. (2006) 'Tri aspekta gorodskogo bilingvizma (foneticheskiy uroven)' [Three aspects of urban bilingualism (at the phonetic level)], in T. Dotsenko, E. Erofeeva, I. Ovchinnikova and T. Chugaeva (eds) ... *Slovo otzovetsa (... It Will Ring the Bell: In Memory of A. Shtern and L. Sakharny*, Perm.

Slavyanskij (2002) *1 Mezhdunarodny congress 'Slavyanskij Pedagogicheskij Sobor' (1st International Congress 'Slavonic Educational Unity')* Tiraspol. Online. Available at: www.voskres.ru/info/tirasp1.htm (accessed 08 July 2007).

Sociological theories (2006) 'Sociological theories of language in the USSR, 1917–1938', Conference at Bakhtin Centre, Russian and Slavonic studies. University of Sheffield, UK.

Sotsialnye (2003–5) *Sotsialnye varianty jazyka–II,III,IV. Proceedings of the international conference in Nizhniy Novgorod (2003, 2004, 2005)*, Nizhniy Novgorod State Linguistic University.

Stavizka, L. (2003) *Korotkiy slovnyk zhargonnoy leksyky ukrainskoy movy* [A Short Glossary of Jargon Lexis in Ukraine], Kyiv: Kritika.

Stebunova (2004) 'Jazykovaya situaziya vostoka Ukrainy: den segodnjashniy i buduschiy' [Language situation in Ukraine: today and tomorrow], in *Russkiy jazyk: Istoricheskiye sudby I sovremennost. II Mezhdunarodny Congress rusistov-issledovateley*, Moskva, MGU, Filologichskiy fakultet. Sekziya XXI 'Russkiy jzyk v novyx geopoliticheskix usloviyax'. Online. Available at: www.philol.msu.ru/~rlc2004/ru/abstracts/?id=21&type=doc (accessed 02 Feb. 2007).

Sternin, I. (1999) 'Nekotorye zhanrovye osobennosti muzhskogo povedeniya' [Some Genealogic Features of Male Communicative Behaviour], in *Zhanry rechi* [Speech Genres], Saratov, vyp2: 184–93.

Timofeev, M. (2001) 'Rzhevskiy, Chapaev, Shtirlits: nazionalnye kharakteristiki voennyx v sovetskix anekdotax (Rzhevskiy, Chapaev, Shtirlits: the national features of army characters in Soviet anec-dotes)', in *Gender: jazyk, kultura, kommunikaziya. (Gender: language, culture, communication). Doklady pervoy mezhdunarodnoy konferentsii*. Moskva, pp. 321–8.

Trasjanka (2007) 'Trasjanka, Surzhyk and Russian – code switching, code mixing or fused lects?', International Symposium, University of Oldenburg, 15–18 June.

Tsyhun, G. (2000) 'Krealizavany pradukt, trasjanka, jak abjekt lingvisitichnaga dasledavannja' [Tra-syanka, a creolized product, as an object of linguistic study], *Skaryna* N6(11) ARCHE. Online. Available at: www.arche.bymedia.net/6–2000/cychu600.html (accessed 07 March 2007).

University (2006–7) 'University Sociolinguistics: Language as a Social Phenomenon, 2006, 2007, 2008', European University in St. Petersburg. Oxford-Russia Fund Summer School.

Uzina, E. (2002) 'O nazionalno-kulturnoy obuslovlennosti flirta' [Flirting as an ethnically and culturally conditioned genre], *Zhanry rechi*, vyp.3, Saratov.

Vakhtin, N. (2001) *Jazyki narodov Severa v XX veke* [The Languages of the Peoples of the North in the XX Century], Sankt Peterburg.

Vakhtin, N. and Golovko, E. (2004) *Sotsiologiya jazyka. Sotsiolingvistika* [Sociology of Language: Socio-linguistics], St Petersburg.

Vakhtin, N., Golovko, E. and Schweitzer, P. (2004) 'Russkiye starozhily Sibiri. Socialnye I simvo-licheskiye aspekty samosoznaniya' [Russian Traditional Communities in Siberia: Social and Symbolic Aspects of Self-Identification], Moskva: Novoe izdatelstvo.

Vakhtin, N., Zhironkina, O. and Romanova, K. (2006) 'Kalampozannja nad doleyu ukrainskoi movu' [Lamentations over the fate of Ukrainian], *Shid-Zahid*, vyp.8:200–208. *Specialne vudannja POR-UBIZHZHJA*, Charkiv-Kiev:Kritika.

Viktorova, K. (2006) 'Jazykovye izmeneiya v processe jazykovogo sdviga (na materiale maloyanisolskogo dialekta rumejskogo jazyka' [Language change in the process of language shift (Maloyanisol dialect of the Rumei language)], Candidate of Philology dissertation, St Petersburg.

Zaliznjak, H. and Masenko, L. (2001) *Movna situaziya Kuiva: den sjiogodnjashny ta pryjdeshny* [Language Situation in Kyiv: The Present Day and the Coming Day], Kyiv: KM Academy.

Zemskaya, E., Kitaygorodskaya, M. and Rozanova, H. (1993) 'Osobennosti muzhskoj i zhenskoj rechi' [Distinctive features of male and female speech], in E. Zemskaya and D. Shmelev (eds) *Russkiy jazyk v jego funktsionirovanii* [The functioning of Russian], Moskva, pp. 90–136.

Zhironkina, O. (2007) 'Lizla baba po lesnitse, upala z drabyny: zametki o jazykovoy situazii na Ukraine' [On the language situation in Ukraine], *Otechestvennye zapiski*, 1(34). Online. Available at: www.strana-oz.ru/?ozid=34&oznumber=1 (accessed March, August 2007).

33

The development of sociolinguistics in the Baltic States

Ina Druviete

Introduction

The Baltic States – the Republic of Latvia, the Republic of Lithuania and the Republic of Estonia – lie on the western edge of the East European plain. The three countries may be regarded as being a cultural, political and economic region despite different historical experiences and an important linguistic division. Latvia has a population of 2.5 million people, Estonia of 1.4 million people, and Lithuania of 3.7 million people.

The present ethnic composition reflects the complicated political and ethno–demographic history of this region. In 2007, the ethnic composition was as follows:

■ *Estonia* – 67 per cent Estonians, 25.9 per cent Russians, 2.7 per cent Ukrainians, 1 per cent Finns.
■ *Latvia* – 58.6 per cent Latvians, 28.8 per cent Russians, 3.9 per cent Belarusians, 2.6 per cent Ukrainians, 2.5 per cent Poles, 1.4 per cent Lithuanians, 0.4 per cent Jews.
■ *Lithuania* – 84.6 per cent Lithuanians, 5.1 per cent Russians, 6.3 per cent Poles, 1.1 per cent Belarusians, 0.6 per cent Ukrainians.

The Latvian and Lithuanian languages belong to the Baltic group of the Indo–European family of languages. The Estonian language represents the Balto–Finnic branch of the Finno–Ugric family of languages. Latvian, Lithuanian or Estonian is the only official State language in the respective countries.

Historical development

Latvians, Lithuanians and Estonians have resided in their present geographical areas for more than 3,000 years. Due to their advantageous geographical position, the territories of Latvia and Estonia have been fought over by Russia and German states since the time these were formed.

402

By the end of the nineteenth century, all three countries were provinces of the Russian empire, and their languages were subject to discrimination (lack of official status, prohibition of use in public administration, secondary schools and courts).

Since then Latvian and Estonian culture and language have developed against the background of the coexistence and rivalry of German and Russian elements, and Lithuanian culture and language against the background of the coexistence and rivalry of Polish and Russian elements.

World War I led to the collapse of the two empires – the Russian and the German – making it possible for Latvia, Lithuania and Estonia to assert their statehood. On 16 February 1918, Lithuania, on 24 February 1918 Estonia, and on 18 November 1918, Latvia declared their full independence.

In 1940, the Baltic States were incorporated into the Soviet Union. After Soviet occupation great changes in ethno-linguistic composition took place. There is no other region in Europe which has survived such massive ethno-demographic changes in the past 60 years.

Since the restoration of independence in 1991, the Baltic States have become rapidly developing democratic states. All three states are members of the European Union and of NATO since 2004.

Language and society research before the first independence period

The development of sociolinguistics in the Baltic States can be analysed in two ways. One approach is to begin with the middle of the twentieth century when sociolinguistics as a branch of linguistics came into being. The other approach allows a broader interpretation including ideas of the relationship between society and language, and language planning and language standardization in particular. This chapter is based on the second approach.

The history of the Baltic States determines this course of action. Over centuries there were two main tasks for people involved in cultural activities: (1) ensuring the survival and use of Latvian, Lithuanian and Estonian in a situation of language competition; and (2) ensuring the linguistic quality of these languages. The Baltic States could serve as models for studying the influence of other languages and cultures on minorities. Since the consolidation of the respective ethnic groups, these have always had direct contacts with a variety of other languages, e.g. Livonian, Estonian, Lithuanian, Belarusian, Russian as neighbouring languages; with Russian, Polish, Swedish and German as languages of cultural exchange and official languages; and with Latin as a language of religious ceremonies for Catholics. Language standardization already existed in the pre-written language period, i.e., until the sixteenth century. When in the seventeenth century the first norm sources appeared, one can talk about more or less conscious language standardization and purification. This process reaches into the field of sociolinguistics since language standardization crystallizes in concrete historical and cultural conditions.

Since the twelfth century when the present-day territories of Latvia and Estonia came under German domination, we can speak about a conscious language policy due to the formation of German-speaking administrative and governmental bodies. In the first Latvian norm sources – grammars and dictionaries of the seventeenth and eighteenth centuries (J. G. Rehehusen, G. Mancelius, H. Adolphy, K. Fuerecker, J. Lange, G. F. Stender, and so on, see Ozols (1965), Grabis (1955)) – the non-acceptance of linguistic interference is observed. Some ideas for the purification of Latvian were expressed in the programme of the *Lettisch-Literarische Gesellschaft* (1824). One task for contemporary sociolinguists is to seek the roots of the political ideas underlying the foundation of practical language standardization in the pre-national period, because the tradition is a very important factor in contemporary approaches.

In Lithuania, the government of the Grand Duchy of Prussia in the middle of the sixteenth century was very interested in the preparation and the publication of religious texts. The better educated and more talented pastors were empowered to prepare the most essential religious literature in the local languages. The work begun by the author of the first Lithuanian book, M. Mažvydas, was continued at the end of the sixteenth century by Jonas Bretkunas. In addition to collections of hymns and sermons, he was the first to translate the entire Bible into Lithuanian. The seventeenth century witnessed a continuation of this collective tradition of producing religious works in East Prussia, as well as linguistic works, exemplified by the first Lithuanian grammar, published by D. Klein in 1653.

The eighteenth century was the time when Lithuanian culture and literature flourished in East Prussia. Here for the first time the pastor M. Merlinas began a linguistic pro-gramme with other pastors on the kind of language to use with the common people. His followers began to gather and publish Lithuanian folklore and folk songs in their lin-guistic tracts, grammars and dictionaries. In the middle of the eighteenth century a com-plete translation of the Bible into Lithuanian was first published, new editions of hymns were prepared, even several grammars and dictionaries. When later, in the nineteenth century, the Lithuanian language became an object of especial interest to Indo-Europeanists, they could rely partially on the linguistic studies of the previous century (Palionis 1967; Sabaliauskas 1979).

The end of the nineteenth century was one of the most critical periods for the exis-tence of the Baltic nations and languages. Latvian, Lithuanian and Estonian had no offi-cial status, their sociolinguistic functions were reduced to a minimum. But the Baltic peoples at this period were consolidated as a nation, national literary languages had been formed, the national literature and press publications had reached a high level and strong national awakening tendencies were felt. The first ideologists of the national awakening devoted equal attention to the legal and linguistic aspects of language policy. The claims for giving official status to Latvian and the struggle against alien influences in Latvian had become a task for the newly-developed Latvian intelligentsia, the so-called neo-Latvians (J. Alunāns, K. Barons, etc.) and their followers (especially A. Kronvalds) (see Ozols 1965). Purifying the language from German elements went hand in hand with creating a modern Latvian word stock and an extensive borrowing from the international word stock. In the 1860s and 1870s the main emphasis was put on the elimination of German influences both in language use and language quality; the negative attitude towards Russian influence began in the 1880s when there were plans to russify the Baltic provinces, including attempts to introduce the Cyrillic alphabet into Latvian spelling.

By the turn of the century the first professionally educated Latvian linguists began to carry out the standardization of Latvian on scientific grounds. These first Latvian linguists (J. Velme, K. Mīlenbahs) were graduates of Tartu University and thus were influenced by German philosophy and sociological linguistics. The concept of an uninterrupted process of language development, of language change as a necessary factor for the living force of the language, the close connection between the language and the sociopolitical background of its speakers, formed the theoretical background for language planning. K. Mīlenbahs, the most prominent scholar of the pre-national period, tried to develop a theoretically grounded system for language development before carrying out practical activities in language standardization. His approach might be described as sociolinguistic in the precise sense of this term (Druviete 1990).

J. Endzelīns who heavily influenced the development of Latvian linguistics for almost half a century, graduated from Tartu University almost 20 years later and had quite a different approach to the development of language, due to considerable influence from neo-grammarian theory. The influence of external factors as a reason for language change was neglected. He did not particularly concern himself with the theoretical issues of language standardization, and so offered concrete proposals which coincided with traditional historically grounded patterns. At the same time a rigorous philological analysis increased the awareness of the lexical treasures of Latvian as well as its value for Indo-European comparative-historical linguistics because of its archaic features.

As a result of cooperation between the two famous Latvian linguists, a very important norm source, *Grammar of Latvian* (1907), was published where the sociological approach of K. Mīlenbahs and comparative-historical approach of J. Endzelīns were successfully connected (Endzelīns and Mīlenbahs 1907).

Estonian culture developed in earnest during the nineteenth-century period of national awakening. Elements of Estonian peasant culture, such as songs and folktales, were collected by the country's first cultural elite after 1850. Between 1857 and 1861, F. R. Kreutzwald compiled and published the Estonian national epic, Kalevipoeg, which was based on various folklore themes. Another achievement of this period was the establishment of Estonia's first regularly published Estonian-language newspaper in 1857.

The national literature had an earlier beginning, in the 1810s, with the patriotic poetry of K. J. Peterson. In the second half of the nineteenth century, Romanticism and love of country found equal expression in the poetry of L. Koidula, Estonia's first woman poet and a key figure in the cultural awakening. The first Estonian song festival was organized in 1869 in Tartu. At the end of the nineteenth century, Estonian theatre also began in Tartu with the formation of the Vanemuine theatre group.

The Russian Empire erased Polish influence on Lithuanians and introduced Russian social and political institutions. Under tsarist rule, Lithuanian schools were forbidden, Lithuanian publications in the Latin script were outlawed. However, the restrictive policies failed to extinguish indigenous cultural institutions and language. The medieval Lithuanian rulers had not developed a written form of the Lithuanian language. The literary Lithuanian language, based on a south-western Lithuanian dialect, came into use during the last quarter of the nineteenth century, replacing the use of the Samogitian, or western Lithuanian, dialect. At the beginning of the twentieth century, the use of Lithuanian was confined mainly to the peasantry, but the language was revived subsequently. However, by the first decade of the twentieth century, Latvian, Lithuanian, and Estonian had reached a rather high level of standardization in spite of the legal restrictions on the sociolinguistic functions of these languages. In the period before independence, there was already established a strong theoretical background for *corpus planning*. *Status planning* could take place only after independence (Piročkinas 1977).

The independence period (1918–40)

The newly established Baltic States came into being under most difficult and unfavourable circumstances. The period from 1914 to the early 1920s can be characterized as one of uncompromising rivalry between languages spread over the territories of these states. Language reasonably was considered a magnificent political and ideological weapon. Almost all the numerous governments during this period issued orders concerning language use.

The minority problem in the Baltic States had always been among the most important factors influencing the development of a socially oriented trend in linguistics. Most of the minority populations belonged to the large nations which not long before had dominated politically, economically and culturally. The first decrees and laws tried to strengthen the positions of the local languages which were considered to be the best means of integrating the society. This concept was reflected in the *Education Laws* and in the *Laws on State Language*.

Language planning during the 1920s and 1930s has not been recognized as an autonomous branch of linguistics. Several linguists, e.g. E. Blese, P. Šmits, J. Jablonskis, P. Jonikas, had contributed to the analysis of social and functional aspects of language, too; however, an intralinguistic, comparative-historical approach to language prevailed mainly due to the authority of J. Endzelīns and K. Būga. Since J. Endzelīns supervised the teaching of young philologists at the University of Latvia, he raised several generations of historically oriented linguists who also themselves taught his findings (Rūķe-Draviņa 1977).

The political system stimulated the development of national culture, education and science, and governmental support was given to linguistics, too. The University of Latvia, the University of Vilnius, the University of Tartu, Ministries of Education, the Culture Foundations, Depositaries of Language Data, and several philological societies were the main organizational centres for scientific research in the Baltic States. Almost all of the leading scholars, also writers, teachers, journalists contributed to the field. Questions of language correctness were widely discussed in the daily press. A great amount of norm sources were published. But it is evident that Baltic linguists were far from in agreement. In Latvia, more than 30 booklets and about 200 articles in the daily press and special journals might be called polemical. Analysis of these linguistic discussions shows that there were two main trends in language standardization. The primary trend was connected with J. Endzelīns and his followers. The theoretical basis for standardization was one based on comparative linguistics and the neogrammarians. The most significant thesis was on regularity of language system and phonetic and morphological laws. The development of language at all levels seemed to be determined by the typology of the proto-language, thus external influences could not be treated as a serious reason for change of the existing norms. The strong opposite views of the representatives of the other trend (E. Blese, P. Šmits, P. Ķiķauka, M. Bruņenieks, F. Garais, etc.– Rūķe-Draviņa 1977) were similar to the famous theses of the Prague Linguistic Circle, known in Latvia, too. These linguists thought that it would be illogical to presuppose that linguistic changes are only destructive occurrences, purposeless and heterogeneous from the viewpoint of the system. Socially oriented Latvian linguists also pointed out that purism is a normal reaction in those periods when national liberation movements occur, but when the existence of nations has not been threatened, reference to historical facts when contemporary usage normally prefers another form may be evaluated as retrospective and antidemocratic. Serious objections were made to the neglect of public opinion about language standardization.

In the 1930s, Latvian, Lithuanian and Estonian formed into well-developed polyfunctional languages with an established system of styles. The Terminology Commissions coined terms in more than 20 branches of science. However, there were no legal bodies for the legal protection of languages, and in the Language Laws there were no articles on the development of language quality. There was a deep gap between *status planning* and *corpus planning* in the 1920s and 1930s. Mutual distrust between linguists and state officials was evident. Reasons for it seemed to be found in the over-estimation of linguistic factors and the under-estimation of legal factors in language maintenance in the situation of language competition.

Sociolinguistics during the Soviet period, 1940–91

The development of sociolinguistics in the Baltic States during the Soviet period has to be analysed against the background of political changes in the region and the political and linguistic goals of Soviet language policy. Its ambigous character is also reflected in sociolinguistic investigations.

On the one hand, the official postulates about the absolute equality of languages and the necessity to create conditions for the evolution and development of all languages were beneficial for *corpus planning*. On the other hand, the resolutely implemented theories about convergence of languages, the benefits of bilingualism ('native' Russian, not vice versa), and ideas about the leading role of Russian and the establishment of Russian as a secondary mother tongue did not allow the fulfilment of this linguistic potential. Strong thematic restrictions were placed on emerging sociolinguistics in the Baltic Republics. Several issues of macro-sociolinguistics, e.g., language shift as a result of collective bilingualism or the role of the language in the life of the nation were considered taboo problems. Even a hint of the linguistic rights of speakers of local languages and the obligation on immigrants to learn them could be classified as a political crime.

For political reasons and administrative pressures Baltic linguists could do nothing about the shrinking of the sociolinguistic functions of languages, therefore the retention of language quality and even its perfection were set as major tasks. The Terminological Commissions had been active, terminological dictionaries in various fields of science and technology were published. As the Baltic languages were in close contact with the Russian language, but had minimal contacts with other European languages, the prevailing issue was the prevention and elimination of language interference. To extend users' knowledge about the structure of their own language and demands for correct speech, linguists paid great attention to popularizing correct language. Practical conferences were organized, TV and radio broadcasts were made. Joint Latvian, Lithuanian and Estonian conferences on language cultivation issues took place. The language situation was similar in all the Baltic states, and therefore cooperation in language policy was a very important factor in avoiding and deterring russification.

During the 1970s, a boom in sociolinguistic investigations in the Soviet Union began. Contrary to widespread opinion, Soviet sociolinguistics did not develop in complete isolation from the Western world; translations of the contributions of the most prominent sociolinguists had been published although supplemented with compulsory criticism in prefaces and footnotes. Baltic linguists had close contacts with exiled scholars who actively worked in sociolinguistics, too (V. Rūķe-Draviņa, e.g. 1977, I. Lehiste, E. Oksaar, e.g. 1992, B. Metuzāle-Kangere, U. Ozolins, e.g. 1999, R. Taagepera e.g. Misiunas and Taagepera 1993, R. Karklina, J. Dreifelds, T. Raun, e.g. 2001, and others; see Metuzāle-Kangere and Ozolins 2005) as well as with foreign scholars (Hogan-Brun and Ramonienė 2005; Maurais 1998; Dini 1997). See also Sabaliauskas (1982). Valuable original investigations by Soviet scholars also appeared, especially concerning social and territorial variability in language, and the linguistic behaviour of an individual. However, macro-sociolinguistics, especially the theory of language policy, was an extremely ideologized field of science. Baltic linguists were enthusiastic to learn different methodological approaches, and used Aesopian language when talking about the unfavourable language situation in Latvia. In order to avoid becoming apologists for the regime and its ideology, ideologically neutral sociolinguistic issues were chosen for investigation, e.g. social aspects of language cultivation.

The first bulky sociolinguistic investigation in the Baltic States took place in 1987 as a part of a Moscow programme, 'The development of the national languages in socialism' (unpublished because of the change of political system). Groups of researchers studied processes of functional bilingualism and multilingualism in various functional spheres. A questionnaire drawn up in cooperation among Baltic scholars contained 62 questions as well as a language test. The conclusions were that the language situation in the Baltic States could be characterized as asymmetrical bilingualism. The Baltic languages had lost several major sociolinguistic functions (including use in parliament, government, the armed forces, railway and air transport) while preserving high mother tongue retention rates. However, a decrease in native language competence among non-Russian minorities had taken place.

In such a situation the struggle for the Latvian, Lithuanian and Estonian languages began. Almost all linguists were involved in it, participating in governmental or non-governmental commissions, explaining language policy issues in the mass media. In the Baltic States the Language Laws were among the first laws of the perestroika-era (1987–89) to be passed together with the legalization of the national flag and anthem. During the process of democratization, a widespread popular movement (demonstrations, petitions, pickets) for official recognition of the priority of the national titular languages developed in all three states. In 1988, amendments to the Constitutions which proclaimed Latvian, Lithuanian and Estonian the official State languages in the respective republics were adopted. In 1989, the Language Laws were adopted in all three Baltic States.

The new political situation created a requirement to carry out sociolinguistic investigations, in the theory of language policy particularly. Theoretical and practical problems of language policy were discussed in the works of A. Blinkena, e.g. 1994/95, O. Bušs, I. Druviete, Dz. Hirša, J. Valdmanis, A. Veisbergs, e.g. 1999 in Latvia (see Joma 2007), A. Rosinas, D. Mikulenienė, V. Ambrazas, L. Grumadienė, e.g. 2005 (Kalėdienė), L. Vaicekauskienė, M. Ramonienė (see Grumadienė 2005), in Lithuania, M. Hint, M. Rannut, e.g. 1995, J. Viikberg, e.g. 2000 (see Rannut 2004) in Estonia. Analyses of ongoing processes in the Baltic States as well as awareness of the language policy experiences in other countries helped to create a new concept of language legislation, which could ensure the preservation of the Baltic languages against the background of ensuring language rights of inhabitants whose native language is other than the official state language.

Independence regained

On 21 August 1991, the Republic of Latvia, the Republic of Lithuania and the Republic of Estonia were proclaimed sovereign states again. In 1992 additions and amendments were made to the 1989 Language Laws. Several additional regulations and decrees were

adopted, e.g. on Official State language proficiency certification regulations, and regulations of the Official State language inspection board. In 1995, new Laws on State Language were adopted in Estonia and Lithuania, and, in 1999, in Latvia. Articles on promoting
language studies were included in all the laws. Research in sociolinguistics is largely
problem-oriented.

In Latvia, the Department of Sociolinguistics was founded in 1992 (Head: Ina Druviete). Since 1995, sociolinguistic research has been carried out on a regular basis. The
main research trends are the complex sociolinguistic analysis of the language situation in
Latvia (I. Druviete, e.g. 1997, 2000, V. Ernstsone, D. Joma, e.g. Ernstsone and Joma
2005, Dz. Hirša, V. Poriņa, D. Strelēvica-Ošiņa), research on EU and national language
policies (A. Blūmane, I. Druviete, J. Sīlis, J. Valdmanis, A. Veisbergs, e.g. 1999), research
of sociolects, slang and youth speech (O. Bušs, V. Ernstsone, L. Lauze, e.g. 2004, 2008,
D. Liepa, L. Tidriķe). Sociolinguistics has been included in the curricula of BA, MA and
doctoral programmes at the University of Latvia, Daugavpils University and Liepāja
Academy. Latvian sociolinguists are members of the State Language Commission under
the auspices of the President of Latvia, of the Latvian Language Expert Commission and
the Commission of Toponyms at the State Language Centre. *The State Language Development Programme* was adopted in 2006. Research in sociolinguistics has been carried on
at the State Language Agency, too. Sociolinguistic methods are increasingly involved in
dialectogy, terminology and semantics (P. Balodis, J. Baldunčiks, e.g. 1989, M. Baltiņa, e.g.
1986, Z. Ikere, A. Stafecka). For a bibliography of the research mentioned in this paragraph,
see Joma (2007).

In Lithuania, language planning is in progress under the auspices of the State Commission of the Lithuanian Language at the Parliament of the Republic of Lithuania
(Head: I. Smetonienė). The Lithuanian Language Commission is composed of researchers from the Lithuanian Language Institute, university professors and representatives of
other institutions. The Commission deals with issues of codification, the use of language
norms, and questions relating to the implementation of the *Law on the State Language*. In
2000, the Government of Lithuania adopted *the Programme of the Lithuanian Language in
the Information Society* for 2000–2006,which deals with newly emerging problems of terminology in computer science. The Institute of the Lithuanian Language is a centre for
research into the Lithuanian language. It gathers data on Lithuanian dialects, analyses the
development of the norms and terminology of the Lithuanian language, and compiles a
database of linguistic phenomena and their assessment (D. Mikulenienė, G. Subačius, e.g.
2001, J. Zabarskaitė). Analyses of the sociolinguistic situation have been regularly undertaken by L. Kaledienė (Grumadienė). Another developing trend is the teaching of Lithuanian as a second and foreign language at Vilnius and Kaunas universities (M. Ramonienė,
I. Savickienė).

In Estonia, the *Development Strategy for the Estonian Language* outlines the development
priorities of the Estonian language for the years 2004–10. The main objective of the
strategy is to realize the opportunities provided by the Constitution and legislation to
secure the protection, sustainability, development, and full-scale use of Estonian as a state
language in all spheres of life on the entire territory of the Estonian state. The Government of the Republic, its ministries, local governments, educational, research, and
development institutions will proceed from the Strategy in planning and organizing their
language-related work. It serves as the basis for the Ministry of Education and Research
to work out the annual action plans. It includes motivation to use good Estonian in all
spheres of life, application of linguistic criteria in employment, tenders and contracts,

etc., stimulation of Estonian language tuition, research and entertainment, including Estonian language popular music; and motivation to use Estonian language software both in established and emerging fields of information technology. The main institutions doing sociolinguistic research are Tallinn and Tartu Universities, the Institute of the Estonian Language (these being research and development institutions); the Estonian Legal Language Centre (creates and administers the database of legal terminology); Võru Institute (research and development institution developing the local Võro language and culture); the Mother Tongue Society (a non-profit society that contributes to the research and planning of the Estonian language); the Association of Estonian-language Teachers (a non-profit society, bringing together teachers of the Estonian language and literature); and the Estonian Terminology Society (a non-profit society that supports and in some domains coordinates terminological work). Main research trends are the analysis, modelling and control of the development of the Estonian linguistic environment (M. Ehala, A. Verschik, e.g. 2005, 2006, M. Rannut, e.g. 2004, Ü. Rannut), and home language surveys (M. Rannut, Ü. Rannut). Sociolinguistic methods in dialectology, grammar and other subfields are widely used (K. Pajusalu, B. Klaas, I. Külmoja, e.g. 2001, U. Sutrop, L. Keevallik, P. Päll, H. Metslang).

Analysis of language situations is an absolute prerequisite for the implementation of the theory-based language policy in a complex ethnodemographic situation such as that in the Baltic States. Cooperation among Baltic sociolinguists still takes place on a regular basis although the systems of language planning and the research institutions and trends of sociolinguistic research are different.

References

Baldunčiks, J. (1989) *Anglicismi latviešu valodā*, Riga: Zinātne.

Baltiņa M. (1986) 'Par normas pazīmēm latviešu literārās valodas vēsturē', *Latvijas Zinātņu Akadēmijas Vēstis*, 1, 66–72.

Blinkena, A. (1994/95) 'The Latvian language: some problems of its development and existence', *ALFA, Vol. 7/8, Actes de language francaise et de linguistique*, Universitas Dalhausiana, Halifax, Canada, pp. 463–9.

Dini, P.U. (1997) *Le lingue baltiche*, ed. E. Banfi, Scandicci: La Nuova Italiam.

Druviete, I. (1990) *Kārlis Mīlenbahs*, Riga: Zinātne.

——(1997) 'Linguistic human rights in the Baltic States', *International Journal of the Sociology of Language*, 127, 161–85.

——(2000) *Sociolinguistic Situation and Language Policy in the Baltic States*, Riga: Mācību apgāds.

Endzelīns, J. and Mīlenbahs, K. (1907) *Latviešu gramatika*, Riga.

Ernstsone, V. and Joma, D. (2005) *Latviski runājošo Latvijas iedzīvotāju lingvistiskā attieksme un valodu lietojums*, Riga: VVA.

Grabis, R. (1955) 'Pārskats par 17. gadsimta latviešu valodas gramatikām. – LPSR ZA Valodas un literatūras institūta Raksti', V sēj. R.: LVI, 205–66.

Grumadienė, L. (2005) 'Language Policy and Sociolinguistic Situation in Lithuania', *Mercator Working Papers, 19*, Barcelona: CIEMEN.

Hogan-Brun, G. and Ramonienė, M. (2005) 'Perspectives on language attitudes and use in Lithuania's multilingual setting. Language and Social Processes in the Baltic Republics Surrounding their EU Accession', Special Issue, *Journal of Multilingual and Multicultural Development*, 26, 5, 425–41.

Joma, D. (ed.) (2007) *Latviešu valoda 15 neatkarības gados*, Riga: Zinātne.

Külmoja, I. (2001) *About the Language of the Russian Diaspora in Estonia. In 100 aastat akadeemilist eesti keele õpet Uppsala Ülikoolis*, Tartu, Uppsala, pp. 98–104.

Lauze, L. (2004) *Ikdienas saziņa: vienkāršs teikums latviešu sarunvalodā*, Liepāja: LPA.
——(2008) *Izpētes materiāla vākšana sociolingvistikā. Metodiski norādījumi*, Liepāja: LiePA.
Maurais, J. (ed.) (1998) 'Les politiques linguistiques des pays baltes', *Terminogramme*, Juillet, Québec.
Metuzāle-Kangere, B. and Ozolins, U. (2005) 'The language situation in Latvia, 1850–2004', *Journal of Baltic Studies*, 36, 3, 317–44.
Misiunas, R. J. and Taagepera, R. (1993) *The Baltic States: Years of Dependence (1940–1990)*, Berkeley, CA: University of California Press.
Oksaar, E. (1992) *Sprache und Gesellschaft*, Mannheim: Brockhaus.
Ozolins, U. (1999) 'Between Russian and European hegemony: current language policy in the Baltic States', *Current Issues in Language and Society*, 6(1): 6–47.
Ozols, A. (1965) *Veclatviešu rakstu valoda*, Riga: Liesma.
Palionis J. (1967) *Lietuvių literatūrinė kalba XVI–XVII a*, Vilnius: Mintis.
Piročkinas, A. (1977) *Prie bendrinės kalbos ištakų*, Vilnius: Mokslas.
Rannut, M. (1995) 'Beyond linguistic policy: the Soviet Union versus Estonia', in T. Skutnabb-Kangas, R. Phillipson and M. Rannut (eds) *Linguistic Human Rights: Overcoming Linguistic Discrimination*, Berlin: Mouton de Gruyter, pp. 170–208.
——(2004) 'Language policy in Estonia', Noves SL, *Revista de Sociolingüística*, 17, 1–17.
Raun, T. (2001) *Estonia and Estonians*, 2nd edn, Stanford, CA: Stanford University Press.
Rūķe-Draviņa V. (1977) *The Standardization Process in Latvian: 16th Century to the Present*, Stockholm: Almquist & Wiksell.
Sabaliauskas, A. (1979) *Lietuvių kalbos tyrinėjimo istorija (iki 1940 m.)*, Vilnius: Mokslas.
——(1982) *Lietuvi Lietuvių kalbos tyrinėjimo istorija (1940–80 m.)*, Vilnius: Mokslas.
Subačius, G. (2001) 'Written standard and spoken standard', in *Baltu filoloģija 10*, Riga: LU, pp. 127–36.
Veisbergs, A. (1999) *Idioms in Latviam*, Riga: LU.
Verschik, A. (2005) 'The language situation in Estonia', *Journal of Baltic Studies*, 36, 3, 283–316.
——(2006) 'Recent contributions to Estonian sociolinguistics', *Estudios de Sociolinguistics*, 7, 122–6.
Viikberg J. (2000) 'Estonian national minorities: past and present', in E. Vēbers (ed.) *Integrācija un etnopolitika*, Riga: University of Latvia, pp. 470–82.

Index

accommodation 10, 12, 172, 365; accommodationist principle 374, 375–76; Arabic 242, 244, 247; the Balkans 376, 378, 380, 381–82; the Caribbean 54, 55; German 264; *see also* the Balkans; language policy and planning

Afghanistan *see* Iranian world

Africa xix; African languages 190, 191, 192, 194, 195, 206, 210, 211, 218, 220; *see also* East Africa; South Africa; West and Central Africa

age: Australian English 151, 153–54; Canada 27; China 70; Italian 330, 331; United States 8, 10, 11–12, 17; *see also* children; young people

Albania *see* the Balkans

alphabets: Arabic 118, 119, 123, 141–42, 226, 247–48; Cyrillic 123, 130, 134, 136, 141, 142, 389, 390, 394, 404; Roman/Latin alphabet 90, 103, 105, 131, 134, 248, 389, 390, 394 (Romanization/Latinization 118, 119, 134, 147; Turkish language reform (TLR) 118, 119); *see also* orthography; written language

anthropological linguistics 286, 395; China 69, 70–72; Mexico 34; Middle East and North Africa 248–49; *see also* ethnicity

Arabic 212; Arabs and Jews in Israel 231; the Caucasus 132; Classical Arabic (*fushaa*) 226, 238, 239, 240, 241–42, 243, 244, 246, 249, 250; dialect 240–41, 242–45, 250; diglossia xix, 239, 240–42, 246, 249; East Africa 216, 219; Egyptian Arabic 239, 241, 251; English 245, 246, 248, 249; Ferguson, Charles A. xix, 238, 240–41; Israel 226, 227, 228–29, 230, 233, 234; language shift 239, 245; Latin alphabet 248; Middle East and North Africa 238–56; minority language 247; Modern

Standard Arabic (MSA) 238, 240, 242, 249, 250; multilingualism 245; numerals 90; official language 216, 217, 227, 233, 234; religion 238, 244, 246–47; revival 240; script 118, 119, 123, 141–42, 226, 247–48; Turks 118; Turkish 118, 119, 120, 121, 123; variationist sociolinguistics 238, 239, 241, 244–45; vernaculars 240–41, 242, 245, 246, 247, 248, 249, 250; *see also* Middle East and North Africa

Armenia *see* the Caucasus

Atkinson, David 341–47, 350–58; *see also* Spain

atlases: the Caucasus 129; German 259; Italy 327, 330, 331, 334; Japan 92; Middle East and North Africa 242, 250

Australia xix, 102, 151–58; Australian English (AusE) xix, 151–54 (age 151, 153–54; gender 151, 153; region 151, 154; socio-economic background 151, 152–53); colony 155, 156; Creole 155; grammar 156; identity 151, 155, 157; language endangerment 155, 157; LOTEs and ethnic varieties 151, 154–57 (Aboriginal languages and Aboriginal Australian English (AbE) 151, 154–56, 157; migrant languages, ethnolects, Pan-ethnic Australian English 151, 154, 156–57); language shift 156, 157; lexicon 154, 156; morphology 153; multilingualism 151; phonology 152, 153–54, 155–56; pragmatics 156; prosody 152–53, 156 (Australian Questioning Intonation (AQI) 152–53, 156)

Azerbaijan *see* the Caucasus

the Balkans xx, 131, 372–84; Albania 117, 372, 374, 375, 376, 381–82, 383;

413